D1727095

Jehovah's Witnesses

Hans Hesse (Ed.)

Persecution and Resistance of Jehovah's Witnesses During the Nazi Regime

1933–1945

EDITION TEMMEN

Die Deutsche Bibliothek – CIP-Einheitsaufnahme

Persecution and resistance of Jehovah's witnesses during the Nazi regime 1933-1945 / Ed.: Hans Hesse. – Bremen: Ed. Temmen, 2001
Dt. Ausg. u.d.T.: "Am mutigsten waren immer wieder die Zeugen Jehovas"
ISBN 3-86108-750-2

Distribution in the US & Canada
Edition Temmen *c/o Courier Press Ltd.,*
4732 N. Lincoln Ave, Chicago, Ill 60625
phone 773-275-5054
Fax 773-275-0596
email: info@edition-temmen.com
www.edition-temmen.com

Title:
Johannes Steyer:
Concentrationcamp Buchenwald

© **Edition Temmen**
Hohenlohestr. 21 – D-28209 Bremen – Germany
Tel. +49-421-34843-0 – Fax +49-421-348094
email: info@edition-temmen.de
www.edition-temmen.de

Production: **Edition Temmen**, Germany

English edition: ISBN 3-86108-750-2
German edition: ISBN 3-86108-724-3

Contents

Part B

Preface

We must be grateful for this book, deeply grateful. In essay after essay we read of the fate of Jehovah's Witnesses in Nazi concentration camps. Some of the essays tell large stories. The other essays tell small stories of a few individuals – stories that illuminate the whole. Part of this work addresses the situation of the Witnesses in Germany. On this I will offer no comment. Rather, permit me in my brief preface to situate the Jehovah's Witnesses within the totality of the Nazis' victims and to speak specifically to what is distinct about their particular experience.

It was John Conway who first suggested that the Nazis victimized some people for what they did, some for what they refused to do, some for what they were, and some for the fact that they were.

To illustrate: political leaders, social democrats, trade unionists, and dissenting clergy were victimized for what they did. Had they not engaged in their activities, they might never have been detained or arrested, harassed or persecuted by the Nazis. Roma and Sinti [Gypsies] were persecuted for what they were; their very being as members of a group was sufficient for the Nazis to subject them to arrest, persecution and, eventually, annihilation. So too, the mentally retarded, physically infirm, and emotionally distraught Germans were murdered because they were an embarrassment to the myth of Aryan Supremacy. »Life not worthy of living,« they were called. Economic calculations directly influenced and were used to justify their destruction; so too, were scientific justifications. The so-called »euthanasia« program was enthusiastically endorsed by many scientists in Germany and even elsewhere.

Jews were victimized not because of what they did, nor because of what they were. They were targeted for destruction because of what their grandparents were. Thus, those who had converted from Judaism a generation before, Christian children of Christian parents, pastors, priests and nuns among them, were defined, segregated, isolated and murdered because they had »Jewish blood« within their veins, the inheritance of their Jewish grandparents.

Alone of all the groups targeted by the Nazis, the Jehovah's Witnesses were victimized because of what they refused to do. They would not enlist in the army, undertake air raid drills, stop meeting or proselytizing. They would not utter the words »Heil Hitler.« Their dissent was irksome, disciplined and systematic. Even in concentration camps, if they signed the following document they could be released:

1   I acknowledge that the International Jehovah's Witness Association is disseminating erroneous teachings and using religion as a disguise merely to pursue subversive goals against the interests of the State.
2   I have therefore completely left that organization and have also spiritually freed myself from the teachings of that sect.
3   I herewith pledge that I will never again participate in the International Jehovah's Witness Association. I will immediately denounce any individual who solicits me with the heresy of the Witnesses or who in any manner reveals his affiliation with the Witnesses. Should Jehovah's Witnesses publications be sent to me, I will immediately deliver them to the nearest police department.
4   In the future, I will obey the laws of the State, and particularly in the event of war, I will

defend the Fatherland with weapon in hand and totally become part of the national community.

5   I have been informed that should I violate today's declaration, I will again be arrested.

One marvels at how few signed such documents.

Survivors of the Holocaust, and even scholars of the Holocaust and ordinary Jews often use the term martyrdom to speak of Jewish victimization. In truth, the Jews were not martyrs during the Holocaust, at least not in its accepted sense, because martyrdom as understood by Jewish tradition entails an element of choice and Jews had no choice. To be more precise, in Lawrence Langer's terms, Jews faced »choiceless choices.« Aside from physically escaping areas under German control or sequestering themselves where they could not be found by the Germans and their many allies, collaborators and informers, Jews were victimized. Conversion could not save them, renunciation of their faith or identity could not save them.

Jews had no choice. Jehovah's Witnesses did. As such, they are martyrs in the traditional sense of the term – those prepared to suffer and even to die for the choice of their faith. Their clear and convincing choice always deepens our understanding of Jewish choicelessness.

Jehovah's Witnesses were isolated and harangued from 1933 onward. Suspicion and harassment turned into bitter persecution as the Witnesses refused to surrender. Twenty thousand among 65 million Germans, the Witnesses entered the spiritual battle against the Nazis as soldiers of Jehovah in the war between good and evil. They taught that Jehovah's forces will defeat Satan. The Nazis could not tolerate such »false gods.« Persecution began immediately in 1933 and continued until 1945. After 1937, Witnesses were sent to concentration camps. Outside the camps, Witnesses were forced to give up their children, jobs, pensions, and all civil rights.

Throughout their struggle, Witnesses continued to meet, to preach, and to distribute literature. Some five thousand Jehovah's Witnesses were sent to concentration camps where they alone were »voluntary prisoners,« so termed because the moment they recanted their views, they could be freed. Some lost their lives in the camps, but few renounced their faith.

Because they understood why they were suffering, they maintained themselves spiritually to a degree unusual among prisoners. Viktor Frankl once wrote, »whoever knows ›why‹ can endure almost any ›how‹.« In many of the articles in this book, we can see an empirical test of Frankl's personal observation. Scholars have pointed out that the survival ratio of Jehovah's Witnesses was higher in the concentration camp than political prisoners and homosexuals. Their sense of community was greater as was their sense of purpose. Because Jehovah's Witnesses rejected »this world,« they did not feel quite as defeated as the political prisoners nor as deprived as the homosexuals incarcerated in the camps.

Certainly, their survival ratio was higher than Jews, most of whom were gassed upon arrival and all of whom stood under a death sentence after 1942 from the moment they entered the camps. There may be other ways of accounting for the higher survival ratio of Jehovah's Witnesses. Their own religious beliefs precluded armed resistance. Committed pacifists, they could even serve as barbers to the SS and work in their homes outside of the camps. The SS did not fear that they would escape. I observe such behavior with great respect for the Witnesses' religious integrity even where I cannot commend such pacifism, especially under such circumstances. My sense of morality would require different behavior. My religion would command more militant action toward such evil. My faith is a »this worldly« faith. The details of this book and its many essays on specific camps and individuals prisoners will give the reader ample opportunity to reflect of Frankl's observation and to test the keenness of his insight.

After years of neglect, Jehovah's Witnesses have begun to document their own history. While for some, this may challenge the integrity of the history that is written, Jehovah's Witnesses are to be commended for confronting this painful past and bringing its material documentation to light. Jews, too, began by documenting their history within the community and its publications. It was only years later that more mainstream publishers began to develop an interest in the Holocaust. I have worked with Jehovah's Witnesses filmmakers and interviewers, I have attended public meetings, written introductions to books, and participated in panels. Never have I have found my freedom of inquiry or expression constrained even by the most subtle of pressures. I presume that is also true of all my non-Witness colleagues. So the appearance of this work under the auspices of its victim group should challenge neither its veracity nor its importance. We need more works on each of the victim groups if we are to understand the full dimensions of Nazi persecution.

My interest in Jehovah's Witnesses was sparked by my distinguished former colleague Sybil Milton who died last week. Both she and her husband Henry Friedlander have contributed to this volume. Her life was a blessing; so too, her memory.

Michael Berenbaum
Ida E. King Distinguished Visiting Scholar of the Holocaust
Richard Stockton College
October 2000

Hans Hesse

Foreword

»Time and again, Jehovah's Witnesses were the most courageous.«[1] — The communist prisoner Gertrud Keen in the Moringen concentration camp used these words to describe the behavior of Bible Students.

The *Deutschland-Berichte* of the exile Social Democratic party in Prague is typical for many other sources. It stated about Jehovah's Witnesses in the Sachsenburg concentration camp: »The Earnest Bible Students' conduct is most astonishing. These ... people showed an implacable spirit of opposition and martyrdom and were unyielding as no other group in the camp.«[2]

Both quotations express great respect for the conduct of Jehovah's Witnesses. Both also reveal that this conduct by the persecuted was considered conspicuous and unusual. In many concentration camps, they represented the majority of prisoners, although in general they usually constituted only 5–10 percent of the prisoners, and nevertheless, this small group was noticeable.

Furthermore, immediately after 1945, concentration camp prisoners wearing the purple triangle were especially remembered. Hanns Lilje, for many years bishop of the Lutheran church in Hanover, emphasized in 1947 that »no Christian community can stand even the slightest comparison with the number of their matyrs.«[3]

Nevertheless, the history of Nazi persecution of this group was increasingly overlooked. The fate of Jehovah's Witnesses is virtually unknown to a wider public today. In some school books, they receive marginal attention, if at all; they are sometimes placed in an incorrect context, included in the »destruction of life not worthy of living.«

Of the approximately 25,000 members of this religious community at the beginning of the Third Reich, nearly 10,000 of them were arrested for various terms. Nearly 2,000 of them were incarcerated in concentration camps. About 1,200 died or were killed, including ca. 250 Jehovah's Witnesses who were executed for refusing military service. In fact, Jehovah's Witnesses were »fought with inexorable severity.«[4]

Not only former fellow concentration camp prisoners emphasized the behavior of Jehovah's Witnesses. Similar analyses are found in historical literature. The most incisive formulation was by Friedrich Zipfel. He stated that the Nazi persecution of the Jehovah's Witnesses »was an unusual process.«[5] Detlef Garbe also pointed to several »very significant peculiarities« in Nazi persecution of Jehovah's Witnesses.[6] The most important are that Jehovah's Witnesses were among the first groups to be persecuted, that Jehovah's Witnesses resolutely and unitedly resisted the Nazis, that the Witnesses were stigmatized and marked as a distinct group by the »purple triangle« in concentration camps, and that they represented the largest number of those sentenced by military tribunals for refusing military service.

An additional characteristic is that they represented the largest number of female prisoners in Moringen, Lichtenburg, and, until 1939, in Ravensbrück concentration camps for women.

All of these facts stand in stark contrast with historiography about Nazi persecution of Jehovah's Witnesses. Until well into the 1990s, researchers showed little interest in this subject.

The classic monograph about this topic by Detlef Garbe was only published in 1993. For the first time, several conferences under the auspices of the Watch Tower Society and various partners (Fritz Bauer Institute in Frankfurt, the concentration camp memorials at Wewelsburg and Neuengamme, as well as the Bundeszentrale für politische Bildung [the Federal Agency for Political Education]) took place in Germany in the fall of 1997 (characteristically as a result of a program in 1994 at the U.S. Holocaust Memorial Museum in Washington, D.C.). These symposia found substantial response and frequent requests for a documentation of the various presentations and lectures. Only the conference at the Wewelsburg District Museum on October 4, 1997, was published under the title *Widerstand aus christlicher Überzeugung: Jehovas Zeugen im Nationalsozialismus* [Resistance out of Christian Conviction: Jehovah's Witnesses under National Socialism].[7]

We have therefore assembled the additional presentations in this anthology. After reviewing the various essays and with increasing distance from the symposia, it was rapidly apparent that it would be desirable to include additional contributions in order to present a comprehensive picture of the status of research about specific aspects of the Nazi persecution of Jehovah's Witnesses.

The first section of this anthology focuses on the history of Jehovah's Witnesses in Nazi concentration camps. Henry Friedlander's essay explains the various categories of concentration camp prisoners and presents a summary of the concentration camp system. Christoph Daxelmüller explores the religious and social behavior of Jehovah's Witnesses in Nazi concentration camps. In addition to these introductory essays, several articles focus on Jehovah's Witnesses in specific concentration camps: Moringen concentration camp for women (Jürgen Harder and Hans Hesse), Niederhagen-Wewelsburg (Kirsten John-Stucke), Sachsenhausen (Antje Zeiger), Moringen as a concentration camp for juveniles (Martin Guse), and Bergen-Belsen (Thomas Rahe).

These specific analyses of the daily realities of Jehovah's Witnesses in the concentration camp system are completed by a series of paintings about the Buchenwald concentration camp made by the surviving Jehovah's Witness prisoner, Johannes Steyer, years after liberation (Johannes Wrobel essay).

Sybil Milton's essay throws an impressive light on the religious association of Jehovah's Witnesses as a »forgotten victim group.«

Even today, there are few documents published about Nazi persecution of Jehovah's Witnesses, let alone a systematic documentation, as Sybil Milton makes clear in her contribution. For the first time, this anthology presents various aspects of Nazi persecution of Jehovah's Witnesses, including translated and facsimile documents. This includes a collection of more than twenty letters by Hans Gärtner, a Jehovah's Witness incarcerated in the Dachau and Mauthausen concentration camp (Angela Nerlich and Wolfram Slupina essay).

The final essays in Part A summarize specific aspects of Nazi persecution of Jehovah's Witnesses. Ursula Krause-Schmitt focuses on women's experiences and Hubert Roser investigates regional aspects of persecution in Baden and Württemberg.

We were gratified to be able to add essays by two additional authors (Hans-Hermann Dirksen and Göran Westphal) concerning the persecution of Jehovah's Witnesses in the German Democratic Republic. This is a very new area of research.

Two additional contributions from the perspective of a historian (Detlef Garbe) and from the viewpoint of a staff member of the Public Affairs department of Jehovah's Witnesses in

Germany (Wolfram Slupina) discuss the reasons for the belated attention to the history of persecution of Jehovah's Witnesses.

The contributions in Part B of this anthology focus on the controversies about the documentary video »Stand Firm Against Nazi Assault« produced by the Watch Tower Society and shown at many symposia and exhibitions and the attendant reservations expressed by public officials and other critics.

The purpose of this section is not to provide expert opinions about different aspects of the documentary video and to reach a conclusive judgement. Our intention is to provide diverse views that can be compared. We are especially grateful to Dietrich Hellmund and Lutz Lemhöfer, who agreed to write their opinions. They did this despite the very tight deadlines given to them.

This section is completed by Gabriele Yonan's expert opinion and an essay by one of the directors of the video documentation, Johannes Wrobel of the History Archive of the Watch Tower Society in Selters. These essays are supplemented by a presentation about responses to the screenings of the documentary video »Jehovah's Witnesses Stand Firm Against Nazi Assault« (Wolfram Slupina).

In her essay, Jolene Chu strives to highlight parallel developments in the persecution of the Jews and of Jehovah's Witnesses.

Two essays introduce and conclude Part B of this anthology; they provide information about Jehovah's Witnesses today (Walter Köbe) and an evaluation of the significance of Nazi persecution by a staff member from the New York headquarters of the Watch Tower Society in Brooklyn and the responsible director of the documentary video (James Pellechia).

To enable the reader to see the totality of Nazi persecution, a chronology was prepared by Jürgen Harder and Hans Hesse. This chronology and the attached bibliography do not claim to be comprehensive or definitive.[8]

This book project could not have been realized without the assistance and support of many others. We would particularly like to thank Dr. Detlef Garbe and Dr. Hubert Roser for their willingness to help and their critical suggestions. We also wish to acknowledge the assistance of Wolfram Slupina and Johannes Wrobel as well as their colleagues from the Watch Tower Society, who provided us with documents, responded to numerous specific questions, and facilitated solutions to technical problems. I would like to thank Karlo Vegelahn for his assistance in producing the bibliography as well as the publishing house EDITION TEMMEN for their supervision of the project.

Special thanks to the team of translators who worked diligently to produce the English version of the original German text: Angelika Diekmann, Shirley Dommett, Audrey Gedminas, Clarissa Hartung, Stephanie Hartung, Anette Loßner, Hanne Mitchell, Ruth Moreno, Silvia Porzelt, Shirley Quo Vadis, Sally Swan, and Brigitte Weiss.

I owe special thanks to Sybil Milton for undertaking the final editorial reading of the translation. She accomplished this with both excellent mastery of the language and diligence. Unfortunately, her editorial work ceased in October 2000 after her sudden death. We mourn the loss of this great researcher and historian in the field of Nazi history. Sybil Milton's approach to the theme of Nazi persecution was a very special one, and with her death, we lose a weighty voice speaking up in favor of other groups persecuted under the Nazi regime, such as the Sinti and Roma.

Finally, I want to thank the many individuals who provided valuable data about the subject of this anthology. I want especially to credit my wife, Dr. Elke Purpus, who critically reviewed portions of this manuscript, but above all for her patience, composure, and support in many critical phases of this project.

Göttingen, Winter 2000
Hans Hesse

Notes

1   Gertrud Keen, video interview with Loretta Walz, in Moringen Concentration Camp Memorial Archives.
2   *Deutschland-Berichte der SPD (Sopade) 1934–1940*, reprint in 6 vols. (Salzhausen and Frankfurt, 1980), v. 4 (1937), p. 707. Quoted here from Detlef Garbe, *Zwischen Widerstand und Martyrium: Die Zeugen Jehovas im »Dritten Reich«* (Munich, 1997), p. 406.
3   Hanns Lilje, *Im finsteren Tal* (Nuremberg, 1947), p. 64.
4   Garbe, p. 9.
5   Friedrich Zipfel, *Kirchenkampf in Deutschland 1933–1945: Religionsverfolgung und Selbstbehauptung der Kirchen in der nationalsozialistischen Zeit* (Berlin, 1965), p. 176.
6   Detlef Garbe, »Die Verfolgung der Zeugen Jehovas im nationalsozialistischen Deutschland – Ein Überblick,« in *Widerstand aus christlicher Überzeugung: Jehovas Zeugen im Nationalsozialismus; Dokumentation einer Tagung*, sponsored by Kreismuseum Wewelsburg, Fritz Bauer Institut, Bundeszentrale für politische Bildung, ed. by Kirsten John Stucke and Andreas Pflock (Essen, 1998), pp. 16–28, quote at 24.
7   Ibid.
8   A number of additional studies are currently being prepared and are as yet not published. These include:
    – Hans-Hermann Dirksen, Die strafrechtliche Verfolgung der Zeugen Jehovas in der DDR. Dissertation at Greifswald University;
    – Karola Fings, »Himmlers Baubrigaden: Eine Studie über KZ-Außenlager und Käftlingseinsatz unter besonderer Berücksichtigung des Einsatz von Häftlingen in den Kommunen« (Ph.D. Dissertation in preparation at the University of Düsseldorf, includes the larger group of Jehovah's Witnesses in »1. SS-Baubrigade«);
    – Brigitta Hack, »Kinder und Jugendliche in der NS-Zeit am Beispiel der Zeugen Jehovas« (Ph.D. Dissertation in preparation at the University of Mainz);
    – Jürgen Harder and Hans Hesse, »Und wenn ich lebenslang im KZ bleiben müßte...« Die Zeuginnen Jehovas in den Frauen-KZs Moringen, Lichtenburg und Ravensbrück, Essen 2001;
    – Christian Herrmanny, »Die Zeugen Jehovas im Spiegel der Printmedien: Eine Untersuchung zur Selbstdarstellung einer religiösen Sondergruppe im Vergleich mit ihrem Bild in Tagespresse und Nachrichtenmagazinen (Master's thesis at Bochum University, in preparation);
    – Waldemar Hirch, »Die Zeugen Jehovas im Visier des Ministeriums für Staatssicherheit der ehemaligen DDR: Observierungs-, Unterdrückungs- und Zersetzungsmaßnahmen gegen eine Glaubensgemeinschaft« (Ph.D. Dissertation in preparation at Stuttgart University);
    – Eva-Maria Tanja Kloos, »Widerstand der Zeugen Jehovas im ›Dritten Reich': Mit Hinweisen zu methodischen Möglichkeiten und praktischen Anwesndungen im Geschichtsunterricht (first state exam for teachers at Pädagogische Hochschule Ludwigsburg);
    – Andreas Pflock, KZ-Herzogenbusch (Ph.D. Dissertation at Hanover University, in preparation); and
    – Robert Reichel, »Jehovas Zeugen in der DDR: Verbot und Verfolgung einer Glaubensgemeinschaft am Beispiel Chemnitz/Erzgebirge« (State exam in history, Freiburg University).

Part A

Henry Friedlander

Categories of Concentration Camp Prisoners

Shortly after Adolf Hitler's assumption of power on January 30, 1933, the Nazis used the emergency decree of February 28, enacted after the Reichstag fire, to invalidate major parts of the constitution of the Weimar Republic. This Decree for the Protection of the People and the State thus revoked the »inviolability of personal freedom,« which had been firmly established in the constitution under article 114. For the Nazi regime, this decree provided the basis for the imposition of protective custody, aimed at political opponents. »Protective custody,« applied until the end of Nazi rule, was in fact a kind of »police detention« for political reasons. Operating outside the supervision of the courts, the police could imprison opponents of the regime even if they had committed no crime and could order unlimited detention as a preventive measure.[1] Thus the notorious concentration camps first appeared shortly after those February days. At first these were improvised, or »wild,« camps, which were relatively soon dissolved. When war broke out, the large concentration camps newly built by the SS in Germany and Austria were the infamous camps Dachau, Sachsenhausen (Oranienburg), Buchenwald, Flossenbürg, Mauthausen, and the women's concentration camp Ravensbrück.[2]

Political prisoners were the first camp inmates. They were termed »prisoners in protective custody,« as they were committed to the camps under the Gestapo's so-called protective custody order.[3] This group of prisoners included communists, social democrats, as well as unpopular liberal journalists and publishers, and sometimes conservative personal enemies of the Nazi bosses. Communists and the social democrats – the so-called »Marxist enemy« – constituted the overwhelming majority of the political prisoners. Starting in 1937, but often also before that time, the Kripo committed criminals and so-called asocials to the concentration camps. One trend was easily observable: although opposition to the Nazi regime decreased, the number of alleged opponents imprisoned in concentration camps increased; obviously, no direct connection between real opposition and imprisonment existed.[4]

The political prisoners wore red triangles. It was a triangle made of red cloth, which had to be sewn to the breast and the right trouser leg. The inmate number was also sewn on white cloth next to the triangle (only in Auschwitz all inmates, with the exception of German and Austrian non-Jewish inmates, had this number tattooed onto their arms). Each category of prisoners had its own color for the triangle. For example, the color for criminals was green, for »asocials« black, and for homosexuals pink. Gypsies wore a brown triangle, whereas Jews wore an upside-down yellow triangle under the triangle of their arrest category, so that the two triangles together formed the Jewish Star of David. Classification by colored triangles, introduced in the camps by the SS, can be seen as a forerunner of today's »color coding« marketing strategies. In the same way, the most advanced technology was used for registering camp inmates. For registration the SS used so-called Hollerith punch cards and Hollerith machines (a forerunner of modern computers), which were provided by Dehomag, IBM's German subsidiary.[5]

A few Jehovah's Witnesses could be found in the concentration camps right from the beginning, but most were committed between 1935 and 1939. During these years the number of Witnesses increased to at least 10 percent of the number of camp inmates. And in some camps their number increased to an even higher percentage. They were not counted among the political prisoners and naturally could not be counted among the criminals. They were an independent group and wore the purple triangle. They were persecuted, arrested, and committed to the camps, all because of their religious conviction. In this respect they occupied an exceptional position in the concentration camps. The purple triangle thus stood only for Jehovah's Witnesses and not for all prisoners of the religious opposition. Unlike Catholic priests, who wore the red triangle of the political prisoners, the Witnesses were not classified as »political« enemies.

The Witnesses did not belong to any of the big German religious denominations — the Protestant or Catholic churches — and they were persecuted not only because of their beliefs but also because of their non-affiliation. This was also an important factor in the concentration camps. While the other inmates, sometimes even the SS, acknowledged their firm conviction, the Witnesses were also viewed as outsiders.

In Nazi Germany the Witnesses were persecuted and committed to the camps because their religious conviction forced them not to join in, that is, they refused to give the »Hitler salute,« to join the Nazi party, and to serve in the Wehrmacht. The totalitarian regime viewed this behavior as politically dangerous, because the refusal to participate was not an individual but a group decision. But since the Witnesses were politically uninvolved German »Aryans,« the SS believed that they could be reformed. For this reason they could be released from the camps as soon as they signed a declaration renouncing their faith, leaving their church, and denouncing their former fellow believers. Most Witnesses did not accept this offer. The ability of the Witnesses to decline their release from custody, and thus to stay »voluntarily« in the camps, was made possible by the fact that each Witness received backing and support from their religious community.[6]

In general, Jews were not committed to the concentration camps during the 1930s. Of course, Jews were arrested and taken to the camps because they were communists or social democrats, or belonged to other proscribed groups, but not just because they were Jews — that tended to be the exception. During the 1930s, the concentration camps were not yet designed to serve as places of detention for Jews and Gypsies, the regime's »biological« enemies.[7] The wave of arrests after Crystal Night was a one-time exception. In 1942, the Reich Leader SS Heinrich Himmler even ordered the transfer of all Jewish prisoners from camps located within the Reich to the East, namely to Auschwitz. In this way even the concentration camps in Germany and Austria were to be »free of Jews.«[8]

The war resulted in a vast increase in the size and number of the concentration camps. Not only did the number of inmates increase in every camp, but also new camps were established to receive the large number of prisoners from all occupied countries. These new inmates were mostly members or potential members of the resistance and wore the red triangle, designed for political opponents, with the first letter of their nation's name imprinted on the triangle. The newly established concentration camps were situated in the border regions of the Reich or in the occupied territories near the Reich's border. The camps Gross-Rosen in Lower Silesia, Auschwitz in Upper Silesia, Stutthof near Danzig, as well as Majdanek in Lublin (originally designed as an SS and police base in eastern Poland) were opened as camps for Polish prisoners. The Neuengamme concentration camp near Hamburg was designed for prisoners from the West. Previously a subcamp of Sachsenhausen, Neuengamme became independent in 1940; in the same way, Wewelsburg, another Sachsenhausen subcamp also became independent with the name Niederhagen. Somewhat later, the camps Natzweiler-Struthof in Alsace and Hertogenbosch-Vught in the Netherlands were also opened for inmates from the West. During the second half of the war, the SS needed additional camps for the exploitation of inmate labor. Thus the camps Vaivara and Klooga opened in Estonia, Riga-Kaiserwald in Latvia, and Cracow-Plaszow in Poland. In the territory of the Reich, the Buchenwald subcamp Dora, where inmates labored on the production of V-weapons in underground caverns, was transformed into the independent Dora-Mittelbau concentration camp. And the POW camp Bergen-Belsen, which had also served as an exchange camp, was converted into a concentration camp at the end of 1944; it was to serve as a reception camp for transports of evacuated inmates from the East.[9]

A great deal changed in the concentration camps during the war. Right in the beginning, members of the SS Death's Head units were drafted into the Waffen-SS; they made up the Death's Head Division and later also served in many different divisions of the Waffen-SS. Those who stayed behind joined the Waffen-SS reserve and thereafter wore the green SS field uniform. During the war, members of the SS often shifted between the Waffen-SS and the concentration camps. Camp guards were often transferred to the fighting units, and those wounded or otherwise unfit for active service were often transferred to the camps. Later many ethnic German SS volunteers were also assigned as guards to the camps.[10]

The use of concentration camp prisoners for forced labor became more and more important during the war. Until 1937 labor was used primarily as punishment. For example, inmates had to carry stones from one side to the other and then reverse the procedure. The excellent documentary *Ein Tag* showed this torture through labor in the camps during the 1930s better than any other film. Later, however, the SS decided to use prisoners as a labor force. The budget of the SS was limited, public funds could be used only for the governmental tasks of the SS (for example, the concentration camps or the security police), and many SS formations (for example, the SD) had to be paid from party funds. As the SS needed money, they wanted to use camp inmates to generate income and founded SS-owned companies in the concentration camps. The Ravensbrück camp was the owner of a toy factory. In Sachsenhausen shoes were tested; the infamous test course at the roll-call square can still be seen there. Various concentration camps had appended factories as, for example, the Gustloff Works at Buchenwald and the Klinker (brick) Works at Neuengamme. But quarries generated the largest income; after all, construction was one of the central fixations of Hitler's Greater German Reich. The SS founded the German Earth and Quarry Works Inc. (*Deutsche Erd- und Steinwerke GmbH*, or DEST), and founded camps at Flossenbürg and Mauthausen in part to take advantage of the nearby quarries.[11] Although productive labor was mainly done by unskilled and thus replaceable inmates, the SS obviously needed skilled workers, and the trained Witnesses were preferred for such skilled work.[12]

The war brought the start of the giant killing operations, at first outside the concentration camps. The assembly line technique of mass murder with gas chambers and crematoria was first introduced in the T4 killing centers Brandenburg, Grafeneck, Hartheim, Bernburg, Sonnenstein, and Hadamar. The first victims were disabled Germans, who were regarded as »not worthy of living.« After the regime observed, in 1940 and 1941, how technically perfect such mass murder could work, it expanded the killings in 1941 to include concentration camp inmates, who were murdered in the T4 centers in a program designated »Operation 14f13.« When the Nazi regime turned from killing the disabled to killing Jews and »Gypsies,« the SS constructed killing centers outside the concentration camps in Kulmhof (Chelmno), and in the camps of Operation Reinhard: Belzec, Sobibor, Treblinka.[13]

But soon mass murder was moved into the concentration camps, which were, after all, organized in such a way that mass murder could take place there. At Auschwitz-Birkenau, and also in the Majdanek camp, mass murder on the T4 model was systematically applied after first being tried out on Soviet POWs in an Auschwitz experiment. There the SS used the already available gas Zyklon B, more dependable than the exhaust gas used at the camps of Operation Reinhard. There the SS also selected healthy young men and women for forced labor, to extract from them last bit of labor. The extermination and forced labor camps, especially Auschwitz-Birkenau, continually provided »human material« that could be wasted in war production.[14] And thus, the concentration camps were integrated into the war industries. In this way, the demand of German industry for cheap labor and the desire of the SS to earn money and to expand its influence complimented each other. The SS and industry made a profit, because camp inmates were far less expensive than other workers. For that reason, the SS Central Office for Economy and Administration (*Wirtschaftsverwaltungshauptamt*, or WVHA) absorbed the Inspectorate of the Concentration Camps as its Office D at the beginning of 1942.[15]

During the years 1943 and 1944, transports of prisoners from the eastern concentration and extermination camps crossed the border of the Reich for forced labor in the German war industry. Everywhere in the Reich, the main concentration camps established subcamps for the armament industry to exploit this new inmate labor force. A great number of these forced laborers were Jewish prisoners, and so the decision of the year 1942 to make the German concentration camps »free of Jews« failed. During the war the great majority of inmates were foreigners. The non-Jewish and non-Gypsy German and Austrian inmates represented a small minority. Because of that, they were an elite class, and the SS employed them as inmate functionaries. The Witnesses, whose number increased as Witnesses were arrested as conscientious objectors, belonged to that elite class and their position also improved. Due to their religious conviction, the Witnesses had the reputation of being especially dependable, and even the SS preferred to use them for confidential tasks.[16]

The end of the German concentration camp system came in the spring of 1945 as the German Wehrmacht faced total defeat. But the end was bloody. The SS did not want to let any living inmates fall into the hands of the Allied troops. Thus began the terrible evacuations, starting with the closing of Auschwitz on January 18, 1945. Vast numbers of prisoners were shot or perished from malnutrition and disease in vastly overcrowded camps and on death marches. This combined with the panic of the SS attempting to reach safety and the simultaneous collapse of the SS command structure.[17] Himmler, who wavered between killing and exchanging prisoners as he attempted to ingratiate himself with the western Allies, even met with the representative of the World Jewish Congress; but he was still not courageous enough to break with Hitler and open the concentration camps.[18] For many inmates the end came too late. As Allied troops liberated the survivors at the end of April and the beginning of May, they observed the results of Nazi policies as they saw, for example, the mountains of corpses at the evacuation camp Bergen-Belsen or on the evacuation ships in the bay of Lübeck.[19]

Notes

1 Nuremberg Docs. PS-775, PS-779, PS-1430, PS-1723. See also Karl Dietrich Bracher, Wolfgang Sauer, and Gerhard Schulz, *Die nationalsozialistische Machtergreifung: Studien zur Errichtung des totalitären Herrschaftssystems in Deutschland, 1933-1934* (Cologne and Opladen, 1960), pp. 82-88.

2 For a summary of history and structure of the Nazi German concentration camps, see the books written just after the war by Eugen Kogon, *Der SS-Staat: Das System der deutschen Konzentrationslager* (Frankfurt, 1946), English ed. as *The Theory and Practice of Hell* (New York, 1950), and Benedikt Kautsky, *Teufel und Verdammte: Erfahrungen und Erkenntnisse aus sieben Jahren in deutschen Konzentrationslagern* (Zurich, 1946), as well as studies published later such as, for example, Klaus Drobisch and Günther Wieland, *System der NS-Konzentrationslager, 1993-1939* (Berlin, 1993); Martin Broszat, »Nationalsozialistische Konzentrationslager 1933-1945,« in Hans Buchheim and others, *Anatomie des SS-Staates,* 2 vols. (Munich, 1967), 2: 11-133; and Henry Friedlander, »The Nazi Concentration Camps,« in *Human Responses to the Holocaust,* ed. Michael Ryan (New York and Toronto, 1981), pp. 33-69.

3 The Gestapo (*Geheime Staatspolizei*) was the newly created political police. Its members were recruited from the detective forces, known as the Kripo (*Kriminalpolizei*). Designated as the Security Police (*Sicherheitspolizei,* or Sipo), both Gestapo and Kripo were headed by Reinhard Heydrich, chief of the SS Security Service (SD). See Henry Friedlander, »The SS and Police,« in *Genocide: Critical Issues of the Holocaust,* ed. Alex Grobman, Daniel Landes, and Sybil Milton (New York, 1983), pp. 150-54.

4 See, for example, Falk Pingel, *Häftlinge unter SS-Herrschaft: Widerstand, Selbstbehauptung und Vernichtung im Konzentrationslager* (Hamburg, 1978).

5 Sybil Milton and David Luebke, »Locating the Victim: An Overview of Census-taking, Tabulation Technology, and Persecution in Nazi Germany,« in *IEEE Annals of the History of Computing* 16, no. 3 (Fall 1994): 25-39.

6 See Detlef Garbe, *Zwischen Widerstand und Martyrium: Die Zeugen Jehovas im »Dritten Reich«* (Munich, 1993), and idem, Der lila Winkel: »Die ›Bibelforscher‹ (Jehovah's Witnesses) in den Konzentrationslagern,« *Dauchauer Hefte* 10 (1994): 3-31.

7 See, for example, Uwe Dietrich Adam, *Judenpolitik im »Dritten Reich«* (Düsseldorf, 1979), and Sybil Milton, »Vorstufe zur Vernichtung: Die Zigeunerlager nach 1933,« in *Vierteljahreshefte für Zeitgeschichte* 43, no. 1 (1995): 115-130.

8 See, for example, Kautsky, *Teufel und Verdammte,* p. 43.

9 For a survey, see Comité International de la Croix-Rouge, Service International de Recherches (International Tracing Service — Internationaler Suchdienst), Vorläufiges Verzeichnis der Konzentrationslager und deren Außenkommandos sowie anderer Haftstätten unter dem Reichsführer-SS in Deutschland und deutsch besetzten Gebieten, 1933-1945 (Arolsen, 1969). See also Elizabeth B. White, »Majdanek: Himmler's Terror Outpost in the East,« *Simon Wiesenthal Center Annual* 7 (1990): 3-21; Angela Fiederman, Torsten Heß, and Markus Jaeger, *Das Konzentrationslager Mittelbau Dora: Ein historischer Abriß* (Berlin and Bonn, 1993); and Eberhard Kolb, *Bergen-Belsen: Geschichte des »Aufenthaltslagers,« 1943-1945* (Hanover, 1962).

10 See, for example, Charles W. Sydnor, *Soldiers of Destruction: The SS Death's Head Division, 1933-1945* (Princeton, 1977). See also the *Dienstlaufbahnkarteikarten* in Henry Friedlander and Sybil Milton, eds., *Berlin Document Center,* vol. 11, parts 1-2, of *Archives of the Holocaust,* 2 vols. (New York, 1992).

11 See Enno Georg, *Die wirtschaftlichen Unternehmungen der SS* (Stuttgart, 1963). See also Hans Marsalek, *Die Geschichte des Konzentrationslagers Mauthausen,* 2nd ed. (Vienna, 1980), and Peter Heigl, *Konzentrationslager Flossenbürg in Geschichte und Gegenwart* (Regensburg, 1989).

12 Detlef Garbe, »Der lila Winkel,« pp. 22-25.

13 See Henry Friedlander, *The Origins of Nazi Genocide: From Euthanasia to the Final Solution* (Chapel Hill, 1995). The murder of the disabled was directed by the Chancellery of the Führer, which hid behind various front organizations, with their headquarters in a confiscated villa at Tiergarten Street No. 4; the killing enterprise was therefore known as Operation T4 or simply as T4.

14 See Eugen Kogon, Hermann Langbein, and Adalbert Rückerl, eds., *Nationalsozialistische Massentötungen durch Giftgas: Eine Dokumentation* (Frankfurt, 1983). See also Hermann Langbein, *Menschen in Auschwitz* (Frankfurt, Berlin, and Vienna, 1980).

15 See Johannes Tuchel, *Konzentrationslager: Organisationsgeschichte und Funktion der »Inspektion der Konzentrationslager,« 1934-1938,* Schriften des Bundesarchivs No. 39 (Boppard on the Rhine, 1991), and idem, *Die Inspektion der Konzentrationslager, 1934-1938: Das System des Terrors,* Schriftenreihe der Stiftung

Brandenburgische Gedenkstätten No. 1 (Berlin, 1994).

16 Detlef Garbe, »Der lila Winkel,« pp. 22–25.

17 See Henry Friedlander, »Darkness and Dawn in 1945: The Nazis, the Allies, and the Survivors,« in *1945 – The Year of Liberation*, publ. of the U.S. Holocaust Memorial Museum (Washington, 1995), pp. 11–35.

18 See, for example, Count Folke Bernadotte, *The Curtain Falls: The Last Days of the Third Reich* (New York, 1945), and Felix Kersten, *The Kersten Memoirs, 1940-1945* (New York, 1957).

19 Eberhard Kolb, *Bergen-Belsen: Geschichte des »Aufenthaltslagers,« 1943-1945* (Hanover, 1962); Rudi Goguel, *Cap Arcona: Report über den Untergang der Häftlingsflotte in der Lübecker Bucht am 3. Mai 1945*, 2nd ed. (Frankfurt, 1982), and Bogdan Suchowiak, *Mai 1945: Die Tragödie der Häftlinge von Neuengamme* (Reinbek near Hamburg, 1985).

Christoph Daxelmüller

Solidarity and the Will to Survive: Religious and Social Behavior of Jehovah's Witnesses in Concentration Camps

Allow me from the outset to raise central questions and to define terminology. Why did Jehovah's Witnesses keep silent for half a century about their suffering and death in Nazi concentration camps? Why did they not use the media to enlighten the public? Why do they not appear in martyrologies of resistance against the violent Nazi regime? Why did it take until 1969, when at least the academic community was made aware of the Witnesses as a result of a short article by the Canadian historian Michael H. Kater?[1] Why did they not claim the same rights as other resistance groups? In 1997, petitioned by relatives, the Berlin Regional Court reversed the sentence of the Reich War Court against Franz Jägerstätter, an Austrian opponent of Nazism, who had been sentenced to death because of his political and religious beliefs. On May 12, 1997, the Department of Justice of the Berlin Senate, declared that the conscientious objector had been sentenced to death as a »political deterrent,« which had also been the case with other verdicts against Jehovah's Witnesses and members of other churches. The Linz Diocese started a beatification process for Jägerstätter, who had been executed on August 9, 1943.[2] But where do Jehovah's Witnesses come in?

Further questions can be added. Why is a folklorist concerned with researching concentration camps and with Jehovah's Witnesses as one of the prisoner groups? The connection between folklore and a more contemporary historical investigation of the concentration camp system is two-fold: on the one hand, the role of devoutness among prisoners, and on the other hand, the loss of devoutness in view of the senseless suffering and death in a man-made hell.[3]

Devout prisoners, such as priests in Dachau, often interpreted sacrificial death as an atonement for the sins of humanity and the era. This necessitates an analysis of devoutness, its fortification and breakdown, a theme that runs not only through the autobiographical accounts of priests from the two major denominations. In an important and leading essay about »Strategies of Devoutness in Subcultures,« based on his paper at the Austrian Folklore conference in Graz in 1989, Roland Girtler pointed out that »real devoutness ... in prison ... would be more likely seen in a negative way.«[4] In the discussion that followed, Girtler went a step further stating that in prison, the devout *Betschwester* (»praying sister«) could be exposed to loss of life and limb. Although the situation cannot be compared, this thesis can also be applied to the concentration camp system in which priests and believers, and not least Jehovah's Witnesses, found themselves exposed to specific harassment and torture because of their religious convictions. Such torture manifested itself as psychological brutality rather than physical violence. The perpetrators insulted the Bible Students calling them »heaven's comedians,« »Bible worms,« or »Jordan-assholes.« In 1935, the SS ordered fifteen Jehovah's Witnesses who had been incarcerated in the Esterwegen concentration camp, to kneel in a circle and sing their »Song of the Faithful« to thank »Jehovah for his generosity.« The camp personnel laughed at the singers' helplessness in view of the stanza: »Thus speaks Jehovah: My arm will help you.«[5]

Devoutness also has a very personal nature, something which has been tabooed in the twentieth century and about which people do not like to speak. Hence the value judgements, for example from Michael Moll, a scholar of German language and literature, for whom Christian concentration camp literature seemed »naive,« »ordinary,« »perverse,« »stupid,« »simple,« »unrealistic,« and »illusory.«[6]

This presents an opportunity to explain the methodical approach. A historian relies on files and archives, on lists and the records of death, and the administration of labor and murder. Very little concerning prisoner cultural activities, such as music, found its way into official records of camp administrations, and when it did, as for example the women's orchestra at Auschwitz[7] or the bands, it was used as an alibi and deception for the outside world.[8] Except for individual activities in the Dachau clergy barracks, there are no records concerning devoutness; it was a hidden and private concern, and, moreover, it was extremely dangerous. The perpetrators were not interested in the structure of a religious life, and the Nazi Sister Pia in Dachau, holder of the NS »Blood Medallion« with the rank of an SS general, remains a mystery in a mysterious world.[9] Nevertheless, devoutness and religiosity proved to be driving forces in the underground and an important aid for survival. When piecing things together archives are a dead end. Instead, we must rely on other, individual reports, which are very subjective, on texts, prisoner statements, and survivors' oral testimony, diary notes, and autobiographies published after liberation. Thus, we must rely on »oral history« or »history from below,« which is less precise than the exact bookkeeping of the camps. However, it is essential to differentiate here between diaries kept during imprisonment and reminiscences revived later during conversations or molded as an autobiography.

Especially survivors' printed literature about concentration camps, which began as thin brochures a few months after liberation in 1945 and subsequently developed in part into extensive inventories of horror, were subject to literary and especially to individual processes for personally dealing with imprisonment and survival, psychologically mastering the past, and giving meaning to lost years and newly regained life, as well as for using memory to contribute to the search for perpetrators.[10] It is obvious that from 1945 to 1950 very detailed and factual autobiographical accounts were published, whereas during the following years — until today — a genre of literature has developed. Even the central documentation center at Yad Vashem in Jerusalem was confronted by the problem of accuracy in survivor testimonies. Already in 1959, one of their most active staff members, Kurt Jakob Ball-Kaduri, initially published his thoughts on this topic in Yad Vashem Studies vol. 3 in Hebrew and English in 1959 and then in German in 1965.[11] He made a very important distinction between »judicial« and »historical« testimonies. »Judicial« truth ought to be so irrefutable as to result in the conviction of the perpetrator, whereas »historical truth« was said to depict the victims subjective view, observing matters that were not of great importance for the jurists. This includes reports about devoutness and solidarity in concentration camps. In the following sections, I am deliberately using statements about Jehovah's Witnesses made by prisoners who did *not* belong to this religious association. This is justified not only by the fact that even today sources about the Witnesses — as well as about homosexuals, Soviet prisoners of war, and prisoners categorized as »asocial« — are anything but satisfactory, but also because of the need for objectivity, with surprising results.[12]

Conflict and Solidarity

The moment one stepped through the camp gate, the first few hours, the first few days in the camp, were the most traumatic for prisoners.[13] Beatings by guards, disinfection, depilation, assignment to frequently overcrowded barracks, nutrition and hygienic conditions were degrading and irritating for civilized persons and today can barely be rationally understood. They entered the camps as strangers, where their names became numbers; they had been torn from families, friends, acquaintances, and other related persons. This traumatic experience could only be moderated if they met other prisoners who initiated them into new survival rituals and cared for these totally disoriented newcomers. Edgar Kupfer-Koberwitz, a journalist and political prisoner, reported an impressive testimony from the Neuengamme concentration camp. A young Jewish prisoner, a Czech tailor, told him early in 1941: »When we Jews from Dachau came to the barrack, the other Jews hid what they had so that they would not have to share. You're shaking your head, but this is the way it was. Outside, we helped each other, but here, where everything is a matter of life and death, everyone wants to save himself first and he forgets about others. But what do you think the Bible Students did? They had to work hard at repairing a water pipe. In this cold weather, they had to stand in icy water all day long. No one understands how they can stand it. They say that Jehovah gives them the strength for this. They urgently need their bread; they are as hungry as we are. But what did they do? They put all the bread together, took one half for themselves and put the other half aside for their fellow believers who had just arrived from Dachau. And they welcomed and kissed them. They prayed before they ate, and they all had radiant and happy faces afterwards. They said that no one was hungry anymore. You see, I said to myself then: These are true Christians, this is the way I had always imagined them. Why can't we be this way? How nice it would have been if our brothers had prepared such a reception for us.«[14]

In his extensive and detailed study about Jehovah's Witnesses in the Third Reich, Detlef Garbe has reconstructed in detail the story of the Bible Students who had been transferred to concentration camps in larger numbers after 1935 and has meticulously depicted their living conditions and survival until 1945.[15] Initially, they constituted a considerable proportion of the total number of »protective custody« prisoners; thus, in October 1933, Jehovah's Witnesses represented 45.9 percent of the 1,350 prisoners in the Moringen women's concentration camp, the second largest group after the communists, and this proportion rose to 89 percent in December 1937.[16] However, the percentage of Witnesses among the camp population dropped noticeably during the war as Jewish deportees and prisoners from occupied countries in northern, western, and eastern Europe increased. In the initial years of the concentration camp system, SS hatred and harassment were aimed especially at Bible Students; this intensified at the beginning of the war because of their refusal to perform military service. Hans Frese recalled: »Some Bible Students were also among those who refused induction into the military because of their faith. One guard was especially crude to them. He invariably cursed them, »these Pharisees who do not want to go to the front so they can brag about being allowed to perform medical service at home, so they are better able to rob the fallen soldiers!«[17]

After 1942, however, their situation noticeably improved: with the internationalization of the camps and the minimal risks of escape, the SS needed older, more experienced prisoners for internal camp administration and organization and Witnesses were used for supervision of outside work crews, labor in SS institutions, as well as for house and office staff. These developments, coupled with the nearly unbreakable solidarity, saved the lives of numerous Jehovah's Witnesses.

Without doubt, Jehovah's Witnesses constituted one of the most resolute communities of solidarity in the conflict zone of the Nazi concentration camps.[18] Nevertheless, it is essential to differentiate between the nature and function of solidly united groups in these conditions, however transitory. To begin with, the individual stages in the development of concentration camps must be taken into consideration, such as the early institutions which served mainly for the consolidation of Nazi power. Among these early institutions, Dachau served as the model concentration camp that provided the pattern for later concentration camps.[19] These camps changed considerably with the outbreak of World War II, and the prisoner society was internationalized with the incarceration of prisoners of war, political opponents from European countries, and above all, by the incarceration of Jews from western and eastern Europe. Finally, we must consider the establishment of killing centers in the East and the subsequent transport of prisoners back to camps within Reich territory as Soviet troops advanced. Furthermore, there is a broad differentiation within the types of internment camps, such as internment camps, transit camps, satellite camps, subsidiary labor camps, and killing centers, small and large scale camps, as well as ghettos.

Moreover, it is a question of endogenous and exogenous factors. Gordon Zahn made a differentiation among victims according to »what they were« (e.g. Jews, Sinti and Roma, Slavs), »what they did« (e.g. criminals, homosexuals, political activists, members of the resistance), and finally »what they refused to do« (e.g. conscientious objectors, Jehovah's Witnesses), although these categories prove to be tenuous.[20] Under this classification system, the clergy of the main Christian confessions, who were mostly imprisoned in Dachau, could be classified both in the second and third categories. In comparison, the sociologist Wolfgang Sofsky differentiates between »*Menschen*« (human beings) and »*Untermenschen*« (inferior persons), thus referring to the perpetrators argumentation and practice. He states that »*Menschen*« had better survival chances, whereas »*Untermenschen*« had minimal survival chances. The first category included »Aryans« from the German Reich and occupied northern Europe, political prisoners, Jehovah's Witnesses, criminals, and asocials; in his categorization, homosexuals are grouped with Jews, Slavs, and »Gypsies,« as well as Soviet prisoners of war and these are classified as »*Untermenschen*.«[21] This categorization also cannot be statistically quantified. Although the essential trait of Jewish prisoners was »being Jewish,« irrespective of other criteria such as national origin (whether Dutch or Hungarian), the classification system and thus the degree of hatred towards each individual prisoner was based on additive factors. »Some German clergy wore the pink triangle for those sentenced on § 175 of the penal code. These unfortunate ones had to suffer harshly from the SS. They were pathologically predisposed individuals who should have been sent to a custodial institution rather than a ›rehabilitation camp.‹ They were individuals with high intellects, but weak willpower, where the female rather than male dominated. They were people who deserved compassion, not loathing.«[22]

Consequently, there was no standardized prisoner belonging to a particular group. The SS worked out a system of symbols, colors, and triangles, a system as simple as it was complete and life-threatening, through which it was possible to categorize and attach almost endless combinations of alleged prisoner offenses, thereby increasing brutality. Numerous testimonies confirm that Kapos and guards knew how to fine tune the spectrum of terror specifically to the prisoner's classification, from public ridicule and cynical humiliation to the threat of corporal punishment and death, to actual physical mistreatment. With the simplicity of Stone Age pictographs, they identified a Jew, a communist, a priest or a Jehovah's Witness, and how they could abuse him physically and psychologically. Thus, prisoners were not subject to standard punishments, but the sum and color of triangles determined treatment, as for example, a priest wearing a triangle for homosexuals or a political prisoner who was also a homosexual and possibly even guilty of a criminal offense and/or of Jewish descent. It can be left to the imagination to calculate the total number of possible combinations, and thus, the variety of violent aggression.

Finally, other partly interchangeable factors led to the emergence of loosely or solidly united groups, utilizing characteristics outside the camp or camp specific determinants. The first type of grouping was determined by national or regional origin, intellectual level, and the resulting motivation to initiate cultural activities in a concentration camp. In addition, there was attachment to an ideological group, i.e. Protestant and Catholic clergymen, Bible Students, communists, social democrats, and members of the resistance. Although social origin (poor, rich) played only a minor role or none at all, it is here that the civilizing processes related to life *before* imprisonment and deportation could lead to the formation of groups inside the concentration camps. Factors intrinsic to the camps included, among others, the situation of deportation and »reception« in the concentration camp; the »barrack, room, table, food, or package cliques,«[23] the work crews, and finally, particular skills as craftsmen but also in musical and artistic fields, which led to entering specific work crews and assignment to camp bands, thereby creating limited possibilities of survival. It is certainly true that the result of belonging to a cohesive group, enabling collective and individual activities during incarceration, including ideological and humanistic ties aimed prospectively for the future, increased the chances of survival in hell; whereas prisoners who lapsed into isolation and passivity, who separated themselves, and looked backwards at life before the camp, were de facto predestined to die.

Nevertheless, here too, the exception became the rule. Let us look at the example of clergy who made differentiations by national and even regional origin as well as denomination among themselves. The heaven of Christian ideology proved to be full of holes, and the slogan of the Roman clergy's universal Catholicism proved a fragile fiction, as is apparent in the case of the Catholic priest Richard Schneider incarcerated in the concentration camp Dachau. In considering his Catholic colleagues, Schneider stated, there was »some aversion to North Germans, particularly east of the Elbe river. … The easygoing Austrians found the Prussian tone offensive.«[24] He at least felt pity for the clergy sent to the camp because of homosexuality.[25]

From a German point of view, the Polish priests in Dachau – the majority of whom were Catholic – found themselves outsiders. According to Schneider, the Polish clergy had certainly made »harrowing blood sacrifices,« and, as a group, were »quite devout,« but some of the lay clergy had set their hearts on »good food and money.« This greed for money was confirmed by German priests who had »worked in Poland, had been arrested there, and transported to Dachau.« On the whole, Schneider felt that the »Polish clergy's attitude to Germans« was one of »discreet hostility.« »From a confessional viewpoint, this was the result of Prussian policy toward Poland on a national level because of the Nazi party's invasion of Poland. They considered any harm done to be correct and theft of food from Germans as no big sin, even if someone took away a whole day's bread ration leaving the person robbed to starve for 24 hours without solid food.«[26]

Not only that, but the German-speaking lay and regular clergy from Czechoslovakia were said to have »many lax elements, who at one time had brought trouble into the camp because of their poor observation of celibacy, and gave offense through their halfheartedness in religious matters.« They seldom went to mass on Sundays, and they read newspapers instead of the breviary. »They read books listed on the Index without hesitation and said that the Index had been repealed for them.«[27] The French secular clergy, similar to the Czechoslovakian secular clergy, were slovenly and nationalistic, always referring to the Germans as »Boches«; even Bishop Gabriel Piguet of Clermont-Ferrand was not an exception.[28] The universal Catholic church splintered into spiritually disharmonious and competing groups and interests in the concentration camp. Some priests, for example, formed a splinter group around Pallotine Josef Kentenich, founder of the Schönstatt movement, who had been arrested for that reason. Schneider said, »His attempt to turn Dachau into a second Schönstadt (sic!) failed because of rejection by a majority of the [incarcerated] priests. The Jesuit Otto Pies received an overwhelming majority against P. Kentenich during the election of a spiritual adviser. This is why P. Kentenich isolated himself with his few adherents, becoming laughing-stocks to some extent. The way in which the Protestant clergy labeled the Schönstadt movement was typical: they called the group ›Our blessed lady's monkeys.‹«[29]

Furthermore, Emil Kiesel, Dachau protective custody prisoner no. 22838, did not speak highly of them.[30] He suffered especially from his clerical colleagues: »To this day I am happy never to have been in a prisoner work crew composed mainly of clergy; I would not have been able to bear it. However, I found so much good among nonecclesiastical prisoners that I was amazed. We got closer to each other as human beings and we were kind to each other.«[31]

Kiesel analyzed the »various group solidarities« in conversation with the Freiburg historian Hugo Ott;[32] he then spoke about his excellent relations with political prisoners, including the communists, socialists, and social democrats. »The communists had a certain predominance because of their seniority in the camp.«[33] Although initially in Dachau, there was some distrust between the communists and clergy resulting from their respective ideologies, Kiesel noted that this situation changed rapidly as they soon realized that externally both groups appeared to be solidly united: »However as time passed, our communist and socialist comrades also noticed that we were prisoners like they were, namely, that we could practice the same comradeship, if not more so. I remember how many relief actions had begun in the priests' barracks, even though we had received only half food rations for a while. ... When our communist prisoners saw that we were not only priests but also human beings on whom you could rely, the relationship between us and these extremely political groups suddenly relaxed.«[34]

The history and the stories about imprisonment, however, reveal that from the basic structure of a future oriented humanitarian ideology in the concrete surroundings of hell – no longer concerned with the goal of realizing paradise in this communist world or in a Christian hereafter – a basic solidarity developed between communists and clergymen, including friendships for life. Dachau prisoner Josef Joos remembered: »At times, the Communists held key positions, and some of them knew how to use this. The Social Democrats toed the line prudently, discreetly, and showed caution, moderation, reasonableness, and humanity. Wherever they held the reins in their hands and for as long as they held them – whether in the camp clerical office, in labor deployment, in the camp library, or in the barracks – they proved their abilities in practical work and especially in human qualities. ... The most interesting person among the communist prisoners was, without doubt, Willi Bader, a transport worker from Ludwigsburg who was block senior in the arrival barrack in 1943–1944. He had one of the earliest Dachau prisoner numbers above his red triangle, namely, prisoner no. 9. This man personified justice and conscientiousness. He was reported to have said: ›Every evening I ask myself whether I have done any injustice to some comrade in the room.‹ He died of typhus in March 1945. The comrades placed some of the first spring flowers on his coffin, in which the burial unit had laid him out. And there were many, including priests, who mourned him.«[35]

Between group solidarity and situational solidarity, there was also the solidarity that arose from absolute misery. This is illustrated by the case of Richard Schneider, born in Hundheim near Wertheim on January 5, 1893, who after May 1, 1930, served as parish administrator in Beuggen, in the Säckingen parish. One year later he was installed there as parish priest. Since he had stated in an election meeting in 1932, »Hitler is no more pure bred than the dogs in Karsau,« he got a taste of the exceptional hatred of the future rulers; nevertheless, this did not stop him from continuing his unyielding criticism of the regime. On November 20, 1940, handcuffed to a Freiburg Jew, he was transported to Dachau, where a prisoner welcomed him in the overcrowded barrack: »I too am from Baden, from Haslach in the Kinzig valley, where Hansjakob comes from.« He was a master painter who had been sent to the concentration camp as a Jehovah's Witness who had refused military service, and he described to Pastor Schneider, the terrible times when he had been beaten and kicked. He was not able to influence Pastor Schneider with his peculiar biblical interpretations, but could infect him with the lice and ulcers that covered his body. During the cold nights, they slept beneath a thin blanket, huddled against each other to stay warm.[36]

Schneider's disapproving attitude towards Jehovah's Witnesses, which was not even mitigated by reference to a common home, nevertheless yielded to the instinct for self-preservation. The only way to bear the cold was to huddle together; thus solidarity occurred as a result of sheer misery.

Devoutness

I thought it was important to illustrate the network of conflicts and solidarities by comparative case studies, thereby illustrating that the limits of prisoner solidarity were narrow and easily strained. It is only against this background that the extraordinary behavior of Jehovah's Witnesses in the concentration camps is apparent.

Hardly any other group of prisoners in Nazi concentration camps showed more distinctly how far pre-camp socialization and civilization patterns determined life and survival in the camps. Their endurance of concentration camp imprisonment was characterized by uncompromisingly placing godly commandments before worldly ones, refusing to give the »Emperor« Hitler what belonged solely to God, declining not only military service but also the use of the Hitler salute and the singing of Nazi songs, the steadfast rejection of food containing blood, and finally, the absolute love of truth. Nevertheless, the almost fundamentalist radicalism with which Jehovah's Witnesses remained true to their religious principles even in the camp, provided fuel for conflict. I have deliberately used the statements of prisoners who did not belong to the Bible Students.

Jehovah's Witnesses' absolute love of truth led to a peculiar situation: Gestapo and SS misused them as informants. The former general secretary of the Lutheran International Union, Hanns Lilje (1899–1977), implicated and arrested for his involvement with the July 20 plot, tells of an encounter with one Jehovah's Witness in his chapter entitled »Comrades«: »The Earnest Bible Students must certainly be included among the religious and Christian groups that made an appearance at this time. Because of their absolute love of truth, the Gestapo readily used them as ›trusties‹ in various prisons. Their love of truth was always so great that they did not even allow for the boundaries of comradeship. Thus it was easy for the Gestapo to supervise other prisoners with their help.«[37]

The religious gap which, in our society at the end of the century, is also a social one – since, among other things, persistent proselytizing activity is feared — does not in any way reduce the deep respect toward Jehovah's Witnesses in the concentration camps. With them, persons found what they had lost, longed for, and sensed could facilitate survival in a deadly environment: an unshakable faith, calmness and composure in enduring suffering, hope for the future, whether reached through the chimney ovens or the gate inscribed with the untruthful words »work makes free.« The survivors' statements are so much alike that it seems as if they had copied each other. They admired the Bible Students' firmness of faith, which never left them in doubt whether there is a God, even though for other prisoners, Jews as well as Christians, He had — in view of this crime — abandoned His creation long ago. Also in Lilje's case, skepticism about the consequences of a literally applied love of truth did not impair his respect for the Bible Students: »They still deserve the kind of respect we owe the ›enthusiasts‹ of the Reformation. Just like them, they made unprecedented blood sacrifices; no Christian community can stand even the slightest comparison with the number of their martyrs. Their massive eschatology enabled them literally to confront death truly unworried, anticipating a better world to come soon. They died in droves until the Gestapo gave up executing them. ... Then, they also served with us and undeniably, carried an element of humanity into the dark house. Not all of them regarded this Evangelical priest kindly, but most of the time they were kind and easy to get along with. Even in their extremely enthusiastic one-sidedness, they were more human than many young SS men who were brutal and shapeless in every respect. Gustav, however, who was responsible for our hallway and whose surname I never got to know, endured eight years of, at times, very hard imprisonment with cheerful Christian composure, unmarked by the brutality of a hostile world. And now, after regaining their freedom, if iron obstinacy appears, once again, to be their predominant characteristic, I must not allow that to prevent me from giving them the praise they deserve. They can claim to be the only large-scale rejecters of military service in the Third Reich, who did this openly and for the sake of their conscience.«[38]

What is almost a summary in praise of Jehovah's Witnesses' steadfastness in the concentration camps is found in Nanda Herbermann's memoirs; she was a protective custody prisoner in the Ravensbrück concentration camp for women, where relatively large numbers of female Witnesses were imprisoned. She got to know two women Bible Students in the camp, »both of whom were white-haired grandmothers nearly seventy years old. They had left their husbands and children and had ended up for their ›faith‹ in the concentration camp, where they lived miserable but heroic lives for more than a decade. They were always gentle and friendly. These two women were assigned to keep the office of the SS senior women's guard clean and also to clean the female guards' roll-call room, the corridors, and office toilets, etc. ... Out of curiosity, I talked with them frequently about their ›faith.‹ There had to be something to it that enabled them to hold so firmly to their beliefs, although they could have signed a declaration stating their resignation from the sect of Bible Students to escape from this hell. Hundreds of these preprinted forms were in the senior guard's office, but the stack of them never decreased in size. Hardly any female Witness signed such a form. I, personally, remember only two cases, two young Dutch women who signed declarations repudiating their faith.«[39]

This is corroborated by Hans Marsálek, who refers to the Mauthausen concentration camp, stating that the Bible Students were the only prisoners »who could definitely have ended their imprisonment by their own action.«[40] During the period from September 29, 1939, when the first group of Jehovah's Witnesses arrived from Dachau, until April 20, 1944, only six German or Austrian Witnesses were said to have been released from imprisonment. »Whether any Jehovah's Witnesses were released after April 20, 1944, is not known, but highly improbable.«[41] According to Marsálek, they were »modest, disciplined, industrious, patient people, who were loyally devoted to their International Association of Bible Students and thus to their faith. They were strictly neutral in illegal political conflicts in the camp. There could be no political cooperation with them, as they refused any activities against the SS, and moreover, none of them intended to escape from the camp.«[42]

Nothing could shake the devoutness of Jehovah's Witnesses in the concentration camps. Particularly with this group, religiousness was the pre-camp motivation' which during incarceration developed into a factor stabilizing identity, dictating their behavior regardless of external circumstances. This resulted in persistent adherence to principles and rituals, to Bible classes, and the work of persuading others, which in a concentration camp could be life-threatening. Their fellow prisoners' attitude to the Witnesses was characterized by reserved fascination. They admired their bravery and stubbornness, and their solidarity and helpfulness; nevertheless, in closer contact, they feared their conversion attempts. For example, Nanda Hebermann stated: »As much as I objected to their view and their faith, they remained firm in their stance, relinquishing nothing, voluntarily enduring superhuman situations even when elderly. Somehow they were naive and their conviction did not match the pace of life in the restless outside world. Still they were well-versed in the Scriptures, not accepting my objections against this or that verse in their Bible. On top of that, they were stubborn and it was impossible to discuss things objectively with them.«[43]

This knowledge of Scriptures also impressed Andreas Rieser, a Catholic priest and prisoner imprisoned in Dachau and later in Buchenwald. He reflected upon the meaning of having a Bible or religious publication in a world of arbitrary camp administrations, where libraries functioned as alibis, cynically supplied with travel literature, although not in an environment that made reading possible. He expressed his admiration for the Witnesses, who put him to shame: »the way these people recited complete chapters of the Holy Scriptures. ... In any case, this unusual acquaintance was a warning for the future: Should you be lucky enough as to be released, read the Book of Books ardently!«[44]

The boundless trust in God, which was never questioned, resulted in an inner optimism and balance that was also noticed by other prisoners. Hebermann said: »Nevertheless, their nature remained cheerful and only a few prisoners in the camp were as optimistic as the Bible Students. They were filled with trust in God that could move mountains. In their barracks, there were no disputes, there was no envy, no jealousy, nor was there disgraceful betrayal among prisoners.«[45]

However, Jehovah's Witnesses were not always assigned their own barracks but were allocated various quarters as prisoner functionaries. For example, in Sachsenhausen they existed together with homosexuals and prisoners from the »Special Department Wehrmacht« in the especially notorious »isolation.«[46] However, wherever they were able to stay together, their readiness for solidarity was particularly obvious and this was decisive for newly arriving prisoners.

Their fellow prisoners remembered Bible Students as honorable, lovable people. Hebermann wrote: »One of the grandmothers who came from Swabia was so pleasant. She had a fresh, kind old woman's face and bright, lively eyes that could still sparkle kindly and cheerfully despite all the horror. When she saw me, she called out ›Nannerle!‹ Her friend, in contrast, was rather sickly and emaciated; the long imprisonment had robbed her of all her strength. But she, too, had this wonderful attitude, although you could see that she was consumed by deep sorrow. Once I found her seated in a hidden corner, weeping and quietly praying: ›O God, help me!

Help my children!‹ I felt so sorry for this lonely grandmother. I could not help her. But since she always suffered from great hunger, I gave her a sizeable piece of cake that evening from a parcel that I had just received. Then, for a moment, her sad expression lifted a bit.«[47]

Here, at the latest, statements begin to be repetitious. Hans Frese, for desertion remanded to military prisons, penitentiaries, and the notorious Moor camps — disputed any solidarity among prisoners — but described the Bible Students, a large number of whom were deported to the Emsland camps after 1935, as »irreproachable in their conduct.« He said that they had »personal courage, openly stood by their views, were not cowards.«[48]

Yet, Jehovah's Witnesses would not have been themselves if, in their unwavering way, they had not attempted to proselytize their fellow prisoners and even some of the guards. When, in 1937 the Esterwegen concentration camp was dissolved, and all of the Emsland camps were placed under the jurisdiction of the Ministry of Justice, numerous Bible Students were transferred there. At times they had to wear white armbands because the guards had been instructed to stop any attempts at proselytizing fellow prisoners. Nevertheless, Jehovah's Witnesses did not let up. In order to differentiate here: Catholic priests also proselytized and baptized since it was within their authority and official responsibilities to do this. A noteworthy daring feat was the ordination of the already mortally ill deacon, Karl Leisner,[49] by the imprisoned bishop Gabriel Piguet of Clermont-Ferrand[50] on December 17, 1944. In the Neuengamme concentration camp, prisoners who were prepared to be baptized by Jehovah's Witnesses were smuggled into work crews assigned to weeding and excavating drainage ditches. There, they would slip, apparently by mistake. Uttering words like: »Now that you have fallen in, you should be dipped in properly,« the Bible Student elder in the work crew grabbed the head of the person willing to be baptized and pushed it under the water, while the SS guards yelled, thinking it was all a joke. Other Jehovah's Witnesses who were at the scene were solemn and prayed silently.[51]

The unwavering stand of Jehovah's Witnesses must not obscure the fact that they also — as this case shows — had to adapt in concentration camps, developing strategies and signals that the perpetrators did not understand. Similar instances have also been reported for believers of other confessions.

In summary, it can be stated that Bible Students came to penitentiaries, prisons, and concentration camps as pacifists. Solidarity among the brothers and sisters guaranteed survival in the death machinery of the concentration camps to only some of the incarcerated Witnesses. Today, we can only roughly estimate the number of those who died in concentration camps and in judicial custody, those slain during Gestapo interrogations, and those who died immediately after liberation because of conditions they had endured in detention. In any case, the number is considerably higher than the rather modest estimates of the Watch Tower Society. As far as is known, about 100-120 Jehovah's Witnesses died in Mauthausen, at least 37 in Neuengamme (near Hamburg), and more than 200 in Sachsenhausen. If we assume that approximately 30 percent of all Bible Students were imprisoned in these three concentration camps, one arrives at the following estimate: Out of the 25,000 to 30,000 persons who professed to belong to the religious association of Jehovah's Witnesses in Germany in 1933, about 10,000 were imprisoned for various durations. Of these, more than 2,000 were remanded to the concentration camps. The death toll among German Jehovah's Witnesses was 1,200, or 60 percent; of these, about 250 were executed by military tribunals for refusing to serve in the military.[52]

In contrast to these estimates, the words of the dead and of survivors speak much more clearly. No other solidly united group was given the same lasting respect as human beings as the

Bible Students, despite the reserve and in fact, openly expressed opposition about their religious convictions. Communists settled their conflicts with Social Democrats, Catholic priests with their Protestant colleagues, prisoners with one another. Hans Frese radically simplified it to a common denominator: »We are not comrades at all; we make each other's life hell. We have to suffer enough from the guards, but our behavior among ourselves is far worse and more unbearable, and in the long run life becomes an ordeal. We have a saying here: ›Conflict among prisoners gives the law its strength.‹«[53] In the prisoners' restless cosmos, however, the Bible Students were an island of peace and hope, equally held in esteem by all prisoners associated with them. Thus, we are compelled to return to the question posed at the outset, asking why, in contrast to other prisoner groups, we waited for nearly half a century before someone started to give an account of the suffering, death, and survival of Jehovah's Witnesses in the Nazi killing machinery — and then, not only to a few experts, but to the general public. Can this possibly be the result of prejudice, an obstacle that we still put in our own way?

Notes

1   Michael H. Kater, »Die Ernsten Bibelforscher im Dritten Reich,« *Vierteljahrshefte für Zeitgeschichte* 17, no. 2 (1969), pp. 181–218.

2   »NS-Todesurteil aufgehoben,« *Altöttinger Liebfrauenbote* v. 97, no. 21 (May 25, 1997), p. 8.

3   Christoph Daxelmüller, »Volksfrömmigkeit im Widerspruch,« in: *Kuckuck: Notizen zu Alltagskultur und Volkskunde* v. 4, no. 2 (1989), pp. 12–16; idem, »Kutur gegen Gewalt: Das Beispiel Konzentrationslager,« in Rolf W. Brednich and Walter Hartinger, eds., *Gewalt in der Kultur*, presentations at the 29th Folklore Conference in Passau 1993, published in *Passauer Studien zur Volkskunde* (Passau, 1994), v. 8, part I, pp. 223–269; idem., »Zum Beispiel ›Konzentrationslager‹: Skizzen zu einer ungewöhnlichen Vermittlungsform,« *Jahrbuch für Volkskunde N.F.* 18 (1995), pp. 11–28; Thomas Rahe, »Jewish Religious Life in the Concentration Camp Bergen-Belsen,« *The Journal of Holocaust Education* 5, nos. 2-3 (1996), pp. 85–121. The research project »Kultur im nationalsozialistischen Konzentrationslagern: Kultur als Überlebenstechnik,« financed by the VW Foundation at the Institute for Folklore of Regensburg University, focuses on »Narrative systems and strategies in oral and published concentration camp survivor reports« (Anita Unterholzner, M.A.); »Jazz and popular music in Nazi concentration camps« (Guido Fackler, M.A.); as well as »Religiosity and Loss of Faith« (Prof. Dr. Christoph Daxelmüller, project director).

4   Roland Girtler, »Strategien der Frömmigkeit in Subkulturen,« in Helmut Eberhart, Edith Hörandner, and Burkhardt Pöttler, eds., *Volksfrömmigkeit*, presentations at the 1989 Austrian Folklore Conference in Graz (Vienna, 1990), Buchreihe der österreichischen Zeitschrift für Volkskunde, N.S., v. 8), pp. 367–388, quotation at p. 382.

5   Valentin Schwan, *Bis auf weiteres* (Darmstadt, 1961), p. 399.

6   Michael Moll, *Gedichte aus nationalsozialistischen Gefängnissen, Ghettos und KZ: Eine kommentierte Anthologie*, unpub. ms. Münster University (1983); idem., *Lyrik in einer entmenschlichten Welt* (Frankfurt am Main, 1988), dissertation Münster University 1987; see Michael Ackermann, ed., »*Unter den Kreuzen von Eisen*«: *Glaube und Literatur in KZ und Exil; Eine Anthologie* (Wuppertal and Zurich, 1989), p. 10.

7   Fania Fénelon, *Das Mädchenorchester in Auschwitz*, 7th ed. (Munich, 1988).

8   For sources, see Guido Fackler, »*Des Lagers Stimme*«: *Musik in den frühen Konzentrationslagern des NS-Regimes (1933-1936)*, unpublished Ph.D. dissertation, Freiburg i.B. (1997), pp. 18f.

9   See Eugen Weiler, ed., Die Geistlichen in Dachau (vol. 2) sowie in anderen Konzentrationslagern und Gefängnissen. Personal Papers of Pastor Emil Thoma, Tengen-Wiechs, n.d. (1982), pp. 397f.

10   See Michael Pollak, *Die Grenzen des Sagbaren: Lebensgeschichten von KZ-Überlebenden als Augenzeugenberichte und als Identitätsarbeit*, Studien zur Historischen Sozialwissenschaft vol. 121 (Frankfurt am Main and New York, 1988); Thomas Rahe, »Die Bedeutung der Zeitzeugenberichte für die historische Forschung zur Geschichte der Konzentrations- und Vernichtungslager,« *Beiträge zur Geschichte der nationalsozialistischen Verfolgung in Norddeuschland* 2 (1995), pp. 84–98.

11   Kurt Jakob Ball-Kaduri, »Wert und Grenzen von Erinnerungen und Zeugenberichten als jüdische Quelle der

Hitler-Zeit,« *Zeitschrift für die Geschichte der Juden* 2 (1965), pp. 159-168.

12 Fackler, p. 36.

13 See Viktor Emil Frankl, »Psychohygiene im Notstand: Psychotherapeutische Erfahrungen im Konzentrationslager,« *Hygiene* (Vienna) I (1950-52), pp. 177-186; idem, *... trotzdem Ja zum Leben sagen: Ein Psychologe erlebt das Konzentrationslager* (Munich, 1977, 1979, 1982); and idem, *Ein Psychologe erlebt das Konzentrationslager* (Vienna, 1947).

14 Edgar Kupfer-Koberwitz, *Die Mächtigen und die Hilflosen: Als Häftling in Dachau*, v. 1: *Wie es begann* (Stuttgart, 1957), p. 286; see Detlef Garbe and Sabine Homann, »Jüdische Gefangene in Hamburger Konzentrationslager,« in: Arno Herzig in cooperation with Saskia Rohde, ed., *Die Juden in Hamburg 1590 bis 1990*, v. 2 (Hamburg, 1991), pp. 545-559, quotation at p. 549; see Edgar Kupfer-Koberwitz, *Als Häftling in Dachau*, series of the Bundeszentrale für Heimatdienst 19 (Bonn, 1956).

15 Detlef Garbe, *Zwischen Widerstand und Martyrium: Die Zeugen Jehovas im »Dritten Reich«* (Munich, 1994), pp. 394-478; see David J. Diephouse's review in http://h-net.msu.edu/german/books/reviews/diephouse1.html (October 8, 1997); see also Detlef Garbe, »Die ›vergessenen‹ Opfer,« in: *Verachtet – verfolgt – vernichtet* (Hamburg, 1988), pp. 5-13; idem, »›Gott mehr gehorchen als den Menschen‹: Neuzeitliche Christenverfolgung im nationalsozialistischen Hamburg,« ibid., pp. 172-219.

16 See essay by Harder and Hesse in this anthology.

17 Hans Frese, *Bremsklötze am Siegeswagen der Nation: Erinnerungen eines Deserteurs an Militärgefängnisse, Zuchthäuser und Moorlager in den Jahren 1941-1945*, ed. with supplementary essays by Fietje Ausländer and Norbert Haase, DIZ series, v. 1 (Bremen, 1989), p. 79.

18 See Christine Elizabeth King, *The Nazi State and the New Religions: Five Case Studies in Non-Conformity* (New York and Toronto, 1982); idem, »Strategies for Survival: An Examination of the History of Five Christian Sects in Germany, 1933-1945,« *Journal of Contemporary History* 14 (1979), pp. 211-233.

19 See Fackler, p. 36.

20 *Awake!*, April 8, 1989, p. 12.

21 Wolfgang Sofsky, *Die Ordnung des Terrors: Das Konzentrationslager* (Frankfurt am Main, 1993), p. 140.

22 Richard Schneider, »Bericht des Pfarrers Richard Schneider über seine Erlebnisse im Konzentrationslager Dachau,« in: *Freiburger Diözesan-Archiv* 90, Dritte Folge 22 (1970), pp. 24-51, quote at p. 41.

23 Fackler, p. 209.

24 Schneider, pp. 40f.

25 Ibid., p. 41.

26 Ibid., p. 40.

27 Ibid., p. 41.

28 Ibid., p. 42.

29 Ibid., pp. 42-43. Josef Kentenich SAC was deported to Dachau on March 13, 1941 and liberated on April 6, 1945. Because of his protest against the dissolution of a Jesuit monastery, Jesuit father Otto Pies was incarcerated at Dachau on August 2, 1941, and liberated on March 27, 1945.

30 (Emil Kiesel), »Schutzhäftling Nr. 22838 KZ Dachau,« in: *Freiburger Diözesan-Archiv* 90, Dritte Folge 22 (1970), pp. 52-58, quote at pp. 55f.

31 Ibid., p. 58.

32 Hugo Ott, interview (with Emil Kiesel, supplemented by the author), in: *Freiburger Diözesan-Archiv* 90, Dritte Folge 22 (1970), pp. 59-81, quote at p. 69.

33 Ibid., p. 69.

34 Ibid., p. 70.

35 Josef Joos, *Leben auf Widerruf: Begegnungen und Beobachtungen im K.Z. Dachau 1941-1945* (Olten, 1946), p. 83.

36 Schneider, p. 29.

37 Hanns Lilje, *Im finstern Tal*, 2nd ed. (Nuremberg, 1948), pp. 58f. Making confession to Catholic clergy was considered a popular method of spying; thus, Franz Ballhorn wrote in his diary on November 27, 1942: »The consequences of militant atheists' spying have already been oppressive measures, blasphemy, slaps in the face, and punishment transports. For many informers, confession is merely a ritual to draw out secrets which are passed on twisted and distorted. This does not stop our Servants of God from following the apostles' call, here where they are fully in His anguished breath«; quoted in Ackermann, p. 45.

38 Lilje, p. 59.

39 Nanda Hebermann, *Der gesegnete Abgrund: Schutzhäftling Nr. 6582 im Frauenkonzentrationslager*

Ravensbrück (Nuremberg, Bamberg, and Passau, 1946), p. 178.

40 Hans Marsálek, *Die Geschichte des Konzentrationslagers Mauthausen: Dokumentation*, 3rd ed. (Vienna, 1995), p. 281.

41 Ibid.

42 Ibid., p. 282.

43 Hebermann, p. 178.

44 Josef Fattinger, *Kirche in Ketten: Die Predigt des Blutes und der Tränen: Zeitgemäße Beispielsammlung aus den Jahren 1938 bis 1945* (Innsbruck, 1949), p. 36.

45 Hebermann, pp. 178f.

46 Alfred Hellriegel with Harry Naujoks, *Mein Leben in Sachsenhausen 1936-1942: Erinnerungen eines ehemaligen Lagerältesten* (Cologne, 1987), p. 183.

47 Hebermann, p. 179.

48 Frese, p. 79.

49 Karl Leisner, born in Münster on February 29, 1915, was deported to Sachsenhausen on March 16, 1940, and to Dachau on December 14, 1940. The ordination took place on December 17, 1944. Leisner briefly survived liberation on April 29, 1945; he died in the Planegg sanitorium on August 12, 1945. See Weiler, p. 406. For Leisner, see Otto Pies (SJ), »Karl Leisner,« in Weiler, pp. 967ff.; idem, *Stephanus heute: Karl Leisner, Priester und Opfer des KZ* (Leipzig, 1964); idem, *Geweihte Hände in Fesseln: Priesterweihe im KZ* (Kevelaer, 1959).

50 Gabriel Piguet, born on February 24, 1887, as a member of the resistance was initially deported to Natzweiler (Struthof) concentration camp on August 20, 1944 and Dachau on September 6, 1944. On April 24, 1945, he was evacuated on one of the so-called death marches with more than a hundred fellow prisoners to the Tyrol, where he was released; see Weiler, p. 521.

51 Garbe, *Zwischen Widerstand und Martyrium*, p. 478.

52 Ibid., pp. 485-488.

53 Frese, p. 56.

Jürgen Harder and Hans Hesse

Female Jehovah's Witnesses in Moringen Women's Concentration Camp: Women's Resistance in Nazi Germany

Introduction

Detlef Garbe analyzed the ratio of men to women in the Jehovah's Witnesses group, concluding »that among the Witnesses proportionally far more women participated in resistance activities than within other religious, social, and political groups, such as the banned parties.«[1] However, there are no specialized studies about female Jehovah's Witnesses, although two essays by Detlef Garbe and Christl Wickert have been published on this subject.[2] Furthermore, there are no specialized studies about the Witnesses as a prisoner group in the women's concentration camps.[3] The same research deficit also applies to the history of the Moringen women's concentration camp.[4] To be sure, a large number of studies have been published during the last few years about women's resistance under the Nazi regime.[5] The female »Bible students«, however, have always been considered a marginal group. This does not reflect the significance of this group, especially in the concentration camps. Until the outbreak of war, they formed the largest prisoner group in the women's concentration camps in Moringen, Lichtenburg, and Ravensbrück.[6] Moreover, communist women prisoners in Moringen openly expressed their respect for the Witnesses: »Time and again, Jehovah's Witnesses were the most courageous.«[7] »They invariably refused to do certain types of work and therefore had to endure very harsh punishments, including denial of food.«[8] They also »talked openly to the camp commandant, telling him to his face that ›Hitler is anti-Christ and devoted to the Devil.‹ As punishment, their Bibles were taken away, but they knew the Bible by heart; they spoke texts out loud together, and assisted each other if some passages had been forgotten.«[9]

Current research does not reflect the availability of archival sources. We have examined 327 prisoner files from the Moringen women's concentration camp,[10] and also analyzed 349 personal forms.[11] The first section of this essay, therefore, focuses on the history of the Moringen women's concentration camp in more detail. This article will then analyze the situation of female Jehovah's Witnesses in Moringen.

1. Moringen Women's Concentration Camp

Moringen is a small town situated near the Solling Hills, in the Northeim rural district near Göttingen. The buildings of the current state hospital are located in the center of the town.

Since 1732, the site had been used for various purposes: initially it was an ophanage; after 1838, it became a »police work house«;[12] in 1885 it was chosen as a »provincial workhouse.« After 1933, three successive concentration camps existed at Moringen: first, it served as an »early« concentration camp with a protective custody section for women from April to No-

Aerial photo of Moringen concentration camp, in the thirties.
Source: Niedersächsisches Landeskrankenhaus Moringen

vember 1933;[13] second, it became a concentration camp for women from 1933 to 1938; and third, it functioned as a »protective custody concentration camp for juveniles« from 1940 to 1945.[14] In 1944, the workhouse closed; until then the workhouse and concentration camp existed concurrently in different sections of the building. After 1945 the barracks of the »protective custody camp for juveniles« and the rest of the building were used as a camp for Polish displaced persons and, after 1948, it again became a provincial workhouse.

A total of 4,300 persons were deported to the Moringen concentration camps. For many, the Moringen concentration camps were the crossroads leading to death and annihilation. It is believed that approximately 10 percent of the prisoners died as a result of inhuman housing conditions in the Moringen juvenile concentration camp.

1.1 Early History

The »protective custody section for women« in the »early« concentration camp at Moringen was the precursor of the Moringen women's concentration camp. Since June 1933, women had been incarcerated as concentration camp inmates in a room of the workhouse hospital. The first two women were the Communists Marie Peix and Hannah Vogt.

As the number of imprisoned women continuously increased, initially from the Hildesheim district and after October 1933 from all Prussian regions except the Rhine province, the so-called women's section of the workhouse became a concentration camp for »protective custody prisoners.« From the first, these women as well as the female workhouse inmates were housed

Courtyard where roll call was held in the early period of Moringen concentration camp.
Photo probably taken in the 1920s. Source: Niedersächsisches Landeskrankenhaus Moringen

separately from the other prisoners. It was a camp within a camp with a separate courtyard (roll call yard is not the correct term) for daily exercise, and with its own administration, etc. Although the SS had no access to this building complex, the »protective custody section for women« nevertheless was part of the concentration camp. Peculiar to Moringen was the relationship between the workhouse and concentration camp. This was exemplified by Hugo Krack, director of the workhouse. The workhouse was responsible for the food supply, housing, »spiritual activity,« and »job creation.« The SS only retained supervision of the male concentration camp prisoners. However, the workhouse director supervised female concentration camp inmates. Although the women's section probably was part of the concentration camp, de facto it was run autonomously by the workhouse director.

With the closing of the men's camp, Hugo Krack became director of the women's concentration camp in November 1933. At that time, there were already 141 women prisoners.[15] With the closing of the men's section,[16] the jurisdiction of the women's camp increased within a few months. After March 1934,[17] when the protective custody section for women at the Brauweiler concentration camp closed, the Moringen women's concentration camp became the central

The women's concentration camp is behind the wall with the clock tower.
Photo probably taken in the 1920s. Source: Niedersächsisches Landeskrankenhaus

women's concentration camp in Prussia. In October 1935, women from Saxony, Thuringia, Hessen-Darmstadt, Bremen, Hamburg, and Braunschweig, but not from Prussia, were also incarcerated in Moringen.[18] After February 1936, women from Bavaria were also brought there.[19] However, no decree has yet been discovered designating Moringen as the central women's concentration camp for the entire Reich.

1.2. The Camp Population

A total of ca. 1,350 women were confined in the Moringen concentration camp during the five years it remained in operation. This number was determined as follows: taking an average of 90 women imprisoned per month, with an average term of four months, would yield a total of 270 women prisoners in Moringen in one year and 1,350 in five years. These figures are probably the upper limit.

This estimate is corroborated by the fact that meanwhile 856 women's names are identified. If these names are added to those names derived from other sources, the total is approximately 1,100 women.[20] This figure is very close to our initial estimate of 1,350 women prisoners. In Lichtenburg, by comparison, there were probably 1,415 women incarcerated during one and a half years.[21] These Moringen statistics differ considerably from the figures stated in existing literature.[22]

1.3. Daily Life (House Regulations, Clothing, Food, Quarters, Labor)

The conditions of detention in Moringen differed considerably from those in the later women's concentration camps. Food was considered utterly inadequate. One female prisoner noted that meals were »very poor, very meager, the most unpleasant I have ever known in my life.«[23] The »house and labor regulations« were essentially based on standard directives in penitentiaries. The director had the following measures available as punishment: reprimand, limitation or denial of privileges permitted under the house regulations, ban on receiving or sending letters and parcels, and isolation in a disciplinary cell.

At this time, inmates in Moringen did not wear uniforms, in contrast to clothing distributed in later women's concentration camps.

The concentration camp inmates were housed in large dormitories and day rooms. In the day rooms, they sat back to back, closely packed on benches without backrests. The prisoner Hanna Elling described this: »Sitting on hard stools without backs was very strenuous. But we figured out how to help ourselves. Almost everyone had her ›backrest.‹ We sat back to back and leaned on each other.«[24] At night, the inmates were taken to dormitories in the attic. Since there was no possibility of heating these rooms, icy cold penetrated through openings in the loose roofing tiles during winter.

The women worked the whole day darning men's clothing, knitting, or working for Winter Welfare (*Winterhilfe*). This monotonous work, during which they were not allowed to talk at all or only in very low voices, was interrupted by a daily half-hour walk in the courtyard. During the summer, some concentration camp inmates were assigned to harvesting at the workhouse farm.

The staff of women guards was recruited from the *NS-Frauenschaft* (Nazi Women's Group). For labor outside the workhouse, the concentration camp director used male guards from the workhouse.

The monotony and uncertainty about their release oppressed the prisoners. This resulted in suicide attempts, but there were also many instances of solidarity among the inmates, corroborated by presents that were made in the camp as gifts for birthdays and similar occasions. Moreover, so-called families were established, groups of women who shared packages and food. Parcels were also sent to prisoners in other concentration camps.

1.4. Prisoner Groups

Before we examine the Jehovah's Witnesses prisoner group in detail, we will first provide a comparative statistical survey.[25] Further, we must define and discuss the term »prisoner group.« In Moringen, prisoners categories did not yet exist unlike the later camps, nor did inmates receive triangular insignias designating the reasons for their arrest (political prisoners - red triangle, criminals - green triangle, Jehovah's Witnesses - purple triangle, or »asocials« - black triangle). Nevertheless, it is possible to identify prisoner groups that can be compared, although it must be explicitly stated that this division is somewhat artificial. There are no problems in defining prisoners who were Jehovah's Witnesses; the same is true for Social Democrats, returning refugees, Communists, and others. Nevertheless, it is extremely difficult to classify the group imprisoned for making »disparaging remarks.« This group included women imprisoned in Moringen because of »inflammatory speech,« »disparaging remarks,« »subversive comments,« »defamation of the Führer,« »depraved behavior,« and »deprecating the Winter Welfare campaign.« Most of these prisoners had been victims of denunciation.[26]

Furthermore, there is not always a clear differentiation between prisoner groups. Several specific instances may illustrate this problem.

1. Several women were confined in the Moringen women's concentration camp for performing abortions. The camp director asked the Gestapo whether they should be classified as »professional criminals,« because they had performed numerous abortions for payment or

whether they should be designated »political prisoners.« The Gestapo identified them as »politicals,« because they had committed a »crime against state population policy.«[27]

2. In another case, a lesbian from Berlin was denounced and imprisoned in Moringen because of »subversive remarks.« She had ostensibly said that Hitler had relations with his deputy, Hess. As a Jew, she was forced to emigrate.[28]

3. Among the so-called violators of racial laws (*Rassenschänder*, literally »race defilers«) was an Aryan secretary employed at the Reich chancellery who, like Lotti Huber, for example, lived with a Jewish man above the age of 60.[29]

4. A porcelain producer was denounced by her son for »antisocial business behavior,« in order to force her from the management. She was imprisoned in the Moringen women's concentration camp. The factory owner had met with her »class enemies« from Berlin Wedding and, as her diary shows, she had considered this as a humiliation.[30]

In general, these problems of definition will never be fully resolved, without destroying comparisons. These cases must still be evaluated.

An analysis of the two sources used in our research reveals the following distribution of prisoner groups:

	1)	% [31]	2)	% [32]	Total	%
Communists	77	23.5	68	19.5	145	21.4
IBV[33]	71	21.7	239	68.5	310	45.9
»Disparaging Remarks«[34]	55	16.8	38	10.9	93	13.8
Returned refugees	39	11.9	–	–	39	5.8
Prostitutes	28	8.6	–	–	28	4.1
»Race Defilers«	24	7.3	2	0.6	26	3.8
»Professional Criminals«	20	6.1	2	0.6	22	3.3
Socialists	10	3.1	–	–	10	1.5
»Welfare«	3	0.9	–	–	3	0.4
Total	**327**	**100**	**349**	**100**	**676**	**100**

The most surprising fact is that Jehovah's Witnesses constituted 45.9 percent, forming the largest prisoner group. This statistical analysis also confirms that in 1937–1938, the prisoner categories of Jewish returning refugees, prostitutes, Social Democrats, and welfare cases, and the small number of »professional criminals« barely existed. »Welfare cases« were evidently a special classification that no longer applied in later years.[35] The possible explanations for other groups are puzzling. The transport lists for inmates to the Lichtenburg concentration camp differentiate only between »political prisoners,« »protective custody prisoners,« and »female professional criminals.« The last transport from the Moringen concentration camp on March 21, 1938, consisted of 107 »protective custody prisoners« and 57 »professional criminals.«[36] One possible explanation is that Hugo Krack, the Moringen camp director, did not count »professional criminals« as concentration camp inmates. In one committal case, to Moringen concentration camp initiated by Bremen welfare officials, Krack classified the prisoner as disciplinary, even though the file was part of the concentration camp.[37]

In any case, explanations are still inadequate and uncertainties are partly attibutable to lacuna in archival sources. We must remember that we have limited data for only about 50 percent of the »protective custody prisoners« in the Moringen women's concentration camp.

2. Female Jehovah's Witnesses

Female Jehovah's Witnesses can first be identified in Moringen women's concentration camp in 1935. They were distributed between 1935 and 1938 as follows:[38]

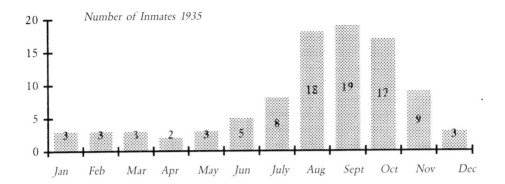

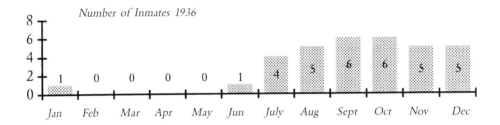

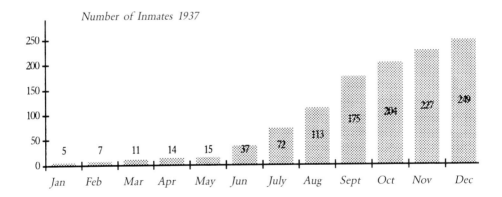

Reports by camp director Hugo Krack about the total number of prisoners are correlated to the number of female Jehovah's Witnesses (the lower figure) for 1937:[39]

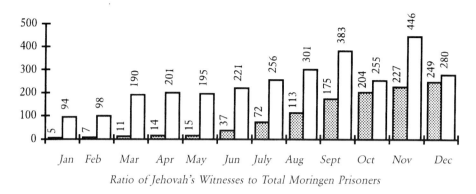

Ratio of Jehovah's Witnesses to Total Moringen Prisoners

In June 1937, the proportion of Jehovah's Witnesses to the total inmate population was 17 percent, in July 28 percent, in August 38 percent, in September 46 percent, in October 80 percent, in November 51 percent, and in December 89 percent. Thus, three waves are observed and will be discussed in the conclusion.

2.1. Places of Origin

The places of origin of the imprisoned women reveal an unusual distribution between urban and rural areas, that is typical for this prisoner group. Prior to their imprisonment, only about 12 percent of the Witnesses in Moringen lived in cities, such as Berlin, Hamburg, or Munich. Except for some local Witness strongholds in Frankfurt am Main, Dresden, and Leipzig, the vast majority of women came from small towns or villages. In particular, the anonymity of big cities made Witness religious activity easier. In smaller towns, it was more difficult to conceal the dissemination of literature in mailboxes and under doormats, missionary activities, and clandestine meetings with fellow believers, from the local population and the authorities. Furthermore, the women and their families were already known as Witnesses before 1933, and especially in provincial and village surroundings, they were closely watched by neighbors and governmental authorities. Thus, many women could be easily arrested during Witness operations, or fell victim to denunciations by their neighbors.

It is also significant that many Witnesses in Moringen came from the eastern areas of Germany, mainly from Saxony.[40]

2.2. Social Structure

The Jehovah's Witnesses imprisoned in Moringen were on average about 45 years old, and thus clearly older than inmates from other prisoner categories.

Approximately half of the Jehovah's Witnesses (52.3 percent) imprisoned in Moringen were married. Of 310 Witnesses incarcerated there, 118 had children.[41] At the time of their arrest, 27 mothers were already single parents.[42] The incarceration of these women had inordinately severe consequences for their children. They were either taken to relatives or associates, or custody was assumed by state welfare authorities. It must be emphasized that these measures also affected large numbers of children of married women, whose husbands had often already been arrested and confined in prisons and concentration camps. In one case, the record proves that the parents lost custody of their child because of their activities as Jehovah's Witnesses.[43]

The social background of the Witnesses was similar to the political prisoners. Approximately one-third had been employed before their arrest:[44] 30.3 percent of these women worked in domestic service, 26.6 percent in the textile business,[45] and 31.2 percent had been workers. Thirteen of the 109 women had jobs that did not match these categories. Five women worked as traveling saleswomen, and six were employed as accountants or clerks. One woman had managed a business until the mid-1920s,[46] and another was a retired post office official.[47] The husbands of those women who were not employed, as far as it can be determined, were either workers or craftsmen.

The vast majority of the Witnesses had attended elementary school, and only a small minority had attended secondary schools.[48] This corresponded to women's educational possibilities at that time.

Thus, it can be concluded that the vast majority of Jehovah's Witnesses in Moringen came from »simple« backgrounds, but that the Jehovah's Witness religious association was not only a »poor man's religion,« as is sometimes asserted in existing literature. We must remember that poverty and the economic ruin of many Witnesses was caused by Nazi persecution.

2.3. Reasons for Confinement of Jehovah's Witnesses in Moringen Concentration Camp

An analysis of the *Schutzhaftbefehle* (warrants for protective custody arrest) found in the personal files suggest the following causes for incarceration in Moringen.

a) Distribution of Literature

Most Jehovah's Witnesses had been arrested for »distributing illegal literature« for the International Bible Students Association and participating in meetings of their religious community.[49] They were either arrested in protective custody and awaited sentencing in court, or the police together with the Gestapo agreed that they were to be arrested and remanded immediately to a concentration camp, if a judicial warrant for their arrest seemed to be uncertain.[50]

b) Missionary Activity

After the religious association of Jehovah's Witnesses had been banned, women still continued to distribute brochures and leaflets from door to door and also talked to strangers to persuade them about their religious beliefs.[51] The women, in part, produced their own propaganda material directly. For example, Elfriede N. personally wrote a leaflet that she displayed while visting homes. One of these circulars was found on her when she was arrested, and was quoted by the Liegnitz district police in their application to the Berlin Gestapo for protective custody: »As one of Jehovah's Witnesses and followers of Jesus, I am here according to his command and proclaim that God's Kingdom is drawing near. We live in times when Jehovah God, the father of the Lord Jesus, will set up a kingdom. The judgment of the world draws near, and now the rulers of this world will be thrown out. All people have to take sides with God if they would like to gain life in the future battle of God, the Almighty. The Bible shows us the way to escape death. And this is life eternal, that they should acknowledge the only true God and the one whom you sent, Jesus Christ.«[52]

The justification for an arrest warrant for »protective custody« of Lina F., issued on July 9, 1937, included the suspicion that she advertised her religious association, thereby justifying her imprisonment: »Despite previous punishment for illegal activity for the International Bible Students Association, there is strong suspicion that she is again publicizing the teachings and ideals of the IBV (International Bible Students Association) through illegal verbal propaganda, thereby disregarding responsibilities to the national community. It is necessary to arrest her in protective custody because the security of the state is directly endangered.«[53]

c) Subscription to Publications

Some Jehovah's Witnesses were no longer active in public after their association was prohibited, but instead concentrated on private »Bible study.« Even if they had not worked openly for the International Bible Students Assocation, they were nevertheless persecuted because their religiously motivated support for their religion was equated with political activities. Thus, the mere receipt or distribution of Bible Student literature within their own religious community was defined as subversive. If discovered, this generally resulted in arrest and, as in the case of Maria K., in arrest and committal to the Moringen women's concentration camp. The »request for protective custody« by the Dresden Gestapo on August 28, 1937, stated: »K. was arrested on August 20, 1937, transferred to the state prosecutors' office in Dresden on August 24, 1937, and returned to the police prison the same day because a magistrate's arrest order had been issued. K. had received and read prohibited IBV (Witness) literature until the beginning of 1937. I request her transfer to a concentration camp.«[54]

d) Private Meetings with Brethren and Sisters in the Faith

Many Jehovah's Witnesses withdrew from public missionary activity and the distribution of literature because of increasing stress from persecution, and limited their religious activities to a private level. Although the state did not have to fear these private meetings, the police and special courts considered these gatherings as subversive, endangering »public peace and order.«

For example, a Munich special court considered Sophie F.'s regular personal conversations with a brother in the faith as sufficient cause to justify a prison term. However, before being sent to prison, Sophie F. was remanded to Moringen. The warrant for her protective custody arrest stipulated the »reasons« for sentencing her to prison: »Mrs. F. is a fanatic adherent of the International Bible Students Association. On December 17, 1936, the Munich special court sentenced her to 3 months imprisonment because she had met three times each week with Max Sch., railroad mechanic, Truderingstr. 99/I, in order to discuss Bible Students' beliefs.«[55] Since she could not be accused of any other crime, the Bavarian political police emphasized the extraordinary danger of this religious group in their justification: »Because of the subversive attitude and recklessness of the Earnest Bible Students, it is the duty of the state to remove any opportunity for these elements to sabotage national interests of the German Reich by imprisoning them in protective custody and thus securing public peace and order.«[56]

e) Central Mailing Addresses

After late 1934, the authorities imposed intensified postal surveillance on all »Bible Students known to the authorities,« in order to obtain a general idea of their contacts and also to prevent mail distribution of the *Watchtower* and other literature. The Witnesses thus estab-

Hulda Schubert, a Jehovah's Witness, born 1875. The photo was taken in Moringen concentration camp. Source: Lower Saxony HSTA Hanover, Hann. 158 Moringen, Acc. 105/96, No. 284.

lished an extensive network of secret mail drops.[57] The men and women involved in these mail drops were individuals who had not previously been publicly active as Jehovah's Witnesses.[58]

The brochures and texts from Germany and abroad, called »spiritual nourishment« by the Witnesses, were first collected at central mailing addresses, and then distributed by courier to other localities, where dissemination to individual communities was organized. After autumn 1934, it grew increasingly difficult to obtain an adequate supply of new literature by mail from abroad, and thus the Witnesses turned to couriers to smuggle literature across Reich borders.[59] These deliveries occured at the German-Czech border as well as at the French and Dutch borders.[60] Additional literature was smuggled through the Saarland until March 1935 and for some time even across regular Swiss border checkpoints into Germany.[61]

Archival sources indicate that at least two women Witnesses had been imprisoned in Moringen for significant participation in such activities. In one case, for example, the justification for protective custody read: »The dressmaker Hedwig D. ... was arrested during the operation against followers of the International Bible Students Association, pursuant to the decree of August 28, 1936. D. has confessed that she provided a central mail address for her brother-in-law, who had been active as district leader of the IBV [International Bible Students Association], although she knew that the IBV had been banned.«[62]

f) Production and Distribution of Literature

Jehovah's Witnesses established illegal printing operations in various localities, in order to attract new members and to distribute literature smuggled in small quantities across the borders into the German Reich. Where printing was not possible because of the absence of equipment, Witnesses prepared carbon copies by typewriter or used simple duplicating machines.[63] The couple Ida and Fritz H. from Bunzlau participated in duplicating and distributing Bible Student literature. They had been arrested by the Liegnitz Gestapo regional office on July 3, 1937.[64] The next day the regional Gestapo office recommended »protective custody« to the Gestapo in Berlin. The note detailed, in passing, that »the couple H. have been conspicuous as ardent Bible Students [Witnesses] for some time in the Bunzlau region. Already in 1934, both of them had been denounced to the police as producers and distributors of Bible Student leaflets.«[65]

In the ensuing trial at the Breslau special court, they were acquitted and secured their

Anna Bäume, a Jehovah's Witness, born 1875. *The photo was taken in Moringen concentration camp. Source: HSTA Hanover, Hann. 158 Moringen, Acc. 105/96, No. 10.*

Liddy Klotsche, a Jehovah's Witness, born 1874. The photo was taken in Moringen concentration camp. Source: HSTA Hanover, Hann. 158 Moringen, Acc. 105/96, No. 185.

freedom for a while, although they immediately resumed their previous activities. In early May 1935, they were discovered distributing handbills, resulting in the search of their apartment. The police discovered approximately 850 advertisement inserts. After another unsuccessful prosecution at the Breslau special court, protective custody and their detention in a concentration camp was requested for both.[66]

g) Reorganization of Local Groups after Waves of Arrest

Many of the women Witnesses incarcerated in Moringen had participated in the reorganization following the mass arrests of 1936 and 1937. They initially held leading positions on a local level and after mid–1936 also assumed similar functions on a regional level.[67] Hermine K. from Baden-Baden was one of the women involved in this reorganization. In 1935, as a travelling representative for a corset factory in the Baden-Baden area, she tried to convert customers to Witness beliefs and was probably been denounced by one of her clients; she was arrested for the first time in summer 1935 and sentenced to six weeks in prison.[68]

After serving her term, Hermine K. was released from prison and immediately resumed activities for the Witnesses. She started working in home care, since this job enabled inconspicuous communication with various individuals. However, the authorities had placed her under surveillance because of her initial conviction and periodically inspected her activities; she thus again fell under suspicion. The grounds for her subsequent arrest cited her activities: »During control checks, it was discovered that her clients included a remarkable number of Bible Students, even former leading members of this sect. It can be assumed that she did not provide home care, but used her visits for prohibited meetings.«[69]

Immediately after her imprisonment, referring to her previous activity, official application was filed for »protective custody« and remanding her to the Moringen concentration camp.

h) Noncompliance with Salutations, Military Service, Air-raid Protection, and Refusal to Participate in Elections

Many of the Jehovah's Witnesses in Moringen passively rejected compliance with state requirements. Their protective custody arrest warrants frequently mentioned their refusal to participate in elections, to give the »Nazi Salute,« and truancy from »air-raid drills.« Further, comments rejecting military service during interrogations by the police and Gestapo, in conjunction with other charges, could result in the incarceration of female Witnesses in a concentration camp.[70]

Moreover, in the case of Berta H., her general attitude of noncompliance was considered evidence of potential risk to the state and, in June 1937, a protective custody warrant was issued after she had completed serving a two-month jail sentence. »The jail sentence did not convince H. to renounce the false IBV [International Bible Students] doctrine. She does not recognize state institutions and government measures. She rejects participation in elections, the military service law, and refuses the German greeting. She also refuses to acknowledge the protective custody order and refuses to sign it. H. is unteachable and it can certainly be assumed that, if released, she will continue to support the goals of the illegal International Bible Students Association. I therefore request the extension of protective custody and transfer to a concentration camp.«[71]

2.4. »Declaration of Commitment«

Current literature places special importance on the so-called »declaration of commitment,« (»Verpflichtungserklärungen«) that Witnesses had to sign if they abjured their beliefs.[72] Four such »declarations« were discovered in the prisoner personal files in Moringen. Three of them have the following text: »I pledge, after release from protective custody, to abstain from all subversive and treasonous activities against the State. I have been informed that I cannot claim compensation from the State for being taken into protective custody. If my own security seems threatened, I may voluntarily enter political custody.«[73]

This »declaration« was dated December 14, 1937.[74] Just six days later, on December 20, 1937, other »declaration« texts had already been used in Moringen. After December 20, 1937, the following typewritten addendum was attached to the initial text: »I have been informed about the consequences of renewed activity for the International Bible Students Association. It was brought to my attention that abstaining from propaganda is by no means sufficient, but that I am expected to completely free myself spiritually from the International Bible Students Association. I have been informed that the arrest warrant will be completely annulled only if my conduct is irreproachable, and that otherwise I may expect to be arrested on the slightest provocation.«[75] Thus, this text intensified the earlier declaration. Until then, the declaration had to be signed by all concentration camp inmates and the same wording was used for all prisoners. This December 20 text indicates the adoption of a distinctive procedure, applicable only to Jehovah's Witnesses at Moringen.

This raises two additional questions: 1. How frequently were these »declarations« signed since, in the case of Moringen, only the first version needs to be taken into consideration, since the concentration camp was already being dissolved on December 15, 1937, and thus the new version could not have gained much importance? 2. What connection did signing this »declaration« have on being released from Moringen?

For the first question, it can be established that Moringen held a total of 310 Jehovah's Witnesses. Personal files survived for 71 prisoners,[76] and the first page of the personal file (personal form) exists for 239 prisoners.[77] The latter pages were sent to the Lichtenburg concentration camp. These forms do not indicate that a single Witness had signed a »declaration.« It is assumed that 39 of the 71 women with complete personal files signed »declarations« and had been released before the Moringen women's concentration camp closed. This means that 13 percent of the Witnesses signed such declarations. This figure corresponds roughly to Garbe's data about the Esterwegen concentration camp in 1935.[78] These figures are, however, rather puzzling. Only in the four previously mentioned cases is there any direct reference to the term »declaration.« In all other instances, Hugo Krack stated that a »commitment form« (»Verpflichtungsschein«) had been signed. The existence of this »commitment form,« in turn, cannot be established from the surviving personal records. In one case, we were able to compare the documents from the Gestapo office with the Moringen personal file. Krack, director of the Moringen concentration camp, wrote to the Düsseldorf Gestapo on the day that the Witness Katharina Thoenes had been released, that a signed »commitment form« had been included in the file.[79] He did not mention that a »declaration« had been signed. The »commitment form« is missing in the Düsseldorf files. There is, instead, the »declaration,« dated June 19, 1937, and signed in Moringen concentration camp two days before Katharina Thoenes was released.[80] There is thus reason to believe that the terms »commitment form« and »declaration« refer to the same document. If this were not the case, the percentage of Jehovah's Witnesses who had signed such »declarations« would fall to about 1 percent. This is unlikely and also affects the second question posed above.

For the second question, we can determine that in at least two cases, the »declaration« or »commitment form« had not been signed, although a release had been ordered.[81] In one case the »declaration« had been signed, but the prisoner was not released.[82]

Consequently, it is clear that the »declarations« in Moringen did not have the same significance that they held in the later concentration camps. The individual »conduct« of Jehovah's Witnesses was decisive in Moringen. This conclusion can be documented from the quarterly conduct reports that camp director Hugo Krack wrote the relevant Gestapo offices; in most cases, these reports formed the basis for prisoner releases.

2.5. Conduct Reports

Every three months, concentration camp director, Hugo Krack, had to write conduct reports about concentration camp prisoners to the Gestapo offices that had initiated prosecution. These conduct reports usually ended with recommendations that influenced decisions about the release of the prisoner. In most cases, the decision conformed with Krack's recommendation. Thus, these reports provided Krack with a significant means of repression and control and he used it often.

In order to prepare these conduct reports, Krack established a system of informants among the inmates.[83] The guards, of course, also registered every remark and the conduct of the inmates, reporting their observations to Krack, if necessary. In addition, Hugo Krack, personally interrogated the concentration camp inmates at regular intervals. The women did not necessarily remember these talks as interrogations, but rather as informal conversations. The concentration camp director attached importance to the psychological value of having such conversations in a favorable setting. It is probable that the prisoners did not understand the purpose of these conversations or the significance of their daily behavior.

For the Witness prisoner group, this led to a very homogeneous picture. In the beginning of his reports, Krack usually stated that the respective Witness had »behaved well« or »orderly« and »worked hard,«[84] but then he wrote that the Witnesses were still »pathologically fanatical,«[85] and »unteachable,« and that their »attitude« had not changed.[86] Krack therefore often »left« the release of a Witness »to the discretion [of the Gestapo].«[87]

Some of the reports reveal how humiliating it must have been for some of the imprisoned women who, in desperation, decided to »renounce the ideas of the IBV,« as Krack phrased it:[88] »By (signing) this (declaration), she publicly repudiated the faith in front of other IBV members in the camp.«[89] »I have the impression that she completely changed her mind and has spiritually absolutely freed herself from the ideas of the Bible Students.«[90] »She is cured of these ideas and thus has signed the attached declaration.«[91] »She recognized that their ideas are erroneous.«[92] »While the other Bible Students, out of fanaticism, could not be moved to work despite severe punishments, she deliberately broke with these women immediately.«[93] Marie L. »absolutely freed herself from the ideas of the IBV. She also publicly acknowledged this and declared that she unconditionally pledges loyalty to the National Socialist state.«[94] Meta E. »affirmed to me that she realized that the ideas of the Bible Students are subversive. She stated this publicly.«[95]

Concentration camp director Krack initiated these public humiliations, so that these women would provide »a fine example«[96] and »model.«[97] Krack then recommended the release of these Witnesses »for educational reasons.«[98] At the same time, he explicitly emphasized the need to implement his recommendations: »I therefore urgently request her release, so that the other Bible Students will see that conversion results in release.«[99]

Sometimes Krack also doubted the success of his repressive »educational efforts.« To be sure, he had accepted a pledge from one Witness to stop »subversive activities,« but he still recommended that she be placed under surveillance, »since these women were dominated by considerable fanaticism and her promise is probably only lip service.«[100]

Krack believed that signing the »declaration« was not enough. He wanted the Witnesses to behave accordingly already in the camp. Thus the »declaration« was symbolic of a specific desired compliant behavior to the Nazi regime. The Witnesses should confess publicly and not simply sign a declaration, irrespective of content. Clearly public »repudiation« was more humiliating than signing a declaration, which, at this time, was still relatively inconsequential and ultimately did not obligate them. As already explained, only a few Witnesses followed this path.

2.6. Bible Students' Resistance in Moringen

An overwhelming majority of the Witnesses incarcerated in Moringen did not succumb to the camp director's efforts to convert them. Instead, they showed absolute solidarity and also attempted to continue »professing« their beliefs in the camp.

In the spring of 1935, the number of Jehovah's Witnesses in Moringen concentration camp was still relatively small and they were thus housed together with women from other prisoner categories. Taking advantage of these conditions, individual Witnesses tried to convert other prisoners to their beliefs. Maria C. was discovered doing missionary work, and her punishment by the camp commandant was recorded in her personal file. She was imprisoned in the Moringen concentration camp because she had participated together with two other Witnesses in an Altona meeting on January 11, 1935, to talk about religious teachings.[101] All three participants at this meeting were arrested by the police and interrogated. A request was filed with the Gestapo in Berlin »to take them into protective custody,« and Maria C. was transported to Moringen the same day.

Like other Witnesses, she did not allow imprisonment in a concentration camp to stop her preaching and missionary work required by her religious beliefs' and she apparently continued this activity without delay in the camp. She was discovered doing this, and camp director Hugo Krack punished her with solitary confinement. The director prepared a written report of her conduct on June 14, 1935, including this incident; the report was to be used at a hearing reviewing her detention: »C. has been interned in the concentration camp since January 11, 1935. She belongs to the International Bible Students and is especially fanatic. I was compelled to place her in isolation because she had tried to spread her ideas among other prisoners. She also refuses to give the required German greeting. ... She informed me that she would never give up her ideas even if she had to stay in a concentration camp all her life (sic!).«[102]

This report reveals that director Hugo Krack still viewed the phenomenon of missionary work as an exceptional occurrence at that date, since he referred only to the specific woman and did not refer to the attitude of the entire prisoner group, in contrast to his later »conduct reports.« The camp authorities clearly had limited knowledge about the beliefs of Jehovah's Witnesses, since even a superficial examination of their religious teachings revealed that especially missionizing to gain new members was one of the key tasks of their preaching.

After 1936, the Witnesses in Moringen collectively resisted the commands of camp authorities. Since the women's concentration camp in Moringen had been created, the camp management tried to secure work orders for the imprisoned women. During the winter of 1936–1937, the »women's protective custody camp« in Moringen was required to repair and to alter old clothing donated to the Winter Welfare campaign.

Winter Welfare work was of central importance to the Nazis. On the one hand, immense funds and quantities of material goods were gathered that served to assist those in need, according to the propaganda, but in reality it served mainly to finance preparations for war. On the other hand, the Winter Welfare campaign became an instrument for control and surveillance of German public opinion. Adolf Hitler, in a speech inaugurating Winter Welfare, described its goal and contents as »the belief in national solidarity,«[103] »educating for a German national community,«[104] as well as »teaching the German people to become true National Socialists.«[105]

Anyone who attempted to escape the collections and work for Winter Welfare was considered politically unreliable and was kept under closer surveillance by the authorities. The Witnesses in Moringen considered the labor assignment of sewing for Winter Welfare as direct support of the Nazi regime, and they therefore refused this work as a group in winter 1936. Hugo Krack finally understood the willingness of Jehovah's Witnesses to resist as a group-phenomenon after they had behaved with solidarity. After this date, Witnesses were no longer punished as individuals, but disciplinary measures were directed against all women in this group.

To prevent the spread of noncompliance among all prisoners in the camp and to put the Witnesses under pressure, Hugo Krack isolated them from prisoners with different arrest categories. In a conduct report about one Witness, dated December 1936, the camp director described these incidents: »K. was placed here as one of the Jehovah's Witnesses. She, as well as the other Witnesses here, is intractable. On the contrary, they have a rebellious nature and refuse sewing for Winter Welfare, that I ordered to be carried out in the camp on a large scale. Thus, I felt compelled to isolate the Bible Students in a punishment cell for disciplinary reasons. I leave it up to your judgment, if she should be released under these circumstances.«[106]

An inquiry by the husband of one Witness at the Essen field office of the Düsseldorf Gestapo district office revealed that camp director Krack had already prohibited prisoner mail at the beginning of November.[107] This ban on outside contact, initially declared for the entire camp for three weeks because of »some prisoner improprieties,« continued only for the Witnesses, after they had been physically separated from the other prisoners. Moreover, Witnesses were prohibited from receiving parcels and money for an indefinite period.[108] Thereafter, they could receive neither psychological nor financial support from relatives or friends, since this punishment had cut them off completely from the outside world. Various inquiries by the women's relatives, and Hugo Krack's written reports, reveal that this quarantine of the Witnesses continued for several months.[109]

The records reveal that the camp director did not limit his punishment to harsher imprisonment conditions, but also got personally involved in the »Bible Student problem« by passing a letter from Katharina T.'s husband to the Düsseldorf Gestapo denouncing him as a Jehovah's Witness: »Enclosed please find a letter to the Bible Student T. that I confiscated. The letter is from her husband in Moers. The contents indicate that the entire family is treasonous, and I, therefore, consider it necessary to inform you about the letter.«[110]

Although the imprisoned Jehovah's Witnesses were under enormous strain, since they could not receive information about the fate of their families and friends, and many of them had to cope with the unusual circumstance of being imprisoned, the Witnesses' prisoner group remained almost totally united in refusing to work in any way for Winter Welfare.

Hugo Krack, director of the concentration camp, relented against the Witnesses' tenacity and their continued resistance. In February 1937, he recommended the release of Helene K., and that she should be kept under police surveillance: »K., along with the other incarcerated Bible Students from Saxony, persist in their beliefs despite all punishments and tenaciously refuse to participate in Winter Welfare work. The prohibition of letters and money imposed on them for months has proved to be pointless. I do not believe that K. and the other Bible Students will change. Since they have already been incarcerated in the camp for a relatively long time, I am requesting that you release them, but place them under more severe police surveillance once they are free.«[111]

There is no evidence in the files that Helene K. was released from the Moringen concentration camp.

Also, during the following months until the Moringen women's concentration camp was closed in spring 1938, the camp authorities were not able to stop the »Bible Student problem.« In contrast to earlier years, after 1937 Jehovah's Witnesses were usually no longer released from detention in this camp, because they continued to refuse any work for the Nazi state. Moreover, the persecution of the Witnesses intensified. Since they could not be released from imprisonment and, simultaneously, increasing numbers were arrested in »protective custody« and remanded to Moringen, the group of Jehovah's Witnesses increased enormously among the camp population. After fall 1937, they constituted more than 70 percent of all women prisoners at Moringen.

2.7. Moringen – Lichtenburg – Ravensbrück

At the end of 1937, the women's concentration camp in Moringen was dissolved. The first transport left Moringen for the Lichtenburg concentration camp on December 15, 1937. On February 21 and March 21, 1938, two additional transports followed. A total of 500 women were transferred to the new concentration camp.[112] As previously mentioned, Jehovah's Witnesses were the largest group of concentration camp prisoners. Therefore, they also formed the largest prisoner group in the Lichtenburg concentration camp.[113] There are still no detailed descriptions of the Witness prisoner group either in the Lichtenburg or in the Ravensbrück concentration camp.[114]

It is important to mention one document that has not received much attention in scholarly literature, but that is significant for the persecution of Jehovah's Witnesses in Nazi Germany. On March 6, 1944, Dr. Robert Ritter applied to the President of the Reich Research Council (*Reichsforschungsrat*)[115] »to grant financial support for the fiscal year 1944-1945 for field research on asocials and criminal biology.«[116] After reviewing his current projects, Ritter described his future research. He stated under item 2: »An examination of the genealogical origin of Bible Students has begun in Ravensbrück women's concentration camp, to obtain data about the genetic value of Bible Student families.« What does this sentence really mean? It is probably connected to Himmler's opinion about Jehovah's Witnesses since the beginning of 1943.[117] Himmler was fascinated by the Witnesses' »religious fanaticism«[118] and wanted to utilize this missionary zeal to bring »the idea of defenselessness to the peoples of the Soviet Union.«[119] This fits the logic of »consistent delusion«[120] of Nazi ideologists like Heinrich Himmler to scientifically authenticate these »positive characteristics.« And Robert Ritter was assuredly the right person to uncover possible »positive racial characteristics.«

It seems rather unlikely, but is still possible, that Ritter wanted to open a »new area of research« on his own initiative, to justify the persecution of Jehovah's Witnesses by proving a linkage between Witnesses and »asocial elements« or »asocial families,« his original research topic. However, we cannot completely exclude this possibility.

Nevertheless, it must be noted that there was obviously some attempt to investigate Jehovah's Witnesses based on the scientific methods of Nazi racial biology in Ravensbrück.[121]

3. Conclusion

In summary, our detailed research about Moringen confirms Detlef Garbe's data and conclusions.[122] There were three waves of arrests resulting in an enormous increase of prisoners in the Moringen concentration camp after the summer of 1937. After the second wave of arrests in 1936, more women assumed leading positions[123] and were arrested one year later. But there is an even greater need for analysis here. The justifications for protective custody warrants must be analyzed by year when the person was detained. The same is true for places of origin. Moreover, the proportion of male to female Jehovah's Witnesses in concentration camps should be examined more carefully. A preliminary analysis reveals that in 1935 the proportion of Jehovah's Witnesses in Moringen, a woman's concentration camp, was between 10 percent and 20 percent. In 1936 it dropped to about 5 percent, and again increased to 89 percent in

1937. Comparable figures for Jehovah's Witnesses show that their proportion was generally between five and ten percent.[124]

The analysis of the social structure of Jehovah's Witnesses must be intensified, especially to make comparisons with other concentration camp prisoner groups. We are certain, for example, that the Witnesses were on average 45 years old and thus definitely older than the Communists, on average 37 years old.

It is also remarkable that the Witnesses in Moringen already displayed the same noncompliant behavior and attitude as in the later women's concentration camps. On the one hand, they were disciplined and industrious; but on the other hand, as a group, they consistently refused work or doctrines that conflicted with their religious convictions.[125]

Historiography about the resistance has not reached any consensus about how the religiously-motivated resistance of Jehovah's Witnesses should be evaluated.[126] There is obviously some danger of creating a hierarchy, with politically motivated resistance considered more valuable than religiously motivated resistance. However, resistance by Jehovah's Witnesses reveals that the boundaries between political and religious resistance are flexible.[127]

Resistance by the Witnesses was not gender specific. As with political groups, male Jehovah's Witnesses had a dominant role. Moreover, the question of why so many women became active Witnesses must also be considered. One possible explanation may be that entire families were Jehovah's Witnesses.

There is still a paucity of analysis about this subject. It is, however, unambiguous that female Witnesses assumed a significant, previously ignored, role in anti-Nazi resistance.

Notes

1 Detlef Garbe, *Zwischen Widerstand und Martyrium: Die Zeugen Jehovas im »Dritten Reich,«* 3d ed. (Munich, 1997), p. 503 and note 62, includes data about the high ratio of women among Jehovah's Witnesses.

2 Detlef Garbe, »Kompromißlose Bekennerinnen: Selbstbehauptung und Verweigerung von Bibelforscherinnen,« in Christl Wickert, ed., *Frauen gegen die Diktatur: Widerstand und Verfolgung im nationalsozialistischen Deutschland* (Berlin, 1995), pp. 52–73; Christl Wickert, »Frauen im Hintergrund: das Beispiel von Kommunistinnen und Bibelforscherinnen,« in: Helga Grebing and Christl Wickert, eds., *Das »andere Deutschland« im Widerstand gegen den Nationalsozialismus: Beiträge zur politischen Überwindung der nationalsozialistischen Diktatur im Exil und im Deutschen Reich* (Essen, 1994), pp. 199–224. The master's thesis by Jürgen Harder, »Widerstand und Verfolgung der Bibelforscherinnen im Frauen-KZ Moringen,« typed manuscript, (Göttingen: University of Göttingen, 1997), is also relevant.

3 See Claus Füllberg-Stolberg, »Bedrängt, aber nicht völlig eingeengt – verfolgt, aber nicht verlassen: Gertrud Pötzinger, Zeugin Jehovas,« in: Claus Füllberg-Stolberg and others, eds., *Frauen in Konzentrationslagern: Bergen-Belsen – Ravensbrück* (Bremen, 1994), pp. 321–32.

4 See Ino Arndt, »Das Frauenkonzentrationslager Ravensbrück,« *Dachauer Hefte* 3 (1987), pp. 125–57; citations from the dtv edition (Munich, 1993). See also Hans Hesse, »Und am Anfang war Moringen ...?,« *Gedenkstättenrundbrief der Stiftung Topographie des Terrors*, 3, no. 75 (1997), pp. 13–21. Hans Hesse, Das Frauen-KZ Moringen, Göttingen 2000. Hans Hesse/Jürgen Harder, »Und wenn ich lebenslang im KZ bleiben müßte ...«. Die Zeuginnen Jehovas in den Frauenkonzentrationslagern Moringen, Lichtenburg und Ravensbrück, Essen 2001.

5 See Ingwer Schwensen, »Auswahlbiographie Frauenforschung zum Nationalsozialismus,« *Mittelweg 36* (Zeitschrift des Hamburger Instituts für Sozialforschung), no. 2 (1997), pp. 34–42.

6 For Lichtenburg, see Garbe, *Zwischen Widerstand und Martyrium*, p. 403 and note 335.

7 Moringen Concentration Camp Memorial Archives: Loretta Walz video interview with Gertrud Keen.

8 Dachau Concentration Camp Memorial Archives: Centa Herker-Beimler interview.

9   Lichtenburg Concentration Camp Memorial Archives: Ilse Gostynske, no. 805.

10   Hanover, Lower Saxony State Archives (hereafter HSTA Hanover): Hann. 158 Moringen, Acc. 105/96, nos. 1–327.

11   HSTA Hanover: Hann. 158 Moringen, Acc. 84/82, no. 6, personal forms for female prisoners in protective custody in Moringen, letters A–K; no. 7, letters L–Z, 1937–1938. These personal forms contain the following data: prisoner's name, date of birth, profession, and reason for arrest. These records had been returned to Moringen in 1938, after the prisoners had been transferred to Lichtenburg concentration camp.

12   Wolfgang Ayaß, *Das Arbeitshaus Breitenau* (Kassel, 1992). The Breitenau workhouse has many parallels with Moringen, until the concentration camp opened. See Gunnar Richter, ed., *Breitenau: Zur Geschichte eines nationalsozialistischen Konzentrations- und Arbeitslagers* (Kassel, 1983); and Dietfrid Krause-Vilmar, *Das Konzentrationslager Breitenau: Ein staatliches Schutzhaftlager 1933–34* (Marburg, 1997).

13   For analyses of the »early« concentration camps, see Klaus Drobisch and Günther Wieland, *System der NS-Konzentrationslager 1933–1939* (Berlin: 1993); Hans Hesse, *Das frühe KZ Moringen*, Göttingen 2000; Klaus Mlynek, »Der Aufbau der Geheimen Staatspolizei in Hannover und die Errichtung des Konzentrationslagers Moringen,« in: *Hannover 1933: Eine Großstadt wird nationalsozialistisch* (Hannover, 1981), pp. 65–80. About one-third (33 percent) of all concentration camp inmates were housed in workhouses in Prussia; about 20 percent of concentration camp prisoners throughout the German Reich were held in workhouses.

14   Martin Guse and Andreas Kohrs, *Die »Bewahrung« Jugendlicher im NS-Staat: Ausgrenzung und Internierung am Beispiel der Jugendkonzentrationslager Moringen und Uckermark* (Hildesheim, 1985, Diplomarbeit); Guse and Kohrs, »Zur Entpödagogisierung der Jugendfürsorge in den Jahren 1922–1945,« in: Hans-Uwe Otto and Heinz Sünker, eds., *Soziale Arbeit und Faschismus* (Frankfurt, 1989), pp. 228–49.

15   HSTA Hanover: Hann. 180, Hannover 752, sheet 1951 (pagination illegible). At the same time, 176 men were incarcerated in the concentration camp.

16   They were sent to the Emsland and Oranienburg concentration camps.

17   HSTA Hanover: Hann. 158 Moringen, Acc. 84/82, no. 2, p. 9.

18   Ibid., p. 72.

19   Arndt, »Ravensbrück,« p. 129.

20   HStA Hanover: Hann. 180, Hannover 752, p. 1951: For example, in November (?1937), Friedrich Flohr, commandant of the »early« concentration camp, submitted a report about the camp population including reference to 141 women prisoners. However, very few individual names are known. The same is true for December 1937. This »surplus« was added to the number of women whose names are known.

21   Arndt, »Ravensbrück,« p. 131; Klaus Drobisch, »Frauenkonzentrationslager im Schloß Lichtenburg,« *Dachauer Hefte* 3 (1987), pp. 101–115.

22   Arndt, »Ravensbrück,« pp. 129f. Arndt estimates that the number of inmates per month varied between 50 and 70 women. These statistical differences can be explained by the fact that Arndt did not use the files at HSTA Hanover, Hann. 158 Moringen, Acc. 84/82, no. 1ff.

23   Moringen Concentration Camp Memorial Archives: Loretta Walz video interview with Gertrud Keen.

24   Hanna Elling, quoted in Jutta Freyberg and Ursula Krause-Schmitt, *Moringen-Lichtenburg-Ravensbrück: Frauen im Konzentrationslager 1933–1945* (Frankfurt, 1997), p. 29.

25   Two archival sources were analyzed for these statistics: (1) HSTA Hanover: Hann. 158 Moringen, Acc. 105/96, 327 individual prisoner files; and (2) idem: Hann. 158 Moringen, Acc. 84/82, no. 6, forms for female prisoners, letters A–K; no. 7, letters L–Z, 1937–1938. These files contain a total of 349 names and include data, such as, date prisoner arrived, date of birth, profession, education, date of release, reasons for arrest, and conduct in the concentration camp.

     After the prisoners had been transferred to Lichtenburg concentration camp, the first page of inmate personal files had been returned to the Moringen concentration camp administration. These pages illustrate the last phase of Moringen as a women's concentration camp. It must be realized that in contrast to the information in (1), these women were not released, but were remanded to Lichtenburg concentration camp. The average term of imprisonment refers only to Moringen. In 1937, releases from concentration camps did not take place as frequently as in 1934. A comparison of names from both records did not reveal any overlap.

26   The number of women sent to concentration camps because of denunciations was very large. However, no definitive statistics are available.

27   HSTA Hanover: Hann. 158 Moringen, Acc. 105/96, no. 33, file B. B., pp. 4f.

28   Ibid., no. 47, file E. C., p. 3 (back).

29   Ibid., no. 9, file E. B.

30 Ibid., no. 245, file H. M., p. 1.

31 HSTA Hanover: Hann. 158 Moringen, Acc. 105/96, no. 1–327, personal files.

32 HSTA Hanover: Hann. 158 Moringen, Acc. 84/82, no. 6, personal forms of female protective custody prisoners, letters A-K; no. 7, letters L-Z, 1937–1938.

33 IBV stands for *Internationale Bibelforschervereinigung*, »International Bible Students Association,« i.e., Jehovah's Witnesses.

34 The definition of this group is problematical.

35 It is possible that these cases are hidden in another category.

36 HSTA Hanover: Acc. 84/82, no. 9, lists female protective custody prisoners transferred to Lichtenburg concentration camp, December 1937 – March 1938.

37 HSTA Hanover: Hann. 158 Moringen, Acc. 105/96, no. 89, file S. F.

38 Figures based on HSTA Hanover: Hann. 158 Moringen, Acc. 105/96.

39 Statistics based on HSTA Hanover: Hann. 158 Moringen, Acc. 84/82, no. 2. Krack did not submit figures for October 1937. This number is derived from HSTA Hanover: Hann. 158 Moringen, Acc. 84/82, no. 6 and 7.

40 It was possible to establish from Witness prisoner personal files that 49.8 percent of the Witnesses came from the so-called eastern territories, such as East Prussia, Pomerania, and Saxony. This can be explained by the history of the Witnesses. After 1923, the Witness main office was the »Magdeburg Bible House,« where a large printing plant was opened, thereby facilitating missionary activities, particularly in Saxony.

41 These 118 mothers had a total of 245 children, averaging two children per woman.

42 They were either widowed, divorced, or single.

43 HSTA Düsseldorf: RW 58 - 8433, p. 4.

44 109 women = 34 percent.

45 Twelve of the 29 women in the textile business worked as tailors.

46 HSTA Hanover: Hann. 158 Moringen, Acc. 105/96, no. 133, file Emma H.

47 HSTA Hanover: Hann. 158 Moringen, Acc. 84/82, no. 7, file Martha S.

48 Information about the education of 292 women could be found in the files: 280 had attended only elementary school (96 percent) and twelve women went to secondary schools, such as commercial schools or commercial high schools. Two of the twelve women attended an academic secondary school for girls.

49 HSTA Hanover: Hann. 158 Moringen, Acc. 105/96, no. 90, file Luise F., p. 2, »warrant for protective custody arrest,« dated October 5, 1937. »Mrs. F., since 1937 a member of the International Bible Students Association, continued considerable activity for this sect after it was banned and contributed to its organizational unity by distributing illegal IBV literature as well as by participating in meetings of this secret society.«

50 HSTA Hanover: Hann. 158 Moringen, Acc. 105/96, no. 133, file Emma H., »warrant for protective custody arrest,« dated May 13, 1935. »H. declared that she will continue to witness and to distribute literature of the Bible Students should she again receive some. This individual is known as a fanatic member of the sect, even after its dissolution ... It has been decided not to take her to court, because no order of commitment to prison can be expected.«

51 HSTA Hanover: Hann. 158 Moringen, Acc. 105/96, no. 258, file Elfriede S., »application for protective custody« by the Liegnitz police, dated August 4, 1935. »S. tried to convince people from house to house. She made herself an identification card that she used during her soliciting activities.«

52 HSTA Hanover: Hann. 158 Moringen. Acc. 105/96, no. 253, file Elfriede N., p. 2, »application for protective custody,« dated April 29, 1935.

53 HSTA Hanover: Hann. 158 Moringen, Acc. 105/96, no. 87, file Lina F., p. 6.

54 HSTA Hanover: Hann. 158 Moringen, Acc. 105/96, no. 201, file Helene Maria K., »request for protective custody,« dated August 28, 1937.

55 HSTA Hanover: Hann. 158 Moringen, Acc. 105/96, no. 91, file Sophie F., p. 3, »arrest warrant for protective custody,« dated December 19, 1936.

56 HSTA Hanover: Hann. 158 Moringen, Acc. 105/96, no. 91, file Sophie F., p. 3.

57 Elke Fröhlich, *Die Herausforderungen des Einzelnen: Geschichten über Widerstand und Verfolgung* (Munich, 1983), v. 6 of *Bayern in der NS-Zeit*, pp. 138f.

58 For conspirative techniques by Jehovah's Witnesses, see Garbe, *Zwischen Widerstand und Martyrium*, pp. 215-231.

59 Ernst Wiesner's report in: *1974 Yearbook of Jehovah's Witnesses*, pp. 141f.; Manfred Gebhard, ed., *Die Zeugen Jehovas: Eine Dokumentation über die Wachturmgesellschaft*, licensed edition of first edition published by Urania Verlag in Leipzig (Schwerte/Ruhr, 1971), p. 178.

60 Gerhard Hetzer, »Ernste Bibelforscher in Augsburg,« in: Martin Broszat, ed., *Herrschaft und Gesellschaft im Konflikt*, v. 4 of *Bayern in der NS-Zeit* (Munich, 1981), pp. 621-643; Garbe, *Zwischen Widerstand und Martyrium*, p. 225.

61 Garbe, *Zwischen Widerstand und Martyrium*, p. 225.

62 HSTA Hanover: Hann. 158 Moringen, Acc. 105/96, no. 48, file Hedwig D., p. 5, »justification for protective custody« by the Berlin Gestapo, dated March 18, 1937.

63 Until 1937, Altona, Kiel, and Bremen were known as duplication centers in northern Germany for *Wachtturm*. See Elke Imberger, *Widerstand »von unten«: Widerstand und Dissens aus den Reihen der Arbeiterbewegung und der Zeugen Jehovas in Lübeck und Schleswig-Holstein 1933-1945*, dissertation (Neumünster, 1991), pp. 320f.; *1974 Yearbook of Jehovah's Witnesses* (New York: Watch Tower Bible and Tract Society, 1973), pp. 139f.; Reiner Möller, »Widerstand und Verfolgung in einer agrarisch-kleinstädtischen Region: SPD, KPD und ›Bibelforscher‹ im Kreis Steinbrug 1933-1945,« in: *Zeitschrift für Schleswig-Holsteinische Geschichte* 144 (1988), pp. 125-228, 212; Inge Marßolek and René Ott, *Bremen im Dritten Reich: Anpassung, Widerstand, Verfolgung* (Bremen, 1986), pp. 303f.

In other parts of Germany, literature was printed or duplicated partly with the simplest tools in Berlin, Munich, Karlsruhe, and Mannheim until 1936-1937. See Manfred Gebhard, ed., *Die Zeugen Jehovas: Eine Dokumentation über die Wachturmgesellschaft*, p. 175 (see note 59); *1974 Yearbook of Jehovah's Witnesses*, p. 112; Manfred Koch, »Die kleinen Glaubensgemeinschaften,« in: Erich Mathias and Hermann Weber, eds., *Widerstand gegen den Nationalsozialismus in Mannheim* (Mannheim, 1984), pp. 415-434. Garbe believes that production of literature, rather than courier work, had been increasingly performed by women. Garbe, *Zwischen Widerstand und Martyrium*, p. 227.

64 HSTA Hanover: Hann. 158 Moringen, Acc. 105/96, no. 144, file Ida H., »request for protective custody,« dated July 4, 1935.

65 Ibid.

66 Ibid.

67 *1974 Yearbook of Jehovah's Witnesses*, pp. 160, 179; Imberger, *Widerstand »von unten,«* pp. 305, 312; Garbe, *Zwischen Widerstand und Martyrium*, p. 253.

68 HSTA Hanover: Hann. 158 Moringen, Acc. 105/96, no. 188, file Hermine K., p. 4 b, » request for protective custody,« dated July 9, 1937.

69 Ibid.

70 HSTA Hanover: Hann. 158 Moringen, Acc. 105/96, no. 73, file Marie E., p. 3, »request for protective custody,« dated August 10, 1937, »She rejected governmental requirements, such as the military service law, air-raid drills, and participation in elections using the rationale that she could not burden her conscience. She also cannot accept the greeting ›Heil Hitler,‹ because all salvation emanates from God.« Ibid., no. 186, file Meta K., p. 5, »protective custody order« dated July 15, 1937, »she does not acknowledge the German greeting, nor does she participate in elections. She has given her unswerving allegiance to her God. She refuses to accept and sign the protective custody order.«

71 HSTA Hanover: Hann. 158 Moringen, Acc. 105/96, no. 124, file Berta H., p. 5, »protective custody order,« dated June 11, 1937.

72 Garbe, *Zwischen Widerstand und Martyrium*, 302ff. Garbe uses the term »retractions« (»Revers«). The text of this »declaration« in Moringen is not known.

73 HSTA Hanover: Hann. 158 Moringen, Acc. 105/96, no. 83, file Alma F.

74 The second identical »declaration« was dated June 18, 1937. HSTA Hanover: Hann. 158 Moringen, Acc. 105/96, no. 311, file Rosina S. Ibid., no. 10, file Anna B. contains another »declaration« dated December 4, 1937.

75 HSTA Hanover: Hann. 158 Moringen, Acc. 105/96, no. 309, file Herta S.

76 HSTA Hanover: Hann. 158 Moringen, Acc. 105/96, nos. 1-327.

77 HSTA Hanover: Hann. 158 Moringen, Acc. 84/82, no. 6 personal forms of female inmates in protective custody, letters A-K; no. 7, letters L-Z, 1937-1938.

78 Garbe, *Zwischen Widerstand und Martyrium*, p. 305, and note 324. »It is believed that in Esterwegen, 13 of 120 imprisoned Witnesses had signed in 1935, or approximately one in ten.« Normally the figures were much higher. According to Düsseldorf Gestapo files, more than half signed. See Garbe, note 333.

79 HSTA Hanover: Hann. 158 Moringen, Acc. 105/96, no. 317, file Katharina Thoenes, p. 34, letter dated June 21, 1937.

80 HSTA Düsseldorf: RW 58-8433, p. 59.

81 HSTA Hanover: Hann. 158 Moringen, Acc. 105/96, nos. 40 and 144.

82 HSTA Hanover: Hann. 158 Moringen, Acc. 105/96, no. 88, file Berta F. On November 6, 1937, she had signed the »declaration,« but no order had been issued to release her; concentration camp director Krack sent a reminder on December 23, 1937, that Berta F. had renounced her faith and therefore was to be released. The case became more complex when Berta F. withdrew her renunciation, see letter from Krack dated January 8, 1938: »Since she does not want to free herself from these ideas, she cannot expect to be released for the moment.« One month later, she was nevertheless released.

83 Statements by former concentration camp inmates.

84 See, for example, HSTA Hanover: Hann. 158 Moringen, Acc. 105/96, nos. 310, 317, 57, 146.

85 Ibid., no. 102.

86 Ibid., nos. 310, 117, 144.

87 Ibid., nos. 310, 96.

88 Ibid., no. 239.

89 Ibid., no. 284.

90 Ibid., no. 57.

91 Ibid., no. 73.

92 Ibid., no. 84.

93 Ibid., no. 91.

94 Ibid., no. 213.

95 Ibid., no. 70.

96 Ibid., nos. 70 and 86.

97 Ibid., no. 91.

98 Ibid., nos. 284, 84, 213, 91.

99 Ibid., no. 124.

100 Ibid., no. 102.

101 HSTA Hanover: Hann. 158 Moringen, Acc. 105/96, no. 40, file Maria C., »request for protective custody« from Gestapo local office in Altona, dated January 14, 1935.

102 HSTA Hanover: Hann. 158 Moringen, Acc. 105/96, no. 40, file Maria C., report [of conduct] by camp director Krack, dated June 14, 1935.

103 Adolf Hilter speech inaugurating Winter Welfare in 1933–1934, see Ernst Wulf, »Das Winterhilfswerk des Deutschen Volkes,« in: Schriftenreihe der NSDAP, Gruppe II: Deutsche Arbeit (Berlin, 1940), p. 12.

104 Ibid., p. 11.

105 Ibid., p. 12.

106 HSTA Hanover: Hann. 158 Moringen, Acc. 105/96, no. 178, file Helene K., p. 13, Krack's report dated December 15, 1936.

107 HSTA Düsseldorf: RW 58-8433, file Katharina Thoenes, letter from Heinrich Thoenes to the Essen field office of the Düsseldorf Gestapo district, November 26, 1936; HSTA Hanover: Hann. 158 Moringen, Acc. 105/96, no. 317, file Katharina Thoenes, p. 14, letter from Essen field office of the Düsseldorf Gestapo district to Moringen concentration camp administration, dated December 2, 1936.

108 HSTA Hanover: Hann. 158 Moringen, Acc. 105/96, no. 317, file Katharina Thoenes, p. 15, Krack's letter to the Düsseldorf Gestapo, dated December 4, 1936.

109 HSTA Hanover: Hann. 158 Moringen, Acc. 105/96, no. 291, file Minna S., p. 10, inquiry from her husband on January 20, 1937: »The person signing this asks for immediate response, since I sent my wife ten marks some weeks ago, and I have not heard anything. I would like to know if she is still in the camp and whether she received the money.«

110 HSTA Hanover: Hann. 158 Moringen, Acc. 105/96, no. 317, file Katharina Thoenes, p. 13, letter from Krack to Düsseldorf Gestapo, dated November 30, 1936.

111 HSTA Hanover: Hann. 158 Moringen, Acc. 105/96, no. 178, file Helene K., p. 15, report by Krack, dated February 12, 1937.

112 HSTA Hanover: Hann. 158 Moringen, Acc. 84/82, no. 8.

113 Garbe, »Kompromißlose Bekennerinnen,« pp. 52-73; Drobisch, op. »Frauenkonzentrationsalger im Schloß Lichtenburg,« p. 103.

114 Füllberg-Stolberg, »Bedrängt, aber nicht völlig eingeengt,« passim.

115 Robert Ritter was a »criminal biologist« one of the leading »scholars« in the Third Reich who, with their pseudo-scientific research, opened the way to death for tens of thousands of people (especially his »racial examinations« on Sinti and Roma meant death in a Nazi concentration camp for the majority) who were

considered »racially inferior« by Nazi ideologists. See Joachim S. Hohmann, *Robert Ritter und die Erben der Kriminalbiologie* (Frankfurt, 1991); Michael Zimmermann, *Rassenutopie und Genozid: Die nationalsozialistische »Lösung der Zigeunerfrage«* (Hamburg, 1996); Michael Burleigh and Wolfgang Wippermann, *The Racial State: Germany 1933–1945*, 5th ed. (Cambridge, 1996); and Henry Friedlander, *The Origins of Nazi Genocide: From Euthanasia to the Final Solution* (Chapel Hill, 1995).

116 BAK: R 73/14005. Information courtesy Stefanie Endlich.

117 Garbe, *Zwischen Widerstand und Martyrium*, pp. 461ff. and especially pp. 468ff.

118 Ibid., p. 468.

119 Ibid., p. 469.

120 In accordance with the title of Wolfgang Wippermann, *Der konsequente Wahn. Ideologie und Politik Adolf Hitlers* (Gütersloh: 1989).

121 No further information has been found about Ritter's work on the Witnesses, and it is not known whether his questionnaires were the same as for Sinti and Roma.

122 Garbe, »Kompromißlose Bekennerinnen,« pp. 52–73; on Jehovah's Witnesses in Hamburg, see idem., *Zwischen Widerstand und Martyrium*, pp. 501ff.

123 Ibid., p. 61.

124 Ibid., p. 64.

125 A report published by exile SPD mentioned the age and special position of the Witnesses, based on their consistent noncompliance in the camps. The May 1937 issue of *Deutschland-Berichten* published in Prague stated: »The old Witnesses gave the guards no end of trouble. They neither gave the Hitler salute nor could they be stopped from saying prayers.« Quoted in Garbe, »Kompromißlose Bekennerinnen,« p. 64.

126 See Garbe, *Zwischen Widerstand und Martyrium*; and Wickert *Frauen gegen die Diktatur* for additional bibliographical references.

127 See Wippermann, *Der konsequente Wahn*, p. 222; Marßolek and Ott, *Bremen im Dritten Reich*, p. 308.

Kirsten John-Stucke

Jehovah's Witnesses in Wewelsburg Concentration Camp

Recent attention to the persecution of Jehovah's Witnesses in Nazi Germany has uncovered new historical findings about concentration camps, which have contributed to revising the history of the Wewelsburg concentration camp. Before examining the special position of Jehovah's Witnesses as prisoners at Wewelsburg, the significance of Wewelsburg as a site of SS rituals and terror will be described in the context of the work of the Wewelsburg Memorial and Documentation Center.

The documentary exhibition »Wewelsburg 1933–1945, Cult and Terror Center of the SS« opened in 1982 at the Wewelsburg District Museum. This was the result of several years of intensive discussion about how to handle the history of Wewelsburg between 1933 and 1945. In 1977, the district council passed a resolution to set up a documentary exhibition »as a warning for the living and to honor the memory of Niederhagen concentration camp victims.«[1] Prof. Karl Hüser of Paderborn University was commissioned to undertake basic research, since no serious investigation of this subject existed. The exhibition documented SS activities and the history of the concentration camp at Wewelsburg.[2]

In 1934, Reich Leader of the SS, Heinrich Himmler, rented Wewelsburg castle from the District of Büren, for his own purposes. Himmler considered his SS (*Schutzstaffel*) a select racial elite, which he wanted to train as a »National Socialist military order of Nordic men.« This required creating training centers to ensure the standardized education of SS leaders. Thus Wewelsburg castle was chosen, since Himmler had known it from the election campaign in Lippe. He was fascinated by the triangular shape of Wewelsburg castle, which had been built as an auxiliary residence by the Prince Bishops of Paderborn between 1603 and 1609, in Weser Renaissance style. However, there were only very vague ideas about a »Reich Leaders' School at Wewelsburg.« Moreover, young SS academics were hired to complete ideological research which would support Nazi philosophy. In 1936, Himmler transferred the development and maintenance of Wewelsburg castle to the Society for the Promotion and Care of German Cultural Monuments (*Gesellschaft zur Förderung und Pflege deutscher Kulturdenkmäler*) that he had founded, thereby freeing himself of accountability to the Nazi party. He then started to implement his ideas to convert Wewelsburg into a pseudo-religious center for SS rites. The north tower would be rebuilt to contain two »cult areas«: the former ground floor chapel was to be a »Hall for the SS Supreme Leaders« and the cellar was to become a »crypt.« The renovation work for the »crypt« and »Hall for the SS Supreme Leaders« was completed mostly by concentration camp prisoners, whereas plans for a large domed room on the upper floor were never realized.[3] Until 1938, workers from the Reich Labor Service were employed in this reconstruction, but they were then reassigned to building the West Wall fortifications. After 1939, Himmler used concentration camp prisoners for rebuilding Wewelsburg; after 1940, they constituted a subcamp of Sachsenhausen concentration camp. Until Wewelsburg became independent, construction and maintenance costs were paid by the Society for the Promotion and Care of German Cultural Monuments. To ease financial pressures on the Society, the subcamp

View of Wewelsburg castle from the south-east. Photo credit: Johannes Büttner, 1990.

was sold to the state in 1941 and the Reich took over all expenditures for the autonomous Niederhagen concentration camp.

Although there are a few scattered written records from Nazi organizations, the SS, and other Nazi institutions, that enable us to reconstruct SS activities at Wewelsburg,[4] there are virtually no records for the history of the concentration camp. Although we can reconstruct the organization of the camp from records in archives and other memorials, these do not explain conditions inside the camp. Furthermore, official documents or Nazi records about Wewelsburg are not available, since they were destroyed before the end of the war.[5] In addition, using Nazi documents as historical sources entails the risk that actual events have been consciously distorted and described in misleading language. A particularly crass example is the death certificates of Wewelsburg concentration camp prisoners. The causes of death cannot be accepted without reservation. In some cases, it is noticeable that the cause of death was deliberately misrepresented to disguise a violent death.[6]

Thus, historians are dependent on other sources to understand the prisoners' living conditions and social structure inside the concentration camp. These include oral or written survivor testimony. Although memoirs are always subjective, this is an advantage, since camp conditions and hardships can only be described by those who have experienced them. When the Wewelsburg documentation exhibition opened in 1982, there were very few oral or written memoirs available. The records of witness depositions and interrogations at the Wewelsburg trials of 1952 and 1970–71 were only consulted later.[7] Moreover, it took many years of intensive work before contacts with survivors were established, and they could be interviewed.[8] These oral history sources provide the basis for research about conditions in Wewelsburg concentration camp.

However, one must bear in mind that these sources are based on elderly survivors' recall of events that had occurred 60 years earlier, and thus may contain errors in statistics and dates that do not affect the reliability of other details. Instead, statements made today include necessary reflection about these events, whereas earlier survivor memoirs often describe their surroundings from narrow personal perceptions.[9]

Jehovah's Witnesses have provided most oral histories and written memoirs about Wewelsburg concentration camp, and also most of the witness depositions at the second Wewelsburg trial. This is probably surprising, because they did not constitute the largest group of prisoners at Wewelsburg. The largest prisoner groups included Soviet forced laborers (the so-called *Ostarbeiter*) and prisoners of war. However, it has not yet been possible to meet survivors from Russia or Ukraine. Only the names are known of the 734 Soviet citizens who died in Niederhagen concentration camp. Nevertheless, Jehovah's Witnesses, although not the largest prisoner group in Wewelsburg, assumed a special place among the prisoners because of their solidarity. Even after the war, they kept in touch with one another because of their solidarity and religious beliefs.

Historical research about the conditions and behavior of Jehovah's Witnesses is facilitated by the availability of numerous written and oral narratives.[10] Jehovah's Witnesses were almost the only group of prisoners at Wewelsburg during two phases of the camp's history: from February to August 1940 when Wewelsburg was a subcamp of Sachsenhausen concentration camp; and later as the prisoners' residual crew (*Restkommando*) after the dissolution of Niederhagen concentration camp from April 1943 to April 2, 1945, when Niederhagen was liberated by the Americans. For both periods, the behavior of prisoners wearing purple triangles can be analyzed in detail. The first Jehovah's Witnesses came as forced labor from Sachsenhausen to Wewelsburg on February 16, 1940. They replaced a group of so-called BV »preventive custody« prisoners (*Befristete-Vorbeuge-Häftlinge*), who, except for a short gap from the beginning of war in September to December 1939, had been incarcerated at Wewelsburg since May 1939. The prisoners were initially housed in a tent below Wewelsburg castle, and later a small camp with barracks was built at the adjacent Kuhkampsberg. An attempted escape by two preventive custody prisoners in May 1939 ended fatally for one prisoner. Another attempted escape by two prisoners occurred in January 1940; one prisoner was shot by a soldier and later died in the hospital and the other was shot in the back by *Kommandoführer* Plaul. In order to divert public attention from the camp, Himmler decided to replace the initial prisoners with Jehovah's Witnesses. They were known for never trying to escape. Additional prisoner transports of Jehovah's Witnesses arrived, and about 220 Witnesses were incarcerated at Wewelsburg after May 1940. The Witnesses were selected from the prisoners at Sachsenhausen and Buchenwald concentration camps because of their professional skills as carpenters, stonemasons, painters, and bricklayers, since Himmler wanted to remodel Wewelsburg into a pseudo-religious SS site. Most of the Witnesses were not new prisoners, but had previously endured several prisons and concentration camps.[11]

Most of the Witnesses had been imprisoned during the first waves of arrests in 1936–1937 as well as in 1938. As the following two biographies show, Jehovah's Witnesses had already experienced several forms of discrimination before their incarceration; these ranged from social ostracism to loss of employment and complete deprivation of livelihood. This is exemplified by the case of Georg Klohe, assigned as prisoner clerk (*Schreiber*) with the first Witness transport in February 1940. Klohe was arrested by the Gestapo in July 1936 en route to Leipzig to meet Erich Frost, the Witnesses' district overseer for Saxony. He was caught in the wave of

View of the former concentration camp from the gatehouse. Belgian military vehicles are parked on the roll call yard. Photo credit: Gilbert Eylan, ca. 1946–1947.

persecution following the September 1936 Lucerne convention (see chronology at end of volume). Klohe lost his job with the AEG (*Allgemeine Elektrizitäts-Gesellschaft*, General Electric Company) because of his refusal to conform to Germanic standards and made his living as a travelling salesman. He also produced illegal phonograph records with biblical maxims and readings. Klohe was sentenced to two-and-a-half years in prison, because of illegal activities for the International Bible Students Association, that had been already banned in 1933. After serving his sentence, he was remanded to Sachsenhausen and from there to Wewelsburg concentration camp. Klohe remained at Wewelsburg until the camp's liberation.[12] The second case was that of Max Hollweg, who was ostracized before he was arrested and sent to a concentration camp. Hollweg refused to join a Nazi organization and as a result was repeatedly dismissed from various jobs. Apprenticed as a stonemason, he worked as a plasterer, an unskilled laborer, and as a day laborer. Although under police surveillance because of continual job changes, Hollweg participated in illegal activities of the International Bible Students Association. He participated in the national letter and flyer campaign of June 1937, the »Open Letter – To Germans who believe in the Bible and love Christ.« Max Hollweg was imprisoned during the ensuing wave of arrests and, after several prison stays, transferred to Buchenwald concentration camp. From there he was transported on May 25, 1940, to Wewelsburg, where he remained until the end of the war.[13]

Since Witnesses constituted the entire Wewelsburg prisoner population during this early phase, prisoner functionaries were chosen from their ranks. In other concentration camps, Witnesses usually did not perform such functions, in part because they believed that these were

»worldly« positions. They refused, at their own risk, to carry out SS measures. They had no choice in Wewelsburg. The position of camp elder was particularly controversial. This function was initially taken by Georg Klohe. In his memoirs, Klohe described that he thought it over for a long time whether he could accept this position and sought spiritual support from his fellow Witnesses.[14] This position was soon assumed by Otto Martens, a Witness from Kiel. Martens' role as camp elder is controversial. Evaluations about his personality differed widely. Thus, many Witness statements given as evidence at the Wewelsburg trial evaluated Otto Martens as an unfair person in a position of responsibility. Rumors about him alleged that he renounced his faith and subsequently joined the navy. He was ostensibly transferred to a submarine unit and drowned during an attack. The heretic, in a manner of speaking, received his just reward.[15] Max Hollweg described Otto Martens' role differently. Hollweg depicted Martens as his spiritual mentor and defended his often rigid behavior.[16] As camp elder, Martens frequently had to make difficult decisions that sometimes had negative consequences for his own religious brethren. Moreover, he tried to impose some discipline on his fellow prisoners to avoid attracting SS attention or anger. Martens was prepared to beat and punish his fellow prisoners to prevent something worse from happening to them. Hollweg doubts that Martens repudiated his religious beliefs. Martens remained as camp elder until April 1943, when Niederhagen concentration camp was dissolved. He was subsequently relocated to a subcamp on the coast, where he ostensibly lost his life. No precise evidence about Otto Martens' fate has been discovered.

Jehovah's Witnesses stood out because of their strong solidarity. Such solidarity was an intrinsic part of their beliefs and life style before incarceration; they previously lived in closely-knit groups and continued this behavioral pattern in the camp. They organized into fixed »parcel groups« that shared parcels with food and clothing parcels with poor or destitute prisoners. They cared for each other during illnesses. Their shared beliefs gave them a deep sense of cohesiveness, intensified by their common knowledge of German and their similar ordeals of discrimination and persecution before incarceration. In this camp period, there were three deaths; the mortality rate increased dramatically when additional prisoner groups arrived at Wewelsburg in September 1940. A total of 107 prisoners died in 1941; the number of deaths increased to 868 men in 1942.[17] The rapid rise in mortality demonstrated the increasing prisoner population, as well as the deterioration of living and labor conditions in Wewelsburg. In the summer of 1940, the prisoners already moved into a newly built protective custody camp. The barracks were overcrowded and an oppressive congestion prevailed everywhere. Food rations were so inadequate that the average number of calories for a prisoner doing hard labor was about 900 calories. The so-called »nettle commandos« (Brennessel-Kommandos) were ordered to gather nettles to make soup.[18] Although prisoners at first even had or had been sent warm underwear, during the war camp clothing became increasingly inadequate and of poor quality. Prisoners working in construction crews tried to place empty cement bags between their skin and clothing. The SS punished this severely. Prisoners working at a building site or in a quarry without warm clothing, even in the harshest winter weather, were constantly vulnerable to illness and death from exposure or frostbite. Weakened or ill prisoners could rarely survive such tortures. In addition, prisoners constantly feared mistreatment by the SS. Prisoners with professional skills had an advantage. Stonemasons, glaziers, and bricklayers were often assigned to work under a roof, which at least protected them from inclement weather. Many of the Witnesses were craftsmen, explicitly chosen for construction work at Wewelsburg. Skilled workers were often treated better by the SS, because they were not so easy to replace as unskilled labor.

The remaining prisoners, together with their relatives,
in front of the former workshop barrack after the camp was liberated in April 1945.
In the background, the fence and watchtower can be clearly seen.

When additional prisoner transports arrived at Wewelsburg, some of the prisoner-functionary positions, such as block elders and Kapos, were given to political, »asocial,« or preventive custody (BV) prisoners. The jobs of camp elder and camp clerk, however, always remained in the hands of the Witnesses. On September 1, 1941, the Sachsenhausen subcamp became the independent Niederhagen concentration camp. Consequently, responsibility was transferred from the Society for the Promotion and Care of German Cultural Monuments to the state. This change had no particular significance for the prisoners. Until summer, the prisoners were still registered in the Sachsenhausen prisoner files, and they now received new prisoner numbers. In the summer of 1942, a separate registry office was set up, where only death registers were kept, and a crematorium was built at the camp. The number of dead prisoners rose to such an extent that it was no longer possible to transport corpses to the Bielefeld or Dortmund crematories without causing a stir.[19]

At first, Jehovah's Witnesses were housed together in barracks. As increasing numbers of Soviet prisoners arrived at Wewelsburg, the Witnesses were separated and dispersed in several different barracks. The SS assigned German-speaking prisoners as room elders (*Stubenälteste*) in the barracks occupied by Soviet prisoners, so that their orders could be more easily communicated and obeyed. Further, the SS had noticed that putting Witnesses together in one barrack only resulted in reinforcing their unity. However, the success the SS anticipated by separating the Witnesses, thereby decreasing their solidarity, did not materialize. Instead, the Witnesses tried to preach and convert their fellow prisoners. Their obvious sense of mission and their demonstrative courage in professing their faith provoked SS anger. On the one hand, Witness prisoners, because of their obedience and honesty, were frequently chosen for jobs requiring trust; whereas on the other hand, they suffered exceptional SS harassment because of their resolute faith. In this connection, a group of Witnesses who already at Buchenwald had refused military service repeated their refusal at Wewelsburg, and consequently had to endure the special hatred of *Arbeitsdienstführer* (work crew supervisors) Rehn and *Kommandoführer* (labor crew leader) Friedsam at Niederhagen concentration camp. Despite their refusal, 27 Witnesses received draft notices in January 1941 and were transferred to neighboring military garrisons. After four or five weeks, 26 of them returned to Wewelsburg, only one had been willing to sign the declaration abjuring their beliefs.[20] The SS threatened them with the worst possible mistreatment. Statements from the victims as well as from fellow prisoners, attested to the fact that SS maltreatment in the weeks that followed was intended to kill these prisoners. The 26 Witnesses were assigned to the forest (*Waldsiedlung*) penal work crew. There, together with »asocial« and protective custody prisoners, the Witnesses had continuously to carry rocks at the double up a steep slope; the SS brutally beat and abused them. They were housed in a barrack that had only dirty straw spread on the floor. They were denied medical care. The Witnesses who were not involved did their best to help their brethren. Although it was prohibited, they tended their wounds, provided them with additional food rations collected from other Witnesses, and gave them emotional support and comfort by Bible readings. According to their own testimony, this solidarity and religious faith enabled the 26 Witnesses to survive six months in the penal labor commando, while remaining true to their beliefs. The other prisoners in the penal labor crew were unable to cope with SS mistreatment, and at least two prisoners attempted to escape and were shot by the SS guards.[21]

This incident illustrates the Jehovah's Witnesses solidarity. Their shared faith enabled them to develop collective strategies facilitating survival in extreme camp conditions. In contrast to the Witnesses, other prisoner groups seldom developed collective behavioral strategies, except for the political prisoners — who, as socialists and communists, shared the same ideology and political goals, namely, victory over the Nazis. The BV »preventive custody« prisoners, the »asocials,« and especially the Soviet prisoners of war did not have common backgrounds before their incarceration in the camps and thus found it difficult to develop collective strategies. Their conduct was characterized by individual concerns or personal friendships rather than by religious solidarity.[22]

To be sure, such strong group cohesion could also induce duress on an individual. Whoever did not agree with the opinion of the group had to count on being ostracized. This was disastrous for those affected, since they were still considered Jehovah's Witness prisoners, but were excluded from the benefits of collective measures (parcel groups, medical support, spiritual sustenance). We should not underestimate the extent to which individual Witnesses yielded to peer pressure out of fear of »exclusion.«[23]

Group solidarity could be endangered by disparate behavior and opinions. A closer examination of the behavioral patterns of Jehovah's Witnesses in Wewelsburg permits us to examine the contradictions and conflicts within this basically united group. The disputes that occurred between Witnesses in larger concentration camps, such as Ravensbrück and Buchenwald, about the ramifications of biblical interpretations for forced labor in armament production, cannot be found in Niederhagen concentration camp. After 1942, concentration camps were increasingly involved in armament production. This meant that Jehovah's Witnesses had to decide whether as objectors to military service and as pacifists, they could take part in manufacturing weapons and producing uniforms or equipment for the German army.[24] There were no predetermined limits for these decisions resulting in heated arguments in the camps.[25]

The workshop barrack where the last prisoners had been housed.
The barrack has since been torn down. Photo credit: Kirsten John-Stucke, July 1996.

Wewelsburg concentration camp was not involved in armament production. The concentration camp was created in 1939 to provide labor for Himmler's ideological building project. The prisoners were used in construction work at the Wewelsburg castle, in the village, and in the camp. The main activities were working in stone quarries, making roads, and building houses. After the defeat at Stalingrad in winter 1942–1943, all economic forces were concentrated in the armaments industry, causing the cessation of construction work at Wewelsburg. The Führer decree of January 13, 1943, resulted in the discontinuation of all »construction work unessential for the war.«[26] In mid-March 1943, a commission authorized by Oswald Pohl, head of the SS Central Office for Economy and Administration (WVHA), arrived at Wewelsburg to inspect the concentration camp and its economic facilities for building an armaments factory there. Thus, there were plans to produce munitions at Wewelsburg, but they were rejected. The concentration camp was dissolved. A residual crew (*Restkommando*) of 42 prisoners (forty Witnesses and two political prisoners) remained in Wewelsburg.

Thus, Jehovah's Witnesses at Wewelsburg did not take part in disputes about arms production. There are no records about discussions whether construction work at Wewelsburg was »unbiblical« or not. The castle was to be used for pseudo-religious, ideological cult celebrations. Nevertheless, it would be one-sided to claim that there were no disagreements; there are references to Wewelsburg in survivor accounts and documents from Witnesses who had been transferred from Wewelsburg to Ravensbrück. Their reports disclose that there were problems with authority exercised by Witnesses who served as prisoner-functionaries. Besides the camp elder, other Witnesses are accused of having acted unjustly and lacking solidarity.[27] Even if this report is interpreted with critical reserve, there are several similarities to other eyewitness accounts.[28] One can therefore conclude that in Wewelsburg, as in other concentration camps, discussions and disagreements about behavior, standards of conduct, and interpretations of scripture occurred. This is hardly surprising, if one considers that the Witnesses in the camps were cut off from the outside world for a long time and had to rely on themselves.[29] *Watchtower* publications could rarely be smuggled into the camp and therefore Witness communities had to rely on their memories. The Witnesses attempted to obtain Bibles by exchanging other valuables, or by smuggling Bibles into the camp. For Jehovah's Witnesses, reading and studying the Bible, together with preaching, were indispensable elements of their faith and the basis for daily decisions in the camp. Thus, Max Hollweg also emphasizes that every Witness in the camp exercised his own free will, according to his conscience and his understanding of scriptures.[30]

Witnesses regularly held Bible classes in Wewelsburg, despite the risk of severe punishment if discovered. During those periods when Witnesses were the only, or almost the only, prisoner group in Wewelsburg, such meetings could be organized more easily than during the period when Niederhagen concentration camp held between 1,000 and 1,500 prisoners. In the residual crew (*Restkommando*), which existed from April 1943 until liberation by the Americans, Witnesses were able to strengthen their religious bond by intensive Bible study. At that time, Niederhagen was an auxiliary camp under the jurisdiction of Buchenwald concentration camp. During the day, Witnesses could move around relatively freely in the camp and, at times, even in the village in order to reach their work places. The SS realized that they were obedient prisoners, who posed no risk of escape. The Witnesses used these lapses in vigilance; thus, Georg Klohe organized a *Watchtower* study group and they built an illegal print shop for *The Watchtower*. The Witnesses had already successfully established contact with the outside world and smuggled letters in Niederhagen concentration camp. After 1942, they were also able to obtain Witness literature, their »spiritual food.« Until the winter of 1942–1943, *The Watchtower* was printed by Julius Engelhard in Oberhausen-Sterkrade. It was then sent via several other locations to Sophie Horstmeier in Eickhorst, who brought the paper to the Witness sisterhood at Bad Salzuflen.[31] On Saturdays, women Witnesses took the last train to Salzkotten and then walked from there through the woods to Wewelsburg. At the nursery near the train station, they hid letters and copies of *The Watchtower* under large stones. On Sunday morning, they returned with the first train to Bad Salzuflen.[32] The Wewelsburg Witnesses organized a temporary printing plant, after the illegal print shop was located in the winter of 1943.[33] They recovered a typewriter from the ruins of a building. They obtained stencils, paper, and printing ink from female Witnesses. Max Hollweg manipulated an electrified fence, so that several Witnesses could crawl out at night from the fenced barracks area and smuggle materials back into the camp. He also succeeded in installing an electrical safety catch on the gate between the SS barracks and the prisoners' barrack. A red lamp lit up in the prisoners' barrack when the gate was opened. Thus, the Witnesses were warned of visits by SS guards and were able to hide suspicious material. This warning system also enabled Witnesses to sneak wives and female friends of prisoners into the barracks.[34] The Witness sisterhood distributed illegally printed publications. This courier system existed under the noses of the SS until the camp was liberated.[35]

The exceptional conduct of Jehovah's Witnesses in Wewelsburg concentration camp is exemplified by their illegal printing plant. The Witnesses usually obeyed camp regulations on religious grounds, but they were also willing to violate these rules to maintain their religious beliefs. Thus their behavior can be considered religiously motivated resistance. The wider latitude they had as residual crew (*Restkommando*) enabled them to pursue their faith. Their behavior was not directed to real political goals, but was based solely on their steadfast beliefs.

This example reveals how research about prisoner biographies at Wewelsburg has developed; it also specifically enables us to evaluate the role of the Witnesses in Wewelsburg. Although several years ago there were no references about the illegal printing activities of the Witnesses in Wewelsburg other than a notice in the *1974 Yearbook of Jehovah's Witnesses*,[36] there is now detailed documentation in the collected survivor interviews and written memoirs that corroborates their resistance. Finally, even the existence of »mail drops« could be substantiated by interviewing Wewelsburg residents.[37] Survivor reports provide an insider view of the concentration camp, conversations with Sophie Horstmeier reveal the perspective of female Witnesses who smuggled *The Watchtower*, and the experiences of Wewelsburg residents confirm that they knew about prisoner resistance. These disparate pieces of a mosaic form a picture that is still incomplete, but which nevertheless can be evaluated from various points of view.

Notes

1   Kreistagsbeschluss, 1977.

2   Karl Hüser, *Wewelsburg 1933–1945: Kult- und Terrorstätte der SS*, 2d ed., no. 1 of the publication series of the Kreismuseum Wewelsburg (Paderborn, 1987).

3   Karl Hüser and Wulff Brebeck, *Wewelsburg 1933–1945: Kultstätte des SS-Ordens*, 2d ed. (Münster, 1995), pp. 18f.

4   SS construction records and individual SS researchers' reports exist. They built a library, a pre-history museum, and carried out archeological excavations as well as genealogical research. However, the occult ideological dimensions of Wewelsburg have not been adequately researched. The documentary film »Die schwarze Sonne« (Black Sun) by Rüdiger Sünner presents the occult background of national socialism. This film uses the sunwheel motif from the »Hall for the SS Supreme Leaders« from the Wewelsburg north tower. The twelve-spoke sunwheel is believed to have been modelled on bronze ornamental brooches worn by Alemannic and Franconian women after the 3rd century. This ornament was based on Roman swastika clasps. It was also interpreted as the »black sun« in occult and mythical beliefs.

5   A rumor persists in Wewelsburg that several boxes of concentration camp records have been stored on a local farm. They are said to have been destroyed shortly before the Wewelsburg trials 1970–71 (as reported in the *Neue Westfälische Zeitung*, February 2, 1971). Nothing is known about the contents of these files and their significance.

6   Kirsten John, »*Mein Vater wird gesucht...*«: *Häftlinge des Konzentrationslagers in Wewelsburg* (Essen, 1996), pp. 97, 107. If death by unnatural means was suspected, the SS had to inform the state attorney. To avoid this, camp doctors frequently utilized formulas, such as »suicide by hanging« or »shot while trying to escape.«

7   The archives of the *Zentralstelle im Lande NRW für die Bearbeitung von nationalsozialistischen Massenverbrechen in Konzentrationslagern* (Central Office of Northrhine Westphalia for Investigating Nazi Crimes in Concentration Camps), Cologne State Attorney, for the second Wewelsburg trial at the Paderborn district court, are held at the Kalkum branch of the Hauptstaatsarchiv Düsseldorf (hereafter abbreviated as HStA Düsseldorf-Kalkum), Rep. 118, nos. 855–935). The trial is Landgericht Paderborn, Prozeß-Unterlagen betr. KL Niederhagen-Wewelsburg, AZ: 24 JS 2/69 (Z). A caveat for using witness interrogations is that questions to eyewitnesses are sometimes slanted and that transcriptions occasionally contain distorted descriptions. Nevertheless, most of these documents are correct. See Johannes Tuchel, »Die NS-Prozesse als Materialgrundlage für die historische Forschung: Thesen zu Möglichkeiten und Grenzen interdisziplinärer Zusammenarbeit,« in: Peter Steinbach and Jürgen Weber, eds., *Vergangenheitsbewältigung durch Strafverfahren? NS-Prozesse in der Bundesrepublik Deutschland* (Munich, 1984), pp. 134–144.

8   Most interviews were conducted in 1992, during a survivors' meeting on the tenth anniversary of the founding of the Wewelsburg Documentation. Transcribed interviews, memoirs, and documents used in

this article are found in the Kreismuseum Wewelsburg Archives.

9   James Edward Young, *Beschreiben des Holocaust: Darstellung und Folgen der Interpretation* (Frankfurt, 1992), pp. 49–69. In evaluating such material, emotional influences, attempts to adapt to contemporary views, or repression must be considered.

10 Until 1931, members of the religious association of Jehovah's Witnesses were known as *Ernste Bibelforscher* (»Earnest Bible Students«). This label continued and was used especially by the Nazis.

11 See Kirsten John-Stucke, »Der ›lila Winkel‹ in Wewelsburg,« in: *Widerstand aus christlicher Überzeugung – Jehovas Zeugen im Nationalsozialismus: Dokumentation einer Tagung,* ed. Kreismuseum Wewelsburg and others (Essen, 1998), pp. 41f.

12 Georg Klohe memoirs and notes, 1969.

13 Max Hollweg, *Es ist unmöglich von dem zu schweigen, was ich erlebt habe: Zivilcourage im Dritten Reich* (Bielefeld, 1997); interview with Max Hollweg, May 16, 1992.

14   Georg Klohe memoirs.

15 HStA Düsseldorf-Kalkum, Rep. 118, nos. 855–935, witness depositions; see also illegal leaflets by Jehovah's Witnesses in Wewelsburg, 1943.

16 Hollweg, *Es ist unmöglich*, p. 99.

17 Hüser, *Wewelsburg*, p. 96.

18 Letter from Friedrich Klingenberg, former Witness prisoner, June 28, 1992.

19 The creation of a registry office and a crematorium were contemplated in a letter sent by the Central Office for Reich Security (RSHA) to the Inspectorate of the Concentration Camps (Office D of the Central Office for Economy and Administration), see Hüser, *Wewelsburg*, pp. 98ff.

20 During the war, those who refused military service could be sentenced to death for »undermining military morale.« Concentration camp prisoners remained under SS authority and thus could not be condemned (as for example the »Wewelsburg objectors«). As soon as they signed the declaration abandoning their faith as a »false doctrine,« they could be released from concentration camps, but were then answerable to a military court. Their release from imprisonment was almost always followed by an enlistment notice for military service; this was a certain death sentence for religiously motivated pacifists, and thus very few signed the declaration.

21 HStA Düsseldorf-Kalkum, Rep. 118, nos. 855–935, Witness depositions.

22 Falk Pingel, *Häftlinge unter SS-Herrschaft: Widerstand, Selbstbehauptung und Vernichtung im Konzentrationslager* (Hamburg, 1978), p. 19.

23 Detlef Garbe, »Der lila Winkel: Die ›Bibelforscher‹ (Zeugen Jehovas) in den Konzentrationslagern,« in: *Dachauer Hefte*, no. 10 (1994), p. 16.

24 Garbe, »Der lila Winkel,« pp. 3–31.

25 Thus, a disagreement about manufacturing skis for the German army resulted in a minority split within the Jehovah's Witnesses group at Buchenwald. The majority refused to make skis, whereas a smaller group of prisoners decided to continue making skis, resulting in their ostracism by the larger group. In Ravensbrück concentration camp, the majority of Witnesses refused to work with angora rabbits, because the wool was used as lining for pilots' jackets. However, there was no resistance to this at Neuengamme concentration camp, where 15 female Witnesses worked at breeding angora rabbits.

26 Hüser, *Wewelsburg*, pp. 101f. The architect Hermann Bartels, however, managed to preserve his entire construction department, intending to complete his, meanwhile megalomaniac, building plans immediately after the »final victory.« His project would have wiped out the entire village, since he envisioned Wewelsburg as a pseudo-religious cult center at the center of a gigantic structure (ca. 600 meter radius).

27 Illegal leaflets by Jehovah's Witnesses; originals in private collection, copy at the Kreismuseum Wewelsburg. The treament of 26 Witness refusing military service is explicitly mentioned and the camp elder is accused of »betraying« a brother.

28 Hollweg, *Es ist unmöglich*, p. 99.

29 In these illegal pamphlets, the camp elder is referred to as *Inselältester* (»island elder«).

30 Conversation with Max Hollweg, November 20, 1997.

31 Sophie Horstmeier was in contact with Georg Klohe, to whom she regularly wrote.

32 Conversation with Sophie Horstmeier, February 17, 1998.

33 J. Engelhard was executed. S. Horstmeier was also arrested and sentenced to four years' imprisonment for »undermining the military.«

34 Similar testimony provided by former Witness prisoners Heinrich Schürmann, May 16, 1992, and S.

Horstmeier, February 17, 1998. Hollweg, *Es ist unmöglich*, pp. 126ff.

35 The Witnesses ensured the silence of the political prisoners by threatening them with denunciation to the SS.

36 *1974 Yearbook of Jehovah's Witnesses* (New York, 1973), p. 201.

37 Interview with Anna H., Wewelsburg resident, in 1993.

Antje Zeiger

Jehovah's Witnesses[1] in Sachsenhausen Concentration Camp

Oranienburg was already in 1933–1934 the site of a so-called »wild« concentration camp, where about 3,000 prisoners were detained in a defunct brewery.[2] At the same time, SS guard units assigned to Columbia House in Berlin were stationed in Oranienburg. Moreover, SS Reich Leader Heinrich Himmler's plans provided for »the construction of a large camp, near Greater Berlin, with possibilities for considerable expansion.«[3] When the Sachsenhausen concentration camp was to be put into operation in July 1936, based on the Dachau model, prisoners were transported from Esterwegen to Sachsenhausen to construct the camp; initially they were housed in temporary improvised barracks.[4] From its opening in 1936 until liberation in April 1945, there were probably a total of about 200,000 prisoners who had passed through the camp.

Oranienburg was also the location of the Inspectorate of the Concentration Camps,[5] responsible for the administration of all concentration camps (arrest conditions, organization of prisoner forced labor, coordination of the mass murder of Jews, Sinti and Roma, Soviet prisoners of war, and the disabled, etc.).

Some Jehovah's Witnesses were among the first prisoners from the Esterwegen concentration camp. Within the first months, other prisoners came from the Lichtenburg concentration camp.

During the Sachsenhausen trial in 1947, the former prisoner Bruno Röhr testified that there were already 20 Witnesses in the camp when he was transported to Sachsenhausen in March 1937.[6] At first, Jehovah's Witnesses, known as Bible Students in the camp, were not recorded separately at Sachsenhausen because of their small number. However, they were subsequently registered separately in camp statistics, when their numbers increased as a result of the April 1937 Gestapo circular direction that Jehovah's Witnesses who had served their jail sentences be remanded, under certain circumstances, into »protective custody« at concentration camps[7] and after the wave of arrests following the mailing of the »Open Letter« on June 20, 1937.[8] Originally the Witnesses probably received a blue marking, and later in 1937–1938, they were given purple triangles as standardized markings. In Sachsenhausen, the purple triangle was also worn by Seventh Day Adventists, Baptists, pacifists, and possibly also by supporters of the New Apostolic community,[9] who, however, were rarely committed to a camp.

Jehovah's Witnesses were characterized by strong organizational structures and solidarity also at Sachsenhausen. At first, Witnesses were very low in the camp hierarchy. They were vulnerable to constant harassment and the worst mistreatment until 1942, when conditions for the Witnesses generally improved in the concentration camps. The SS believed that Jehovah's Witnesses were just as dangerous as Communists.

Statistics and Social Structure

Disparate material is available for Sachsenhausen camp statistics. There is, however, no statistical material from SS provenance for the years 1940–1945. Statistical data is available for 1937 and 1939.[10] There are daily »notes about prisoner variations« from 1937, or »reports about changes« from 1938 and 1939, based on the same sources: the »administration of prisoners, money, and possessions,»[11] as well as daily reports on prisoner arrivals from the camp Political Department.[12] For 1936, only a few Political Department reports about arrivals during November and December have been preserved. Data for 1940–1943 are based on presumably incomplete receipts from the property warehouse.[13] No comparable sources have been located for 1944 and 1945.

The difficulty of reconstructing the statistical composition of Sachsenhausen was already obvious immediately after liberation. Statistical summaries based on existing sources were prepared for the Sachsenhausen trial, held in Berlin-Pankow in 1947.[14] These may not always be completely accurate for the years 1940–1945.[15] This list was also used to determine the percentage of Jehovah's Witnesses in Sachsenhausen, since after June 1938 the percentage of Witness prisoners constantly decreased with the arrival of large numbers of other prisoners.

The first statistical registration of Witnesses on May 5, 1937, listed 26 at Sachsenhausen. By the end of May 1937 the number of Witnesses had risen to 32, or 1.4 percent of a total of 2,263 inmates. The Witnesses reached their highest percentage in May 1938 with 10.7 percent, equivalent to 314 prisoners. With the tremendous increase in the number of Sachsenhausen prisoners from 2,920 in May 1938 to more than 9,200 in June 1938, the Witnesses dropped to 3.4 percent of all prisoners. In April 1945, there were between 230 and 250 Witnesses out of a total of ca. 36,654 prisoners, or less than 1 percent.[16]

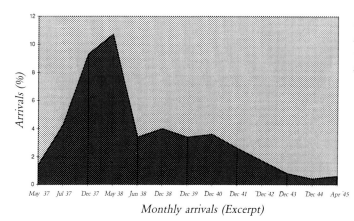

Percentage of Witness prisoners based on total number of prisoners

Monthly arrivals (Excerpt)

So far, information by name has been traced for more than 650 prisoners from Germany,[17] 29 from Austria,[18] 152 from the Netherlands and Belgium,[19] 6 from Poland,[20] 3 from France,[21] and 2 from Czechoslovakia.[22] Moreover, there were additional Polish, Belgian, Czech, Soviet (including Ukrainian) Jehovah's Witness prisoners in Sachsenhausen for whom no personal data is available.

There is some data about another 180, mostly German, Witnesses, who were deported to Sachsenhausen subcamps (especially Wewelsburg and Neuengamme), and were therefore briefly included in the statistics of the Sachsenhausen main camp. More than 980 Jehovah's Witnesses can be linked to Sachsenhausen during its entire existence.[23]

For the period from 1938 to 1942, 168 deaths of prisoners wearing the purple triangle can be documented; there are a few individual death certificates in 1943.[24] This included 128 German, 20 Dutch, 16 Austrian, and 1 Czech Witness. Particularly during the winter of 1939–1940, nearly every fourth Witness died; 13 of them died from dysentery between February and May 1940. There are also records of two suicides.

Death Statistics

Year	Number of deaths
1938	6
1939	34
1940	97
1941	6
1942	22
1943	3
Total	**168**

Most prisoners whose arrival dates could be established lost their lives within ten to eleven months after their transfer to the Sachsenhausen concentration camp. The number of violent deaths as a result of mistreatment could, however, not be established. Two thirds of the deceased were below the age of 50. Data about the arrival dates of 550 Witnesses could be traced for the period 1936–1943. There is proof of 22 prisoner transfers to other camps and 34 releases during this time.

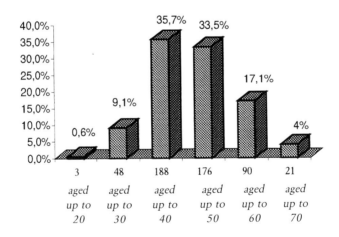

Data about 526 prisoner arrivals was used to establish prisoner age structure for the period 1936–1943, since each prisoner's age was registered at entry.[25] The youngest person was 18, two of the oldest were 68. The majority of the prisoners, 108 of them, fit into the 35–39 age group, and 101 prisoners belonged to the 40–44 age group.

The statistical average is 41 years[26] and thus there is no significant difference from the 40.8 years established for Neuengamme.[27]

Age Structure of Jehovah's Witnesses at the Sachsenhausen Concentration Camp

Age	Number of Prisoners	Percentage
up to age 20	3	0.6
up to age 30	48	9.1
up to age 40	188	35.7
up to age 50	176	33.5
up to age 60	90	17.1
up to age 70	21	4.0
Total	**526**	**100**

Similar to the figures for Neuengamme (20 percent), 21.1 percent of the prisoners at the Sachsenhausen concentration camp were older than 50 when they arrived. However, the proportion of those below the age of 30 (9.7 percent) is higher than the figure for Neuengamme (7.5 percent).[28] There are no comparable figures available for the age at arrival for all prisoners at the Sachsenhausen concentration camp.

Comparative figures for prisoner age at time of arrival are available for Buchenwald for January 30, 1941,[29] and for the Sachsenhausen subcamp at Wewelsburg in spring 1941.[30] It is clear that the age structure of Jehovah's Witnesses in Sachsenhausen is more comparable to the age structure of the total number of prisoners at the Buchenwald concentration camp.

Comparison of Average Age[31]

Age	A	B	C
up to age 20	1.9%	0.0%	0.0%
up to age 30	15.3%	3.3%	5.5%
up to age 40	32.6%	23.0%	28.8%
up to age 50	31.4%	45.4%	43.9%
up to age 60	15.4%	23.3%	20.3%
up to age 70	3.3%	5.0%	1.5%

A: All prisoners
B: Witnesses in Buchenwald
C: Witnesses in Wewelsburg

For Jehovah's Witnesses in Sachsenhausen we can assume a high incidence of marriage. Data on 235 individuals (143 from death records, and 92 from property warehouse receipts for the period 1940–1942) were usable. More than 70 percent of the imprisoned Witnesses were either married or widowed.

Marital status		D	E[32]
	Total	Percent	Percent
Married or widowed	168	71.5%	74%
Unmarried or divorced	67	28.5%	26%
Total	**235**		

D: Witnesses in Sachsenhausen
E: Witnesses in all camps

Information about the number of children was found only in property warehouse receipts.

Marital status		D	E[33]
	Total	Percent	Percent
No children	38	41.3%	44%
One child	17	18.5%	17%
Two or more children[34]	37	39.8%	39%
Total	**92**		

D: Witnesses in Sachsenhausen
E: Witnesses in all camps

It is interesting that seven prisoners indicated a prison as their wife's address.

In order to determine their occupations, 168 death certificates for Jehovah's Witnesses were evaluated for the years 1938–1943. Information about an additional 47 Witnesses were found in trial documents, including witness depositions and partly also in memoirs, resulting in a total of 208 useable data elements. In the event of multiple entries for one individual, the first entry was recorded.

Occupations	Number	Percentage
Employees	11	5.2%
Civil Servants	8	3.8%
Factory/farm workers	50	23.7%
Skilled workers	25	11.8%
Craftsmen	65	30.8%
Farmers	11	5.2%
Self-employed	17	8.1%
Retired/Disabled	5	2.4%
Others	19	9.0%
Total	**211**	

Most of the incarcerated Jehovah's Witnesses belonged to the lower and lower middle classes.

Exclusion

Prisoners committed to Sachsenhausen underwent a form of »welcoming ceremony« that pre-saged subsequent conditions. Prisoners were usually taken to the camp in police vehicles or buses from the Berlin-Alexanderplatz police prison. Numerous prisoners also arrived by train at Sachsenhausen train station, and were either placed on trucks or had to walk the last few miles, usually accompanied by considerable mistreatment. New prisoners were initially taken to the Political Department. Although they were interrogated about the reason for their arrest, the answers were generally meaningless as, in most cases, extreme physical force was used.[35] »Three older Jewish prisoners ... also two Witnesses, and a doctor from Berlin were soon so terribly injured that they lay on the concrete floor in front of us with bleeding faces, bruised legs, and crushed hands. ... Punches and blows rained down on them from all sides.«[36]

This »welcoming ceremony« also included offensive insults of Witness beliefs, such as »Bible worms,« »heaven's comedians,« »paradise birds,« »religious Bolsheviks,« etc.[37]

In November 1937, a police vehicle took Herbert Baron, together with prisoners belonging to other categories, from Berlin to Sachsenhausen. The 27-year-old Baron was arrested for belonging to the International Bible Students Association. After arrival, new prisoners had to practice exercise drills, as they did not have sufficient experience in forming and breaking ranks. Another method used to wear down new prisoners was forcing them to squat with their hands crossed behind their heads, the notorious »Saxon greeting.«

Harald Abt, transported to Sachsenhausen in 1940, was warned on arrival that he would be »sent to Jehovah« within 14 days, if he continued to follow his faith. He then had to remain squatting for four hours with his arms stretched out in front of him. Afterwards, the custom-ary procedures of showering, receiving clothing, and shaving took place. Especially in winter, prisoners were showered in their prison clothes.[38]

Frequently families, informed about the release of their relatives, came to pick them up at the prison and found the Gestapo waiting there with »protective custody« warrants, even though the prisoners had already served their sentence.

A 48-year-old grinder from Borsig Works in Hennigsdorf was arrested on September 16, 1936, since he had copies of *The Watchtower*. He had thus violated the May 21, 1935, ban on Witness literature and its distribution, and was charged under the Law for the Protection of the People and State. He was sentenced to one year and three months in prison by a Berlin special court and served his sentence at Berlin-Tegel prison. The prison administration officially in-formed the family about the forthcoming date of release. »He was to be released at noon. I waited in vain until 12:30 p.m., and then went to the porter, only to learn that my father had been picked up by the Gestapo at 9.00 a.m. For nine months, we did not know where my father was.«[39] Since his father did not sign the declaration abjuring his faith and showed no willingness to leave his religion, he was transferred to the Sachsenhausen concentration camp on April 3, 1938. He was incarcerated there until April 21, 1945, when the camp was evacuated.[40]

Two weeks before he was remanded to Sachsenhausen in 1938, a new circumstance affected Jehovah's Witnesses in the camp and also explained why the family remained uninformed about the father's fate for a protracted period of time. The new camp commandant Hermann Baranowski, replicating the system at Dachau, issued new regulations on March 20, 1938, for the »quarantine« of Jehovah's Witnesses, political recidivists, and prisoners assigned to penal labor companies.[41] The penal labor crew was headed by SS Staff Sergeant Bugdalla. Further, Knittler, Fickert, Sorge, and Schubert — and later also Beerbaum and Braun — were appointed

SS block leaders of »quarantine« and acquired reputations for exceptional brutality.[42]

»Isolation« was a separate camp fenced off from »normal« camp activities. For this purpose, Barracks 3, 4, 19, and 20 were separated and the windows whitewashed to prevent people from looking in or out. After late September 1938, these barracks were renumbered 11, 12, 35, and 36. Almost all Jehovah's Witnesses at Sachsenhausen were taken to »isolation,« with few exceptions.[43]

The »personal freedom« of Witness prisoners was further restricted by this change of location. This included complete prohibition of mail, temporary denial of medical treatment, exclusion from receiving drugs, withholding warm clothing, temporary ban on buying things, longer work hours, and occasional denial of food; only the slightest grounds were needed for these restrictions.[44]

During the first winter of war, scarlet fever and dysentery spread as a result of very poor nutrition, mostly turnip soup (for lunch), bread, and imitation coffee, and because of inadequate sanitary facilities. At first prisoners were denied treatment. Prisoners were allowed medical care only after more serious illnesses proliferated.[45]

At the beginning of 1939, »isolation« prohibitions were eased to some extent. However, letters were not allowed to consist of more than five lines. Moreover, all outgoing letters were stamped: »The prisoner remains, as before, a stubborn Bible Student and refuses to reject the Bible Students' false teachings. For this reason, the usual privileges of correspondence have been denied him.« This regulation remained in force until the second half of 1944, but was sometimes suspended in individual cases.[46] The other regulations remained completely in force. The Witness prisoners were first allowed to leave »isolation« at the end of the summer of 1941, when Soviet prisoners of war arrived at Sachsenhausen.[47]

Terror

Numerous cases are known of Jehovah's Witness prisoners being severely mistreated in »isolation,« because the Witnesses usually did nothing to deflect or mitigate the expected tortures by giving more moderate answers.

As a result of arbitrary nocturnal surprise raids, block leaders inspected prisoners' quarters and punished them for »inadequate« cleaning with »sport.« This meant that prisoners were terrorized with calisthenics until they collapsed and remained lying on the ground outdoors. Frequently, water was then poured over these prisoners, often causing their death during winter.

Prisoners unable to work because of illness or other reasons were assembled in the so-called standing commando (*Stehkommandos*). They stood in front of the barracks all day long and in all kinds of weather. At times probably 2,000 prisoners were assigned to this commando in Sachsenhausen.[48] This often included many prisoners with purple triangles.[49] Prisoners in the standing commando often collapsed, since Witness prisoners included numerous elderly and ill prisoners, as well as World War I veterans who, as a result of their injuries, wore artificial links.[50] »May 17 is deeply engraved in my memory. It was the last day for Diedrich (Diedrich Mindermann, a Witness). He was so weak that he could no longer stand. I tried to hold him by standing back to back with him, our arms linked. It was all right for a while, but then two brothers had to support him; he collapsed, however, and lay there until roll call. ... He died at my side.«[51]

Special practices were employed against Jehovah's Witnesses, since the SS considered their resistance, remaining believers despite ill-treatment, a provocation. So-called »baptism,« pushing prisoners into water-filled pits, trucks, etc., took place in all seasons, but had especially dramatic consequences in winter.[52] At certain fixed intervals, block leaders »determined« when a »chosen one« would renounce his faith. Georg Schullian, an 18-year-old apprentice clerk, was sent to Sachsenhausen in 1937 and died there in April 1940. He was frequently the victim of block leader Beerbaum's ill-treatment. He was tortured to such an extent that he actually repeated the derogatory words suggested by an SS officer against his faith. However, he recanted these words immediately afterwards.[53]

Johann Ludwig Rachuba, a miner and one of the first Sachsenhausen prisoners in 1936, became a symbol of stalwart religious behavior. With almost stoic composure, he endured all the tortures of his tormentors. They constantly punished him in various ways, such as whipping, jailing, hanging from a post, and standing at the gate without supper in the evening. Among other things, Bugdalla ordered that Rachuba be buried up to his neck in dirt and that two SS men, one of them Bugdalla, relieve themselves over him. He was still alive when they later dug him out, but had suffered severe physical damage from hypothermia. Other cases of prisoners being buried alive are also known. The reasons for Rachuba's punishment were his missionary activities, recorded in the disciplinary roster as »publicity for Jehovah.« He was also accused of laziness, since he was unable to work rapidly because of previous ill-treatment.[54]

The first winter of war in 1939–1940 was remarkable for the 11,000 prisoners at Sachsenhausen. From November 1939 to May 1940, about 400–600 prisoners died each month. During this period, 94 Jehovah's Witnesses also died at Sachsenhausen; this meant that nearly every fourth imprisoned Witness perished.[55]

Furthermore, at that time, there were also many premeditated killings.

After April 1940, prisoners were locked into very small broom or storage closets. All the gaps were sealed with wet blankets and the keyholes crammed with paper. Between five and fifteen prisoners were left in the closet for several hours until they died an agonizing death from suffocation.[56]

On January 17, 1940, two Witnesses were executed on Heinrich Himmler's personal orders.[57] When Himmler visited the camp prison, he passed the cells of Franz Welz (incarcerated at least since March 1939) and Robert Ziebold (in Sachsenhausen since 1937 or 1938). Himmler felt that both prisoners lacked the necessary respect, since undisturbed by his presence they had continued praying.

Camp commandant Baranowski's sadistic abuse was the decisive factor in sentencing 50-year-old Franz Welz, a stone mason, to the camp cellblock. Welz could only move with crutches following severe injuries to both legs in World War I. Baranowski removed the crutches, demanding that Welz move without them since he could rely on God's help as a Jehovah's Witness. After this incident, Welz no longer saluted. It is not known whether, because of his physical handicap, he could have given the required salute at all. Robert Ziebold, a 35-year-old driver, joined in this refusal to salute.[58]

Both men were initially removed from their prison cells to »isolation,« probably in Barrack 36; because they had snubbed Himmler, they were then whipped 25 lashes while tethered to a whipping stand. Other Jehovah's Witness prisoners reported that shortly thereafter, the two men were executed by firing squad. The SS prison overseer Eccarius confirmed this execution during the Sachsenhausen trial.[59]

The whipping stand, where prisoners were flogged as they counted aloud the number of strokes, was as infamous and feared as being suspended on a post with hand's tied, and feet not touching the ground. These tortures were already reported in 1938 by Zürcher.[60]

The Witnesses confronted constant terror with unshakable faith. The maltreated prisoners were cared for in the infirmary by this cohesive group as much as circumstances allowed.

Refusing Military Service

Apart from Jehovah's Witnesses sentenced for violating the law of February 28, 1933, Witnesses usually faced the death penalty, and in less severe cases prison sentences, for »undermining military morale« by refusing military service.[61]

Military jurisdiction, rescinded after World War I, was re-established in May 1933 as part of the preparation for war. Jehovah's Witnesses faced new difficulties with passage of the law on compulsory military service in 1935.[62] Military service was publicized as »honorable for the German nation« and »as loyalty of the individual to his race.« Jehovah's Witnesses, however, only accepted unreserved loyalty toward God, including the obligation to remain neutral in this »ephemeral« world.[63] Apart from the fact that military service contradicted the directive for non-violence, the oath of allegiance presented another problem. Any concession allowing exemption was rejected by Hitler, since in the event of war, namely, in »times of national emergency, personal convictions were to be put aside for higher ethical purposes.« Refusing military service became a more serious offence when war began,[64] and resulted in the third major wave of arrests of Witnesses, following earlier increases in arrests during the summer of 1937 and spring of 1938.

These facts are significant for Sachsenhausen, since the first public executions for refusing military service occurred there. The first execution by firing squad was of the 29-year-old Jehovah's Witness August Dickmann, incarcerated in Sachsenhausen since November 1937 because of his activities for the Bible Students Association.[65]

A few days after the outbreak of the war, his wife sent Dickmann a draft notice that had been sent to his home address. He was ordered to report to the Political Department of the camp, probably on September 5, 1939, and declare his willingness for military service.[66] After he refused, he was beaten, then sequestered for several days in a jail cell. Meanwhile, his case was reviewed in Berlin. As a warning, his execution was ordered for September 15, 1939, and was to be carried out before the entire camp. Sachsenhausen then had 8,500 prisoners, including 367 Jehovah's Witnesses.[67] The Jehovah's Witnesses were to be lined up adjacent to the execution wall. August Dickmann, his hands bound, took his position in front of the wooden execution wall, and Camp Commandant Baranowski read the execution order — according to several eye witnesses in a dramatic way —, that had apparently been signed by Himmler. The firing squad was commanded by Rudolf Höss, then Adjutant and Protective Custody Camp Leader at Sachsenhausen and later Commandant of Auschwitz. The firing squad consisted of between three and six SS men. After the execution was over, Höss following Baranowski's signal fired another bullet at Dickmann, who already lay on the ground. Four Jehovah's Witnesses, among them Heinrich Dickmann (August Dickmann's brother), had to place the body into a coffin. Heinrich Dickmann had been imprisoned at Sachsenhausen for six months.

The prisoners were dismissed, except for the Jehovah's Witnesses. Baranowski attempted to use the impact of the execution. He demanded that the Witnesses sign a declaration renouncing their religion and threatened to shoot all who would not sign. The antithesis happened: two Witnesses stepped forward to reverse signatures that had been previously given. The Witnesses were punished with so-called »sport,« exercises that taxed their physical abilities to the limit.

Harry Naujoks, a former political prisoner and camp elder, reported that the other prisoners considered the execution arbitrary and without judicial authority, resulting in their broad solidarity with the Witnesses.[68]

There was also other criticism of this police justice. Even before the execution order, precautions were taken to prevent judicial intervention, e.g. the judiciary were not to be informed about cases of undermining military morale. If the Gestapo approved an execution, it was supposed to be carried out in the nearest concentration camp.

The judiciary learned about two executions on September 8 and 11, 1939, from the press. Press coverage about August Dickmann's execution resulted in intervention by the Ministry of Justice. Reich Minister of Justice Gürtner sent his reservations about the rivalry between judicial and police authority to Hitler, via the head of the Reich Chancellery. In response, Hitler, who probably had been informed afterwards, stated that the executions had been carried out on his personal orders, since the courts were not able to cope with war-time conditions.[69]

Draft notices were also sent to incarcerated Jehovah's Witnesses in concentration camps, including Ernst Seliger. Since Seliger had been arrested before the war, he could not be punished retroactively for undermining military morale.[70]

Even after this, Gestapo ordered executions continued, although they were usually for refusal to perform labor assignments.[71] When Jonathan Stark, a 17-year-old apprentice commercial artist refused to take the oath to »Führer and state« during enrollment in the National Labor Service, he was deported to Sachsenhausen in October 1943 and was immediately assigned to a penal detail. On November 1, 1944, the 18-year-old was hanged because he had continued to adhere to his convictions despite repeated interrogations by the camp commandant.[72]

Labor Deployment

There are about 200 statements by Jehovah's Witnesses about labor deployment in Sachsenhausen, that permit limited analysis of specific aspects of labor allocation. It is no longer possible to arrange these reports chronologically.[73]

Prisoners were often assigned to »good« or »bad« labor crews because of their categories. Initially, the SS considered Jehovah's Witnesses as very dangerous prisoners. Therefore, the Witnesses were originally assigned to labor crews requiring hard physical labor, such as excavation and transport; this was intended to increase pressure on the entire group.[74] In general, Jehovah's Witnesses were careful and conscientious workers as long as the work did not support the war. However, they not only refused direct military service but also any labor deployment related to armaments production, although noncompliance varied in different concentration camps and even in the same camp.[75] Despite the risks of harsh punishment, even death sentences, the Witnesses strictly refused to perform any activities that did not conform with their beliefs.[76] In many labor crews, it was often fortunate for other prisoners when a Witness (and not a »preventive custody« prisoner) was assigned as prisoner functionary, because Witnesses did not strive for personal status or power, since such behavior diverged from their attempted neutrality. This attitude, together with helpfulness and an unshakable faith, often helped prisoners in extreme situations, such as the seriously ill in the infirmary, or prisoners in solitary confinement in the cellblock facing an uncertain fate. Three Witnesses were assigned work as trusties in the cellblock.[77]

There were also divergent views on the compatibility of certain activities and religious convictions in Sachsenhausen. Several Jehovah's Witnesses were assigned to build the firing range in the main camp, and did not refuse to do this. On the other hand, at the satellite camp in Rathenow (Arado Works), one Dutch Witness refused to construct a firing range. As a result, he was to be transferred to the main camp for execution.[78]

One prisoner, assigned to the paintshop of the SS factory Deutsche Ausrüstungswerke, even refused to paint war toys, an assignment he felt was incompatible with his beliefs.[79] Refusing assigned work often had lethal consequences. Some prisoners were executed for refusing to work and for sabotage. This is why the 31-year-old Dutch Witness Willem van Klaveren was hanged, only a few days before the camp was evacuated.[80]

Since Jehovah's Witnesses prisoners were mostly skilled craftsmen,[81] at first they were often assigned to skilled labor. Already in the summer of 1936, Witnesses transferred from Esterwegen to Oranienburg were assigned to the construction detail. During the first few years, Witnesses were assigned to nearly all work related to the construction and extension of the new Sachsenhausen camp site (as, for example, enlarging the prisoners' camp, technical installations, and building officers' quarters). This work required heavy physical labor for excavations, felling and moving trees, and other transport work. The penal detail, which also included Jehovah's Witnesses, had to »run to the SS camp with full or empty trucks« on tracks they had previously built. The prisoners »hauled sand from the SS camp to the greenhouse along this strenuous path, circling the entire camp to reach the other end of the camp.« The Witness Herbert Baron reported that 4–6 prisoners had to push one of the 20 trucks each of which held 1.5 cubic meters.[82]

During later years, new Witness prisoners were often assigned to the shoe-testing work crew, testing shoes for various purposes, or they were assigned to the forest crew, felling trees.[83]

Eventually, even the SS realized that Witnesses absolutely refused only certain labor assignments, but otherwise carried out their work conscientiously and reliably. After 1941–1942, the situation improved, not only because the Witnesses were released from »quarantine,« but also in part because the Witnesses had an unquestionable advantage compared to most new prisoners during the later years, since they already knew the camp.

They later received work assignments that ensured them relatively good and securer conditions. They received new assignments in the infirmary, the kitchen, and clothing warehouse, etc. At least two Witness prisoners were assigned as servants for more than 30 officers' quarters.[84]

Even an official change in attitude can be documented. Following a visit to the estate of his physician and masseur, Dr. Kersten, in Hartzwalde (near Oranienburg), Heinrich Himmler wrote on January 6, 1943, to SS Lieutenant General Oswald Pohl (head of the SS Central Office for Economy and Administration) and Heinrich Müller (Chief of the Gestapo), that Jehovah's Witnesses were »incredibly fanatical, self-sacrificing and obedient.« Himmler suggested that they be assigned increasingly to special tasks.[85] It should also be mentioned that after 1943, female Witness prisoners from Ravensbrück worked as maids and governesses in SS homes.[86]

There were also groups of Dutch and Polish Jehovah's Witnesses in the Rathenow subcamp; Dutch, Austrian, and German Witnesses assigned to the Lichterfelde subcamp for construction work for the Central Office for Reich Security, and at least ten Dutch, German, and Polish Witnesses allocated to the *Klinkerwerke* (brick works). In the latter, for example, a Dutch Witness held the position of foreman on a road construction detail. There are references to Witnesses as foremen in other subcamps. Thus, in 1944, they were assigned as foremen on construction details in the Marienfelde subcamp and were also assigned as barbers in the main camp.[87]

Individual Witnesses are mentioned in connection with other subcamps. For example, at the Niemegk subcamp a Jehovah's Witness held the position of camp elder. Other Witnesses are also found for the subcamps at Glau, Hauptzeugamt, and Lieberose.

Since skilled craftsmen were always needed for building new camps, Jehovah's Witnesses were repeatedly assigned to such labor crews because of their willingness to work and their low risk of flight. Thus, Sachsenhausen was a transfer point to other concentration camps for many Witnesses.

After February 13, 1940, a total of 243 Jehovah's Witnesses (103 from Sachsenhausen and 140 from Buchenwald) were assigned to construct the Wewelsburg subcamp (near Paderborn), which initially was placed under the administrative jurisdiction of Sachsenhausen. When Wewelsburg became an independent concentration camp on September 1, 1941, the percentage of Jehovah's Witnesses at Sachsenhausen dropped from 4.6 to 2.5 percent.[88]

After February 29, 1940, 50 Jehovah's Witnesses were included on several transports assigned to build the Neuengamme concentration camp near Hamburg. It became an independent camp in June 1940.[89] Several transports to Dachau between August 28 and September 16, 1940, included 98 Witness prisoners.[90]

The new camp commandant Hans Loritz, appointed after Baranowski's death in 1940, had already utilized Witness prisoners in special labor companies at Dachau and continued this practice in Sachsenhausen. Consequently, from August to December 22, 1941 and May to July 1942, small work crews — each consisting of 12 to 25 prisoners, mostly Jehovah's Witnesses — traveled to Wolfgangsee. There they built houses for SS officials, including for the Sachsenhausen camp commandant and for SS Lieutenant Colonel Arthur Liebehenschel, on the staff of the Inspectorate of Concentration Camps in the SS Central Office for Economy and Administration (WVHA). These prisoners enjoyed an atypical freedom of movement there compared to the usual conditions they encountered.[91] »Soon, in the warm summer evenings, we prisoners marched 100 meters from our log cabin down to the lake to go for a swim; the SS senior colonel took the lead and I carried the accordion.»[92] This exceptional situation changed when the prisoners were relocated back to Sachsenhausen. The usual jail conditions were again in force.

On October 15, 1942, the first SS company for railroad construction, which however, included only a few Witnesses, left the Sachsenhausen concentration camp for Düsseldorf to complete various jobs on SS buildings.[93]

In February 1944, Heydrich's widow, whose husband had headed the Central Office for Reich Security before his death, requested a group of 15 prisoners (German, Dutch and Czech Jehovah's Witnesses) for labor on her Jungfern Breschan estate. This detail included Reinhold Lühring, who later become the estate manager.[94]

Religious Commitment and Solidarity

Jehovah's Witnesses violated the usually strictly observed camp regulations because of their staunch devotion to their religious convictions. This faith was their motivation in the daily struggle for survival. They considered the restrictions of detention, mistreatment, and bigotry as divine trials, that could not be averted by escape. Group support was imperative for their unyielding stance. Definite organizational structures were established in the camps, resulting in some protection for their actions. At great personal risk, they provided food or saved some of their own rations for fellow believers who fell ill.

Their untiring missionary activities, which they pursued even at their own extreme risk, conferred meaning to their lives as prisoners. Their preaching was particularly successful with Soviet, Polish, and Ukrainian prisoners. »Some of them were secretly baptized right in the camp–in the infirmary bathtub.«[95] Many of those who converted merely wanted to share the group's amenities, but such adherents usually did not remain very long.

The declaration to renounce their faith was presented to Jehovah's Witnesses at regular intervals. The Dutch Jan Steinfurt, incarcerated at Sachsenhausen from 1942 to 1945, was summoned once a month to the Political Department to demand his signature. Another Dutch Witness who signed the declaration, recounted that he was released immediately.[96] The prisoners' wives and children were ordered to come to the camp to induce the prisoners to sign, since the presence of families increased psychological pressure on the prisoners.

Presumably most of the 34 prisoners released in 1938 and 1939 signed this declaration.[97] Prisoners who returned to their barrack after signing the declaration renouncing their faith were under great stress, since they were excluded from the group. When the dockworker Paul Balzereit from Kiel, who had been senior German spokesman for the International Bible Students Association until 1936, signed a renunciation declaration, he was ordered to the camp gate for release. However, he was compelled to return to the barrack later that evening and was subsequently released on April 29, 1939.[98]

During the first years in concentration camps, Jehovah's Witnesses had no religious literature available, what they called their »spiritual food.« They were also restricted in their missionary activities and could only »witness.« In 1937, however, there was considerable confusion when a prisoner thought he had ascertained the time of the battle of Armageddon.

The Witnesses sequestered in »isolation« had a Lutheran Bible. It had reached the »isolation« area first via the officers' quarters and then probably via the gardener's wife. Selected brothers were responsible for »spiritual support.« In each of four barracks, the Witness responsible received the Bible briefly in order to memorize certain sections and then transmitted these passages to fellow prisoners. There were probably no meetings. The designated Witness spoke individually to each imprisoned brother and encouraged them.[99] When the SS, following a lead, thoroughly searched barrack 36 for the Bible, they were unable to find it. Barrack elder Albin Lüdke, a Communist, had hidden it in his closet, since he did not expect to be searched. He was especially admired by the Witnesses in the barrack for his loyalty and helpfulness.[100]

Karl Schurstein, 44 years old, was active as a preacher after May 1939. He probably managed to smuggle copies of The Watchtower into the camp by hiding them in his artificial leg. When he was transferred to Dachau in the summer of 1940, he appointed Ernst Seliger, the pharmacist in the prisoner infirmary, as his successor. Seliger had been in Sachsenhausen since July 1937.[101]

Erich Frost, department head of the German International Bible Students Association, then 39 years old, a concert pianist and composer, was also taken to Sachsenhausen. In 1940, at the request of his fellow brethren, Frost composed a marching song and other pieces of music. This song, with different words, is still in the Witnesses' songbook today.[102] Shortly thereafter, the SS also became aware of Frost's talent as a concert pianist and assigned him to play for their entertainment at evening gatherings. In addition, Frost also composed other pieces of music.

After the Witnesses had left the »isolation,« they managed gradually to bring more publications into the camp; these were eagerly duplicated in various work areas, particularly in the infirmary. In 1941, seven issues of *The Watchtower,* other publications, and probably even Zürcher's book *Kreuzzug gegen das Christentum* (»Crusade against Christianity«) were smuggled into the camp.[103]

After 1942, they regularly held Bible classes on Sunday afternoons in barrack 59 and presumably all Jehovah's Witnesses participated. Spotters were organized as far as the camp gate to report the presence of SS men and to protect the Witnesses from discovery and harm. »A report was received that we regularly held religious meetings in our barrack and had Bibles and other religious publications. ... All morning, SS block leaders searched cabinets and straw mattresses on our beds. They did not find much, but a few brothers had carelessly hidden some notes in their beds.«[104] Fourteen Witnesses were found guilty and flogged with 25 cane strokes.

For their »spiritual sustenance,« Bible Student prisoners built a network outside the camp together with their religious »brothers and sisters« who had not yet been imprisoned. The acquisition of religious literature, Bibles, and other publications as well as the majority of correspondence was transmitted through a group operating under Willi Fritsche in Berlin. Although several active adherents were arrested in 1942, they still received religious material directly from the European central office in Bern, known as »mother.« This group also had close contact with the Ravensbrück women's concentration camp and the Hartzwalde estate mentioned earlier, so that communications existed between Witness prisoners in Sachsenhausen, Ravensbrück, Hartzwalde, and the female Witnesses in the Oranienburg SS houses.[105] Correspondence was sent via messengers, who also employed civilians in their labor crews. In addition, even some SS members assisted Jehovah's Witnesses as couriers. Also, prisoners being transported often took letters with them in specially prepared inconspicuous objects, such as hollowed out tools.[106]

Ernst Seliger was in charge of the clandestine center for distributing literature, located in the infirmary. Copies were also made there. Every six to eight weeks contact was established with several subcamps, containing small groups of Witnesses, to exchange publications and letters.[107]

There had already been a massive search of the imprisoned Witnesses in 1942, resulting in numerous punishments by whipping. During the morning of April 27, 1944, an »event on a grand scale« occurred: a state police investigation against the Witnesses.[108] It lasted several days and began when all Witness prisoners were ordered to leave their labor assignments to report to the gate. »Some of the block leaders chased the brothers, requiring them to run ahead of them with their arms raised, and held their pistols, ready to fire, aimed at the brothers.«[109] Since the Gestapo had already completely rounded up Witness groups in Berlin and in Dresden, they were well informed about the connections, and searched the work sites, where they found some religious publications. Ernst Seliger was the main focus of the police investigations that also targeted other Witnesses. Consequently, Seliger and other Witness prisoners were transferred from the infirmary. When the investigation was nearly finished, there was apparently treachery within their own ranks, resulting in a search of the infirmary. This uncovered additional publications and letters from Ravensbrück, although a Communist fellow prisoner in the infirmary had already destroyed most of the dangerous material. The prisoners responsible for »pulling strings« were to be punished the next Saturday with whipping, which, however, inexplicably did not transpire.

Already on April 26, 1944, a similar investigation had already occurred in the Lichterfelde subcamp (Berlin). Twelve ringleaders were identified and initially punished by being locked up in the »delousing.«[110] Another similar operation occurred at the main camp, probably shortly before the camp's evacuation in April 1945.

Death Marches[111] and Liberation

The final phase of the evacuation of the eastern camps began when the Soviet offensive crossed the Vistula river. After February 1945, when the Red Army also crossed the Oder river, an evacuation plan had been prepared for the Sachsenhausen concentration camp.

The last surviving list for Sachsenhausen dated January 15, 1945, from Office D of the SS Central Office for Economy and Administration (WVHA), stated that there were 52,924 male and 13,173 female prisoners.[112] At that time, most prisoners were probably in the Sachsenhausen main camp, so that it was extremely overcrowded and living conditions had deteriorated drastically. Even the prisoners could clearly see the signs of the approaching end: numerous incoming and departing transports, the systematic liquidation of many prisoners, and increasing bomb attacks on Oranienburg.

By January 1945, the Witnesses expected an early evacuation and agreed that, when it finally occurred, all Witnesses would meet in camp barrack 4.[113]

Because of the chaotic situation on April 20, 1945, the evening before the evacuation, the meeting location was changed to the tailor's workshop. After most of the male Witnesses had already assembled there, a few women arrived during the night. Moreover, the Witnesses probably also took all religious publications, *Watchtower* issues, and several Bibles with them.

Approximately 33,000 prisoners left the camp in columns of 500 prisoners each; they were grouped by nationality and had very few supplies. Additional guards were recruited among the political and »preventive detention« prisoners.

Despite the predetermined column size and their grouping by nationality, Ernst Seliger, mentioned earlier, was able to convince the camp Deputy Commandant Höhn, who had taken charge of the evacuation, that the 230 Jehovah's Witnesses, including 17 or 18 women, could march together. Circumstances let to them having four carts. These mainly carried SS officers' baggage, but also included two crates belonging to the camp deputy commandant, that probably contained valuables confiscated from numerous prisoners on arrival. The Jehovah's Witnesses also transported sick and weak prisoners on these carts, among them the Dutch Witness representative Robert Winkler.

The SS corporal, designated as transport leader, forced the group to walk for 18 hours. No deaths occurred among the prisoners, although several Witnesses were between the ages of 65 and 72. The SS guards received orders to shoot prisoners who could not keep pace and fell behind the column. In other evacuation columns, numerous prisoners who fell behind their group were shot.

The group spent the night in two barns in Bechlin, a village today incorporated in Neuruppin. Since the owners of the farm were also Jehovah's Witnesses, known to a member of the column, neighbors and local residents provided food and shelter.[114]

The following day the column marched 28 kilometers, reaching the village of Rägelin. Members of the group kept trying to obtain food and were often successful because of their efforts with local residents. Since the column continued walking, those who obtained food had to run after the group.

Despite the circumstances, they did not neglect their missionary activities. It was later reported that farmers and even German soldiers heard about »God's Kingdom and also about the concentration camps.«[115]

Marching via Christdorf (near Wittstock), the Jehovah's Witnesses probably reached the so-called Below Forest, part of the Wittstock town forest, on April 26, 1945. More than 18,000 prisoners from the main camp and the »Heinkel works« subcamp were camped in the open, crowded together under close guard without food or water and without shelter or sanitary facilities. The Witnesses built shelters and split up into nine, later into ten, groups of 20-25 men with an overseer for each group in charge of distributing food, making announcements, and organizing meetings. Meanwhile another 18 Witnesses arrived from the »Heinkel« subcamp.

Female prisoners, also evacuated from Sachsenhausen in large numbers, did not camp in the forest but were housed in barns in the nearby village of Grabow. This also applied to the few Witness »sisters.«

Jehovah's Witnesses were provided with almost no food. Thus, 230 people apparently received only two small cans of corned beef and two bowls of flour. Shortly thereafter, because of their trustworthiness, some Witnesses were ordered as helpers to the SS leaders' kitchen and were thus able to provide the group with additional food. Since there was a shortage of water, some Jehovah's Witnesses dug out their own well. Eight men were assigned as guards, changing shifts every hour, to prevent confrontations, including thefts and fights, which assumed alarming proportions at night. It is remarkable that even in this extreme situation, they developed various activities devoted to their faith. For example, the seriously ill Dutch Witness Arthur Winkler, translated Dutch issues of *The Watchtower* into German, crouching on the ground while wearing gloves because of the cold. Others followed this example by copying the translations. Finally the Witnesses resumed studying religious texts in groups. »Group studies refreshed the brothers' hearts so that the atmosphere was excellent. How utterly different it was in the large camp out there! Hunger was increasing, so that grass, herbs, tree bark, and tree roots were cooked and eaten. As a result, unrest and dissatisfaction increased as did the steadily increasing number of deaths; each day about 100-110 people died. Burglary, thefts, and fights were thus the order of the day.«[116]

Representatives of the International Red Cross followed the numerous columns of prisoners and were later able to distribute food packages to the prisoners. On April 28, Jehovah's Witnesses also received some packages which, among other things, included coffee, tea, sugar, and canned milk. The following day, the group was again on the march, simultaneously with other columns. The women who had been accommodated in Grabow rejoined the group, bringing food with them.

On May 2, 1945, the Witness prisoners reached a wooded area near Schwerin, by way of Meyenburg, Friedrichshagen (near Parchim), and Crivitz. The increasing sound of battle and air raids indicated the Allies' advance. SS personnel deserted the group. Prisoners who had been forced to serve as camp guards threw their weapons away.

On May 3, 1945, the group was free but remained in the forest camp with the same group structure. All the Witnesses survived because of their solidarity and extensive mutual help, although many other prisoners fell victim to the strain and shootings.

Additional Jehovah's Witnesses, who had worked in Ravensbrück, probably joined the group. They had been taken back to Sachsenhausen on the day the camp was abandoned and had also been on a death march, but by a different route.

After the forest camp near Crivitz was dissolved on May 6, the group was initially housed in an infantry horse stable.

On May 9, 1945, 47 Dutch, Belgian and French belonging to the group were moved to the Hagenow Air Base.[117] Thirty-two Dutch as well as all Belgian and French Jehovah's Witnesses were transferred to Lüneburg on May 15. At first, eight sick Dutch men stayed behind. On May 19, 1945, the Polish Jehovah's Witnesses were also taken to Hagenow.

On May 15, the remaining Witnesses used eight heavily laden horse-drawn wagons to move into the Hindenburg barracks, after stopping at another barracks.[118] At least 102 members, mostly German Witnesses, were still at the first barracks. They had found huge quantities of paper, also typewriters and mimeographs for making large numbers of copies, in the office of the first barracks. Most stayed at the Hindenburg barracks until June 4, 1945. They reported that between the date of liberation and June 4, they produced and circulated 130,000 pages of religious content. Some Jehovah's Witnesses as well as other former prisoners stayed in Schwerin until mid-November 1945.

Summary

This essay is the first analysis of Jehovah's Witnesses in the Sachsenhausen concentration camp. Jehovah's Witnesses were among the first groups persecuted by the Nazis. As early as 1936, Witnesses were included among the first prisoners in Sachsenhausen.

The SS viewed the unbreakable tenacity of Witness beliefs and values as dangerous defiance of Nazi ideology. This is why the Witnesses first became the foremost object of hatred, permanently exposed to SS terror. Despite prohibitions and physical violence, the Witnesses asserted their beliefs with religious radicalism and maintained their self-respect, even under the extreme conditions of the concentration camp.

Their existing outside structures continued and were transferred to daily life in the camp. Their solidarity was remarkable and many owed their life to it. They maintained solidarity and unity in all situations.

Most of them were arrested because of nonconformist behavior, such as disregarding various regulations that conflicted with their beliefs, and their rejection of any politically-oriented behavior. Very few were arrested and incarcerated in concentration camps because of refusing military service or rejecting military-related work.

The group always remained a minority during the whole time the Sachsenhausen concentration camp existed. In May 1938, every tenth prisoner was a Jehovah's Witness. Less than one percent of the Witnesses included other religious nonconformists (Adventists, Baptists, pacifists), who were placed in the same prisoner classification. Apart from Witnesses from the German Reich, there were also small groups of foreigners; among them, the Dutch were the largest group. The average prisoner age was 41.

We can assume that at least 200 Jehovah's Witnesses, about one fifth, died in Sachsenhausen. Three of them were executed.

Jehovah's Witnesses applied their organizational structures to everyday camp life. Many Witnesses imprisoned at Sachsenhausen came from other concentration camps and therefore, inevitably had experienced incarceration.

At first, Jehovah's Witnesses in Sachsenhausen had the lowest status among the prisoner hierarchy. At first, setting up »isolation« was intended to reduce proselytizing by the Witnesses. They were also segregated by other SS restrictions, such as the general prohibition of receiving mail and denial of medical treatment. Moreover, there were physical hardships, as for example, assignment to labor crews with low survival chances. Also in Sachsenhausen, their opinions varied about the compatibility of certain work assignments with their religious convictions.

Although they strictly followed most camp regulations, the Witnesses deliberately violated them by smuggling religious publications as well as correspondence.

Once the SS leaders realized the Witnesses reliability, diligence, and honesty, they put these characteristics to use for their own advantage. They also wanted later to use their religious fanaticism and nonviolence for political purposes in pacifying occupied territory.

The SS assigned Witnesses to labor crews for constructing SS buildings or establishing new concentration camps. These indicate SS changes in attitude towards the Witnesses. Moreover, the SS could rely on their low risk of escape. The situation eased when, in the autumn of 1941, Jehovah's Witnesses were allowed to leave »isolation.« This improved conditions as a whole. Jehovah's Witnesses were increasingly assigned as prisoner functionaries and given better labor details.

Witness noncompliance was based solely on religious beliefs and was not political, so that they could not associate with other prisoner groups in their resistance. In their opinion, a change in living conditions, for which they also hoped, could only be achieved by divine intervention. Also, during the death marches, their mutual solidarity, and probably clear differentiation from other prisoner groups, ensured the survival of the whole group.

At first, opportunities to practice religion were severely restricted. Gradually, they were able to smuggle religious publications into the camp, and to copy and distribute them. Their preoccupation with their faith, group Bible studies, and later with issuing daily texts and other religious literature distracted them from the negative prospects of life and strengthened their determination to survive. Therefore, despite enormous personal risk they unwaveringly tried to carry on missionary work among other prisoners. Several people were even baptized by Jehovah's Witnesses in Sachsenhausen.

The uncompromising conduct of some Jehovah's Witness, such as August Dickmann, executed in front of the entire camp, or Johann Ludwig Rachuba, who received extraordinary physical abuse, left fellow prisoners with deep sympathy but also admiration. Even when prisoners belonging to other categories did not share their convictions, most of them respected and recognized the Witnesses' attitude.

For many of Jehovah's Witnesses in Sachsenhausen, their suffering did not end in May 1945. At the beginning of the 1950s they were often imprisoned once again for several years in the German Democratic Republic.

Notes

1 The religious association of Bible Students, whose members have called themselves Jehovah's Witnesses since 1931, was founded in Pittsburgh in the late 1870s. The organization today has about 5.6 million active members throughout the world, including about 170,000 in Germany. *1989 Yearbook of Jehovah's Witnesses*, (1989), p. 36; hereafter cited as *Jahrbuch* with corresponding year.

2 Martin Knop, Hendrik Krause, and Roland Schwarz, »Die Häftlinge des Konzentrationslager Oranienburg,« in *Das Konzentrationslager Oranienburg*, ed. Günter Morsch (Berlin, 1994), p. 54.

3 Falk Pingel, *Häftlinge unter SS Herrschaft* (Hamburg, 1978), p. 250.

4 *Sachsenhausen: Dokumente, Aussagen, Forschungsergebnisse und Erlebnisberichte über das ehemalige Konzentrationslager Sachsenhausen* (Berlin, 1986), p. 18.

5 First established in Berlin, it was located in Oranienburg after 1938. In 1942, it was merged with Office D of the SS Central Office for Economy and Administration. Because it was located in Oranienburg, Sachsenhausen concentration camp had a model status. For the history of the Inspectorate, see Johannes Tuchel, *Konzentrationslager: Organisationsgeschichte und Funktion der Inspektion der Konzentrationslager 1934-1938*, Schriftenreihe des Bundesarchivs, vol. 39 (Boppard, 1991), and Tuchel, *Die Inspektion der Konzentrationslager 1938-1945: Das System des Terrors* (Berlin, 1994), p. 20.

6 Fritz Sigl, *Todeslager Sachsenhausen: Ein Dokumentarbericht vom Sachsenhausen-Prozeß* (Berlin, 1948), p. 42.

7 Martin Broszat, »Nationalsozialistische Konzentrationslager 1933-1945,« in: Martin Broszat, Hans-Adolf Jacobsen, and Helmuth Krausnick, *Anatomie des SS-Staates*, vol. 2 (Munich, 1989), p. 73; Lothar Gruchmann, *Justiz im Dritten Reich 1933-1940: Anpassung und Unterwerfung in der Ära Gürtner* (Munich, 1988), pp. 599-620; Detlef Garbe, *Zwischen Widerstand und Martyrium: Die Zeugen Jehovas im »Dritten Reich«* (Munich, 1993), pp. 286-296.

8 See Franz Zuercher, *Kreuzzug gegen das Christentum: Eine Dokumentensammlung* (Zuerich, 1938), pp. 192-195.

9 Sachsenhausen Archives, R 33/26a: For Baptists and Adventists, see Paul Buder, »Mein Lebenslauf,« p. 53. Ten religious groups have been established so far at Sachsenhausen concentration camp. See Reimer Möller, »Widerstand und Verfolgung in einer agrarisch kleinstädtischen Region: SPD, KPD und ›Bibelforscher‹ im Kreis Steinburg 1933-1945,« in *Zeitschrift für Schleswig-Holsteinische Geschichte* 114 (1988), p. 166.

10 Sachsenhausen Archives: R 205 and R 206, copies of files 1367/1/17 and 23 from Moscow »Special Archives.«

11 Sachsenhausen Archives: R 202 and R 205, copies from Moscow »Special Archives« files 1367/1/16, 1367/1/20, and 1367/1/24. For 1936, see R 205 copies from Moscow, file 1367/1/16. From the beginning of 1937, the Political Department has lists of arrivals and later »reports about changes« in registering prisoner monies and securities. Jehovah's Witnesses were listed under the designations IBV (International Bible Students Association), Bifo or Bibelforscher (»Bible Student«), and in one case as a Jehovah's Witness.

12 Political Department arrival reports for 1937 are located in Brandenburgisches Landeshauptarchiv (hereafter cited as BLHA): record group Pr. Br. Rep. 35 H (Sachsenhausen concentration camp), vol. 32, 1938-1939. See also Sachsenhausen Archives R 203, copies from Moscow »Special Archives« files 1367/1/21 and 1367/1/22.

13 Sachsenhausen Archives, R 209-219: Property Warehouse (*Effektenkammer*) receipts, copies from Moscow »Special Archives,« 1367/1/30-41. These warehouse receipts include personal data, such as: family name, first name, date and place of birth, wife's address, number of legitimate and/or illegitimate children, the oldest child's address, and address(es) for notification of death and heirs, as well as the date this form was completed.

14 See Sigl, *Todeslager Sachsenhausen*, fn. 6.

15 Sachsenhausen Archives, R 214 M 58, pp. 1-14; R 232 M 158, pp. 47-117, copies from Archives of the Russian Federation (hereafter cited as GARF), files 7021-104. For 1941, there are statistical statements for individual dates in April, July, and October. The difference in the total number of prisoners is less than ten. See BLHA, record group Pr. Br. Rep. 35 H: Sachsenhausen concentration camp, vol. 2, pp. 8-44.

16 The figure of 230 Jehovah's Witnesses is found in »Memorandum über den Auszug der Zeugen Jehovas aus dem Konzentrationslager Sachsenhausen.« It is not clear whether these figures include prisoners from the Heinkel factory subcamp. The »Memorandum« was published in three parts in the magazine *Trost* on

September 1, September 15, and October 1, 1945, vol. 23, no. 551-553. There is also evidence in various memoirs that individual Witnesses marched to Schwerin.

17 Prisoners came from all parts of Germany and their number may also include some Austrians.

18 Sachsenhausen Archives, R 209, 211, 219: analysis of property warehouse receipts as well as material from the Dokumentationsarchiv des österreichischen Widerstandes (hereafter DÖW), Vienna: files 14587; 14640; 17559; 17654; 18051; 18084; 18144; 18490; 18553; 18555; 18649; 18761. Partial copies in Sachsenhausen Archives R 89/14 and Johann Holzner, Anton Pinsker, Johann Reiter, and Helmut Tschol, eds., *Eine Dokumentation über die Opfer des Nationalsozialismus in Nord-, Ost- und Südtirol von 1933 bis 1945* (Innsbruck, 1977), pp. 56f., 86.

19 Details based on property warehouse receipts and death registers in the Oranienburg registry office (Standesamt Oranienburg). These were supplemented by documents and memoirs from the archives of the Wachttoren-Bijbel-en Traktaatgenootschap in Emmen, Netherlands (hereafter abbreviated as AWT).

20 Archives of the Main Commission for the Investigation of Nazi Crimes against the Polish People, Warsaw: file no. 16, pp. 136, 142, 146, »Liste der Zugänge vom 26. Februar 1945 vom KL Sachsenhausen nach Mauthausen.«

21 Cercle européen des Témoins de Jéhovah anciens déportés et internés, July 13, 1997, and *Watchtower* (August 15, 1980), pp. 5-10.

22 Standesamt Oranienburg: Death Register.

23 This is true especially for 1940 and 1941 and is corroborated by the few preserved statistics for 1941. Research about camp statistics for 1940-1945 establishes that the highest number of Witnesses were listed in August 1941 with 522 individuals. This figure, however, includes 243 prisoners from the subcamp at Niederhagen; 139 of them were transferred directly from Buchenwald to Niederhagen. These prisoners were only under the command of the Sachsenhausen administration, as described by Max Hollweg. The same is also true for transports to Dachau between August 28 and September 16, 1940, when 32 of 98 Witnesses were registered as prisoners of Sachsenhausen, only because their subcamp was under the administrative jurisdiction of Sachsenhausen.

24 This summary also includes three Adventists. The deaths were identified in the Death Register at the Standesamt Oranienburg and in BLHA: record group Pr. Br. Rep. 35 H (Sachsenhausen concentration camp), no. 3.

25 A total of 550 arrivals were recorded, for 24 of them the dates of birth could not be determined.

26 A date could be determined for only 35 out of 152 Dutch Witnesses and 12 out of 29 Austrian Witnesses.

27 Garbe, *Zwischen Widerstand und Martyrium*, p. 466.

28 Ibid.

29 Ibid., p. 467.

30 Kirsten John, *»Mein Vater wird gesucht...«: Häftlinge des Konzentrationslagers Wewelsburg* (Essen, 1996), p. 42. About 100 prisoners had come from Sachsenhausen and were probably registered a second time at this later date.

31 Table based on John, *»Mein Vater wird gesucht,«* p. 44.

32 Rüdiger Lautmann, Winfried Grikschat, and Egbert Schmidt, »Der rosa Winkel in den nationalsozialistischen Konzentrationslagern,« in: *Seminar: Gesellschaft und Homosexualität* (Frankfurt, 1977), pp. 325-365 (about the fate of the homosexuals).

33 Ibid.

34 Of these 37 prisoners, 10 had two children; 14 had three children; 7 had four children; 2 had five children; 1 had six children; 1 had seven children; and 2 had eight children.

35 Heinrich Lienau, *Zwölf Jahre Nacht: Mein Weg durch das »Tausendjährige Reich«* (Flensburg, 1949), pp. 49-53; and Arnold Weiss-Rüthel, *Nacht und Nebel: Ein Sachsenhausen-Buch* (Berlin and Potsdam, 1949), pp. 41-47.

36 Weiss-Rüthel, *Nacht und Nebel*, p. 44.

37 Sachsenhausen Archives R 122/16: Walter Hamann, »Erinnerungsbericht« (Dec. 1970), p. 31 and Wilhelm Lange, »Lagerbericht« (n.d.), p. 9; Garbe, *Zwischen Widerstand und Martyrium*, p. 400.

38 Harald Abt, »Erinnerungsbericht,« in *Watchtower* (April 15, 1980), p. 6; and Frankfurt: Studienkreis Deutscher Widerstand, Dokumentationsarchiv, file AN 707: Herbert Baron, »Jahre des Grauens« (1977), p. 2.

39 Sachsenhausen Archives, R 122/16: Gerda Steinfurth, »Erinnerungsbericht« (November 8, 1995), p. 1.

40 Sachsenhausen Archives, R 122/16: copies of Wilhelm B.'s personal papers.

41 Sachsenhausen Archives R 136: Statement by Paul Wauer (Capri, May 21, 1945), p. 3, copy from Rijksinstituut

voor Oorlogsdocumentatie, Amsterdam; also *1974 Yearbook*, p. 169; and Garbe, *Zwischen Widerstand und Martyrium*, pp. 404 ff..

42 Sachsenhausen Archives, R 122/16: Werner Edling, »Erinnerungsbericht« (September 21/October 19, 1995); and Harry Naujoks, *Mein Leben im KZ Sachsenhausen: Erinnerungen des ehemaligen Lagerältesten* (Berlin, 1989), p. 109.

43 Sachsenhausen Archives: The »Veränderungsmeldungen« include barrack assignments; *1974 Yearbook*, p. 169; Garbe, *Zwischen Widerstand und Martyrium*, pp. 403f.

44 Sachsenhausen Archives, R 122/16: Heinrich Dickmann, »Erinnerungsbericht« (March 13, 1994), Werner Edling, »Erinnerungsbericht« (September 21/October 19, 1995).

45 Apart from the fact that rations were scanty, the food was of such poor quality that a foul smell spread over the whole camp when food pails were moved. Harald Abt, »Erinnerungsbericht,« in *Watchtower* (April 15, 1980), p. 9; Sachsenhausen Archives, R 136: statement by Paul Wauer (Capri, May 21, 1945), p. 3, copy from Rijksinstituut voor Oorlogsdocumentatie.

46 Sachsenhausen Archives, Photo Archive 1996 – 850: photocopies from AWT of personal letters from Walter Hamann, dated June 11, 1944, and Gijsbertus van der Bijl, August 27, 1944, to their families.

47 Lienau, *Zwölf Jahre Nacht*, p. 123; Gerhard Oltmanns, »Erinnerungsbericht,« *Watchtower* (October 1, 1968), p. 600; Naujoks, *Mein Leben im KZ Sachsenhausen*, p. 266.

48 Naujoks, *Mein Leben im KZ Sachsenhausen*, p. 166.

49 Sachsenhausen Archives, R 122/16: In May 1940, more than 60 Witnesses (one-seventh of all Witness prisoners) were assigned to this commando. See Walter Hamann, »Erinnerungsbericht« (Dec. 1970), p. 22.

50 BLHA, record group Pr. Br. Rep. 35 H (Concentration camp vol. 8/2): see Paul Bonnemann deposition, and others, in the trial vs. Suhren and Pflaum; and Harald Abt in *Watchtower* (April 15, 1980), p. 10.

51 Walter Hamann, »Erinnerungsbericht« (Dec. 1970), p. 22.

52 Studienkreis Deutscher Widerstand, Dokumentationsarchiv, Frankfurt, file AN 707: Herbert Baron, »Erinnerungsbericht« (1977), »Jahre des Grauens,« p. 5; Sachsenhausen Archive, R 33/26a: copy of Paul Buder, Erinnerungsbericht »Mein Lebenslauf« (n. d.), p. 25; BLHA, record group Pr. Br. Rep. 35 H (Sachsenhausen concentration camp), vol. 8/2, Emil Hartmann, »Erinnerungsbericht« (July 13, 1948), p. 332.

53 Sachsenhausen Archives, R 33/26a: Paul Buder, »Mein Lebenslauf« (n. d.), p. 28; and R 122/16: Werner Edling »Erinnerungsbericht« (September 21/October 19, 1995).

54 Sachsenhausen Archives, R 33/26a: Paul Buder »Mein Lebenslauf« (n.d.), pp. 65f., reprinted in John, »*Mein Vater wird gesucht*, p. 142; and Sigl, *Todeslager Sachsenhausen*, p. 43.

55 From January 1939 to December 1940, a total of 131 deaths of Witnesses were recorded.

56 BLHA, record group Pr. Br. Rep. 35 H (Sachsenhausen concentration camp) vol. 8/2, Testimony by Paul Bonnemann in the trial vs. Suhren and Pflaum; Sachsenhausen Archives R 136: statement by Paul Wauer (Capri, May 21, 1945), p. 3, copy from Rijksinstituut voor Oorlogsdocumentatie; Garbe, *Zwischen Widerstand und Martyrium*, p. 410.

57 Standesamt Oranienburg, death register, no. 374 and 380: The cause of death was recorded as »shot because of insubordination.«

58 Sachsenhausen Archive, R 3326a: copy of Paul Buder, »Mein Lebenslauf« (n. d.), p. 28; and R 122/16: Werner Edling, »Erinnerungsbericht« (September 21/October 19, 1995).

59 Sigl, *Todeslager Sachsenhausen*, p. 43.

60 Erich Frost, »Erinnerungsbericht« (March 7, 1971), p. 75, in private collection; Studienkreis Deutscher Widerstand, Dokumentationsarchiv, Frankfurt, AN 707: Herbert Baron, »Jahre des Grauens« (1977), p. 8; Zürcher, *Kreuzzug*, p. 151.

61 »Verordnung über das Sonderstrafrecht im Kriege und bei besonderem Einsatz (Kriegssonderstrafrechtsverordnung/KSSVO) vom 17. August, 1938,« KSSVO/*Reichsgesetzblatt* (1938), I, 1455.

62 Military Service Law of May 21, 1935, *Reichsgesetzblatt* (1935) I, 609ff. The law provided for exemption from military service in peace time, only in cases of complete unfitness as well as for ordained persons. Jews and Sinti and Roma were deemed unworthy of military service, see Garbe *Zwischen Widerstand und Martyrium*, pp. 344f.

63 About the necessity of neutrality, see Garbe, *Zwischen Widerstand und Martyrium*, pp. 52ff.

64 Garbe discovered that during the first year of war, there were 152 trials against Jehovah's Witnesses out of 1,087 proceedings for »subverting the military.« A total of 117 cases resulted in the death penalty: 112 or 95 percent of these cases involved Jehovah's Witnesses. A total of 200–250 German and Austrian Witnesses were executed. Garbe, *Zwischen Widerstand und Martyrium*, p. 365.

65 *1974 Yearbook*, pp. 165-169; Naujoks (1989), p. 143 (according to »Erinnerungsbericht« Heinrich Dickmann, in: *Watchtower*, July 1, 1972, p. 398); see also Garbe (1993), pp. 411-414.

66 BLHA, record group Pr. Br. Rep. 35 H (Sachsenhausen concentration camp) vol. 8/2: Emil Hartmann, »Erinnerungsbericht« (July 13, 1948), p. 334.

67 Sachsenhausen Archives, R 206: report dated September 15, 1939, copy from Moscow »Special Archives,« file 1367/1/23.

68 Naujoks, *Mein Leben im KZ Sachsenhausen*, p. 143.

69 On September 3, 1939, Hitler instructed Reich Leader SS Heinrich Himmler to maintain domestic order by all possible means. Heydrich was also authorized to punish any attempt to undermine »German unity and the will to fight.« Any incidents were to be reported to him immediately, as head of the Security Police, and dissident »elements were to be brutally liquidated« by »ruthless action« without consideration of the individual. To avoid delays, local and district and local police had been instructed to send all cases to the state police, without notifying the judicial authorities, i.e., investigating judges. See Lothar Gruchmann, *Justiz im Dritten Reich, 1933-1940: Anpassung und Unterwerfung in der Ära Gütner* (Munich, 1988), pp. 677-679.

70 Ernst Seliger in *Watchtower* (July 15, 1975), p. 424.

71 See section on »Labor Deployment.«

72 *1974 Yearbook*, p. 183; Annedore Leber, *Das Gewissen steht auf: 64 Lebensbilder aus dem deutschen Widerstand 1933-1945* (Mainz, 1984), p. 12; »Erinnerungsbericht« Maria Stark (1996).

73 Sachsenhausen Archives: based on oral history documents, including memoirs, interviews, and correspondence with survivors as well as documents from trials against former SS men stationed at Sachsenhausen. A few original prisoner identity cards were also available.

74 Wolfgang Sofsky, *Die Ordnung des Terrors: Das Konzentrationslager* (Frankfurt, 1997), 146; and Garbe *Zwischen Widerstand und Martyrium*, pp. 475ff.

75 Garbe, *Zwischen Widerstand und Martyrium*, p. 424.

76 Sachsenhausen Archives, R 132: copy from AWT of Adrianus Kamp »Erinnerungsbericht« (1996).

77 Sachsenhausen Archives: Letter from Michael Vermehren, July 17, 1996, p. 2.

78 Sachsenhausen Archives, R 132: copies from AWT of Pieter Broertjes »Erinnerungsbericht« (n. d.) and Jan van den Berg, »Erinnerungsbericht« (1995).

79 Wolfgang Szepansky, *Dennoch ging ich diesen Weg* (Berlin, 1985), p. 176.

80 Four members of the van Klaveren family perished in Sachsenhausen. Sachsenhausen Archives, R 132: copies from AWT Adrianus Kamp (1996); Wilhelm Lange »Lagerbericht« (n. d.), p. 10.

81 See »Statistics and Social Structure.«

82 Studienkreis: Deutscher Widerstand - Dokumentationsarchiv, Frankfurt, file AN 797: Herbert Baron, »Jahre des Grauens« (1977), p. 7; and Sachsenhausen Archives, R 122: Werner Edling, »Erinnerungsbericht« (September 21/October 19, 1995).

83 Copies from private collection of Erich Frost, »Erinnerungsbericht« (n. d.), p. 66; and copies from AWT of Arie Kaldenberg, »Erinnerungsbericht« (91/95) and Gijsbertus van der Bijl (n. d.), Sachsenhausen Archives, R 132.

84 Erich Frost, »Erinnerungsbericht« (March 7, 1971), p. 69, from private collection; copy from AWT of Klaas de Vries, »Erinnerungsbericht,« Sachsenhausen Archives, R 132.

85 Published in *1974 Yearbook*, p. 196; Garbe, *Zwischen Widerstand und Martyrium*, pp. 451f. In 1944 another change in attitude towards Jehovah's Witnesses was evident. Himmler suggested using German Jehovah's Witnesses as missionaries: »In this way we can prepare the groundwork to use German Witnesses in Russia in the future, and will thus have missionaries to pacify the Russian people by spreading Witness teachings.« (Letter from Heinrich Himmler to SS Lieutenant General Kaltenbrunner dated July 21, 1944, probably not preserved in the original, but excerpted in: Friedrich Zipfel, *Kirchenkampf in Deutschland, 1933-1945: Religionsverfolgung und Selbstbehauptung der Kirchen in der nationalsozialistischen Zeit* (Berlin, 1965), p. 201; and Garbe, *Zwischen Widerstand und Martyrium*, p. 458.

86 *1974 Yearbook*, p. 197; Änne Dickmann, »Erinnerungsbericht« (1994); and Wilhelm Lange, »Lagerbericht« (n. d.), p. 9.

87 Sachsenhausen Archives, R 122: Otto Hartstang, Erinnerungsbericht (October 10, 1995); and R 132: Jan van den Berg, Erinnerungsbericht (1995), copy from AWT.

88 Internationaler Suchdienst, ed., *Verzeichnis der Haftstätten unter dem Reichsführer SS (1933-1945)* (Arolsen, 1979), p. 271.

89 Ibid., p. 268.

90 Sachsenhausen Archives, R 214 M 56: copy from Moscow »Special Archive.«

91 Sachsenhausen Archives, R 136: Statement by Paul Wauer (Capri, May 21, 1945), 5, copy from Rijksinstituut voor Oorlogsdocumentatie; Gerhard Oltmann's diary (n. d.), 117-120. Staatsarchiv Münster, 6 Ks 1/61, vol. 390.24 (XXIV), pp. 177f.: statement by Paul Marquardt dated March 25, 1960, in the trial vs. Baumkoetter and others.

92 Erich Frost was allowed to write his first longer letter home, see Erich Frost, »Erinnerungsbericht« (March 7, 1971), pp. 69ff.

93 Gerhard Oltmann's diary (n. d.), pp. 117-120; Erich Frost »Erinnerungsbericht« (March 7, 1971), pp. 76f., in private collection.

94 1974 Yearbook, p. 198; Sachsenhausen Archives, R 132/15: AWT copies; Hennes Pieper, in Vrijuit (May 3, 1997); Aart Bouter »Erinnerungsbericht« (April 9, 1990).

95 Harald Abt, Erinnerungsbericht, in Watchtower (April 15, 1980), p. 10; Louis Piechota, »Erinnerungsbericht,« in Watchtower (August 15, 1980), p. 7.

96 Sachsenhausen Archives, R 132: from AWT Jan Steinfort, »Erinnerungsbericht« (91/95), and Hermanus de Haan, »Erinnerungsbericht« (December 2, 1995).

97 See charts on »Statistics and Social Structure.«

98 Sachsenhausen Archives, R 33/26a: copy of Paul Buder, »Mein Lebenslauf« (n. d.), p. 48.

99 Ernst Wauer, in Watchtower (August 1, 1991), p. 27.

100 Sachsenhausen Archives: Werner Edling, »Erinnerungsbericht« (September 21/October 19, 1995).

101 1974 Yearbook, p. 194; and Ernst Seliger, in Watchtower (July 15, 1975), p. 424.

102 Private collection: Erich Frost, »Erinnerungsbericht« (March 7, 1971), pp. 67f.; Gerhard Oltmanns, »Erinnerungsbericht« (n. d.), pp. 110-114; and Songbook of Jehovah's Witnesses.

103 1974 Yearbook, p. 194; and Harald Abt, Erinnerungsbericht, in Watchtower (April 15, 1980), p. 10.

104 Private collection: Erich Frost, »Erinnerungsbericht« (March 7, 1971), p. 75.

105 There were also family links to Ravensbrück as wives, mothers, and/or sisters were imprisoned there and male relatives were also sometimes incarcerated in the Ravensbrück »men's camp.«

106 Wilhelm Lange, »Lagerbericht« (n. d.), p. 9.

107 The subcamp Lichterfelde was supplied once a week with letters and Biblical texts by 37-year-old Paul Grossmann, who worked there. See 1974 Yearbook, pp. 202ff. A Dutch Witness prisoner used the pretext of essential medical or dental care in the main camp to receive letters and publications from prisoners in the infirmary. See Sachsenhausen Archives, R 132: Johannes Steinfort, »Erinnerungsbericht« (91/95), from AWT.

108 Wilhelm Lange, »Lagerbericht« (n. d.), p. 1; Sachsenhausen Archives, R 122/16: Walter Hamann report »KzLg. Sachsenhausen - 1944,« (1970). Odd Nansen first became aware of these events on April 28, 1944. Odd Nansen, Von Tag zu Tag: Ein Tagebuch (Hamburg, 1949), p. 158. There were similar Gestapo operations in other concentration camps between the end of April and the beginning of May 1944.

109 Wilhelm Lange, »Lagerbericht« (n. d.), p. 1.

110 Wilhelm Lange »Lagerbericht« (n. d.), p. 3; 1974 Yearbook, p. 203.

111 For »death marches,« see Antje Zeiger, »Die Todesmärsche,« in: Günter Morsch, Befreiung: Sachsenhausen 1945 (Berlin, 1996), pp. 64-72.

112 Tuchel, Konzentrationslager, 212, document 37.3 »Die letzte Übersicht über die Zahl der Wachmannschaften und der KZ-Häftlinge aus der Amtsgruppe D vom 15. Januar 1945.«

113 Apart from the assumption that the prisoners would be evacuated, there were numerous rumors about what would happen to the prisoners as the Allies approached. For death march of Jehovah's Witnesses, see especially »Memorandum über den Auszug der Zeugen Jehovas aus dem Konzentrationslager Sachsenhausen vom 21.4. bis 3.5.1945,« Trost (note 16); Sachsenhausen Archives R 122/16: Walter Hamann, »Erinnerungsbericht« (Dec. 1970), pp. 27-31; and Louis Piechota, in Watchtower (August 15, 1980), pp. 5-8.

114 The owner of the farm, Gustav Edling, and his son, Werner Edling, were imprisoned as Witnesses in Sachsenhausen concentration camp from 1937 to 1940.

115 »Memorandum,« Trost (Bern, September 15, 1945), p. 4.

116 Ibid., p. 6.

117 See Wilhelm Lange, »Memorandum Teil II« (n. d.), p. 3 (unpublished).

118 Bundesarchiv Berlin, Stiftung Archiv der Parteien und Massenorganisationen, SAPMO DY 55 V 278 2/146: »Verzeichnis der in Schwerin befindlichen Bibelforscher (Hindenburg Kaserne)« includes 102 names, the majority had been incarcerated in Sachsenhausen. Moreover, numerous prisoners received new identity

papers, including Jehovah's Witnesses such as Otto Raschke, »Vorläufiger Personalausweis,« July 15, 1945. Dutch Witnesses were also registered in Hagenow. Copies from AWT in Sachsenhausen Archives, Photo archive 97.130.010.16: Police registration for Ferry Slegers in Hagenow, dated May 15, 1945.

Martin Guse

»The Little One … He Had to Suffer a Lot«: Jehovah's Witnesses in the Moringen Concentration Camp for Juveniles

In August 1940, young men were first consigned to the so-called »police protective custody camp for juveniles« in Moringen near Göttingen, Germany. This was a special concentration camp for juveniles which existed until April 1945. A corresponding camp for young women, aged 13 to 25, was established by the Nazi police state in the immediate vicinity of the Ravensbrück concentration camp for women. It existed from June 1942 to April 30, 1945. The police and SS named this camp after the vast region known as »Uckermark.«

Reinhard Heydrich, Chief of the Security Police and SD, first called for special camps for the incarceration of so-called »wayward,« »criminal,« and »noncomformist« youngsters in September 1939. This idea was developed in the Central Office of the Reich Criminal Police (RKPA), under the direction and control of its deputy director, Paul Werner. At a meeting of the Reich Defense Council (*Reichsverteidigungsrat*) chaired by Göring on February 1, 1940, the topic under review was the »supervision of youth.« The discussion focused on the increasing likelihood of growing »degenerate« conduct and juvenile delinquency for youngsters influenced by the war. On this occasion, Heydrich's demands were explicitly supported by Reich SS Leader Heinrich Himmler.[1]

After this meeting, the Reich Defense Council authorized the RKPA in Berlin to set up so-called protective custody camps for juveniles. A jurisdictional struggle lasting several months ensued between the police and the Ministry of Justice, during which the Ministry of Justice first sought to obtain a clearer definition of the juveniles at issue and also for clear legal command once they had been incarcerated in these camps. The police ultimately prevailed. An estimated 1,400 male youngsters were detained in Moringen between 1942 and the end of the war without judicial rulings, but were incarcerated on Nazi administrative orders or Gestapo protective custody arrest warrants.[2]

Himmler's reason for encouraging the building of a concentration camp for juveniles was based on his opinion that »reformatories do not achieve their goal.«[3] Himmler's statement temporarily ended many years of debate about the capability or ostensible »non-capability,« of bringing up youngsters placed in state juvenile institutions. The Reich Youth Welfare Law (*Reichsjugendwohlfahrtsgesetz* or RJWG) of July 5, 1922, created, for the first time, unified national regulations for public correctional education in Germany.[4] Paragraph 73 of this law provided for the »detention« of youngsters who were considered incorrigible, »impossible to raise properly,« or conspicuous in reformatories. A »detention« law was never passed either in the Weimar Republic or in Nazi Germany, although social workers engaged in lively discussions about it. The demand to separate youngsters who were considered intractable or impossible to raise properly and to transfer them from reformatories to »juvenile detention institutions« without correctional objectives but serving only to ensure manpower, ultimately failed in the Weimar Republic. This failure occurred because of the absence of a clear definition of »deprav-

Commandant's office in Moringen concentration camp.
Source: Niedersächsisches Landeskrankenhaus Moringen.

ity,« failure to identify the group to whom it would apply, unclear confinement procedures, and uncertain funding. Discussions about whom this law would affect included definitions of the clientele, as »malcontents,« »severe mental inferiors,« or »psychologically unbalanced.« For decades, biologists, welfare officials, and physicians had applied social Darwinism to welfare and social work, idealizing »healthy, noble, and productive« individuals in contrast to the »subnormal, immoral, and unfit.« During the economic recession, the social security net crumbled because of insufficient public funds, increasing the substantial gap between educational maxims stressing social adjustment and actual conditions in reformatories. During the 1920s and 1930s, social Darwinianism became more influential in welfare circles: »The quick passage of national legislation for the detention of the asocial, coupled with rehabilitation, must be emphatically demanded. Only then can cases of antisocial behavior – incorrigible individuals incapable of reform – be transferred to detention, in their own interest and in the interest of the community. ... Without this detention law, welfare correctional education promotes dangerous negative selection in terms of racial hygiene. We deliberately damage future generations, if we care for and guard at great cost and in splended institutions these mentally inferior elements, who will irrefutably descend into crime, begging, vagrancy, or prostitution, who on reaching legal age at 21 are then left to their own fate and given the chance to procreate, thereby enabling genetic defects to continue in ever more individuals and generations.«[5]

During the winter of 1932-1933, emergency decrees to cut costs in public institutions resulted in the release of countless youngsters, age 19 or older, from reformatories and welfare institutions, without the legislators giving any consideration to other possible options. Countless youngsters, both female and male, faced an uncertain future without further supervision.

In social work circles, the proclivity intensified to blame the youngsters for their learning difficulties in custodial care, and terms like »impossible to raise properly« and »inferior genetic material« became increasingly common.[6]

Moreover, in Nazi Germany, welfare groups continued to call for a detention law. This was achieved in part by the establishment of state »detention institutions« in Hamburg, Berlin, Baden, and the Rhineland.

Although legal provisions for regulating correctional education were formally unchanged in Nazi Germany, they were undermined and distorted by the new orientation of the Führer principle and Nazi state racism. The selection and exclusion of the »genetically inferior« was encouraged. The evaluation of youngsters in correctional institutions was increasingly based on genetic and racial criteria. The Law for the Prevention of Offspring with Hereditary Defects from July 14, 1933, resulted in the sterilization of innumerable youngsters in Nazi correctional homes.[7] Pedagogic experts and specialists in child upbringing increasingly demanded »special treatment« for residents in correctional schools who were allegedly »genetically damaged« or »racially alien,« as well as for noticeable incorrigibles who became conspicuous in the »institutional community.« The opening of the juvenile concentration camp took place simultaneously with preliminary work for a law regarding »aliens to the national community« (*Gemeinschaftsfremdengesetz*); this law was to give legitimacy to the incarceration of social outsiders in concentration camps, based on the 1920s and 1930s debates about detention.[8] However, the law was never implemented because of the war. Nevertheless, juvenile concentration camps provided welcome places of experimentation for the police and SS within the framework of earlier developments. The extensive acceptance of a social policy based on race and the separation of individuals considered »part of the community« from those deemed »alien to the community« contributed to the general radicalization of practices in German correctional homes. Many welfare and social workers viewed the juvenile concentration camps in Moringen and Uckermark as welcome substitutes for the long-requested detention law.

Drawing on many years of debates about cost-efficient »detention« of youngsters who were allegedly incapable of a proper upbringing, and referring to the »preventive custody decree« (*Vorbeugehafterlaß*) of December 14, 1937,[9] which enabled the police and SS to apprehend the »asocial« and »work shy (idlers),« male juveniles were initially imprisoned at the camp Moringen/ Solling in August 1940. The RKPA looked for a suitable site and based on their previous experience, rented the provincial work house in Moringen, a building that had already been used as a concentration camp for men and women by the police and SS between 1933 and 1938. Until late 1941, youngsters were housed in the former men's section of the Moringen work house in a multi-story stone building. In 1941, the SS erected new barracks, the so-called »Camp II,« as a cost-effective and expedient solution to the space problem that arose with the steadily increasing number of prisoners.

In order to give the camp the appearance of legitimacy, various ministries issued decrees formally regulating the arrest of male youngsters.[10] State youth welfare offices and regular *Kripo* (criminal police) detectives received the authority from the RKPA to recommend which troublesome youngsters should be placed in so-called »custody camps for juveniles.« Youth welfare offices received precise instructions for identifying »asocial« and »criminal« male and female youngsters for detention, and the number of agencies authorized to arrange custody increased considerably in the following years. Decrees containing vague language and guidelines that could be interpreted freely, allowed officials immense leeway to punish youngsters who demonstrated »unacceptable« behavior.[11] The privilege of formally requesting the detention of youngsters in

Aerial photo of Moringen concentration camp, in the thirties.
Source: Niedersächsisches Landeskrankenhaus Moringen.

juvenile concentration camps expanded rapidly from the criminal police (*Kripo*) and youth welfare offices to judges in guardianship courts, prisons, judicial offices, or district HJ (Hitler Youth) leaders. Consequently, corrective educational institutions and youth welfare offices, with regional differences, made frequent use of applications for the confinement of difficult and unsatisfactory youngsters. Paul Werner, deputy director of the RKPA, noted in a 1944 report that 50 percent of the first 1,000 prisoners in Moringen had previously been in juvenile institutions, and 716 boys had previous convictions for offenses against property.[12]

It is particularly noticeable that request forms for juvenile detention contain relatively brief accounts of a youngster's negative behavior or characteristics. Frequently, the enumeration of offenses or ostensible character flaws was skillfully utilized to construct a rationale for stigmatizing and criminalizing individuals, thereby corroborating the grounds for urgent confinement in a juvenile concentration camp, without possibility of appeal. It was routine to use vague language for behavior and to categorize the juveniles as »work shy,« »innate criminal,« and »community aliens.« The assessment of the »pupils« and the justifications for their confinement were actually a declaration of pedagogical bankruptcy. For example, an employee of the youth welfare office in Kattowitz, in a request dated July 18, 1944, suggested breaking one boy's »defiant attitude during puberty« by confining him in a concentration camp for juveniles.[13]

Inevitably, this mainly affected youngsters who, under the influence of the war, had tried to evade the increasing regimentation of all aspects of life, and those who came into conflict with the norms and values of the Nazi state. The increasing number of cases of »refusal to work,«

»staying away from work,« »wandering about,« theft, and sexually permissive lifestyles, were considered by the police and SS as »conduct deleterious to the national community.« It must be noted that, under the influence of the war and the resulting militarization of all aspects of life and work, the standard definitions of the terms »asocial« and »criminality« were extended considerably, especially when it seemed that state authority was being attacked by so-called internal enemies.[14]

When the Ministry of Justice complained that they had been excluded from arrests intiated by the police, the SS and police responded with tactical compromises. One such concession in 1944 gave guardianship court judges the right to convene hearings. Nevertheless, the police and SS partially won the competition for jurisdiction by setting up juvenile concentration camps. Subsequently, there were frequent public reports about the camps. The RKPA staff, the camp commandant, and the »camp's senior instructor« — a social worker in SS uniform — taught welfare training sessions and lectured at academic conferences of welfare associations and judicial officials. The social worker in an SS uniform defined his position as »a duty, because of his responsibility to the nation, solemnly to implement measures for segregating pernicious elements, neither as punishment nor reprisal, but, from the need, as in the case of lepers, to protect the healthy, peaceful sector of human society.«[15]

Until the war ended, the charade of a supposed final attempt to correct and train youngsters was maintained, although their actual situation, including increasing fatalities from malnutrition-related illnesses, was concealed. Moringen was merely considered as an object for SS and police propaganda, who recorded their new assignment as a complete success. The fact was concealed that that political »protective custody« of young males had already occurred in 1942 in Moringen.[16]

The reasons for incarceration in the Moringen concentration camp were many and varied, ranging from the previously mentioned pedagogical bankruptcy (»impossible to raise properly,« »uncontrollable,« or »delinquency«), to »refusal to work,« »loafing at work,« and »sabotage.« Others were confined for refusal to serve in the Hitler Youth. The RKPA, Gestapo, and SS also made arrests on racial grounds (for Sinti and Roma as well as Jews) and for eugenic reasons (the disabled and individuals likely to be sterilized), as well as homosexuals (i.e., male prostitutes), or because of insubordination, opposition, or direct resistance. Approximately 20 youngsters were confined in Moringen because they were fans of Anglo-American swing music and belonged to the Hamburg »Swing Youth«. Still others had been arrested because of their family relationship (*Sippenhaft*), such as 16-year-old Rainer Küchenmeister, whose father had been executed as a member of the »Red Orchestra« resistance group.[17]

The historian Heinrich Muth accurately classified the so-called protective custody juvenile camp in Moringen as a »general concentration camp for juveniles.«[18] He had studied only the archival records in the 1980s, but had no knowledge of actual camp conditions.

Direct governmental measures against Jehovah's Witnesses after 1933 also tangibly affected youngsters (children and teenagers). For example, they frequently encountered the arrest of one or both parents in a concentration camp, the denial of employment or business licenses for their one or both parents, and the cancellation of public stipends, such as state stipends to families with several children.[19] After the Nazi's assumed power, children of Jehovah's Witnesses confronted new ideological school curricula. Based on their religious beliefs about the exclusiveness of divine law, young Witnesses rejected any participation in ritualistic demonstrations of loyalty to the secular state, as for example, refusing to use the Hitler salute, disregarding mandatory attendance for saluting the flag or participating in parades during their daily school routine. They refused to render obeisance to the Nazi state, considering this as idolatry and blasphemy. This resulted in constant and escalating conflict with teachers and authorities, who responded with public humiliation, beatings, expulsion from school, and denial of apprenticeships.

As the detention of their parents in concentration camps intensified in 1936, the first children and teenage Witnesses were forcibly removed to juvenile detention centers. These centers were used in Nazi Germany specifically as punishment for nonconformist and opposition juveniles. Youth welfare offices began to place young Witnesses in »protective custody,« applying paragraph 56 of the Reich Youth Welfare Law (RJWG). This meant that officials would monitor and advise parents about raising their children. Detlef Garbe noted that »in practice, protective custody meant surveillance of parental conduct by youth welfare offices and their staff, resulting in complete control and operating also as social and political punishment.«[20] Moreover, parental custody was frequently invalidated under paragraph 1666 of the German Civil Code (BGB), resulting in state guardianship of minor children, since a Christian upbringing would inevitably lead Witness children to »spiritual and moral neglect.« Detlef Garbe described in detail the court proceeding against Mr. and Mrs. Z. from Hamburg. Parental custody was removed because they »maintained their belief in an international religious group« and »because the spiritual welfare of their children was acutely jeopardized.«[21] In his verdict, the presiding judge mentioned that removal of parental custody was politically motivated: »For years, the parents emphasized spiritual values at home ... making life in the national community virtually impossible.« Later, the Hanseatic Legal and Court Journal [*Hanseatische Rechts- und Gerichtszeitschrift*] formulated and legitimized this policy: »Custody must be removed from parents if they teach their children sanctimonious fanaticism, thereby alienating them from the ideas of the Nazi state.«

Youth welfare offices and their employees were thus given a lever to use against Jehovah's Witnesses, although it was nearly impossible for them to prove that the general welfare of such children and teenagers was endangered daily. Instead, they reported about caring and exemplary parents, and »industrious, attentive, well-mannered, and enthusiastic« children. Despite »exemplary conduct in school,« the youngsters »refusal to give the Hitler salute« was used to vilify these youngsters as religious fanatics, with »abnormal tendencies« and »incorrigible.« Therefore, the matter did not really involve parental neglect, but only an alleged gross indifference to the »German national community.« Welfare offices and guardianship courts considered the state's right to instruct children as having precedence over that of the parents. On June 21, 1937, the Gestapo issued a decree that enforced custody of Jehovah's Witnesses throughout the Reich.

In general, governmental agencies were appointed as guardians, although individual guardians were designated in certain specific situations. The children and teenagers concerned were generally placed in »politically unobjectionable« foster families, and above all in state correctional institutions.[22]

In addition to parents and schools, a law dated December 1, 1936, designated the Hitler Youth as the official state youth organization responsible for the »upbringing of German youth.«[23] Jehovah's Witnesses' refusal to send their children to the Hitler Youth, mandatory after 1939, resulted in additional cases removing parental custody.[24]

Detlef Garbe legitimately describes this as unequivocal »child abduction,« used as coercion to break resistance by Jehovah's Witnesses. Welfare offices and their staffs, played a decisive role in implementing state ideological measures, that were not devised for the »welfare of the child.«

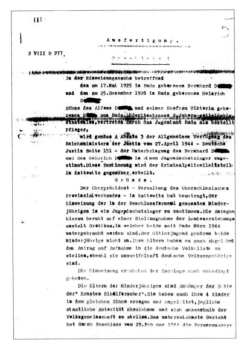

Ruling by the Ruda Local Court about removing Bernhard and Heinrich D. to Moringen. Source: Archiwum Panstwowego w Katowicach, Poland.

In reality, they knowingly and deliberately destroyed countless families, causing extended separation of parents from their children above the age of six, and strictly prevented any possible contacts by refusing to reveal the child's new location.

In the new environments of correctional institutions and foster families, youngsters were exposed to various coercive measures, such as ideological reeducation, humiliations, and beatings. Male and female children who resisted again became conspicuous to welfare personnel, and could be labelled »incorrigible« resulting in deportation to one of the three juvenile concentration camps: the Moringen and Uckermark »juvenile protective custody concentration camps,« or the Polish »juvenile detention camp« in Litzmannstadt.

A revealing case file about two brothers, Bernhard and Heinrich D., demonstrates the aggressive practices of youth welfare offices. In this case, both the district juvenile correctional institution and the Kattowitz district youth welfare office petitioned that Witness children labelled »delinquent« be transferred to the Moringen juvenile concentration camp. Nineteen-year-old Bernhard D. and his 17-year-old brother, Heinrich D., came from Ruda. Their parents, Alfons and Viktoria D., lost custody in February 1944, and the two boys were temporarily transferred to a juvenile institution. »The parents belong to the Earnest Bible Students sect. They have raised their four children in the teachings of this sect. Because they reject national and racial goals and refuse to obey the law, their teaching is subversive and dangerous to the state.«[25] The father, Alfons D., was deported to Auschwitz, after refusing to apply for enrollment on the »German Ethnic List.«[26] The two sons had been confined in the Grottkau Nazi juvenile correctional institution since late March 1944. On August 7, 1944, the youth welfare

Translation of the document on p. 102:
Official Copy
2 VIII D 277.
Ruling
Regarding the confinement of
   Bernhard D., born in Ruda on May 17, 1925, and Heinrich D., born in Ruda on December 25, 1926,
   sons of Alfons D. and his wife, Viktoria, née G., from Ruda, Lüderitzstrasse 2, Jehovah believers, stateless, represented by the Ruda Youth Welfare Office as appointed guardians.
   Based on the general regulations of the Reich Minister of Justice dated April 27, 1944, section A paragraph 3, published in Deutsche Justiz, page 151, we herewith agree to the confinement of Bernhard D. and Heinrich D. in a protective custody camp for juveniles. Permission is given to the Criminal Investigation Department, Kattowitz.
Justification
   The provincial governor of the Upper Silesian region in Kattowitz has petitioned for approval to commit the above-named minor children to a protective custody camp for juveniles. This request is based on a report by the Grottkau regional reform school where both boys have been placed since late March 1944. Both minors do not belong to the Hitler Youth. Their parents have also refused enrollment on the German Ethnic List, although they are ethnic Germans without any doubt.
   Committal seems to be absolutely necessary in this situation. The parents of the minors are members of the Jehovah's Witness sect. They have also raised their four children according to this creed and taught them to reject any governmental authority and to remain separate from the national community. The undersigned court has awarded ... custody of these minors under formal order issued on February 29, 1944. It simultaneously ordered the minors be provisionally placed in a reform school. However, this was not successful with both boys. The minors still refuse to join the community. They refuse to give the German salute, have a casual and indifferent attitude when the flag is raised, and thus are not acceptable in a reform school community, because they do not want to conform to the existing order. When the district youth welfare office specialist visited the institution and came across the boys working in the garden, they did not acknowledge his presence, and even acted as though he was not present because he wore a Hitler Youth uniform. Both minors have become so firmly rooted in the subversive ideas of the Earnest Bible Students that they do not wish to be freed from them. Corrective education cannot succeed with them. On the contrary, the boys pose a threat to the institution since their negative attitude might be imitated and cause a revolt. An attempt to change their views must be made through intervention in a protective custody camp for juveniles. It seems that only strict and severe measures might be successful. It is for this reason that the requested detention has been approved.
Ruda, August 11, 1944
Local Court
signed: Dr. von Horn, Regional Court Judge.
Order issued by:
Court registrar of the Local Court

office conceded that the boys »undoubtedly« seemed »well-behaved and did not cause any of the usual problems connected with upbringing.« However, the institution justified their request for confinement as follows: »Their passive political attitude made them a great danger to the institutional community. The boys always remained at ease during flag-raising and would not use the ›Heil Hitler‹ salute. For them, the war was the work of Lucifer, a fallen son of God. God did not allow them to participate in any form of warfare, not even as medics. The enlightened had to endure the consequences of such actions and beliefs. The boys confronted such martyrdom, not just passively, but with joy. Correctional education has failed to free them from their religious obsession. These minors have an advanced form of pathological religious fanaticism. In Bernhard's case, religious mania is so extreme that physicians have already considered placing him in a psychiatric institution. ... Thus, I am requesting the incarceration of these youngsters in a protective custody juvenile concentration camp.«[27]

Four days later, the Ruda Local Court, represented by Regional Court Judge Dr. von Horn, upheld the district youth welfare office's petition. Moreover, it confirmed the grounds for arrest based on its own investigation of the daily routine in the Grottkau juvenile home, stating: »When the district youth welfare office specialist visited the institution and came across the boys working in the garden, they did not acknowledge his presence, and even acted as though he was not present because he wore a Hitler Youth uniform. Both minors have become so firmly rooted in the subversive ideas of the Earnest Bible Students that they do not wish to be freed from them. Corrective education cannot succeed with them. On the contrary, the boys pose a threat to the institution since their negative attitude might be imitated and cause a revolt. An attempt to change their views must be made through intervention in a protective custody camp for juveniles. It seems that only strict and severe measures might be successful. It is for this reason that the requested detention has been approved.«[28]

On August 31, 1944, the Kattowitz Gestapo got involved in the matter and ordered the youngsters, for the last time, to renounce their faith and request inclusion in the German Ethnic List. Bernhard and Heinrich D. unequivocally refused. The Gestapo cancelled their incarceration in Moringen — the reasons for this cannot be found in the surviving records — and ordered their deportation to other concentration camps, thereby closing their case file. Further research revealed that Bernhard and Heinrich D. were deported to Gross-Rosen and later to the Buchenwald concentration camp. Their sisters, Rosa and Edith, were placed under arrest conditions in a monastery near Oppeln.

Former Moringen prisoners recounted that a relatively large group of Jehovah's Witnesses were incarcerated in the concentration camp for juveniles. Moreover, they could still remember the Witnesses resolute refusal to work in the army weapons factory (MUNA) in Volpriehausen; this factory was one of the largest Moringen labor details, and the SS demanded harsh punishment for noncompliance. Werner Christ from Vienna remembered: »The youngsters confined in Moringen because of their religious outlook always made us, the other inmates, sit up and take notice. Despite bitter and onerous persecution, these people maintained such consistent beliefs that, in the end, the SS labelled them camp idiots. They refused to work in the armament plants, which in any other camp would have resulted in death sentences. Even when they had been brutally beaten, their convictions did not change. I once witnessed a newly arrived prisoner stating the following at the entrance to MUNA in Volpriehausen: ›This plant produces grenades. Grenades kill people, and human beings were not made to kill each other but to live in peace!‹ Of course, this was reported and punished. This didn't worry the Bible Students, since they wanted to be assigned only to unimportant work.«[29]

The unwavering beliefs of one Jehovah's Witness impressed the former political prisoner, Erwin Rehn. He stated: »And Meyer had just turned 18, and could be drafted, when we were still in Camp II. And thus he was kept with us. He did not report for induction into the army. Meyer, a Bible Student, was newly assigned to MUNA, and he stood at the entrance to the shaft and said: ›I won't touch that! I don't touch guns, no weapons. I don't touch ammunition. I'm not allowed to.‹ The SS then made fun of him and said: ›Now get to work!‹ But he replied: ›No. I'm not going to touch that!‹ The SS replied: ›So that you can go to heaven. You'll be going there without delay.‹ Then they filled his pockets with grenades, put them in his shirt, both defused and live grenades. But he removed them all and threw them away. They then beat him till he was motionless. We thought he was dead, but he was tough ... Later he was again assigned to MUNA, and was allowed to sweep the work area; they never tried to force ammunition into his hands again.«[30]

Jonathan Stark from Ulm, prisoner 1140 in Moringen concentration camp for juveniles, executed in the Sachsenhausen concentration camp on November 1, 1944. Source: Watchtower History Archive, Selters, Germany.

The SS and army developed violent techniques that deliberately involved completely insecure and easily manipulated prisoners against the unwavering resistance by Jehovah's Witnesses. The ammunitions plant was placed under army management. »In any case, reports kept arriving, either from guards or civilian workers, that he had refused to do this or that task. Thus the head of the labor detail tried to terrorize him, and encouraged other prisoners to beat him up since his refusal to work meant more work for them. They were evidently already angry at him because they had said: ›He is trying to get out of work and we have to put up with that!‹ They didn't understand what it meant to be a Bible Student. ... I only know that they beat him to a pulp. He lay there without making a sound since it wouldn't have made any difference.«[31]

Life for Jehovah's Witnesses in the concentration camp meant disciplinary reports resulting in punishment and beatings. Former prisoners told me about rumors that had circulated in the camp that one of the Witnesses was beaten to death in MUNA by either the SS or the army. Ex-prisoner Werner Koepke had suspected what would happen to his two fellow prisoners at their release from the camp. He said, »When we marched out to work, they were standing in front of the guardhouse in civilian clothing. Rumors circulated that ›They'll never be released!‹ The little one ... he had to suffer a lot. He was whipped repeatedly by S ... He really suffered. I heard that he had torn up his draft notice. That was probably what enraged S. He had said: ›You are fighting for Germany, and this one, doesn't feel like it.‹ People claimed that the Bible Students would only have to sign and they would have been released. Either they were placed on trial, and may even have received the death penalty.«[32]

Werner Koepke's concluding speculation can be confirmed in the archival record for at least two Jehovah's Witnesses who had been imprisoned in Moringen concentration camp: Erich Meyer, born on June 14, 1925, in Rheydt, was arrested in Mönchengladbach in September 1942. From the end of 1942 until the summer of 1943, he was incarcerated in Moringen and assigned prisoner number 839. He was sentenced to death for refusing military service and the SS transported him to the Berlin-Charlottenburg police prison where he was executed at the beginning of 1945.[33]

Jonathan Stark was assigned inmate number 1140 in Moringen. The 17-year-old came from Ulm where he had graduated from art school. He had lost his job as a lithographer because of his religious beliefs. He was conscripted for the Reich Labor Service on October 1, 1943, but refused to take an oath to »Führer and State.« After initial Gestapo interrogations, he was finally arrested on November 23, 1943, and transferred to the Stuttgart police prison. There he met inmate Walter Schumann who later remembered secret conversations with the young man. »He was not in the least sad about his imprisonment and candidly told me that he belonged to the Bible Students organization, and his deep personal conviction did not allow him to swear an oath to Adolf Hitler. His name was Stark and he came from Ulm. He knew what awaited him: Welzheim concentration camp. Several of his fellow believers were already incarcerated there. He mentioned that his family had remained secretly in contact with them, and he had been informed in detail about their treatment there. Initially, he was imprisoned at the Reich Labor Service and coerced in various ways to swear the oath. Since he had remained firm, he was handed over to the Gestapo for further treatment. Stark continued in his report: ›But, another official arrived during my interrogation, a fat, unpleasant person, who screamed that I was a disloyal scoundrel and it would be best if I were shot without delay. The young man had been informed about his father's imprisonment and told that he, too, ought to be executed; in fact, all Bible Students (should receive death penalties). Yet, none of this intimidated young Stark. It was evident that he was prepared to be a martyr and, if necessary, to die for his beliefs.«[34]

Jonathan Stark was not transferred from the Stuttgart police prison to Welzheim, but in early 1944 was instead deported to the Moringen juvenile concentration camp. There the SS assigned him to the political prisoners group, the so-called (Ge)Stapo prisoners, and he was housed in the corresponding cell block. He was transported to the Sachsenhausen concentration camp in the fall of 1944 and placed in Block 14, awaiting execution. On November 1, 1944, at the age of 18, Jonathan Stark was hanged.[35]

Another Jehovah's Witness, Emil Wohlfahrt, born on May 22, 1928, in Carinthia was also incarcerated as a political prisoner in Moringen from December 1, 1944, until the camp was dissolved. He was assigned inmate number 1365.[36]

Like all other prisoners, Witnesses incarcerated in the so-called protective custody juvenile camp in Moringen experienced an organizational structure similar to concentration camps for adults. Police councillor and SS Major Karl Dieter was camp commandant until 1944; he was then recalled because of an investigation of camp commandants suspected of corruption.[37] SS block leaders for the Moringen concentration camp were recruited from the Waffen SS and the SS Security Service; the 130 member guard unit belonged to the SS Death's Head unit.[38] The SS and civilians handled daily affairs in the commandant's office and the camp was placed

Entrance to MUNA armaments factory in Volpriehausen.
The Witnesses consistently refused to work there. Source: Detlef Herbst, Volpriehausen.

under the direct jurisdiction of the Inspectorate of Concentration Camps (Office D – Concentration Camps of the SS Central Office for Economy and Administration) in Oranienburg for 15 months in 1942 and 1943.[39] All general regulations for concentration camps also applied to Moringen, as well as Ravensbrück, Stutthof, Flossenbürg, Auschwitz, or Mauthausen. In fact, both so-called protective custody camps for juveniles were listed in the telephone directory for concentration camps.

For inmates, daily life in the camps was organized in a standardized daily routine focused around military drills.[40] The oppressive routine was couched in absolute dogmas, proclaiming »work, cleanliness, order, punctuality, and discipline« and their brutal implementation through countless regulations, roll calls, and punishments. In a lecture, the camp's so-called »senior instructor« mentioned 51 different types of authorized »disciplinary measures.« These included, among others: infringements during the frequent roll calls (for example, head counts, locker checks, bed inspections, examinations for cleanliness, and inspection of eating utensils), violations against camp regulation (such as, escape attempts or establishing impermissible contacts), unsatisfactory work performance, and thefts of food. Any form of deviant conduct or resistance by the prisoners was precisely registered by the oppressive apparatus, based on official and unofficial sanctions and persecution. Prisoners found the withholding of privileges and disciplinary penalties especially painful, above all deprivation of food, standing at attention for many hours, and whippings, as well as so-called »punishment sport.« Major concerns in Moringen, similar to all other concentration camps, included the unlimited exploitation of labor with utterly insufficient food and inadequate medical care. The prisoners' ten to twelve hour workday was utilized primarily for armaments production and supporting the war effort. Prisoners at concentration camps for juveniles were also assigned farming work or building highways, and also working for companies, such as Wayss & Freitag. Moreover, inmates' wages, usually substantially below standard pay rates, were established by contract between the SS and the companies, and companies remitted these sums directly to the SS. Up to now, the affected former prisoners have not received a single wage payment. This exploitation of juvenile labor ensured considerable profit from withheld wages for both the SS and the business enterprises, and guaranteed a continuous supply of cheap, replaceable labor. After 1942, the number of deaths from malnutrition and starvation increased; thereafter no substantial improvement in conditions occurred. Thus, the SS condoned the potential death of young prisoners.

The juvenile prisoners were also vulnerable to another life threatening danger: pseudo-scientific evaluations by the staff of the Criminal Biological Research Institute (KBI) at the Reich Kripo Offices. The Ministry of the Interior issued a decree on December 21, 1941, announcing that the Institute was attached to the RKPA to increase its authority and to intensify police measures for the »prevention of crime.«[41] Dr. Robert Ritter, director of this Institute and previously instrumental in the genocide of Sinti and Roma,[42] defined the work of the KBI regarding juveniles designated »alien to the community.« »The growth and development of criminals and their offspring can be cut out at the roots by genetic engineering. The great future task of criminal biology is in fighting crime by eugenics.«[43] The decree also explicitly defined the KBI's main task to include the screening and selection of juveniles incarcerated in Moringen.[44] This was to be based on all available data for juvenile inmates; curriculum vita, behavior reports, expert opinions, welfare files, and other data were compiled and listed. Ritter and his coworkers research into »hereditary criminal proclivities« involved repeated and systematic interviews with juvenile inmates, including information about the professions and illnesses of parents and grandparents, the development of puberty, school life, occupation, the prisoners' own illnesses, knowledge of how the youngster had spent his free time, and his circle of friends. In this way, Ritter sought to establish a direct connection between certain professions (pages, messengers, domestics, movie projectionists, shop assistants, auto mechanics' assistant) and criminal tendencies.

Ritter's previous work had suggested patterns that stereotyped entire groups and classified them as »asocial« and »criminal,« and he modified this model to fit the Moringen concentration camp. Observations, tests, and evaluations of Moringen inmates were constantly repeated and expanded. Ritter developed different cell block systems for both juvenile concentration camps. The system in Moringen included certain special features. He codified individual prisoners based upon his personal assessments and character ratings. They were classified into »types,« for example, D Block was assigned to permanent failures (*Dauerversager*); S Block was for disruptive elements (*Störer*), U for the unfit (*Untauglichen*), etc.

SS block leaders prepared regular semi-annual reports about the conduct of individual inmates, which were then forwarded by the camp administration to the KBI. Criminal biologists recorded all camp offenses, such as escape attempts, food thefts, unsatisfactory work, infringements in making beds and neatness, as well as all announced and implemented punishments.

This system of prisoner evaluations and categorization required unconditional subordination and complete obedience. The criminal biologists evaluated any form of rebellion against enslavement and any attempt by youngsters to improve camp living conditions by unauthorized actions, as further proof of »hereditary depravity.« Robert Ritter carried out his pseudo-scientific experiments on living human beings. He considered Moringen juvenile concentration camp to be a »treasure trove for the KBI«; this was mentioned by the president of the Essen Regional Court during a visit to Moringen in 1944.[45] The prisoners' life depended on criminal biologists rating categories. Release from custody was an exception for youngsters. Other »releases,« based on KBI judgments, meant transfer to state hospitals and nursing homes with an uncertain fate for the affected individual; it also meant transfer to a jail or penitentiary, the Reich Labor Service, or army. Furthermore, Ritter and his colleagues arranged for at least 55 transfers to large concentration camps and suggested sterilizations.[46] The camp commandant and camp physician requested sterilizations, that were then carried out by physicians from the Göttingen University Clinic.[47] RKPA reports reveal that at least 123 young people were transferred from Moringen and Uckermark juvenile camps to adult concentration camps based on the »scientists« genetic and criminal-biological predictions.

Youngsters confined in Moringen and Uckermark had no leeway for developing their own personalities. During an important phase of their development, often still in puberty, they were torn from familiar surroundings, robbed of their names, and degraded to mere numbers. The youngsters were, from early morning reveille until evening lock-up in dormitories or barracks, incessantly subjected to demands and requirements, as well as regimentation and punishment. The constant expectation of penalties and punishment led to constant psychological and physical stress, which at best could only be avoided during the few hours of nightly sleep. While still developing physically, the completely frightened boys were helplessly exposed to camp conditions and thus easily exploited by the SS. The cell block system, a cleverly devised system of reporting and punishment, awarded functions such as camp elder, barrack leader, or table senior to control the prisoners and to play them off against each other. Thus, it is not accurate to speak about a homogeneous »prisoner community« in Moringen. Solidarity and friendship were mechanisms for survival and were generally limited to small groups. Some prisoners sought to secure better conditions and privileges in the camp by denunciation or by performing services for the SS. For a few prisoners, self-mutilation and suicide attempts were desperate means of escaping unbearable conditions.[48] Prisoner clothing, made from the simplest denim, and wooden shoes, provided no protection during fall and winter. Illnesses, such as dysentery, typhoid fever, and tuberculosis, increased as a result of inadequate nourishment and wretched conditions in unheated dormitories and barracks. The youngsters also suffered from diphtheria, hepatitis, skin rashes, and bladder infections. The SS transferred prisoners with tuberculosis to a sanatorium in Benninghausen, near Paderborn, to prevent the spread of tuberculosis in the camp and thus protect the remaining prisoners for labor. Twenty-four Moringen prisoners who contracted tuberculosis died at Benninghausen; they arrived there in appalling condition, physically debilitated, and considerably underweight.[49] In Moringen itself, at least 55 youngsters died, mostly as a result of the horrible living conditions, diseases caused by malnutrition, and suicide. Four boys died in traffic accidents en route to labor assignments; four were executed by firing squad or »shot attempting to escape«; and another died under unknown circumstances in the Göttingen hospital.[50] These death statistics were based on surviving archival records. Former prisoners also reported additional unregistered deaths. It is also impossible to determine how many youngsters died during the evacuation march, after Moringen was closed, in early April 1945. Although we cannot conclusively establish an exact number of deaths based on existing archival sources, we can assume that one youngster in ten did not survive Moringen. The permanent emotional and physical damage to survivors is immeasurable.

The formation and development of Moringen reveals the direct and indirect complicity of German welfare authorities as well as scientists such as Ritter in the Nazi persecution and genocidal program. The German welfare system readily complied with tasks assigned by the fascist system, by establishing the rigid separation of youngsters into two groups: those »who belonged to the national racial community« and those defined as »alien.« The youth welfare offices and reform schools became accomplices in fascist disciplinary methods. Youngsters who could not be »broken« by these methods were deported to protective custody concentration camps for juveniles. In this manner, detention in concentration camps under SS control was recognized as an expedient »form of upbringing.« The religious association of Jehovah's Witnesses was particularly affected by these exclusionary social-educational practices.

Notes

1   Bundesarchiv Koblenz (hereafter BAK), R 22/1189. The following participated in the meeting, among others: Reich Ministers Goebbels, Frick, Lammers, Kerrl and Rust; various state secretaries from various ministries; Reich youth leaders; Staff Officer Lauterbacher, as well as Himmler and Heydrich for the police. See Heinrich Muth, »Das ›Jugendschutzlager‹ Moringen,« in *Dachauer Hefte* 5 (1989), pp. 223-252.

2   Institut für Zeitgeschichte, Munich (hereafter IfZ): Muth collection, Analysis of the »Lagerbuch Moringen« at the International Tracing Service in Arolsen, and at the BAK (hereafter cited as »Lagerbuch Moringen.«) The International Tracing Service has refused the author research access to the Lagerbuch.

3   BAK, R 22/1189.

4   *Reichsgesetzblatt* (hereafter RGBl) 1922, I: pp. 633ff.

5   Vossen, *Die FE (Fürsorgererziehung) der über Achtzehnjährigen* (Berlin 1925), p. 104.

6   For the development and background in education in reformatories, see Elizabeth Harvey, »Die Jugendfürsorge in der Endphase der Weimarer Republik: Das Beispiel Fürsorgeerziehung,« in: H. U. Otto and H. Sünker, *Soziale Arbeit und Faschismus* (Frankfurt, 1989), 198-227; and Martin Guse and Andreas Kohrs, »Zur Entpädagogisierung der Jugendfürsorge in den Jahren 1922-1945,« ibid., pp. 228-249.

7   RGBl 1933: I, no. 86, pp. 529-531.

8   See BAK R 22: vols. 943 and 944.

9   See Karl Leo Terhorst, *Polizeiliche planmäßige Überwachung und polizeiliche Vorbeugungshaft im »Dritten Reich«* (Heidelberg, 1985), especially pp. 115ff.

10 Decree of the Reich Minister of the Interior, October 3, 1941, re: »Einweisung in das Jugendschutzlager Moringen,« in *Ministerialblatt für die Preußische innere Verwaltung* (hereafter MBliV) 1941, no. 41, cols. 1773-1774.

11 Circular of the Reich Leader SS and Chief of the German Police, dated April 25, 1944, re: Einweisung in die polizeilichen Jugendschutzlager, in *MBliV*. (1944), no. 19, cols. 437-439; General Regulations of the Reich Ministry of Justice, dated April 27, 1944, re: »Unterbringung in polizeilichen Jugendschutzlagern,« ibid., cols. 437-439; decree of Youth Leader of the German Reich, dated May 5, 1944, re: »Unterbringung Jugendlicher in polizeilichen Jugendschutzlagern,« ibid., cols. 439-441; Circular of the Reich Ministry of the Interior, dated April 26, 1944, re: »Unterbringung in Jugendschutzlagern,« ibid., cols. 445-46; Circular of the Reich Ministry of the Interior, dated October 26, 1944, re: »Unterbringung im Jugendschultzlager,« in: MbliV., 1944, v. 9 (105.), no. 44, col. 1066.

12 Paul Werner, »Die Einweisung in die polizeilichen Jugendschutzlager,« in *Deutsches Jugendrecht*, no. 4 (Berlin, 1944), p. 103.

13 Glowna Komisja Badania Zbrodni Hitlerowskich w Polsce [Main Commission for the Investigation of Nazi Crimes in Poland], Warsaw, microfilm 48.

14 For example, Hitler believed »that even the theft of a handbag committed by minors should be punishable by the death penalty.« See BAK, R 22, v. 1176, p. 225.

15 IfZ, Muth collection, A (Sammlung Ihrig II).

16 See note 2, Lagerbuch Moringen. A decree of the Central Office for Reich Security (RSHA), dated December 4, 1942, announced that youngsters who had been arrested in police detention under protective custody

warrants for longer than three weeks, had to be sent to Moringen and Uckermark »protective custody juvenile camps,« in *Befehlsblatt des Chefs der Sipo und des SD* (Berlin, 1942) v. 3 , no. 56: p. 362.

17 For the story of Rainer Küchenmeister, see the documentary novel: Manfred Flügge, *Meine Sehnsucht ist das Leben: Eine Geschichte aus dem deutschen Widerstand* (Berlin, 1996).

18 Muth, »Jugendschutzlager« Moringen, p. 240 (see note 1).

19 See Detlef Garbe, *Zwischen Widerstand und Martyrium: Die Zeugen Jehovas im »Dritten Reich,«* 3rd ed. (Munich, 1997), pp. 186–220.

20 Ibid., p. 195.

21 Ibid., pp. 196f.

22 In this connection, the case of 13 year old Hans Thoenes from Moers is applicable. His mother had been incarcerated in the Moringen women's concentration camp from August 18, 1936 to February 25, 1937. On February 5, 1937, the Moers Local Court ordered the boy transferred to a juvenile institution, »to save the otherwise useful boy from complete spiritual and moral neglect.« Information courtesy of Hans Hesse, based on North-Rhine Westphalia Hauptstaatsarchiv Düsseldorf (hereafter HSTA Düsseldorf): RW 58, no. 8430, p. 6 Rs.

23 RGBl (1936) I: p. 993.

24 »Jugenddienstverordnung« of March 25, 1939, RGBl (1939) I: p. 710.

25 Archiwum Panstwowego w Katowicach, Sygn. Kattowitz District Administration, no. 6745, p. 2, request for committing the juvenile correctional students Bernhard and Heinrich D. to a protective custody juvenile camp.

26 The »German Ethnic List« (*Deutsche Volksliste*) was part of Nazi Germanization policy in the occupied Eastern territories. Himmler's decree of March 4, 1943, enrolled former Polish citizens on this list and divided them into four groups for determining their degree of Germanness. Group I included ethnic Germans and their relatives, who actively acknowledged their Germanness before the war.« See Hermann Weiss, »Deutsche Volksliste,« in: Wolfgang Benz and others, eds., *Enzykolpädie des Nationalsozialismus* (Munich, 1997), pp. 424f. Jews and Sinti and Roma could not be registered in the »German Ethnic List.« The list created categories for the racial segregation of a large portion of the population.

27 Archiwum Panstwowego w Katowicach, Sygn. Kattowitz District Administration, no. 6745, pp. 2f., request to commit the juvenile correctional students Bernhard and Heinrich D. to a protective custody juvenile concentration camp.

28 Ibid., p. 6.

29 M. Guse Archive: Werner Christ, Gedächtnisbericht (1986); Christ was prisoner no. 700.

30 Conversation M. Guse and A. Kohrs with Erwin Rehn, December 20, 1984.

31 Conversations M. Guse and A. Kohrs with Fritz Laska, November 3 and 23, 1984.

32 Conversation M. Guse, A. Kohrs, and M. Buddrus with Werner Koepke, December 3, 1985.

33 Lagerbuch Moringen; Watchtower History Archive, Selters, Germany: statements by Erich Meyer's brothers/ sisters.

34 Walter Schumann, *Nur vierzehn Tage: Ein Tatsachenbericht* (Stuttgart, n. d.), pp. 107f.

35 Lagerbuch Moringen; Watchtower History Archive, Selters: statement by Jonathan Stark's father, November 21, 1945. See Annedore Leber, *Das Gewissen steht auf: Lebensbilder aus dem deutschen Widerstand von 1933-1945* (Berlin, 1954), p. 20, as well as Silvester Lechner, *Das KZ Oberer Kuhberg und die NS-Zeit in der Region Ulm/Neu-Ulm* (Ulm, 1988), p. 89.

36 Lagerbuch Moringen; Watchtower History Archive, Selters.

37 Muth, »Jugendschutzlager Moringen,« p. 245.

38 BAK Berlin, including Dahlwitz-Hoppegarten Archive: ZB 5237; also the former Berlin Document Center archives now deposited at BAK Berlin-Lichterfelde; and the Auschwitz Memorial Museum Archives.

39 *Trials of War Criminals Before the Nuremberg Military Tribunals Under Control Law No. 10*, v. 5, pp. 298ff., containing report by Oswald Pohl, Chief of the SS Central Office for Economy and Administration, April 30, 1942; and letter from Pohl to Heydrich, May 30, 1942, noting that he had already stated on June 18, 1941, he would be willing to work out a budget for building the protective custody camp for juveniles. See also Glowna Komisja Badania Zbrodni Hitlerowskich w Polsce, Warsaw, and the IfZ: Fa 506/13, pp. 248-249.

40 Lower Saxony Hauptstaatsarchiv, Hanover, and conversations with survivors.

41 MBliV (1942), no. 2, cols. 41-43.

42 Michael Zimmermann, *Rassenutopie und Genozid: Die nationalsozialistische »Lösung der Zigeunerfrage«* (Hamburg, 1996), pp. 172ff.; Joachim S. Hohmann, *Robert Ritter und die Erben der Kriminalbiologie*

(Frankfurt, 1991); and Patrick Wagner, *Volksgemeinschaft ohne Verbrecher: Konzeptionen und Praxis der Kriminalpolizei in der Zeit der Weimarer Republik und des Nationalsozialismus* (Hamburg, 1996), pp. 274ff.

43 Robert Ritter, »Das kriminalbiologische Institut der Sicherheitspolizei,« *Kriminalistik* 16, no. 11 (Berlin, 1942), p. 117.

44 Decree Reich Ministry of Interior, December 21, 1941, in: *MBliV* (Berlin, 1942), no. 2, cols. 41–43.

45 BAK, R 22, v. 1191, p. 584f.

46 RKPA reports and documents document 23 sterilizations. See P. Werner, »Die Einweisung in die polizeilichen Jugendschutzlager,« *Deutsches Jugendrecht*, no. 4 (Berlin, 1944), p. 103. The deputy director of the RKPA mentioned 37 further youngsters who had already been sterilized before they had been sent to Moringen.

47 BAK, R 22, v. 1191, p. 586, lists figures in the inspection report by the president of the Essen Regional Court. See also Lagerbuch Moringen, as well as registrations of transfers to concentration camps in the Lagerbuch Moringen, in the personal archives of M. Hepp.

48 M. Guse collection of survivor interviews.

49 Westfälisches Institut für Regionalgeschichte Archives, Münster, Germany.

50 Lagerbuch Moringen; death list in the Moringen Magistrat Archive; funeral register in the Moringen Magistrates Archive; as well as the death register in Lower Saxon Hauptstaatsarchiv, Hanover: Nds. 721 Göttingen, Acc 93/79.

Thomas Rahe

Jehovah's Witnesses in Bergen-Belsen Concentration Camp

The *Aufenthaltslager* Bergen-Belsen, as it was officially known, was built in the spring of 1943 for a specific purpose in the Nazi concentration camp system.[1] The camp was to serve as an *Aufenthaltslager*, an internment camp, for certain groups of Jewish prisoners temporarily exempted from deportation to the killing centers, since they were to be exchanged for German nationals held by the Allies. This purpose determined the prisoners' social structure and living conditions in Bergen-Belsen, which differed considerably from conditions in most other concentration camps. At first, living conditions were clearly better than in other camps, since Jews designated for exchange were not to be able to describe actual conditions in the camps. In the first few months of Bergen-Belsen's development, Jews comprised almost 90 percent of all prisoners.

Initially, non-Jewish prisoners at Bergen-Belsen were confined to the so-called prisoners' camp (*Häftlingslager*) that had existed from the beginning. At first, this camp housed construction units (*Baukommando*), consisting of prisoners brought from other concentration camps to Bergen-Belsen. After March 1944, this part of Bergen-Belsen housed prisoners from other camps, who were ill or unable to work. After late 1944, this section of Bergen-Belsen increasingly became the destination for numerous prisoner transports evacuated from camps close to the front. The growing number of non-Jewish prisoners at Bergen-Belsen was linked to the increasing number of transports from the East. At liberation, Bergen-Belsen included prisoners from nearly all European nations and from almost all persecuted groups: Jews, Sinti and Roma («Gypsies«), political prisoners, »anti-socials,« Jehovah's Witnesses, and homosexuals.

Despite Bergen-Belsen's specific purpose as a transit and exchange camp for Jews, Jehovah's Witnesses, also known as »Bible Students« (*Bibelforscher*), were found not only among the prisoners liberated on April 15, 1945. A large number of Jehovah's Witnesses were among the first prisoners at Bergen-Belsen, even before the arrival of Jewish »exchange prisoners.«

The Witnesses were among the inmates assigned to repair and build new barracks at Bergen-Belsen. Between April 30 and May 15, 1943, three transports with ca. 600 male prisoners from Buchenwald, Niederhagen-Wewelsburg, and Natzweiler concentration camps arrived at Bergen-Belsen, where construction of the camp began in May 1943. The transport arriving at Bergen-Belsen about May 7, 1943, contained between 100 and 150 prisoners, mostly Jehovah's Witnesses from the dissolved Niederhagen concentration camp.[2] Subsequently two and three further Witness prisoners, previously transported from Niederhagen-Wewelsburg to Buchenwald, arrived at Bergen-Belsen respectively on May 10 and June 2, 1943.[3]

An analysis of this first group of Jehovah's Witnesses sent to Bergen-Belsen reveals the central problem that significantly complicates historical research about Witnesses in Bergen-Belsen. Just before liberation of the camp, the SS succeeded in almost completely destroying all camp files as well as totally burning prisoner registration cards. Unlike Jewish prisoners held as hostages at Bergen-Belsen, there are virutally no parallel records for Jehovah's Witnesses incarcerated at Bergen-Belsen. This makes it extremely difficult to determine the number of Jehovah's

Witnesses incarcerated in Bergen-Belsen. Further, it means that the names of most Witnesses cannot be established, thereby obliterating the starting point for biographical research about this prisoner group.

A few names and some biographical details are available for five Witness prisoners assigned to construction at Bergen-Belsen: Karl Schleicher (born February 23, 1891) and Karl Truckenbrod (born May 24, 1906) were transported from Buchenwald to Bergen-Belsen in May 1943. The other three prisoners were Herbert Schmidt (born January 7, 1913), Erich Golly (born August 18, 1891), and Kurt Ropelius (born September 10, 1904). Herbert Schmidt was arrested in February 1937 and arrived at Bergen-Belsen after imprisonment in Sachsenburg/Sachsenhausen, and Niederhagen-Wewelsburg concentration camps. The fact that Schmidt was transferred as an individual prisoner in a normal passenger train under Gestapo guard may have had something to do with his education and professional experience as an architect, and thus he was considered a useful expert. In Niederhagen he had already been assigned to planning and constructing buildings, and was given similar tasks at Bergen-Belsen.[4]

Erich Golly was first sentenced to six months imprisonment in December 1934 and was rearrested in December 1936. He was deported to Bergen-Belsen from Sachsenhausen, Niederhagen-Wewelsburg, and possibly also Buchenwald concentration camps. A letter that Golly wrote from Bergen-Belsen, dated February 6, 1944, reveals that German Witnesses in Bergen-Belsen were allowed to receive parcels and letters.[5]

The only detailed account about the Bergen-Belsen construction unit (*Baukommando*) is found in Kurt Ropelius's memoirs. »During 1943, the Wewelsburg concentration camp was dissolved and as a professional cook, I was transferred to the Dachau concentration camp for a cooking course. The plan was to reassign me from Dachau to Bergen-Belsen as a cook. Because of the harsh climate in Dachau, I again caught pneumonia with a very high fever, and subsequently developed pleurisy. ... After I recovered to some extent, an SS-Sergeant, who had already tried twice unsuccessfully to get me at Dachau, accompanied me to Bergen-Belsen. This was a small concentration camp. We were separated from the Jewish compound only by a barbed wire fence that ran alongside a footpath used by guards and watch dogs. I was again assigned to work in the SS kitchen under the same tormentor, an SS Staff Sergeant, who had previously mistreated me in the Wewelsburg concentration camp. I was still so weak that I could not even remove the rings from the kitchen stove. The bullying continued. My coworkers were Russians and Poles; whenever an opportunity offered, I witnesses to them (talked about the beliefs of the Witnesses). One brother (Witness), a civil engineer, succeeded in contacting Witnesses outside through a civilian with whom he had to work. They smuggled us spiritual food (Watchtower publications), and also a copy of a letter from a brother who had been sentenced to death. ... Some time later a swollen hernia caused me increasing pain. The physician, an SS officer who daily had to inspect and report on the food, heard about my suffering and offered to operate on my hernia. This took place in the prisoners' infirmary. I later found out that the operation took many hours, since it was the doctor's first. He was able to make two long incisions but then could not stitch them together. The brother (Jehovah's Witness) managing the infirmary, who had assisted the physician, later told me that they quickly sent for a specialist from the Jewish compound, who instructed the SS physician on how to sew it together. I could not regain consciousness because of protracted anesthesia and serious loss of blood. But again Jehovah helped me by sending me a good-hearted prisoner who did everything humanly possible to bring me back to life.«[6]

Although the Witnesses deported to Bergen-Belsen from Niederhagen-Wewelsburg cannot be identified by name, we know something about the social structure of this group. Information about Jehovah's Witnesses in Niederhagen-Wewelsburg is relatively good and this data can be extrapolated to the smaller group later deported to Bergen-Belsen.[7]

Thus it can be established that most Witnesses incarcerated in Niederhagen-Wewelsburg were craftsmen experienced in construction. They were not new prisoners remanded directly to Wewelsburg on arrest or after serving their jail sentences, but had been selected at Sachsenhausen and Buchenwald concentration camps because of their professional skills.[8]

They also differed from other prisoner groups at Niederhagen-Wewelsburg because of their relatively high average age: more than 65 percent were older than 40. »The Witnesses formed very close bonds at Wewelsburg, because of common religious beliefs, the time they had spent

Charlotte Tetzner (1948).
Source: Watchtower History Archive, Selters.

together as prisoners, as well as their common language. Nearly all the Witnesses came from German-speaking regions. As predominantly German-speaking prisoners, the Witnesses increasingly stood apart from other prisoners, since after September 1940 they were outnumbered by the newly arriving foreign prisoners.«[9]

The explicit group cohesiveness among Jehovah's Witnesses at Niederhagen-Wewelsburg is also reflected in their lower mortality rate. Statistics reveal that this bond significantly increased their chances of survival: »Of 306 Witnesses only nineteen died, whereas out of 903 German prisoners of other categories at least 357 persons died.«[10]

The social homogeneity of Jehovah's Witnesses in Niederhagen-Wewelsburg and in other concentration camps can be attributed to the fact that prior to their arrest, they »had lived in closely-knit, strong religious communities and had already formed well-structured networks for mutual assistance and disseminating their beliefs. These structures were transferred into the camps and adapted to meet extreme conditions. Prior to arrival at Wewelsburg, most Witnesses had already experienced SS and Gestapo persecution, thus enabling them to cope with the critical period after incarceration. Based on their previous experiences, Witnesses were able to develop common responses that alleviated some of the extreme demands in concentration camps. They formed cohesive groups for mutual assistance. Packages and transfers of money were always distributed equally; by pooling cash and stockpiling provisions, weaker persons and prisoners without relatives could receive support. They also took care of each other, when ill or injured. [...] At work and in the few free hours before sleep, they held religious discussions. They ›organized‹ Bibles illegally to pursue their study of the Bible. [...] Moreover, they tried to quote Bible texts and pamphlets from memory or to write them down on pieces of paper they had ›organized,‹ which they then exchanged during work or in their barracks in the evening.«[11]

Jehovah's Witnesses transported to the construction unit (Baukommando) at Bergen-Belsen brought their expertise and specific skills with them. They constituted a significantly distinct prisoner group, as Kurt Ropelius indicated, compared to other prisoners, particularly political prisoners from Poland and the Soviet Union. Thus, their transfer from Niederhagen-Wewelsburg to Bergen-Belsen as a relatively homogeneous group meant continuities in their personal networks and shared spiritual solidarity, rather than a rupture with their previous concentration camp experiences. Moreover, the SS camp commandant of Niederhagen-Wewelsburg, Adolf Haas, became the first commandant of Bergen-Belsen and had brought his SS staff with him. Thus, the Witnesses deported to the Baukommando at Bergen-Belsen were already familiar with the SS personnel and their behavior patterns, whereas Polish or Russian fellow prisoners who had been deported to Bergen-Belsen from Natzweiler or Buchenwald had to adapt to very different camp conditions.

The Baukommando was disbanded on February 23, 1944, and the prisoners transferred to Sachsenhausen. The next reference in the surviving archival record to Jehovah's Witnesses at Bergen-Belsen is dated March 5, 1945. It is a list documenting the transport of 26 female Jehovah's Witnesses from Bergen-Belsen to the Dora-Mittelbau concentration camp.[12] These women were part of a group of about 40 female Witnesses that had traversed various camps, including Groß-Rosen and Mauthausen, on their lengthy and agonizing evacuation from Auschwitz in mid-January 1945. They arrived at Bergen-Belsen in the middle or end of February 1945.[13]

Charlotte Tetzner, née Decker, was one of the women in this transport from Bergen-Belsen to Dora-Mittelbau. She had converted to the beliefs of Jehovah's Witnesses in the camps.[14] She had been arrested together with her parents in April 1941; her father, a communist, was sent to Dachau, while she and her mother were deported to Ravensbrück. She experienced a severe personal crisis after receiving news of her father's death at Dachau, resulting in her renunciation of atheism and conversion to the beliefs of Jehovah's Witnesses. Both she and her mother were scheduled to be released in December 1941, but in the camp office Tetzner was presented with a declaration repudiating her beliefs as a Witness. She refused to sign this form and was immediately returned to the concentration camp, although her mother was released. During the months that followed she was repeatedly urged to distance herself from the Witnesses. She was even personally presented to Heinrich Himmler when he inspected Ravensbrück, but to no avail.

Tetzner was transported from Ravensbrück to Auschwitz in March 1942. »Charlotte Tetzner was again classified as a political prisoner, but felt that this no longer applied to her and therefore made a purple triangle which she then sewed on her uniform. She wanted openly to express her connection to the Witnesses, and emphasize her faith. Although this caused considerable trouble with the SS women overseers, they finally gave up and let her keep the triangle.«[15]

Many female Jehovah's Witnesses »evacuated« from Auschwitz to Bergen-Belsen died at Belsen despite their relatively brief stay there.[16] They arrived in Bergen-Belsen when conditions had deteriorated from a «privileged camp« into a death camp, making the camp an unimaginable inferno. In March 1945, more than 18,000 prisoners died there from starvation and epidemics and thus the Jehovah's Witness transport also confronted incredible hardships. In mid-January 1945, these already debilitated women had to walk about 75 kilometers in icy weather from Auschwitz, where they were then transported in open freight cars to the Gross-Rosen concentration camp. They remained there for about two weeks until they were relocated to Mauthausen and three days later, finally reached Bergen-Belsen.[17]

Gertrud Ott's memoirs indicate that religious faith served as an important source of psychological strength in such extreme physical and psychological situations. »Sister Gretel Fricke was able to organize a meeting in the train, which strengthened all of us very much. Our singing and discussion of texts

Marta Lange, a Jehovah's Witness incarcerated in several concentration camps and liberated in Bergen-Belsen. Photo summer 1945. Source: private collection.

and Watchtower articles were a great witness to the political prisoners and accompanying guards, who did not stop us.«[18]

Similar incidents are also documented in Bergen-Belsen in connection with the transport of 26 female Jehovah's Witnesses to Dora-Mittelbau in early March 1945. Witnesses assigned to various barracks in Bergen-Belsen were prepared to volunteer for a labor transport to Dora-Mittelbau, so that the ill could remain behind in Bergen-Belsen. However, they refused to volunteer for this transport, instead assembling in one of the barracks where Elsa Abt said a prayer in which they joined, thereby strengthening their resolve. The SS had no other option than to assemble the transport for Dora-Mittelbau by force.[19]

Nevertheless, the disastrous and chaotic situation in Bergen-Belsen during the final weeks before liberation left virtually no leeway for religious activities. At the same time, these conditions levelled the differences between prisoner groups who all faced a desperate fight for survival. Thus, unlike in other camps, there is no reference to smuggled editions of *The*

Watchtower or other religious texts of Jehovah's Witnesses in the final phase of Bergen-Belsen. The SS made no further attempts to force Jehovah's Witnesses into signing declarations renouncing their religion in the final chaotic days and weeks before liberation at Bergen-Belsen.[20]

Nevertheless, the Witnesses still appeared, even to some of the other prisoners, to be a distinctive group identifiable not only because of their purple triangles. Thus, the French Jewish physician Odette Abadi, who had been deported first to Auschwitz and then to Bergen-Belsen, wrote in her memoirs: »For several days now, Ursula, a 100 percent German Aryan, has lived in our room. She was arrested because she belongs to the Bible Students sect, Jehovah's Witnesses, a sect that searches for the truth in the Bible. They neither embrace antisemitism nor fascism nor Nazism and their adherents refuse to perform any war-related work. ... They are courageous and dignified women, but a bit too submissive for our taste. Kramer (camp commandant of Bergen-Belsen) assigned Ursula to care for his children, which gave her the privilege of being accommodated with medical personnel when she had typhoid fever.«[21]

Although only one transport list still exists for Jehovah's Witnesses incarcerated in Bergen-Belsen, namely the register with 26 names for the transport from Bergen-Belsen to Dora-Mittelbau in early March 1945, several other sources provide indirect evidence of additional transports. This enables us to estimate the number of Jehovah's Witnesses transported to Bergen-Belsen during the final weeks before liberation, or who were liberated there.

Odette Abadi mentions that »about 60« Jehovah's Witnesses were in Bergen-Belsen.[22] Abadi describes a section of Bergen-Belsen that housed only women prisoners, and it can thus be assumed that she is referring only to female Witnesses. Although Abadi, who arrived at Bergen-Belsen from Auschwitz in early November 1944, mentions no precise date for her estimate, biographical research reveals that there must have been additional transports containing women Witnesses to Bergen-Belsen. For example, several Jehovah's Witnesses can be specifically identified by name who were transported from Auschwitz or Ravensbrück to Bergen-Belsen.[23]

Another important statistical source is a letter written two months after liberation on May 19, 1945, from 28 Jehovah's Witnesses in liberated Bergen-Belsen to their religious associates in England. It states: »Out of 31 brothers and 52 sisters, only 3 brothers and 25 sisters are still living here (after two months).«[24] A postscript adds the nationalities of the survivors: »Here in Bergen-Belsen, there are Witnesses from the following nations: Russia, Poland, Hungary, Austria, the Netherlands, Germany, and Slovakia.«[25]

A letter by the Quaker Relief Service transmitting the Witnesses' letter to London, mentions that the majority of Witnesses liberated and still alive in Bergen-Belsen were Polish speaking.[26] Therefore, we can conclude that a large number of Polish or Polish-speaking Witnesses arrived at a very late date at Bergen-Belsen and that these transports cannot be documented by name lists. The list of names of female Witnesses deported from Bergen-Belsen to Dora-Mittelbau on March 4, 1945, also includes many Polish names, and thus, even if they were ethnic Germans, they could speak good Polish.

It is not possible to provide precise data about the social structure of the Witnesses liberated at Bergen-Belsen or to calculate the number of Witnesses who died there before or after liberation, since the SS destroyed most records at Bergen-Belsen. There is only one death certificate for one Polish Jehovah's Witness in Bergen-Belsen: it certifies the death of Gregor Otrembski (born 1887) on February 9, 1945.[27]

More precise statistics about the percentage of different national groups incarcerated in or liberated at Bergen-Belsen exist only for the Netherlands, the result of a survey made by the Dutch Watchtower Society. There were 15 Jehovah's Witnesses from the Netherlands in Bergen-

Waffen - SS.
Konzentrationslager Mittelbau   O.U., den 5.3.1945
Politische Abteilung

274.

Neuzugänge
----

vom K.L. Bergen-Belsen vom 4.3.1945.(Frauen-Biebelforscherinnen)

			geb.		
1.	Stl.	F-15	Abt, Else	2.9.14	Danzig	Buchhalterin
2.	RD	F-18	Aschmutat, Auguste	1o.1.88	Kalleweiten	o.Beruf
3.	RD	F-3o	Baseler, Martha	19.11.o5	Kolberg	o.Beruf
4.	RD	F-35	Birnbaum, Dora	27.9.92	Oederan	Hausfrau
5.	RD	F-32	Bräuer, Hilde	14.8.o6	Zöbletz	Hausfrau
6.	Stl.	F-19	Cienciala, Helene	23.12.21	Goleszow	o.Beruf
7.	RD	F-21	Darsow, Wanda	4.11.o6	Köslin	o.Beruf
8.	Stl.	F-17	Decker, Charlotte	3o.11.2o	Chemnitz	Stenotypistin
9.	RD	F-29	Friedrich, Martha	28.8.93	Lodz	Schneiderin
1o.	Stl.	F-28	Gelbhardt, Janette	14.6.21	Swinice	Hausmädchen
11.	Stl.	F-11	Idkowiak, Irene	1.4.23	Posen	o.Beruf
12.	Stl.	F-26	Jakobi, Alma	3.11.96	Lodz	o.Beruf
13.	Stl.	F-13	Jankowiak, Kazimiera	12.2.14	Szroda	Expedientin
14.	RD	F-34	Lubinus, Annette	15.4.o2	Leer	Haushalterin
15.	RD	F-27	Moser, Maria	13.11.o6	Uttendorf	Verkäuferin
16.	RD	F-31	Nahodil, Barbara	21.3.97	Wien Gerasdorf	Hausfrau
17.	Stl.	F-24	Piechocka, Benigna	29.6.23	Pniewy	Studentin
18.	RD	F-25	Regenfelder, Luise	17.7.97	Schirmdorf	Arbeiterin
19.	Stl.	F-14	Roszyk, Johanna	2o.7.o9	Morowino	o.Beruf
2o.	RD	F-23	Schneider, Auguste	6.1.91	Bad Kreuznach	o.Beruf
21.	RD	F-36	Schnitger, Helene	27.2.oo	Rastede	Hausfrau
22.	RD	F-33	Schröder, Martha	1o.9.87	Parchim	Postbeamtin
23.	Stl.	F-16	Streich, Else	17.5.o3	Döpsalow	o.Beruf
24.	RD	F-22	Thalheimer, Else	6.8.oo	Schweinfurth	o.Beruf
25.	Stl.	F-12	Santulek, Marie	3.3.27	Weichsel	o.Beruf
26.	RD	F-2o	Weinen, Josefine	17.2.o2	Oberhausen	o.Beruf

Verteiler:
Abt.II,
Abt.III,
Arbeitseinsatz   F.d.R.   Der Leiter d.Abteilung II.
Arbeitsstatistik
Häftl. Revier
Häftl.Eig.Verwaltung

                                                  gez. Schurz

                    SS - Rottenführer   SS - Untersturmführer

List of names of the transport of female Jehovah's Witnesses from Bergen-Belsen to Dora-Mittelbau concentration camp on March 4, 1945. Source: Main Commission for the Investigation of Crimes Against the Polish People, Warsaw, sygn. 8 KL Dora.

Belsen who could be identified by name, 10 of them perished there.[28]

Finally, an additional albeit tiny group of Jehovah's Witnesses imprisoned in Bergen-Belsen must be mentioned: Jews, who had already joined the religious community of Jehovah's Witnesses before their arrest and deportation to concentration camps, but had become victims of Nazi persecution because they were Jews. A total of three female Witnesses can be identified by name, who were deported as Jews to Bergen-Belsen. Eva Basz and Olga Slezinger from Hungary were first deported to Auschwitz, where they were marked by yellow stars. However, they insisted on wearing the purple triangle. Both were evacuated together to Bergen-Belsen: Eva Basz was liberated and survived, but the fate of Olga Slezinger is not known.[29]

Rachel Sacksioni-Levee, active as a Witness evangelist in the Netherlands, was arrested because of her Jewish descent, deported to the Westerbork transit camp in May 1944, and subsequently relocated to Bergen-Belsen. A few days after she arrived in Westerbork, she was already seated in a train bound for Auschwitz, when her name was called out and she was returned to the camp. The reason for this and her later deportation to Bergen-Belsen was the same: in Westerbork she claimed to be a diamond worker believing this to be advantageous — as it turned out correctly. She was assigned to a special barrack in the »star camp« section of Bergen-Belsen, where Jewish prisoners were to create a diamond industry for obtaining foreign currency for Nazi Germany. However, when this scheme failed, most of the male diamond dealers and workers were deported to Sachsenhausen. On the next day, December 5, 1944, most of the women in this group, including Rachel Sacksioni-Levee, were transferred as forced labor to the Beendorf subcamp. She survived and returned to the Netherlands after liberation.[30]

Rachel Sacksioni-Levee's memoirs are the most comprehensive source about conditions in Bergen-Belsen from a Witness perspective; they also reveal her precarious special position as both a born Jew and a devout Jehovah's Witness. She succinctly explained: »I was in Bergen-Belsen for seven months, where I witnessed but found no one listening. I was seen as a Jewish apostate and treated with disdain.«[31]

Unlike the Witnesses who arrived in the inferno of Bergen-Belsen during the final months of chaos and mass death, it was still possible for Rachel Sacksioni-Levee in 1944 in the »star camp« to continue Bible study, an essential activity for Witnesses. She recalled: »Since I had no Bible with me, I asked everywhere whether anyone had a Bible. I finally found a doctor who had one and was prepared to sell it to me for two pieces of bread and three rations of butter.«[32]

The section of her memoir about a religious dispute with Chief Rabbi Aaron Davids in the Bergen-Belsen »star camp« is of special interest, since such reports rarely exist for other concentration camps. »There was also a chief rabbi among the prisoners who held religious meetings in our barracks on Saturdays. I confidently stood next to him and asked whether I could ask him some questions, and others subsequently asked if they could also do so. He answered that we should write the questions on paper and he would answer them the following week. I asked him a question about Isaiah 7:14, Micha 5:1, Psalm 110, and if he could explain to me who the Lord is to whom he spoke, and I wrote down several other texts from the Hebrew scriptures. I let him know that I had read the Greek scriptures and how they corresponded to the Hebrew scriptures, etc. Oh, how I looked forward to the next week. And finally he arrived. He responded to somebody who had asked if the world had been created in six literal or spiritual days. He sat there and talked about this for an hour, concluding that there are many who said that they were six literal days and others who claimed they were spiritual days ... but that we did not absolutely know. The second question was: Since when have the people of Israel existed? He answered that when the Jews moved to Egypt there were seventy of them. These began to

Erich Golly with his family, before 1935. Source: private collection.

multiply and that was the beginning of Israel. In this connection, I asked if I might also add something about these questions. The rabbi, however, quickly refused and stated that he would not answer my question here, because ›the people here are not suitable for that.‹ I stated that if he was a servant of God, he had to explain his views in public, so that others might also learn something from the discussion. Thus he could also explain to the others that I advocated erroneous views. However, he could not be persuaded to do this, but I believed he wanted to speak to me alone. I then tried to seek him out, but he avoided me. When he could no longer evade me, he then asked: ›Can you read Hebrew?‹ When I responded in the negative, his reply was: ›First learn Hebrew and then come back!‹ I told him frankly that he had only replied this way because he was unable to answer my questions. I also emphatically told him that I could have provided a far better answer to the two questions in a much shorter time. I remarked that the Bible spoke about a thousand-year day and other similar matters.«[33]

A cautious estimate, based on incomplete records, is that at least 150 to 200 Jehovah's Witnesses were incarcerated at different times in Bergen-Belsen. Most were German, especially the prisoners transported for construction work in 1943. However, after early 1945, a large number of foreign (non-German) Witnesses evacuated from the East through many other concentration camps arrived at Bergen-Belsen, where they were liberated. More precise numbers are available only for the Dutch.

Nevertheless, these figures do not reveal the persecution of Jehovah's Witnesses specifically at Bergen-Belsen.[34] Witnesses were banned and became victims of persecution in all countries occupied by Nazi Germany and their Axis partners. This also applied especially to the Netherlands: of 426 Jehovah's Witnesses arrested during German occupation, about 200 to 250 persons were deported to concentration camps and 117 perished.

Detlef Garbe's research establishes that more than 3,000 prisoners with a »purple triangle« were incarcerated in Nazi German concentration camps; a little less than one-third were foreign (non-German) Jehovah's Witnesses. »Statistical data or estimates by nationality are available for Jehovah's Witness prisoners: 200–250 Dutch, 200 Austrians, 100 Poles, additional groups of between 10 and 50 Witnesses from Belgium, France, the Soviet Union, Czechoslovakia, and Hungary.«[35] The composition of the Witness prisoner group at Bergen-Belsen seems to be representative of the persecution of this religious community in the Nazi concentration camps.

Notes

1   See Eberhard Kolb, *Bergen-Belsen: Geschichte des »Aufenthaltslagers« 1943–1945* (Hanover, 1962); idem, *Bergen-Belsen: Vom »Aufenthaltslager« zum Konzentrationslager 1943–1945*, 5th rev. ed. (Göttingen, 1996); Rolf Keller and others, eds., *Konzentrationslager Bergen-Belsen: Berichte und Dokumente* (Hanover and Göttingen, 1995).

2   Karl Hüser, *Wewelsburg 1933 bis 1945: Kult- und Terrorstätte der SS; Eine Dokumentation*, 2nd rev. ed. (Paderborn, 1987), p. 102.

3   Ibid., 103, 356; Bundesarchiv Koblenz: NS 4 Bu/5, page 12 and NS 4 Bu, vol. 6.

4   Bergen-Belsen Memorial Archives: Interview Thomas Rahe with Herbert Schmidt, February 21, 1997.

5   Bergen-Belsen Memorial Archives: Copies of Erich Golly's personal documents provided by Erich Kraushaar.

6   Watchtower History Archive, Selters: Kurt Ropelius, »Meine Lebensgeschichte,« unpublished manuscript (Berlin, 1971), pp. 16f.

7   See Kirsten John, »*Mein Vater wird gesucht...*«: *Häftlinge des Konzentrationslagers in Wewelsburg* (Essen, 1996), pp. 41ff.

8   Ibid., p. 41.

9   Ibid., p. 42.

10   Ibid., p. 47.

11   Ibid., pp. 136–139.

12   Main Commission for the Investigation of Crimes against the Polish People, Warsaw, Sygn. 8 KL Dora.

13   Elsa Abt, »Zusammen mit meinem Mann den Glauben bewahrt,« in: *Watchtower* (July 15, 1980), pp. 12–15; Charlotte Tetzner's account in: Lore Shelley, ed., *Auschwitz - The Nazi Civilization: Twenty-Three Women Prisoners Accounts* (Lanham, NY and London, n.d.), p. 254.

14   Bergen-Belsen Memorial Archives: copy of Charlotte Tetzner memoirs (1986); Shelley, *Auschwitz*, pp. 247–256; Detlef Garbe, *Zwischen Widerstand und Martyrium: Die Zeugen Jehovas im »Dritten Reich«* (Munich, 1993), pp. 432ff. I would like to thank Dr. Detlef Garbe, Hamburg, for providing bibliographical data about Charlotte Tetzner.

15   Garbe, *Zwischen Martyrium und Widerstand*, p. 434.

16   Bergen-Belsen Memorial Archives: communication from Elsa Abt to Thomas Rahe, May 7, 1997.

17   See Charlotte Tetzner's account in Shelley, *Auschwitz*, 254; Watchtower History Archive, Selters: Gertrud Ott unpublished memoirs (1971), p. 14 and Selma Klimaschewski memoirs (1971), p. 7; see also Abt (note 13). The accounts differ about the route of the evacuation transport. Klimaschewski names Groß-Rosen, Mauthausen, Buchenwald, Bergen-Belsen; Ott mentions the sequence of Mauthausen, Groß-Rosen, and Bergen-Belsen; Abt refers to Groß-Rosen, Mauthausen, and Bergen-Belsen. It can be assumed that this transport with female Witnesses reached Bergen-Belsen via Groß-Rosen and Mauthausen, because of other information about evacuation transports from Auschwitz to Bergen-Belsen. It is improbable that these differences in routing indicate several different Witness transports.

18   Watchtower History Archive: Gertrud Ott memoirs, p. 14.

19   Bergen-Belsen Memorial Archives: Thomas Rahe interview with Marta Ciecierski, née Lange, May 2, 1997.

20 Ibid.

21 Odette Abadi, *Terre de Détresse: Birkenau – Bergen-Belsen*, transl. W. Siano (Paris, 1995), p. 141. Abadi's memoirs are the only account from another prisoner group that mentions Jehovah's Witnesses in Bergen-Belsen.

22 Ibid. Abadi's remark that from time to time several female Witnesses had been shot in Bergen-Belsen cannot be corroborated. All other sources, including testimonies by surviving Witnesses, provide no confirmation for this statement.

23 Watchtower History Archive, Selters: »Prisoner List of Jehovah's Witnesses in Bergen-Belsen,« compiled July 1, 1997, including 75 names as well as the other camps in which these Witnesses were incarcerated before or after Bergen-Belsen. Furthermore, there are other specific examples of additional Witnesses, identified by name, who were also imprisoned at Bergen-Belsen.

24 The letter was printed in the Swiss periodical *Trost* (August 1, 1945), p. 7.

25 Ibid.

26 Ibid.

27 Polski Czerwony Krzyz, Biuro Informazyjne Zarzad Glowny.

28 Information from the Wachttoren Bijbel- en Traktaatgenootschap (Emmen), April 15, 1997.

29 *1996 Yearbook of the Jehovah's Witnesses*, pp. 91ff.

30 Beit Lohamei Haghetaot Archives, Dutch Archive Section: file Josef Weiss, no. 317, includes transport lists for the »star camp«; see also *1986 Yearbook of the Jehovah's Witnesses*, pp. 160ff.; Kolb, *Bergen-Belsen* (1962), pp. 117–121.

31 Herinneringscentrum Kamp Westerbork, 7778–02: Rachel Sacksioni, »Mijn leven in de waarheid voor en na de Tweede Wereldoorlog,« p. 6 (German translation by A. Pflock); and the virtually identical declaration 7778–01: »Verklaring van Rachel Sacksioni-Levee« (June 19, 1947).

32 Sacksioni, »Mijn leven,« p. 6.

33 Ibid., pp. 6f. The identity of the chief rabbi is found in Sacksioni-Levee, »Verklaring,« p. 5.

34 Garbe, *Zwischen Widerstand und Martyrium*, pp. 328ff.

35 Ibid., p. 484.

Johannes Wrobel

The Buchenwald Series:
Watercolors by the Jehovah's Witness
Johannes Steyer

When Johannes Steyer from Wittgensdorf, Germany, died on March 1, 1998, he left 27 impressive watercolor paintings to the Wachtturm-Gesellschaft, History Archive, in Selters/Taunus, Germany. The paintings depict his experience of victimization and persecution in the Third Reich.

Johannes Steyer was born in Röhrsdorf, near Chemnitz, on September 28, 1908. Together with two sisters and one brother, he grew up in poverty, since his father did not earn much as a railroad worker. His mother stayed at home and took care of the family. After attending elementary school, Johannes Steyer went to work straightening needles on knitting machines, a skill he acquired on his own.

He first encountered the Bible Students in 1931, the year when this Christian religious association adopted the name »Jehovah's Witnesses.« He was baptized that same year and became active. Until 1935, Steyer was apparently able to disseminate the Biblical teachings of the Witnesses without Nazi interference. During the 1970s he completed an artistic portrayal from memory of what happened to him after 1935. He was under police surveillance while preaching (painting 1), and denounced to the police (painting 2). It was not long before he was arrested and interrogated (painting 3). Shortly thereafter, he was sent to a concentration camp (painting 4).

On March 5, 1935, Johannes Steyer was arrested and sent to Sachsenburg concentration camp. He was caned with 25 strokes for refusing to salute the swastika flag (painting 8), and was confined to an unlighted cell for 70 days. After Sachsenburg concentration camp was closed in July 1937, he and other prisoners were taken to Buchenwald concentration camp near Weimar, then under construction (paintings 5 and 6). There he was assigned prisoner number 1795. He told friends about painting 5: »This picture shows the construction of Buchenwald concentration camp. We had to do everything, from clearing the forest and laying building foundations to building barracks. Doing everything by hand was hard manual labor. At Sachsenburg, Camp Commandant SS Major (*Sturmbannführer*) Rödel had already told us: ›We'll give you less to eat so that you won't be so daring.‹ This actually occurred in Buchenwald; we were also prohibited from receiving assistance from home. We were thus unable even to buy a dry roll in the canteen, since we were not allowed to receive money. Even on Sundays, all Witnesses had to work until noon – without lunch. Our portions were distributed among the other prisoners.«

The other watercolors depict Johannes Steyer's experiences from his arrest to liberation, impressions which continued to haunt him. (He arranged the watercolors by number in chronological order.) These works include: the exhausting hours standing during roll calls (painting 7), flogging (painting 8), and hard labor (paintings 9 and 10). He once explained painting 8: »An inmate was often missing during roll call. After a long search, the prisoner was finally found, sometimes only the next morning. These prisoners were then beaten or simply shot.

Even the smallest of offenses incurred severe punishments. I was considered an ›incorrigible‹ prisoner, and personally experienced what is depicted in this picture. The reason was my refusal to sign military induction papers.«

Johannes Steyer recorded not only the cruel and inhuman treatment in vibrant colors. He also probably used bright friendly pigments to reveal that his Christian faith was one of hope and deliverance. During his incarceration, he always felt reassured of hope and his yearning for freedom when he saw the first spring flowers, whereas a »hopeless one« found death at the electrified fence (painting 11). He recalled that »despair drove some to suicide. As depicted here, an inmate who couldn't stand it any longer, threw himself on the electrified fence, and volleys of gun-fire ended his life and suffering.«

The harsh concentration camp life and forced labor were made even more onerous by sadistic Kapos, who served the SS (painting 12). They brutally drove their fellow prisoners to the roll call yard (painting 13). Johannes Steyer described the surprise that sometimes awaited them: »As a deterrent to future resistance, prisoners who had been shot while trying to escape were dragged into the roll call yard in front of the assembled prisoners.« (painting 14)

His paintings deal repeatedly with compulsory hard labor, including the prisoner labor details marched out after morning roll call (painting 18). The thoroughly exhausted inmates returned, together with their guards, to the camp every evening (painting 15); some were near death and unable to walk (paintings 16 and 17).

The Buchenwald concentration camp was securely guarded (painting 19). On occasion, instead of reporting to work after morning roll call, prisoners would have to report for an interrogation (painting 20). Prisoners were also summoned by loudspeaker to report to the camp commandant (painting 21). This scene could have taken place in the Sachsenhausen concentration camp, north of Berlin, where Johannes Steyer was transferred on May 8, 1940, after again refusing military service.

Like most Jehovah's Witnesses, Johannes Steyer refused to serve in Hitler's army, and he portrayed himself, in painting 22, refusing to accept military induction papers. He considered Hitler as the »sword of the church,« who was behind the persecution of Jehovah's Witnesses (painting 23). On October 7, 1934, after receiving numerous protest letters and telegrams, Hitler screamed: »This brood will be exterminated in Germany!« (painting 24) The Nazis were, however, unable to completely obliterate this small but unyielding religious community in Germany.

Johannes Steyer was sentenced to death by hanging for refusing military service. He only escaped this fate by luck, when he was assigned to a forced labor unit in Düsseldorf, demolishing rubble and ruins after bomb attacks. He was subsequently transferred to Alderney, Channel Islands, from where he and other Witnesses were transported to Steyr, part of the Mauthausen concentration camp complex in Austria.

The last three watercolors deal with liberation: how »glad tidings« spread through the camp (painting 25), and the Witnesses thanked God that the »power of the evil ones« had been defeated and the SS had fled (painting 26). »Free!« at last, the gate at Buchenwald opened, promising a new future for the survivors (painting 27). Johannes Steyer said in retprospect: »We were beside ourselves and leapt for joy because we secured freedom after ten years. The endless slavery finally stopped. It was as if nature awakening also shared our joy. Flowers bloomed, everything awoke to a new life.«

No. 1: Johannes Steyer, under surveillance, preaching as a Jehovah's Witness.
»We do not want Jehovah God's Kingdom! We have our church and our Führer!«

No. 2: A Nazi denounces him to the police.
»I'll have you arrested!«

No. 3: The Gestapo arrests him for interrogation. »It was said that he would return around noon.«
No. 4: Arrival in a concentration camp involves abuses such as standing or squatting for hours.
»Deported to the CC«.

Im Aufbau_dahinter entehen erste Baraken im Wald.... J. St.

No. 5: Buchenwald concentration camp was still under construction when Johannes Steyer arrived in July 1937. »Under construction – behind this, the first barracks are being built in the woods...«

No. 6: Jehovah's Witnesses are assigned to build barracks, and soon move into one of the barracks they had built in Buchenwald. »Foundations are ready.«

fertiges Fundament... J. St.

Oft ergab es sich, daß beim Zählappell ein Häftling fehlte_ nach langen suchen wurde er gefunden_ manchmal erst am anderen Morgen ...

No. 7: Standing for hours during roll call is part of the strict daily camp routine. »An inmate was often missing during roll call. After a long search, the prisoner was finaly found, sometimes only the next morning.«

No. 8: The SS punishes prisoners for minor offenses, or often just to torment them. »Strapped to the block: 25 strokes because of laziness at work.«

No. 9: The prisoners are mistreated in the stone quarry

No. 10: Johannes Steyer remembers how Jews and Jehovah's Witnesses have to carry stones by hand under the worst conditions. The prisoners who collapse from exhaustion are mistreated by the SS or even killed. »Jehova's Witnesses (Bible Students) – before them a group of Jews – are carrying stones from the quarry.«

.. die ersten Blumen weckten
Freiheitsdrang — ein Hoffnungsloser am
Elektrozaun, wurde noch v. Turm aus erschossen.

No. 11: Despair has driven this prisoner to suicide at the electrified fence. Volleys of gun fire end his life and suffering. »...the first flowers awakened the crave for freedom – hopeless one in the electric fence, was shot from the tower.«

No. 12: The Kapos, or overseers, let themselves be used by the SS to mistreat fellow prisoners. »Assistants to the SS = the Kapos.«

die Handlanger der SS
= die Kapos

No. 13: The Kapos drive the prisoners to roll call. »Get out for roll call!!« (Text in original painting is the wrong way round.)

No. 14: One prisoner shot while trying to escape is dragged to the roll call yard and placed before the rows of prisoners to break their resistance.

No. 17: The prisoners carry the injured with them from work back to the camp.
»Done for the day.«

page 133:
No. 15: In the evening, an exhausted labor
detail returns to camp.

No. 16: Johannes Steyer called this theme:
»Between Life and Death.«

No. 18: »After morning roll call, the columns of prisoners march out to work.«

No. 19: The camp is closely guarded.

No. 20: Periodically, Jehovah's Witnesses are ordered to the Political Department for interrogation.
»I won't come out to work today ... got an interrogation.«

No. 21: The camp commandant sends for prisoners for interrogation. »Prisoner no. 000 is to report immediately to the camp commandant!«

No. 22: Johannes Steyer refuses induction into the military.

Als Schwert der Kirche, schwang sich Hitler gegen Jehovas Zeugen, Juden, Polit.u. Krimis./ Die Absicht war eine getarnte Verfolgung d. Zeugen Jehovas, d. nicht als Christenverfolgung, sondern ___ Kriminell zu betrachten sei.

No. 23: »Hitler with Halo« »As sword of the church, Hitler attacked Jehovah's Witnesses, Jews, political prisoners, and criminals. The aim was a disguised persecution of Jehovah's Witnesses, i.e., not as Christians, but because they were considered criminals.«

No. 24: Hitler's reaction on October 7, 1934, to receiving numerous protest telegrams against the persecution of Jehovah's Witnesses from all over the world: »This brood will be exterminated in Germany!«

No. 25: »Glad Tidings« — The camp is liberated!

No. 26: One prisoner, probably Johannes Steyer himself, thanks God for liberation: »Thanks to the Lord who breaks the power of the evil ones. The SS have fled ... we are free!«

No. 27: The camp gate is open; freedom's »golden light« beckons brightly. »Free!«

Sybil Milton

Jehovah's Witnesses as Forgotten Victims

It is especially appropriate that the subject »Jehovah's Witnesses as Forgotten Victims« is discussed today, since 63 years ago on October 7, 1934, the Witnesses resumed their religious activities in Nazi Germany despite prohibition of their work. On that same date, more than 20,000 telegrams were sent to »Hitler's government« from all over Europe and the United States protesting the persecution of Jehovah's Witnesses. This organized resistance by Witness communities against increasing restrictions on their religious freedom coincided with intensified persecution and repression in Nazi Germany after 1935.

Let me digress for a moment to explain how I discovered this subject. For the past decade, my work as a historian has focused on Nazi Germany and the Holocaust. My article »Women and the Holocaust« included material about Jehovah's Witnesses incarcerated in women's concentration camps.[1] Later, as Senior Historian of the United States Holocaust Memorial Museum in Washington, D.C., I included historical documents about the fate of individual Witnesses in Nazi Germany in several academic and educational publications.[2] Moreover, the initial museum professional staff looked for authentic artifacts and documents for the permanent exhibition and research collection that presented the fate of Jehovah's Witnesses between 1933 and 1945. We used illegally printed Witness leaflets and periodicals, Gestapo and police mug-shots of Witness prisoners, prisoner registration cards from numerous concentration camps, German administrative stamps restricting mail privileges for Witnesses in concentration camps, censored family correspondence, and prisoner uniforms with purple triangle patches and prisoner numbers from Ravensbrück, Sachsenhausen, and Wewelsburg. Despite the inclusion of many of these artifacts in the permanent exhibition, the presentation of the fate of Jehovah's Witnesses is incomplete.

Recently, I published an essay that had been originally presented at the 1995 Weimar conference about concentration camps in Nazi Germany and occupied Europe. It concerned press coverage of early concentration camps during the 1930s in the German and foreign press, including American, Swiss, and French Witness periodicals.[3] I have also co-edited a multi-volume archival documentation series that included facsimile documents from German and Austrian archives, including some material about Jehovah's Witnesses.[4] Despite my publications about the persecution of non-Jewish victims in Nazi Germany, I do not pretend to be an expert about the history of Jehovah's Witnesses.

Until recently, the role of Jehovah's Witnesses as »forgotten victims« of the Holocaust was marginalized; their fate was neglected or limited in various concentration camp memorial museums. In larger memorials (such as, for example, Dachau, Buchenwald, Neuengamme, Ravensbrück, Mauthausen, and Auschwitz), the history of Witnesses is sporadically documented for the specific site. In contrast, smaller regional and municipal memorial museums (as, for example, Düsseldorf, Cologne, and Wewelsburg), present the history of this group more adequately. The complex realities of these camps are usually presented through fragile archeological remnants, such as barracks, crematoria ruins, segments of the protective custody camp and the camp commandant's office, as well as landscaped cemeteries with protestant or catholic chapels. Jehovah's Witnesses are seldom explicitly mentioned in these memorial ensembles. Of course, these posthumous lacunae should not surprise us, since Jehovah's Witnesses fit neither into the ideological views of East European memorials, that still reflect the biases of former communist regimes, emphasizing the political resistance, nor are they effortlessly integrated into western presentations about racial victims that conform to the categorizations of West German restitution legislation. Thus, even today, Witnesses who had refused to join the Nazi German army are usually not eligible for restitution in the Federal Republic. We must explicitly examine why the fate of Jehovah's Witnesses has been neglected, fragmented, and rejected. I would like to suggest several reasons for this pattern of exclusion and disinterest.

The first reason is the intolerance or, at least, the disinterest of German and European society. Until recently, the history of the concentration camps has focused on political prisoners. Although different prisoner groups, such as Jehovah's Witnesses, have also been mentioned, education and research has concentrated on political prisoners. Of course, this is easy to understand. Political prisoners were quantitatively the largest group; after liberation, they organized and led camp survivor associations and organizations. The basic differences between the fate of the biologically defined victims of Nazi genocide and the fate of political opponents is now generally accepted. The Germans killed multitudes, including political opponents, members of the resistance, elites of conquered nations, and victimized others because of their national origin, but always based these murders on the beliefs, actions, and status of those victims. Different criteria applied only to the murder of the handicapped, Jews, and Sinti and Roma (»Gypsies«). Members of these groups could not escape their fate by changing their behavior or beliefs. Those persecuted for biological and racial reasons were usually killed as entire families. This distinction is essential for an understanding of the killing centers. The Christian denomination, Jehovah's Witnesses, tenacious in their opposition to the Nazi regime, was marginalized in this interpretive framework that emphasized political or racial victims. Even today this Christian community is frequently categorized by the derogatory term »sect.«[5] Although this pejorative expression originated in official Nazi usage, uncritical repetition of this term continues to have negative implications today, since it reinforces existing bigotry.

The second reason is a consequence of postwar memorial practices in handling the volatile subject of the Holocaust. Until recently, Nazi terror has been depicted and interpreted in two distinct ways. On the one hand, the history of persecution and the ensuing widening terror and brutality is used as an example of coercive anti-democratic dictatorship. This interpretation, evident in former communist eastern European memorials, focuses on the fate of the political opponents, such as communists, socialists, trade unionists, intellectuals, the clergy, and European resistance movements. On the other hand, Nazi Germany is presented as a racial state in Holocaust museums and exhibitions, concentrating exclusively on the mass murder of European Jews. Many different victim groups simply do not fit into this bifurcated interpretation. Victim groups, such as the Sinti and Roma, but also the Jehovah's Witnesses, are then only mentioned peripherally as »other victims.«

The third reason is that lack of published documentation about Jehovah's Witnesses magnifies the existing bias ignoring the fate of the Witnesses. Basic documents about the increasing persecution of the Witnesses are scattered in many countries in various public and private archives. There is no central collection of such documents, nor is there any one publication that focuses primarily on the Witnesses, in comparison to numerous documentary publications about the persecution of Jewish or political victims.

The fourth reason is that important eye-witness testimony by surviving Witnesses has not been collected. In the first postwar years, it is logical that only brief reports by Jehovah's Witnesses were published sporadically. This can be attributed, in part, to Witness lack of confidence in German and European society; as a result Witnesses presented their testimony only within their own religious communities. The Witnesses' silence was caused by several factors: their distrust of the general populace and government as well as their uneasiness about potential discrimination and retaliation. Furthermore, Jehovah's Witnesses seldom appeared as witnesses in postwar trials; among thousands of victim depositions, Witness documentation was usually found in unsuccessful restitution cases.

Nevertheless, this dismal record can be revised to some extent, since some things have improved during the last five years. Recent academic literature includes the Witnesses. In Germany, articles and monographs by Michael Kater and Detlef Garbe as well as documentary films about the Witnesses have found wider public attention.[6] Moreover, newer historical research and publications in the United States, Austria, and France have also resulted in some improvement.[7]

Immediately after the assumption of power in 1933, the Nazis used violence and terror as well as systematic lists of ostensible enemies; such measures were also directed against Jehovah's Witnesses. Witnesses were affected almost immediately. Since their beliefs did not allow them to render unconditional obedience to any state, they were maligned and assaulted for their »internationalism« (and also as an American corporation). The Emergency Decree for the Protection of the People and the State [*Verordnung zum Schutz von Volk und Staat*] enacted on February 28, 1933, abrogated the basic rights of the Weimar constitution, thereby creating the basis in late April 1933 for raiding and confiscating the Magdeburg Witness printing plant as well as impounding their publications.[8] This decree also prohibited Witness meetings and missionary activities.

Already in 1934, both the German government and the Nazi party attempted to coerce Jehovah's Witnesses into leaving their positions in the civil service and in the private sector. The cumulative escalation of economic restrictions designed to isolate Jews, as well as »Gypsies« and Jehovah's Witnesses in Nazi Germany, initially included boycott, exclusionary legislation, expulsions from professional organizations, and employment discrimination. Unemployment benefits, pensions, and related retirement benefits for Witnesses were curtailed and cancelled. Because of their religious convictions, Witnesses would not vote, would not use the »Heil Hitler« greeting, and refused to join either the State Labor Service or the Nazi welfare organization. The cumulative result of this expanding incremental persecution restricted Witnesses in the availability of potential employment, since they were barred from any assistance by state labor bureaus and exchanges. Although religion provided some solace, Witnesses faced new and mounting economic hardships, since they had been dismissed from their jobs, prohibited from receiving licenses for itinerant trades, and deprived of unemployment insurance payments. This resulted in the pauperization of many Witnesses and their families. They also confronted profound barriers to emigration during the worldwide depression, since few countries accepted Jehovah's Witnesses as refugees of conscience. Scholars ought to investigate the details of this economic persecution and daily deprivations for Witnesses in Nazi Germany, since this is one of the many gaps in our current knowledge; this would require systematic research of civil and criminal court records in German state archives. Detlef Garbe has already begun to do some of this research, but there is still no complete list or analysis of the various civil and criminal cases against Witnesses during the Nazi period. The Law for the Confiscation of Subversive and Enemy Property [*Gesetz über die Einziehung volks- und staatsfeindlichen Vermögens*] promulgated on July 14, 1933, was initially used for the seizure of property, possessions, and assets of proscribed and denaturalized political opponents, thereby impoverishing them. The automatic loss of citizenship, including property rights, made many socialists and communists unwelcome as transients or residents in some countries of exile. This law was also applied to the property of Jehovah's Witnesses as domestic ideological enemies, resulting in the confiscation of their motorbikes, private bicycles, cars, and other vehicles that had been used to distribute clandestine literature inside the Reich, thereby limiting their religious activities and often their ability to make a living. For example, the Jehovah's Witness Franz Josef Seitz had been employed at the municipal bath and hospital in Karlsruhe as a heating maintenance worker and building superintendent for 23 years. After repeated warnings for refusing to use the »Heil Hitler« greeting, Seitz was fired without notice in early January 1936. Seitz appealed the denial of unemployment insurance payments, since he believed that paragraph 90 of the Labor Law applied only to political, but not to religious convictions. His appeal was dismissed, since he allegedly was to blame for his loss of employment. He subsequently refused a compulsory labor assignment, stating that he should receive unemployment insurance compensation since he had contributed to the system for many years. He eventually won a small unemployment stipend on appeal. Seitz was subsequently arrested by the Gestapo in July 1936.

On January 23, 1935, the Reich and Prussian Interior Ministry issued a decree ordering the removal of Jehovah's Witnesses from all civil service employment and also from positions in private industry [*Runderlaß des Reichs- und Preußischen Innenministeriums zur Dienstentfernung von Zeugen Jehovas aus dem Staatsdienst und in der privaten Industrie*]. Increasing cooperation between the Ministries of Labor, Interior, Justice, and the Gestapo resulted in growing unemployment and poverty among German Witnesses, intensified by their subsequent arrest and incarceration in concentration camps. The *1974 Yearbook of Jehovah's Witnesses* published a partial tally: »During Hitler's rule, 1,687 of them had lost their jobs, 284 their businesses, 735 their homes, and 457 were not allowed to carry on their trade. In 129 cases their property had been confiscated, 826 pensioners had been refused their pensions and 329 others had suffered other personal loss.«[9] Current literature about the economic consequences of Nazi policies for Jehovah's Witnesses is fragmentary, since publications have usually emphasized the expulsion of the Jews from the German economy after 1933;[10] to some extent there is also a nascent academic literature about the economic oppression of Sinti and Roma.

Intimidation and retaliation also extended to school age Jehovah's Witness children and youth. School officials removed Witness' children from parental custody to Nazi homes and juvenile correctional institutions, when minors refused to enroll either in the Hitler Youth or the League of German Girls. More than 860 minors were involuntarily separated from their parents under paragraph 1666 of the German Civil Code. This paragraph stipulated that child endangerment was proven, if as a result of the father's custodial care a child was disadvantaged or guilty of immoral and dishonorable behavior. School officials, police, and juvenile and district courts ruled that Witness parents endangered their children's welfare by not conforming to the norms of a Nazified educational system and society. The subsequent fate of these children removed from their families have not been researched, in part because they have been disregarded as survivors in postwar Germany. This topic is seldom mentioned in existing literature about children, although the Nazi war against these Witness children ought to be one component of the growing study of victimized children in Nazi Germany.

The practice of intimidation and reprisal also resulted in the interrogation and arrest of wives, sisters, and daughters in retaliation for the political activities of male relatives who had fled or gone into hiding. The use of female hostages continued after the initial Nazi seizure of power, eventually extending to all of occupied Europe after 1940. By late 1935, 75 percent of all women imprisoned at Hohenstein prison were hostages for male relatives.[11] When Gerhard Seger published in 1934 in Czech exile his well-known account about his experiences and escape from Oranienburg concentration camp, his wife and daughter were arrested in reprisal and released only after international protest. Similarly, Rudolf Meissner, a Jehovah's Witness, learned after emigrating in 1935 that his sister had been arrested as a hostage as leverage against his behavior abroad.[12]

Research barely exists about the relationship between Jehovah's Witnesses in Germany and Witness communities in Switzerland and Austria. Jehovah's Witnesses had already been banned in Austria in mid-June 1935. Nevertheless, we know that German, Austrian and Swiss Witnesses were able to maintain relationships and communications, thus facilitating the production and distribution of illegal publications and also sustaining organizational links. Underground work by Jehovah's Witnesses was similar to the activities of political dissidents in exile. It consisted of collecting money to support colleagues in emigration, sponsoring admission to countries of potential refuge, setting up illegal print shops for flyers and periodicals to be smuggled by courier across the German border, and recruiting new members. Publications about Germans in exile or emigration have mainly concentrated on prominent political, cultural, and scientific personalities, Jews, and political refugees, without including anything about the parallel experiences of Jehovah's Witnesses.

The book burnings of May 1933 also affected literature published by Jehovah's Witness presses. From August 21 to August 24, 1933, 65 tons of Bibles and other Witness publications were incinerated in a public bonfire in Magdeburg. Although Witnesses were prohibited from distributing Bibles according to a decree of the Reich and Prussian Interior Ministry in late January 1936, the Bible as such was not banned to others in Germany. The police, postal authorities, and customs officials confiscated Witness periodicals and publications as »harmful,« and these works were totally banned after April 1933. Nevertheless, they were smuggled into Germany from abroad. Historical analyses of the book burnings and censorship policies in Nazi Germany fail to mention similar prohibitions for Witness periodicals and publications.[13] The Witnesses are not mentioned in the existing literature about Nazi cultural purges and publication prohibitions after 1933. Current scholarship should be more inclusive about such matters. Furthermore, the relationship between Witnesses in Germany and those in adjacent foreign countries has not been researched. The Gestapo was generally well-informed by German diplomats about German refugees and their activities. Usually this involved Jewish emigrants and political exiles. Historical research about German Witnesses who had fled abroad is just beginning.

American, Swiss, and French Jehovah's Witness periodicals, as for example, *Watchtower*, *Golden Age*, and *Consolation*, published numerous articles and letters to the editor about their coreligionists incarcerated in German concentration camps. These articles were mainly based on eyewitness testimonies as well as on material quoted from other journals, such as the *Manchester Guardian*, the *Weltbühne* (Prague), and the *News Chronicle* (London). These reports emphasized the fate of Witnesses and of Jews in the concentration camps. The fate of political prisoners was not covered as often, although Carl von Ossietzky's imprisonment was reported. Issues of *The* Watchtower regularly included extensive and detailed information about the concentration camps: mistreatment, brutality, malnutrition, and poor living conditions.

These articles were often uncompromising and frequently included caricatures. The Catholic Church was portrayed as collaborating with the Nazis, and it was frequently mentioned that Adolf Hitler was a Catholic. In contrast with other newspapers and periodicals, the number of articles about conditions inside Nazi Germany increased in *The Watchtower* during the 1930s. Before 1939, this material was well distributed even inside Germany as a result of Witness underground work.

The topic of Jehovah's Witnesses in the concentration camps is only partially researched. Nevertheless, we do know that Witnesses constituted a high percentage of all prisoners before the war. In the summer of 1935, about 400 Witnesses were imprisoned in Sachsenburg concentration camp; this was about 15 percent of the prisoner population. The Lichtenburg concentration camp for women in 1938 contained 260 Witnesses among the 1,415 prisoners, constituting 18 percent of all prisoners. The Witness did not renounce their beliefs even in the concentration camps. The Hamburg communist Charlotte Gross described how female Witnesses in the Lichtenburg concentration camp refused to listen to a speech by Adolf Hitler: »We tried to convince them that resistance would be pointless and senseless, since they would be forced to listen. However, they explained to us that they had only one leader, Jehovah, and that hearing the speech of another leader would be betrayal!«[14] The Witnesses were compelled to listen to the Führer's speech; they were then whipped by the SS and icy water poured over them. Afterwards the women who became ill were not permitted to see a physician. Moreover, those involved in the protest were deprived of food for two or three days; they were also prohibited from receiving mail or writing letters. Communist prisoners provided the Witnesses with bread, although they considered their demonstrative resistance »unnecessary.« Similar SS brutalities to break the Witnesses' resistance are described in many memoirs.[15] Eugen Kogon commented after the war that »the SS was psychologically never quite equal to the challenge presented by Jehovah's Witnesses.«[16]

Between 1935 and 1939, Jehovah's Witnesses were a separate prisoner category in the concentration camps, sometimes housed in separate barracks and given distinctive markings on their uniforms. The markings used to isolate and identify Witnesses in various concentration camps were not standardized during the first five years. The purple color-coded inverted triangular patch was systematically used only after 1938. Witnesses were assigned a black circular dot and »a yellow band below the knees« in Esterwegen concentration camp;[17] male Witnesses were assigned blue circles to be worn on their chest and blue stripes on their trousers in Lichtenburg concentration camp;[18] and in Dachau in May 1937, they wore »red stripes ... with circles.«[19]

We know very little about prisoner differences by gender in the German concentration camps and even less about non-German Jehovah's Witnesses remanded to concentration camps and prisons after 1939. Their tenacious resistance and non-conformity continued despite extreme duress and limited options in camps.

The last war years brought somewhat improved conditions for some Jehovah's Witnesses, since they were occasionally assigned as farm labor and employed as domestic servants by the SS (including as barbers, cooks, etc.). After the war, this resulted in misunderstandings, especially in the German Democratic Republic, about their ostensible collaboration. Even when only lightly guarded, Witnesses never escaped from the camps since their beliefs did not allow for the possibility of flight.

Trials against Witnesses who refused military service after 1939 resulted in ca. 250 death sentences. Court martial verdicts in the Reich War Court, whose proceedings are located in the

Freiburg Military Archives branch of the German Federal Archives, have been used the first time in recent literature about »the other soldiers.«[20]

Despite new sources, research about Jehovah's Witness in Nazi Germany has barely begun, and the complexities and contours of this subject will have to be explored in future historical research. After more than half a century, we must concede that despite some improvements, the subject of Jehovah's Witnesses is still missing in most literature about Nazi Germany.

Notes

1   Sybil Milton, »Women and the Holocaust: The Case of German and German-Jewish Women,« in: *When Biology Became Destiny: Women in Weimar and Nazi Germany*, ed. Renate Bridenthal, Marian Kaplan, and Atina Grossmann (New York, 1984), pp. 297-333.

2   Idem, *Artifact Poster Set: Teacher Guide*, 2d rev. exp. ed. (Washington, D.C. 1993); and entry »Jehovah's Witnesses« in: Walter Laqueur and Judith Tydor Baumel, ed., *Encyclopedia of the Holocaust* (New Haven: Yale, in press).

3   Idem, »Die Konzentrationslager der dreißiger Jahre im Bild der in- und ausländischen Presse,« in: Ulrich Herbert, Karin Orth, and Christoph Dieckmann, eds., *Die nationalsozialistischen Konzentrationslager: Entwicklung und Struktur*, v. 1 Publikationsreihe der Gedenkstätte Buchenwald, (Göttingen, 1998), pp. 135-147.

4   Sybil Milton and Henry Friedlander, eds., *Archives of the Holocaust*, 26 vols. (New York and London, 1990-1995), see especially vol. 19 *Dokumentationsarchiv des österreichischen Widerstandes*, 363-70 and vol. 20 *Bundesarchiv of the Federal Republic of Germany*, pp. 283f. and 398.

5   Bundesverwaltungsgericht [Federal Administrative Court], decision dated June 26, 1997, 7 C 11.96.

6   Michael H. Kater, »Die Ernsten Bibelforscher im Dritten Reich,« in: *Vierteljahrshefte für Zeitgeschichte*, 17 (1969), 181-218; Detlef Garbe, *Zwischen Widerstand und Martyrium: Die Zeugen Jehovas im »Dritten Reich,«* 3rd rev. ed. (Munich, 1997); idem, »Der lila Winkel: Die ›Bibelforscher‹ (Zeugen Jehovas) in den Konzentrationslagern, in: *Dachauer Hefte* 10 (1994), pp. 3-31; idem, »Sendboten des jüdischen Bolschewismus«: Antisemitismus als Motiv nationalsozialistischer Verfolgung der Zeugen Jehovas, in: *Tel Aviver Jahrbuch für deutsche Geschichte* 23 (1994), pp. 145-171.

7   Christine King, »Jehovah's Witnesses under Nazism,« in: Michael Berenbaum, ed., *A Mosaic of Victims: Non-Jews Persecuted and Murdered by the Nazis* (New York, 1990), 188-193; Sylvie Graffard and Leo Tristan, *Les Bibleforscher et le nazisme 1933-1945* (Paris, 1990); Guy Canonici, *Les Témoins de Jéhovah Face à Hitler* (Paris, 1998); and Dokumentationsarchiv des Österreichischen Widerstandes and Institut für Wissenschaft und Kunst, eds., *Zeugen Jehovas: Vergessene Opfer des Nationalsozialismus?* (Vienna, 1998).

8   National Archives, College Park, Maryland: Record Group 59, 362.1163/ Watch Tower, Boxes 1675-76.

9   *1974 Yearbook of Jehovah's Witnesses* (1973), p. 212.

10 See Helmut Genschel, *Die Verdrängung der Juden aus der Wirtschaft im Dritten Reich* (Berlin, Frankfurt and Zürich, 1966); and Frank Bajohr, *»Arisierung« in Hamburg: Die Verdrängung der jüdischen Unternehmer 1933-1945* (Hamburg, 1997).

11 Milton, »Women and the Holocaust,« pp. 298ff.

12 Leo Baeck Institute, New York, E. J. Gumbel Papers: »Frauen als Geisel,« *Sonderdienst der deutschen Informationen: Das Martyrium der Frauen in deutschen Konzentrationslagern*, no. 41 (June 11, 1936).

13 Dietrich Aigner, *Die Indizierung »schädlichen und unerwünschten Schrifttums« im Dritten Reich*, Sonderdruck aus dem Archiv für Geschichte des Buchwesens (Frankfurt, 1971).

14 Hanna Elling, *Frauen im deutschen Widerstand 1933-1945* (Frankfurt, 1981), p. 104.

15 Wolfgang Langhoff, *Die Moorsoldaten: 13 Monate Konzentrationslager* (Zürich, 1935), pp. 311ff.

16 Eugen Kogon, *Der SS-Staat: Das System der deutschen Konzentrationslager* (Munich, 1983), p. 266.

17 Arthur Winkler, »Im Konzentrationslager Esterwegen,« in: *Trost* (Swiss edition), March 1, 1938, p. 12; »In the Esterwegen Concentration Camp,« in: *Consolation* (August 10, 1938), p. 13.

18 Klaus Drobisch and Günther Wieland, *System der Konzentrationslager 1933–1939* (Berlin, 1993), pp. 206f.

19 *Deutschland-Berichte der Sozialdemokratischen Partei Deutschlands (SOPADE)*, May 1937 (reprint Frankfurt, 1982), p. 686.

20 Detlef Garbe, »›Du sollst nicht töten‹: Kriegsdienstverweigerer 1939-1945,« in: Norbert Haase and Gerhard Paul, eds., *Die anderen Soldaten: Wehrkraftzersetzung, Gehorsamsverweigerung und Fahnenflucht im Zweiten Weltkrieg* (Frankfurt, 1995), pp. 85–104.

Sybil Milton

Jehovah's Witnesses: A Documentation

Documentation about the persecution of Jehovah's Witnesses in Nazi Germany is dispersed among many national and regional archives in Germany, Austria, and the United States. There is no single comprehensive collection of documents available about the repressive treatment of Witnesses.[1] In contrast to other victim groups, there are few published sources about the Witnesses; further, regional and local history literature about resistance and persecution only contains limited primary documentation about the fate of the Witnesses.[2] Moreover, there is no complete list of Nazi decrees affecting the Witnesses in Germany and occupied Europe. The following documents are a representative selection from diverse sources.[3]

Document 1:

Copy of circular from the Reich and Prussian Interior Ministry, Berlin, 30 January 1936, re: Prohibiting distribution of Bibles by Jehovah's Witnesses.[4]

C o p y
Reich and Prussian
Minister of the Interior
III P 3233/10 124
Berlin, 30 January 1936
NW 40, Königsplatz 6

Re: Earnest Bible Students [Jehovah's Witnesses]
In the circular dated 21 May 1935 – III P 3233/10 – I repealed the circular of 13 September 1935, I 3233 A/20.8. Based on existing conditions, I hereby order that former members of the banned International Bible Students Association are no longer permitted to distribute Bibles. Henceforth, I mandate that the police are to take action against the distribution of Bibles or other religious publications, that are otherwise inherently unobjectionable, by former members of the banned International Bible Students Association.
Signed for:
signature

Document 1

2

Abschrift.

Der Reichs- und Preussische Minister des Innern.
III P 3233/10 124 .

Berlin, den 30. Januar 1936.
NW 40, Königsplatz 6

Betrifft: Ernste Bibelforscher.

Mit Rundschreiben vom 21. Mai 1935 - III P 3233/10 - hatte ich den Runderlass vom 13. September 1934 - I 3233 A/20.8. - für hinfällig erklärt. Aus gegebener Veranlassung weise ich darauf hin, dass es hiernach den früheren Mitgliedern der verbotenen Internationalen Bibelforscher-Vereinigung nicht mehr gestattet ist, Bibeln zu vertreiben. Ich ersuche, in Zukunft gegen den Vertrieb von Bibeln, sowie von anderen an sich einwandfreien religiösen Schriften durch frühere Mitglieder der verbotenen Internationalen Bibelforscher-Vereinigung polizeilich vorzugehen.

Im Auftrage:
gez. Unterschrift.

An
die Landesregierungen
(für Preussen: den Herrn stellvertretenden Chef und Inspekteur der Preussischen Geheimen Staatspolizei,
- Zum Schreiben vom 20.1.1936 Nr. II 1 B.1.S. 90/36 -
für Baden: den Herrn Badischen Minister des Innern).

R58/405

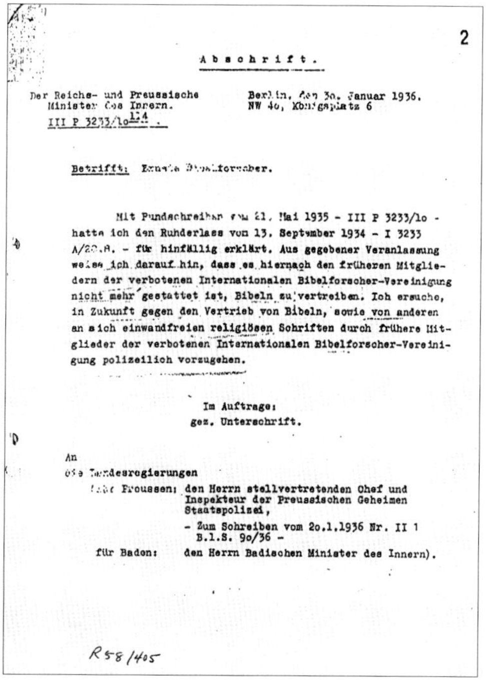

To be distributed to state governments:
— for Prussia: the Deputy Director and Inspector of the Prussian Political Police, reference, letter 20 January 1936, no. II 1 B.1.S. 90/36;
— for Baden: to the Baden Minister of Interior.

Document 2:

Letter by the Gestapo's Regional Office, Dortmund, signed Dr. Hinkmann, to the Chief of Police in Bochum and Dortmund, 7 May 1936, re: Police surveillance of Jehovah's Witnesses.[5]

Prussian Political Police
State Police Office for the Arnsberg Administrative District
- II B -
Dortmund, 7 May 1936
Re: International Bible Students Association

I have been informed that former members and followers of the banned International Bible Students Association (IBSA) are illegally preparing to reestablish themselves, disguised for example, as some sort of natural health practice.

I consider the activities of former members of the IBSA of utmost importance and want to be informed immediately about anything suspicious during surveillance.

Copies for District Administrators enclosed for distribution to local police officials.
(signed) Dr. Hinkmann.

Document 3:

Circular from the Chief of Police in Dortmund, 25 May 1937, re: Freeze on issuing passports.[6]

Chief of Police
II 3
Dortmund, 25 May 1937
To all Police Precincts
Re: Passports for members of the illegal International Bible Students Association.

Passports will no longer be issued for individuals known as Bible Students. Furthermore, a passport freeze should be imposed on all persons known as Bible Students, and passports already issued to them are to be revoked.
Please inform Department II of any such cases. An appropriate notation is to be entered on any relevant passport application.

Document 4:

Circular from the Gestapo Regional Office, Munich, 19 May 1937, re: Protective custody [Schutzhaft] for Jehovah's Witnesses.[7]

Political Police   Munich, 19 May 1937
Gestapo Regional Office Munich
B. No. 49790/37 II 1 B b

To: Police Headquarters, Munich
Police Headquarters, Hof
District Agencies and City Commissioners, except in the Palatinate
District Sub-Office, Reichenhall
  memo to local governments, except in the Palatinate; Chief Mayors; Mayors of cities formerly in administrative districts, except in the Palatinate; Border Commissioners; and Border Offices.
Re: Protective Custody for Bible Students
Reference: Circular of 23 September 1935; B.No. 54216/35 I 1 B.

The circular of 23 September 1935, B. No. 54216/35 I 1 B, is revoked and replaced by the following directive that is effective immediately:

1. Every person who in any way promotes or spreads the interests or unity of adherents of the illegal International Bible Students Association (IBSA) is to be taken into protective custody and immediately brought before a court in order to issue an official arrest warrant.

2. Should an official arrest warrant not be issued or later be cancelled, the individual who has become active for the IBSA can, if necessary, be detained in protective custody for more than

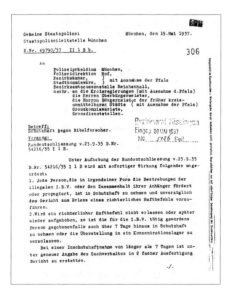

seven days or remanded to a concentration camp.

When a protective custody term is longer than seven days, a precise statement of particulars must be reported in duplicate.

If transfer to a concentration camp is based only on *suspicion* [emphasis in original] of activities for the illegal IBSA, then the application must present the detailed facts on which the suspicion is based. Concerning the duration of protective custody arrest, a strict standard is to be applied especially if the individual in question is a functionary of the IBSA or a recidivist.

If a female individual only claims to be a Bible Student or a male merely states that as a Jehovah's Witnesses, he must refuse military service, work in Reich air raid association, in the compulsory fire department, and other similar organizations, this is not to be considered illegal activities for the IBSA. In such cases, protective custody is not to be imposed unless the individual can be proven, in whatever form, to have been actively engaged for the illegal IBSA. But as soon as a statement is followed by the actual deed, such as refusing the order to enlist in the Reich air raid association, serve in the compulsory fire department, etc., then protective custody is to be imposed. If the order for military service is not obeyed, the individual concerned is to be handed over immediately to the proper armed forces office.

3. All members of the IBSA who are released from prison after serving their sentence, are to be taken into protective custody without delay; transfer to a concentration camp can be requested if an explanation of the facts is submitted.

Signed for:
(signed) S t e p p .

Confirmation of Accuracy:
Copy 5126 to be sent FYI to the district police chief in Bad Kissingen, for informing all sub-stations.

Bad Kissingen, 21 May 1937.
District Office

Document 5:

Arthur Winkler, »In the Esterwegen Concentration Camp,« in: Trost [Consolation] *(Bern), 15 February 1938, pages 12f.*[8]

Diagram of Esterwegen   [Page 12]

Today, we are starting a report about Esterwegen, a German concentration camp in Prussia, written by a Jehovah's Witnesses, who was personally incarcerated there for some time. He personally vouches for the accuracy of his report that he has signed as author. He also drew this sketch of the camp. The reader can see barracks numbered 1 to 9 that house prisoners as well as other barracks, watchtowers equipped with machine guns, the arrangement of patrol paths, and the SS camp.

In the Esterwegen Concentration Camp

I, the undersigned, was a prisoner in the Esterwegen concentration camp in East Frisia, Germany. My reports are based on personal experiences, and in part on what I saw, heard, and personally encountered.

The Gestapo brought me to the camp sketched above, because I am a Jehovah's Witness. Merely the fact that I am a Witness and believe in God's word, gave the Gestapo adequate justification to bring me to this camp. Initially I was brought before an investigative judge; he acquitted and released me, stating: »I do not know what the Gestapo will do with you now.« The Gestapo rearrested me two days later.

Esterwegen is one of the camps under the headquarters in Papenburg. East Frisia contains marshlands as well as about twenty different prison camps, each holding about 1,000 prisoners. There were approximately 1,300 – 1,500 prisoners in Esterwegen Camp when I was there. SS men, Hitler's guard regiment, served as guards. They were all young men, age 20 to 25, who had been trained to behave callously, taught to hate, and to treat — or more accurately to mistreat — their defenseless fellow men.

Prisoners were housed in wooden barracks, approximately 50 meters long by 10 meters wide, partitioned into three rooms. The first room was the ›common room‹, but only in name, since prisoners actually spent their time in the marshes and wherever hard labor was implemented, or wherever abuse was carried out. Meals were also eaten in the ›common room.‹ When I was there, every prisoner could receive 15 marks per week to purchase food and tobacco, which reveals the adequacy of the food provided.

The second room contained dormitories with 50 bunk beds for approximately 150 men.

The beds in this room were three-tiered bunk beds. To illustrate how utterly inadequate this room was for so many men, it must be mentioned that the SS had quarters of the same size, but these rooms held 35 or fewer beds. Periodically, to harass the prisoners, all beds were moved into a heap. It always required considerable time and effort to put everything back in order again. The back room was the washroom.

A sketch of the camp is found above. The upper section of this sketch is the SS camp, for the commandant, officers, and SS men and containing administrative offices, the kitchen, an officers' mess and club, garages, the clothing supply room, and an infirmary.

The lower part of the sketch is the prisoners' camp. The outer wall indicates the perimeter; it was approximately 2 meters high, reinforced at the top with iron bars connected by barbed wire. SS men patrolled the perimeter path inside the walls

---

Im Konzentrationslager Esterwegen

Der Unterzeichnete war selbst Gefangener im Konzentrationslager Esterwegen in Ostfriesland, Deutschland. Meine Berichte sind auf Erfahrungen, Miterlebtes, und stützen sich auf das, was ich teils gesehen, gehört und mitgemacht habe.

Als ein Zeuge Jehovas wurde ich auf Veranlassung der Gestapo in das obige Lager gebracht. Der Umstand allein, daß ich ein Zeuge Jehovas war und Glauben an Gottes Wort ausübte, war für die Gestapo hinreichend Grund genug, um mich in das Lager zu transportieren. Zuerst wurde ich vor den Untersuchungsrichter gestellt; dieser sprach mich frei, entließ mich aber mit den Worten: „Was die Gestapo nun mit Ihnen tun wird, das weiß ich nicht.' Ich wurde denn auf zwei Tage später aufs neue durch die Gestapo verhaftet.

Esterwegen ist eines der Lager, die der Zentralstelle Papenburg unterstellt sind. Ostfriesland ist eine Moorgegend, wo sich etwa zwanzig verschiedene Straflager befinden, jedes Lager mit etwa tausend Gefangenen belegt. Zu meiner Zeit waren im Lager Esterwegen etwa 1300 bis 1500 Gefangene. Die Bewachung erfolgte durch S.S.-Männer, der Hitlergarde. Es waren alles junge Menschen von 20 bis 25 Jahren, die zuvor herangebildet wurden, damit sie entsprechend hartherzig auftreten und mit eingepflanztem Haß ihra Mitmenschen, die völlig wehrlos sind, behandeln oder oft besser gesagt — mißhandeln.

Die Gefangenen sind in Holzbaracken untergebracht, die etwa fünfzig Meter lang und zehn Meter breit sind. Sie sind in drei Abteilungen geteilt. Der erste ist der Aufenthaltsraum, dessen Namen nach, denn der eigentliche Aufenthalt der Gefangenen ist das Moor und überall dort, wo schwere Arbeit verrichtet wird. Oder auch dort, wo mißhandelt wird. Im „Aufenthaltsraum' werden auch Mahlzeiten eingenommen. Wie reichhaltig das Essen verabreicht wird, möge aus der Tatsache ersehen werden, daß zu meiner Zeit jeder Gefangene die Freiheit hatte, sich 15 Mark pro Woche schicken zu lassen, damit er sich Lebensmittel und Tabak kaufen könne.

Der zweite Raum ist der Schlafraum, wo zirka 150 Mann schlafen. In dem Schlafraum sind drei Betten übereinander. Um zu zeigen, daß dieser Raum völlig unzureichend ist für so viel Mann, sei erwähnt, daß die S.S.-Männer ebenso große Schlafräume hatten; hier standen aber keine fünfzig Betten, sondern nur 35 und weniger. Um die Gefangenen zu schikanieren, geschah es von Zeit zu Zeit, daß sämtliche Betten in den Schlafsaal kreuz und quer durcheinander gewürfelt wurden. Es erforderte immer viel Zeit und Mühe, alle wieder in Ordnung zu bringen. — Der hintere Raum war der Waschraum.

Hier folgt nun eine Lagerskizze. Der obere Teil der Skizze, d. h. das S.S.-Lager, ist der Teil für den Kommandanten, für die Offiziere, die S.S.-Männer, die Garagen und die Küche, das Kasino, das Sekretariat, die Kleiderkammer und das Lazarett.

Der hintere Teil stellt das Gefangenenlager dar. Die Außenmauer stellt die Umgrenzung dar; sie ist etwa zwei Meter hoch, oben sind Eisenstäbe befestigt, die mit Stacheldraht verbunden sind. Auf dem Patrouillenweg innerhalb der Mauer patrouillieren die S.S.-Männer Tag und Nacht. Sie sind alle mit Schnellfeuergewehren versehen. Der Stacheldrahtverhau links des Patrouillenweges ist außergewöhnlich dicht durcheinander geflochten, etwa 1,50 Meter hoch und auch breit. Der Stacheldraht ist außerdem mit Hochspannung geladen. An den Stacheldraht angrenzend befindet sich der Todesweg, das ist ein schmaler, weißer Sandweg, auf dem schwarze Tafeln stehen, die einen weißen Totenkopf versehen sind. Die Totenköpfe dienen als Warnungszeichen. Alle, die wissentlich oder unwissentlich diesen Weg betreten, werden vom Turm mit dem Maschinengewehr und auch vom Posten aufs neu erschossen. Wer den Freitod auf diese Weise sucht, oder wer aus irgendwelchen andern Umständen diesen Weg betrat, wird dann nach dem schönen Motto „auf der Flucht erschossen' erledigt. An den beiden äußeren Ecken und in der Mitte ein Eingang des Gefangenenlagers sind Türme angebracht, die von allen Seiten einen Überblick über das Lager ermöglichen und mit Maschinengewehren und großen Scheinwerfern versehen sind, um das Lager bei Nacht sofort in ganz hellen Licht zu versetzen. Die numerierten Baracken sind die Gefangenenbaracken.

Die vorstätlich angewendeten Mittel und Methoden, um die Gefangenen zu zwingen, Zugeständnisse zu machen, damit sie willfährig und aus Furcht tun, was der heutige Hitler-System verlangt, sind folgende:

a) Dem Gefangenen wird fortwährend ein Zustand vollkommener Hoffnungslosigkeit vor Augen gehalten, jeder Anspruch auf Gerechtigkeit wird ihm entzogen, und anderseits versucht man Mitleid zu erregen, indem man den Gefangenen an seine Frau, Kinder, Geschwister, Eltern usw. erinnert.

b) Eine andere Form ist die versteckte und öffentlichter Drohung und Bedrohung, Bearbeitung mit Fußtritten und Faustschlägen, um Angst und Furcht zu erregen und die Gefangenen auf diese Weise zur völligen Aufgabe passiven Widerstandes zu zwingen.

c) Die dritte Form der Bekämpfung, besser gesagt, grausamer Mißhandlung, besteht in der Anwendung brutalster Gewalt. Das Opfer werden zum Beispiel auf eine Pritsche geschnallt und vom den stärksten S.S.-Männern mit einem Ochsenziemer unbarmherzig geschlagen. Zum Schluß wurden dem so Mißhandelten des öftern die Kleider ausgezogen, und er bekam zur Steigerung seiner Drangsal noch weitere 15 Schläge auf den nassen Handtuch auf das nackte Gesäß. Diese Art der Mißhandlung wird im Beisein des Kommandanten, der Offiziere, der S.S.-Männer und oft in der ersten Zeit auch in Gegenwart der Gefangenen durchgeführt. Es geschieht, daß solcher Art Mißhandelte bewußtlos zusammen-

Wir beginnen heute mit einem Bericht über das deutsche Konzentrationslager Esterwegen in Preußen. Der Bericht ist von einem Zeugen Jehovas verfaßt, der selber eine Zeitlang dort interniert war. Wir verbirgt mit seinem Namen die Echtheit seiner Darstellung. Diese Lagerskizze hat er selber gezeichnet. Der Leser sieht hier unten 1 bis 9 die Wohnbaracken der Gefangenen, dann die übrigen Baracken, die Wachttürme mit Maschinengewehren bewehrt, die Anlage der Kontrollgänge und der SS-Lager.

day and night; they were equipped with semi-automatic rifles. Located to the left of the sentries pathway was a densely woven electrified barbed-wire barrier, about 1.5 meters in height and width. Adjacent to the barbed wire was the death strip, a narrow path strewn with white sand, containing black warning signs imprinted with a white skull and crossbones (the death's head). Anyone, who knowingly or accidentally, stepped on to this path was immediately shot by machine guns from the guard towers and by the sentries. Those who chose to commit suicide in this way, or who stepped on to the path for another reason, were disposed of according to the formula: »Shot while attempting to escape.« Guard towers with machine guns and searchlights for instantly illuminating the camp at night, from which the entire camp could be monitored in all directions, were built at both the outermost corners and in the center at the main gate of the prisoners' compound. The numbered barracks were the prisoners' barracks.

The calculated methods used to force prisoners into acquiescence, so that they would willingly submit, out of fear, to the demands of the Hitler system, were as follows:

a) The prisoner was constantly shown his utterly hopeless situation, deprived of any possibility of justice, while at the same time playing on his sympathy by reminding him of his wife, children, siblings, parents, etc.

b) A second method was the use of hidden and open threats of mistreatment, kicking and punching prisoners to make them apprehensive and frightened, thereby forcing them completely to give up any passive resistance.

c) The third form of control, stated unambiguously, cruel mistreatment, involved using extreme brute force. For example, victims were strapped to a plank and beaten mercilessly with a leather whip by the strongest SS men. Afterwards, intensifying the ordeal, the abused was undressed for an additional whipping, fifteen strokes with a wet towel across his naked buttocks. These brutalities were administered in the presence of the commandant, officers, SS men, and at first, also in the presence of other prisoners. Those subjected to such mistreatment often collapsed unconscious.   [page 13]

Usually, those whose backs had been bloodily whipped black-and-blue did not receive any salve to ease their pain or to promote healing the bloody welts. Orderlies who understandably took pity on them, risked maltreatment in the same manner, rather than loss of their jobs, if they gave them anything for relief.

Another common form of maltreatment was the use of manacles and foot-cuffs to block circulation. To increase this abuse, the prisoner was bent over, tied up, and forced to lie on the floor of a small cell for hours. When the shackles were unlocked, his hands and feet naturally swelled. One could later establish the type of torture experienced by the victim from the scars and twisted fingers.

Another type of brutality was described as »sport,« the worst form of military workout. Everyone in the camp, whether healthy or infirm, had to participate in »sport.« These calisthenics were to be done, in the words of the officers and SS men, »until you become mentally numb, you pigs«; that is, until many prisoners lay unconscious on the ground. Buckets of ice cold water were poured over their heads and bodies until they regained consciousness, after which they again had to participate in exercises. When they once again lay unconscious on the ground, the process was repeated, if those in charge felt like it.

Another form of punishment involved locking prisoners in the camp prison (*Bunker*). A *Bunker* was a small narrow cell, without daylight, in which prisoners received even less than the usual insufficient food rations. This punishment lasted one week, two weeks, three weeks, a month, and even longer.

One particular form of harassment had prisoners carrying tree trunks in a circle for many hours, pushing iron handcarts filled with sand, or pointlessly carrying other heavy objects. This was done mainly on foggy days, when the risk of escape was greater, and when no one could leave the camp. All work was done under SS guard, armed with guns and semi-automatic rifles. Moreover, labor commandos assigned to work outside the camp were guarded with machine-guns.

A ›special‹ method of torture had been devised in Dachau Concentration Camp, and tested on prisoners who, wanting to put an end to their torment, had tried to escape. Heavy iron nails were hammered into thick beams, so that the points could be seen from 7 to 10 centimeters on the other side of the wood. The victims were pulled by hook on to these beams, so that their backs came to rest on the nails. This devilish method was used on five people who had attempted to escape from Dachau; all five died, one after the other, in agony on this torture stake.

(To be continued)

Continuation and conclusion of Arthur Winkler, »In the Esterwegen Concentration Camp,« in: Trost (Swiss edition), 1 March 1938, pages 12f. This translation from the German is based on the English article, »In the Esterwegen Concentration Camp,« in: Consolation, 10 August 1938, pages 12–15, slightly retranslated and reedited by Sybil Milton.[9]

[Page 12]

There were prisoners from all classes and ideologies in the Esterwegen concentration camp. There were Reichstag deputies, owners of factories and estates, millionaires, attorneys, senior and subordinate national and communal civil servants, merchants, artisans, laborers, communists, socialists, free-thinkers, Masons, Jews, and Jehovah's Witnesses thrown together at Esterwegen. The major reason why they were sent to a camp was that they held other beliefs than those proclaimed in »Mein Kampf« or in the »Mythology of the Twentieth Century,« and had the courage to state them. Most of these people had convictions or religious faith, and did not want to be hypocrites. Nevertheless, these reasons were insufficient to place these individuals before a normal court. A number of prisoners were older than 60, when I was confined there. One prisoner was 72 years old and there were also two blind persons in the camp, a communist and a Jehovah's Witness.

The prisoners were divided into political prisoners and habitual criminals. All of those specified above, and also homosexuals, were assigned to the section for political prisoners. The political prisoners wore green threadbare uniforms, marked on the backs with large yellow dots. The political prisoners were housed on the right side of the camp street and the habitual criminals, known as »Bevauer« [*Berufsverbrecher*] were put on the left side.

The professional criminals were in preventive detention [*Vorbeugungshaft*]. The SS men and officers stated that this loss of freedom removed the possibility that they would commit crimes, and also that they might be intimidated from recidivism and violating the regulations of the Third Reich. Some of them had already served two or three sentences; others had been punished more frequently. No hope for freedom was given to them.

The prisoners were compelled to work in the marshes every day. On the way to and from the moors, they were compelled to sing songs. Songs were always mandatory whenever they marched, whether inside or outside the camp. They often had to sing while running double time. Drainage channels were being dug in the marshes; then peat is shoveled in rectangular cubes and stacked for drying. In addition, new roads are being constructed. In this way, the extensive East Frisian moors were cultivated — indeed they were made arable through the prisoners sweat, blood, lives, and money. Why? Because the prisoners had to pay for their involuntary detention in the camp, the same as if they were paying for a stay in a sanitorium. Prisoners had the »privilege« of paying more than two marks for every day of their stay in the camp; if unable to pay, their property, including furniture, was confiscated and those entirely destitute had to obtain emergency work and were compelled each week to pay a percentage of their nominal earnings, which can be equated to additional severe punishment. It has also occurred that parents and other family members were held liable for such payment, if they owned property or had the financial means. Prisoners do not receive any monetary or material compensation for the hard labor they performed, but instead must pay for every day in the camp, for the utterly inadequate food, miserable clothing, for the mistreatment endured, for whippings and physical injury; for all of this more than two marks per day had to be paid. It seems that individuals are employed according to their qualifications; thus tailors have to make uniforms for the camp officers and SS men, also for other troops stationed there. Carpenters are compelled to make furniture, partly for the camp but also for other officials, without any payment and often under every type of threat and mistreatment.

When I was in Esterwegen, the socialist Reichstag deputy Dr. [Julius] Leber and his colleague, [Ernst] Heilmann were also there.[10] Dr. Leber and I were both housed in barrack 9 and I had many opportunities to speak with him. One day, he and Heilmann were locked in the dog kennels, and ordered to act as if they were dogs. When any SS man walked in the vicinity of the kennels, they (Dr. Leber and Heilmann) were forced to bark like dogs. Not satisfied with this, Heilmann was required to drink his own urine and Dr. Leber was forced to eat his own excrement. As a result, Dr. Leber contracted a stomach and intestinal illness that physically debilitated him. There was an SS physician in the camp, who rarely believed prisoners with internal illnesses. This was also true with Dr. Leber. Every layman could tell from his change of facial color, his emotional condition, his physical deterioration, and his constant pain that this vile behavior had caused a severe illness. But this was not enough to satisfy the demands of the camp spirit. In addition, the daily routine required fifty or more knee bends, falling on the floor and standing up again, jumping, rolling on the ground, etc.

The Jehovah's Witnesses are the daily targets for every kind of persecution, terror, and brutality. Using the previously mentioned methods, an attempt was made to force them to disavow their belief in their God Jehovah and his Word, the Bible. They did not receive any Bibles, on principle, in the camp; nor are bibles given out in prisoners anymore. Attempts were made, with every possible and impossible means, to force them to sign a sworn statement, declaring that they no longer want to be Witnesses, that they will never again resume contact and association with the Witnesses, and that they will no longer read any literature from the Witnesses.

In order to ridicule them in front of other prisoners, Witnesses are called »paradise birds,« »heaven clowns,« »Jesus grasper,« and also occasionally they are called »Jehovah.« Those who do not capitulate and remain unwavering in their faith are forced to wear a yellow band below the knee, as a blatant symbol of identification and to show they were assigned to a punishment company. In the opinion of the SS, the Witnesses were the worst traitors, incorrigible, and the scum of humankind.

The brutality mentioned in issue no. 370 are not the only ones committed against Witnesses. The report leader [an SS functionary, ed.] Tarré attacked a number of Witnesses in the prisoner bathhouse. They were forced to undress and Tarré personally sprayed them with squirts of ice cold water. Cold water under special atmospheric pressure was squirted on their sex organs and at their abdomen. During this maltreatment, they were constantly asked whether they still wanted to remain a Witness and they were threatened with the continuation of these measures unless they renounced their faith. Since no one abandoned their beliefs, he continued this sadism until the victims were completely exhausted. This bestial behavior resulted in abnormal swelling of the sex organs as well as excruciating pain; the prisoners eventually ended up in the infirmary. Tarré showed up there every day to inquire if they were still Jehovah's Witnesses and threatened them with further all possible additional tortures, if they remained steadfast in their faith.

Not only were wrist cuffs that cut off circulation used, but also fingers were simultaneously secured in a crooked position. These hideous tortures were frequently repeated, so that the martyred individuals had crippled fingers, which I personally observed, but they went even further, causing the complete paralysis of the prisoners' hands. The names of these victims can and will be published, if we can obtain their consent.

About two weeks before 28 September 1935, it was announced what would be done on that date to Jehovah's Witnesses who refused to sign the previously mentioned declaration. The most brutal would pale into insignificance compared to what would now be done. There were daily threats about 28 September. Even prisoners were incited to threaten recalcitrant Witnesses, in order to instill fear from every possible side. But what happened? Report leader Tarré, an arrogant and pompous brute, who had always tried to come up with new methods of torture and who would, if possible, have deprived prisoners of any time for rest and contemplation, had a motorcycle accident on the afternoon of 27 September. Apparently he had planned his opening move at evening roll call on 27 September. The SS liked such preliminaries as the beginning of systematically prearranged larger campaigns. Instead of coming to the camp, Tarré was taken to the hospital. He broke his arm in the motorcycle accident. As a result, 28th September was one of the quietest days ever for Jehovah's Witnesses in the camp.

Witnesses were usually assigned the most menial work. Jehovah's Witnesses and Jews were always assigned to the latrine commando. The sewage tanks had to be cleaned by hand regularly, and of course, clothing, as a result, became soiled with excrement.

It was reported to me that Esterwegen camp was closed a while ago. SS report leader Tarré is now a prisoner in Dachau concentration camp. Since this camp is notorious even outside Germany, Tarré can have a good opportunity to reflect daily on how bitter those cruelties are that he once indulged in, but also to consider how brutally he had once behaved.

What is the real purpose of this sadism? All these acts of torture are intentional, premeditated, and implemented on orders of the German government. I am saying »at the command of the German government,« because the camp commandant told us this when we were released and warned us not to divulge anything about experiences in the camp, since we would endanger others who would then be sent to the camps and we knew what would happen to them there. These hideous methods of the Inquisition were to instill prisoners with fear and terror, so that any thought of opposing the current system will be suppressed, and any thought of resistance or free expressions of opinion will be prevented.

What is said here is cruel, but it is the truth. But how much harder is it for the many thousands and hundreds of thousands who become victims of this gruesome brutality! It would embitter them, if this factual report is not believed. I will not talk about the cruelties inflicted by Gestapo officials in Gestapo basements and jail cells, nor the many acts of terror committed by the SA and SS. A sermon by a priest in a Cologne prison at Christmas 1935 stated that 2.5 million people share our fate. How many must there be now, considering that the number of camps and prisons has grown? There are perhaps some people who believe what the German government says. The German government rejects all publications about actual conditions in German concentration camps as lies and atrocity propaganda by the enemy. What has the German government done to be believable and defend itself in international public opinion? Every now and then they permit foreign commissions to inspect concentration camps. But these visits are fraudulent and a miserable travesty, as these commission never learn the truth, not even from the prisoners, who cannot risk telling the truth in the presence of their torturers, because they would later be tortured to death. I myself witnessed how foreign commissions were informed about Esterwegen as a »training camp,« where prisoners were schooled for three months. When a prisoner already in the camp for a long time, not knowing the true state of affairs, answers the commission that »I have been here for 20 months,« the commandant complacently and falsely informs the commission that this was an exceptional case and the prisoner was incorrigible. The same chicanery also took place about food. There was usually good food when a commission visited the camp or a lot of meat was carried to the prisoner kitchen during the commission's visit. Once they had left, obviously with good impressions, all the meat was again carried away from the camp. If the food in the camps is really as good as was told to the commissions, why do prisoners need money to purchase food?

If what the German government states that all exposés about conditions in camps, prisons, and penitentiaries are lies, then there is one way to prove the German government's claims, and that is that those known as maltreated should be freed and given their passports, so that they might personally refute what was reported about them abroad. But the opposite occurs. The first thing that the Gestapo did after I was freed was to rescind my passport and place me under police surveillance. Although my wife, who is a foreign national, likewise ordered and paid for her passport, she never received it because I intended to go to my relatives abroad to recuperate. We never received a refund for the fees paid for my wife's unissued passport.

The Third Reich is notorious for a system of informants under the Gestapo, that is, the German secret [non-uniformed] state political police. The spies are persons bought by the Gestapo, who are not necessarily convinced representatives of National Socialism. A large percentage are hypocrites, which I experienced personally. They are traitorous paid instruments of the Gestapo and the Third Reich. They are in the camps, in prisons, in every city, in every place, and are also found abroad. They spy on fellow human beings, to deliver them to the brutal Gestapo. They are one of the reasons that freedom of expression and mutual trust have disappeared in Germany.

I am familiar with all of these dangers and intrigues, the notorious deeds of the Third Reich. I also know that by publishing these facts I am making myself vulnerable to further persecution by the Gestapo. Nevertheless, I will not be silent, but will make the truth about the Third Reich known, a truth that it suppresses with all means at its disposal. In the interests of humanity, I consider it my duty to state that the numerous publications about the Third Reich and conditions in the German concentration camps are absolutely true. It should be a warning for all honest good-willed people to prevent becoming victims of a dictatorship, not to grant support to arrogant, deceptive, and presumptuous purveyors of force pretending to be beneficent rulers, ostensibly promoting a new society for the benefit of all.

This is not a complete comprehensive report, but deals only with details and personal impressions, so that the reader can get an approximate view of the situation. In order to corroborate this evidence of the truth and to vouch for its authenticity, I assume complete responsibility and have tenaciously taken up the battle against lies, slander, and brutality. I am certifying the accuracy of this report with my own signature in order to encourage all who stand for truth and justice and who wish actively to participate in this fight.

Arthur Winkler

Document 6:

Regulations for the removal of mail privileges, printed on the back of a letter from Ravensbrück women's concentration camp.[11]

»The prisoner remains, as before, an intractable Bible Student and refuses to repudiate the false teachings of the Bible Students.

For these reasons, the usual mail privileges of writing letters have been denied to her.«

Document 7:

Decision of the Karlsruhe District Court, Civil Law Chamber I, in Karlsruhe v. [Franz Josef Seitz] and Willi Seitz, 15 April 1937, case no. 1 ZFH 33/37, re: Removal of parental custody for the minor male son, Willi Josef Seitz.[12]

District Court, Civil Law Chamber I   Karlsruhe, 15 April 1937
1 ZFH 33/37   Re: Parental custody of Willi Josef Seitz,
                                        born 11 March 1923

Sentence:

The complaints of the heating maintenance worker Franz Josef Seitz, residing in Karlsruhe at Kriegsstrasse 171, against the decision of the Karlsruhe Magistrate's Court B III of 6 April 1937 is rejected and liability for court costs are [to be born] by the plaintiff.

Grounds:

On 6 April 1937 the Karlsruhe Magistrate's Court B III withdrew parental custody and rights from the stoker Franz Josef Seitz for his son Wili Josef and simultaneously ordered that the boy be placed in the observation station of the reformatory at Schloss Flehingen. The circumstances that caused this ruling are found in the detailed account of the Magistrate's Court.

The father appealed, requesting a reversal of the sentence. He disputes that the prerequisites for prosecution under paragraph 1666 of the Civil Code are established. The spiritual and physical welfare of his son is not endangered and he does not abuse his rights of custody. The son has been strictly raised and has a religious personality. Since his suspension from school, he has become apprenticed. Complaints about his son were not present when he attended school, nor in his apprenticeship. He does not deny that his son refused to participate in national ceremonies, to use the German greeting and to raise or salute the flag. This cannot be attributed to parental influence. He did not order his son to do this and left the decision about his behavior up to his son's discretion. He had formerly belonged to the Association of Earnest Bible Students and today still professes this belief. The details of the complaint are referenced from the records.

According to the allegations' which the father will not deny, the youth had refused to participate in national school ceremonies, to salute the flag, to use the German greeting, and to sing national songs. The boy informed the school director that he would not be a soldier and wrote two essays revealing his opinions about contemporary events. The minor

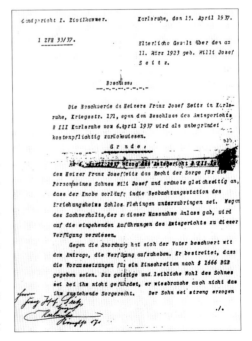

is incapable of feeling German, of appreciating the deeds of great German men, or cognizant of his duties to his compatriots and country, based on his conduct and the beliefs expressed in his two school essays. It is the unequivocal duty of parents to educate their children in a manner that does not alienate them from their German nature, to raise their children with German customs and beliefs that morally and intellectually reveal the spirit of National Socialism in the service of the Volk and the national community (preamble and paragraph 2 of the Law about Hitler Youth, 1 December 1936, Reichsgesetzblatt 1, p. 913). This violation of parental duties is a subjective infraction of para. 1666. The court is convinced, against the father's statement, that the son's beliefs are the result of parental influence. The father today still acknowledges that he is a Jehovah's Witness. He was fired from his job because of his activities as an Earnest Bible Student and was also prosecuted and punished for this. The mother has the same views as the father. It is clear that the minor did not get his beliefs independently, but his behavior and views are those of his parents. Moreover, the minor has been suspended from school, and it would be impossible for him to secure further education essential for a job.

These factors provide the preconditions for the magistrate's court to intervene based on paragraph 1666 of the civil code. The appeal is denied, since the sentence of the magistrate's court is commensurate with the particulars of this case.

The court order under para. 1666, part 1.2 is deemed temporary, but under para. 1666, part 1.1 it is an irrevocable ruling, and this does not contravene the circuit court (*Kammergericht*) ruling of 24 August 1934.

Signed: von Frankenberg   Hug   Krämer
Stamped with the registrar's seal of the District Court, Karlsruhe

Document 8:

Court Martial [Feldurteil] verdict by the 3rd Senate of the Reich War Court, Berlin, 11 July 1940, re: Franz Zeiner, a Jehovah's Witness who resisted induction into the armed forces, is sentenced to death for undermining military morale [Wehrkraftzersetzung].[13]

[page 1]

In the Name of the German People!

Court Martial Verdict

In the criminal case vs.
        Private Franz Zeiner,
        Reserve Infantry Battalion I/482
for undermining military morale
the 3d Senate of the Reich War Court in its session on 22 June 1940, with the following participating judges:
        Senate President, Dr. Schmauser, presiding judge
        Rear Admiral Arps
        Colonel Galle

Colonel Selle

Senior War Court Councillor Dr. Block

Prosecuting counsel:

Senior War Court Councillor Dr. Bischoff

As registrar:

Chief Inspector of the Reich War Court Hotje

has sentenced the defendant to death for undermining military morale, to permanent loss of civil rights, and to dishonorable discharge and separation from the military.

In the Name of the Law.

[page 2]

Grounds

I.

The defendant was born out of wedlock on 23 January 1909 in Zeltweg (Styria) to a woman employed as an unskilled construction laborer. He was brought up by strangers. After graduating from primary school, he worked as an unskilled laborer for various firms and also worked as a farm laborer. He was periodically unemployed. He later received a homestead.

Since 1935, the defendant has been living with a divorced woman. He has not married, since this woman is nearly blind and therefore permission to marry has not been granted.

The defendant has not been politically active. He has no prior convictions.

The defendant was raised as a Catholic. In 1933, he became aware of the teachings of the Earnest Bible Students at a lecture. Thereafter, he read Witness publications and became a fervent adherent of these beliefs, without however joining the Association of Earnest Bible Students. His partner also affirms her belief in this doctrine.

II.

On 22 January 1940, the defendant underwent a medical examination for the draft and was found fit for service in the First Infantry Reserve. On 17 April 1940, he was called up for Infantry Reserve Battalion I/482 in Mistelbach, and instructed to report on 20 April 1940.

He did not comply with the notice to report. On 20 April, he wrote a letter to the Draft Registration Office in Vienna X, stating that as a true Christian, that is, a follower of Christ, he could not and would not bear arms. God prohibited killing. He had pledged to do God's will as written in the Holy Bible.

He was again summoned to the draft registration office, and repeated his refusal to serve, although he was immediately informed about the grave consequences.

Moreover, during subsequent judicial questioning and during the trial, he asserted his beliefs, despite repeated reprimands and despite his being informed of the grave consequences of his actions.

III.

The defendant is a German national. He is 31 years old. The official notice for active military service makes him a soldier effective on the date of his being drafted. As such, he is required to complete military service. He was aware of this.

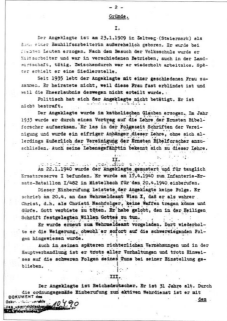

[page 3]

By nevertheless repeatedly and stubbornly refusing to perform military service, he has sought to evade this duty. The fact that he has acted on religious convictions is not material to his guilt under criminal law. There is no evidence of temporary insanity or diminished mental capacity.

The defendant is, therefore, to be punished for the crime of undermining military morale, under Section 5, paragraph 1, No. 3 of the KSSVO.

IV.

In principle, this sentence carries the death penalty. Under paragraph 2, sentences to be served in a prison or penitentiary may be considered in less serious cases. This does not apply in this case. It is true that the defendant has not acted out of cowardice or similar motives. However, his stubbornness and inflexibility eliminates the possibility of a milder sentence. This type of implacable opposition to military service is dangerous propaganda can undermine the willingness of others for military service. Therefore, the death penalty must be implemented.

Military service is honorable for the German people. Since the defendant refuses to perform the honorable duty of a German, he may not retain his civil rights. He is thus permanently deprived of his civil rights under paragraph 32 of the Criminal Law.

He is also sentenced to dishonorable discharge from military service based on paragraph 31 of the Military Code of Justice.

signed:　　　Schmauser　　　Arps　　　Galle　　Selle　　　Block

The President of the Reich War Court　　　　　　　　Berlin, 11 July 1940
as the supreme judicial authority

Confirmation of sentence.
I hereby confirm the sentence.
The sentence is to be implemented.

signed: Bastian, Admiral

Distribution List: B III a and b = 32.

Notes

1   Detlef Garbe, *Zwischen Widerstand und Martyrium: Die Zeugen Jehovas im »Dritten Reich«* (Munich, 1993), pp. 29-40.

2   See Günther Högl, ed., *Widerstand und Verfolgung in Dortmund 1933-1945* (Dortmund, 1992), pp. 297ff., devotes only 3 out of 479 pages to the Witnesses, although there are respectively 11 pages on the catholic church and 9 for the protestant churches.

3   See Sybil Milton, »Jehovah's Witnesses as Forgotten Victims,« in this volume.

4   Bundesarchiv R 58/405, fol. 2, reproduced as facsimile in Henry Friedlander and Sybil Milton, eds., *Bundesarchiv of the Federal Republic of Germany, Koblenz and Freiburg* (New York and London, 1995), p. 308.

5   Högl, 298, from the Dortmund Police Archive.

6   Högl, 299, from the Dortmund Police Archive.

7   Bundesarchiv R 58/264, fol. 306, reproduced as facsimile in Friedlander and Milton, pp. 283f.

8   These Witness newspapers are found in the U.S. Holocaust Memorial Museum library collection and in the Library of Congress, Washington, D.C. For further information on Esterwegen, one of the Emsland camps, see Aktionskomitee Emslandlager e.V., ed., *Auf der Such nach den Moorsoldaten: Emslandlager 1933-1945*, 3rd ed. (Papenburg, 1991); Dokumentations- und Informationszentrum Emslandlager e.V., ed., *Die Emslandlager in Vergangenheit und Gegenwart; Ergebnisse und Materialien des Internationalen Symposiums* (Papenburg, 1985); Erich Kosthorst and Bernd Walter, *Konzentrations- und Strafgefangenenlager im Emsland 1933-1945: Zum Verhältnis von NS-Regime und Justiz; Darstellung und Dokumentation* (Düsseldorf, 1985); and Elke Suhr, *Die Emslandlager: Die politische und wirtschaftliche Bedeutung der Emsländischen Konzentrations- und Strafgefangenenlager 1933-1945* (Bremen, 1985).

9   The English translation in *Consolation*, 10 August 1938 was reedited and revised by Sybil Milton based on the original German-language version in *Trost* (Swiss edition), 1 March 1938, p. 12f.

10 Julius Leber (b. 1891 Biesheim, Upper Alsace – d. 1945 in the Berlin-Plötzensee prison) was a protective custody prisoner in Esterwegen concentration camp, March – April 1935. Ernst Heilmann (b. 1881 Berlin – d. 1940 in Buchenwald concentration camp) was sent to Papenburg and Börgermoor/Esterwegen concentration camps from mid-September to the end of 1933 and again from October 1935 to February 1937. See Martin Schumacher and others, ed., *M.d.R.: Die Reichstagsabgeordneten der Weimarer Republik in der Zeit des Nationalsozialismus; Politische Verfolgung, Emigration und Ausbürgerung 1933-1945* (Düsseldorf, 1992), pp. 482ff. (Heilmann) and pp. 783ff. (Leber).

11 Sigrid Jacobeit, ed., *Ravensbrückerinnen* (Berlin, 1995), p. 63.

12 U.S. Holocaust Memorial Museum Archives, RG 32.008.01, Willi Seitz; translated by Sybil Milton.

13 Dokumentationsarchiv des österreichischen Widerstandes, Vienna, DÖW file 10490, reproduced in facsimile in: Elisabeth Klamper, ed., *Dokumentationsarchiv des österreichischen Widerstandes, Vienna* (New York and London, 1991), pp. 363ff.

Angela Nerlich and Wolfram Slupina

Rescued From Oblivion:
The Case of Hans Gärtner[1]

The preparation of the exhibition »Jehovah's Witnesses Stand Firm Against Nazi Assault« in approximately 500 German cities and towns resulted in local historical research, especially of the Nazi period.[2] During the past months, we have each week recorded about 100 personal narratives, that had previously not been known to the Wachtturm-Gesellschaft History Archive in Selters/Taunus, Germany.

Intensive local research about the persecution of Jehovah's Witnesses under the Nazis occurred when the exhibition was shown in the Lorsch Altes Rathaus (old town hall) from September 9 to 14, 1997. As a result, we discovered the fate of sixteen Jehovah's Witnesses. We had already known the names of seven additional individuals, but knew nothing about what had happened to them. This was cleared up through research. The Jakob Kindinger e.V. History Workshop in Bensheim assisted us. One case study, first shown in the Lorsch exhibition, illustrates the many biographical narratives that have been rescued from oblivion by research.

Hans Gärtner's Ordeal: Childhood and Family Background

Hans Gärtner was born in Lorsch (Bergstrasse) on August 17, 1906, as the first of five children (one son, four daughters). His mother, Margarete Gärtner (née Metz), died in 1917 at the age of 36, shortly after the birth of her fourth daughter. His father, who operated a fruit and vegetable business, died only one year later in 1918. After the death of their parents, the four daughters were split up and sent to various relatives, whereas Hans Gärtner was entrusted to friends, the Bierbaum family in Lorsch. Appolonia Ludwig, one of his sisters, retrospectively characterized her brother as a humorous person with a zest for life. Already as a child, Hans Gärtner liked to draw and play music.

He was a Catholic and later converted to Protestantism. On April 15, 1920, he began his apprenticeship as a barber at the Rhein hair salon in Lorsch.[3] On April 15, 1923, he passed his barber's apprentice examination and continued to work as an assistant in the Rhein hair salon until April 30, 1925.[4] On May 4, 1925, he took a job in Heinrich Lampert's barbershop at Obergasse 21 in Zwingenberg.[5] In August 1927, Hans Gärtner went to Kirchheimbolanden for further professional training, but returned to Lampert's barbershop on May 1, 1928, remaining there until October 13, 1929.[6] Gärtner returned to Kirchheimbolanden (Palatinate), and after additional training received a master barber's certificate. It was in Kirchheimbolanden that Gärtner first encountered »Bible Students,« and joined them soon thereafter.

In the early 1930s, Hans Gärtner was one of Jehovah's Witnesses (also known as Bible Students) when he returned to Lorsch. On January 2, 1933, at the age of 26, he got married in Zwingenberg to a factory worker, Dorothea Karoline Schuch.[7] After the wedding, his mother-in-law purchased a shop at Obergasse 3 (Marktplatz 11) in Zwingenberg, where Hans Gärtner set up his own barbershop. Thereafter, the family lived in the apartment above the shop on Obergasse 3 in Zwingenberg.

The photo shows the five siblings as young adults. Source: Private collection

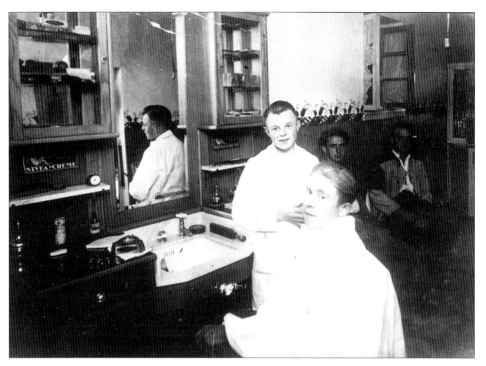

Hans Gärtner as an assistant in the Rhein hair salon. Source: Private collection

Persecution Begins

On October 18, 1933, the Hessen State government »dissolved and banned the International Bible Students Association, effective immediately,« citing Paragraph 1 of the Emergency Decree of the Reich President for the Protection of Volk (People) and State, issued on February 28, 1933. This decree ordered that »the immediate confiscation and seizure of the organization's property be started. Enforcement is to be reported to our office. An inventory of the impounded and confiscated items must be sent to the state police and forwarded to us.«[8]

In November 1933, Hans Gärtner was also affected. His name turned up on a list of Jehovah's Witnesses from the Zwingenberg region, compiled by the state police station (Landesgendarmeriestation) in Zwingenberg on November 3, 1933.[9] Just one day later, the Hessen State government implemented these directives and nineteen of the publications of the International Bible Students Association were confiscated at Gärtner's residence.[10]

Johannes Gärtner, Jr., who never knew his father Hans Gärtner, learned later from his mother that his father had consistently refused to return the »Hitler salute,« and thus renounce his beliefs. The Nazis were aware that the young master barber did not conform to the ideology of those in power, and it soon became clear that he would face difficulties. His wife and his mother-in-law, both of whom did not share his beliefs, insisted that he could return the »Hitler salute,« gritting his teeth, keeping a clenched fist inside his pocket, and do it anyway, even if he was privately unwilling to disregard his beliefs. Hans Gärtner repeatedly replied, »I will not be a hypocrite before the Lord.«[11]

Hans Gärtner in the 1930s.
Source: Private collection

Hans Gärtner with his wife Dorothea Karoline.
Source: Private collection

The Zwingenberg police wrote to the Hessen District Administration in Bensheim on March 4, 1935, that a Witness meeting had been observed in Zwingenberg. Hans Gärtner was included on the list of participants; they also mentioned Christian Kaltwasser,[12] whom Gärtner would again meet more than two years later in the Dachau concentration camp.[13]

First Protective Custody Arrest

Gärtner's daughter, Liesel, was born on April 3, 1935. Three weeks later, on April 24, 1935, the Nazis placed Hans Gärtner in protective custody arrest or investigative detention pending trial, initially in the Darmstadt state prison and subsequently in the Langen magistrate's court jail (Amtsgerichtsgefängnis). During these nine weeks, he was also interrogated.[14]

On April 27, 1935, the local chapter of the Nazi party in Zwingenberg wrote to the Nazi district party leadership in Bensheim, charging the imprisoned Jehovah's Witness: »For some time now, Gärtner's shop has served as a hide-out for enemies of the state and the national racial community. I hereby request that you immediately take steps to close the above-mentioned shop. Closing this shop is urgently required in the interest of party and state, so that this hotbed of Marxism finally disappears.« The letter was signed by local chapter leader Dickler, who would later symbolically be called to account for his complicity in the fate of Hans Gärtner. On April 30, 1935, the Nazi district party leader in Bensheim forwarded this letter to the Hessen District Administration in Bensheim, recommending that Hans Gärtner's shop be closed as quickly as possible.[15] The Hessen District Administration in Bensheim,

Gärtner's house. Gärtner's former barbershop is now a hardware store.
Source: Wachtturm-Gesellschaft, Selters

however, could not legally justify closing the shop on grounds of policing trade and, in a letter to the Darmstadt Gestapo, dated May 6, 1935, inquired whether closing the business was politically advisable. They recommended continuous police surveillance of the shop by the gendarmerie and local police.[16] The Darmstadt Gestapo replied on May 10, 1935, stating their reluctance to close the shop since it was not justified politically. Their letter, however, ended with the sentence: »Continued surveillance of his shop is obvious.«[17]

On June 17, 1935, Hans Gärtner was sentenced to one month in prison for his activities as one of Jehovah's Witnesses.[18] The three weeks he had already served in investigative custody were subtracted from the sentence. The grounds for sentencing included the following: »After the ban, he was repeatedly present at meetings in Götz's home ... He admitted that he had received publications from unknown persons in Switzerland, and that he had given them to Voltz and other unnamed Witnesses.«[19] He spent an additional nine days in the Langen state and magistrate's court prison. He was released on June 26, 1935. Nearly one year later, on June 1, 1936, his son, Johannes Gärtner, Jr., was born.

Second Protective Custody Arrest

In a report dated August 13, 1936, the Zwingenberg police forwarded a report through the Hessen District Administration in Bensheim to the Darmstadt Gestapo, about prohibited activities by regional Jehovah's Witnesses and house searches conducted in this district.[20] Gärtner, the Zwingenberg barber, was also mentioned in this report as an active Witness, who had already been imprisoned in 1935. Moreover, this report stated that Johannes Gärtner along with two other Jehovah's Witnesses had been taken into protective custody.

This letter was sent on August 15, 1936, to the Hessen District Administration in Bensheim along with the protocols of the interrogations of Hans and Dorothea Gärtner.[21] On September 19, Hans Gärtner became so ill that he was transferred, as a protective custody prisoner, to the Darmstadt district court prison. In a report dated October 15, 1936, the Darmstadt Gestapo summarized the previous activities of known Jehovah's Witnesses in Zwingenberg and its surroundings. This report mentioned that Hans Gärtner had been »found guilty of illegal activities.« Among other things, he was accused of listening to a speech by the President of the Watch Tower Society on Radio Toulouse in the spring of 1936.[22] On November 30, 1936, he was sentenced to six months in prison, less time served in investigative custody.[23] He remained in prison until February 16, 1937. The official justification for his arrest was that Hans Gärtner had listened to foreign broadcasts.

Several weeks before his release, the Nazi District Party leadership again apparently requested that the Hessen District Administration in Bensheim close Hans Gärtner's shop. On January 9, 1937, the Bensheim District Administration replied, as previously in 1935, that unfortunately there was no legal justification for closing the shop, although they shared the Nazi Party's view. Therefore, as in 1935, the Bensheim District Administration forwarded the Nazi Party's request to close the shop to the Darmstadt Gestapo, asking them to determine whether closing the shop would be warranted for political reasons.[24]

On March 19, 1937, the Darmstadt Gestapo once again refused the request of the Hessen District Administration in Bensheim.[25] The District Administration in Bensheim forwarded a copy of this letter to the Nazi District Party leadership in Bensheim on March 22, 1937, where it apparently had been received by April 1, 1937. Simultaneously, the District Administration in Bensheim mailed instructions to the Zwingenberg police to continue surveillance of Hans Gärtner's shop for illegal Jehovah's Witness meetings.[26] The Nazi Party District leadership in Bensheim again wrote the Hessen District Administration on April 7, 1937, stressing the urgency of closing Hans Gärtner's shop.[27] The District Administration in Bensheim replied on April 12, 1937, noting that the Darmstadt Gestapo's negative decision remained binding.[28]

After Hans Gärtner's release on February 16, 1937, which had occurred during the aforementioned exchange of letters, he was able to stay with his family for four months. During that period, he visited his sisters and talked to them and his other relatives about his biblical convictions. Appolonia Ludwig remembers that, early in the summer of 1937, he once told her, as if he had a premonition of the suffering that lay ahead of him: »Engrave in your memory what you should think about when I have passed away: I know what I'm dying for; the others don't.«[29]

Third Protective Custody Arrest and Concentration Camp

On May 26, 1937, the Zwingenberg police compiled a list of the fifteen known Jehovah's Witnesses in and around Zwingenberg; Hans Gärtner was included.[30] Shortly thereafter, he was arrested a third time.

His third imprisonment resulted from the following incident: While taking a walk one Sunday, Hans Gärtner met his former employer, the barber Lampert. When Lampert used the »Heil Hitler« greeting, Hans Gärtner simply replied: »This greeting is out of the question for me. Good afternoon!«[31] Lampert, who had envied the young master barber's success and popularity with his customers, denounced Gärtner,[32] and on June 14, 1937, Hans Gärtner began his third term of protective custody from which he never returned.[33]

Prisoner No. 12362 in Dachau Concentration Camp

Gärtner was taken at first to Bischofshofen, and then transferred to the Dachau concentration camp, arriving there on June 26, 1937.[34] The list of his personal effects, signed by Hans Gärtner, still exists. He received prisoner number 12362 and was assigned to road construction.

From the time he arrived in Dachau until late 1937, Hans Gärtner stayed in touch with his family by mail; eight of these letters still exist.[35] His letter to his wife on January 1, 1938, indicates that he had again met Christian Kaltwasser in Dachau.[36] They had both been observed at a secret meeting two years earlier, and would be incarcerated concurrently for about one year.

Hans Gärtner maintained contact with his family, as far as possible, by mail.[37] Existing documents show that contact between this family man and his wife and children was interrupted on April 1, 1938, by the complete prohibition of all mail privileges, and later repeatedly curtailed by drastic restrictions.

After her husband's imprisonment, Dorothea Gärtner managed the barbershop with the help of her brother and an assistant until July 1939. (Hans Gärtner periodically refers to this in his letters.) Once during this period, the Nazis attempted to remove everything from the shop. Hans Gärtner's corpulent mother-in-law, who was not one of Jehovah's Witnesses, stood in the shop door with an ax in her hand and threatened: »Hans Gärtner worked hard to get this shop, for his children. I'll kill the first one of you who comes in here.«[38] Apparently, the woman's threat sounded convincing, since the Nazis withdrew empty-handed.

During the summer of 1939, Dorothea Gärtner evidently asked the Bergstrasse District Barbers' Guild whether assistants were available for her husband's barbershop. The guild responded on July 15, 1939, informing the young woman that no apprentices were available, and recommended that she close the shop temporarily. The shop apparently had to be closed during the second half of 1939.

Although he was already confined in a concentration camp, Hans Gärtner was nevertheless examined in 1939 for fitness for military service. His service record indicates that he was considered unfit for military service. A remark under the heading »religion« states: »Gottgl. (BiFo),« which means »Believer (Bible Student).«[39]

Dorothea Gärtner received a signed postcard from her husband with a pre-printed text instructing her to report her husband »as temporarily absent« for the May 17, 1939, census of inhabitants, employment, and enterprises.[40]

In Mauthausen

Hans Gärtner was transferred to the Mauthausen concentration camp on September 27, 1939. In late 1939, his wife received a postcard, with a drawing by her husband, that read: »I am with you in my thoughts, and walk with you on the Malchen.«[41] On January 8, 1940, Dorothea Gärtner received a printed notice, informing her that her husband would be allowed to receive a package. However, the parcel could weigh only one kilogram (2.2 pounds), rather than the standard five kilogram (11 pound) package.

Hans Gärtner and his wife hoped that his imprisonment would end in late April 1940, because of some hints by several SS officers, and that this family man would be able to return home. At the beginning of 1940, Dorothea Gärtner visited her sister-in-law, Appolonia Ludwig, and told her among other things: »Hans will be coming home soon.«[42]

In January 1940, Dorothea Gärtner, who was not a Jehovah's Witness, was allowed to visit her husband in the Mauthausen concentration camp, probably because the Nazis hoped she would exert a strong ideologically conformist influence. However, Hans Gärtner remained loyal to his ideals. Shortly thereafter, when he weighed only 40 kilograms (88 pounds), his food rations were reduced.

Return to Dachau until Death

On February 18, 1940, Gärtner was transferred back to Dachau. There he received the new prisoner number 1227.[43] On one occasion, when the starving prisoner implored an SS officer for a piece of bread, instead of receiving bread, one of his fingers was cut off.[44] In his last letter from Dachau to his wife, dated March 31, 1940, he apparently referred to this atrocity circumspectly: »... my physical affliction, that you know of. ...«[45] In this letter, he advised his wife to sell the barbershop, since he apparently would not have been able to continue work because of this »affliction«. Furthermore, the Hessen Craftsmen's Chamber had meanwhile made headway in permanently closing his shop. Hans Gärtner wrote about this in his letter of March 31, 1940: »A few weeks ago, the Hessen Craftsmen's Chamber informed me that I have been deleted from the barbers' list and that therefore they will repossess my license that is at home.« His family was thus deprived of their means of making a living, although they did not share his religious convictions.

Three weeks later, on April 26, 1940, Hans Gärtner died in the Dachau concentration camp, shortly before his awaited release. He was only 33 years old.

His Family Continues to Suffer

The telegram announcing Gärtner's death was sent to his foster parents, the Bierbaums in Lorsch, not to his wife. They, in turn, delivered the horrible news to Dorothea Gärtner, then only 30 years old. The official cause of death was listed as »circulatory impairment/heart failure.«

Hans Gärtner's widow petitioned to be given her husband's wedding ring and, since this first request remained unanswered, she asked a second time on June 10, 1940. Moreover, she also requested the transfer of her husband's corpse or urn. Her letter was received in Dachau on June 15, 1940. She was then advised that Hans Gärtner had not handed over a wedding ring, and that the urn could be requested from the Munich crematorium. However, the widow could not financially afford to request that her husband's ashes be sent to her.

In 1945, after Hitler's dictatorship ended, the town of Zwingenberg interceded on her behalf, and wrote to the former Dachau concentration camp on December 30th, to request a compassionate response to her inquiries. Since this was unsuccessful, two of Hans Gärtner's sisters went to Dachau to find out more about their brother's fate, and if possible, to see his grave and retrieve any of the decedent's remaining belongings. However, they failed too. Instead, they were only able to see a tied up sack from a distance, and were told by some former SS men, whom they had met, that this supposedly contained their brother's corpse. Two former SS men told them: »All we can tell you is that he is over there, in that heap.«[46] His mortal remains have never been buried.

The Town of Zwingenberg Rehabilitates Hans Gärtner

In 1947 or 1948, a symbolic gesture of contrition was made, when former local chapter leader Dickler from Zwingenberg, who had denounced Gärtner before the Nazi district party leadership in Bensheim and recommended closing his shop in April 1935,[47] was forced to carry a sign stating »I am to blame for the death of Hans Gärtner,« while ringing a cow bell to attract attention, throughout the entire town of Zwingenberg. The procession was escorted by American soldiers, who tried to incite the then 10-year-old Johannes Gärtner, Jr., to throw stones at Dickler and beat him with a stick, which the boy, however, refused to do. Still carrying the sign and ringing the cow bell, Dickler was subsequently driven by American army truck from Zwingenberg to Bensheim, where he was released. This spectacle was reported in detail with accompanying photographs.[48]

To this day, a street in Zwingenberg, Hans-Gärtner-Weg, is named after this Jehovah's Witness.[49] A memorial stone in the cemetery at the foot of the Melibokus commemorates the integrity and courage of this man who died for his convictions.

Nevertheless, very few knew about Hans Gärtner's life and suffering. Even in his hometown, it was not known that he died courageously for his religious beliefs as one of Jehovah's Witnesses. An inquiry at the Zwingenberg town archive in April 1997, concerning the identity of Hans Gärtner, after whom a street had been named, revealed only the erroneous information that he had belonged to a political fringe group and was thought to have been a Communist. Historical research has saved his story from oblivion.

Above: The street sign for Hans-Gärtner-Weg in Zwingenberg.
Below: Hans Gärtner's memorial stone.
Source: Wachtturm-Gesellschaft, Selters

The Letters[50]

The letters Hans Gärtner wrote to his family give us a poignant glimpse into his story. They are reproduced in chronological order. The original wording and spelling is reproduced in facsimile in the German edition, but this was not possible in an English translation. All letters and postcards, except the postcard dated September 24, 1939, carry the concentration camp's censorship cachet (stamp). All letters, except for the postcards dated February 6, 1938, March 23, 1938, and September 24, 1939, and the letters dated July 2, 1939, September 3, 1939, December 2, 1939, and March 31, 1940, carry one of two stamps: »Requests for release from protective custody submitted to the camp authorities are useless,« or, »The prisoner remains, as before, a stubborn Bible Student and refuses to reject the Bible Students' false teachings. For this reason, the usual correspondence privileges have been denied him.« Letters with the latter stamp have been explicitly identified.

Letter no. 1

Letterhead Dachau concentration camp (Barrack 2, Room 5), dated July 16, 1937
Stamp: Mail Censor's Office (Postzensurstelle).
Requests for release from protective custody submitted to camp authorities are useless

Dear wife and children: I am still fine, which I hope is true for all of you. I thank you from my heart for your dear gifts and the letter, that everything is going well for you. I will write soon. Warm regards and kisses to you all, your husband.

Letter no. 2

Letterhead Dachau concentration camp (Barrack 2, Room 5), dated July 26, 1937
Stamp: Mail Censor's Office (Postzensurstelle).
Requests for release from protective custody submitted to camp authorities are useless

Dear wife and children: My health is ok. How are you and the children? I received your letter and the money order for 3 Marks, for which I thank you again from the bottom of my heart. How is the shop doing, and are all of the customers still coming? My dearest wife, let me know exactly how much you are paying for the assistant's salary, lodging, board, sick pay, and other expenses. Is your brother still helping in the shop? Do you have enough for you and the children? Are the children healthy and active, and can little Hans walk yet? Is mother all right again, and is father still working? What are Ludwig and Friedel doing; are Heiner and Anna healthy? Dear wife, don't lose heart, and just keep the shop going as well as possible. Also, I wish you a happy 28th birthday. Send me something soon. *Money.* [emphasis in the original] Received card dated July 22, 1937. Warmest regards from your husband.

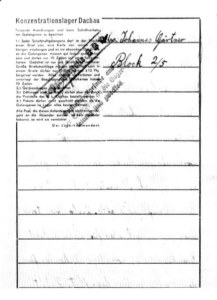

Letter no. 3

Letterhead Dachau concentration camp (Barrack 2, Room 5), dated August 9, 1937
Stamp: Mail Censor's Office. Requests for release from protective custody submitted to camp authorities are useless

Dear wife and children: I received your letter of July 30 and was very glad to learn that you are all still healthy and that the shop continues to provide your livelihood. Six Marks have yet to be paid for the children's underwear that Babette got in Lorsch. Furthermore, there are still two unpaid bills from Mr. Weilmünster; one for 5.50 and a second for 10.80 Marks. Let me know whatever concerns the business, and carry on as well as you can. Dearest wife, don't lose courage, since I know how hard it is for you to manage everything. I have one request, my dear wife, send me 5–10 Marks next time. Apart from that, I am still healthy. Greet and give heartfelt kisses to our dear children for me. My greetings to assistant Roth, Mr. Weilmünster, all our customers, father, mother, Heiner and Anna as well as Friedel, Ludwig, Marie and Jakob, Fritz and Liesbeth in Pfungstadt. Many greetings and kisses and I hope to see you very soon, I remain your dear husband.

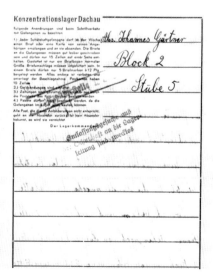

177

Letter no. 4

Postcard printed with letterhead Dachau concentration camp (Barrack 2, Room 5), dated August 28, 1937

Stamp: Mail Censor's Office. Requests for release from protective custody submitted to camp authorities are useless

Dear wife and children: My health is still alright. Thank you from the bottom of my heart for the birthday card. Dear wife, how are you and the children and the business doing? Please answer soon with whatever you want to send me. Regards and kisses, Hans.

Letter no. 5

Postcard printed with letterhead Dachau concentration camp (Barrack 2, Room 5), dated September 12, 1937

Stamp: Mail Censor's Office. Requests for release from protective custody submitted to camp authorities are useless

Dear all: Received payment of 5 Marks. Thank you very much. Please write me soon, how things are going for you, the children, and the shop; and how is everything for for [sic] the others? Kindest regards to you, children, and all, Your husband.

Letter no. 6

Letterhead Dachau concentration camp (Barrack 2, Room 5), dated September 20, 1937
Stamp: Mail Censor's Office. Requests for release from protective custody submitted to camp authorities are useless

Hans Gärtner writes on cover sheet under address: Letters to me are to be written only in ink.

All my dears: Dear wife, received your letter of 12 September 1937, from which I can see that you and the children are healthy. Thank God for this in silent prayer, that He has helped you through every difficulty until now. Don't lose courage and continue to run the shop as well as you can for your livelihood. As far as taxes, I have receipts and daily records for 1936 showing that I paid all quarterly sales taxes. Daily receipts are written in the big book; receipts for taxes and bills for 1936 are filed in the green folders. I don't understand why they are asking for an additional amount of 28.85 Marks for 1936. Just settle financial matters as well as you can. I can't change anything about all of this now. Dear wife, can't little Hans walk yet? Bathe him often in saltwater and add a lot of calcium to his food. And how is Liesel, she probably asks about me a lot. I would be delighted to see all three of you. I ask one thing of you dear wife, send me a few Marks again and five 12-Pfennig stamps. Trust in God, the Almighty, be of good courage and don't lose heart. Hopefully, we'll see each other soon at home again. Hoping to see you as soon as possible, with warm regards to you and the children, your husband. Regards also to the whole family as well as Mienchen and Marie. Write.

Letter no. 7

Letterhead Dachau concentration camp (Barrack 1, Room 4), dated November 20, 1937 Stamp: Mail Censor's Office. Requests for release from protective custody submitted to camp authorities are useless

Dear wife and children: This is my reply to your letter of October 24, 1937, and see that you are still healthy. I am especially delighted by one thing about our dear children, that little Hans can finally walk. I often have envisage him in front of me, limping. Liesel probably asks about me a lot. Teach the children only good things, and be a good maternal example for them in everything. Have neither hatred nor envy toward others, above all not toward my business rivals.* Dear wife, endure the unavoidable patiently and humbly, with dignity. Trust in God Almighty completely, be of good cheer and entreat him daily to support you in everything, for God does not abandon those who totally trust in him. As for the shop, do the best you can financially. I am still healthy thanks to God. I also thank you for the three 12-Pfennig stamps that you enclosed. I did not receive your last letter, but only got one 12-Pfennig stamp that you had enclosed. Did any of my relatives or sisters visit you during my absence? If it is possible for you, *send me 5 Marks.* [sic] Hoping to see you as soon as possible, with warm regards and kisses to you and the dear children, your husband. Greet the whole family.

* Note: One of his colleagues had played a decisive role in Hans Gärtner's final arrest.

Letter no. 8

Letterhead Dachau concentration camp (Barrack 8, Room 4), dated December 19, 1937 Stamp: Mail Censor's Office. Requests for release from protective custody submitted to camp authorities are useless

All my dears! Dear wife, My health is still ok, thank God. Have you received my letter and Christmas voucher card about receiving a package? Still don't have an answer. How is your health, also how are the dear children and father, mother, Andreas, and all other family members? How are things with the shop, is it continuing the same, and how are you getting along financially? Dear wife, I wish you and all my darlings – Happy Holidays. Send me a few Marks and think of me. I implore you for an immediate answer how things are going at home. Greet all the customers for me. Other than that, I can't think of anything else for today. Hoping to see you very soon, I greet and kiss you and our dear children, your husband. Greet father, mother, and all family members. Greet the assistant and Mr. Weilmünster, and my sisters. Do they visit you? Please reply.

Konzentrationslager Dachau

Folgende Anordnungen sind beim Schriftverkehr mit Gefangenen zu beachten:

1.) Jeder Schutzhaftgefangene darf in der Woche einen Brief oder eine Karte von seinen Angehörigen empfangen und an sie absenden. Die Briefe an die Gefangenen müssen gut lesbar geschrieben sein und dürfen nur 15 Zeilen auf einer Seite enthalten. Gestattet ist nur ein Briefbogen normaler Größe. Briefumschläge müssen ungefüttert sein. In einem Briefe dürfen nur 5 Briefmarken à 12 Pfg. beigelegt werden. Alles andere ist verboten und unterliegt der Beschlagnahme. Postkarten haben 10 Zeilen.
2.) Geldsendungen sind gestattet.
3.) Zeitungen sind gestattet, dürfen aber nur durch die Poststelle des K. L. Dachau bestellt werden.
4.) Pakete dürfen nicht gesendet werden, da die Gefangenen im Lager alles kaufen können.

Alle Post, die diesen Anforderungen nicht entspricht, geht an die Absender zurück. Ist kein Absender bekannt, so wird sie vernichtet.

Der Lagerkommandant.

Abs: Johannes Gärtner

Block 8/4

Entlassungsgesuche aus der Schutzhaft an die Lagerleitung sind zwecklos

Prozessstelle

Meine lieben alle! Dachau, den 19. 12. 1937. Liebe Frau, gut geht mir's bis jetzt noch gesundheitlich, Gott sei dank. Hast Du meinen Brief u. Weihnachtsbestellkarte wegen Paket erhalten? Habe nämlich noch keine Antwort. Wie steht es bei Dir Gesundheits halber u. bei den lieben Kindern u. Vater, Mutter, Andreas u. allen andern Familiengliedern? Wie geht es im Geschäft zu, geht dasselbe noch weiter u. wie kommst Du denn Finanziel damit aus? Liebe Frau, ich wünsche Dir

u. Euch lieben alle frohe Feiertage. Schicke mir ein par Mark u. denkt an mich. Ich bitte um sofortige Antwort wies zu Hause alles zu geht. Grüße die ganze Kundschaft von mir. Sonst wüßte ich für heute nichts weiter. In der Hoffnung auf baldigstes Wiedersehn grüßt u. küßt Dich u. unsere lieben Kinder Dein Mann. Grüße Vater Mutter u. alle Familienglieder. Grüße den Gehülfen u. Herrn Weilmünster, u. meine Geschwister. Bekommst Du Besuch von Ihnen? Bitte Antwort

Letter no. 9

Letterhead Dachau concentration camp (Barrack 8, Room 4), dated January 1, 1938
Stamp: Mail Censor's Office. Requests for release from protective custody submitted to camp authorities are useless

All my dears: I received your letter of December 28, 1937, dear wife, with deepest gratitude and can see that you, the dear children, and all family members are still in good health. As for the package, I can tell that you all took great care and effort, and even pinched and scraped on your own food. I thank you sincerely for the tasty contents. Surely father, mother, and other family members contributed to it, for which I thank you all from my heart. I thank you all for your special efforts concerning a request. As to money, I know quite well that things aren't going so well. Therefore I thank you in advance since you all want to help sending me 5 Marks. You, my dear wife, trust in God Almighty with your whole heart and pray to Him daily, as he helps you out of all your troubles. Give my condolences to the Germann and Kolb families. Send my regards to aunt Minchen in Viehweg and Marie in Mittelgässchen, to all the customers, and to assistant Peter Jökel, who has replaced me completely. Now be of good courage, resolute, and work diligently, for it will be rewarded. In the hope of seeing you all very soon, I greet and kiss you, the children, and all family members. Your dearest Hans. It is snowing hard here. A blessed 1938 to all of you. Greetings from Kaltwasser. *Reply.* [sic]

Letter no. 10

Postcard printed with letterhead Dachau concentration camp and handwritten addenda »3K« (Barrack 8, Room 4), dated January 23, 1938

Stamp: Mail Censor's Office. Requests for release from protective custody submitted to camp authorities are useless

Dear wife and children! I received your letter of January 13, 1938, along with three 12-Pfennig stamps, with heartfelt thanks and can see that you, the dear children, and all of you are still doing well, thank God. Also my condolences to grandmother. Thank you very much, dearest wife, for the money. Greet Mr. Weilmünster, the assistant, and all the customers. Letter *follows,* [sic] your beloved husband. Greetings to you and the dear children. Greet all the family members.

Letter no. 11

Postcard printed with letterhead Dachau concentration camp and handwritten addenda »3K« (Barrack 8, Room 4), dated February 6, 1938

Stamp: Mail Censor's Office. Requests for release from protective custody submitted to camp authorities are useless

All my dears! I could see from your card of January 30, 1938, dearest wife, that you are all still healthy, thank God, still doing well, which is also true for me. It gave me great joy that my sisters have not forgotten us. Take courage, dear wife, and trust God. Only He will help. Write me about how things are going in the shop, whether the customers are all c(oming). Regards and kisses, your dear husband.

Letter no. 12

Letterhead Dachau concentration camp and handwritten addenda »3K« (Barrack 12, Room 4), dated February 20, 1938
Stamp: Mail Censor's Office. Requests for release from protective custody submitted to camp authorities are useless

All my dears! This is my letter I previously promised. Dear wife: my health is still quite good, »thanks and praise to God.« How are you and our dear children doing; are you all still healthy and happy? How often I picture you together on a nice Sunday walk and in my mind, I hear your joy and laughter together at home. How are father, mother, uncle Andras, little Ludwig, Mariechen and her beloved, and our neighbors, the young Heinrich Schuch family? How is everything going with the shop and is it financially ok? Are the business people all coming and what about the customers? Are you satisfied with the assistant? What's new in the shop and with the entire family? Dear wife, be of good courage and hold on, patience and love to our children. Also love and honor father and mother in oder to have a long life, trust in God Almighty and entreat his help. Write my address correctly and when sending money, write my exact address on the back of the small stub. I am asking for a few Marks. I greet and kiss you all, Hans.

Letter no. 13

Postcard printed with letterhead Dachau concentration camp and handwritten addenda »3K« (Barrack 19, Room 2), dated March 6, 1938
Stamp: Mail Censor's Office. Requests for release from protective custody submitted to camp authorities are useless

Dear all! I thank you from my heart for the money you sent by money order.[*] How are you, dear wife and children and dearest parents-in-law? All the good you are showing me will be richly rewarded. How are things going with the shop? Please write immediately. In the hope of seeing you again very very soon, greetings, Hans.

*Note: The original receipts of the three specifically mentioned money orders sent to Dachau concentration camp are in the private collection of Johannes Gärtner, Jr.

Letter no. 14

Postcard printed with letterhead Dachau concentration camp and handwritten addenda »3K« (Barrack 19, Room 2), dated March 23, 1938
Stamp: Mail Censor's Office Dachau concentration camp

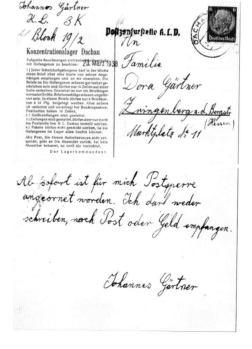

My mail is restricted from now on. I am neither allowed to write nor to receive mail or money. Johannes Gärtner.

Letter no. 15

Letterhead Dachau concentration camp 3K (Barrack 15, Room 4), dated April 1, 1938
Stamp: Mail Censor's Office
Note: This is the first letter to carry the stamp: »The prisoner remains, as before, a stubborn Bible Student and refuses to reject the Bible Students' false teachings. For this reason, the usual correspondence privileges have been denied him.« The letters with this stamp are only one page long, rather than the usual two page letters.

Dearly beloved wife and children! Have you been ill, since I have not received any news from you since my last letter? My dears, how are you all doing? I am still doing well. I thank you from my heart for the money you offered me in your last letter, but don't forget my name, date of birth, barrack and room number on the back of the small stub. Also warmest congratulations to our Liesel. In the hope of being with youagain as soon as possible, regards and kisses to all you dear ones, Hans. Greet the customers.

Letter no. 16

Letterhead Dachau concentration camp and handwritten addenda »3K« (Barrack 19, Room 2), dated June 2, 1938
Stamp: Mail Censor's Office. Requests for release from protective custody submitted to camp authorities are useless

All my dears: I received your letter dated May 25, 1938, dear wife, for which I thank you from my heart. I can't tell from the contents, dear wife, how things are going with the shop, for you and the dear children. Are things going so badly with the shop, as I gather from your mother's letter of March 11, 1938, that you are going to work to pay the assistant. If so, I ask you, since you are unable to keep it up any longer, to give it up until I come back to you, my dearest. In case you cannot sell the equipment, then please store it somewhere. But keep my tools until I come home. Dear wife, how are you and my dear little children doing; are you all still healthy? Or have any of you fallen ill? How are mother and father and all the other family members? I wish my little Hans a happy second birthday from my heart, and our Liesel a happy 3rd birthday, and also you very soon. Be of good courage and don't lose heart. In the hope of seeing you again very soon, regards and kisses to all you dear ones, Hans.

Letter no. 17

Letterhead imprinted Dachau concentration camp 3K (Barrack 15, Room 4), dated January 1, 1939
Stamp: Mail Censor's Office
Note: Denial of correspondence privileges as in letter no. 15

All my dears! I had my greatest joy when they gave me your Christmas greetings. A sign of life from you again after nine months. As of today, I am allowed to write one letter and to receive one letter from you per month. My health is, thank God, still alright, which I also assume for you and the children. How are father and mother and the other family members? How are things with our shop and customers, and household finances. Liesel from Auerbach wrote me in March, although I could not answer her. I cannot write much, although I want to be grateful for this. Wish you all a blessed New Year. God be with you all and see you very soon, regards and kisses, Hans.

Letter no. 18

Letterhead imprinted Dachau concentration camp 3K (Barrack 15, Room 4), dated February 8, 1939
Stamp: Mail Censor's Office
Note: Denial of correspondence privileges as in letter no. 15

Dearly loved wife and children! Received your letter of December 1, 1939, with great joy and heartfelt thanks. I rejoiced most about our dear children, that they are still well. Otherwise, I'm still healthy, which I think must also be true for all of you dear ones. Please write me monthly about the shop's earnings and family affairs. Persevere with me, and have courage and faith. Regards and kisses to all you dears, from Hans. Greet all the family members, customers, and acquaintances.

Letter no. 19

Letterhead imprinted Dachau concentration camp 3K (Barrack 15, Room 4), dated March 5, 1939
Stamp: Mail Censor's Office
Note: Denial of correspondence privileges as in letter no. 15

Beloved wife and children! Received your dear letter of February 19 with greatest and thankful joy. More than anything I rejoiced about your words concerning our little children, family and shop, that you can support yourself. Sincere congratulations to Marichen and Jakob, and give them back the 35 Marks, as best you can. I know your great worry and need. Be of good courage and hold out. Who owns Schak & Wolfs' house? What about Mrs. Fuchs and the cacti? See you again very soon, with warmest regards and kisses, Hans.

Letter no. 20

Letterhead imprinted Dachau concentration camp 3K (Barrack 15, Room 4), dated May 7, 1939
Stamp: Mail Censor's Office
Note: Denial of correspondence privileges as in letter no. 15

Beloved wife and children! I was very happy to receive your Easter card, for which I sincerely thank you. My health is still doing well, which also is possible for you. What else is new in the shop, family? Dear wife, be of good courage and await »me«; for you will be richly rewarded for this. If I come, then unexpectedly. Dear wife, send me 15 Marks right away. Let me know everything else in a letter. See you again very soon. Regards and kisses, your dear Hans.

Letter no. 21

Preprinted postcard from Dachau concentration camp (Barrack 15, Room 4), with the following text:

»For the May 17, 1939, census of inhabitants, employment, and enterprises, I am to be listed as temporarily absent on the residential list and the supplementary card for origin and education under Section B. All entries about me must be precise, especially on page 3 of the household list. The questions concerning profession are to be answered by my last employment.«

Handwritten signature: »Your husband, Hans«

Letter no. 22

Letterhead imprinted Dachau concentration camp 3K (Barrack 15, Room 4), dated June 4, 1939

Stamp: Mail Censor's Office

Note: Denial of correspondence privileges as in letter no. 15

All my dear! Received your dear letter and Pentecost card with great joy and see that you are all still doing well. Dear wife, have courage and don't lose heart, for all your worries will soon end. I thank you sincerely for the money lent to me by Marichen. Write my sister Susanna, that she might send me some money. Please answer soonest. Greetings and kisses to all you dearest ones and to my friends.

Letter no. 23

Letterhead imprinted Dachau concentration camp 3K (Barrack 15, Room 4), dated July 2, 1939

Stamp: Mail Censor's Office

Note: This letter does not have any other stamps, but is only one page long.

Dearest beloved wife. Children! Until now, dear wife, I am still healthy, which is hopefully also possible for you my dears; or is someone ill, since you did not write me this month? How are things with you, the dear children, parents and family members? How are the shop and customers? Also, I wish our little Hans a happy birthday on June 1. For today be greeted and kissed. Hans. Please answer right away. [Send] twelve Pfennig stamp and some money.

Letter no. 24

Letterhead imprinted Dachau concentration camp 3K (Barrack 19, Room 3), dated September 3, 1939

Stamp: Mail Censor's Office

Note: This letter does not carry any other stamp, but is nevertheless only one page long.

My dearest beloved. Thank you from all my heart for the birthday card. Our mutual happiness is not at all indifferent to me; however, my dear, I cannot possibly fulfill your request. You will soon understand that I had only the best in mind for you and the children. Hold out a bit more with me, we will see each other quite soon. Regards and kisses to all you dears, Hans. Reply.

Letter no. 25

Postcard printed with letterhead Dachau concentration camp 3K (Barrack 15, Room 4), dated September 24, 1939

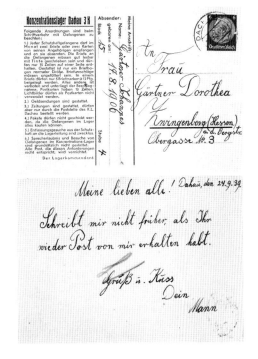

All my dears! Do not write me before you have received mail from me again. Regards and kisses, your husband.

Note: This card has no stamp from the camp officials. On September 27, 1939, Hans Gärtner was transferred to Mauthausen concentration camp.

Letter no. 26

Letterhead Mauthausen concentration camp (Barrack 15, Room 1), dated December 2, 1939
Stamp: Mail Censor's Office

All my dears: It is now possible for me to answer your September letter with my new address. My health is still holding up; I hope the same is true for you, my dear ones. I was quite surprised at what you told me about your present situation and the business. I would have liked so much to answer you immediately, but was not possible. What other income do you have besides from newspapers. That sentence from my last letter is to be understood: »Don't be sad, nor should you begrudge your neighbor's happiness and contentment. The day for our great family happiness is coming ever closer, peace and joy. Hold out still a bit longer with me. Have patience, love, perseverance, and honesty. Your joy will be immense when I am again with you, my

Meine Anschrift:
Name: Gärtner Johannes
geboren am: 17.8. 1906
Block 15.   Stube 1

Mauthausen, den 2. 12. 1939

dears. Rent out the shop with equipment for 30 Marks monthly, but not my tools. Oil and store the good electrical hair cutter, the razors, scissors, hair clippers, sharpeners, curling iron, spirit stove, and hair dryer until I return. Use my pullovers as winter clothing for our dear children. How are father, mother, and all family members? All you dear ones think of me in the coming days; in love, patience, and great peace, we want to look to the future together full of hope and confidence. I wish you great peace and rich blessings from God for the holidays. Your husband thinks of you with love and faithfulness, wishing you and the dear children a blessed New Year. Greet father, mother, Andreas, Heiner and family, Marichen and family, and my sisters warmly. Regards to everyone. Answer very soon.

Letter no. 27

Letterhead imprinted Dachau concentration camp 3K (Barrack 29, Room 1), dated March 31, 1940
Stamp: Mail Censor's Office

All my beloved ones. Usually it is possible for me to write only 5 lines every three months. A few weeks ago, the Hessen Craftsmen's Chamber informed me that I have been deleted from the barbers' list and that therefore they will repossess the license that is at home. Due to these circumstances and also my physical affliction, that you know of, I am forced to sell. Do this and make use of the money for you and the children. I no longer can properly pursue my profession anyway, but it will be healthier. How is your health, you, the children, parents, and everyone? In hopes of seeing you very soon, Your dear Hans. Don't send me mail or money before I have let you know my new prisoner number.

Note: In this letter, Hans Gärtner used old German script, which he also used in his first card in 1937. The writing style shows his poor condition. The letter carries no signature. Three weeks later, on April 26, 1940, Hans Gärtner died in Dachau concentration camp.

Notes

1 Angela Nerlich conducted interviews with Johannes Gärtner, Jr., Hans Gärtner's son, and with Appolonia Ludwig, one of Hans Gärtner's sisters, in May 1997. The interviews were not taped, but accurate quotations from Hans Gärtner, Sr., recalled by these individuals, are included in this biography. This essay is based on material held in their private family collection, unless otherwise noted. Copies are available at the Wachtturm-Gesellschaft (History Archive) in Selters/Taunus, Germany. The events occurred for example in Zwingenberg, located about 20 km. south of Darmstadt.

2 See the essay »›Jehovah's Witnesses Stand Firm Against Nazi Assault‹—Touring Exhibitions and Video Presentations, 1996–2000,« in this anthology.

3 Certificate for Advanced Training, labor book issued by the Lorsch Mayor's Office, April 19, 1920.

4 Darmstadt Craftmen's Chamber (Handwerkskammer Darmstadt), apprenticeship certificate.

5 Handwritten reference by Heinrich Lampert, barber, Zwingenberg, August 25, 1927.

6 Hans Gärtner's labor book, issued by the Lorsch Mayor's Office, April 19, 1920. Gärtner was »listed in the 1920 register as entry no. 43.«

7 Marriage certificate issued on January 2, 1933, by Zwingenberg (Hessen) Registry Office.

8 Hessisches Staatsarchiv Darmstadt (hereafter HStA Darmstadt): Department G 15, Bensheim, no. Q 132, letter from Hessen State Ministry, Department Ia (Police) to district administrations, police headquarters, police offices, and state police headquarters in Darmstadt, October 18, 1933.

9 HStA Darmstadt: Department G 27, Darmstadt, no. 396, List of members of the International Bible Students Association in this district, November 3, 1933.

10 HStA Darmstadt: Department G 15, Bensheim, no. Q 132, List of confiscated books, Zwingenberg police station, November 4, 1933.

11 Interview with Appolonia Ludwig, May 18, 1997.

12 Christian Kaltwasser was one of the seven individuals previously mentioned, about whom nothing more than their names was known.

13 See letter 9.

14 HStA Darmstadt: Department G 27, Darmstadt, no. 396, Darmstadt Special Court verdict in the case against Franz Egle and 12 colleagues, June 17, 1935.

15 HStA Darmstadt: Department G 15, Bensheim, no. Q 132, letter from Zwingenberg NSDAP local chapter to NSDAP district party leadership in Bensheim, April 27, 1935.

16 HStA Darmstadt: Department G 15, Bensheim, no. Q 132, letter from Hessen District Administration in Bensheim to the Darmstadt Gestapo, May 6, 1935.

17 HStA Darmstadt: Department G 15, Bensheim, no. Q 132, letter from the Darmstadt Gestapo to the District Administration in Bensheim, May 10, 1935.

18 HStA Darmstadt: Department G 15, Bensheim, no. Q 132, Report by the Darmstadt Gestapo, October 15, 1936. January 17, 1935, mentioned as the date of the sentence in the »register of persons residing in the Zwingenberg police district, who were members of the International Bible Students Assocciation,« May 26, 1937, obviously is a typing error. Correct is: June 17, 1935, the same date as mentioned in the record about the seven co-defendants.

19 HStA Darmstadt: Department G 27, Darmstadt, no. 396, Darmstadt Special Court verdict in the case against Franz Egle and 12 colleagues, June 17, 1935.

20 HStA Darmstadt: Department G 15, Bensheim, no. Q 132, letter from the Zwingenberg police to the Darmstadt Gestapo, August 13, 1936.

21 HStA Darmstadt: Department G 15, Bensheim, no. Q 132, interrogation protocols for Hans and Dora (Dorothea) Gärtner, Zwingenberg, August 13, 1936.

22 HStA Darmstadt: Department G 15, Bensheim, no. Q 132, Darmstadt Gestapo report, October 15, 1936.

23 HStA Darmstadt: Department G 15, Bensheim, no. Q 132, »register of persons residing in the Zwingenberg police district, who were members of the International Bible Students Association,« May 26, 1937.

24 HStA Darmstadt: Department G 15, Bensheim, no. Q 132, letter from Hessen District Administration in Bensheim to NSDAP district party leadership in Bensheim, January 9, 1937, and the Gestapo in Darmstadt.

25 HStA Darmstadt: Department G 15, Bensheim, no. Q 132, letter from Darmstadt Gestapo to Hessen District Administration in Bensheim, March 19, 1937.

26 HStA Darmstadt: Department G 15, Bensheim, no. Q 132, letter from Hessen District Administration in Bensheim to NSDAP district party leadership in Bensheim, and to the Zwingenberg police, March 22, 1937.

27 HStA Darmstadt: Department G 15, Bensheim, no. Q 132, letter from NSDAP district party leadership in Bensheim to Hessen District Administration in Bensheim, April 7, 1937.

28 HStA Darmstadt: Department G 15, Bensheim, no. Q 132, letter from Hessen District Administration in Bensheim to NSDAP district party leadership in Bensheim, April 12, 1937.

29 Interview with Appolonia Ludwig, May 18, 1997.

30 HStA Darmstadt: Department G 15, Bensheim, no. Q 132, »register of persons residing in the Zwingenberg police district who were members of the International Bible Students Association,« May 26, 1937.

31 Interviews with Johannes Gärtner, Jr., May 10, 1997, and Appolonia Ludwig, May 18, 1997.

32 Hans Gärtner's later letters from Dachau concentration camp demonstrate his good relationship with his customers.

33 In letter no. 7, November 20, 1937, Gärtner tells his wife that he had no hatred for his former colleagues. This might be an allusion to being denounced by Lampert, who had earlier been his employer.

34 Dachau Concentration Camp Memorial Museum, Archives: original Dachau prisoner card registry.

35 See letters nos. 1–8 from Hans Gärtner in Dachau concentration camp to his wife, July 16, 1937; July 26, 1937; August 9, 1937; August 28, 1937; September 12, 1937; September 20, 1937; November 20, 1937; and December 19, 1937.

36 See letter no. 9.

37 See letters nos. 10–25 and no. 27, from Hans Gärtner in Dachau concentration camp to his wife, dated: January 23, 1938, February 6, 1938, February 20, 1938, March 6, 1938, March 23, 1938 (dated through the postage cancellation stamp), April 1, 1938, June 2, 1938, January 1, 1939, February 8, 1939, March 5, 1939, May 7, 1939; letter no. 21 is undated; June 4, 1939, July 2, 1939, September 3, 1939, September 24, 1939, March 31, 1940, and letter no. 26, the only letter written to his family from Mauthausen concentration camp, dated December 2, 1939.

38 Interview with Appolonia Ludwig, May 18, 1997.

39 »Gottgl.« is the abbreviation for »Gottgläubig« or »believer,« and »BiFo« is the abbreviation for »Bibelforscher,« translated here as »Bible Student« or Jehovah's Witness.

40 Letter no. 21, undated.

41 Malchen is the highest mountain in the Bergstrasse region (located between Darmstadt and Heidelberg), and is known today as Melibokus. The family lived at the foot of this mountain.

42 Interview with Appolonia Ludwig, May 18, 1997.

43 Dachau Concentration Camp Memorial Museum, Archives: original Dachau prisoner card registry.

44 Interview with Appolonia Ludwig, May 18, 1997. She had obtained the information from Christian Kaltwasser, who had been imprisoned with Hans Gärtner in Dachau for about one year and knew about his suffering.

45 See letter no. 27.

46 Interview with Appolonia Ludwig, May 18, 1997.

47 HStA Darmstadt: Department G 15, Bensheim, no. Q 132, letter from Zwingenberg NSDAP local chapter to NSDAP district party leadership in Bensheim, April 27, 1935. See note 15.

48 Neither originals nor copies of these stories could be located; these details are based on survivor testimony.

49 It was renamed Hans-Gärtner-Weg, at the latest, in early 1947.

50 This material is from a private collection. Copies are available at the Wachtturm-Gesellschaft, History Archive, Selters/Taunus, Germany.

Ursula Krause-Schmitt

Resistance and Persecution
of Female Jehovah's Witnesses

Katharina Thoenes was 31 years old when, on October 9, 1935, she was imprisoned for the first time. Her prison sentence of one month was relatively short in contrast to other verdicts at that time. Nevertheless, it was an example of Nazi injustice, violating basic rights to freedom of religion. Katharina Thoenes was married to Heinrich Thoenes, a miner, and had a ten-year-old son. The young family lived in Moers.

Eight months after her release, Katharina Thoenes was re-arrested, denounced by the director of the Moers elementary school. She was remanded to the women's concentration camp in Moringen. For the next five years she would not see her husband and her son.

There were two reasons for issuing »a protective custody arrest warrant« against her. First, Katharina Thoenes was accused of holding »prohibited Jehovah's Witnesses meetings« in her apartment. The Gestapo's proof was based on denunciations which mentioned »frequent visits to the apartment in question« and »closed windows and doors.«[1]

The second more serious reason was that Katharina Thoenes did not want to surrender her son to the enticements and distortions of the Nazi system, but instead raised him according to her beliefs and values. These alternative values, basically anti-military, were considered »subversive,« since the Nazi state wanted total control of every individual. Therefore, her beliefs were punished in a draconian manner. Katharina Thoenes was separated from her family, from her son, because »she had forbidden her 11-year-old son to use the German salute in word and deed at school. All measures at school to influence the young person's upbringing were rejected, since she claimed that the ›State has no right to decide my child's beliefs; I will not allow the State to enslave me.«[2]

The Nazi state opposed this »subversive upbringing« of children and in several cases, responded by incarcerating female Jehovah's Witnesses in concentration camps. If a trial occurred, this justified harsher sentences. Of course, the fathers of Witness families also played a major role in raising their children. However, in daily life, mothers usually directly encountered the results of Nazi instruction. Their children told them first about harassment in the classroom, the schoolyard, and on their way home from school. The mothers tried to protect their children, encouraging them to refuse to give the Hitler salute, in order to shelter them from the abhorrent and corrupting requirements of the Nazi state.

Psychologists, such as Bruno Bettelheim, have pointed out that the daily requirement for using the »Hitler salute« was an important factor in building a »national racial community,« and as preparation for war. The salute was a public display of loyalty required from every member of society from childhood on and refusals resulted in severe penalties. The »Hitler salute« meant that those who were critical of the regime were pressured daily to renounce their personal convictions and thus despise themselves for conformity: »Thus, every anti-Nazi became a martyr many times each day or had to lose self-respect.«[3] For both male and female Jehovah's Witnesses, the »Hitler salute« was more than just a public display of loyalty: it was blasphemy, as well as the worship of a human being forbidden by the Bible. In order to remain loyal to their beliefs, the Witnesses had to refuse to render the salute. The upbringing of their children involved more that just adherence to doctrines; the children were to be raised as persons of integrity whose self-respect was not to be broken. They had to pay a very high price for this attitude. Several years after the Nazi dictatorship was created, adherence to the central tenet and universal command: »You shall not kill!« resulted in a life and death decision for youngsters raised as Witnesses. The majority of Witnesses rejected military service, and military tribunals allowed them no leniency, unless they renounced their faith.[4]

In August 1936, Katharina Thoenes was taken to the Moringen concentration camp, close to Göttingen. Moringen was the first central women's concentration camp in Nazi Germany. It was established in summer 1933, during the first years of the Nazi dictatorship; political prisoners were the largest group, mostly Communists who had participated in anti-Nazi resistance actions. From the accounts of women were imprisoned in Moringen, we know that a large group of female Jehovah's Witnesses were incarcerated in a separate hall. The actual number of imprisoned female Witnesses during the first years of the Nazi dictatorship first became apparent when the archives of the Berlin Documentation Center, which were under American administration until 1991, were opened to German scholars. The female Bible Students comprised 45.9 percent and were the largest group of concentration camp prisoners during the early phase of Nazi rule. In December 1937, the percentage of female Jehovah's Witnesses soared to 89 percent.[5] According to more recent research, every fifth inmate in the Lichtenburg women's concentration camp, established in 1938 after Moringen became too small, was a female Witness.[6] Finally, two barracks were reserved for German prisoners wearing the purple triangle, female Witnesses, in the compulsory multinational society of the Ravensbrück concentration camp, which held ca. 130,000 women and children during the war years.[7]

In Moringen, camp director Krack especially harassed the female Witness prisoners. This was also apparent in the prisoner file of Katharina Thoenes. Krack not only censored her monthly correspondence with her husband and son, but he denounced her to the Düsseldorf Gestapo because of the »entire family's subversive attitude,« which in turn resulted in further persecution. He denied Katharina Thoenes mail privileges with her immediate family. Her husband and son were not informed about this and were extremely worried about their wife and mother, since her letters no longer reached them. In January 1937, her son Hans could no longer bear the uncertainty and addressed a letter to the director Krack: »Since November 1936 I have not received any sign of life from my beloved mother, and this is a cause of greatest anxiety for me. This is why I am taking the liberty of addressing the administration to ask how my beloved mother is doing. She is innocent, she has done nothing wrong. Is she still alive? I am enclosing a stamp and request that I receive news about my beloved mother. I appeal to your compassion. You also had a mother whom you loved, and therefore I expect to receive a few lines from my beloved mother, if she is still alive and well.«[8]

We do not know whether Katharina Thoenes was at least able to exchange a few words with her husband and son before she was remanded to the court prison in Kleve on February 17, 1937. Eight days later, the district court sentenced her to ten months in prison. Immediately after the trial, Katharina Thoenes was compelled to return to the Moringen concentration camp, and her file now carried the infamous entry »additional arrest« (*Überhaft*). This note can also be found on many Jehovah's Witnesses arrest files and meant that the Gestapo retained all rights for supplementary decisions. »*Überhaft*« often meant irrevocable relocation to a concentration camp and therefore it was the equivalent of an arbitrary death sentence. Katharina

Thoenes' »protective custody« was interrupted in June 1937 »on a probationary basis,« in the cynical language used on the Gestapo order. In reality, this did not mean her release, but that she had to begin serving her prison sentence.

I could not find anything further about the fate of Katharina Thoenes and her family. It is possible that her son was removed from her custody. After 1937–1938, it was standard for Jehovah's Witnesses that the Nazi state usurped custody of their children. No other anti-Nazi group suffered as much as the Witnesses from measures directed against their families. Removing their children was one of the most important measures in the Nazi arsenal of persecution. In 1974, the Watchtower Bible and Tract Society estimated that in at least 860 cases, children were separated from their parents; it is probable that the actual number of affected children is somewhat larger.[9] The removal of children and the years of separation without any contact, as well as the especially draconian upbringing in Nazi homes and families to compel the children to participate in the »national community,« represented individual tragedies that can hardly be expressed in words.

When Katharina Thoenes was incarcerated in the Moringen concentration camp, there was a demonstration of collective resistance by female Jehovah's Witnesses. They refused to perform sewing assignments for the Winter Welfare. At least, this is how director Krack described it. It is more likely that the work was connected with something that the women could and would not perform because of their faith. It is possible that, during such work, they would be forced to listen to speeches by the Führer; it is also possible that the products sewn were intended for the German army or Reich Labor Service, demands that they would have refused because of their beliefs. The penalties imposed were severe: All female Witnesses lost mail and package privileges for an indefinite period.

There is also documentation about collective acts of resistance by Jehovah's Witnesses in the Lichtenburg and Ravensbrück concentration camps. In October 1938 in Lichtenburg, they refused to listen to a broadcast of Hitler's speech. Political prisoners tried to convince them that such resistance was »useless« and the SS would react with brutality. But the women remained unyielding. The Communist inmate Charlotte Groß from Hamburg reported this incident and its consequences: »Most of the Bible Students were housed on the top floor. The SS began to place water hoses along the front of the house. Therefore we knew what they were planning and tried again to convince the women not to engage in useless resistance, but to no avail. Evening came and the prisoners took their seat in the castle courtyard. Suddenly there was a great commotion. The SS forced the Witnesses to leave the hall by hosing them with water, and outside they were beaten. They arrived at the assembly place dripping wet and were not allowed to sit down. They had to remain standing in wet clothing for more than one hour and to listen to the Führer's speech. It was October and already rather cold. Afterwards, they were not permitted to check into the infirmary, and moreover, they were deprived of food for two or three days.«[10]

Other inmates reported that the Witnesses would call out, »There's war! There's war!« and quote the Bible against war. And Maria Zeh, a Communist from Stuttgart, recalled that a few days later she found the corpse of a Witness, who had been beaten to death, in the Lichtenburg dungeon.[11]

I want to comment on the phrase »useless resistance,« used by Charlotte Groß, since this could easily be misunderstood as a disparaging observation. The term »useless« can only be understood against the background of total SS control in the concentration camps, their attempt to break every prisoner, and to impede any individual or group demonstration through tremendous cruelty. The political prisoners believed that demonstrative resistance could be »useless,« if it resulted in open conflict with the SS. The political prisoners gave practical advice to the Witnesses in Lichtenburg, namely, that they should not risk their lives. This warning did not apply to fighting to retain self-respect, which was crucial for survival. All concentration camp prisoners faced a daily struggle between life and death: not to let one's spirit be broken by SS terror, not to lose beliefs — whether political, ethical, or religious — and to develop survival strategies for oneself and others. Almost all accounts by fellow prisoners about the behavior of female and male Jehovah's Witnesses in concentration camps state the utmost respect for their undeviating beliefs. At times, this respect is mixed with a lack of understanding about the roots of such unyielding power of resistance.

In Ravensbrück, the Witnesses refused any work that benefitted the war. They refused to sew uniforms in SS tailor shops. When, instead, they were ordered to sew »bags,« they examined the patterns more closely that evening in their barracks and decided that these bags would be used to hold ammunition. Their refusal to work was punished with three weeks of punitive arrest in the camp jail. They refused to unload hay for army horses, to wrap packages of bandages, and to build air-raid shelters. In summer 1940, Camp Commandant Koegel cynically assigned this work to the Jehovah's Witness barracks, well aware that they would refuse. Nanda Herbermann, a Catholic prisoner, described the consequences: »The commandant, extremely irritated, ordered ten strokes of the whip for each Bible Student. Everyone had to report for punishment. Even today, I still see the procession of mostly elderly, lovable mothers. ... They were driven like a crowd of animals, each prisoner had to stand in line to be strapped to the whipping block, and then it started, one after the other. ... But they prayed, quietly and humbly. ... When they left the camp jail, they tried to maintain their composure as far as possible. Many crawled, their elderly and battered bodies doubled-up and bent with pain. Many of these women were sixty and older ... some of these elderly mothers did not survive this beating.«[12]

Collective resistance by Jehovah's Witnesses in Ravensbrück also included the fall 1942 refusal to breed angora, since they had discovered that the wool would be used for army clothing. The Witnesses assigned to the horticultural work crew »Kellerbruch« joined the protest, when they found out that the vegetables being harvested were sent to an SS military hospital. As punishment, about 90 women had to stand in the jail courtyard for three days and three nights; afterwards they were all flogged 25 times and forced to endure 40 days arrest in unlighted jail cells. The Communist prisoner, Margarete Buber-Neumann, barrack elder in barrack 17 for Jehovah's Witnesses, described the subsequent transfer of the »ring leaders« to Auschwitz. Moreover, some of the women were executed by the SS in Ravensbrück.[13]

There were also resistance acts that were controversial among the female Witnesses in Ravensbrück, such as the principle refusal of some women to stand for roll call and the refusal by a small group of Witnesses to accept tiny pieces of blood sausage that, for a while, enriched meager food rations on Sundays. The SS responded to this refusal by removing 20 grams of margarine from their rations. This had catastrophic consequences for the affected women because of endemic malnutrition. Their rejection of food is one of the few examples demonstrating that their strength arose from their faith, and that sometimes this could be inimical to self-preservation and the determination to survive.

Usually religious faith strengthened personal stability, increasing the possibilities for self-assertion in the concentration camps.[14] Female Jehovah's Witness supported each other through religious certainty, explicit group solidarity, and mutual assistance. They shared food rations, nursed their coreligionists back to health even under the most difficult circumstances, and cleaned their barracks, thereby, to some extent, under difficult hygienic conditions inhibiting the spread of infectious diseases and lice. Since labor was essential for survival, they tried to get assigned to work crews that had nothing to do with war. They tried to perform this work as conscientiously as possible. However, if they were assigned to anything connected to the war, they would refuse as individuals or, as previously discussed, as a group.

Maria Günzl, a Social Democrat, who survived Lichtenburg and Ravensbrück concentration camps, dedicated a touching poem to her fellow inmates, female Jehovah's Witnesses.[15]

»Of the hundreds of women Bible Students
shall be said to their honor and respect
that their religious songs on Sunday afternoon
uplifted the hearts and minds of all camp prisoners.

They always remained faithful to their belief
that deliverance was near.
Despite all tortures in the camp prison, the dark house,
where crowded together by the hundreds,
they received only bread and water as punishment.
Because they did not make garlands on Hitler's birthday,
they were tortured and persecuted.

When after weeks of horrible agony, they
were freed from the torture cell,
they tottered down the camp street as living corpses.
We felt for them:
We wept and grieved about
what had been done to them.«

Notes

1   Lower Saxon Main State Archive Hanover (hereafter HSTA Hanover): Hann. 158 Moringen, Acc. 105/96, file Katharina Thoenes. I would to thank Hans Hesse for this reference. See also, Jutta von Freyberg and Ursula Krause-Schmitt, *Frauen im Konzentrationslager 1939-1945: Moringen, Lichtenburg, Ravensbrück* (Frankfurt, 1997).

2   HSTA Hanover: Hann. 158 Moringen, Acc. 105/96, file Katharina Thoenes.

3   Bruno Bettelheim, »Die psychische Korruption durch den Totalitarismus,« in: *Erziehung zum Überleben: Zur Psychologie der Extremsituation* (Stuttgart, 1980).

4   Detlef Garbe, »Kriegsdienstverweigerung der Zeugen Jehovas,« in: *Zwischen Widerstand und Martyrium* (Munich, 1993).

5   See Jürgen Harder and Hans Hesse's essay in this volume.

6   Klaus Drobisch, »Frauenkonzentrationslager im Schloß Lichtenburg,« *Dachauer Hefte* 3 (November 1987).

7   Ino Arndt, »Das Frauenkonzentrationslager Ravensbrück,« *Dachauer Hefte* 3 (November 1987); and Garbe, »Die Häftlinge mit dem ›lila Winkel‹« chapter in: *Zwischen Widerstand und Martyrium*.

8   HSTA Hanover: Hann. 158 Moringen, Acc. 105/96, file Katharina Thoenes.

9   Garbe, »Kinder aus Bibelforscher-Familien als Objekte staatlicher Zwangsmaßnahmen,« in: *Zwischen Widerstand und Martyrium.*

10 Stephanie Sieck, *Aus der Vergangenheit kann man doch – muß man doch lernen! Charlotte Groß: Lebenslauf einer Antifaschistin*, interview and photo documentation (Hamburg, 1979).

11 Studienkreis Deutscher Widerstand, Frankfurt, Dokumentationsarchiv des deutschen Widerstandes 1933–1945: AN 3683, reminiscences of Maria Zeh.

12 Nanda Herbermann, *Der gesegnete Abgrund: Schutzhäftling Nr. 6582 im Frauenkonzentrationslager Ravensbrück* (Nuremberg, 1946).

13 Margarete Buber-Neumann, *Als Gefangene bei Hitler und Stalin: Eine Welt im Dunkel* (Stuttgart, 1958).

14 Sybil Milton, »Deutsche und deutsch-jüdische Frauen als Verfolgte des NS-Staats,« *Dachauer Hefte* 3 (1987).

15 Maria Günzl, *Trost im Leid* (Stuttgart, 1976).

Hubert Roser

The Religious Association of Jehovah's Witnesses in Baden and Wurttemberg, 1933–1945[1]

Research about the history of Jehovah's Witnesses in Nazi Germany has increased during the past several years. There are two main reasons for this trend. On the one hand, there is a continuing trend in contemporary German history to focus on the fate of »the forgotten victims« of Nazi dictatorship. Although research has focused almost exclusively on Jews for several decades, increasing public and scholarly attention is being given to Jehovah's Witnesses, as well as to Sinti and Roma, homosexuals, and the so-called »anti-socials« (the collective Nazi term for marginal social groups, such as beggars, homeless, »work shy,« and prostitutes).[2]

These groups became the targets of Nazi repression for very different reasons. Whereas Nazi racial ideology did not even grant Jews or Sinti and Roma the right to live, homosexuals, »anti-socials,« and Jehovah's Witnesses were ultimately persecuted because of their nonconformist social behavior. Similar to the mentally and physically handicapped, they were associated with inferior members of the Nazi »racial community« who, for »eugenic« reasons, were to be ruthlessly »eliminated,« if necessary. The fact that the unyielding opposition of Jehovah's Witnesses was only based on their wish to freely exercise their religion was inconsequential for Nazi governmental attitudes. Their demonstrative readiness to oppose the behavioral standards of the »racial community« was decisive and clashed with the Nazi regime's demand for complete control. The consequences are well known: every second member of this religious association, then comprising approximately 25,000 members, was persecuted after 1933; thousands were incarcerated in prisons and concentration camps, sentenced to death, or cruelly murdered.

Furthermore, beginning in 1996, the Watchtower Society set in motion a radical about-face in dealing with their identity and history. Following decades of isolation, they now pursue and support research and preservation of the past without hesitancy, both through their own symposia and video presentations, and through cooperation with professional historians. The results of these efforts are reflected in this anthology. It is not surprising that their increasing willingness for discussion and dialogue is directly linked to their unequivocal wish for equality with other religious communities and for recognition as a corporation under public law.[3] It is part of a general process of »social opening« by Jehovah's Witnesses as a result of the current discussion about »sects,« and this greater public transparency of the religious association can only be welcomed.

To some extent, the impetus for researching the history of the Jehovah's Witnesses began in 1993, when Detlef Garbe's Hamburg dissertation was first published. Meanwhile it is one of the most important books of the more recent social history of the Nazi period.[4] This monograph effectively synthesizes the results of diverse local and regional literature.[5] Furthermore, Garbe's dissertation initiated and inspired a series of new studies focusing on Jehovah's Witnesses refusal to serve in the military[6] and conditions of daily life in the concentration camps.[7]

The nearly complete absence of comparable studies for Baden-Wurttemberg[8] prompted the research center »Resistance Against the Nazis in Southwest Germany« in the summer of 1997, to focus on the fate of religious minorities in the Third Reich. This institution, created nine years ago by Professor Rudolf Lill at Karlsruhe University, consists of a small group of contemporary historians researching resistance against the unjust Nazi regime in Baden and Wurttemberg between 1933 and 1945.[9]

After completing studies about »July 20, 1944,« the White Rose, and assistance to Jews persecuted by the Nazi regime,[10] to name just a few, two publications are currently being prepared dealing with daily life, persecution by the Nazi state, and resistance by smaller religious groups to the state's totalitarian demands. An anthology concerned with Jehovah's Witnesses was published in spring 1999,[11] and this will be followed by a larger comparative publication, examining the fates of religious minorities under the Nazis. Apart from Jehovah's Witnesses, small Christian religious groups, such as the Seventh-Day Adventists, Quakers, Baptists, Methodists, and Anthroposophians, will be analyzed in detail.

Common to all these groups was that the exercise of their faith (which differed from the German majority), the maintenance of spiritual solidarity, and their loyalty to institutional and organizational structures in times of distress were understood as opposition to the Nazis and as political resistance aimed at totalitarian authority. The Nazi regime often responded with brute force to such attempts to draw away from totalitarian reach and to maintain certain essential areas of privacy; this coercion was inappropriate to the numerical significance of these various groups. The consequences were restricted freedom of movement, prohibition of the active exercise of faith in many — but not all — cases, persecution and, finally, physical extermination in prisons or concentration camps.

In this respect, Jehovah's Witnesses were one among many victim groups. In addition to the comparative severity of their persecution, what makes them stand out from all other groups, is the radicalism and perseverance with which they, as a collective community, opposed the Nazi regime. Of all the religious minorities in Germany, except for the Jews, Jehovah's Witnesses had to pay the heaviest price in blood. They were the only religious group in the concentration camps stigmatized by the Nazis with their own marking: the purple triangle. This in itself shows that the government judged them as particularly implacable opponents.

Even though Jehovah's Witnesses were among the first victims of Nazi persecution, they initially underestimated the terrorist potential of the Nazi movement, and believed that they could save themselves by conforming to a certain degree during the period following the »seizure of power.«[12] They shared this ultimately fateful misperception with nearly all other social and political groups in Germany, from the extreme right, including both churches, to the social democrats. During the consolidation of the Nazi regime, when the Nazi party was able to eliminate systematically all remaining political opponents without much resistance, no one remained who was willing to stand up for democracy. People vacillated more or less between open demonstrations of loyalty, a wait-and-see attitude, and partial opposition. Sooner than many other opposition circles and more resolutely, the Jehovah's Witnesses realized that, in the long run, no divergent religious movement would be able to survive alongside National Socialism.

It can be proved beyond any doubt that from the turn of the year 1934–1935, the »Earnest Bible Students« in Baden-Wurttemberg also acted with increasing energy against the numerous restrictions and prohibitions of the Nazi state. I would like to illustrate this point using several specific cases. Furthermore, I would like to show how the Nazi state felt obliged to respond to such »insubordination.« Finally, I would like to make clear why remembering this fundamental resistance by a small group to the Nazi regime is significant for us today.

In Baden alone, from the end of 1934 to 1937, more than 200 male and female Jehovah's Witnesses had to appear before and answer to the Mannheim Special Court,[13] which had been set up in March 1933 for sentencing political offenders. This figure can be stated with relative precision since, apart from slight gaps, the investigative files and proceedings of the Mannheim Special Court have been preserved in their entirety.[14] What was their »crime«?

Those familiar with the religious doctrines of Jehovah's Witnesses[15] know that active Witnesses (inactive members are unknown to the community) can hardly be satisfied by studying the Bible or other religious literature at home. This worship at home was exactly what the Nazi regime considered religious »activity,« and each »member of the national community,« regardless of the religion to which he or she may have belonged, was entitled to this private domain, even the Jews initially. Nevertheless, holding meetings with others having similar views and exchanging ideas, using one's home for such meetings, receiving publications with religious content, and forwarding them to fellow believers or sympathizers, or going from door to door to »bear witness« to others was susceptible to prosecution and, as a rule, severely punished by the Nazi state.

Moreover, in practice the limits were rather flexible, and judicial latitude was common. Owning a Bible and reading it, whether alone or in the company of others, was not punishable in itself, as it came under constitutionally guaranteed religious freedom that was never formally abrogated by the Nazis. Even the distribution or sale of Bibles door to door was not always prosecuted after 1933, thereby resulting in the same non-uniform administration of justice as in the days of the Weimar Republic.[16] »Interpreting« the Bible according to their own doctrines was, however, considered affirming the beliefs of Jehovah's Witness and therefore punished as »support« of a prohibited and subversive organization.[17] Consequently, the freedom of movement for Jehovah's Witnesses was unequivocally restricted.

In February 1936, during a Gestapo interrogation, Luise Bingenheimer, a housewife and Jehovah's Witness from Mannheim, explained why she could not simply bow to the Nazi ban: »Our faith is being made impossible by the government. It is of no value for me to sit at home by myself reading the Bible. We have been prohibited from doing what is essential for us: meeting together with other people to convince them about the truth.«[18] This statement was not necessarily connected to political beliefs or even opposition against the government.

What did the Nazis do to stop, or at least restrict, Jehovah's Witness activities, that had worried them increasingly? Witnesses who actively stood up for their faith and who did not flinch away from publicly bearing witness were generally sentenced to several weeks or months in prison. This occurred mainly after the autumn of 1936, when the Gestapo arrested some of the leading underground functionaries, incidentally also unconvering networks of conspiratorial Bible-reading groups throughout Germany; the courts sentenced them to several weeks or months imprisonment. Whoever was willing to remain silent and withdraw into inactivity, whatever the reason, remained essentially untouched. The Gestapo or local party organizations kept them under surveillance and spied on them for a while, but in most cases this slackened as the Nazi regime decided not to mercilessly »destroy« every opponent. Those willing to conform could count on leniency. A number of Jehovah's Witnesses, also in southwestern Germany, obviously followed this unwritten rule of behavior and, thereafter personally restrained themselves. Their number cannot be clearly determined.

Actually, and this should be emphatically stressed, the overwhelming majority of Jehovah's Witnesses did not give in, but unswervingly continued their opposition. Following their religious principles, most Jehovah's Witnesses ›stood firm against Nazi assault,‹ even in the face of great danger.[19] The »eternal bond« between them and their God, Jehovah, would remain inviolable, extending even beyond death.

In countless cases, Jehovah's Witnesses who had just been released from prison fearlessly resumed their activities. Two extreme, but by no means atypical cases, illustrate this behavior. Nothing was more urgent for the unemployed stonemason Wilhelm Friedrich Soulier, for example, than to continue preaching publicly about »God's Kingdom,« immediately after he had been released from investigative arrest on September 26, 1936. He had been sentenced by the Mannheim Special Court.[20] Soulier visited a Karlsruhe resident in Pfauenstrasse for this very purpose; the man immediately noticed Soulier's poor health after his release from custody. Soulier remarked that he »had no reason to complain. Now that he had been released, he was obliged to proclaim God's Kingdom, and that was more difficult« than the time in prison.[21] Another Jehovah's Witness, Karl Dochat, a metal grinder from Pforzheim, who had just been arrested in his home by the Gestapo, replied to officials that he had expected »to be hunted and also found.« At the same time, he announced that after he had served his sentence, he would continue advocating his faith.[22]

The Nazi police and judiciary simply labeled such »unteachable« religious advocates as »fanatics« or »stubborn Bible Students.« After mid-1936, the Nazis focused special attention on local and regional underground »leaders.« They hoped to muzzle them permanently in order to secure the regime's authority. In most cases, once the Gestapo got hold of them, a one or two-year prison term was usually followed by several years in concentration camps, where many died. Those Witnesses sentenced to several months or years in prison after 1937 at the latest, and who did not sign the »declaration« repudiating the »false doctrines of the Earnest Bible Students,« inevitably ended up in a concentration camp.

The apparatus of Nazi persecution also felt compelled to ruthlessly »discipline« another »target group.« Whoever proved particularly unyielding during Gestapo interrogations, under torture, or in court, and was not willing to divulge the names of fellow believers, referring to a ruler in heaven rather than a temporal »leader« on earth, almost always had to serve several additional years in »protective custody« after completing their prison sentences. Soulier, the Karlsruhe stonemason mentioned earlier, refused any response to both the Gestapo and the judge, and, after serving his prison term, was initially remanded to the Kislau concentration camp in Baden on November 5, 1937, and subsequently transferred to Sachsenhausen, where he died of unknown causes one year later.[23]

A variation of the fundamental refusal of Jehovah's Witnesses, evident during the first three war years, was the refusal to go to war for Germany and to kill others. Those who, despite repeated conscription demands, decided not to renounce their faith and report for military service risked prosecution before the Reich War Court, resulting in death sentences. Hundreds of young men, including Jehovah's Witnesses, who had refused conscription and military service, were in a terrible quandary: either they had to violate their conscience and thus relinquish the prospect of »eternal life,« or they could jeopardize their earthly lives, which had really only just begun.

In southwestern Germany, a number of Jehovah's Witnesses refused military service because of their religious beliefs, thereby expediting their deaths. One case is typical, that of Otto Friedrich Dups, a farmer from Sulzfeld (Kraichgau, north Baden). As early as 1935, he already served four months in prison for »activities for the proscribed Bible Students' sect.« On December 7, 1939, the Reich War Court sentenced him to death by hanging for »undermining military morale,« based on Section 5, Paragraph 1, of the Decree on Extraordinary Criminal

Regulations in Wartime (*Kriegssonderstrafrechtsverordnung*), enacted on August 17, 1939. He was executed in Berlin-Plötzensee on December 22, 1939.[24] In his farewell letter to his family, written on December 22, he stated: »My dearest ones, you are informed about everything. I have written to you about everything necessary. You, my dear ones, know what a Christian must do.«[25]

Andreas Maislinger, a political scientist from Innsbruck, who has researched the history of Jehovah's Witnesses in Austria,[26] and who, meanwhile, has focused on postwar reaction to National Socialism and resistance, has extensively studied the total rejection of military service of Jehovah's Witnesses. His research focused on the case of Franz Jägerstätter (an Austrian Catholic »martyr,« 1907–1943), who was executed for refusing military service.[27] Maislinger's conclusions are equivocal. On the one hand, he basically acknowledges Jägerstätter's decision favorably. On the other hand, he is critical that such an uncompromising attitude, placing his own life on the line for his faith, ultimately meant that Jägerstätter »abandoned« his young wife and small children.

I would like to refrain from such basic moral judgements. The ultimate price of an individual's faith is a personal decision made under specific and unique circumstances, and therefore cannot be measured against absolute moral criteria. Much less can one's conscience remain entirely immune from daily tribulations that can influence decisions, resulting in individual decisions that take completely different paths. In my opinion, this is as true for democratic as dictatorial situations. A heuristic conclusion may be drawn from the theory, that there would be no more wars if everybody refused to serve in the military, which undoubtedly looks promising at first glance.

The first thing we can learn from the attitude of Jehovah's Witnesses in Nazi Germany is that a small group, relying on their faith and resolute solidarity, succeeded in withdrawing from the Nazi regime's totalitarian grasp, albeit at a high price. Those who feel that they would not be strong enough to follow such a course may examine alternatives about how they might behave in a similar situation. In any case, it is important to pay our respect to the resistance offered by Jehovah's Witnesses. Second, it should be an obligation for us, the generations born after the Third Reich, to ensure that people will never again have to die to remain true to their conscience.

Notes

1   Revised texts of my lectures in Munich on November 1, 1997, and in Augsburg on November 17, 1997, at the opening of the Watchtower Society (Selters/Taunus) traveling exhibition »Jehovah's Witnesses Stand Firm Against Nazi Assault.«

2   See, for instance, the prolonged public discussion about a central memorial in Berlin for the victims of Nazi crimes. Authoritative studies about various non-Jewish groups are Burkhard Jellonnek, *Homosexuelle unter dem Hakenkreuz: Die Verfolgung von Homosexuellen im »Dritten Reich«* (Paderborn, 1990); Michael Zimmermann, *Rassenutopie und Genozid: Die nationalsolzialistische »Lösung der Zigeunerfrage«* (Hamburg, 1996); Wolfgang Ayass, *»Asoziale« im Nationalsozialismus* (Stuttgart, 1995); and Patrick Wagner, *Volksgemeinschaft ohne Verbrecher: Konzeptionen und Praxis der Kriminalpolizei in der Zeit der Weimarer Republik und des Nationalsozialismus* (Hamburg, 1996).

3   See Informationsdienst der Zeugen Jehovas, ed., *Jehovas Zeugen: Antworten auf häufig gestellte Fragen* (Selters, 1996), p. 5; Detlef Garbe, »Die Verfolgung der Zeugen Jehovas im nationalsozialistischen Deutschland:

Ein Überblick,« in: Kreismuseum Wewelsburg, eds., *Widerstand aus christlicher Überzeugung: Jehovas Zeugen im Nationalsozialismus; Dokumentation einer Tagung*, Historische Schriften des Kreismuseums Wewelsburg, Beiheft 1 (Essen, 1998), pp. 24ff.

4   Detlef Garbe, *Zwischen Widerstand und Martyrium: Die Zeugen Jehovas im »Dritten Reich*,« 3rd rev. ed. (Munich, 1997); and idem, »Im Westen vergessen, im Osten verschmäht: Verweigerung und Widerstand der Zeugen Jehovas in der Geschichtsschreibung,« in: *Informationen: Zeitschrift des Studienkreises Deutscher Widerstand 22*, no. 46 (1997), pp. 27ff.

5   For individual titles, see bibliography at the end of this book.

6   See Norbert Haase, *Das Reichskriegsgericht und der Widerstand gegen die nationalsozialistische Herrschaft* (Berlin, 1993), pp. 95-99; Gerhard Paul, *Ungehorsame Soldaten: Dissens, Verweigerung und Widerstand deutscher Soldaten (1939-1945)* (St. Ingbert, 1994), pp. 47-51; Detlef Garbe »*Du sollst nicht töten*«: Kriegsdienstverweigerer 1939-1945,« in: Norbert Haase and Gerhard Paul, eds., *Die anderen Soldaten: Wehrkraftzersetzung, Gehorsamsverweigerung und Fahnenflucht im Zweiten Weltkrieg* (Frankfurt, 1995), pp. 85-104; Hermine Wullner, ed., »*... kann nur der Tod die gerechte Sühne sein*«: Todesurteile deutscher Wehrmachtgerichte; Eine Dokumentation (Baden-Baden, 1997), pp. 297-312.

7   Kirsten John, »*Mein Vater wird gesucht ...*«: Häftlinge des Konzentrationslagers in Wewelsburg (Essen, 1996); Kirsten John-Stucke, »Der ›lila Winkel‹ in Wewelsburg,« in: Kreismuseum Wewelsburg, eds., *Widerstand aus christlicher Überzeugung*, pp. 39-53; Jürgen Harder, *Widerstand und Verfolgung von Bibelforscherinnen im Frauen-KZ Moringen*, University of Göttingen, 1997; and the memoirs of Max Hollweg, *Es ist unmöglich von dem zu schweigen, was ich erlebt habe: Zivilcourage im »Dritten Reich«* (Bielefeld, 1997).

8   An exception is Manfred Koch, »Die kleinen Glaubensgemeinschaften,« in: Erich Matthias and Hermann Weber, eds., *Widerstand gegen den Nationalsozialismus in Mannheim* (Mannheim, 1984), pp. 415-434.

9   See Michael Kißener, »Widerstand gegen den Nationalsozialismus: Zur Einrichtung einer Forschungsstelle an der Universität Karlsruhe,« in: *Staatsanzeiger für Baden-Württemberg*, no. 96 (November 28, 1992).

10 See Rudolf Lill and Michael Kißener, eds., *20. Juli in Baden und Württemberg* (Konstanz, 1994); Rudolf Lill, Klaus Eisele, ed., *Hochverrat? Neue Forschungen zur »Weißen Rose*,« rev. new ed. (Konstanz, 1999); Michael Kissener, ed., *Widerstand gegen die Judenverfolgung* (Konstanz, 1996). Angela Borgstedt is currently completing a national project at the Berlin Center for Research on Antisemitism about the so-called »helpers of Jews.«

11 Hubert Roser, ed., *Widerstand als Bekenntnis: Die Zeugen Jehovas und das NS-Regime in Baden und Württemberg* (Konstanz, 1999).

12 See Garbe, *Zwischen Widerstand und Martyrium*, pp. 87-107.

13 For the Mannheim Special Court, see Christiane Oehler, *Die Rechtsprechung des Sondergerichts Mannheim 1933-1945* (Berlin, 1997).

14 Generallandesarchiv Karlsruhe (hereafter GLA), record group 507; the related Stuttgart files were, however, completely destroyed during the war.

15 See Garbe, *Zwischen Widerstand und Martyrium*, pp. 43-57.

16 Garbe, *Zwischen Widerstand und Martyrium*, pp. 78f. Until 1935, especially the Konstanz state prosecutor was unsure how to proceed in a number of cases. A violation of trade regulations could not be proven. At the most, a fine was imposed for disturbing Sunday's rest. GLA 507/5889: report by the Konstanz district office, December 19, 1935.

17 Decree by the Baden Secretary of the Interior, May 15, 1933, in: *Badischer Staatsanzeiger*, no. 114 (March 15, 1933). As in all other German states, the legal basis was the President's Decree for the Protection of the People and the State of February 28, 1933, enacted immediately after the Reichstag fire to prevent ostensible communist assaults.

18 GLA 507/851, p. 15: interrogation of February 18, 1936.

19 The documentary video *Stand Firm Against Nazi Assault* (78 minutes) has been distributed by the Watchtower Society in many languages since late 1996.

20 GLA 507/2113: Soulier had been sentenced to two months in prison because of his activities as a Jehovah's Witness. The sentence was considered served because of his term in investigative arrest.

21 GLA 507/2428: Protocol of interrogation, early November 1936.

22 GLA 507/2141: Gestapo headquarters interrogation protocol, Karlsruhe, late 1936.

23 GLA 507/2428-29: indictment by special court, November 19, 1936, and invalidation of this verdict after 1945.

24 GLA 507/1210: Situation report (*Lagebericht*) of the Senior State Attorney (*Oberstaatsanwaltschaft*) in

Heidelberg to the Baden Attorney General (*Generalstaatsanwalt*), Karlsruhe, January 22, 1940; Hermine Wüllner private collection, Sandhausen near Heidelberg: documents about Otto Friedrich Dups. The case is covered in detail in Bernd Breitkopf and Kurt Hochstuhl, *Sulzfeld: Von Bauern, Steinhauern und Edelleuten* (Ubstadt-Weiher, 1997), pp. 260f.

25 Watchtower History Archive, Selters/Taunus: copies of this letter and other documents relating to Dups.
26 Andreas Maislinger, »Die Zeugen Jehovas (Ernste Bibelforscher),« in: Dokumentationsarchiv des Österreichischen Widerstands, ed., *Widerstand und Verfolgung in Tirol 1934-1945: Eine Dokumentation*, v. 2 (Vienna, 1984), pp. 369-383; idem, »Andere religiöse Gruppen,« in: Dokumentationsarchiv des Österreichischen Widerstands, ed., *Widerstand und Verfolgung in Salzburg 1934-1945: Eine Dokumentation*, v. 2, (Vienna, 1991), pp. 323-353.
27 Andreas Maislinger, »Franz Jägerstätter,« in: Fred Parkinson (ed.), *Conquering the Past, Austrian Nazism Yesterday and Today* (Detroit: 1989), pp. 187ff. The extensive literature meanwhile published about Jägerstätter includes: Georg Bergmann, *Franz Jägerstätter: Ein Leben vom Gewissen entschieden, von Christus gestaltet*, 2nd ed. including the entire unpublished literary estate (Stein a. Rh., 1988); Norbert Haase, »Gott mehr gehorcht als dem Staat: Franz Jägerstätter vor dem Reichkriegsgericht. Eine Dokumentation,« in: *Tribüne: Zeitschrift für das Verständnis des Judentums* 29 (1990), pp. 198-206; Erna Putz, *Franz Jägerstätter: »... besser die Hände als der Wille gefesselt. ...,«* new ed. (Grünbach, 1997); Erna Putz, *Gefängnisbriefe und Aufzeichnungen* (Linz, 1987); Alfons Riedl and Josef Schwabeneder, eds., *Franz Jägerstätter: Christlicher Glaube und politisches Gewissen* (Munich, 1997); and Manfred Messerschmidt, »Aufhebung des Todesurteils gegen Franz Jägerstätter,« in: *Kritische Justiz* 31 (1998), pp. 99-105.

Hans-Hermann Dirksen

Jehovah's Witnesses in the German Democratic Republic

The preceding articles cast a sobering light on a dark chapter of German history. It took a long time until the full extent of Nazi terror and persecution was understood, and longer still until historical research began to be assembled. At present, it still cannot be estimated when these studies will be completed. Today, it is necessary to consider and evaluate tragedies that took place not just over twelve years, but over a forty year period of additional oppression and persecution. In the case of the German Democratic Republic (hereafter GDR), we encounter completely new and subtler forms of state repression and violence. It is essential for us to ask whether we are willing to begin this historical research, and capable of doing so. If we compared the development of research about the GDR with that of Nazi history in the Federal Republic of Germany, we would be now at the beginning of the 1950s. At that time, only several years had elapsed since the end of the Third Reich and the Federal Republic very reluctantly began an unbiased investigation of Nazi terror with the help of historians, although the wounds experienced were still too deep. Further, research was not to appear as a form of »victor's justice,« particularly since historians in West Germany examined that history far less emotionally than in the East. Is it expedient to encumber German people growing together? Or will GDR history only be examined 50 years from now?

The answers to these questions can only be found by looking at the victims, for example, at the victims belonging to the religious community of Jehovah's Witnesses. This group, persecuted under the Nazi regime, had to submit to continued persecution in eastern Germany. This became evident with their official prohibition in 1950 in the GDR. In 1945, Jehovah's Witnesses were released from concentration camps and prisons, only to find themselves again incarcerated five years later. They were sometimes sentenced by the same courts, and sometimes even sent to the same prisons. After 1945, when local congregations were once again organized, the head of the »Bible House« in Magdeburg emphasized that the leaders of parishes should have spent some time in a concentration camp or prison. Research confirms that the campaign of arrests before the 1950 ban was primarily directed against these leading preachers. Therefore, it is not surprising that, based on our current knowledge, over 300 Witnesses had to serve long terms of imprisonment during the Nazi period as well as in the GDR. For example, individuals such as the district preachers Fritz Adler, Hans Albert, and Oswald Dietrich accumulated a total of almost 24 years imprisonment under both systems.[1]

How was this possible? It was undoubtedly possible because of a lack of objectivity in historical research and, all the more so, because of the suppression of such history. This occurred, even though the fate of this religious association under the Nazis was well-known in both West and East Germany. During the immediate postwar years, there is seldom a report about the concentration camps that does not mention Jehovah's Witnesses at least peripherally.[2] East German public awareness primarily highlighted the Nazi persecution of »anti-fascist democratic fighters,« making it no major problem to silence the fate of a small group, such as the Jehovah's Witnesses.[3]

Extensive research and publication can prevent the suppression and erasure of history and its lessons. Amnesia about the past inhibits conscience and understanding. Injustice can be more easily overlooked if it is not objectively recognized. This lesson can be drawn clearly from the belated research about Jehovah's Witnesses under National Socialism. This example certainly shows the importance of studying history. Thus, historical research cannot be postponed even for one generation. It is necessary to collect and organize the scattered documents and to record survivor testimonies in order to study them. Doing this will provide proof to fall back on when »evidence« is needed. Finally, it must be said that remembering and rehabilitating the victims is considerably more important than the reputations of the perpetrators. Moreover, objective research usually results in information. There are two groups: perpetrators and victims. To refuse to do this research to protect and help the perpetrators is inevitably the first step toward forgetting. The only concession to be made to perpetrators is to distinguish the degree of their culpability. Information and reports supplied to, and communications with the Ministry for State Security (MfS), which did not result in serious harm, such as imprisonment, must surely be judged differently from denunciation, which resulted in numerous convictions. Finally, the case of the Jehovah's Witnesses shows that it is possible for individuals to personally reject and protest inhumane behavior.

Research about the persecution of Jehovah's Witnesses in the German Democratic Republic is another new and enormously important aspect of historical research. Studying and analyzing this history has not been possible until now, and it is therefore not surprising that there are no publications about it. Consequently, this aspect of GDR history has virtually sunk into oblivion. It is possible to study this material now that archives have become accessible. Such opportunities for research should be taken full advantage of to prevent a repeat of what happened in East Germany: on the one hand, renewed bans, arrests, and convictions only a few years after the end of Nazi rule; and on the other hand, the memory of the victims being obliterated.

The First Postwar Years

After the war ended and the concentration camps were liberated, Jehovah's Witnesses began their religious activities again. This can be seen in the first organizational directives: »When carrying out this work that is now beginning, it is necessary that every publisher receives a territory suitable to his abilities and then works in this territory alone ... and he will work this territory completely and thoroughly with the main objective of establishing study classes. Recent publications of Jehovah's Witnesses should be used to study the Holy Scriptures. This should be done systematically. The territories should be worked over and over again by the same publisher. Every company publisher will receive a small personal territory from the territory servant and he should cover this thoroughly while looking for men of good will.«[4]

In Magdeburg, the religious organization was reestablished as an association on September 9, 1945[5] and registered with the Magdeburg Local Court on September 22, 1945.[6] Permission for the activities of this religious organization also posed no problem for the local Soviet military administration in Halle. After enrollment in the official association register, the Magdeburg school authorities, responsible for religious questions, issued an authorization on October 13, 1945: »This is to certify that the Russian Military Administration allows the International Bible Student Association, German Branch (as a registered association), to conduct religious services.«[7]

Moreover, the property of the old Bible House in Magdeburg was returned. Throughout the Soviet Occupation Zone, new congregations, known as groups, were established. Jehovah's Witnesses also attempted to resume preaching of their doctrine in an organized way, and also to hold public meetings and lectures. The Witnesses were convinced they would find fertile ground for their preaching because of the rampant general despair and hopelessness. Their missionary zeal was also strengthened by their awareness that they had acted appropriately under National Socialism: They went into the concentration camps rather than participate in the Hitler regime and they accepted the death penalty rather than take part in war.[8] The Soviet Military Administration in Germany (SMAD) and also the East German authorities soon developed political interest in the Witnesses, because of their public missionary work.

Difficulties with local SMAD commandants ensued. The Soviets could not understand the missionary zeal of Jehovah's Witnesses and, therefore, it was often left to the whim of the local commanding officer as to whether they would permit public lectures and public preaching from house to house. It must be noted that the Potsdam agreement guaranteed the freedom to practice religion in principle.[9] This explicitly established the right to engage in religious activities throughout Germany. This argument frequently helped local groups of Jehovah's Witnesses in revoking local bans. Jehovah's Witness representatives from Berlin and Magdeburg also called on the »Tulpanow Department,« the SMAD office of information in Berlin, that was also responsible for religious affairs in the Soviet Occupation Zone, because of the unclear situation.[10] In 1947, these conversations resulted in written confirmation from SMAD that the Jehovah's Witnesses were a recognized religious organization: »Notice: The administration of the ›Bible Students‹ sect (Jehovah's Witnesses) is hereby informed that they are among the religions permitted within the Soviet Occupation Zone. Head of the Department for Public Organization, signed Major Wassiljew.«[11]

This confirmation, however, did not provide any further assistance with certain local SMAD commanding officers. Confirmation from Karlshorst did not determine the mood of these local commanding officers.[12]

Permission for religious services caused constant problems, especially in Saxony. Each commanding officer had the power to censor, control, and command. It was possible that in one district religious services in private homes were prohibited and could only be held in public places. In the adjacent district, on the other hand, all religious services in public places were forbidden and only those in private homes were allowed. In another district, preaching from house to house was banned. In a nearby district, there were no objections, but services could only be conducted by a local resident. Even though state constitutions had meanwhile been passed guaranteeing the free and undisturbed practice of religion, local authorities curtailed this freedom by issuing regulations that religious functions could only take place in facilities belonging to the church. Any other permission had to be requested for each individual meeting. In this way, regular religious services of Jehovah's Witnesses were placed on the same level as theatrical performances and public festivals. If these regulations were not observed, the religious services were stopped and the preachers in charge were punished or even arrested. Sometimes the authorities only claimed that no permit existed as a pretext for intervening. For example, the preacher in Freiberg, Richard R. from Lößnitz, received notification to pay a fine on October 24, 1947: »As the responsible company servant of the Jehovah's Witnesses, Freiberg group, you delivered a public biblical lecture in Bartz's Restaurant in Langhennersdorf on October 10, 1947, from 8.35 p.m. until 10 p.m. This lecture was not approved by the Soviet city and district commandant nor by the local police. To hold such lectures, you must receive stamped permission from the district commandant as well as a letter of authorization from the district police. Since you gave lectures without both of these documents, you are liable to prosecution. Evidence: Notification by the Langhennersdorf police dated October 11, 1947. I am issuing you a fine of 10 Reichsmarks, for this violation of the regulations of the Freiberg district administration and Municipal Council concerning ›meetings requiring permission,‹ of September 15, 1947. Should this fine not be paid, a sentence of two days in prison must be served.«[13]

At first, German authorities just received orders from the Russian commandants, but as they continued getting stronger, especially with the increasing transfer of important duties to members of the SED (Socialist Unity Party), they became directly involved in hindering Jehovah's Witnesses. Already in the spring of 1946, city and district information offices in Saxony received initial reports about the activities of the Witnesses.[14] There are numerous investigative reports by information offices that indicate increasing concern about the growing number of followers of this religious organization. On March 18, 1947, the Freiberg information office reported, for example: »If Freiberg's women are called upon to participate in a large demonstration for peace, only 150 to 200 persons show up, but when Jehovah's Witnesses issue invitations for a meeting, we are astonished that 90 percent of the 800 people in attendance are women.«[15]

These reports particularly displeased responsible SED government officials. They clearly indicated that Witness meetings provided the population with an incentive that might prove detrimental for Party (SED) political activities. Jehovah's Witnesses were portrayed as a political rival in the fight for the masses in such reports, and it is possible that their real size was overestimated. Moreover, it was recognized that the followers of this religious organization were completely neutral to socialist reconstruction that was now starting.[16] They did not participate in political organizations, referenda, and elections. This would not be tolerated and in late 1948, the SED central secretariat authorized the so-called Department K 5, the precursor of the State Security, to undertake nationwide surveillance of Jehovah's Witnesses throughout the Soviet occupation zone.[17] Reports came from the entire Soviet Occupation Zone, which merely showed that Jehovah's Witnesses congregated and talked about the rapid approach of God's Kingdom. Moreover, their neutrality was described. Except for Saxony, all state authorities confirmed the non-political and purely religious motives of Jehovah's Witnesses.

But it was precisely this neutrality and political abstinence that led the SED leadership to classify Jehovah's Witnesses as one of the enemies of socialism.[18] Although the SED was still interested in maintaining the impression of religious freedom, they attempted to impute subversive tendencies to Jehovah's Witnesses. At the beginning of 1949, the reports of Department K 5 changed. Descriptions such as »activities hostile to the state« or »sect hostile to reconstruction« appeared. These phrases had nothing to do with the unchanged activities of the Witnesses, but illustrated how their activities were being depicted or described. The state governments as well as the highest party and national leaders were also considering restricting Jehovah's Witnesses activities. Thus, in the fall of 1949, the Politburo decided to implement specific measures against Jehovah's Witnesses.[19] The Politburo announced that Jehovah's Witnesses, a »sect under American influence,« was foreign to East Germany and that they opposed the progress of socialism through their activities hostile to reconstruction. A major operation was planned to restrict the Witnesses' activities and to influence public opinion against the Witnesses: »The behavior of Jehovah's Witnesses in the Soviet Occupation Zone shows with increasing clarity, that this organization is an especially subtle form of propaganda by American monopoly capital. In specific situations, it was established that this organization was even used for espionage. On the other hand, membership in this organization has increased rapidly within the last few months, which is especially visible in the democratic mass organizations (the DFD or Democratic Women's Association, and FDJ or Free German Youth), partly even in the Party itself. To counteract this development and to fight this insidious propaganda, the following measures are necessary:

1. All specific proof of American imperialist propaganda by Jehovah's Witnesses must immediately be exposed by the press and radio. The Department of Culture and Education, Mass Propaganda, and the Secretariat for Women's and Youth Affairs are hereby instructed to observe the Jehovah's Witness movement attentively and continuously to make material available to the press and radio. This propaganda should not take issue with Witness religious issues, but should only fight the political consequences or political statements of this American imperialist propaganda.

2. Sale of Jehovah's Witness publications in the Soviet Occupation Zone is only possible with an SMAD license stamp on the publication. All unlicensed publications must be confiscated immediately.

3. At the request of the DVdI (German Administration of the Interior), all state and municipal administrations must be instructed not to permit public facilities (town halls, classrooms, etc.) to be used for Bible Student meetings.

4. Confidential instructions are to be issued by the party executive or the zonal directorate to state party executive boards and democratic organizations that party or organizational facilities are not to be made available to Jehovah's Witnesses. Moreover, the party press and democratic mass organizations press is to receive instructions that ›Jehovah's Witness‹ members can no longer be accepted.

5. All public meetings, if they do not purely serve church purposes, are to be registered, including the ›Jehovah's Witnesses.‹ All unregistered meetings are to be prohibited and dissolved.

6. Wherever legal regulations protecting the democratic order are violated by ›Jehovah's Witness‹ speakers or agitators, statutory penal laws must be applied.

7. The Church Departments of the Ministries for National Education are instructed to prepare a list of all ›Jehovah's Witness‹ functionaries, listing their names, cities of residence, and precise addresses. This will enable investigation and surveillance of these functionaries.

8. The Secretariat of Youth Affairs is instructed to work out precise measures together with the Central Council of the FDJ (Free German Youth) implementing these guidelines in areas where the influence of the Bible Students on youth is especially strong. The FDJ is to take special care arranging quality cultural meetings in this field.

9. The Department of Women's Affairs, in conjunction with the DFD, is instructed to prepare proposals for working among female ›Jehovah's Witnesses.‹

›Jehovah's Witnesses‹ who appear in mass organizations with American imperialist propaganda are to be removed from these organizations.«[20]

At the end of 1949 and the beginning of 1950, newspaper articles appeared identifying Jehovah's Witnesses as »Witnesses for Wall Street«[21] or later, even as »agents of American monopoly capital.«[22] As a result of measures by the *Volkspolizei* (East German Police), systematic and sensational prohibitions dissolving the Jehovah's Witnesses occurred throughout the German Democratic Republic. Meetings and even larger congresses in many localities were dispersed or broken up by the *Volkspolizei*, with short-term arrests following. Dramatic scenes occurred, especially when the *Volkspolizei* arrested leading preachers and speakers, and frequently up to one thousand Witnesses who had attended the meetings, assembled in front of the *Volkspolizei* building chanting: »Release our imprisoned brothers.«[23] Even Bible studies in private homes were increasingly controlled and dissolved.

In February 1950, Jehovah's Witnesses, especially the Bible House in Magdeburg, submitted a lengthy petition to the government of the GDR, drawing attention to these abuses. They thought that these problems only came from some individual »lower-level bureaucrats,« who were using public agitation to incite persecution of Jehovah's Witnesses. At that time, it was not understood that the incipient persecution of Jehovah's Witnesses was the result of a direct order from the SED Politburo and consequently, any petition or plea for assistance was useless. These attempts were not few in number: the Witnesses tirelessly wrote to politicians, government representatives, and other institutions in the East as well as in the West to attract attention to their situation. On July 10, 1950, numerous copies of the previously mentioned petition were mailed in printed form from the Jehovah's Witnesses Berlin office to East and West Germany.[24] In autumn 1950, when the annual district convention of Jehovah's Witnesses from the GDR was to take place in West Berlin, the GDR government feared that Jehovah's Witnesses would use this public event to attract widespread attention to their suppression in East Germany. Moreover, the first elections of the new German Democratic Republic were to be held in mid-October. It was anticipated that the Witnesses, on the whole, would not participate in these elections. The government even feared that the Witnesses would try to stop others from participating in these elections. All the more so, since many other citizens and church leaders were skeptical about these elections, for purely political reasons, and because of the newly created »National Front« block parties. Apparently, the number of Jehovah's Witness followers and their influence were significantly overestimated.[25] On the other hand, party and state leaders were not willing to reach an agreement with the Witnesses and tolerate them as a free religious organization in the GDR. This contradicted the party and state leaders' understanding of absolute dominance, based on the assumption that the rise of socialism in the GDR would initially lead to a considerable »increase in class conflict.« If one wanted to remain victorious, any resistance against socialist progress and any person holding a different opinion had to be removed. In the interim, Jehovah's Witnesses had been banned in Poland during the summer of 1950, after extensive house searches and arrests. Prominent Jehovah's Witnesses in Poland were to be placed on trial without delay.[26] When the Witnesses in East Germany heard about this, they realized that their freedom would also soon come to an end in the GDR. Therefore, five years after their liberation from Nazi concentration camps, they once again prepared to work illegally.

The Ban

Only a short time later, on August 30, 1950, there was a sudden wave of arrests. About 400 leading Witness preachers were arrested between 4 a.m. and 6 a.m. by the State Security throughout the entire GDR.[27] On the same day, the Bible House in Magdeburg was raided by the State Security in large numbers, who forced their way into the building in the early morning, arrested 27 male Witnesses, and confiscated the whole complex.[28] Only one day later, on August 31, 1950, Steinhoff, then Minister of the Interior, informed the German branch office of the Watchtower Bible and Tract Society in Magdeburg that the Witnesses had been removed from the list of authorized religious organizations and were henceforth banned. At the same time, he announced punishments for further activities. His explanation stated: »The activities of ›Jehovah's Witnesses‹ during the last ten months have clearly proved that they have continually misused the name of a religious organization for unconstitutional purposes. Throughout the entire territory of the German Democratic Republic as well as in Greater Metropolitan Berlin, they have pursued systematic agitation against the existing democratic order and its laws under the cloak of religious meetings. Further, they have continually imported and distributed illegal publications, whose contents violate the Constitution of the German Democratic Republic as well as efforts to maintain peace. At the same time, it has been established that ›Jehovah's Witnesses‹ have served as spies for an imperialistic power.«[29]

Steinhoff thus interfered directly with the freedom of religious belief and the undisturbed practice of religion guaranteed by Article 41 of the GDR Constitution. He also violated Article 9 of the Constitution, which guaranteed all citizens the right to publicly express their opinions and that there would be no censorship of the press. While some Jehovah's Witnesses were questioned in the interrogation cellars of State Security prisons under inhumane conditions,[30] many other Witnesses had to acknowledge receipt of a copy of Steinhoff's decree with a codicil that they would no longer support this religious organization. Although the ban was issued on August 31, 1950, no one initially knew anything about it. Since newspapers at that time incessantly published virulent articles against Jehovah's Witnesses, along with alleged resolutions from the working population, the ban could be presented as the government's compliance with the »workers request.«[31] The ban and wave of arrests were covered in the press on September 5, 1950, almost one week later.[32] Utilizing this propaganda subterfuge, the SED wanted to avoid giving the impression that religious persecution was directed by the government. The SED did not want to appear hostile to religion in any way just before the upcoming October 1950 elections.[33]

As already pointed out, the preliminary proceedings against the Jehovah's Witnesses arrested in the operations on August 30, 1950, were carried out exclusively by the State Security. Other investigative agencies were not involved. This was possible because the investigative proceedings were based on Allied Control Council Directive 38, which had been proclaimed for denazification in postwar Germany.[34] The Soviet Military Administration had appointed the previously mentioned Department K 5 for denazification. After the Ministry for State Security was founded in February 1950, it assumed jurisdiction of Department K 5. Denazification had already been completed by 1950. Control Council Directive 38 included a section that was to prevent a revival of National Socialism. This enabled prosecution of anyone spreading tendentious rumors or fomenting war after 1945.[35] Although Nazi rumors had been the intended target, the GDR used this passage to fight its political enemies. This proved successful because investigations and preliminary proceedings could be carried out exclusively by State Security. Control Council Directive 38 was also used, because of these advantages, in preliminary judicial proceedings against Jehovah's Witnesses. None of the Witnesses who had been interrogated in preliminary proceedings ever saw a prosecutor or a judge, let alone a defense attorney.[36] All investigations were carried out by members of the Ministry for State Security.

A further problem for party and state leaders was that they could not be certain that the local court holding jurisdiction would really sentence Jehovah's Witnesses according to their wishes. Therefore, at a meeting about the forthcoming trials, the Attorney General of Saxony-Anhalt in Halle raised the question, whether it would even be worthwhile to conduct such trials, since Jehovah's Witnesses were particularly well-known and would only be portrayed as martyrs.

A Wave of Trials before East German Criminal Courts

Therefore they decided first to hold an impressive show trial before the GDR Supreme Court in Berlin, which could serve as a model for all subsequent trials in district courts.[37] A certain number of Witnesses were transferred to Berlin for this purpose. On September 27, 1950, after pre-trial investigation had been completed, the Minister for State Security, Zaisser, personally handed the completed investigative report to Attorney General Melsheimer, who accepted it verbatim and forwarded it on September 30, 1950, to the Supreme Court for filing an indictment.[38] The introduction stated: »All persons charged are members of the so-called Watch Tower and Tract Society with headquarters in Brooklyn, United States, and refer to themselves as ›Jehovah's Witnesses.‹ This organization pretends to be a religious organization, concerned only with religious matters. Investigations have established that this is a cleverly disguised American imperialist espionage organization at whose order the widely branched suborganizations of the Watchtower Society operate.«[39]

Hilde Benjamin was the presiding judge for the trial. A short time after she received the indictment, she issued the order to proceed, together with two associate judges from her criminal division, and set October 3 and 4, 1950, as the trial date. It became obvious that neither the Attorney General's office nor the Supreme Court had checked, even in part, the pre-trial investigation and evidence collected by the Ministry for State Security. They assumed that the pre-trial investigation and results were correct. On October 4, after hearing the evidence and witness testimonies, the Jehovah's Witnesses were sentenced for alleged espionage, war mongering, and boycott campaigns to terms varying from eight years to life imprisonment. The former district preacher, Fritz Adler, and the head of the legal department of the Bible House in Magdeburg, Willi Heinicke, were sentenced to life imprisonment. The Supreme Court stated in its opinion that the Jehovah's Witness organization had headquarters in Brooklyn in the United States, and was centrally led from there. From there, followers could be manipulated in any way, and using religious pretexts, they could reach every family and even every individual; the latter did not realize that the Witness made systematic notes about everything he observed and that those notes were evaluated by the organization and then sent to America, where they were subsequently forwarded to American intelligence via Brooklyn. Without any proof, they claimed that Jehovah's Witnesses had delivered regional maps to Brooklyn, on which the location of firms, post offices, fire departments, police stations, Soviet military headquarters, bridges, underpasses, airports, air-traffic centers, factories, and companies had been marked, containing especially invaluable material for American intelligence. Further, important addresses of mayors, police presidents, directors of regional and local courts, judges, state attorneys, and police officers had been forwarded to Brooklyn in order to also denounce these progressive East German citizens. The literature of Jehovah's Witnesses was described as propaganda leaflets against the Soviet Union, the people's democracy, and the German Democratic Republic. This propaganda supposedly promoted war-mongering and imperialist tendencies and influences. Moreover, the court considered the Witnesses' nonparticipation in the elections of October 15, 1950, and that they had not signed petitions promoting peace, as special agitation for boycotts.[40] The Supreme Court used the previously mentioned Control Council Directive 38 and article 6, paragraph 2 of the GDR Constitution as the basis for punishment.[41] For the first time, the Supreme Court interpreted article 6, paragraph 2, as valid criminal law, even though this programmatic article had not been designated for application as a mandatory part of criminal law. Hilde Benjamin stated that if paragraph 1 of the Criminal

Code specified that elements of a felony punishable with prison sentences of one year to life imprisonment are to be considered a crime, then it must be concluded that this would also apply to crimes against article 6 of the GDR Constitution. The fact that paragraph 1 of the Penal Code only defined the difference between a crime and an offense was ignored by Hilde Benjamin. Also, espionage was not mentioned in article 6, so that punishment for espionage based on article 6 constituted a violation of the elementary rules of criminal law.[42]

Nevertheless, this basic Supreme Court ruling, as well as the indictment by the Ministry for State Security, became the basis for hundreds of trials that were held before East German district courts during the next few years.[43] Many additional trials followed rapidly after the Supreme Court's ruling in mid-October. Starting in mid-October, especially in Mecklenburg, trials were held almost daily before the Schwerin Regional Court, with trial days also held in Greifswald, Neubrandenburg, and Rostock. By the end of October 1950, all Witnesses who had been arrested in Mecklenburg had been brought to trial. In early November 1950, the wave of trials reached Thuringia and Brandenburg. At the end of November, a series of show trials began in Saxony.

For example, on November 29, 1950, the fourth largest criminal division, under the senior presiding judge Kühnrich of the Zwickau District Court, sentenced nine Jehovah's Witnesses under order 201. The case involved four Witnesses from the Plauen district and five Witnesses from the Zwickau region. Oswald Dietrich and Hans Albert were sentenced to life imprisonment; both had already been incarcerated in concentration camps for many years. The other defendants were sentenced to terms of nine to twelve years imprisonment, and two respectively received terms of two and three years imprisonment.[44] The verdict stated: »All defendants deny having participated in boycott propaganda, promoting hatred between nations, and war-mongering. They maintain that their congregation and preaching activities were based solely on the Bible and thus they had attempted to influence the public only in a religious sense. ... They definitely reject the charge of war-mongering, since only ›Jehovah's Witnesses‹ have always been against war and for peace. They were the only ones who had not used weapons and had urged people throughout the world never to reach for weapons.«[45]

Nevertheless, the court viewed all charges, such as espionage, war mongering, and boycott propaganda, as proven. Indeed the court had to apply a »liberal evaluation of evidence«: »The defendant Dietrich sent a street map of Plauen to the Bible House in Magdeburg on which the group territories and the boundaries of the sect had been marked. The defendant Albert had sent reports and letters, mentioned in actual depositions, to Magdeburg. In these reports, he mentioned the names of important persons in the city of Plauen. We may assume that the other reports by this defendant to Magdeburg, whose contents he can no longer recall, also contained important statements about other ›incidents,‹ faithful to his secret espionage instructions. The importance of what these two defendants have done can only be understood if one realizes the role that the United States plays in world politics at the present time. Every specific detail about persons, buildings of all kinds, companies, streets, and organizations are like pieces of a mosaic, which, when put together, form a very precise picture of the economic and political condition of the German Democratic Republic, and of its personnel.«[46]

This meant that even the organization of Witness groups in the Plauen region was considered a state secret, and its transmission was considered to be espionage for the West. The delivery of such information to the West could, however, not be proven. Also the penalty assigned clearly showed that the sentence was not based on the specific behavior of the defendants, but that merely belonging to the religious organization of Jehovah's Witnesses was sufficient justification for severe punishment. Even basic legal precepts were altered: »In determining the sentence, the court took into consideration the public danger of each defendant's crime and the global consequences of these deeds. It would be erroneous to assess individual deeds without taking world affairs into consideration. Based on these considerations, specific deterrence should be rejected and general deterrence applied. Furthermore, when considering such dangerous acts as those committed by the defendants, in case of doubt the generally accepted principle is: ›When in doubt, favor the defendant.‹ This should be replaced by: ›When in doubt, favor progressive and peace-loving humanity as a whole.‹«[47]

Furthermore, the remarks of the district court were extremely direct: »It is better to punish nine defendants severely than to underestimate their actions and punish them only lightly, because this would allow a great number of their fellow believers to also become criminally liable and would sacrifice all mankind in a new imperialist war (sic), if the activities of this sect are not suppressed. The sentences were increased insofar as all defendants showed no repentance for their behavior and, faithful to their secret instructions, did not make a complete confession. To the contrary, at the main trial the defendants clearly demonstrated that they would resume and continue their activity at any time.«[48]

The defense attorney appealed this sentence for all defendants. The appeal trial took place on April 4, 1951, before the Dresden Higher Regional Court. All appeals were dismissed as being without merit.

The culmination of this wave of trials was Saxony-Anhalt. The first trial there began in mid-December; the defendants were Jehovah's Witnesses who had been arrested at the Bible House in Magdeburg. There were also convictions of Jehovah's Witnesses in East Berlin. The peculiarity in this case was that the GDR Constitution was not valid in East Berlin and therefore article 6 of the Constitution could not be used as the basis for sentences. Consequently, Jehovah's Witnesses in East Berlin could only be sentenced as warmongers and inciters of rumors under Control Council Directive 38.[49] This wave of trials became known as the »first operation against Jehovah's Witnesses.« It lasted approximately until the summer/autumn of 1951, depending on how quickly the courts sentenced individual Witnesses.

The State Security's New Methods

A decade of difficult times began for those Witnesses who had not been arrested. One consequence of the ban was that many Witnesses lost their jobs.[50] They were also denied recognition as victims of fascism, which provided pensions to all former concentration camp inmates. On the one hand, virtually all of the leading preachers, as well as those Witnesses who had already accumulated experience under the Nazi prohibitions, had been arrested and sentenced. On the other hand, many of the Witnesses who had assumed leadership in the group had only joined the Witnesses a few years earlier. Nevertheless, they continued their activity underground. They sent couriers to West Berlin to obtain magazines, such as *The Watchtower* and *Awake!*, as well as information and instructions for religious services that they then delivered to the individual groups or smaller study groups. Further, they carried out preaching activity secretly. Whoever was caught had to reckon with arrest and a long prison sentence. It was even more difficult for couriers, Jehovah's Witnesses who assumed leading functions with groups, or who served as circuit overseers. They could count on sentences of ten to fifteen years in prison.

The SED government and the State Security realized that the activities of Jehovah's Witnesses would not really be substantially suppressed by the August 1950 operation and subsequent show trials, since the *Volkspolizei* repeatedly reported about Witnesses' activities. Because of the ban, they could no longer easily determine who had assumed leadership in the individual groups. They therefore decided to infiltrate Jehovah's Witnesses with informants and confidants (known in German as *GM* or *Geheime Mitarbeiter*).[51] They had already used informants earlier, but it was now done on a much wider scale. State Security developed so-called operative proceedings (known in German as *OV* or *Operative Vorgänge*) that coordinated and directed the surveillance of individual groups. This method produced good results, since they were now in a better position to expose the leading servants, and especially the circuit servants, and have them arrested by State Security. They realized, however, that whenever a leading preacher was arrested someone else immediately took his place and that they would need substantial effort to prove his activities and have him arrested. Therefore, after 1956, the Ministry for State Security used a new tactic in their fight against the Witnesses, namely uncertainty and division: »The goal of the operation is to create insecurity and division within the sect. This is to achieve disintegration of the sect of ›JW‹ from within. These methods proved successful in certain districts so that the members are suspicious of each other.«[52]

The Ministry for State Security started to compromise certain leaders of the Witnesses before their fellow believers in order to produce uncertainty and distrust. In adddition, the Ministry for State Security tried to bring former Jehovah's Witnesses together to create a nominal opposition to this religious organization. They were to produce publications disparaging the teachings and leadership of the Witnesses. After »de-Stalinization« in 1956, the hard line policy of arrests and sentences for Jehovah's Witnesses could no longer be the only measures for persecuting the religious organization, and the GDR could no longer afford merciless persecution of religion because of foreign policy concerns. As a result, fostering internal disintegration became an even more important method for fighting Jehovah's Witnesses.

The building of the Berlin Wall on August 13, 1961, resulted in a changed situation. It is interesting that the Jehovah's Witnesses already feared, because of Khrushchev's 1958 Berlin declaration, that their supply routes to West Berlin could suddenly be cut off. For this reason, after 1959–1960, they began to make arrangements for selecting a separate leadership for East German Jehovah's Witnesses, which could go into effect in case of this event. This group was to ensure that contact with the Wiesbaden branch office and the supply of religious literature would not be interrupted. A leadership of three Jehovah's Witnesses was formed; the entire German Democratic Republic was divided into five districts, each headed by a district servant. This district servant had separate circuit servants for each individual sub-district. The Jehovah's Witnesses were therefore fully prepared when the wall was erected in 1961. Changes were also made in the distribution of literature. Since publications could no longer be easily imported from West Berlin, it was decided to start duplicating literature in East Germany. Microfilm or sample copies of the latest periodicals were brought into the GDR and then copied there. Initially, copying was done by typewriter; later, simple mimeographs were used until they were finally able to acquire their own copying and printing machines to simplify and increase the work.[53]

The ZOV »Swamp«

A few years after the wall had been built, the Ministry for State Security noticed that the Witnesses had appointed leaders in East Germany. Therefore, in March 1963, they created a new »central operational procedure,« under the pseudonym »swamp« and using the German acronym ZOV (*Zentraler Operativer Vorgang*), to discover the identity of these leaders and where they were active.[54] The goal of this operation was to liquidate the leaders, i.e., to arrest and convict them, thereby leaving the Jehovah's Witness religious organization in the GDR without direction. Until November 1965, the Ministry for State Security used informers (Unofficial Collaborators, known in German as *IM* or *Inoffizielle Mitarbeiter*) to discover the Witness leadership in the GDR. This procedure should have been completed much earlier and have led to arrests, but the inadequate results of this investigation meant that they were unable to identify the exact number of persons in the new Witness leadership. To achieve better results, the Ministry for State Security developed a new procedure. They attempted to infiltrate the Witnesses with informers, who were not to occupy simply any position in the organization, but who had been specially trained to assume leadership positions, thereby effectively penetrating the organization. This strategy worked so well, that they believed that, if existing leaders were arrested, their »Unofficial Collaborators« had a chance to move up into responsible positions and would therefore be able to control the entire organization of Jehovah's Witnesses in the GDR. Finally, on November 23, 1965, they were ready. The district authorities of the Ministry for State Security arrested seventeen leading Jehovah's Witnesses in Dresden, Erfurt, Berlin, and Halle and interrogated them for months. Eventually, pretrial investigations were compiled and eight criminal trials were held before different GDR district Courts. On July 25, 1966, this trial series began with the main trial against L., the leader of the Jehovah's Witnesses, and two co-defendants, before the Dresden District Court. The trial lasted six days. On August 5, 1966, the sentences were handed down.

L. was sentenced to twelve years in prison and the two other Witnesses each to eight years.[55] The sentence resulted from their organizational activity for maintaining the religious association, including smuggling literature and reports to the Berlin branch office of Jehovah's Witnesses about the preaching activity. The sentence was no longer based on article 6 of the Constitution, but on the criminal law amendment act of 1958. After the criminal law amendment act came into effect, sentences in the GDR were no longer based on article 6.[56]

On December 22, 1966, the last verdicts in this trial series were issued by the Halle District Court against three Jehovah's Witnesses, who were sentenced to from five to ten years in prison.[57]

Disintegration

After the leading Witness members had been arrested, the Ministry for State Security issued new work orders for the ZOV »swamp,« specifying new methods for dealing with Jehovah's Witnesses.[58] When dealing with Jehovah's Witnesses, special attention was to be given to winning over new informers (Unofficial Collaborators) in responsible positions, as well as to intensifying the work of disintegration.[59] In time, the Ministry for State Security successfully infiltrated informers into responsible positions in the religious organization of Jehovah's Witnesses in the GDR and thus received extensive information about their structure and work.

Disintegration activities were intended to cut the connections between the six new leaders of Jehovah's Witnesses in the GDR and their counterparts in West Germany and America. The disintegration strategy, which had been started a few years earlier and was to discredit leading Jehovah's Witnesses in West Germany and America, was to be continued. The goal was to make the Witnesses in the GDR think that branch offices in the West were only using them, not concerned for either their interests or their well-being. The State Security deviously used former Jehovah's Witnesses, who had been visited and recruited shortly before their release from prison, and/or those who had chosen to turn away from Jehovah's Witnesses. They promised them special positions or advantages in the GDR. The recruitment of such individuals was necessary, since only these individuals had special knowledge about the teachings and principles of Jehovah's Witnesses. The Ministry for State Security knew that effective disintegration could not be successful by simply discrediting the leaders, but that a pseudo-scientific confrontation with their teachings was also necessary in order to be taken seriously by the Jehovah's Witnesses. For this purpose, the Ministry for State Security used the association »Christian Responsibility« founded in Gera.[60] Willy Müller, its director, was recruited by the Ministry for State Security during his second arrest, and in 1959 he started writing slanderous letters to Jehovah's Witnesses he knew. After »Christian Responsibility« was created, he also published his own magazine called *CV* (from the German acronym for *Christliche Verantwortung*). The Ministry for State Security never intended to create their own religious organization of Jehovah's Witnesses in the GDR. They merely wanted to foment disintegration and split off members from the religious organization of Jehovah's Witnesses. »Christian Responsibility« was administered by officers from the Ministry for State Security, and the journal *CV* had to be submitted and approved by the Ministry for State Security before it could be published. Frequently, officers at the Ministry objected to something in the magazine that had to be changed.[61] The activity of »Christian Responsibility« continued until the end of the German Democratic Republic, with a circulation of about 6,000. There is no evidence that this journal had much influence on Jehovah's Witnesses. The obvious slanderous character and poor scholarly quality of the articles achieved just the opposite, making the recipients of this journal even more determined in their beliefs. In 1970, Urania published a book that professed to be a documentation about Jehovah's Witnesses.[62] In fact this publication was the work of the State Security.[63]

As from early 1967, as a result of continuing de-Stalinization and the political situation in East Germany, Jehovah's Witnesses were no longer prosecuted before courts for their activities. Nevertheless, their preaching activities and the distribution of their literature were still viewed as hostile enterprises. After 1970, Jehovah's Witnesses caught preaching were penalized with a fine according to the administrative offense law. In 1975, a law relating to associations was drafted and administrative fines were based on this law.[64] This specified that an individual Witness was active on behalf of an unregistered and therefore prohibited association, and had therefore violated the law relating to associations. The administrative fines of about 200–300 Marks increased if the Witness was detected preaching for the second or third time. This procedure, using administrative fines, lasted until the end of the GDR in 1989.

It is interesting that many of the affected Jehovah's Witnesses considered this form of persecution in the 1970s and 1980s to be onerous. This feeling resulted from the awareness of being under constant surveillance and from the subliminal threat. During these years Jehovah's Witnesses assumed that they were constantly being watched by State Security. This particular tactic was used by State Security officers during discussions with Jehovah's Witnesses, who were to have the impression of being constantly observed. Furthermore, they did not know by whom they were being watched. It could be by an unknown member of the Ministry for State Security, a neighbor, a colleague at work, or an infiltrated informer claiming to be a fellow believer. This constant distrust against everyone was meant to completely isolate and exclude Jehovah's Witnesses socially. It would thus be wrong to claim that there was no further persecution of Jehovah's Witnesses during the 1970s and 1980s. And no one knew whether the situation in the GDR would again become worse.[65]

Military Service

A further aspect of the persecution of Jehovah's Witnesses appeared on January 24, 1962, when military conscription was introduced,[66] and increased when beginning on September 7, 1964, military service could be performed in so-called construction units.[67] With this arrangement, the party and state leadership thought they had made enough concessions for those who refused military service for religious reasons. Since service in these construction units was under military control, this did not establish an alternative for Jehovah's Witnesses. Therefore, there were large numbers of arrests and convictions of young Jehovah's Witnesses every May and November, the usual dates for each year military conscription. As a result of their attitude towards war, Jehovah's Witnesses did not accept military service and therefore they were punished for their refusal to serve. This began shortly after the Military Service Law was enacted. Jehovah's Witnesses were usually sentenced to one year and eight months in prison. Moreover, if they had served earlier and subsequently become Jehovah's Witnesses, they could be drafted in the reserves. A Witness who refused to serve in the reserves was usually sentenced to six months in prison. Criminal prosecution against Jehovah's Witnesses changed only in 1986, and thereafter they were no longer punished for refusal of military service. The state continued to try to draft them, but the authorities did not react when they did not report for conscription.

Recognition

In 1989 after the reunification of Germany (the *Wende*), the new GDR government reconsidered the religious association of Jehovah's Witnesses. They recognized that the persecution and ban of Jehovah's Witnesses in the GDR had not been justified. Therefore, the GDR government decided to recognize the Jehovah's Witnesses and confirmed this recognition on March 3, 1990. From this date, the Jehovah's Witnesses religious association was again permitted and recognized for the short time the GDR still existed.[68]

Conclusion

It must be said that the persecution of Jehovah's Witnesses was pursued with great intensity in the German Democratic Republic. This persecution was conducted by using various methods during the whole existence of the GDR. According to our information, about 4,000 Witnesses were sentenced to prison terms, fifteen of them to life imprisonment. An additional 1,000 were in pre-trial detention. About 300 Witnesses suffered imprisonment under both the Nazis and the East Germans. Fifty-eight Witnesses died in prison, some shortly after their »early« release from prison.[69] This early release was to avoid their dying in prison, thereby possibly damaging the reputation of the GDR prison system. The reason for the persecution of Jehovah's Witnesses was their wish not to be involved in politics. The GDR, however, announced: »We are not persecuting the practice of religion, but religion must not be used for purposes hostile to the State.« Neutrality to political reconstruction or compulsory military service was considered hostile to the State. The fact that the headquarters of the Jehovah's Witnesses was in the United States, »the main enemy of socialist reconstruction and world peace,« was in itself considered hostile to the state. Therefore, Jehovah's Witnesses were automatically considered to be in the camp of »monopoly capitalists« and »war provocateurs.«

The special situation of Jehovah's Witnesses as a victim group is currently recognized by the application of the Law for the Compensation of SED Injustice (*Unrechtsbereinigungsgesetz*); this law enables people who were sentenced and imprisoned for political reasons in the GDR to be rehabilitated and financially compensated. Jehovah's Witnesses who were punished because of their practice of religion or because of their refusal to serve in the military, are rehabilitated today without question. In order to be granted rehabilitation, it is enough to prove that they were sentenced as Jehovah's Witnesses in the GDR. The situation is completely different for the former perpetrators, such as judges and prosecutors. If preliminary investigations or indictments are not terminated because the statute of limitations, there is nearly always an acquittal. It is claimed that premeditated perversion of justice cannot be proved with certainty. Set in the values and ideology of the time, judges and prosecutors are said to have had no option.[70] This reasoning is not convincing, especially when everyone could clearly see that Jehovah's Witnesses, when they preached about the intervention by God on Judgement Day, were not war agitators. It is equally clear that, when they made small maps marking the streets in which to preach, they were not committing espionage. All courts ignored the fact that none of the Jehovah's Witnesses wanted to bring about political change or overthrow the state, much less betray it to the »imperialists.« How easily legal indifference can blur knowledge about the horrors of persecution!

After the mid-1960s, the SED wanted to stop public persecution of Jehovah's Witnesses, so that international attention would disregard the fate of Jehovah's Witnesses in the GDR. In fact it proved to be true that the numerous arrests of Jehovah's Witnesses in the GDR attracted lots of attention, making them martyrs in the Federal Republic of Germany.[71] Also, East German authorities never managed to disband the organization. Without attracting much attention, they only punished the innocent practice of faith, such as preaching or holding meetings. It can actually be proven that the persecution of Jehovah's Witnesses in the GDR was forgotten. Moreover, the Federal Republic took a new direction in their dealings with the GDR, not constantly pointing to ongoing injustices, giving such things less emphasis, in order not to endanger the peaceful coexistence. Therefore, the persecution of Jehovah's Witnesses in the GDR has become a virtually unknown history.

It is crucial that the special history of Jehovah's Witnesses in the GDR be rescued from oblivion and it will be interesting to see whether the forgotten history of Jehovah's Witnesses in the GDR can be brought back into public awareness.[72]

Notes

1   *Berliner Zeitung* (May 26, 1964) states that Fritz Stieler served 22 years in prison and Wilhelm Engel spent 23 years in prison.

2   See, for example, Walter Bartel and Stefan Heymann, eds., *Konzentrationslager Buchenwald: Bericht des Internationalen Lagerkomitees* (Weimar, 1949), v. 1: »On July 27, the first 91 political prisoners, including 7 Bible Students arrived from Sachenhausen concentration camp.« (p. 14) »In 1934, the Bible Students protested the ban on their activity, sending 20,000 protest telegrams directly to Hitler. This resulted in the arrest of their functionaries at Magdeburg in the autumn of 1934. There were continuous arrests from this time until the main action in 1936. The first Bible Students arrived with the first prisoners in Buchenwald. Until the autumn of 1938, their number had increased to 450. They had to spend hard years and the penal work crew, created in 1937, consisted mostly of ›blue circles,‹ as they were then called, because their clothing was marked by big blue circles. Their main work consisted of carrying stones and they were usually assigned

to perform the heaviest jobs. The Bible Students' behavior was anti-fascist the entire time, even though some outsiders occasionally caused problems for the prisoner functionaries managing the camp.« (pp. 136f.)

See also Fritz Sigl, *Todeslager Sachsenhausen: Ein Dokumentarbericht vom Sachsenhausen-Prozeß* (East Berlin, 1948). »The former prisoner Bruno Roer, who had been imprisoned in Sachsenhausen as a member of the International Association of Consequent (sic) Bible Students, testified, ›When I came to Sachsenhausen in 1937, there were already 20 prisoners incarcerated there because of their religious convictions. Later, after 1938 and 1939, there were 500 prisoners. Conditions were considerably worse for us than for the other prisoners incarcerated in the camp. From 1938 until 1942, more than 200 prisoners incarcerated for their religious beliefs died in the barracks.‹« (pp. 42f.)

3 See Olaf Groehler, »Der Umgang mit dem Holocaust in der DDR,« in: Rolf Steininger, ed., *Der Umgang mit dem Holocaust* (Vienna, 1994), pp. 233f.

4 Wachturm Bibel- und Traktat-Gesellschaft (Watchtower Bible and Tract Society), »An alle Verkündiger der Theokratie« (Brooklyn, NY, 1946), p. 3.

5 Bundesarchiv Berlin (hereafter BAB): Record Group 11, Ministry of the Interior, Hauptverwaltung Deutsche Volkspolizei 860, pp. 150ff.

6 Amtsgericht Magdeburg, Vereinsregister No. 819, September 24, 1945.

7 Wachtturm-Gesellschaft, History Archive: O-Doc. 13/10/45.

8 In January 1946, there were only 3,655 Jehovah's Witnesses. Already in March 1947, there were 6,315 Witnesses and in April 1948, this increased to 13,094. In April 1949, there were 17,264 and shortly before the ban, 23,220 individuals had joined the Jehovah's Witnesses. Statistics based on monthly *Informator*, the internal newsletter of Jehovah's Witnesses in Germany.

9 *Das Potsdamer Abkommen* (East Berlin, Staatsverlag, 1984), pp. 182, 187. In paragraph III. A., point 10, it states: »The freedom of speech, press, and religion is granted, taking into consideration the requirement of upholding military security. Religious organizations are to be respected.«

10 Colonel Tulpanow headed the SMAD department of propaganda and censorship, later the information department.

11 Wachtturm-Gesellschaft, History Archive: O-Doc. 24/6/47.

12 See *1974 Yearbook of Jehovah's Witnesses*, p. 222: »Presenting this document at places where interferences occured helped in some instances, but other officials seemed to feel that the headquarters was far away and that they were their own lords.«

13 Notice of punishment issued by Freiberg district police, Sa(xony), Reg. No. 09.03/1/47 A/H, dated October 24, 1947, UaP; document in author's collection.

14 For example: The federal official for records of the State Security Service of the former German Democratic Republic (hereafter BStU), Ministry for State Security (MfS), Allg. P (Leipzig) 501/63 vol. 5, p. 63. The Leipzig information office requested the field service on April 4, 1946: »An association with the name ›Jehovah‹ is supposedly conducting services or religious meetings in Leipzig. It could also be an association which has Jehovah as a part of a longer organization name. In general, it must be discussed how activities of religious organizations take place.«

15 Staatsarchiv Dresden: Record Group MinPräs. No. 1355, p. 214.

16 Staatsarchiv Dresden: Record Group MdI No. 235, p. 7: At the end of May 1948, the Annaberg district reported about the Jehovah's Witnesses: »They do not participate in the democratic reconstruction and refuse any political participation. During the petition for a referendum, they not only did not sign up, but also opposed the referendum. In their house to house propaganda, they untiringly visited every household and family.«

17 BStU, MfS Central Archive: Allg. S 726/67, p. 7: On September 22, 1948, Bruno Haid, then a member of the SED central secretariat, personnel department, wrote to the vice-president of the German Administration of the Interior (German: DVdI) Erich Mielke, requesting all material about the activities of religious sects (Jehovah's Witnesses) and all political agitation by the church.

18 BStU, MfS Central Archive: Allg. S 726/67, p. 19: On December 6, 1948, the head of Thuringia's Department K 5 reported that »although incoming reports allow us to establish that the meetings themselves do not contain anti-democratic propaganda, it is nevertheless clear that this sect's negative view of all public issues, means that those being wooed – and these are not simply elderly women, but usually members of the working population – will be lost for our tasks.«

19 BAB: DY30 IV 2/2/44, SED Central Committee, Politburo decisions, Politburo meeting on September 13, 1949.

20 Ibid., attachment No. 2.

21 *Neues Deutschland*, September 16, 1949. The author of this article, Stefan Heymann, was a member of the state and national board of directors of VVN; he had earlier recognized the fate of Jehovah's Witnesses in Nazi Germany and praised their antifascist behavior (see note 2).

22 »Agenten des amerikanischen Monopolkapitals am Werk,« *Thüringer Volk*, February 2, 1950.

23 BStU, MfS Central Archive: AU 477/59, vol. 12, pp. 25f.: For example, the *Volkspolizei* closing of the circuit assembly in Elsterverda at the beginning of July 1950.

24 BStU, MfS Central Archive: AU 477/59, vol. 12, p. 3. After it became known, on July 29, 1950, the Post Ministry ordered that this letter was not to be forwarded, but should instead be confiscated.

25 Some reports estimated more than double the actual number of Witnesses.

26 »Die Sekte der Zeugen Jehovas: eine Agentur des amerikanischen Spionagedienstes,« *Trybuna Ludu*, June 29, 1950.

27 BStU, MfS Central Archive: HA XX/4 825, p. 46: By the end of 1950, there were more than 800 arrests.

28 BAB: HVDVP no. 860, pp. 158ff: Report by Paulsen, director of the *Volkspolizei* in Saxony-Anhalt, to the central administration of the German *Volkspolizei*, September 2, 1950. Paulsen could only refer to the statements of the State Security, since the *Volkspolizei* was not involved in the entire operation: »Under the responsible leadership of the State Security, without notifying the LBdVP (state *Volkspolizei* officials), me, or my deputy, the offices of the Watchtower Society in Magdeburg were occupied by members of the State Security on August 30, 1950, at 4 a.m.«

29 Wachtturm-Gesellschaft, History Archive: O-Doc. 31/8/50.

30 Some Witnesses, such as Erich Poppe from Meißen, even died as a result of mistreatment during pre-trial detention by the State Security. Usually the MfS utilized psychological attrition. For example, the light was left on overnight in prisoner cells. Nightly controls were constantly carried out, so that prisoners could not sleep. They would be interrogated at night, until shortly before morning roll-call. They then would be returned to their cells. Their bed, however, would be folded back and locked. It was strictly forbidden to sleep during the day; the explanation for this was that prisoners should have time to consider their crimes. In this way they wanted completely to break the prisoners psychologically. When the Witness Hildegard Heinsdorff was arrested in Brandenburg on August 30, 1950, they considered her especially dangerous because she had been employed by the state administration, and she was therefore confined for six months during preliminary investigation in an unlighted cell.

31 For example, the article »Propagandisten des Krieges,« *Neue Zeit*, August 26, 1950, reported: »We believe that in the entire religious history of mankind, there have never been such ›preachers‹ who have agitated so ruthlessly for war. This agitation appears especially ruthless, when it is done as openly as in our Republic.« An article »Apostel des Untergangs,« *Berliner Zeitung*, August 26, 1950, mentioned: »The activities of ›Jehovah's Witnesses‹ unrestrictedly serve the enemies of our democracy and are busy accumulating victims for the American imperialistic war of atomic extermination, who desire suicidal doom. Their extensive literature comes from the American zone and their sources of money are to be found in the United States. The leaders and instigators of this religiously embellished organization are enemies of mankind, and our own safety demands that we take this into account.«

32 »Zeugen Jehovas verboten,« *Neues Deutschland*, September 5, 1950, B, 207; »Jehovas Zeugen verboten,« *Landeszeitung Schwerin*, September 5, 1950; and »Jehovas Zeugen verboten,« *Neue Zeit*, September 5, 1950.

33 This is why September 4, 1950, is usually given as the date when Jehovah's Witnesses had been banned in the GDR.

34 Kontrollratsdirektive (hereafter KD) 38, October 12, 1946, in *Zentralverordnungsblatt* (1947), pp. 203ff.

35 KD 38, paragraph II, Article III A III, specified that: »Whoever had endangered or is still endangering the peace of the German people or world peace after May 8, 1945, by means of propaganda for National Socialism or militarism or by inventing and spreading tendentious rumors, is considered an activist.«

36 Some Witnesses received a court appointed defense counsel shortly before the main trial.

37 There is no evidence who made this decision in existing sources.

38 BStU, MfS Central Archive: AU 477/59, vol. 1, no page number.

39 Ibid.

40 Sentence by Supreme Court of the GDR, October 4, 1950, Az: 1 Zst. (I) 3/50, printed in *Neue Justiz* (1950), pp. 452ff.

41 Article 6, systematically incorporated into the second paragraph of the second part of the 1949 Constitution, is entitled »the rights of citizens« and stipulated that:

»1. All citizens are equal before the law.

2. Boycott agitation against democratic institutions and organizations, agitation for murder against democratic politicians, display of religious, racial or national hatred, military propaganda as well as war propaganda and all other actions which are directed against equality, are considered crimes in the Criminal Code. Democratic rights under the Constitution do not include propaganda for boycotts.

3. Whoever is punished because of this crime, cannot be employed in public service nor hold leading positions in commercial and cultural life. He loses the right to vote or be elected.«

42 This expedient was necessary because the Allies had invalidated existing (Nazi) espionage laws.

43 *Landgerichte* (regional courts) were subsequently renamed *Bezirksgerichte* (district courts). It is difficult to find equivalent Anglo-American court designations that make this distinction clear.

44 Urteil Landgericht Zwickau: Az: 4 gr. 13/50.

45 Ibid., p. 10.

46 Ibid., p. 15.

47 Ibid., p. 16.

48 Ibid.

49 See for example, Urteil des Landesgerichts Berlin, December 22, 1950, Az: 35 PKMs 50.50. Both defendants were sentenced to five and six years imprisonment only on the basis of Control Council Directive 38. See note 27.

50 For example, Stern Radio in Leipzig dismissed the Witness Georg Br. on October 10, 1950, on the following grounds: »Your undemocratic behavior forces us to terminate your employment immediately.« In this case undemocratic meant not participating in elections and not voting.

51 See Ministry for State Security (MfS) instructions No. 1/51/V from Erich Mielke, dated January 9, 1951: »It is only possible to find the leading functionaries and most dangerous agents of this sect if emphasis is placed on recruiting GM [secret confidants] and informants with the right perspectives.« Quoted in: Gerhard Besier, *Pfarrer, Christen und Katholiken* (Neukirchen, 1992), pp. 150f.

52 BAB: DY 30 IV 2/14/250, p. 281.

53 Information by Johannes Wrobel, Wachtturm-Gesellschaft, History Archive, Selters/Ts.

54 BStU, MfS Central Archive: AOP 15388/89, vol. 1.

55 Urteil Bezirksgericht Dresden, August 5, 1966, Az.: 1 BS 17/1966.

56 The sentence was for continued common transfer of information under § 15 Strafrechtsergänzungsgesetz (hereafter StEG) and ongoing coordinated propaganda and agitation activities endangering the state according to § 19 I, subsection 1 and 2, and II, III StEG in conjunction with § 47 and 73 of the penal code.

57 Urteil Bezirksgericht Halle, December 22, 1966, Az.: 1 Bs 11/66.

58 BStU, MfS Central Archive: AOP 15388/89, vol. V, pp. 6ff.

59 Ibid., p. 4.

60 Ibid., p. 7.

61 See Andreas Fincke, »Zwischen Widerstand, Ergebenheit und diplomatischem Lavieren,« in: *Materialdienst der Evangelischen Zentrale für Weltanschauungsfragen (EZW)* no. 8 (Stuttgart, 1994), pp. 217ff; Klaus-Dieter Pape, »Wie entstand die Zeitschrift ›Christliche Verantwortung‹ in der DDR?« in: *Materialdienst* no. 1 (1995), pp. 18ff; and Falko Schilling, »Zur Zeitschrift ›Christliche Verantwortung‹,« in: *Materialdienst* no. 4 (1995), pp. 121f.

62 Manfred Gebhard, ed., *Die Zeugen Jehovas* (Berlin, 1970).

63 Gerhard Besier and Stephan Wolf, eds., *Pfarrer, Christen und Katholiken* (Neukrichen, 1992), p. 84. The MfS archives were used in this study.

64 Decree about the creation and activities of associations, November 16, 1975, *DDR Gesetzblatt* (1975), Part I, p. 723.

65 During the ban, Martin Jahn, one of the Jehovah's Witnesses, conducted a number of training courses (the so-called Kingdom Ministry Schools) for leading preachers of Jehovah's Witnesses in the Chemnitz region. Subsequently, a fine of 1,000 marks was imposed upon him. He noted: »The freedom of those with responsibilities in the congregations was greatly curtailed because of continued surveillance. We found that the constant surveillance was a great psychological burden, even though the MfS did not step in. We also knew that we were listened in on, so we constantly had to watch what we would say in our homes. It was especially difficult to explain this to our children. In our preaching work, we no longer had to worry constantly about being arrested or receiving a fine. During the years before the reunification of Germany, we had heard that specific camps were being built for the incarceration of political and religious enemies.«

66 *DDR Gesetzblatt* (1962), Part I, p. 2.

67 *DDR Gesetzblatt* (1964), Part I, p. 129.

68 Wachtturm-Gesellschaft, History Archive: O-Doc. 3/3/90.

69 Information provided by Johannes Wrobel, Wachtturm-Gesellschaft, History Archive, Selters/Ts.

70 For example, the sentence by the German Federal Supreme Court on November 16, 1995, Az.: 5 StR 747/94, p. 20: »The values of the GDR at the time the acts were committed are decisive for determining whether it was an unbearable arbitrary deed.«

71 Gerhard Finn, *Die politischen Häftlinge der Sowjetzone 1945-1959* (Pfaffenhofen, 1960), p. 90.

72 It is important to realize that it is rather late to achieve this. Moreover, the passage of time has created a *fait accompli*. The few survivors of the large show trials of the 1950s are mostly in their 70s today, and were then young men about 20 years old. The leading Witnesses of that time have long since died.

Göran Westphal

The Persecution of Jehovah's Witnesses in Weimar, 1945–1990[1]

Jehovah's Witnesses were not recognized as a religious association in the German Democratic Republic. After the war and the end of National Socialism, they hoped to be able to practice their religion freely, and because of their experiences during the war, to proclaim their beliefs more convincingly. Yet, even before the GDR was created, they were under government surveillance and disadvantaged compared to other religious groups. Almost as long as the GDR lasted, the practice of religion was forbidden. Despite the constitutionally guaranteed rights of freedom of religion, in October 1949, almost a year after the founding of the East German State, all activities by Jehovah's Witnesses were prohibited. In the years thereafter many members in responsible positions were arrested and sentenced to long terms of imprisonment. Subsequently, although open persecution against Jehovah's Witnesses stopped, they still, for example, had to contend with employment disadvantages. It was only in March 1990 that the ban was lifted by the Council of Ministers of the German Democratic Republic and Jehovah's Witnesses were recognized as a religion.[2]

Despite the ban, Weimar, compared with other cities, had a large number of Jehovah's Witnesses, who maintained their convictions and, corresponding to their beliefs, organized their ministry between open activity and underground illegality. After the ban in 1950, Jehovah's Witnesses were rarely the subject of public debate in the GDR, although there were a few private conversations about encounters with them. Even religious newspapers seldom mentioned them.[3] The public in general took no notice of this group. Even since the political change, public opinion has been influenced by limited knowledge, apathy, prejudice, or incorrect and biased media presentations.

The Jehovah's Witnesses who have lived in Weimar in the years since the war, and who can remember details, are becoming elderly. Therefore, I wanted to collect their life stories, events, and experiences, and to document the unique situation of this small but active religious organization during their ban.

1945–1950: From Newly Regained Freedom to Renewed Ban

On April 11, 1945, with the liberation of the Buchenwald concentration camp, 250 Jehovah's Witnesses left the camp along with the other prisoners. Karl Noske,[4] Ernst Georg Pietzko,[5] and Anton Baumeister[6] were among them. After their liberation, they lived in Weimar and began to rebuild the Weimar congregation. The family of Karl Noske had already moved there shortly after his imprisonment. One of the Jehovah's Witnesses who had resettled in Weimar described the situation after the war: »There was a sigh of relief after the war, and we believed that the Bible Students, as they were then known, were now free and that we could finally behave accordingly. But in retrospect we discovered that this was only short-lived from 1945 to 1950.«[7]

Aware of the urgency of their proclamation, some zealous Jehovah's Witnesses were not always very tactful in their preaching work in a few isolated instances.[8] In November 1945,

August H., returned to Weimar from imprisonment in Russia. Sometime later, his wife joined him there. He was a refugee from present-day Czechia. During World War II while in the military, he left the Catholic church because of his disappointment with it. August H., now 81 years old, wrote in his memoirs about his first years in Weimar: »For a while we lived in the Bodelschwingstraße, then in Belvederer Allee. There we came into contact with Jehovah's Witnesses through their preaching work. One brother was Anton Baumeister, who had been in the Buchenwald concentration camp, and another brother was Wilhelm Timm. Both have unfortunately meanwhile died. At my job, I met Brother Robert Peters who conducted a Bible study with us. Also present were Brother Hupel and his wife, and we took turns having the study in their home and ours. We were baptized at the last convention in Arnstadt in 1950.«[9]

Robert Peters, who with his wife and three children came as a refugee to Weimar at the beginning of 1946, later recalled in a letter to his son Manfred Peters that the congregation was made up of nine evangelists.[10] As a result of increased preaching and conducting Bible studies during the years 1945-1950, the number of evangelists grew quickly. There were about 60–70 active Witnesses in 1950. Although a police surveillance report from February 1950 estimated the membership as high as 800, according to information given by one of the »Members of the Board of the sect,« this was not accurate.[11]

The firmly organized group had difficulty in finding places for congregation meetings. As the public was invited to lectures, the locations had to provide adequate seating for many people. At first Jehovah's Witnesses were able to meet in the restaurants »Felsenkeller« in Humboldtstrasse and »Schwanseebad,« then in the »Birkenhaus« restaurant in Leibnizalee, later at the »Lagerbierhalle« at Herderplatz, where seating for 200 people was available, and finally in a room at Ackerwand.

An excerpt from a speech by Manfred Peters explains how preaching was prepared and the preaching work organized: »It was very exciting for the brothers when the Theocratic Ministry School was introduced. It was then still known as the ›Course in Theocratic Ministry.‹ Only brothers were enrolled in the school, which aimed to train them as capable public speakers. The whole congregation felt for such young brothers as Rolf or Peter Brüggemeier, or Albert Lehmann, when they delivered their first short talk. Brother Anton Baumeister as school overseer insisted on compliance with time limits. He was a very capable speaker, as he had used his eight years in a concentration camp to learn how to present precious truths effectively. With determination, he walked up on stage and firmly ordered ›time up‹ after six minutes.«

The result of this instruction was evident: Regularly on early Sunday mornings in summer, preaching took place in surrounding towns. On foot, bicycle, or, if possible, by bus, the evangelists went to Buttelstedt or Gaberndorf. They had already in advance rented a room in an inn to hold a public lecture in the afternoon. This was announced publicly and by personal invitation. Two brothers requested the town crier's bell from the mayor, as well as permission to announce the lecture with a loud voice. Many interested persons came.[12]

Most of those who came to the talks were refugees from former eastern regions of Germany. A police report from February 1950 confirmed this: »Eighty percent of those present at the meetings were new citizens.«[13] Earlier generations of families or individuals active in today's congregations, namely H., Hupel, Wermuth, and Timm, were refugees. Mario Wermuth, for example, is a third generation Jehovah's Witness. His paternal grandparents came from Silesia, the maternal grandparents from Königsberg. They had their first contact with Jehovah's Witnesses in Weimar: »Jehovah's Witnesses rang at my grandparents' door. Soon thereafter, my grandparents visited the congregation for the first time and were suspicious, since no collection plates were passed around. Even before the ban, they regularly went to the Witnesses.«[14]

The Soviet Military Administration in Germany (SMAD) initially accommodated the requests of Jehovah's Witnesses,[15] but soon became leery of independent churches and sects. They were not used to handling numerous religious groups and had difficulties in differentiating between them. Their relationship with Jehovah's Witnesses was especially difficult. The Soviet Military Government was aware that this religious group had been persecuted in fascist Germany and that many of its members had been imprisoned in concentration camps. After the war the SMAD recognized their organization and gave them the status of a non-profit organization.[16] Former concentration camp prisoners were recognized as victims of the Nazi regime, entitling them to an additional pension. Nevertheless, Jehovah's Witnesses were still disadvantaged. In part, Catholic and Protestant churches, concerned about their own relationship with the SMAD, added to the mistrust against other religious groups by pointing out that Witness beliefs deviated from the Bible. Rolf Brüggemeier wrote about this in an unpublished letter to the editor of the CDU newspaper *Thüringer Tageblatt* on August 29, 1950: »As long as we Jehovah's Witnesses still had to inform the Russian authorities about our gatherings, we often heard, not only here in Weimar, but also in other cities: ›You good, you know there is a God, but pastor not know, pastor always make politics, pastor write piles of letters and criticize you.‹ If today we do not have the same favorable relationships with German democratic authorities, we know quite well that the same Pharisees have once again been involved.«[17]

The churches were consulted by the authorities, to a certain extent, on how to deal with religious groups. The efforts of the German branch of the Watchtower Society in Magdeburg, to secure a fair position for full-time ministers regarding food rations, are confirmed by an extensive correspondence with various Thuringian officials in 1946 and 1947.[18] Only in Thuringia, ministers of the Jehovah's Witnesses did not have the same status for food rations as did the official clergy of the two major churches, who received level three food stamps for workers. The Protestant consistory of the church province of Saxony in Magdeburg was asked to comment about this. In their response, they challenged the presentation of the Watchtower Society regarding the limited range of services of Protestant pastors, nevertheless, they refused to estimate the extent of service by ministers of the Watchtower Society.[19] On February 24, 1948, the executive department for church matters of the Thuringian Minister President's office sent the state church council in Eisenach a »register of all sects and independent churches in the state of Thuringia.« It did not include either an address or activities of the Jehovah's Witnesses in Weimar.[20] In April 1948, the state government requested the Protestant church to support it when dealing with applications of religious organizations to be recognized by the government. The Regional Church Council replied that it had no knowledge about the »extent or importance of different sects,« and pointed to the jurisdiction of the state for recognizing religious communities. In summary, the church resisted state attempts to utilize it against the Watchtower Society and to a large extent it withdrew and made neutral statements.

In June 1948, the presidential department of the state of Thuringia requested the German branch of Jehovah's Witnesses in Magdeburg to submit its statute and a report about the number of members. As requested, the branch office sent the state government its organization statute as well as a »report about the development of the organization of Jehovah's Witnesses dedicated to the service of God in Germany after the Nazi period.«[21] The report provided the following information about the development of the organization in East Germany: »On October 31, 1946, the number of local congregations in the Russian Zone including Berlin was 368. The number of evangelical preachers increased to 5,000 in the eastern zone and 7,800 in the three western zones, or a total of 12,800. On October 31, 1947, there were 9,200 active ministers in 522 groups ... in the eastern zone. On May 31, 1948, there were 12,900 ministers in 567 organized congregations.«[22]

The branch also used this report to explain its neutrality toward political decisions and its loyalty to the law, emphasizing that Jehovah's Witnesses were not enemies of Communism: »The ministry of Jehovah's Witnesses is based exclusively on the Bible and follows biblical guidelines, namely the methods of Jesus Christ and the apostles as set out in the scriptures. These are laid down in the statutes of Jehovah's Witnesses in the form of sermons, which include Bible-based talks, collective Bible study, and the house to house missionary work. ... In obedience to God's foremost law, the organization of Jehovah's Witnesses is exclusively dedicated in its service to God and consistently remains neutral regarding all worldly disputes between nations, political parties or other movements. It does not support any faction in current political questions, nor does it endorse specific political actions.«[23]

In September 1949, the Jehovah's Witnesses particularly felt the government's negative and hostile attitude when they tried to organize a gathering of 700 delegates. The written contract signed in early June by the management of the FDGB hall (Independent German Federation of Trade Unions) to rent a room was canceled. Despite the numerous and persistent efforts of Jehovah's Witnesses to find a replacement location, the meeting could not be held in Weimar. Similarly, the agreement with the German railroad administration for special trains was not fulfilled, although payments had already been made. Official memoranda from the office of the Minister President commented on this: »Two representatives of the local community of Jehovah's Witnesses, the leading one being the craftsman Robert Peters, Weimar, Cranachstr. 1, visited me regarding the following matter. According to their documents, the Weimar community of Jehovah's Witnesses had a written contract with the FDGB hall in Weimar to rent the large assembly hall on September 11, 1949, for a zone meeting of Jehovah's Witnesses (700 delegates, including guests from the west zones and foreign countries). A short while ago the management of the FDGB hall informed the community that the contract could not be kept as this hall was needed for a VVN meeting (Association of Victims of the Nazi Regime) on the same day. Mr. Peters is of the opinion that the cancellation of the contract was not legally valid. Nevertheless, a lawsuit was not in his interest, as it would not be decided before September 11, since they needed this room or other suitable facilities. Mr. Peters visited a second time to inform us that his negotiations with the city administration had been useless. Mr. Peters visited a third time to inform us that Mr. Lepin had also not been able to give a favorable response. This had been stated to him without any adequate explanation. He saw the continuing failure of his efforts as added proof that Jehovah's Witnesses are confronted by hostility and hate and are unprotected by the constitution.«[24]

As a result of these efforts, the office of the Minister President, after consulting the district police station in Weimar, made the following note on September 9, 1949: »The DVdI (German Department of the Interior) has given orders to inform Jehovah's Witnesses that their meeting is to be canceled in favor of the VVN memorial meeting. Schools as well as other public buildings are not to be made available for the events of Jehovah's Witnesses. Special trains for the transport of delegates also cannot be made available, using as justification that the transport system does not allow for this because of the harvest. We realize that Jehovah's Witnesses have already published a flyer to protest against the difficulties they have encountered in holding their zone meeting. The flyer was probably also sent to the West.«[25]

The founding of the GDR in October 1949 brought no relief to Jehovah's Witnesses. The authorities continued to keep them under surveillance as before. Jehovah's Witnesses were known by their public activities and continued to be closely observed and mistrusted. This interest in them was not as a religious group, but because they were viewed as a growing threat to the peaceful development of a democratic society and as agents of the class enemy. An internal police »report about antidemocratic, reactionary activities of religious sects, churches, and clergymen« dated February 6, 1950, stated: »The antidemocratic and reactionary activities of different sects, churches, and clergymen have experienced such an upsurge that we deem it necessary to watch them more closely than before. ... It is obvious that these religious circles have departed from the field of religion to lead an open war against the present order in line with their western instigators. ... The ›Jehovah movement‹ especially continues to expand and, although their propaganda is supposed to be politically neutral, it is continually getting more cynical and hateful. ... Therefore, it is necessary that precautions are taken to severely punish such reactionary activities.«[26]

This report described »the Bible Students as the ... strongest ... sect in Thuringia,« with 800 members in Weimar.[27] Evidently, they deliberately exaggerated the numbers, since the actual number of Jehovah's Witnesses was fewer than one tenth of that number in 1950. The report gives an exact list of names, dates of birth, addresses, and places of employment of evangelists taking the lead. It also lists meeting places.

In June 1950, the Department of Information, which was part of the Ministry of Interior, wrote: »Jehovah's Witnesses, as agents of US imperialism, are a serious political threat; intense activities by Jehovah's Witnesses after their district meeting. Around Easter, Jehovah's Witnesses held four district meetings in Thuringia. After these they greatly intensified their activities. ... Thousands of flyers in Weimar invited the public to the numerous meetings of Jehovah's Witnesses. Jehovah's Witnesses have also intensified their activities at their places of employment. A number of larger companies of the state-owned economy report that Jehovah's Witnesses do not participate in the trade union elections, although they are members of the FDGB. A large number of letters of protest were sent by leading officials of the sect to government departments and to the *Volkspolizei* (police), to voice their opinion about unconstitutional violations by the *Volkspolizei* and government.«[28]

The obstacles and drawbacks that Jehovah's Witnesses faced throughout the GDR were assuming ever greater proportions. Full-time ministers did not have the same legal status as did those from the major churches. Use of public facilities was denied, meetings for worship were either disturbed or prohibited, literature was confiscated, and Jehovah's Witnesses were dismissed from state or privately owned companies. On July 10, 1950, the Berlin office of Jehovah's Witnesses published a petition against this unjust treatment: »To the authorities, organizations, and persons in public offices.« In the name of all Jehovah's Witnesses in East Germany, it protested against the disadvantages they faced and, by quoting articles from the GDR Constitution, pointed to the unlawful behavior of the national authorities. The petition demanded in particular:

»We request immediate measures be taken to end the slanderous campaign of political and religious abuse in the press and radio against Jehovah's Witnesses.

»... that full-time ministers have ... the same legal rights and advantages as the clergy and ministers of other religious organizations ...

»... that Jehovah's Witnesses regain unrestricted equality before the law with other religious organizations, to be allowed to use schools and municipal halls ...

»... that clear and unambiguous instructions be given to the police to immediately and permanently restore freedom of religious services ...

»... to prevent further confiscation of Watchtower lectures and other Bible based literature ...

»... to prevent further dismissals of Jehovah's Witnesses from national and municipal companies, factories, etc ...

... to take all necessary steps to restore Jehovah's Witnesses to the same status in law as enjoyed by other religious organizations and their clergy and to secure equal protection of the laws for freedom of assembly, speech, press, and worship ... thereby enabling us to take the necessary steps to gain the favor of Jehovah.«[29]

Mario Wermuth remembers his grandparent's experience of an attempt by the police at that time to disturb and break up a meeting. They were able to save literature from confiscation by smuggling it out of the hall just in time.[30] In Weimar, no Jehovah's Witnesses were dismissed for religious reasons, which was the result of the disparate treatment of this religious organization by individual state governments. One pragmatic reason for this could be that most Jehovah's Witnesses were craftsmen valued as reliable workers. In his unpublished letter to the editor dated August 29, 1950, Rolf Brüggemeier wrote about this: »Jehovah's Witnesses earn their living by means of hard work, and every single company and place of employment acknowledges them to be prudent and progressive workers. Even in Weimar, on May 1st, two Witnesses were awarded a bonus.«[31]

The official propaganda increased. Different reports in the press caused party groups and trade union leadership in state-owned concerns to demand measures against activities of Jehovah's Witnesses. In a letter dated August 30, 1950, the social security office of Weimar wrote to the Thuringian state government: »The personnel of the social security office of Weimar has taken a position about Jehovah's Witnesses and have come to the unanimous conclusion that such activities hostile to the people can no longer be tolerated in the political rebuilding of our state. ... Although the constitution guarantees freedom of religion and belief, this does not apply to such elements. The activities of Jehovah's Witnesses solely serve the enemies of democracy and result in new victims to American imperialistic war preparations. ... Therefore, the personnel of the Weimar social security office demand an immediate ban.«[32]

The government of the GDR seemed to find popular approval in their further actions against this religious organization. The situation was reaching a climax. On August 30, 1950, leading Jehovah's Witnesses were arrested in the state of Thuringia. A Weimar newspaper reported about this in a small note in bold print the next day: »The Ministry for State Security advises that a number of persons disguising themselves as ›Jehovah's Witnesses‹ have been arrested, because of conducting war propaganda, supporting fomenters of war and criminal activities against peace, as well as their connections with the secret service of an imperialistic power, and because of hostile activity against the German Democratic Republic.«[33]

In Weimar, before dawn on August 30, ten men and two women were arrested. For the individuals concerned this came suddenly and unexpectedly. Among them were Robert Peters and Anton Baumeister who had already been in custody in the Buchenwald concentration camp during the Third Reich. At first their relatives received no information about their whereabouts or additional actions by the authorities, until it became known that a trial would be held in Erfurt.

In the GDR, newspaper articles were then published supporting the claim of the sect's hostile character toward the nation. More protest resolutions from the staffs of Thuringian companies were published which saw the peaceful rebuilding of their country threatened and demanded immediate action by the government: »Exposing the criminal activities of the ›Jehovah's Witnesses‹ sect, which is aimed against the German Democratic Republic and peace, has given rise to great indignation among the inhabitants of the state of Thuringia. Numerous declarations of protest and staff meetings demanded that severe measures be taken to expose agents disguised as Jehovah's Witnesses and to put an end to their activities. A protest resolution by the staff of the Henry Pels plant in Erfurt stated, among other things: The constitution guarantees every citizen of our republic the freedom of speech, freedom of the press, freedom of assembly, and freedom of religion. The policy of our government shows that the constitution has been strictly and earnestly upheld. But we are not of the opinion that the democratic freedoms are meant to lend a hand to Anglo-American imperialism. Recent months have shown that a certain agency has disguised itself under a religious cover to pursue its activities unhindered. The development and activities of Jehovah's Witnesses have recently shown that consciously among their ranks, an agency is at work against the GDR for Anglo-American imperialism. We strongly disapprove of the disguised agency among the ranks of Jehovah's Witnesses and demand that the government of the GDR take immediate measures to end their secret service activity once and for all.«[34]

Similarly, the trade union leadership at the Reich railway in Erfurt sent a statement to the Ministry of the Interior that they had observed agents of American imperialism freely pursuing their hostile activities against the nation. The laborers of the Erfurt radio and telecommunications (RFT) company, demanded that immediate measures be taken against the activities of Jehovah's Witnesses. Employers of the Blausiegel Rubber manufacturing plant in Erfurt demanded forceful intervention against the »sect« that had connections to the secret services of an imperialistic power.[35]

A climax of all state activities against this religious organization was the ban on their meetings and preaching activities. On September 5, 1950, under the headline: »Finally: Jehovah's Witnesses Banned,« the front page of the *Abendblatt* reported: »Berlin, September 4. The Department for Information advises: Based on the unanimous approval of the cabinet, Dr. Steinhoff, the Minister of the Interior of the German Democratic Republic, announced: The religious sect ›Jehovah's Witnesses‹ (Bible Students) are banned within the territory of the German Democratic Republic based on article 6(2) of the GDR Constitution. All activities of this sect or furtherance of its aims are forbidden and are liable to prosecution.«[36]

Despite increasing difficulties and disadvantages, the Weimar Jehovah's Witnesses were completely surprised by the ban. Sixty to seventy Jehovah's Witnesses in Weimar and 21,000 throughout the GDR were affected by this prohibition.

1950–1960: From Trials to Amnesty

On November 2 and 3, 1950, sixteen Thuringian Jehovah's Witnesses were placed on trial before the regional court in Erfurt.[37] The twelve defendants from Weimar were Robert Peters (locksmith), Anton Baumeister (carpenter, already imprisoned for eight years in Buchenwald concentration camp), Gottfried Mutschink (businessman), Franz Kassing (installer of heating systems), Albert Lehmann (tailor), the Hans brothers (precision mechanics), and Alfred Noske (apprentice technical draftsman), whose father had also been incarcerated in Buchenwald, Wilhelm Timm (laborer), Herbert Kunisch (skilled locksmith), Hugo Güttler (farmer), Ilse Fuchs (housewife), and Martha Rost (retired).

The *Abendblatt* reported the charges: »The defendants are accused of espionage, incitement to boycott, and war propaganda as ordered by American imperialists, of threatening the peaceful development of the German people and world peace, by agitating against the Stockholm Appeal to outlaw atomic weapons, and of their fraudulent attempts to hinder the inhabitants of the GDR from participating in elections and the fight for peace. Furthermore, they have slandered the peoples of the Soviet Union and people's democracies, thereby causing considerable harm to the progressive and peaceful development of the German people, and have threatened the security of the GDR by building an illegal organization. ... To compensate its members for their criminal behavior and gain more followers, the ›company servant‹ Peters ... has introduced imported Care packages from West Germany. ... In addition to the ›company servant‹ Peters, the defendants ... Hans Noske, Güttler, Kunisch, and Timm have above all been involved in espionage by searching out the addresses of prominent persons in office and by providing reports about state-owned companies. All defendants participated in antidemocratic slander. ... In May 1950, the ›company servant‹ Peters called for disobedience against GDR laws and regulations in a meeting of the members and agitated in a public meeting against the state's authority. Mutschink resisted inspection by the Volkspolizei, thereby hurting one of the police. ... Timm independently wrote a slanderous antidemocratic pamphlet and distributed it with the help of Kunisch.«[38]

The public was excluded from the trials. According to Manfred Peters, the assigned defense counsel displayed no effort for his clients and barely explained the procedures to them. The defendants received no written charges. They had no opportunity to defend themselves legally.[39] Their sentences were read on November 3, 1950. Their prison sentences ranged from a year in prison to fifteen years in a penitentiary.[40] Robert Peters, viewed as the leader, received the highest sentence. Gottfried Mutschink was sentenced to twelve years in a penitentiary. Hans Noske and the pensioner Martha Rost were each sentenced to one year in prison. Being under age, the 17-year-old Alfred Noske was sentenced to two years probation. A report in the *Abendblatt* stated that all defendants accepted the sentences.[41] Manfred Peters described the decision about Anton Baumeister's sentence: »Eight years in a penitentiary were proposed for Brother Anton Baumeister. In his last words he said laconically: ›Eight years are behind me and eight years are ahead of me. That's fair enough!‹ Thereafter the court retired for deliberation. He received ›only‹ six years. Evidently the communists didn't want to be equated to the Nazis.«[42]

According to Konrad Ettel, some prison and penitentiary guards who had formerly been imprisoned in concentration camps as communists, and had suffered there together with Jehovah's Witnesses, were now assigned to guard their former fellow prisoners.[43] Even Erich Honecker, who had been in the Brandenburg-Görden prison from 1937 to 1945, had gotten to know Jehovah's Witnesses there.[44]

In general, Jehovah's Witnesses reacted with »stoic understanding« to their sentences. They had the firm conviction that the GDR »wasn't going to last that long. Hitler had been in power for twelve years, and surely the communists would be less. We never asked why we were persecuted here and not in the West.«[45] Imprisonment was the climax of persecution, and in this Jehovah's Witnesses saw confirmation that biblical prophecies were being fulfilled and that they were living in the time of the end.

They had to begin serving their sentences immediately. Family members were denied access to see or speak with their relatives after they had been condemned. Manfred Peters recalls about his father's sentence: »My father was first in the Brandenburg-Görden prison, later in Bautzen. He was in solitary confinement for three years and was given no work assignment. My mother could visit him for half an hour every three months. Other visits were prohibited. My father seldom spoke about that time. Several times he was put in a bunker for owning pages of the Bible. Most of the Jehovah's Witnesses were in Brandenburg. He had no contact with them. It seemed like a reward that after three years he was allowed to work in the prison. Later he was in prison cells with others, but I do not know if they were spiritual brothers. He was treated correctly. During pretrial detention, he was interrogated under strong lights.«[46]

Robert Peters himself described the conditions of his imprisonment as far more inhumane in a letter dated April 1968 to the Association of War Disabled in Pforzheim: »First a cellar for nine prisoners, 40 cubic meters in size, no daylight, sanitary facilities and food in a catastrophic state, thereafter 13 months solitary confinement, until August 1955 = five years without physical activity on starvation rations. Then suddenly heavy manual labor, in the high temperatures of summer, exposed to the sun, unloading coal wagons, after four weeks a heart attack, later work in the laundry. In summer 1956 again unloading coal wagons, when a circular piece of wood, weighing 30 kilograms, fell on my head, during the 1958 flu epidemic? despite having a fever, I had to continue working on a milling machine for many days, since there was a complete absence of doctors and medical personnel, until one night I vomited enough blood to fill half a bowl. I have had problems with my lungs ever since.«[47]

His father's jail sentence had no negative consequences for Manfred Peters. Before the arrest, his father had been able to find him an apprenticeship as a bookbinder. Everybody in the company knew the reason for his father's arrest. During his apprenticeship, Manfred Peters was left in peace about this. His mother continued to raise him and his two sisters in the beliefs of Jehovah's Witnesses. This did not endanger her.[48]

Also August H.'s employer knew that he was a Jehovah's Witness. Before their baptism, he and his wife had formally left the Catholic Church and had not participated in elections. They had to give a statement about this. As August H. made no excuses and did not conceal his beliefs, they were known as Jehovah's Witnesses. For the same reason he left the trade union. There were disadvantages for the family when they were living four people to one room and needed a larger apartment. Although there were appropriate apartments, they had to wait for half a year before they were assigned one.[49]

After the trials, the property of the Watchtower Society was confiscated and became state-owned property throughout the GDR. An »inventory of confiscated items from the Jehovah's Witness sect« shows that, from the rented facilities of the congregation in Weimar, there were two speakers' podiums, 123 chairs of all kinds, 30 benches, and 39 items of furniture, such as lamps, curtains, and stoves.[50] The head of the department of the Office for the Protection of State-Owned Property in Weimar decided on December 15, 1950 on the disposition of these articles: »1. According to an order by the Minister of the Interior of the German Democratic Republic, the confiscated items of the ›Jehovah's Witness‹ sect are to be used as inventory for offices and furniture, as has been suggested by district administrators or mayors, which required the consent of the Minister of the Interior of the state government. Primarily state-run companies, MAS (Machine Lending Stations) with facilities for cultural activity and assembly are to be considered.

»Confiscated typewriters are to be given to administrations, social organizations, and state-owned companies.

»Cash is to be transferred to account number 170 with the National Bank in Berlin.

»Illegal publications are to be handed over to the institutions of the Ministry of State Security, or to be destroyed with their consent.«[51]

Later correspondence between authorities proves that most of the items were quite old and damaged and could seldom be reutilized. The police in Apolda filed an application to use the curtains for their rooms. There were disagreements about a typewriter confiscated in Erfurt, that the Ministry of State Security at first did not want to give it to the Erfurt city council. The 31 Pfennigs confiscated from the congregation in Suhl by State Security was forwarded in a letter to the head of the department with the explanation that it did not pay to transfer this sum to the National Bank in Berlin.[52]

The number of 60 to 70 active Witnesses in Weimar decreased as a result of the arrests. All men that had responsible positions in the congregation were under arrest. Young people who had been Jehovah's Witnesses for only a few years now had to shoulder responsibility for the congregation. The now smaller congregation was divided into study groups that met in private homes. As there were not enough qualified men, women conducted these study groups. It was difficult to regularly obtain study literature, such as *The Watchtower* published twice a month. For security reasons most Jehovah's Witnesses were not allowed to know who was responsible for this and where it came from. During the forty year ban in the GDR, each new issue of *The Watchtower* appeared regularly.

There were new arrests in Weimar from 1950 to 1952. This time, it affected Jehovah's Witnesses who had only recently assumed leadership positions and had been observed by State Security. Rolf Brüggemeier was arrested in November 1950. His brothers, Peter and Hans-Joachim, and their mother were arrested on March 14, 1951. The arrest of Peter Brüggemeier occurred in the interlude between his theoretical and practical examinations as an apprentice baker, so that he could not, at first, finish his apprenticeship. He recalled: »I went to the cellar of the State Security building in the Erich Weinert Street. The cell was three steps one way and three steps the other. I thought to myself, ›just as a criminal deserves.‹ At first I did not know why I had been arrested, as I had not been a Witness very long. They could arrest my mother and my brother Jochen only that afternoon. The interrogations were only at night. I was blinded by the light of a desk lamp and thus could not see anybody. I was also threatened with a pistol. Otherwise the treatment was actually quite fair. I was transferred to Erfurt in June. There I had a ›toilet experience,‹ the toilet paper was a firm, smooth paper used for notes just like cardboard. The trial began in August. I was only supposed to see the written indictment briefly, but totally unexpected, I managed to smuggle it to another Jehovah's Witness who was not on trial, so that ›suddenly it was just gone.‹«[53]

The indictment by the senior state attorney dated July 21, 1951, to the Erfurt Regional Court, criminal division I (consisting of three judges and two lay assessors), accused Peter Brüggemeier and his brother: »Both defendants Peter and Hans-Joachim Brüggemeier, like their mother, were proclaimers of the sect and, after its ban, responsible for one group. Moreover, they held forbidden meetings and eagerly participated in the slander of progressive, peaceful nations. The defendant Peter Brüggemeier practiced his provocative slander among his fellow workers and distributed infamous slander from western imperialism (sic!). Both hid large quantities of slanderous pamphlets to distribute among the population for purposes of agitation. They received their spiritual food from the slanderous reports of RIAS (radio in the American sector) and the western press, as well as slanderous publications from the ›Jehovah's Witness‹ headquarters in Brooklyn. ... All of the defendants are inflexible enemies of the progressive and peace-loving policy of our German Democratic Republic and the Soviet Union. They all knew that this sect was hostile to the state and, by their criminal activities, they have alienated themselves from society.«[54]

Again, after only one day in court, their convictions were read. The justification for sentencing dated August 24, 1951 stated: »They are completely suspect. From 1949 to 1951, they have continued to incite boycott against democratic institutions in Weimar and its vicinity. They further propagated hatred against nations, thereby propagadizing for National Socialism, and harmed the peace of the German people by inventing and spreading biased rumors. Despite the ban on the treasonous ›Jehovah's Witnesses‹ by the German Democratic Republic government on October 2, 1950, they illegally continued the activities of this sect and, in part, have rebuilt it, as well as importing illegal propaganda material of this sect from West Berlin after October 2, 1950. Crimes under article 6, section II, article 3, section A III of Control Council Directive 38.«[55]

Peter Brüggemeier was sentenced to six years in prison, his brother and mother each to eight years in jail. She was taken to the women's prison in Waldheim in Saxony. Peter reported about his jail sentence: »Jochen and I were sent to the prison in Untermaßfeld. I was immediately put to work. It was nice work for a shoe factory. We were three men in one cell. We slept on straw sacks, that were filled once a year. Sometimes a mouse came. Every day we were given a 20 minutes ›break.‹ The entire work unit contained Jehovah's Witnesses, there were about 40 of us. Later we were split apart to break our solidarity. This attempt was revoked when Jehovah's Witnesses discussed their beliefs with other prisoners. Nothing happened to those who obeyed the prison regulations. We were quiet like sheep. Sometimes they tried to exert pressure on us: ›Either you eat blood sausages or you get to eat nothing at all!‹ Then they cut the blood sausages into little pieces and put them into the soup, so that we wouldn't notice it. In 1952, we were transferred to Cottbus on three or four trucks and placed in large jail cells. We were supposed to build an airport there. We refused, as it was to be used for military purposes. I was there for one and a half years. It was during this time that I learned the most. Bibles were prohibited, but an older, more experienced Witness taught me many things. In Cottbus, I suddenly discovered that one of the persons who had previously interrogated me, was now a prisoner. He must have done something wrong. Then for two days I came to Mildenberg. That must have been a mistake. I was transferred to Gransee and was supposed to go by ›Grotewohl Express‹ to the prison in Bützow. This was the name of the last wagon of the train, which was reserved for prisoners. A bustling old prison guard brought me to the train station. We missed the train, since we had left too late. There were more fleas than anything else in Bützow. I also worked as a baker for two months in Brandenburg prison. On February 28, I was released, fourteen days earlier than I had expected.«[56]

August H., who had taken a leading role in the congregation after Peter Brüggemeier's arrest, recalled: »Sometime in 1951, I was appointed group servant. I had to care for 40–50 spiritual brothers. This meant that I was very busy after work to keep everything together. Of course, I was continually under Stasi surveillance. But I was already used to this because of my experiences with the Nazis. My dear wife also had much to do. We had to copy many things by typewriter, to pass it along to others. Yes, it was a very difficult time, but with the help of our heavenly Father we were able to do many things which would not have been possible otherwise. Obtaining literature was only possible with the help of Jehovah. During this time, I was on the go immediately after work, also in outskirts. We had to maintain contact with the others. There were meetings with the responsible brothers and the circuit servant.«[57]

Because of these activities for the Witnesses, August H. was also arrested. He wrote about this in his memoirs: »Then the day came when the State Security picked me up at work. The Stasi picked me up at work at three in the afternoon, one day after our wedding anniversary. It was September 26, 1952. If my wife hadn't been pregnant and if we did not have children, they would also have arrested her. This is what the State Security told me during my interrogation in Erfurt. My first interrogation took place on the day of my arrest and lasted for 12 hours, in my jail cell from six in the evening to six in the morning. I was not allowed to sleep. We were six people with a crooked bunk with just enough room for all of us. Easing nature was only possible in the cell, always light, about midnight we were allowed to go outside for ten minutes, since nobody was allowed to see us. Saturdays we could shower with cold water. Since I had been a (Soviet) prisoner of war (in the Crimea), I was already familiar with a lot of things, such as the food, and it was thus easier for me to cope with many things. ... I had been arrested without an arrest warrant. They had also searched our house without a warrant, it looked like a bomb had hit it. In the presence of our children, everything was tossed out of the closets.«[58]

August H. had to endure many humiliating interrogations, while an angry State Security officer threatened him with a gun, because he would not betray the names of his spiritual brothers. Shortly thereafter the Erfurt trials for him and other Jehovah's Witnesses took place; they had many parallels to the previous trials: »The trial occurred six months later. I was briefly able to see the written indictment shortly before my trial started. Then it was taken away from me again. The public was excluded from the trial; they were only allowed when my sentence was being read. My wife was also present. Earlier we had been told that we would be sentenced under article 6 and Control Council Directive 38. ... After my conviction, I was allowed to speak briefly with my wife in the presence of a judge. We talked about the name of the child we were expecting. They barely allowed her to discuss this with me.«[59]

The following excerpt from his memoirs shows that despite indictment and impending sentence, August H. remained unyielding and kept his humor: »During the trial, the state attorney had the judge ask me if I knew where I was. He asked and I answered: ›Yes, before the party court of the SED.‹ This was like a bomb and I was asked why I would say something like that. I replied, ›because you are wearing the big party badge.‹ I learned that they haven't worn it since then. But instead of being sentenced to seven years, I received eight years.«[60]

His wife was unable to work because of four children at home, and had to survive on 180 Marks welfare. When August H. sent her some of the money he had earned in prison, they deducted it from her welfare payment. August H. reported about an attempt to destroy the unity of the Witnesses at the Gräfentonna prison: »One day all Witnesses were taken from work at the same time and placed in one cell. They had something special planned. We were twelve brothers in one cell and they must have thought that because of overcrowding we wouldn't get along. We also had to ease nature in this cell. This was not easy, you have to learn to bear this. There was only one bucket which was emptied only once a day. Also there was no running water in the cell, only one bowl and a pitcher with water for twelve men. They watched us closely and waited for us to get into fights. Days and months passed and nothing happened.«[61]

August H. had the possibility of being released earlier, since he had reached a work quota of 130 percent. Therefore his wife filed an application for her husband's release, which was granted after he had served four and a half years of his sentence. On December 20, 1956, August H. was allowed leave the penitentiary in Bützow.

Other Jehovah's Witnesses still in prison were also released in the second half of the 1950s. However, there were also new arrests. Rolf Brüggemeier was arrested a second time in 1957 and was later expelled to the Federal Republic of Germany. After their release, Franz Kassing, Hans Noske, Hugo Güttler, and Ilse Fuchs left the German Democratic Republic. The police had recommended that they leave the GDR. For this reason some congregations in the GDR closed or were combined with other congregations.[62]

Manfred Peters' mother filed several applications for the release of her husband, but they were always refused. In 1960, he was finally and unexpectedly released from prison after ten years and three months. Manfred Peters recalled: »My mother received a telegram from him saying: ›Will arrive at 11.30 p.m.‹ We had no idea what this could mean. Just to be certain, we went to the train station and my father got off the train. He was wearing new clothes and was carrying a suitcase as if he were returning from a trip.«[63]

The reason for his early release was a partial amnesty that Walter Ulbricht promulgated on September 12, 1960, as chairman of the newly-founded state council of the GDR. Life sentences were also reduced. In general, the early releases brought Jehovah's Witnesses no relief, since they were still viewed as enemies of socialist society. Yet the accusations made for propaganda reasons, that Jehovah's Witnesses were acting for American imperialism, diminished. There were no more convictions based on incitement to boycott or preparations for war.

There were about 50 Witnesses in the Weimar congregation at the end of the 1950s.

1960–1980: Between Intimidation and Tolerance

Jehovah's Witnesses continued to be prohibited and their activities were kept under intensive surveillance by the State Security, until the political changes of 1989. The State Security had a department in their Erfurt district office solely for the surveillance of Jehovah's Witnesses. They were the only ones authorized to keep Jehovah's Witnesses under surveillance and to interrogate them. By acting independently, the police would have overstepped their authority. The charges remained of not supporting the state, possessing and distributing prohibited literature, and sending reports about their preaching activity to the Federal Republic of Germany. After 1960, Jehovah's Witnesses no longer confronted such severe persecution as before, and although the danger of new arrests continued, it had diminished. Manfred Peters described these changes in dealing with Witnesses: »In the sixties, the State Security could no longer assert that we were agents of imperialism. The public would not have believed this. Further, they could acquire all of Watchtower Society literature in the West and thus learn about our beliefs. But we were not sure. We always had to be cautious.«[64]

Because of the previous strain of persecution, about 30 Jehovah's Witnesses left the Weimar congregation and emigrated to the Federal Republic of Germany. The closing of the German internal border on August 13, 1961, therefore drastically changed the congregation's situation. Manfred Peters talked about this in his speech: »Until the building of the Berlin Wall on August 31, 1961, there was the possibility of getting quickly into the West. Afterwards, this was no longer possible. I would like to say that this was good for the congregations in the GDR, and also for the Weimar congregation. Now all the publishers remained and the congregation could develop normally.«[65]

After their release, Jehovah's Witnesses were kept under special surveillance for ten years by the State Security. They were not supposed to speak about their sentences in public. Robert Peters was not able to adjust to these precautions. In some of his conversations he carelessly spoke about his sentence. »My father went to the barber and carelessly said that it had been ten years since he had last been to a barber. Then, of course, he was asked why, and then he spoke about his long years in prison. This could have been dangerous for him. It was hard for him to understand this. Once he said: ›I was better off in the cell than I am here. There at least I could speak freely.‹ He was about 60 years old and couldn't find any work. There was nothing to hold him here any more. Before the wall was built, my father emigrated to the West.«[66]

Manfred Peters believes that people like his father were missing from the Weimar congregation. Those who had maintained their beliefs despite persecution would have been encouraging examples of unwavering faith for young people.

Young male Jehovah's Witnesses again had to show their unfailing faith, when in November 1964 they were to be inducted into the National People's Army (the GDR had introduced compulsory military service on January 24, 1962). Refusal to perform military service could be punished with a prison sentence of up to five years. In the military districts of Erfurt, Gera, and Suhl, prison sentences were usually 22 months long and were considered offenses warranting general sentencing.[67] Because he refused military service, Konrad Ettel was sentenced by the first criminal division of the Erfurt Military Court. He served his sentence from November 1973 until September 1975 in Gräfentonna and Eisenach. In the GDR, sentences varied by court jurisdiction. Konrad Ettel reported that Jehovah's Witnesses in Berlin were sentenced to fewer months. They were imprisoned together with other Witnesses to cause dissension among them. They failed to stop Jehovah's Witnesses from speaking with fellow prisoners about their beliefs and the reason for their arrest. Every prisoner had the right to request a Bible, but applications from Jehovah's Witnesses were always denied. »The Bible in the hands of Jehovah's Witnesses was viewed as worse than a gun in the hands of a criminal.«[68]

Businesses made efforts to change the views of Jehovah's Witnesses and encouraged them to participate in social activities. But finally they accepted that, for religious reasons, the Witnesses did not participate in certain social events. Others often failed to understand their determination because of the disadvantages that resulted. Jehovah's Witnesses stood up for their beliefs and their attitude as released prisoners was known in any case.

Typical experiences at their places of employment are found in Christel Timm's report. Her uncle Wilhelm Timm had been one of those sentenced in 1950: »In time my employer knew that I was one of Jehovah's Witnesses. Since I was working in a private laundry, I incurred no disadvantages. Later when I worked in a state-owned company, there were some restrictions and I received only small or no awards.«[69]

Manfred Peters reported about his experiences: »In the state-owned company, I was in a different wage group than other politically active employees. I did not belong to any party, I never participated in the May demonstration, and I received smaller bonuses. I was not promoted, but then that was not what I wanted. Maybe then, I would have become a supervisor of others, necessitating political activities. I used company possibilities to enhance my qualifications. At first I was a book binder, then a machine compositor, printer, and finally an offset printer. We always had to expect to be treated differently.«[70]

August H. wrote about State Security attempts to prevent him from speaking about his sentence and from obstructing his obtaining further job qualifications: »I had to quit my job as an auto mechanic for health reasons and I then worked in the Limona beverage combine as a mechanic. I had to write a curriculum vitae with explanatory comments for this. The bosses knew me because I had repaired their private cars. One day I received a letter from the authorities informing me that my sentence was being erased. The company must have also received a copy of the letter since they requested that I rewrite my vitae without mentioning the sentence. I then informed them I was not going to change what I had written: it stays because that is how it happened. Nonetheless, I received quite a few bonuses and I was awarded a monetary bonus as best worker. I was not allowed to take the final exam for a master craftsman's certificate, nor were my daughters allowed to do so. We were never given a reason for this refusal.«[71]

After serving his prison sentence, Peter Brüggemeier returned to a private bakery and finished his apprenticeship. The owner was very accommodating, but soon left the GDR. Then Peter Brüggemeier worked in the state-owned »Backwaren« (baked goods) company. He stated right at the start in the cadre departement, that he would not wear a May carnation nor participate in political elections, and, therefore, he did not expect to receive any bonuses. All his workmates knew his convictions. He said that he could have become production manager if he would have participated in social activities. Peter Brüggemeier worked for 20 years in this company.[72]

Konrad Ettel, who for many years was a colleague of August H., did not report any significant disadvantages at his place of employment: »After my release, the cadre department was glad that I was there again. I did not have to sign a note promising not to speak about prison events. I had to report regularly to the district military command and to the police. We were kept under constant surveillance. At first, I received fewer bonuses. Then I said: ›If there is some work to do, you know where to find me, but when it comes to bonuses, you forget me.‹ Thereafter I received bonuses.«[73]

Beginning in the mid–1960s, Jehovah's Witnesses met twice a week for their meetings. The congregation was still divided into small study groups, that studied Watchtower articles or met for the Ministry School. The infrastructure consisted of individual families to whom other Jehovah's Witnesses came. Care was taken not to disregard the ban on gatherings, so that in the beginning, six persons at most met as a group. Konrad Ettel explained: »We did not want to provoke the State Security.«[74] There were about eight to ten such groups in Weimar. The study groups met in appropriate apartments. The Brüggemeiers and Manfred Peters described how these meetings were organized and how precautionary measures were taken: »Everyone came and left inconspicuously. If study was to start at 6 p.m., for instance, the first person arrived at least one hour earlier, the others drifted in gradually. They left again, one at a time, in the same manner. We were all wearing slippers, the housewife wore an apron, and there was coffee and cake on the table. Everything was supposed to look like a private family gathering. If a stranger would ring the doorbell, we always had something on hand to hide the literature.«[75]

Three Witnesses described how they arranged the difficult procurement of »Watchtower literature« after the Berlin Wall was built:

»Yes, in part it was distributed by hand from one person to the next, but also via mail; a number of items got lost. At that time many things were copied by hand and passed on. Answers were written down because literature was to be passed on to other congregations. It was then taken to acquaintances. We always received the most important things.«[76]

»Literature was copied by typewriter or duplicated by mimeograph machine. Only those in charge knew how literature was exchanged between different congregations. Discretion was taken very seriously. Everybody wrote down answers to the study materials on a separate piece of paper. That is why study at that time was more intense than today, when notes or remarks can be written next to the text.«[77]

»In the 1970s, we had special literature. We received a thinner edition of *The Watchtower*, containing only the main articles or summaries of other articles were closely printed without illustrations. Watchtowers, copied by hand, were passed around every day.«[78]

One operation, water baptism, required complete discretion and dependability. It symbolized dedication to God and required complete immersion. Therefore it could only be done in a bathtub in an apartment. Somebody who baptized others made himself vulnerable to prosecution. For safety reasons, the baptizer came from a different city and was not known to the person to be baptized. As an identification sign, one had to give a password at the door. At baptism, only the nearest relatives could be present. Manfred Peters did these baptisms in Erfurt and did not know the individuals he baptized. He was baptized in 1954 together with four others in the Noske family bathtub.[79]

Arrangements for the annual Memorial required good organization by all Witnesses. The sacrificial death of Christ was celebrated on Nisan 14 (the Babylonian-Assyrian name for the month March/April) after sunset. This date was also known by the State Security, but they did not know where it would be celebrated and who would participate. Manfred Peters reported about this in his 1995 speech: »The annual Memorial was something the State Security did not like. In preliminary interrogations, they already warned some brothers that they would stop it. But they were not able to do this. Although the police stood in many hallways and on street corners to intimidate us, Jehovah's Witnesses met in their apartments to obediently and thankfully remember the death of their savior. We often felt like the Israelites in Egypt when they celebrated their first Passover. Afterwards they were led into freedom, and so were we!«[80]

It sometimes happened that mailmen or insurance agents, who had business near houses that were being kept under surveillance, were asked for their identification by the police. The policemen did not always know why they had to do these checkups. Jehovah's Witnesses could easily be identified in the controls, since they carried a handwritten statement in their passports saying that in case of an accident they would refuse all treatments with units of stored blood. On the day of the Memorial, Jehovah's Witnesses had to leave early and alone to avoid police controls. The Brüggemeiers reported about one year when all Witnesses in their study group could go to their apartment to attend the Memorial unhindered: »From our window, we could already see people suspiciously walking up and down our road in the afternoon. We have a big garden which at that time could still be reached through a house on a different street. That is something that the State Security had not considered. All brothers and sisters used this route to come to us. After the Memorial was finished, everybody left the house using the main entrance; the the State Security were still standing in front of our house and could not explain that.«[81]

One of the basic Witness activities is their missionary preaching work. This preaching work brought them into contact with the public, had to be organized with meticulous security. Manfred Peters and the Brüggemeiers explained the system they used:

»People were spoken to sporadically in private, for example, in every house only one family. If we saw a uniform or a phone in the hallway, this was a signal that somebody from the police or a government office lived there. Then we made excuses that we had mistakenly found an incorrect name. Otherwise, we would identify ourselves as Christians and spoke with other people about the Bible. This often resulted in nice conversations. At that time the territory assigned to each Jehovah's Witness was larger than today. For instance, in every street only two houses were called on or always the apartment on right hand side of the ground floor. It could be that at the second visit we were disappointed because the householder had already informed himself about us and knew that our activity was forbidden. We also gave an informal witness on the street, while shopping, and even at our place of work.«[82]

»We only tried to call at houses where the house numbers contained, for example, the number ›One.‹ That was important as we could easily remember where we had called before and that other Witnesses would not unintentionally call there again. We made as few notes as possible and carried no literature except for Bibles licensed in the GDR. When something seemed suspicious to us, we made excuses like: ›Somewhere in this area there is supposed to be a car for sale.‹ In those times, few came into ›the truth‹ (i.e. accepted the beliefs of Jehovah's Witnesses).«[83]

Complaints by residents who felt bothered by the Witnesses' visits were also used to further intimidate them. These individuals, however, never appeared in person nor were their addresses given. Some policemen visited by Witnesses reported them to the police.

The State Security was partially informed about public activities and meetings in homes by surveillance and interrogations. Konrad Ettel noted that the State Security certainly knew about their preaching work: »The Stasi told us what they knew. They would easily reveal, if they wanted to act against us.«[84] August H. wrote about surveillance and knowledge of the State Security: »We were kept under constant surveillance, even at home, as I found out later. There were so-called house books, in which everybody had to be registered that lived in the house, and we, as guests, also had to sign them, since visitors from a different town spending the night also had to be registered, and this was checked by the police. At times we were also watched from the street. I found out about this later. For a time I also had the house book, and then the State Security often came and asked questions about the occupants. Then I told them that I was sorry but I had no contact with them and they had to ask them directly. They left again. I got to know the State Security. Yes, they told me where I had been and when. Yes, we were practically watched around the clock, it was difficult. We always had to change meeting places.«[85]

In the interrogations, the teachings of Jehovah's Witnesses were not supposed to be discussed. The State Security was only interested in names and the structure of the organization. Manfred Peters described how such interrogations went: »I was frequently interrogated by the State Security. They came to my place of employment and asked the director to send for me and demanded a room. There, for two hours, two men interrogated me. I kept silent. We viewed Jehovah as our father, and the organization as our mother. We had the principle: We can always talk about our father, but we have to be silent about our mother. My wife was also interrogated. Or we received a postcard with a written summons to the police and there an employee of the State Security was waiting for us.«[86]

Jehovah's Witnesses were concerned about being arrested or sentenced to pay a fine during these interrogations. The Brüggemeiers told about an incident when the State Security had been able to infiltrate their study group with an informer: »In the 1970s, an approximately 30-year-old man came to our meetings. He was also baptized. He was on a disability pension and therefore could travel to the West and return with literature. He was very zealous and always wanted to go to a different study group. His conduct seemed so suspicious to us that we asked him outright: ›Are you a Stasi spy?‹ He did not deny it, but never came again.«[87]

Jehovah's Witnesses also noticed the influence of the State Security Police in securing permission for visits to the Federal Republic. Bettina Brüggemeier, who had been on disability pension since 1969, wanted to go to a convention (a gathering lasting several days, often with tens of thousands of visitors). The State Security knew when the Watchtower Society planned such conventions. Mrs. Brüggemeier received travel permission only after the convention was over. She said that sometimes she could go, and she assumed that the State Security sometimes overlooked some convention dates. In 1974, Peter Brüggemeier's firm approved his request for a trip to West Germany, in order to attend the funeral of his mother who had been living in the Federal Republic since 1959. Then the trip was not allowed in any case.[88]

Towards the end of the 1970s, Jehovah's Witnesses had a foretaste of being able to practice their religion freely, when for the first time they could hear tape recordings of large conventions. For this purpose, they would meet in two study groups in order to take advantage of this opportunity from early in the morning until late at night. In his speech, Manfred Peters remembered: »Yes, with good instructions from the organization we dared to do more. We received the tape recordings of circuit and district conventions. Then on the weekends, we would sit tightly packed, 15–20 persons in one apartment, and listen to the delicious samples of spiritual feasts provided by Jehovah. During the breaks, the sisters would show that they were good hosts by serving coffee and cake. The study directors had to refocus our attention back to the actual reason for coming together. With some, a certain tiredness set in. At other such meetings, the elders had to call on the sisters not to be so overly kind in their hospitality.«[89]

At this time, the Weimar and Apolda congregations were combined. In Apolda the women had taken the lead in the congregation since there had been no qualified men available. At the end of the 1970s about 120 Jehovah's Witnesses belonged to this growing congregation.

1980–1990: From Relief to Recognition as a Religious Organization

The relationship between the state and the Witnesses during the 1980s is best described as a »constant roller coaster.« They often considered how tolerant the State Security had become in their dealings with them. Decreasing pressure made Witnesses bolder. They assumed that the Protestant peace campaign, »swords into plowshares,« in 1982 was one of the reasons why the state was making concessions to them.

Supplying literature had become somewhat easier after the 1980s. Because of the somewhat easier travel regulations, individual Jehovah's Witnesses could travel to the Federal Republic, mostly to visit relatives. They would bring back literature from these trips, although this was frequently confiscated by border controls. Visiting fellow believers from the Federal Republic of Germany would also bring literature along with them. The Brüggemeiers can remember, in the mid-1980s, receiving a summons to the police because friends they had invited had been denied entry at the border. The police had found *The Watchtower* and other publications on them. The Brüggemeiers were threatened with arrest by the Stasi, and they considered this a real danger. Most of the time, Jehovah's Witnesses from the West had to pay a fine or were denied entry into the GDR.[90]

Konrad Ettel stated that the congregation was always »up to date« on literature. Nevertheless, they still had to continue copying this literature. He was assigned by the congregation to do this: »My predecessor, who had done this work before, moved into a newly-built apartment and could no longer copy the literature. There wasn't enough room in his new apartment to do this and there was no stove in which he could have destroyed documents in case of danger. From then on my wife and I, for many years, developed microfilms which a courier brought. We copied the ›Kingdom Ministry‹ for three congregations. Each study group had one copy. Once a month we would produce 36 copies of six pages (in DIN A 5 format, or 148 x 210 mm size). So it would not become obvious, different Witnesses would buy the required huge amount of photographic paper. I received contributions from the congregation to defray my expenses.«[91]

Mario Wermuth reported about another reason why it was important for the preaching activity to have a suitable residence: »At first I lived only in one part of an apartment. At 19 years of age, I was appointed as a book study conductor, and, therefore, had to find another apartment. This shared apartment would not have been suitable for theocratic (religious) purposes, since the neighbors would have noticed the regular meetings.«[92]

The entire Weimar congregation had no opportunity to meet regularly. For security reasons usually no more than ten persons would meet in book study groups. Jehovah's Witnesses, therefore, used family festivities such as weddings or graduations to meet in larger groups. The only possibility where all 90 Witnesses could meet freely was at funerals.[93]

The directive of the Watchtower Society to wear formal dress to the meetings, as was done everywhere else, brought about a great change. Many Jehovah's Witnesses considered this distinctive clothing as reckless. Manfred Peters said that many first had to purchase a jacket, a tie, and formal shoes. Peter Brüggemeier wondered if he should even follow this directive. Jokingly his wife remembers the thought: »My husband, the proletarian, with a tie!« For security reasons they would sometimes put a board game on the table, but the State Security did not intervene. In the mid-1980s, Jehovah's Witnesses even dared to sing during their meetings. Mrs. Brüggemeier said: »It got better until we even could sing.« The directive not to copy songs by hand anymore was at first confusing. At first some thought something terrible must have happened. The directive could be followed in good conscience, since the branch office in Selters/Taunus had sent song books. Today Manfred Peters views these directives as the flowing transition from prohibition to freedom.[94]

In the matter of refusal to do military service, the GDR proved unyielding until a few years before the great change. Jehovah's Witnesses were often drafted after they had married and had their first child. Mario Wermuth stated that this happened a number of times among his friends. They also had difficulties regarding premilitary training. Since this was incorporated in apprenticeships, Jehovah's Witnesses refused to take part in it, and thus some could not complete their job credentials. Mario Wermuth said that in 1979 he was the last apprentice who was accepted without having to participate in this premilitary training. Ralf Pfeifer, who began his apprenticeship one year later, could not finish it because of his refusal.[95]

The Brüggemeiers and Konrad Ettel reported about the private relations of the police and the members of the State Security to Jehovah's Witnesses:

»We had relatively few problems because of not participating in elections. A neighbor was a police officer; she was well-disposed towards us. She was also an election assistant. Until the Wende (reunification of Germany in 1989), we were observed by the State Security from the house across the street. Despite this, we did not feel insulted. We had good relations with our neighbors. We were always a topic for the National Front community resident's committee. We were also on the agenda of the SED district board. A neighbor would report afterwards: ›It went against you again.‹ Probably because of our neighbors, we had fewer retaliations. We were put under surveillance but left in peace.«[96]

»The Weimar area was always a little more liberal than Gera, for example. Our preaching activity was an example of this. A number of times I preached in homes of the state security and police. We would converse, but I was never reported because of it. Some told me: ›What you are doing is good. We wish you much success.‹ In my apartment building, I had a good neighborly relationship with an ardent communist.«[97]

Mario Wermuth, who worked in a small company at that time remembers an unusual incident with a police officer, responsible for the residential area: »In 1989, I applied to visit my sick grandmother in the West. Consequently, the police came to my company to ask my boss about me. He confused me with the boss. He asked me if Mario Wermuth worked here, what was my opinion about him, and if he was reliable. I told him all about myself. I could visit my sick grandmother.«[98]

In Weimar, fines were seldom imposed because Jehovah's Witnesses had participated in illegal preaching work. In other cities, such as Dresden, fines were imposed more often. Mario

Wermuth reported that his wife was summoned to the police where she was threatened with a fine of 500 marks because of her preaching activity.

When the inner German borders were opened on November 9, 1989, Jehovah's Witnesses from Weimar realized that now there would be a way to have their organization recognized. Soon thereafter, East German Jehovah's Witnesses, at the behest of the Selters branch office, applied for recognition of their religious organization with the Secretary of State for Church Affairs of the GDR government. On March 14, 1990, the Council of the GDR, Office for Church Affairs located in Berlin, recognized the religious organization of Jehovah's Witnesses as a religious organization with legal status under article 39 section II of the Constitution.[99] With this registration, the almost forty year long illegal activity by Jehovah's Witnesses came to an end. After the Wende (reunification of Germany), the Weimar and Apolda congregation numbered some 140 evangelists.

Notes

1   This text is a synopsis of my paper for the first state exam for teaching in the Theological Faculty in the Department of Religion at Friedrich Schiller University in Jena. This essay was condensed and revised for this anthology, and includes new data about the August 1950 ban of Jehovah's Witnesses.

2   Thus, Jehovah's Witnesses acquired a better legal position than in the old German federal states, where every congregation (parish) must be registered as an association.

3   The Thuringian church periodical *Glaube und Heimat* did not report about numerous arrests of Jehovah's Witnesses in Weimar on August 30, 1950, and the subsequent ban of this religious group on August 31, 1950. For the ban, see Hans-Hermann Dirksen's essay in this anthology.

4   Karl Noske remained in Weimar for one year after the war, but retained his place of residence there. As circuit overseer, he was responsible for many assemblies. He escaped arrest in 1950, since he was not in Weimar because of his travels. Thereafter he moved to the Federal Republic of Germany. He died in 1978.

5   Ernst Georg Pietzko, born December 9, 1917 in Hindenburg, Upper Silesia. He stayed only a short while in Weimar, as the branch office appointed him district overseer (with full-time responsibilty for several circuits.) He and his wife were arrested is Stralsund in 1951. He died on March 24, 1978.

6   Anton Baumeister, carpenter, born November 1, 1902 in Augsburg. He had spent eight years in prison and concentration camp. Even after a further jail sentence in the GDR, he remained in Weimar. He died in 1977. Konrad Ettel, who had moved to Weimar in 1971, recalls a remark of Anton Baumeister: »Buchenwald, that was my university.« Transcript of conversation with Konrad Ettel, September 19, 1997.

7   Written report Christel Timm, September 1997.

8   Transcript of conversation with Manfred Peters, September 8, 1997.

9   Private collection, memoirs August H., September 1997.

10   Private collection, speech for dedicating Kingdom Hall Manfred Peters, 1995.

11   Thüringisches Hauptstaatsarchiv Weimar (Thuringian Central State Archive, Weimar; hereafter ThHStAW), State of Thuringia, Ministry of the Interior 1112, p. 5.

12   Private collection, speech by Manfred Peters for the dedication of the Kingdom Hall, 1995.

13   ThHStAW: State of Thuringia, Ministry of Interior 1112, p. 5.

14   Private collection, speech by Manfred Peters for the dedication of the Kingdom Hall, 1995; autobiographical memoirs August H., September 1997; transcript of conversation with Mario Wermuth, September 18, 1997.

15   ThHStAW: State of Thuringia, Office of the Minister President 904–910, p. 140.

16   A report by the German branch office of the Watch Tower Society stated: »The confiscated properties had been returned to the Society with the permission of the SMA (Soviet Military Administration). ... As part of restitution, the German branch of the International Association of Bible Students ... was again registered in September 1945 under no. 819 in the official associations' register of the Magdeburg Local Court.« ThHStAW:

State of Thuringia, Office of the Minister President 904-910, p. 123. In a note to the files dated December 1949, Jehovah's Witnesses are included among the »legal independent churches and sects.« ThHStAW: State of Thuringia, Ministry of Interior 1200, p. 24.

17 ThHStAW: State of Thuringia, Office of the Minister President 904-910, p. 140.

18 Ibid., pp. 76-77, 91.

19 Ibid., p. 87.

20 Archives of the Protestant Church in Thuringia: State Church Council A 818, v. 2, 1948-1972, »Sects and other church communities.«

21 ThHStAW: State of Thuringia, Office of the Minister President 904-910, p. 121.

22 Ibid., p. 123.

23 Ibid.

24 Ibid., p. 126.

25 Ibid., p. 124. German Administration of the Interior (DVdI): In mid–1946 the SMAD ordered the founding of a German central administration, at first leaving the beginnings and the duties of the DVdI unclear. Until the founding of the GDR its most important purpose was organizational assistance in training, standardization, and centralization of various police departments. Later it also organized the State Security.

26 ThHStAW: State of Thuringia, Ministry of Interior 1112, p. 3.

27 Ibid., p. 5.

28 ThHStAW: State of Thuringia, The Minister President – Department of Information 67/1.

29 ThHStAW: State of Thuringia, Ministry of Interior 1200, p. 112.

30 Conversation with Mario Wermuth, September 18, 1997.

31 ThHStAW: State of Thuringia, Office of the Minister President 904-910, p. 138.

32 ThHStAW: State of Thuringia, Ministry of Interior 1200, p. 42.

33 *Abendblatt: Das Blatt für Politik, Kultur und Wirtschaft für Mitteldeutschland*, August 31, 1950.

34 *Abendblatt*, September 1, 1950.

35 Ibid.

36 *Abendblatt*, September 5, 1950. In fact the ban had already been issued on August 31, 1950. See the essay by Hans-Hermann Dirksen in this anthology.

37 *Abendblatt*, November 2, 1950. Manfred Peters, whose father was one of the principle defendants, states that there had been only one day of proceedings. Conversation with Manfred Peters, September 8, 1997.

38 Ibid.

39 Conversation with Manfred Peters, September 8, 1997. Apart from the newspaper articles, there are no other written sources about the trial. The Office for Rehabilitation Affairs in Erfurt noted that the file for the rehabilitation of Alfred Noske reveals that the criminal case was based on a sentence of the Erfurt Regional Court of November 3, 1950. Letter from the presiding judge of the Erfurt Regional Court dated October 14, 1997. The State Attorney's office in Erfurt has replied to a letter that the criminal case against Alfred Noske are held under the file number StKs 12/50. This file is still at the Erfurt branch of the Gauck office. Letter dated November 25, 1997.

40 In a Berlin trial against Jehovah's Witnesses in October 1950, two Witnesses were sentenced to life imprisonment. See *Abendblatt*, October 4, 1950.

41 *Abendblatt*, November 5, 1950.

42 Private collection: Speech dedicating Kingdom Hall, Manfred Peters, 1995.

43 Conversation with Konrad Ettel, September 19. 1997.

44 Conversation with Manfred Peters, September 8, 1997.

45 Conversation with Bettina and Peter Brüggemeier, September 15, 1997.

46 Conversation with Manfred Peters, September 8, 1997.

47 Private collection: Letter of Robert Peters 1968, Manfred Peters.

48 Ibid.

49 Written report by August H., September 1997.

50 ThHStAW: State of Thuringia, Office for the Protection of the State-Owned Property LK 570.

51 Ibid.

52 Ibid.

53 Conversation with Bettina and Peter Brüggemeier, September 15, 1997.

54 Private collection: Documents from the indictment and criminal trial, Peter Brüggemeier.

55 Ibid.

56 Conversation with Bettina and Peter Brüggemeier, September 15, 1997. Blood as food and in transfusion are prohibited for Jehovah's Witnesses. They strictly adhere to the Jewish dietary rules in Leviticus 17:10: »As for any man who eats any sort of blood, I shall indeed cut him off from among his people.«

57 Private collection: biographical memoirs August H., September 1997.

58 Ibid.

59 Ibid.

60 Ibid.

61 Ibid.

62 Conversation with Manfred Peters, September 8, 1997.

63 Ibid.

64 Ibid.

65 Private collection: Speech dedicating Kingdom Hall, Manfred Peters, 1995.

66 Ibid.

67 Prison sentences up to 24 months were for routine offences. In contrast, sentences longer than 24 months were for major crimes to which severe sentencing applied. Conversation with Konrad Ettel, September 19, 1997.

68 Ibid.

69 Report by Chritstel Timm, September 12, 1997. Even though, from our point of view today, the rarely granted awards and bonuses might seem superficial, they then had a great value in employment. They were regarded as personal recognition and appreciation of work performed, and were also welcome added income. The following experiences describe conditions in the GDR.

70 Conversation with Manfred Peters, September 8, 1997.

71 Private collection: biographical memoirs August H., September 1997.

72 Conversation with Bettina and Peter Brüggemeier, September 15, 1997.

73 Conversation with Konrad Ettel, September 19, 1997.

74 Comments by Konrad Ettel, November 1997.

75 Conversation with Bettina and Peter Brüggemeier, September 15, 1997.

76 Private collection: biographical memoirs August H., September 1997.

77 Conversation with Manfred Peters, September 8, 1997.

78 Conversation with Bettina and Peter Brüggemeier, September 15, 1997.

79 Conversation with Manfred Peters, September 8, 1997.

80 Private collection: Speech dedicating Kingdom Hall, Manfred Peters, 1995.

81 Conversation with Bettina and Peter Brüggemeier, September 15, 1997.

82 Conversation with Manfred Peters, September 8, 1997.

83 Conversation with Bettina and Peter Brüggemeier, September 15, 1997.

84 Comments by Konrad Ettel, November 1997.

85 Written report by August H., September 1997.

86 Conversation with Manfred Peters, September 8, 1997.

87 Conversation with Bettina and Peter Brüggemeier, September 15, 1997.

88 Ibid.

89 Private collection: Speech dedicating Kingdom Hall, Manfred Peters, 1995.

90 Conversation with Bettina and Peter Brüggemeier, September 15, 1997.

91 Conversation with Konrad Ettel, September 19, 1997.

92 Conversation with Mario Wermuth, September 18, 1997.

93 Comments by Günther Golling, July 1997.

94 Conversations with Bettina and Peter Brüggemeier, September 15, 1997, and Manfred Peters, September 8, 1997.

95 Conversation with Mario Wermuth, September 18, 1997; Comments by Ralf Pfeifer, October 1997.

96 Conversation with Bettina and Peter Brüggemeier, September 15, 1997.

97 Conversation with Konrad Ettel, September 19, 1997.

98 Conversation with Mario Wermuth, September 18, 1997.

99 *Neues Deutschland*, March 21, 1990.

Detlef Garbe

Social Disinterest, Governmental Disinformation, Renewed Persecution, and Now Manipulation of History?

Considerations about Belated Work on the Persecution of Jehovah's Witnesses

Jehovah's Witnesses, who were subjected to relentless persecution in the Third Reich, are among the so-called forgotten victims of the Nazi regime. For decades they were ignored in commemorations held for the victims of National Socialism, despite the fact that a considerable number of Jehovah's Witnesses suffered persecution and death, even though they were a relatively small religious group. Of the 25,000 persons professing to be Jehovah's Witnesses (International Bible Students Association) in Germany at the beginning of the Third Reich, about 10,000 were imprisoned for varying lengths of time; more than 2,000 of them were sent to concentration camps. The death toll among Jehovah's Witnesses in Germany was about 1,200, of whom about 250 were executed mostly by military courts because of their refusal to perform military service.

Taking everything into consideration, it has been established that no other religious movement resisted the pressure to conform to National Socialism with comparable unanimity and steadfastness.[1] Jehovah's Witnesses, already banned a few months after the Nazis came to power, were among the first groups to be persecuted, and of all religious groups, except for Jews, proportionately the most brutally persecuted by the Nazi regime. They comprised the largest number of military service objectors to be sentenced by Wehrmacht courts during World War II. In the concentration camps, Jehovah's Witnesses in the prewar years represented on average 5 to 10 percent of all prisoners, and at times, in certain concentration camps (Fuhlsbüttel, Lichtenburg, and Moringen), they were even the largest prisoner group. They formed a separate ideological prisoner category designated after 1938 by a »purple triangle« on the prisoners' uniforms.

Nevertheless, the persecution of Jehovah's Witnesses was »a very peculiar phenomenon« as noted more than thirty years ago by Friedrich Zipfel, the first historian to be interested in this subject.[2] Moreover, their persecution generally caused little or no interest in historiography or by the public until the 1990s.

My essays deals with the question of why public acknowledgement of Jehovah's Witnesses as a victim group has been denied them for so long. One of the main reasons for the silence about the history of the persecution of Jehovah's Witnesses is that little notice has been taken of alleged (or actual) peripheral groups in general. As with other groups stigmatized as »sects,« Jehovah's Witnesses also encounter enormous social resentment. However, there are many additional factors in the case of this religious association, necessitating a more basic explanation. The first topic in this essay will be the various approachs to the history of Jehovah's Witnesses in postwar Germany, the German Democratic Republic, and the Federal Republic of Germany, focusing especially on the histories written in these regions of the country. Then, I will consider the factors that stood in the way of Jehovah's Witnesses dealing with their own history.

Forgotten in the West

As is well known, Germans, both East and West, generally have found it very difficult to accept their historical heritage. In the postwar years, they were at first preoccupied with clearing the rubble left from the war, with accepting refugees and displaced persons, finding their way in a new political order, and with reconstruction. In the East, divided because of the continually intensifying bloc confrontation, the populace was soon absolved and exculpated from responsibility for the past because of the revolutionary tradition of the ruling party and their antifascist legacy. Also in West German regions, where the western allies assisted with developing a democracy, the majority of the population did not want to hear the reports of concentration camp survivors, irrespective of whether they had been persecuted for political, racial, or religious reasons. These reports reminded them of their own guilt, on omissions or silent toleration of the injustices of Third Reich after 1933 — that they had ignored the persecution of dissidents, opponents of the regime, the Jewish population, Roma and Sinti, and, after the outbreak of the war, against prisoners of war and foreign forced laborers.

Thus, the official politics, in both East and West, claimed to have overcome the Nazi era.[3] The self-designated ›workers and peasants' republic‹ propagated »antifascism,« which was usually not really interested in dealing with the past; the great majority of the victims, Jews and those impressed for forced labor from numerous European countries, disappeared behind the image of heroic communist resistance fighters, which served primarily as a weapon in international class conflict. On the other hand, the Bonn Republic, extolled itself as an antitotalitarian form of government, as an embodiment of freedom, and mentioned the ideals of the military opponents of July 20, 1944. At the same time, they recommended themselves to the Western powers as military allies in the power struggle against the bloc of nations under Soviet hegemony after the end of the Second World War. Rearmament and American nuclear weapons followed. Shortly after the end of war, in the West, vigorous anti-Communism was superimposed over a readiness to deal with the past. Even though the government repeatedly presented their accomplishment of complete alienation from the Nazi regime to foreign countries, the early Federal Republic gave much more attention, seen as a whole, to the reintegration and reinstatement of those persons from the administration, the wartime economy, and the armed forces, than to the rehabilitation of the victims of Nazi persecution. As offices and political establishment were again filled with representatives of the traditional elite, the perceptible desire of the very early postwar years for purification and starting anew became overlaid by an increasing atmosphere of collective refusal to remember and by social restoration.[4]

Initially in the 1970s, but especially in the 1980s, a far reaching change began, which had its origin in the change of generation and thereby in the more unbiased reappraisal by a younger generation whose personal lives were not directly burdened by the Nazi past, but also in the easing of political tensions, with the increasing meaninglessness of ideological pretensions which had set the tone for preoccupation with the Nazi period during the Cold War. Interest in the Nazi past, which had increased substantially by this time, produced a large number of books and numerous efforts at reappraisal. The search for clues in various places which, for example, would shed light on the history of Jewish communities or on the network of forced labor camps that extended throughout all of Germany during the war years, led to the creation of memorials. Academic investigation of this history now also focused more intensively on local and regional history and discovered the daily lives of the »ordinary people« under the Nazi regime as a subject for research.

Until then, preoccupation with »persecution and resistance« had, for the most part, been limited to the July 20, 1944 failed coup and its participants (the officers, aristocrats, and bourgeois opponents of the regime); to the Confessional and Catholic Churches, as well as to the student resistance of the »White Rose.« During the first postwar decades, contemporary history in West Germany substantially conformed to the need for legitimacy by major social organizations. In order to emphasize their own distance from the Nazi regime, institutions such as political parties, trade unions, and churches researched their own role in the resistance. Just the publications about the »church struggle« and »church response to the Nazi challenge« could fill special libraries. The result was a perspective that identified resistance against the Nazi regime with »the churches, trade unions, and the parties.« Resistance by individuals and groups who could not be classified with these large organizations, particularly if they lacked general social acceptance or still lack it today, disappeared from view for a long time. Only with the change of paradigms at the end of the 1970s did resistance in working class circles, non-conformist scenes, forms of noncompliance, and youth protest groups (Edelweiss Pirates and Swings) came into focus. At that time, investigations also began into the fate of forgotten persecutees, such as Roma and Sinti, homosexuals, and victims of Nazi euthanasia. This was soon followed by research into the racial, eugenic, and social bases of Nazi genocide. Neverthe-less, Jehovah's Witnesses remained largely ignored even in those years of a robust expanding re-evaluation of history, since they were included neither in resistance historiography, nor in the investigation of Nazi social and health policies.

Even, when in retrospect, one considers that the history of the small religious bodies in the Nazi era was not a major topic for contemporary historians, or for church historians,[5] the marked indifference of historical scholarship, nevertheless, appears surprising. The smaller free churches and marginal religious groups were almost always omitted in general descriptions of the resistance and even in separate studies about Christian opposition.[6] Not one academic publication about the extraordinary fight for survival by Jehovah's Witnesses in the Third Reich was published in the first two postwar decades. However, the persecution of Jehovah's Witnesses did initially find coverage in the publications of the briefly influential »Vereinigung der Verfolgten des Naziregimes« (VVN, Association of those Persecuted by the Nazi Regime), that had been set up in all German states after liberation and which, initially, tried to include »Bible Student comrades« among their ranks.[7] The appreciation of Jehovah's Witnesses found in the memoirs of concentration camp survivors on the whole stood in explicit contrast to public and academic disinterest. In descriptions by former political and Jewish prisoners of the horrors of the concentration camps which appeared in great number, particularly in the early postwar years, the Witnesses were often mentioned as »a most remarkable group ... in the concentration camps«.[8] In this literature, they were described more or less comprehensively, and depending on the political views of the author, were treated either with respect because of their unyielding posture in the camps, or with incomprehension because of their fanaticism.[9]

The first scholarly essay about Jehovah's Witnesses, based on a broad examination of sources (with emphasis on Berlin), was written by Friedrich Zipfel in 1965 within the framework of his comprehensive investigation into the »persecution of religion« in the Nazi period; it was published under the somewhat misleading title *Kirchenkampf in Deutschland* (»Church Struggle in Germany«).[10] Four years after Zipfel, the Canadian historian Michael H. Kater published a comprehensive essay in *Vierteljahrshefte für Zeitgeschichte*, about »The Earnest Bible Students in the Third Reich,« which, for the first time, also included the confrontations between National Socialism and the Bible Students in the 1920s.[11] A comprehensive account of Jehovah's Witnesses in Nazi Germany has only been available since 1993.[12] Three years later, Kirsten John published a study about Witnesses in the Wewelsburg concentration camp, which was especially significant since Jehovah's Witnesses constituted the majority of prisoners in this camp.[13] A monograph about Jehovah's Witness prisoners in the concentration camps, however, is lacking to this day.

An inadequate perception of the fate of the persecuted is also revealed by the subject of restitution. It is true that Jehovah's Witnesses basically were included in the regulations of the Federal Indemnification Law which, in article 1, recognized claims based »on the grounds of belief,«[14] but Jehovah's Witnesses who had been sentenced by Wehrmacht courts for refusing military service, or their heirs, were usually not awarded compensation. In these cases, the Federal Supreme Court rejected persecution »based on beliefs,« because the reason for punishment was not belief but the lack of readiness to render »statutory military service,« and therefore no »specific Nazi injustice« had occurred. In a basic ruling on June 24, 1964, the Federal Supreme Court stated that the refusal by a Witness to render military service could not be classified as justified resistance, because »there were surely many who ... were convinced that the war started by the Nazi regime was a criminal war of aggression. They, nevertheless, complied with their induction order and fulfilled their military duty.«[15] Consequently, according to the peculiar logic of the Federal Supreme Court, it cannot be said that a Witness »in refusing to obey the call to military duty, resisted the demand to commit a crime.« Even the existence of wrongdoing was rejected, because even with the imposition of the death sentence upon those who refused military service, Wehrmacht judges could — according to the Federal Supreme Court in 1964! — have been guided »exclusively by the conviction that it was necessary to protect the defense of the German people in war.«

It took a long time for the Federal Republic to disassociate itself from this decision. Following a precedent issued by the Federal Social Court of September 11, 1991, by which the death sentences of the Wehrmacht courts were, according to the circumstances, to be basically considered as »obvious injustice,«[16] the German Federal Parliament passed a resolution in May 1997 after time-consuming debates, which stipulated that convictions for »refusal to serve in the military,« »desertion,« and »damage to military discipline« were unjust and awarded the victims a one-time lump sum compensation.[17]

Despised and Persecuted in the East

The silence and discrimination in the West was juxtaposed to renewed persecution of Jehovah's Witnesses in East Germany. At first, though, it had appeared totally different there. Because the victims of fascism were exalted in the new social order, Jehovah's Witnesses could initially count on certain concessions during the first postwar period in the Soviet occupation zone. They reestablished their German headquarters at the administration building and printing plant in Magdeburg, which had been restored after seizure by the Gestapo. Former concentration camp prisoners became leaders of their missionary preaching work. Soon, however, the Soviet and, later, the GDR authorities reacted with restrictions. On August 30, 1950, the administration building of the Watch Tower Society in Magdeburg was occupied by strong police forces, and the employees arrested. On the next day, the religious association was prohibited. Dr. Steinhoff, GDR Minister of the Interior, stated as grounds for the ban: activity for »unconstitutional purposes, systematic agitation against the existing democratic order and its laws under the cloak of a religious association, as well as the importation of illegal literature.« The main accusation stated that »the Jehovah's Witnesses worked for the secret service of an imperialistic power.«[18] The indictment against nine leading functionaries of Jehovah's Witnesses, presented at the trial before the Supreme Court of the GDR on October 3 and 4, 1950, claimed that the accused were members of »a criminal organization in the pay of the American warmongers, disguised as a religion« and »agents of American intelligence aiming for the systematic disintegration of our country with the aim of destroying it.«[19]

Several days before the ban, the SED had already begun a widespread campaign of defamation primarily using the press. Thus, for example, the *Tägliche Rundschau*, widely distributed in the GDR, carried the headline »Jehovah's Witnesses Must Disappear!« in its September 3, 1950 edition, and reported on an alleged »wave of protest« in the population against the religious association. In a protest resolution by the staff of the VEB Paper Manufacturing Works Perfecta in Bautzen, it was claimed that: »Proof of the real nature of the Jehovah's Witnesses is that the majority of their adherents fundamentally refuse to sign the Stockholm peace appeal for outlawing the atom bomb and thereby clearly and consciously express that they are ready, the same as the Western business magnates and monopolists, for a new world war and fresh genocide.«[20]

In the first few days after the ban, more than 500 Jehovah's Witness functionaries were arrested. Other members were handed the prohibition order and had to acknowledge receipt by signing a rider that they would no longer work for this religious association.[21] Numerous former concentration camp prisoners were also affected by the repressions.[22] According to existing statistics, from 1950 to 1961 in the GDR, a total of 2,891 Jehovah's Witnesses had been arrested, 2,202 of whom (including 674 women) received sentences (averaging 5.5 years) for seditious activity, espionage, and so-called warmongering. At least 50 Jehovah's Witnesses who, without exception, had already been incarcerated under the Nazi regime, died in prison.[23] The status accorded Jehovah's Witnesses as »victims of fascism« in the early postwar years was generally rescinded as was the grant of an »honorary pension« paid in the GDR to victims of Nazi persecution.[24]

Against this background, it is hardly surprising that Jehovah's Witnesses were, for the most part, simply ignored in GDR resistance historiography. Since mentioning the group in works about the history of the concentration camps could, in part, hardly be avoided, the conceptual language was simply altered. Thus, for example, »prisoners from religious groups,« »ministers,« or »sectarians« were used, when Jehovah's Witnesses were meant.[25]

In order to counteract the GDR's awkward situation that the Jehovah's Witnesses who sat in their prisons by the hundreds were former victims of the Nazis, government agencies decided in 1970 to publish an extensive »Documentation about the Watch Tower Society,« which also included full details about the behavior of Jehovah's Witnesses from 1933 to 1945.[26] This book was published under the name of Manfred Gebhard, but compiled by unnamed authors with the support of the Ministry for State Security; it was also published the following year, 1971, in a licensed edition in the Federal Republic.[27] It provided many details and insider information, while at the same time clearly accommodating ideological interests. The purpose of this publication was evident; the »Documentation« was to legitimize the ban and prove that the measures taken against Jehovah's Witnesses in the GDR were not »persecution because of belief,« but concerned »the prosecution of individuals, who had been used by the Wachtturm-Gesellschaft exploiting religious feeling for slander, antidemocratic agitation, enemy intelligence activity, and political abuse of the Bible and of religion and, thus, committed sedition.«[28]

This presentation resulted in a history of the Watch Tower Society as an organization »serving psychological warfare,« »bought by big capital,« and thus part of the »worldwide dispute between imperialism and socialism.« Consequently, the authors of the »Documentation« had the impudence to utilize Gestapo assessments of the situation for their construction of an alleged cooperation between the U.S. State Department and the Watch Tower Society, in which the religious group's international ties were blamed for Nazi animosity.[29]

Disputing Jehovah's Witnesses opposition to the Nazi regime was the focus of the »Documentation.« By means of selective choice of sources, through distorted quotations, by referring to the Nazi press after 1933, to Gestapo interrogation records, or to petitions for clemency from leading members, a picture emerged, according to which the ban of the Witnesses in 1933 rested on a misunderstanding or »political forgery.« Whereas in reality, the functionaries of the Watch Tower Society were »fascist compromised religious-political adventurers« who sought the »approval of the Nazis« and had later shown themselves ready for a »mass betrayal of their own brothers in faith to the Gestapo.«

Although this documentation, concocted by GDR State Security, can clearly be seen as a product of a certain epoch, its characterization of the Witnesses still has considerable significance today, since it remains one of the few publications on this subject found in libraries, and, therefore, its conclusions have been partly embraced, unverified, by critics of Jehovah's Witnesses up to the present.[30]

The persecution of Jehovah's Witnesses in the GDR eventually ended with the social revolution in autumn 1989. This persecution, however, clearly decreased in general after the end of the Ulbricht era — except for sentencing those refusing military service, only reprimands and monetary fines were handed down in the 1970s and 1980s[31] — but, until the end, it was centrally coordinated by Ministry for State Security Main Department XX. (Even in the 1980s, the Stasi opened an operation named »Sumpf« (swamp), directed against ostensible enemies, primarily the so-called east department of the Watch Tower Society in Selters/Taunus.) After a forty year ban, Jehovah's Witnesses were re-registered and formally recognized as a religious association in the GDR by the government under Hans Modrow on March 14, 1990.

Furthermore, revised versions of the 1970 documentation published in the GDR under the name of Manfred Gebhard are also found on the right. A peculiar harmony with Stasi propaganda is displayed in several parts of a book issued in 1995 in the series »Pro Fide Catholica« by the publishing house Anton A. Schmidt (Durach). The book carried the title »The Secret Power Behind Jehovah's Witnesses« and was authored by Robin de Ruiter, a »Dutch researcher and writer.« He also found a close connection between the Watch Tower Society and the U.S. State Department under the direction of the Minister and »high ranking Freemason« Cordell Hull. By simultaneous references to racial and antisemitic propaganda writings of the 1920s and 1930s by August Fetz or Julius Kuptsch, as well as to the GDR documentation by Gebhard, the old conspiracy theory was restated,[32] in which Jehovah's Witnesses were influenced by »freemasonry« and stood »in the service of Zionism.« As evidence for his obscure theses, De Ruiter quotes yet again the »Protocols of the Elders of Zion,« which were part of the standard repertoire of National Socialism.[33]

Against this ideological background, it is not surprising that Jehovah's Witnesses became, like many other Nazi victims, an object of neo-Nazi agitation. Thus the Institute for Historical Review in California, which can be considered part of the American neo-Nazi scene, in a circular published in 1980 under a Swedish cover address, attacked the position of Jehovah's Witnesses towards the Third Reich and attempted to justify Nazi persecution as defense measures. The pamphlet alleged that similar to the Jewish World Congress through its President Chaim Waizmann in 1939, the Watch Tower president Joseph Franklin Rutherford had already declared war on Germany five years before. Without hesitation the persecuted were branded as persecutors.[34]

Between Historical Explanation and Manipulation of History: The Participation of the Jehovah's Witnesses Information Service

Although it is correct to attribute widespread silence about the persecution of Jehovah's Witnesses in the Nazi era to many years of disinterest in the West or to the ban and disinformation in the East, it must also be stated that the long-standing refusal to deal with this subject is, to a large extent, caused by the structure and peculiarity of the »Watch Tower Bible and Tract Society.« The exclusive claim of this controversial religious association, whose »Governing Body« lays claim to the sole truth and its doctrine, which in rational terms is barely understandable particularly for those unacquainted with the Bible, has probably contributed to the neglect of this subject, and also to the group's isolation from the outside world. Research efforts, as far as they went, met with reluctance from the Watch Tower Society for a long time. Outsiders could not obtain access to the archives of the Watch Tower Society. Not only anxiety and bad experiences, in particular with journalists primarily concerned with dubious »exposures,« but also the wish for a monopoly on the interpretation of their own history, had contributed to this uncooperative attitude.

Meanwhile a major change has occurred here. For about five years, the Watch Tower Society has increasingly opened up about historical questions.[35] This is accompanied by public relations at considerable expense and with great commitment. This is seen especially in exhibitions and the video documentary »Jehovah's Witnesses Stand Firm Against Nazi Assault,« produced in 1996 by the Watch Tower Society and distributed world-wide in numerous languages. The purpose of the Information Services of Jehovah's Witnesses, founded in 1996, is to bring their survivors and victims into public awareness. Whereas the Watch Tower Society several years ago saw »no benefit at all in historical assessments,«[36] it now makes reference to the results of the historical research and uses it to obtain attention.

Similar activities are taking place in many European countries. There also, Jehovah's Witnesses take pains to shed light on the persecution of their religious association. Thus, a traveling exhibition compiled by the European Circle of Former Deported and Interned Jehovah's Witnesses (»Cercle Européen des Témoins de Jéhovah Anciens Déportés et Internés« based in Boulogne-Billancourt) earned considerable praise in 1995–96; it could be seen in many cities in France.[37] Moreover, recently documentations by Guy Canonici[38] and Matteo Pierro[39] about the Nazi persecution of Jehovah's Witnesses have been published in France and Italy.

There is also a distinct change noticeable in public acknowledgment of this subject. Jehovah's Witnesses are no longer omitted in redesigned memorials. Proof of this are the new exhibitions at Buchenwald and Neuengamme, reorganized in 1995, as well as the comprehensive recognition of Jehovah's Witnesses in the United States Holocaust Memorial Museum that opened in 1993 in Washington. Jehovah's Witnesses are also occasionally memorialized in the naming of streets. Thus in the immediate vicinity of the Plötzensee memorial in Berlin-Charlottenburg is a street named Emmy-Zehden-Weg since 1992, a reminder of her fate; she was executed on June 9, 1944, after being sentenced by the People's Court for concealing three Witnesses who had refused military service. At the Brandenburg central commemoration on the anniversary for victims of National Socialism, which was held at the Sachsenhausen memorial on January 27, 1998, the persecuted group of Jehovah's Witnesses received central attention. In numerous German cities mayors and other public officials have opened the traveling exhibition »Stand Firm Against Nazi Assault,« produced in three sets by the Jehovah's Witnesses Public Affairs Office.

The Watch Tower Society has several motives behind these efforts after decades of self-imposed restraint. Their current substantial commitment is to gain recognition and draw public attention to Jehovah's Witnesses as one of the groups of Nazi victims. As in comparable cases of other groups counted among the so-called forgotten victims and who have, mainly in the last ten to fifteen years, successfully drawn some public attention (as for example, Sinti and Roma and homosexuals), the incentives are not only and not primarily about dealing with the past, but also with present matters of concern. In a press release issued by the Jehovah's Witnesses Information Services on November 6, 1996, the statement refers to »present parallels of the public stigmatization of Jehovah's Witnesses comparable to the purple triangle,«[40] as well as a repetitious »rebuttal of religious competitors,« probably meaning the Protestant and Catholic churches. Dr. Gabriele Yonan, a scholar of religion, is quoted with the sentence: »It must not happen again, that Jehovah's Witnesses are discriminated against.«[41]

Against the background of the debates about the »Scientology Church« and its ruinous effects on followers drawn under its influence, Jehovah's Witnesses and other small distinctive religious groups termed »sects« find themselves at present in the vortex of a discussion which intends to put all these groups on the same level. Therefore, the Watch Tower Society is concerned with improving its social reputation. The religious association would like to free itself from the stigma of the term »sect«; it desires recognition as a religious association on par with other churches and religious bodies. Endeavors to gain recognition of the persecution of Jehovah's Witnesses are, in my opinion, also to be seen in this context. A strong controversy has errupted about the issue of granting them privileges of a »corporation under public law.«[42] After the state of Berlin refused corporate rights to the »religious association of Jehovah's Witnesses in Germany,« which the Witnesses believed had been granted to them in 1990 through re-registration under the Modrow government, the Witnesses took legal action. Whereas the Berlin Administrative Court in 1993 and the Higher Administrative Court in 1995 affirmed that the religious association had fulfilled all constitutional requirements for granting corporate rights and, as a consequence, this legal status should not be denied,[43] their claim was denied by the Federal Administrative Court in a decision of June 26, 1997, since the Jehovah's Witnesses religious association, with its active refusal to participate in voting at elections, contradicts organizational principles of democracy for public order in the federal and state systems. The litigation is still pending as the Jehovah's Witnesses have appealed to the Federal Constitutional Court.

Another feature must also be taken into consideration, namely a modification of the doctrine respecting imminent expectation published in the *Watchtower* in 1995. Accordingly, for the more than five million Jehovah's Witnesses who are active in the worldwide preaching, the certainty that God will create a new world »before the generation that saw the events of 1914 passes away«[44] has given way to trust in the promise that this occurrence will take place »shortly« at an unforeseeable time lying only in God's hands.[45] The history of religion teaches that the history of one's own religious identity gains significance when future expectations alone are no longer the exclusive motivating force.

It is a well known phenomenon, and appropriately frequently deplored, that present disputes are often fought out in interpretations of the past. Reference to the suffering experienced by Jehovah's Witnesses in Hitler's Germany because of their loyalty to their convictions and the boldness with which they confronted the regime, can in today's Germany — sensitized to the subject of Nazi persecution — influence how Jehovah's Witnesses are perceived, despite the existence of negative prejudices. The Watch Tower Society is not unfamiliar with the tendency of other groups to use the history of resistance for self-description, or of the early apologetic writing of the history of the »church struggle« that was not free from this inclination.[46]

A tendency to manipulate the past, however, is also shown by some critics of Jehovah's Witnesses, of whom no critical analysis of historical findings is demanded, but merely the prerequisite of a disparaging judgment in the dispute with present day activities of Jehovah's Witnesses. Contrary to such rationales, it must be emphasized that the duty of history writing is to reconstruct past events based on sources and on empirical evidence. The question of the evaluation of the behavior of Jehovah's Witnesses in the Third Reich should not be contingent on polemics about controversial activity by the present day Watch Tower organization. Research results based on an evaluation of broad empirical materials, and which corroborate the extraordinary intensity of the persecution, do not become false because the Watch Tower Society, in contrast to earlier years, is now trying to improve its public image by referring to the persecution of Jehovah's Witnesses in the Third Reich. On the other hand, of course, the human, and in many respects moving, actions of Jehovah's Witnesses in Nazi Germany and dismay about the suffering inflicted upon them should not suspend the use of the same critical criteria for their history that are valid for evaluating the behavior of commission and omission as well as the goals of all groups and individuals during the Nazi era, or in any other period.

The problem of evaluating the attempts by the leadership of the religious association at the start of Nazi rule — in petitioning the authorities, through negotiations, and diplomatic interventions — to obtain the reversal of prohibitions or restrictions is especially controversial. Special significance is therefore attached to the convention held in Berlin-Wilmersdorf on June 25, 1933, during which approximately 7,000 Jehovah's Witnesses in attendance adopted a declaration drafted by Watch Tower President Rutherford himself. This declaration aimed at convincing those in power that the Witnesses had purely religious and unpolitical goals, as well as the absurdity of their alleged »disloyalty« and other accusations lodged against them; for this purpose, the manifesto used a line of argumentation that stressed certain similarities with the »high ideals« of the Nazi state, thereby causing a somewhat anti-Jewish style.

Despite the Watch Tower Society's new openness in questions about the the past, it has not yet decided to distance itself from the policy of conformity pursued in 1933. It is true that the declaration of June 25, 1933, is no longer idealized by the Watch Tower Society as a »vehement protest against the Hitler government.«[47] But the fact that in times of hardship in 1933, resulting from a situation that was not as clear to contemporaries as it is to us today, concessions were made to »the spirit of the times« is still not admitted today. Fortunately, however, a recent edition of *Awake!* concerning the desire, also expressed within the religious group, for an explanation went into detail about the Wilmersdorf declaration. It was admitted as »regrettable« that the passage about »commercial Jews of the British-American empire« was »misunderstood« as an expression of alleged anti-Jewish hostility and has thus »given cause for any offense.«[48] But the Watchtower organization has not decided to admit that during the first months of the Third Reich the »visible organization of Jehovah,« as others, sought accommodation to preserve their existence, requesting that believers temporarily discontinue all missionary activities and thus, did not act from the first with the decisiveness which characterized their later behavior under Nazi rule,[49] presumably because the authority of the Governing Body in Brooklyn and its permanent claim of acting »by inspiration and authority from the Most High«[50] is at issue.[51]

In order to cast doubt on the steadfastness of Jehovah's Witnesses under the Nazi regime, apart from the Wilmersdorf Convention, reference is frequently made to the leadership members Franke and Frost, who were said to have betrayed their fellow believers to the Gestapo. The »exposé« published in 1961 by *Der Spiegel* under the title »Väterchen Frost« (»Jack Frost«) was explicitly slanted to certain interests: For the purpose of denigrating the former manager of the German branch office and the former editor responsible for the German editions of *Watchtower* and *Awake!*, historical facts were distorted, in the way that the Watch Tower Society is often accused of doing. Frost's persecution was described by *Der Spiegel* in the following words: »Following interrogations by the Gestapo, Frost was allowed to exchange his prison cell for forced labor in Emslandmoor, was released, and later temporarily in Sachsenhausen concentration camp during the war and ... finally landed in an SS-construction brigade offshore from France on the rocky island of Alderney.«[52] What cynical language: »was allowed« and »temporarily.« Not only were the notorious Emsland camps depicted here as harmless and the continuous concentration camp internment of Frost until the end of the war denied (Alderney was a satellite camp of Neuengamme concentration camp), but history was openly falsified. The alleged release from the Gestapo refers to the customary release after serving a judicially ordered sentence after 1937, and for non-recanting Jehovah's Witnesses, their subsequent remand or transfer to concentration camps.[53] In fact, Frost had not spent one single day in freedom after his arrest on March 21, 1937.

Since 1961, referring to the *Spiegel* article, the so-called betrayal by [leading] Jehovah's Witnesses Frost and Franke has been alluded to time and time again. In the GDR documentation from 1969 it is stated that Frost »without any apparent inducement by the Gestapo, let alone because of beatings, began to talk of his own volition.«[54] However, Frost, and there is no reason to doubt his statements after all we have learned from the archives, was severely tortured, »beaten into unconsciousness and revived with buckets of water« during the interrogations at the Gestapo headquarters in the Prinz-Albrecht-Straße.[55]

The Lasting Significance of Resistance by Jehovah's Witnesses

The Jehovah's Witnesses victims, who for the sake of their faith suffered persecution and were prepared to risk death rather than participate in military action, deserve our utmost respect and admiration and our society would do well not to deny this to them. However one analyzes the individual motive and conduct of Jehovah's Witnesses, in contrast to the overwhelming majority of the German population, at no point did they support Nazi rule. Rather, the stand taken by Jehovah's Witnesses would have, according to Klaus Drobisch, »been befitting« for the majority of the population.[56]

Nevertheless, it should not be ignored that Jehovah's Witnesses, in their conflict with the regime, fought for the freedom of their own organization and worship, but not for freedom for everyone in a more comprehensive or political sense. The resistance of Jehovah's Witnesses set itself up against the ban already imposed on their society in 1933 and against the prohibition of their religious activity and thereby the preaching of the message of the impending arrival of the divine kingdom. In effect, this meant for them the prohibition of their faith; they rendered active and organized resistance against this massive form of hostile governmental regulation.

The continuous insubordination of Jehovah's Witnesses who were firmly determined to remain resolute, come what may, to be sure disturbed the Nazi regime, which was intent on the uncontested transformation of all fellow Germans into the national community, but their intentions and goals were not set at changing the political order. Certainly Jehovah's Witnesses sought a revolution but this would be brought about by God and, instead of the present rulers, no government formed by another political power but Christ, as sovereign of the divine kingdom, should enter. Thus the resistance of Jehovah's Witnesses is not to be subsumed under the political resistance. Their behavior during the Nazi regime defies the usual classifications, because zealous believers made a conscious decision to oppose the Nazi regime at the risk of their lives and indeed were not »resistance fighters.« With their resistance, they did not want to act as a »beacon« for others, but wanted to give »witness« to their faith. Nevertheless, they carried out their fight with utmost determination and exemplary courage. For them, subjection »under a demon« was equivalent to sacrificing »real life.« Therefore, it must be considered that Jehovah's Witnesses, in the cognizance of their chosenness, saw the victory of God over satanic power in the last battle of »Armageddon.« Those who saw themselves on the threshold of God's kingdom and awaited the promised resurrection of the dead, were certain that surrendering their own lives, which their resistance might entail, would not last a long time.

Consequently, in their own perception, the success of their activities was verified not by undermining the regime, but as evidence of their religious faith. The effort to courageously maintain their faith, to stand the »test of integrity« placed upon them and thus prove themselves true Witnesses of their God Jehovah, stood clearly in the foreground of their actions. By their deeds and their refusal to compromise, Jehovah's Witnesses wanted to help faith in the imminent coming of God's kingdom penetrate among others. »Resistance« was for them an act of faith, an imperative of belief. By that means they showed what power can be mobilized by faith, power which the Nazi regime, with all its means of force, could not break.

When one observes the martyrdom of Jehovah's Witnesses, rich in victims, in the Third Reich from a scholarly historical perspective, one must come to the conclusion: They did not put up resistance against the dictatorship because of antifascist or democratic beliefs. Although it is true that the courageous stand of Jehovah's Witnesses in the Third Reich deserves respect and esteem, it is at best a restricted and limited model in a democratically constituted society. In this connection, it must be mentioned that Jehovah's Witnesses did not resist only Nazi authority, and in no way was the Nazi state exclusively attacked and exposed as a tool of Satan. The refusal to salute the flag, of (forced) membership in political organizations and, in particular, of military service, also brought Jehovah's Witnesses in many other countries, and at all times, into situations of conflict.[57] And with reference to Rutherford's satanic triad, »commerce, politics, and churches,« the Watch Tower Society viewed political governments in general as tools in the hand of the devil, which also explains journalistic hostility to them in nondictatorial states. This only changed in 1962 when the Watch Tower Society abandoned

Rutherford's concept of supreme authorities; since then, they reidentified the superior authorities spoken of in Romans 13 with secular governments and thereby awarded them a God approved function of order in the »old world.«

I would like to end this article on a personal note with a slight variation of my statement at the world premiere on November 6, 1996, of the video »Jehovah's Witnesses Stand Firm Against Nazi Assault«: As a non-Witness, I have engaged myself academically for over ten years with the history of Jehovah's Witnesses. My critical reserve toward from the doctrinal and organizational structure of the Watchtower Society remains unaltered. At the same time, I am deeply impressed with thankfulness and great respect for those Jehovah's Witnesses whose faith in God and trust in the promises of the Bible gave them the strength to maintain respect for life even at that horrific time. All of us, Jehovah's Witnesses and non-Witnesses, must not forget the history of the purple triangle prisoners. It was—despite all mistakes and confusions—a beam of light in a dark age.

Notes

1   The purpose of this essay is not to present the history of persecution of Jehovah's Witnesses in Nazi Germany. For this reason, I have not provided detailed references for statistical data. For this, please refer to my various publications on this subject, especially my book, in its third revised edition: *Zwischen Widerstand und Martyrium: Die Zeugen Jehovas im Dritten Reich* (Munich, 1997); also my recently published essay, »Die Verfolgung der Zeugen Jehovas im nationalsozialistischen Deutschland: Ein Überblick,« in: *Widerstand aus christlicher Überzeugung: Jehovas Zeugen im Nationalsozialismus—Dokumentation einer Tagung*, eds. Kreismuseum Wewelsburg, Fritz Bauer Institut, and Bundeszentrale für politische Bildung, compiled by Kirsten John-Stucke (Essen, 1998), pp. 16–27.

2   Friedrich Zipfel, *Kirchenkampf in Deutschland 1933-1945: Religionsverfolgung und Selbstbehauptung der Kirchen in der nationalsozialistischen Zeit* (Berlin, 1965), p. 176.

3   See Jürgen Danyel, ed., *Die geteilte Vergangenheit: Zum Umgang mit dem Nationalsozialismus und Widerstand in beiden deutschen Staaten* (Berlin, 1995).

4   See Norbert Frei, *Vergangenheitspolitik: Die Anfänge der Bundesrepublik und die NS-Vergangenheit* (Munich, 1996); Detlef Garbe, »Äußere Abkehr, Erinnerungsverweigerung und ›Vergangenheitsbewältigung‹: Der Umgang mit dem Nationalsozialismus in der frühen Bundesrepublik,« in Axel Schildt and Arnold Sywottek, eds., *Modernisierung im Wiederaufbau: Die westdeutsche Gesellschaft der 50er Jahre* (Bonn, 1993), pp. 693–716.

5   Literature about the persecution of the small religious groups in the Third Reich is generally scanty. There is no well-researched general history to this day. A comparative examination of five small religious associations has been completed by Christine E. King, *The Nazi State and the New Religions: Five Case Studies in Non-Conformity* (New York and Toronto, 1982).

6   For example, Jehovah's Witnesses and other small religious bodies were not mentioned at all in the chapter »Christians in Resistance« in the commendable anthology by Richard Löwenthal and Patrik von zur Mühlen, *Widerstand und Verweigerung in Deutschland 1933 bis 1945* (1st ed., 1982).

7   Carl Dominik from Schleswig represented the persecuted Jehovah's Witnesses on the board of the VVN for the British zone formed in May 1948. During 1949, there was a wave of Jehovah's Witness departures from the VVN. The reasons given were that, on the one hand, the VVN had taken on a party political character which made it impossible for Jehovah's Witnesses, on the basis of »Christian neutrality,« to continue membership and, on the other hand, reference was made to the repressive measures taken against Jehovah's Witnesses in 1949 who lived in the Soviet occupation zone or in the German Democratic Republic.

8   Heinrich Christian Meier, *So war es: Das Leben im KZ Neuengamme* (Hamburg, 1946), 31f.; on the special characteristics of this prisoners' group, see Detlef Garbe, »Der lila Winkel: Die ›Bibelforscher‹ (Zeugen Jehovas) in den Konzentrationslagern,« *Dachauer Hefte* 10 (1994), pp. 3–31.

9   See Garbe, *Widerstand und Martyrium*, pp. 40f.

10 See note 2.

11 Michael H. Kater, »Die Ernsten Bibelforscher im Dritten Reich,« *Vierteljahrshefte für Zeitgeschichte* 17 (1969), pp. 181–218.

12 See note 1.

13 Kirsten John, »*Mein Vater wird gesucht*«: *Häftlinge des Konzentrationslagers in Wewelsburg* (Essen, 1996).

14 For many years it was debated under the compensation and restitution rights whether the Jehovah's Witnesses could be included among the so-called persecuted groups, which the Nazi regime »intended to bar« completely »from the cultural or economic life of Germany« (Art. 51, paragraph 4 of the Federal Indemnification Law). After various controversial supreme court decisions on this subject, the interpretation of the law of restitution finally confirmed that Jehovah's Witnesses, on the basis of the indiscriminate persecution which based itself solely on membership in this organization, were to be recognized as a persecuted group. Apart from the Witnesses, only the »Jews, including so-called Mischlinge of the first degree« and »Gypsies after December 8, 1938,« fell under this restitution ruling. See *Bericht der Bundesregierung über Wiedergutmachung und Entschädigung für nationalsozialistisches Unrecht* (October 31, 1986), printed matter 10/6287, p. 11.

15 Bundesgerichtshof, IV ZR 236/63, sentence of June 24, 1964.

16 Bundessozialgericht, 9a RV 11/90, sentence of September 11, 1991.

17 Decision of the Deutscher Bundestag, May 15, 1997, 13th Election period, 175th session.

18 The prohibition order is printed in Rolf Nobel, *Falschspieler Gottes: Die Wahrheit über Jehovas Zeugen* (Hamburg, 1985), p. 101.

19 Quoted in *Die Tat*, no. 38, October 14, 1950.

20 *Tägliche Rundschau*, September 3, 1950.

21 See lecture by the attorney Hans Hermann Dirksen, »1945–1950: eine Zeit zwischen Illusion und Hoffnung für Jehovas Zeugen,« December 16, 1997, p. 4.

22 The *1951 Yearbook of Jehovah's Witnesses* reported that a Witness received the GDR police, who had come to arrest him, in the striped »zebra clothing« which he had worn in Nazi concentration camps. Thereupon an arrest was avoided, at least for the moment. See *1951 Yearbook of Jehovah's Witnesses* with its report about 1950 (ed. Watch Tower Bible and Tract Society, 1951), p. 135.

23 Figures based on the table »Überblick zur Geschichte der Zeugen Jehovas in der DDR 1949-1990,« by Johannes Wrobel, Wachtturm Bibel- und Traktat-Gesellschaft, History Archive (December 1997). I have taken further information for the inadequately investigated persecution of Jehovah's Witnesses in the GDR from the manuscript of a lecture by Martin Jahn »Standhaft trotz staatlicher Verbote: Jehovas Zeugen 1933 und 1950« (Freiberg, December 1997).

24 See Olaf Groehler, »Integration und Ausgrenzung von NS-Opfern: Zur Anerkennungs- und Entschädigungsdebatte in der Sowjetischen Besatzungszone Deutschlands 1945 bis 1949,« in: Jürgen Kocka, ed., *Historische DDR-Forschung: Aufsätze und Studien* (Berlin, 1994), pp. 105-27.

25 For example, see Komitee der Antifaschistischen Widerstandskämpfer in der Deutschen Demokratischen Republik, ed., *Die Frauen von Ravensbrück*, compiled by Erika Buchmann, (Berlin, 1959), pp. 146f.; *Todeslager Sachsenhausen: Ein Dokumentarbericht vom Sachsenhausen-Prozeß* (Berlin, 1948), pp. 42f., 206.

26 Manfred Gebhard, ed., *Die Zeugen Jehovas: Eine Dokumentation über die Wachtturmgesellschaft*, licensed first editon (Leipzig: Urania Verlag, 1970 and Schwerte [Ruhr], 1971), pp. 134-142, 153-213.

27 The documentation was based on a manuscript by the author which he compiled at the end of the 1960s, after he had left the Jehovah's Witnesses. Confronting the Staatssekretariat für Kirchenfragen (State Secretariat for Church Issues) in the GDR, the editor, who no longer participated in the writing of the documentation, emphatically distanced himself from its adulterations and falsifications and called it a mistake that he had agreed to the use of his name without knowing the results. See Garbe, *Widerstand and Martyrium*, 20. For the cooperation of department XX of the MfS in this book, see Gerhard Besier and Stephan Wolf, eds., »*Pfarrer, Christen und Katholiken*«: *Das Ministerium für Staatssicherheit der ehemaligen DDR und die Kirchen*, 2nd ed. (Neukirchen-Vluyn, 1992), p. 84.

28 Gebhard, *Zeugen Jehovas*, p. 255.

29 Ibid., pp. 67f., 75f.

30 See, for example, Rolf Nobel, *Falschspieler Gottes: Die Wahrheit über Jehovas Zeugen* (Hamburg, 1985), esp. the chapter headed »Von Märtyrern und Verrätern,« pp. 196-199.

31 The harsh sentencing of those who refused military service ended in 1985, because the GDR abandoned calling up Jehovah's Witnesses for military duty.

32 For an analysis of völkisch antisemitic polemics against Jehovah's Witnesses, see Detlef Garbe, »'Sendboten des jüdischen Bolschewismus': Antisemitismus als Motiv nationalsozialistischer Verfolgung der Zeugen Jehovas,« *Tel Aviver Jahrbuch für deutsche Geschichte* 23 (1994), 145-171; and the recent remarkable essay by Manfred Gebhard and Dr. Hans Jonak von Freyenwald, »Ein faschistischer Apologet gegen die Zeugen Jehovas,« *Beiträge zur Geschichte der Arbeiterbewegung* 39, no. 1 (1997), pp. 20-39.

33 Robin de Ruiter, *Die geheime Macht hinter den Zeugen* (Durach, 1995), pp. 87ff.

34 *Jehovah's Witnesses Declare War Against Germany!*, rh 224, Taby 1980. This pamphlet, published by the Institute for Historical Review, also used nationalistic sources from the 1920s and 1930s as well as the Gebhard »Dokumentation über die Wachtturmgesellschaft.«

35 The Watch Tower Society has also been more open in the past few years about several other questions. Thus, since May 1996, it is left to the conscience of individual believers, whether they choose to render civilian service, which previously, was viewed as linked to military service and as a violation of Christian neutrality.

36 Comp. Garbe, *Widerstand und Martyrium* (note 1), p. 38, note 117.

37 *Mémoire de Témoins 1933-1945*, ed., le Cercle Européen des Témoins de Jéhovah anciens déportés et internés (Louviers, 1995).

38 Guy Canonici, *Les Témoins de Jéhovah face à Hitler* (Paris, 1998).

39 Matteo Pierro, *Fra Martirio e Resistenza: La persecuzione nazista e fascista dei Testimoni di Geova* (Como, 1997).

40 Press release by Jehovah's Witnesses Information Services, November 6, 1996, p. 3f.

41 Ibid., p. 4.

42 Religionsgemeinschaft der Zeugen Jehovas in Deutschland, ed., *Anerkennungsverfahren der Religionsgemeinschaft der Zeugen Jehovas in Deutschland 1990-1997* (Selters/Taunus, 1997).

43 It is true that both courts rejected the interpretation of law presented by the Jehovah's Witnesses religious association that corporate status had already been attained on reregistration in the GDR, along with the activation of the GDR church tax law on September 29, 1990. The religious association could however »request from the defendant state of Berlin, ... that they be awarded this legal status.« (OVG Berlin, Decision of December 14, 1995, Az. OVG 5 B 20.94, p. 14).

44 For decades, the Watch Tower Society preached, based on the prophecy of Jesus recorded in the 24th chapter of Matthew's Gospel, verse 34, that »for this wicked world ... the end will come, before all who are a part of this generation will have passed away« and that for this reason »there cannot be many more years before the prophesied end« (*Awake!*, April 8, 1969, p. 13f.) With increasing distance from the date 1914, the year which according to the teaching of Jehovah's Witnesses, Christ had taken up his reign, and the unavoidable decrease in the »1914 generation« because of old age, a modification eventually became overdue.

45 See the changes in the editorial pages of the semi-monthly magazine *Awake!*; the old version referring to the 1914 generation was printed for the last time on October 22, 1995 (see also surroundling articles in *Watchtower*, November 1, 1995).

46 See Friedrich Baumgärtl, *Wider die Kirchenkampf-Legenden* (Neuendettelsau, 1958).

47 *Wachtturm*, July 1, 1961.

48 »Jehovah's Witnesses – Courageous in the Face of Nazi Peril,« *Awake!*, July 8, 1998, pp. 10-14 (quote at p. 14).

49 Garbe, *Widerstand und Martyrium*, pp. 87ff., refers to attempts by the Watch Tower Society for the »adaptation of the Society to national conditions« in a memorandum of the Bibelforschervereinigung, April 26, 1933.

50 As formulated by the Watch Tower president Rutherford in his 1937 book, *Enemies. The proof that definitely identifies all enemies, expases their methods of operation, and points out the way of complete protection for those who love righteousness*, ed., Watch Tower Bible and Tract Society (Bern, 1937), pp. 72f.

51 On the question of the submission required from believers, there are still no signs of an opening to be seen. Jehovah's Witnesses are still obliged to show an unconditional and unquestioning loyalty to the Governing Body. This applies in cases where something appears that is not understandable or with which one does not agree at the moment. In these cases, *The Watchtower* recommends: »Thus, loyalty includes waiting patiently until further understanding is published by the faithful and discreet slave.« (*Watchtower*, March 15, 1996, pp. 15f.)

52 *Der Spiegel*, no. 30, July 19, 1961, pp. 38f.

53 Garbe, *Widerstand und Martyrium*, pp. 300f.

54 Gebhard, *Zeugen Jehovas*, p. 182.

55 Erich Frost, letter to the Neuengamme survivor association, July 15, 1969, in the archives of the Forschungsstelle für Zeitgeschichte, Hamburg, Hans Schwarz personal papers, 13-7-04. It must be remembered that special caution is needed when evaluating Gestapo interrogations. Gestapo protocols are not reliable sources that accurately record actual conversations. In interrogations, the whole Gestapo arsenal was put into use: deception, psychological exhaustion, and physical violence. I have also found a few documents during my research that contrast with the self-depiction of Watch Tower Society leaders, at least as it is conveyed in their publications. My interest as a historian is the history of a religion and not evaluations of the personality of individual functionaries based on moral criteria. I therefore have no interest in any exposé as in Spiegel, since from the first, there was something exceedingly oppressive attached to reaching conclusions based on Gestapo protocols, given the circumstances which accompanied them.

56 Klaus Drobisch, »Rezension von Garbe, Zwischen Widerstand und Martyrium,« in: *1999: Zeitschrift für Sozialgeschichte des 20. und 21. Jahrhunderts* 11, no. 1 (1996), pp. 115ff.

57 Jehovah's Witnesses were affected by repressive measures in numerous countries after the end of the war. From 1945 until the early 1990s, they were prohibited in 23 African, 9 Asian, 8 European, 3 Latin American, and 4 island nations. See *Jehovah's Witnesses — Proclaimers of God's Kingdom* (New York, 1993), p. 676.

Wolfram Slupina

Persecuted and Almost Forgotten

> *Wilt thou show wonders to the dead?*
> *shall the dead arise and praise thee?*
> *Shall thy loving kindness be declared in the grave?*
> *or thy faithfulness in destruction?*
> *Shall thy wonders be known in the dark?*
> *and thy righteousness in the land of forgetfulness?*[1]

The National Socialists cruelly persecuted Jehovah's Witnesses without mercy.[2] Using an extremely sophisticated killing machine, they attempted to consign the Witnesses to oblivion by systematically exterminating them. Despite their political neutrality, Jehovah's Witnesses were among the first to be banned and persecuted by the Nazis, who came to power in 1933.[3] Their fate could historically be compared to the Holocaust of the Jews. Of all the Christian associations the Nazis targeted, they were by far the most severely and mercilessly persecuted.[4] Germany was to become a »land of forgetfulness« for them.[5] After all the parishes of the 25,000[6] Jehovah's Witnesses and their associates throughout Germany publicly distributed a letter on October 7, 1934, drawing attention to the oppression they faced and explaining the Christian basis for their spiritual resistance, Hitler vowed: »This brood will be exterminated in Germany!«[7] That was more than 65 years ago. Jehovah's Witnesses are still here, but Hitler and his Nazi party are not. Michael H. Kater documented this as follows: »The Third Reich knew how to deal with internal resistance only with brutal force and even then was unable to overcome the forces of rebellion among the German people, and was unable to master the problem of the Earnest Bible Students from 1933 to 1945. Jehovahs Witnesses emerged from their period of persecution in 1945 weakened but spiritually unbroken.«[8]

On October 16 and 17, 1996, in Bad Urach, the Landeszentrale für Politische Bildung Baden-Württemberg organized a workshop concerning the January 27 Memorial Day for the Victims of the Concentration Camps. One history teacher commented: »It is impossible to forget what happened in the concentration camps,« whereupon I replied: »The example of Jehovah's Witnesses proves the contrary. They were viciously persecuted by the Nazis and put into concentration camps with other victims. Among those groups were the Communists, whom the Nazis stigmatized as ›political‹ prisoners with a red triangle.[9] Later, these individuals who had suffered the same cruel persecution as Jehovah's Witnesses, in turn, threw them into prisons and jails in the GDR.«[10] Over 300 persons were imprisoned, first by the Nazis because of their religious convictions and later by the Communists under GDR rule. Of the 60 Jehovah's Witnesses who died or were killed during their imprisonment in the GDR, 23 had already been imprisoned under the Nazi regime.[11] Obviously people had already forgotten after only a short interval what had transpired under the Nazis. They went on to persecute the Witnesses anew in parts of the same country. Under those circumstances, how could Jehovah's Witnesses have possibly assembled a historiography of the sufferings which they had just endured under the Nazis?

266

In recent years, Jehovah's Witnesses have repeatedly been forgotten on lists of Nazi victim groups.[12] Hence, Detlef Garbe justifiably includes them among the »forgotten victims,«[13] although his statistical evidence shows that they were »not a negligible group in prewar years. As a rule, they made up between five and ten percent of the total inmate population of the concentration camps, sometimes even more. In some camps there were times when they were even the largest prisoner group.«[14] Friedrich Zipfel wrote: »Hardly an analysis has been made or a book of memoirs written about the concentration camps in which there is not a description of the strong faith, the diligence, helpfulness, and fanatical martyrdom of the Earnest Bible Students. In contrast, general literature about the resistance seldom includes Jehovah's Witnesses opposition before their imprisonment and seldom mentions them at all or, at most, in passing. However, the activity and persecution of the Bible Students is a very unusual case. Ninety-seven percent of the members of this small religious group became victims of Nazi persecution. One third of them were killed, either by execution, or by other violent acts, hunger, illness, or forced labor. The severity of this persecution was without precedent and was the result of uncompromising faith which defied Nazi ideology.«[15] In 1994, based on her research, Brigitte Oleschinski concluded that »there were groups whose depressing litany of persecution, for vastly different reasons, met so little interest on both sides of the inner-German border that the persons concerned were not even protected against new accusations. ... Based on their ideology, some of them challenged the Nazi system with radical opposition that had no equivalent in the two major Christian churches. Today, these same people still have to fight for appropriate acknowledgement of their sufferings and achievements in the current wide-ranging historiography about the resistance.«[16]

That Jehovah's Witnesses have been forgotten as a victim group is even more incomprehensible since the Nazis stigmatized them with a purple triangle as a distinct prisoner category. They usually had to wear this on the left side of their chest above their black prisoner number.[17]

Similarly, Jehovah's Witnesses are not mentioned in writings about conscientious objectors in the Third Reich, and are thereby deliberately »forgotten,«[18] despite the fact that they were the largest segment of this group, numbering several hundred,[19] including about 250 German and Austrian Jehovah's Witnesses and thus they provided the largest number of victims.[20] Garbe documents that »in the Third Reich, they were the only group which as a whole publicized refusal of military service and consistently practiced it.«[21] Hanns Lilje already reached this conclusion in 1947 when he observed: »They can claim to be the only large-scale rejecters of military service in the Third Reich, who did this openly and for the sake of their conscience.«[22] Recently, the book »Soldaten für Hitler« [Soldiers for Hitler] stated in the chapter entitled »The Resistance«: »The refusal to serve in the military was usually based on pacifist and religious motives. Since the Protestant as well as the Catholic Church actively supported military service, there were only very few Christians associated with a church who, following their personal conscience, refused military service and therefore deliberately went to the scaffold. The resistance of Jehovah's Witnesses is not well known, they had been banned just a few months after Hitler came to power, and were persecuted with merciless severity. None of the other religious communities so unanimously and uncompromisingly resisted Nazi coercion, such as compulsory oaths or the obligatory Hitler greeting. None of them paid with such a high price in blood.«[23]

Is the fact that official and other organizations do not mention the Witnesses a sign of being deliberately ignored? Or is it perhaps just forgetfulness? Could this today once again perhaps result in exclusion, discrimination, and stigmatization that ushers in new persecution of a minority here in Germany?

The following question, which Jehovah's Witnesses are often asked, needs a detailed answer. Why did it take more than fifty years to document the self-sacrifice and suffering of their fellow-believers? Did they forget or perhaps want to forget the horrible suffering themselves?

From 1933 to 1945, when most of the world's population did not yet know names like Auschwitz, Buchenwald, Dachau, and Sachsenhausen, Jehovah's Witnesses already revealed the existence of these concentration camps in their publications. At great risk, reports about imprisoned Jehovah's Witnesses were smuggled out of the camps.[24] Based on comprehensive documentation about the concentration camps in Germany in the book »Kreuzzug gegen das Christentum« [Crusade against Christendom] by the Jehovah's Witness Franz Zürcher, the Polish writer Hulka-Laskowski reached the following conclusion: »I am full of heartfelt sympathy and admiration for these courageous people who give such a superb witness to their faith. If there were half a million such Protestants and Catholics in Germany, this unfortunate country would look different.«[25]

The historian Detlef Garbe correctly states: »Unlike other ›forgotten victims,‹ individual Jehovah's Witnesses usually do not feel that their persecution during National Socialism was a stigma in their life which had to be concealed in postwar Germany. Rather, their experiences under persecution became an integral part of their identity. For them, liberation from the ›Nazi yoke‹ was a sign of God's saving grace, and hence an acknowledgement of and a recompense for their faithfulness and ›integrity.‹«[26]

For Jehovah's Witnesses to write a documentation out of hatred, revenge, or for the sake of compensation, goes against their religious ethic.[27] Detlef Garbe correctly states: »Clearly, the effort to stand firm in their faith, to survive the ›trial,‹ and thus prove themselves to be true witnesses of their Lord Jehovah was the underlying motive for their actions. ... ›Resistance‹ [whether intellectual, spiritual, or religious resistance or resistance as a result of Christian conviction, an aggressive form of refusal; therefore not to be ›mistaken for a political expression of resistance‹[28]] was an affirmation of their faith.«[29]

During the past 50 years, Jehovah's Witnesses have documented and acknowledged this »declaration of their faith« by publishing more than 250 memoirs, biographies, or names of survivors and victims, chronicling their triumph, courage, and faith.[30] They have done this in 128 different languages with an average of 22,103,000 copies printed of each account.[31] Therefore, Jehovah's Witnesses must disagree with Detlef Garbe's statement that »only in very few instances were they interested in informing the public, and thus their memoirs were limited to family and other fellow believers.«[32] The reasons why Jehovah's Witnesses did not research their past down to the smallest detail until now are different than those stated by Garbe.[33]

First, the Witnesses—in contrast to other victim groups—could have ended their incarceration and persecution at least temporarily and under certain conditions by signing a special »declaration« disavowing their beliefs.[34] Thus, they were in some way personally responsible for their ordeals and in a certain sense did this of their own free will. This was not in order to be later celebrated as heroes but only because of their uncompromising faith and desire to serve their God. After liberation from the concentration camps, they did not pity themselves or harbor feelings of revenge. Thus, Jehovah's Witness victims did not commence legal proceedings against their persecutors. They had gone through these experiences because of their uncompromising and unshakable faith. They preferred to use their recovered freedom for their beliefs. Nazi persecution had greatly impeded care for their parishes and their preaching activities. Besides their concern for their own families, they had the additional task of reorganizing the remaining parishes and Bible-based preaching.[35] If they had become too immersed in the past they had just survived, it would have hindered or even paralyzed this important work. Unlike other religious associations, they did not have to go through a so-called rehabilitation process, since they could not be blamed for making concessions to the Nazi system. Their regained freedom literally spurred them on. They looked ahead. With raised heads, they could resume their religious activities. They felt that they lacked the time for historical documentation.[36]

Jehovah's Witnesses were not the only group to adopt this view after the war. The publication *Dreißig Jahre Dokumentationsarchiv des österreichischen Widerstandes (1963–1993)* [Thirty Years of the Documentation Archives of the Austrian Resistance] states: »Undoubtedly, it would have been reasonable and necessary to start documentation of resistance and persecution as early as 1945. The memory of what had just happened was still clear, a lot of the material which got lost in subsequent years was still available, access to material in archives would probably have been simpler, and above all, many of the historical protagonists would still have been alive. ... However, in the difficult postwar period and reconstruction and beginning boom of the 1950s, different issues predominated, mostly economic. There was little time for and interest in historical consciousness, documentation, or in coming to terms with the past.«[37]

Furthermore, in the immediate postwar years and even decades later, most political and religious spokesmen did not question the Witnesses' firm stand. At that time, their persecution under Nazi dictatorship had not yet been forgotten.

A few specific examples will document this. Thus, Pastor Martin Niemöller (from 1947 to 1964, president of the Protestant Church in Hessen and Nassau), who had also been arrested by the Nazis on July 1, 1937, and had spent years in various concentration camps,[38] wrote about Jehovah's Witnesses in 1946: »We Christians of today stand ashamed before a so-called sect like the Earnest Bible Students, who by the hundreds and thousands went into concentration camps and died because they declined service in war and refused to fire on humans.«[39] In 1947, Hanns Lilje, who was Lutheran state bishop in Hanover for many years, stated with respect that »no Christian community can stand even the slightest comparison with the number of their martyrs.«[40] The Social Democrat Hans Flatterich wrote in his 1945 memoirs about imprisonment shared with the Witnesses in the Neuengamme concentration camp: »With what steadfastness these people [Jehovah's Witnesses] endured the cruelest ill-treatment year after year. And yet, they did not renounce and compromise their beliefs and even here in the camp they always tried to win other inmates for their beliefs. I must admit, I was forced to give these people my deepest respect.«[41] Already in 1937, the *Deutschland-Berichte*, published by the exile Social Democratic Party in Prague, reported positively about Jehovah's Witnesses in the Sachsenburg concentration camp: »The Earnest Bible Students' conduct is most astonishing. These ... people showed an implacable spirit of opposition and martyrdom and were unyielding as no other group in the camp. Right from the beginning, we political prisoners decided not to rebel and to comply with all the instructions of the camp authorities. The SS would not have put up with much and were just waiting for us to give them a reason to intervene. So we gave the Hitler greeting as ordered, etc. The Earnest Bible Students, however, could under no circumstances be moved to do so. Their belief in Jehovah prohibited this, and they adhered to it strictly. A number of them even refused to accept release from the camp. Some declared that they wanted to stay in the camp until they were again allowed to exercise their religious activities.«[42]

The actual start of persecution and prohibition of Jehovah's Witnesses goes back to the late 1920s. Already two years prior to January 30, 1933, the date when Adolf Hitler was named

Chancellor, the basis for subsequent massive persecution was already established. On March 28, 1931, the Reich President issued an emergency decree, which at the initiative of church leaders restricted the activities of Jehovah's Witnesses in Bavaria.[43] During 1932 this also extended to Württemberg and Baden. Between the major churches and the Nazi party, there already existed »a common interest in combatting the Bible Students which continued after January 30, 1933, and was another step toward their mutual arrangement.«[44] In 1933, under the Nazis, when a general ban extended throughout the whole German Reich, it was again representatives of the Protestant and Catholic churches who welcomed this prohibition.[45] Garbe states: »It was precisely this temporary flank protection of the Nazi state by the larger churches during the period of the regime's stabilization that spared them persecution on a larger scale« and which »encouraged« persecution of the Witnesses.[46] Guenter Lewy is even more explicit. He described historical developments as follows: »On April 13, when the Earnest Bible Students were banned in Bavaria, the churches even accepted the order of the State Ministry of Education and Cultural Affairs to denounce each member of this sect that continued practicing the proscribed religion. The developing totalitarian state left the special interests of the Catholic Church untouched; under these circumstances, it was not hard for the church to make peace with them.«[47] Thus stigmatization, exclusion, and persecution to the point of extermination were consciously accepted. The conflict on the religious level was seemingly decided in favor of the large churches because of the support of their political allies. But in the end this false victory for the churches proved to be a moral and spiritual defeat. This also must not be forgotten!

This look into the past becomes even more frightening when we realize that today similar developments can be clearly seen. As at the end of the 1920s and the beginning of the 1930s, the major churches and their sect experts have initiated desperate campaigns against Jehovah's Witnesses and other denominations, because of the considerable losses within their own ranks.[48] In this connection, the importance of the terms »sect« or »cult« is noteworthy.[49] Martin Kriele, professor for Political Science and Public Law at the Cologne University, points out that »this term, which normally has a neutral meaning in a pluralistic state, has [recently] been turned into a pejorative battle slogan. This term marks them with the stigma of being intellectually primitive and politically intolerant. ... And yet, this process clearly shows a new trend toward state control of ideologies. The enlightenment, historically linked with the fight for freedom, accepted by the majority, now insists on monopoly. Sects ... are not to be banned but ostracized with governmental authority, for example, resulting in the denial of non-profit status for their associations, loss of matriculation at universities, or the denial of recognition as a corporation under public law; further, that their members could be barred from the civil service. A judicial precedent is proposed, which would permit the application of the criteria mentioned above. ... Under our constitution, the religious debate is the concern of free social groups, not of the state. The Federal Ministry refers to alleged wishes of ›the churches.‹ These are allowed ideological debate. However, they should counteract the impression that they are using the first opportunity they could get to return to controlled ideology with state assistance. Political parties mediate between state and society. Some share in the disparagement of sects. For example, the Young Union [CDU] depicts people belonging to a sect as insects, who should be killed with a fly swatter. They should make it clear that they are acting as a group in society and that they do not support state ideological control.«[50] When referring to the present, the historian Sybil Milton writes: »The Christian denomination, Jehovah's Witnesses, tenacious in their opposition to the Nazi regime, was marginalized in the interpretive framework that emphasized political or racial victims. Even today this Christian community is frequently categorized by the derogatory term ›sect.‹ Although this prejorative expression originated in official Nazi usage, uncritical repetition of this term continues to have negative implications today, since it reinforces existing bigotry.«[51]

In Nazi Germany, newspapers publicizing »state ideological control« carried articles entitled »Enemies of the State in religious Guise,«[52] »The most dangerous sect: Earnest Bible Students before the Special Court,«[53] or they classified the Witnesses as a »subversive organization.«[54] Could these be newspaper headlines and declarations printed today? Witness for example, the *Darmstädter Echo* of June 7, 1997, which, under the headline »Eimuth Considers Jehovah's Witnesses Enemies of the Constitution,« states: »According to Kurt-Helmuth Eimuth, sect expert of the Protestant Church in Hessen and Nassau,[55] Jehovah's Witnesses are an anticonstitutional organization.«[56] Eimuth used similar ideas at a hearing of the Bavarian parliament in June 1997.[57]

Eimuth was also appointed by resolution of the German parliament on May 9, 1996, to the Enquete Commission on »So-called Sects and Psychogroups.«[58] Eimuth, as one of the Commission's experts, was invited to a public hearing on March 13, 1997.[59] His book, *Die Sekten-Kinder* (Children in Sects), was used by the Commission as a basis for assessing Jehovah's Witnesses.[60]

In their minority opinion about the interim report of the Enquete Commission, two members, Angelika Köster-Loßack (a Bundestag member) and Hubert Seiwert (Professor at the Institute of Religious Science at Leipzig University), addressed the problem quite frankly: »According to ddp [a German press agency] with regard to ›sects, psycho cults and new religious movements,‹ the sect expert of the Protestant Church in Berlin-Brandenburg spoke in favor of ›using the Office for the Protection of the Constitution to observe and assess these groups. The epd [Protestant Press Service] said that the sect expert of the Protestant Church in Hessen and Nassau [i.e., Eimuth] depicts Jehovah's Witnesses as an ›anticonstitutional organization.‹ Taking such statements into consideration, the possibility of religious and ideological minorities being labeled once more as anticonstitutional and enemies of the state, seems very real and must therefore be made a subject of debate.«[61]

After analyzing the same facts with regard to the investigation by the Enquete Commission, Gerhard Besier (Professor of Historical Theology and Religion at Heidelberg University) wrote: »Among the experts of the commission, we also find so-called commisioners of the churches for ideological issues, a problematic conflict of interest. It seems obvious that the shrinking major churches must have an interest in eliminating any competitors.«[62]

As Kriele remarked, the word »sect« in most cases also means »denial of status as a corporation under public law.«[63] During the Third Reich, this was the basis for massive persecution. Zipfel wrote: »Minor religious associations considered either troublesome or dangerous by the Nazis had to bear the brunt of the oppressive measures of the state police. Unlike the Catholic and Protestant churches, these associations did not have the status of a corporation under public law. ... On the other hand, these denominations had very little legal protection. ... The main criteria for the application of oppressive measures was the loyalty of the organization towards the state. If this was included in their respective religious creeds and as long as their members complied with governmental restrictions, the denominations were spared during the first persecution. If not, these groups were first banned as an organization, which was then followed by the persecution of its members by the police on the basis of § 5 of the Decree of the Reich President to Maintain Domestic Peace of December 19, 1932, together with § 1 of the Reichstags fire decree and the use of penal provision in § 4. The ›International Association of Earnest Bible Students,‹ the ›Watch

Tower Bible and Tract Society,‹ was the first religious association to suffer the sustained oppressive measures of the Nazis.«[64] Since, during the 1920s and 1930s, smaller religious associations did not have the status of a corporation under public law, there was no protection for them in the governmental structure. Consequently, they became religious and political fair game. Have these tactics been forgotten today?

After Germany's unification in October 1990, the question of the legal status of Jehovah's Witnesses in the territory of the former GDR had to be cleared up. The last meeting of the GDR Council of Ministers stated on March 14, 1990: »OFFICIAL RECOGNITION: The ›Religious Association of Jehovah's Witnesses in the GDR,‹ with its headquarters in Berlin, capital of the German Democratic Republic, is officially recognized. This official recognition gives the religious association legal capacity and authorizes it to exercise its activities under article 39 (2) of the GDR constitution.«[65] Such official recognition gave the religious association full legal capacity. Article 19 of the Unification Agreement explicitly stated that administrative decisions issued in the GDR before this agreement would remain in effect. The official recognition of this religious association was such an administrative act and is therefore still valid.

After unification, the name changed from »Religious Association of Jehovah's Witnesses in the GDR« to »Religious Association of Jehovah's Witnesses in Germany.« It should be mentioned that the legal status of the »Religious Association of Jehovah's Witnesses in Germany« still needs to be resolved. In the GDR, religious associations had their own legal status which does not exist in the legal system of the Federal Republic. Unification forced the religious associations which already had official recognition in the GDR to apply for a new legal status conforming to the West German legal system. This can either be the status of a corporation under public law or that of a registered association. For this reason the religious association of Jehovah's Witnesses initiated legal proceedings to obtain a legal status recognized by the German legal system.

Recognition as a corporation under public law is necessary so that the religious association can appropriately represent its members as a whole. The need for this is especially acute because of the horrible persecution of Jehovah's Witnesses under the Nazi regime and because of the almost forty years of persecution that followed under the dictatorial GDR system.[66] This would enable Jehovah's Witnesses to enjoy the same rights already granted to more than thirty other religious associations.[67] However, the Senate of Berlin turned down the application for recognition as a corporation under public law. This rejection resulted in a lawsuit. On October 25, 1993, the Berlin Administrative Court stated in its decision that this religious association must be recognized as a corporation under public law. The Senate of Berlin filed an appeal.[68]

On December 14, 1995, the Higher Administrative Court in Berlin upheld the court decision of the Berlin Administrative Court. The Higher Administrative Court had no doubts that the religious association of Jehovah's Witnesses met the constitutional requirements for a corporation under public law and must therefore be recognized as such.[69] The State of Berlin filed another appeal against the Higher Administrative Court decision.

Surprisingly, on June 26, 1997, the Federal Administrative Court overturned the previous decisions that had been in favor of the Witnesses. The court decision explained: »The plaintiff fails to show loyalty toward the democratic state which is indispensable for a lasting cooperation. According to the actual statements of the Higher Administrative Court, Jehovah's Witnesses' attitudes towards the state are basically positive, not negative, but as a matter of principle they refuse to participate in political elections. This refusal—as well as their refusal of military service and alternative service—is an expression of their strict adherence to a command of their faith, namely the biblical commandment of ›Christian neutrality‹ in political matters.«[70] This line of reasoning is not new. Refusal to perform military service and refusal to participate in political elections were the reasons why Jehovah's Witnesses were excluded, deprived of their personal rights and cruelly persecuted in the Third Reich, as well as under communist rule in the GDR.[71] One wonders if these historical facts were forgotten in the court's opinion.

Under the headline »Doubtful,« the *Frankfurter Allgemeine* stated: »The Federal Administrative Court was in a predicament because the lower courts had awarded the status. Since it wanted to decide differently, it had to read more into the law, than what the law contains.«[72] According to *Neues Deutschland,* it »hardly bothered anyone that the court [had created] ›new law‹ by arbitrarily requiring stricter rules than—until now unwritten—principle of allegiance to the law. The judges ›conjured up new criteria out of a hat‹ (*Tagesspiegel*).« The Newspaper stated: »Nowhere did the court decision mention that fascist rule took such a heavy toll of lives from the members of this religious association, even compared to other victim groups. The comment of the archbishopric Berlin ›that anti-church tendencies could increase if Jehovah's Witnesses now presented themselves as martyrs‹ thus appears suspect. After all, during the Nazi period the official church was just as aloof in this case as it was with regard to the persecution of the Jews. ... Today they [Jehovah's Witnesses] rank among the ›forgotten‹ victims. To this day there are still no regulations for their restitution. In the Soviet Occupational Zone, the persecuted Witnesses were recognized as victims of fascism. However, in 1950, the religious association was banned in the GDR. The members were deprived of the status as victims of the Nazi regime. They were again persecuted. Critical reserve toward the beliefs of this religious association should not permit the sufferings of those with the ›purple triangle‹ to fall into oblivion.«[73]

On August 13, 1997, Jehovah's Witnesses filed a constitutional complaint with the Federal Constitutional Court in Karlsruhe against the Federal Administrative Court decision of June 26, 1997, arguing that this court verified a violation of constitutional rights, namely an infringement of constitutional rights under article 3, the principle of equality, and of article 4, religious freedom.[74] On September 20, 2000, there was a hearing before the Federal Constitutional Court.[75] The verdict was announced on December 19, 2000, and overturned the decision of the Federal Administrative Court.[76] Christian Geyer, writing for the English edition of the *Frankfurter Allgemeine Zeitung* on December 22, 2000, reported under the heading »Christian Neutrality: Ruling Emphasizes Separation of Church and State«: »Germany's Federal Constitutional Court has used the Jehovah's Witnesses' lawsuit, in which they seek status as a public corporation, to bring much-needed clarity to the relationship between religion and the modern state. ... ›Whether a religious society's application for corporate status is denied will be determined not by its beliefs but by its behavior.‹ That is the key statement in this judgment, from which everything else follows: insistence on adherence to the rule of law on the one hand and, on the other, rejection of the German Federal Administrative Court's newly developed and nebulous criterion of ›state loyalty,‹ ... The ›vague concept‹ of ›state loyalty‹ runs afoul of the high court judges because it leaves open an extraordinarily large number of interpretations, going so far as to include the expectation that a religious society ›must either adopt certain state goals as its own or view itself as counsel to the state.‹ This, in the view of the court, not only endangers legal certainty but also tends to reduce the distance between the state and religion to a point neither required nor permitted by German state church law. ... In a first reaction to the judgment, the Central Committee's spokesman on church policy, Hermann Kues (who is also the spokesman on church policy for the joint Christian Democratic Union and Christian Social Union parliamentary group), declared that it would be ›a catastrophe‹ if the Jehovah's Witnesses were to attain legal recognition. He trusts in the knee-jerk reaction that he expects his use of the word ›sect‹ to elicit and fails to realize that many Christian statements about the secular world might be viewed as similarly isolationist, immoral and sectarian. Instead, Kues would force upon Christianity a task that the state, according to the verdict in Karlsruhe, may simply not demand of it: ›Christianity attempts to shape people into responsible citizens.‹« [77] The Federal Administrative Court was instructed to reconsider the application of Jehovah's Witnesses. Thus the final legal status of the religious association still remains unsettled.[78]

The public controversy about so-called »sects and psychogroups,« as well as the discussion about their status as a corporation under public law, has given rise to negative media coverage that has obscured historical facts about the Witnesses.[79] As a result, individual members and the religious association itself have experienced disadvantages and discrimination, which should not be ignored. Some examples to illustrate this:

— A swastika and »1933« were spray-painted on the door of the Kingdom Hall in the Saarlouis parish. This happened after a television broadcast on February 4, 1993.[80]
— The Jehovah's Witness parish in Bad Segeberg received a threatening letter in 1993. Among other things, it stated: »In conclusion, you will hear from us and see us again, but our actions won't be against you alone, but against all sects and religions that are taking advantage of people!«
— During New Year's Eve on December 31, 1993, a wall of the Kingdom Hall in the Kiel-Mettenhof parish was spray-painted with the following words in black: »Get rid of Sects.« There had already been graffiti on the walls one and a half years earlier.
— On August 22, 1995, unknown persons repeatedly sprayed red paint on the entrance of the Kingdom Hall of the Günzburg parish, including the word »Satan.«
— In 1995, the Jehovah's Witnesses parish in Malchin received repeated bomb threats by mail. Criminal charges were filed against unknown individuals.[81]
— Mr. B. M. asked the Junge Union Deutschlands, Enzkreis/Pforzheim District Group, for documents about Jehovah's Witnesses. He was told: »We have nothing in writing that would give explicit information about their activities. ... Since Jehovah's Witnesses and their ›machinations‹ have always been viewed suspiciously, this is surely not without good reason ...«
— In Chemnitz, on June 10, 1997, three skinheads attacked Mr. M. K., a Jehovah's Witness, while he was engaged in his missionary work. One of the skinheads claimed that »Jehovah's Witnesses ... sexually molested children.« Mr. K. was seriously injured and had to be hospitalized.[82]
— On July 14, 1997, Mr. H.-J. Sp. received a call from Mrs. R. from the mail editorial service of Telekom in Cottbus. In agreement with the Telekom's legal department she informed him that from now on, Jehovah's Witnesses would no longer be registered under the entry »churches, religious associations.« This was based on the July 1997 decision of the Federal Administrative Court Berlin. Jehovah's Witnesses would subsequently be registered alphabetically among private individuals.
— On July 15, 1997, the chief editor of the *Darmstädter Echo* informed the parish of Jehovah's Witnesses in the city of Mühltal that the newspaper would no longer publish the times of their religious services. The parish was promised the following, obviously in anticipation of the results of the Enquete Commission: »We are closely following the work of the Bundestag

Enquete Commission on »So-called Sects and Psychogroups.« Should they reach new conclusions in about 18 months, we might be willing to review today's decision.«

— In July 1997, Mr. V. J. B., a Jehovah's Witness, was informed by the community Sasbach that the local paper would no longer announce the religious services of Jehovah's Witnesses along with the services of other churches. Even a meeting with the mayor could not change that decision.

— A representative of Jehovah's Witnesses visited the editorial office of the *Hannoversche Allgemeine Zeitung* on September 8, 1997. He wanted to speak about the possibility of publishing an objective report by a journalist about Jehovah's Witnesses. The responsible editor said that the publishing of this article had been discussed by the editorial office and rejected by the majority. The reason stated was: »Jehovah's Witnesses are a sect and on the same level as Scientology.« The editorial office would under no circumstances publish anything about or from Jehovah's Witnesses.

— Biased TV broadcasts that present a twisted picture of Jehovah's Witnesses are shown in schools. Teachers extensively discuss these programs with the students pointing out how dangerous Jehovah's Witnesses are. The viewpoint of the religious association is not presented for discussion, as a fair and orderly curriculum would require.

— In November 1997, massive pressure from parents prevented an exhibition by Jehovah's Witnesses in the Realschule Gerolzhofen, entitled »Jehovah's Witnesses Stand Firm Against Nazi Assault.« As a substitute, the city provided rooms in the Bürgerspital.[83]

— Some state property registries and probate courts in the new federal states have questioned the power of attorney of the chairman of the religious association. In cases of real estate purchases or in matters regarding an estate, they often do not make entries in official registers.

— »After massive complaints from readers,« the local paper in Eschede is no longer willing to announce events of the local Jehovah's Witness parish.[84]

— Following an agreement, Mr. H. N. (a Jehovah's Witness) wanted to take care of F. W., whose parents are also Jehovah's Witnesses. The guardianship court of the Aurich local court rejected the request because he »belongs to the sect or the religious association of Jehovah's Witnesses, and even has a leading position. This group of persons is generally excluded from matters pertaining to the care of somebody.«[85]

— In March 1998, a notice was received from the editorial office of the daily newspaper *Südkurier* that »in the whole region where the Südkurier is distributed, Jehovah's Witnesses will no longer be included in the announcements for religious services.« In comparison with other religious associations, this is discrimination.

— At first, members of the Enquete Commission thought it important to talk about »so-called« sects, to show their unbiased openness, today this is generally shortened to »sects« in public. The state, required to show religious and ideological neutrality, accepts this without protest.[86]

— One member of the Berlin Senate submitted an official inquiry for discussion, as to which of the accusations against the religious association of Jehovah's Witnesses were known to the Senate of Berlin and which were used in the successful lawsuit against its recognition as a corporation under public law. The representative of the Senate Interior Department expressed himself in a discriminatory way against the religious association.[87]

— On February 2, 1999, the facade of the Kingdom Hall in Breese was spray-painted in black with the slogans »We want a zone free of Jehovah's Witnesses,« »Jehovah's Witnesses out!« This was the sixth time within a short period of time that the Kingdom Hall had been damaged.[88]

These are only a few of the many examples of discriminatory acts against Jehovah's Witnesses in Germany today. One could claim that the foregoing experiences have very little to do with the subject »Persecuted and Almost Forgotten.« Nevertheless, these occurrences are very significant. They are indications of the sad deterioration of public opinion in recent times. This is aggravated by the fact that eyewitnesses who immediately after the war were able to give comprehensive verbal accounts of the persecution during the Nazi period, are becoming scarce. In many cases, those still alive are no longer able to contribute to historical documentation. Back in 1945, Theodor Heuss, who became the first President of the Federal Republic of Germany in 1949, referred to this problem, when he spoke about the victims of National Socialism. In a speech given at a celebration of the government of Baden-Württemberg, he said: »We, the living survivors still have our firsthand impressions. We knew this person and that person no longer with us today. We know about the tortures which killed him. There are even many here today in this house who have suffered from persecution, humiliation, imprisonment, detention in jails, or concentration camps. By their existence, their reports, and their influence, they are the accusing witnesses of those terrible years. But they also, like us, will one day no longer be here. Names and reminiscences will fade. Then, will all this be forgotten, perhaps becoming heaps of material only for historians and novelists. This is exactly what must not happen.«[89]

A new generation represents our country. Many young people do not know that the Bible Students, as they are named at memorial sites, and Jehovah's Witnesses are one and the same prisoner category. Not a few consider National Socialism as heroic and deliberately forget the atrocities connected with it. The philosopher Karl Jaspers presciently warned about this shortly after World War II: »There is a danger. That of not wanting to know, forgetting, and even the not believing (there are still people that deny the realities in the concentration camps). Further, there is the evil of those who by their obedience are ready to be used as tools—and finally an indifference that finds tranquility in the present and future, and the passivity caused by a deep feeling of powerlessness, along with surrender to ostensible necessities.«[90] However, Jehovah's Witnesses have preserved until today their religious and ethical position which gave them the strength to resist Hitler's cruel system. They can serve as examples today, even as they did in the past.

On January 27, 1998, the State of Brandenburg held its main commemoration for the victims of National Socialism, especially Jehovah's Witnesses, at Sachsenhausen. Steffen Reiche, Minister of Science, Research, and Culture, emphasized that »Today's event involves more than just reminiscing about and acknowledging the victims. It directly affects the present. The conduct of Jehovah's Witnesses in the camps and prisons displayed virtues, which, today as in the past, are indispensable to the continued existence of a democratic constitutional state, namely their steadfastness against the SS and their humanity towards fellow prisoners. Considering the increasing brutality of our society towards foreigners and towards persons of different political or ideological opinions, these virtues have become imperative for the citizens of our country.«[91]

There is a need for greater historical documentation about the »forgotten victims« so that, on the one hand, the persecuted will not be forgotten in the future, and on the other hand, there is a lesson that can be taught to future generations. Jehovah's Witnesses want to continue to contribute to this work.

Historians, memorial sites, and a number of politicians appreciate and support the initiative of bringing the story of Jehovah's Witnesses, as a »forgotten« group of victims of National Socialism out of obscurity. Thus, they join in sending a positive signal against a negative trend and assign the story of Jehovah's Witnesses as victims of National Socialism an important role in society.

The world premiere of the video documentary »Jehovah's Witnesses Stand Firm Against Nazi Assault« on November 6, 1996, was held at the Ravensbrück Memorial and attended by numerous representatives of various public institutions, historians, and survivors.[92] The Prime Minister of the State of Brandenburg, Manfred Stolpe, stated in his introductory remarks that »the Government of the State of Brandenburg ... is interested in a clear and comprehensive presentation of the history of Jehovah's Witnesses in the concentration camps. ... Your video presentation is an important step towards informing the public about the role of your religious association under the Nazi regime. It would surely be beneficial if the video were included in the pedagogical program of the Memorials at Ravensbrück and Sachsenhausen, thus being accessible for visitors.«[93]

On May 7, 1997, the Moringen Concentration Camp Survivors Association organized an event entitled »Persecution of Jehovah's Witnesses under the Nazi regime, 1933-1945.« Highlights of this program included interviews with surviving Jehovah's Witnesses, as well as papers by the historians Hans Hesse and Jürgen Harder. The video »Jehovah's Witnesses Stand Firm Against Nazi Assault« was screened. This was accompanied by an impressive exhibition, which emphatically documented the sufferings of female Jehovah's Witnesses, the largest group of victims in the concentration camps for women.[94]

An outstanding contribution in the effort to focus attention on Jehovah's Witnesses as a victim group was the academic conference »Spiritual Resistance Out of Christian Conviction: Jehovah's Witnesses under National Socialism« held in Wewelsburg castle on October 4, 1997. It was organized by the District Museum Wewelsburg and the Fritz Bauer Institute, a center of study and documentation of the history and consequences of the Holocaust, as well as by the Bundeszentrale für politische Bildung along with specialists from the United States and Germany. The meeting was well received.[95] This was followed by another symposium in Wewelsburg castle on October 5, with the topic »History and the Present: Jehovah's Witnesses in Germany.« »Spiritual Resistance Out of Christian Conviction« was also discussed at a later meeting on October 17 at Wewelsburg. The same theme was discussed on October 7 at the Neuengamme Memorial, on October 8 in the Museum für Hamburgische Geschichte, and on October 10 and 11 in the Bürgerhaus Frankfurt-Bornheim. All these meetings included an exhibition on the subject.[96]

Similar symposia were held at concentration camp memorials in Buchenwald (October 21–31, 1997),[97] Sachsenhausen (January 27, 1998),[98] and Bergen-Belsen (April 18, 1998; the exhibition »Stand Firm Against Persecution« included additional panels for this concentration camp memorial from April 18 until June 21, 1998).[99] Dr. Volkhard Knigge, director of the Buchenwald Memorial, stated appropriately at the opening of the exhibition »Stand Firm (Persecution of Jehovah's Witnesses 1933–1945)«: »Possibly, the fact that such ›simple people‹ did not yield to the totalitarian demands of the Nazi state is one reason why the persecution by the Nazi regime has been forgotten for so long—in both parts of Germany. The exhibition ... wants to put an end to this long obscurity. For this reason, the Buchenwald Memorial has welcomed the exhibition. It helps us with the efforts we have been making since 1989–90 to recall groups of forgotten victims into collective memory. Along these lines, I am to convey the greetings of the

Prime Minister of the Free State of Thuringia, Dr. Bernhard Vogel, for the Thuringian Government. With sincere sympathy, the government takes note of these efforts to remember.« Apart from panels documenting the individual fate of Jehovah's Witnesses, Buchenwald was the first exhibition to include watercolors by a former Buchenwald Witness prisoner, Johannes Steyer, prisoner no. 1795.[100]

On January 27, 1998, survivors, as well as representatives of Jehovah's Witnesses, were invited to the Commemoration for the Victims of National Socialism in the State Parliament of Baden-Württemberg. During the public discussion there with eight survivors and representatives of victim groups, Deputy Prime Minister of the State Parliament, Frieder Birzele, interviewed Gertrud Wulle, a surviving Jehovah's Witness. As at Brandenburg, efforts are now being made by the government to acknowledge Jehovah's Witnesses as victims and to include them in events, in an effort to prevent them from being forgotten. And rightly so!

The history of Jehovah's Witnesses clearly demonstrates that amnesia can quickly turn into persecution with all its negative consequences. This should never be forgotten! Karl Jaspers wrote about National Socialism: »What has happened serves as a warning. To forget means to be guilty. We have to continually remind ourselves of this. It happened and might possibly reoccur at any time. Only knowledge can prevent that.«[101]

Publications of the Watch Tower Society containing life stories and recollections of, or naming, Witness survivors:

Elsa Abt (incarcerated for 7 years, Watchtower [WT], April 15, 1980, pp. 12-15; 1994 Yearbook of Jehovah's Witnesses [YB] p. 202; Jehovah's Witnesses—Proclaimers of God's Kingdom [JWP], p. 453)

Harald Abt (imprisoned for 14 years, WT April 14, 1980, pp. 6-12; YB94 pp. 202, 224, 247; JWP p. 453)

Alfred Antoni (The Golden Age, January 29, 1936, pp. 274f.)

Maria Appel (YB74 pp. 187-190)

Rolf Appel (YB74 pp. 187-190)

Walter Appel (YB74 pp. 187-190)

Adolphe Arnold (concentration camps in Schirmeck, Dachau, Mauthausen, Awake! [AW], September 22, 1993, pp. 15-19, JWP p. 451)

Emma Arnold (Schirmeck concentration camp, solitary confinement, AW September 22, 1993, pp. 15-19; JWP p. 451)

Gustav Auschner (AW April 8, 1989, p. 14)

Emma Auschner (her sons Kurt and Rudolf Auschner were sentenced to death, YB74 p. 185)

Wilhelmina Bakker (YB86 pp. 142, 154)

Georg Bär (YB74 pp. 153f., 154, 182f.)

Eva Ballreich (her husband Heinrich was sentenced to death, YB74 pp. 185f.)

Paul Balzereit (YB74 pp. 109-111, 131, 148ff.)

Wilhelm Bathen (YB74 p. 175)

Sandor Beier (YB74 p. 201)

Jacob van Bennekom (executed, Rotterdam prison, Amersfoort concentration camp, WT April 1, 2000, pp. 24-27)

Gijsbert N. van der Bijl (from 1941 to 1945 in Buchenwald; WT January 1, 1998 pp. 25-29)

Franz Birk (YB74 pp. 191, 200)

Wilhelm Blascheck (YB89 p. 123)

Richard Blümel (WT August 1, 1967, pp. 472-475)

Marinus de Boer (YB86 pp. 164ff., 168)

Albertus Bos (WT April 1, 2000, pp. 27f.)

Friedrich Boschan (YB74 p. 113)

Helmut Brembach (YB74 pp. 114, 139ff.)

Victor Bruch (concentration camps in Buchenwald, Lublin, Auschwitz, Ravensbrück, JWP p. 452)

Josef Buchner (Mauthausen concentration camp, YB89 pp. 113, 131f.)

Otto Buchta (died in Mauthausen concentration camp, YB2000 pp. 164f.)

Paul Buder (YB74 pp. 145, 167)

Karl Bühler (sentenced to death, YB74 pp. 185f.)

Frieda Bühler (YB74 pp. 185f.)

Tjeerd de Bruijn (YB86 pp. 124, 126, 146)

Gretel Bürlen (WT May 1, 1997, p. 26)

Ludwig Cyranek (beheaded in 1941, WT May 1, 1989, pp. 11ff.; AW April 8, 1989, pp. 15f.; YB74 pp. 179-181; YB89 pp. 106f., 110f.)

Ruth Danner (WT January 15, 1998, p. 6)

Josephine Darmstadt (YB74 p. 138)

Franz Desch (concentration camps in Mauthausen, Gusen, YB89 p. 132)

Änne Dickmann (WT July 1, 1972, pp. 395-399; Jehovas Zeugen — Menschen aus der Nachbarschaft. Wer sind sie? [JZM], Selters/Ts. 1995, p. 18)

August Dickmann (executed because of conscientious objection by a firing squad in the Sachsenhausen concentration camp in 1939, WT July 1, 1972, p. 398; WT August 1, 1991, p. 28; WT May 1, 2000, p. 32; AW April 8, 1989, p. 14; AW February 8, 1993, p. 21; AW May 8, 1993, p. 6; YB74 pp. 166-169; JZM p. 18)

Heinrich Dickmann (WT July 1, 1972, pp. 395-399; YB74 pp. 167ff.; JZM p. 18)

Minna Dietrichkeit (YB74 p. 178)

Heinrich Dietschi (YB74 pp. 154, 159-161)

Klara Dietschi (YB74 p. 161)

Hans Dollinger (YB74 pp. 148ff.)

Evert Dost (YB86 p. 143)

Heinrich Dwenger (YB74 pp. 74, 154)

Bro. van de Eijkhoff (YB86 pp. 134, 158)

Hermann Emter (YB74 p. 162)

Julius Engelhardt (YB74 pp. 181f., 201)

Leopold Engleitner (arrested in 1934, YB89 pp. 94ff., 112f.)

Emilie (Mielchen) Ernst (WT May 1, 1997, p. 26)

Elisabeth Ernsting (YB74 p. 201)

Peter Esch (Buchenwald, AW April 8, 2000, p.31)

Gertrud Franke (JWP p. 451; YB74 pp. 117, 179)

Konrad Franke (WT March 15, 1963, pp. 180-183; WT December 1, 1983, p. 31; WT May 1, 1989, p. 12; WT May 1, 1997, p. 27;

YB74 pp. 109, 133-138, 191f.; JWP p. 451)

Max Franke (JWP p. 451)

Franziska Frey (YB74 p. 181)

Friedrich Frey (YB74 p. 169)

Franz Fritsche (WT November 1, 1979, p. 12; YB74 pp. 199, 201f.)

Erich Frost (WT April 15, 1961, pp. 244-249; WT March 15, 1998, p. 21; WT May 1, 1989, p. 12; YB74 pp. 152, 158, 198)

Carl Göhring (YB74 p. 126)

Peter Gölles (YB89 pp. 103f., 106, 125-129, 134; JWP pp. 450, 454)

Jan Gontkiewicz (Majdanek, Buchenwald concentration camps, YB94 p. 204)

Leen de Graf (died in Ladelund, Wachttoren, November 1, 1945, p. 208)

Alfred Graichen (WT Aug. 1, 1997, pp. 20-25)

Rudolf Graichen (WT Aug. 1, 1997, pp. 20-25)

Teresa Graichen (WT Aug. 1, 1997, pp. 20-25)

Helene Green (YB74 p. 187)

Bernhard Grimm (1942, executed in Berlin-Plötzensee at the age of 19; JZM p. 4)

Paul Großmann (YB74 pp. 152, 203f.)

Heinrich Halstenberg (YB74 p. 145)

Walter Hamann (YB74 p. 205)

Martin Harbeck (YB74 pp. 112, 131f., 157, 179)

Elise Harms (WT October 15, 1981, pp. 26-30; YB74 p. 183)

Johannes Harms (WT October 15, 1981, pp. 26-30; AW June 8, 1985, p. 11; AW April 8, 1989; p. 16, AW August 22, 1995, p. 5; YB74 pp. 183f.)

Martin Harms (YB74 p. 183)

Emil Hartmann (YB74 p. 183)

Kurt Hedel (YB74 p. 176)

Richard and Gerhard Heide (YB89 pp. 83, 123)

Steve Heiwegen (YB86 pp. 143, 151)

Max Henning (Buchenwald concentration camp, WT June 1, 1996, pp. 20-24)

Elfriede Henschel (died in prison, AW February 22, 1998, pp. 12-17)

Horst Henschel (AW February 22, 1998, pp. 12-17; YB74 pp. 122ff.)

Hugo Henschel (sentenced to death, AW February 22, 1998, pp. 12-17; YB74 pp. 122ff.)

Liesbeth Henschel (mother of Horst Henschel, AW Feb. 22, 1998, pp. 12-17; YB74 pp. 122ff.)

Christine Hetkamp (YB74 pp. 181f.)

Hildegard Hiegel (YB74 p. 113)

Wilhelm Hirsch (executed as conscientious objector, JZM pp. 4f.)

Julius Hochgräfe (YB74 p. 147)

Sister Höhne (YB74 p. 185)

Elisabeth Holec and her mother (both in the Ravensbrück concentration camp where the mother died, YB89 pp. 111f.)

Maria Hombach (3½ years in solitary confinement, WT May 1, 1989, pp. 10-13; YB74 p. 180; JWP p. 451; JZM p. 19)

Hansi Hron (née Buchner, YB89 pp. 106-110)

Carl Hultman (YB86 p. 145)

Hans Jäger (YB74 pp. 192f.)

Éva Josefsson (Auschwitz, Bergen-Belsen, WT June 1, 1998, pp. 28-31)

Piet Kalkmann (died in the Neuengamme concentration camp, Wachttoren, November 1, 1945, p. 208)

Otto Kamien (AW February 8, 1993, p. 20)

Bro. Kapinus (YB2000 p. 164)

Willi Karger (YB74 pp. 192f.)

Franz Kassing (YB74 p. 153)

Heinrich Kaufmann (YB74 p. 163)

Martha Kaufmann (YB74 p. 163)

Evert Kettelarij (WT April 1, 2000, p. 27)

Ludwig Kinicki (arrested in 1944, died in the Gusen concentration camp, YB94 p. 204)

Karl Kirscht (YB74 p. 177)

Grete Klein (YB74 pp. 130f.)

Willi Kleissle (YB74 p. 144)

Georg Klohe (YB74 pp. 152f.)

Erwin Klose (AW November 22, 1992, pp. 19ff.)

Heinrich Kluckhuhn (YB74 pp. 158, 160)

Helmut Knöller (YB74 pp. 117f., 170f.)

Johann Kölbl (YB74 p. 113)

Anton Kötgen (YB74 p. 150)

Franz Kohlhofer (YB74 p. 144)

Gusti Kornelius (YB74 pp. 127f.)

August Kraft (was arrested on May 25, 1939, died in the Mauthausen concentration camp, YB89 pp. 99-102, 132; JWP p. 450)

Karl Krause (Gusen concentration camp, YB89 pp. 132f.)

Johann Kuderna (YB89 p. 105)

Joseph Kulczak (WT January 1, 1999, p. 23)

Annemarie Kusserow (Hamburg-Fuhlsbüttel penitentiary, WT September 1, 1985, pp. 11, 14)

Franz Kusserow (WT September 1, 1985, pp. 13ff.; JWP p. 449)

Hilda Kusserow (Ravensbrück concentration camp, WT September 1, 1985, pp. 14f.; JWP p. 449)

Hildegard Kusserow (WT Sept. 1, 1985, p. 13)

Karl-Heinz Kusserow (Dachau concentration camp, WT September 1, 1985, p. 14)

Wilhelm Kusserow (publicly executed in Münster, WT September 1, 1985, p. 14; JWP p. 449)

Wolfgang Kusserow (executed for refusing military service like his brother Wilhelm, AW August 22, 1995, p. 5)

Elisabeth Lange (YB74 p. 172)

Wim Laros (YB86 p. 145)

Willi Lehmbecker (YB74 p. 128)

Max Liebster (WT October 1, 1978, pp. 20-24; AW April 8, 1989, p. 7)

Simone Liebster (née Arnold, for 22 months in a Nazi reform school as a teenager; father and mother were in a concentration camp; AW September 22, 1993; pp. 15-19)

Elfriede Löhr (WT November 1, 1979, pp. 8-14; YB74 pp. 159ff.; JWP p. 450; JZM pp. 18f.)

Walter Lübke (YB74 p. 211)

Reinhold Lühring (YB74 p. 198)

Bernard Luimes (WT April 1, 2000, pp. 27f.)

Franz Massors (sentenced to death, YB74 pp. 190f.)

Hubert Mattischek (in three concentration camps, among them Dachau and Mauthausen, YB89 pp. 115-118)

Willi Mattischek (Mauthausen concentration camp, YB89 pp. 115ff.)

Berta Maurer (YB74 p. 173)

Gottfried Mehlhorn (WT May 1, 1997, p. 27)

Franz Merck (YB74 p. 134)

Hildegard Mesch (YB74 p. 152)

Stefan Milweski (Majdanek, Buchenwald concentration camps, YB94 p. 204)

Piet van der Molen (Amersfoort concentration camp, YB86 pp. 157ff.)

Alois Moser (was in seven prisons and concentration camps, e.g. in Mauthausen, YB89 pp. 113, 131f.; JWP p. 451)

Charlotte Müller (WT May 1, 1997, pp. 24-29)

Alfred Mütze (YB74 p. 111)

Hans Naumann (AW May 22, 1983, pp. 23-27)

Oldřich Nesrovnal (Dachau, YB2000 p. 167)

Johannes Neubacher (WT January 15, 1996, p. 4; JZM p. 19)

Marta Neuffer (YB74 p. 179)

Otto Niedersberg (YB74 pp. 113f.)

Bozena Nováková (YB2000 pp. 168ff.)

Johann and Hermine Obweger (YB89 pp. 123ff.)

Gertrud Oehme (WT May 1, 1997, p. 26)

Gerhard Oltmanns (WT October 1, 1968, pp. 598-602)

Jan Otrebski (imprisoned for four years, YB94 p. 202)

Gertrud Ott (Auschwitz, Groß-Rosen, Bergen-Belsen concentration camps, JWP p. 452; YB74 pp. 200f.)

August Peters (WT November 1, 1962, pp. 668ff.; JWP p. 452)

Johann Pichler (in 1939 executed by a military detachment for refusing military service, YB89 pp. 119ff.)

Louis Piéchota (WT August 15, 1980, pp. 5-10)

Hans and Marie Poddig (YB74 pp. 127, 131f.)

Bernhard Polmann (executed, WT April 1, 2000, pp. 24, 28; YB86 pp. 166f.)

Gertrud Pötzinger (Ravensbrück concentration camp, WT August 1, 1984, pp. 25-31; JWP pp. 452, 661, 663; JZM p. 19)

Martin Pötzinger (Dachau, Mauthausen concentration camps; died in 1988, AW April 8, 1989, p. 13; AW October 22, 1999, p. 16; WT December 1, 1969, pp. 729-732; WT September 15, 1988, p. 31; YB74 p. 138; JWP pp. 452, 661, 663)

Hermann Raböse (WT March 1, 1987, p. 22)

Johann Rainer (YB89 pp. 114f.)

Antonie Rehmeijer (WT April 1, 2000, pp. 27f.)

Ernst Rehwald (sentenced to death, YB74 p. 185; AW February 8, 1993, pp. 21f.)

Hans Rehwald (sentenced to death, YB74 p. 185; AW February 8, 1993, pp. 21f.)

Helene Rehwald (AW February 8, 1993, pp. 21, 23)

Josef Rehwald (JZM p. 18; AW February 8, 1993, pp. 20-23; WT May 1, 1997, p. 27)

Paul Rehwald (AW February 8, 1993, pp. 21, 23)

Franz Reiter (execution by guillotine in Berlin-Plötzensee in 1940, YB89 pp. 121ff.; JWP p. 662)

Magdalena Reuter (née Kusserow, 4 years in the Ravensbrück concentration camp, WT September 1, 1985, pp. 10-15; AW September 8, 1990, p. 20)

Julius Riffel (YB74 pp. 161, 178ff.)

Anton Rinker (YB74 pp. 190f.)

Erwin Rinker (JZM p. 18)

Wilhelm Röger (YB74 pp. 177, 202)

Kurt Ropelius (YB74 p. 206)

Max Ruef (prison, wife and child died, YB74 pp. 121f.)

Rachel Sacksioni (Westerbork, Bergen-Belsen concentration camps; two of her children died while she was in the concentration camp, YB86 pp. 160ff.)

Josef Scharner (WT March 15, 1968, pp. 187-190; YB74 p. 190)

Wilhelm Scheider (1939-1945 in different concentration camps; died in 1971, WT March 1, 1987, p. 22; JWP p. 453; YB94 pp. 203, 208)

Franz Schipp (imprisoned for 3 years, YB94 p. 202)

Hermann Schlömer (YB74 p. 129)

Grete Schmidt (WT February 1, 1989, pp. 25f.)

Hermine Schmidt (WT March 1, 1987, p. 22; JZM p. 19)

Horst-Günter Schmidt (JZM p. 19)

Auguste Schneider (YB74 pp. 162, 173)

Therese Schreiber (YB89 pp. 101, 104ff.; JWP pp. 450, 454)

Max Schröer (YB74 p. 198)

Max Schubert (YB74 pp. 115f.)

Gertrud Schulze (YB74 p. 200)

Karl Schurstein (8 years imprisonment, killed by the SS in Dachau in 1944, JWP p. 452)

Karl Schwarzer (WT August 1, 1991, p. 29)

Willi Seitz (YB74 p. 121)

Ernst Seliger (WT July 15, 1975, pp. 423–426; YB74 pp. 189, 202f.; JWP p. 452)

Hildegard Seliger (WT July 15, 1975, pp. 423–426; JWP p. 452)

Olga Slézinger (Auschwitz concentration camp; died in Bergen-Belsen, WT June 1, 1998, pp. 29f.)

František Šnajdr (Mauthausen, YB2000, p. 171)

Sigurd Speidel (in 1943 beheaded in the Berlin-Moabit prison for refusing military service, JZM pp. 4f.)

Sister Stadtegger (Ravensbrück concentration camp where she died, YB89 p. 102) and her husband (YB89 p. 102)

Jonathan Stark (YB74 p. 183)

Valentin Steinbach (YB74 p. 172)

Ludwig Stickel (YB74 p. 116)

Hans Stossier (sentenced to death, AW October 22, 1994, pp. 9, 13)

Ida Strauß (YB74 p. 158)

Arthur and Anni Strenge (YB74 pp. 119ff.)

Heinrich Strohmeyer (YB74 pp. 158, 160)

Alois Stuhlmiller (YB86 p. 154)

Hans Sturm (his mother, uncle, aunt, sister and her husband and daughter were imprisoned, AW June 8, 2000, pp. 18-20)

Hans Thomas (YB74 p. 138)

Herman Tollenaar (Oranienburg concentration camp, YB86 pp. 142, 145)

Martha Tünker (YB74 p. 201)

Ilse Unterdörfer (WT November 1, 1979, pp. 8-14; YB74 pp. 113, 157f., 160, 172, 199f.; JWP p. 450)

Ernst Varduhn (YB74 pp. 152f.)

Heinrich Vieker (YB74 p. 129)

Cor de Vreede (YB86 pp. 148f.)

Eliza de Vries (YB86 p. 143)

Klaas de Vries (YB86 p. 146)

Albert Wandres (WT September 1, 1965, pp. 537-542; YB74 pp. 134, 146ff., 162; JWP p. 450)

Willi Wanner (AW April 22, 1986, pp. 13-16)

Eduard Warter (WT March 1, 1987, pp. 21-24)

Ruth Warter (WT March 1, 1987, pp. 21-24)

Ernst Wauer (WT August 1, 1991, pp. 25-29)

Paul Wauer (YB74 p. 198)

Josef Wegscheider (in 1939 executed by a military detachment for refusing military service, YB89 pp. 119ff.)

Family Weigand (couple with four children, Eva, Georg, Johannes, Konstantin, AW October 22, 1988, pp. 18-21)

Arnold Werner (YB86 pp. 138, 142)

Albert and Margaret West (WT March 1, 1989, pp. 10-13)

Gregor Wicinsky (YB2000 p. 167)

Ernst Wiesner (YB74 pp. 141f., 163)

Emil Wilde (YB74 pp. 125f.)

Sister Wilde (tortured to death by the Gestapo, YB74 pp. 125f.)

Robert Arthur Winkler (Esterwegen, Vught, Sachsenhausen concentration camps, died in 1972, Trost, February 15, 1938, pp. 12f.; Consolation August 10, 1938, pp. 12-15; WT March 15, 1967, pp. 186-190; YB74 pp. 147, 151ff., 180f; YB86 pp. 154-158, 168; JWP p. 453)

Paulina Woelfle (imprisoned for 5 years, YB94 p. 202)

Franz Wohlfahrt (5 years in Rollwald; his father and his brother were executed by the Nazis, YB89 pp. 115, 118; JWP 451; AW October 22, 1994, pp. 8-15)

Maria Wohlfahrt (née Stossier, AW October 22, 1994, pp. 8-13)

Paul Wrobel (WT June 15, 1973, pp. 176-179)

Gosse Wulder (YB86 pp. 145f.)

Gertrud Wulle (née Pfisterer, YB74 p. 179; WT May 1, 1989, p. 12)

Emmy Zehden (beheaded in Berlin-Plötzensee in 1944, JZM p. 4; AW January 22, 1997, p. 31)

Wessel Thomas Zevenhek (Vught, Sachsenhausen, Neuengamme, Wöbbelin concentration camps; description of his detention in a letter to the editor, Wachttoren, November 1, 1945, p. 208)

Franz Zürcher (YB74 pp. 153f.)

Jehovah's Witnesses-Victims of the Nazi Regime in Germany

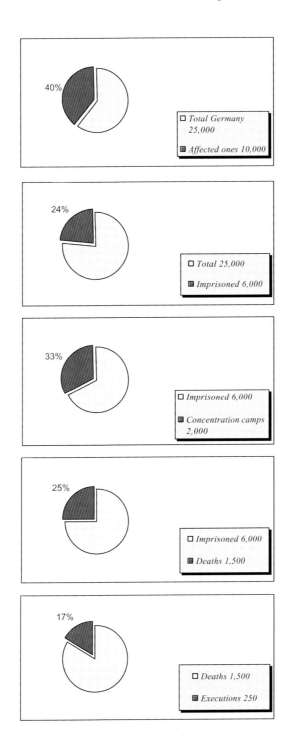

Notes

1   Psalms 88: 10-12, *The Holy Bible Containing the Old and New Testaments. King James Version*, ed. American Bible Society (New York, n. d.).

2   Jehovah's Witnesses started bearing their biblically based name in 1931; see Isaiah 43:10-12, *Die Heilige Schrift, Elberfelder Bibel*, 16th ed. (Wuppertal-Elberfeld: R. Brockhaus, 1954). The reading »Jehova[h]« for the tetragrammaton JHWH (6,828 instances in the Hebrew and Aramaic text of the Bible; see Rudolf Kittel, ed., *Biblia Hebraica* [Stuttgart: 1973]; Karl Elliger and Rudolf Wilhelm, ed., *Biblia Hebraica Stuttgartensia* [Stuttgart: 1967-77]; E. Jenni, *Theologisches Handwörterbuch zum Alten Testament*, 3rd edition [1978-79], vol. 1, col. 703f.) goes back to the Dominican monk Raymund Martini (c.1220 - c.1285), who, already in 1278, chose this form of God's name in his volume *Pugio Fidei adversus Mauros et Judaeos*; see Leipzig edition, 1687; on the pronunciations of the tetragrammaton, see Wilhelm Weidmüller, »*Der rätselhafte Gottesname ›JHWH‹: ›Jahwe‹? - ›Jehova‹? - ›YeHuàH‹? - ›I-E-U-A‹?*« in: *Archiv für Geschichte des Buchwesens*, ed. Historische Kommission des Börsenvereins des Deutschen Buchhandels e.V., v. VI (Frankfurt, 1966), cols. 1407-1426; George Wesley Buchanan, »The Tetragrammaton: How God's Name Was Pronounced,« in: *Biblical Archaeology Review*, 21, no. 2 (March-April 1995), pp. 30f., 100. Jehovah's Witnesses do not reject the pronunciation Jahwe, which is preferred by most Hebraists, but they continue to use the pronunciation Jehovah because the original pronunciation has not yet been scientifically established. However, they reject the Jewish tradition of replacing the tetragrammaton with the words »Lord« and »God,« which originates from a misunderstanding of Leviticus 24:16; see Wilhelm Weidmüller, col. 1412f.; *The Divine Name that Will Endure Forever* (Brooklyn, New York: Watch Tower Bible and Tract Society of New York, 1984), pp. 6ff.; *New World Translation of the Holy Scriptures with References* (Brooklyn, New York: Watch Tower Bible and Tract Society of New York, 1984), Appendix 1A, p. 1561. Before 1931, they were commonly known as Bible Students (or Earnest Bible Students), a name derived from their corporation called International Bible Students Association. Non-Witnesses continued using this name after 1931, and it still remains in the name of the original British corporation International Bible Students Association. The individual members of this religious association are called Jehovah's Witnesses. See *Jehovah's Witnesses - Proclaimers of God's Kingdom* (Brooklyn, New York: Watch Tower Bible and Tract Society of New York, 1993), pp. 149-158, 229.

3   See Detlef Garbe, *Zwischen Widerstand und Martyrium: die Zeugen Jehovas im »Dritten Reich*,« 4th edition (Munich, 1999), pp. 16, 96, 116; Brigitte Oleschinski, »Religiöse Gemeinschaften im Widerstand,« in: *Widerstand gegen den Nationalsozialismus*, ed. Bundeszentrale für politische Bildung, Schriftenreihe vol. 323 (Bonn, 1994), p. 197; Friedrich Zipfel, *Kirchenkampf in Deutschland 1933-1945* (Berlin, 1965), p. 175.

4   See Detlef Garbe, *Zwischen Widerstand und Martyrium,* 11; Philip Friedman, *Das andere Deutschland: Die Kirchen*, pamphlet no. 2 (Berlin, 1960), p. 23; Reiner W. Kühl, »Widerstand im Dritten Reich: Die ernsten Bibelforscher in Friedrichstadt,« in: *Unterhaltung für Friedrichstadt und die angränzende Gegend*, Mitteilungsblatt der Gesellschaft Friedrichstädter Stadtgeschichte 27 (1985), p. 165; Friedrich Zipfel, *Kirchenkampf*, pp. 175, 203f.; Michael H. Kater, »Die Ernsten Bibelforscher im Dritten Reich,« *Vierteljahrshefte für Zeitgeschichte* 17, No. 2 (1969), p. 181.

5   Based on incomplete data, from 1933 to 1945 about 10,000 out of the approximately 25,000 Jehovah's Witnesses and their associates in Germany (of whom, 20,000 were active evangelists) were immediate victims of the Nazis (loss of employment, loss of pension, children abducted, sentenced to pay fines or serve jail terms, etc.). According to recent research, nearly 6,000 of these (more than 445 from Austria) were in prisons and/or concentration camps. Almost 2,000 (recent research indicating more likely closer to 1,500), including 150 Austrians, lost their lives; more than 300 of them (at least 48 from Austria) were executed. The total number of the affected Witnesses is considerably higher, when the victims from other countries are included. See *1934 Yearbook of Jehovah's Witnesses* (New York, 1933), p. 101; *1974 Yearbook of Jehovah's Witnesses* (New York, 1973), pp. 182, 212; »*Then is Finished the Mystery of God*« (New York, 1969), p. 121; *Watchtower*, vol. 105, no. 19 (October 1, 1984), p. 8; *Jehovah's Witnesses—Proclaimers of God's Kingdom* (New York, 1993), pp. 659-665, 720; Garbe, *Zwischen Widerstand und Martyrium*, p. 350 (footnote 118), pp. 491-500; idem, »›Sendboten des Jüdischen Bolschewismus‹: Antisemitismus als Motiv nationalsozialistischer Verfolgung der Zeugen Jehovas,« *Tel Aviver Jahrbuch für deutsche Geschichte: Nationalsozialismus aus heutiger Perspektive* 23 (1994), p. 170; Eugen Kogon, *Der SS-Staat: Das System der deutschen Konzentrationslager* (Berlin, 1947), p. 51; Marley Cole, *Zeugen Jehovas: Die Neue-Welt-Gesellschaft* (Frankfurt, 1956), p. 121; Eberhard Röhm, *Sterben für den Frieden, Spurensicherung: Hermann Stöhr (1898-1940) und die ökumenische Friedensbewegung* (Stuttgart, 1985), p. 213; Wolfgang Benz, »Kirchen: Selbstbehauptung und Opposition,«

in: *Informationen zur politischen Bildung: Deutscher Widerstand 1933-1945*, ed. Bundeszentrale für politische Bildung (1994), p. 21.

6   In 1933 there were 19,268 active Jehovah's Witnesses in Germany. That year, 24,843 persons attended the Memorial, including 123 persons from Saarland. The number of active Witnesses does not necessarily include associated children and elderly so that a total number of 25,000 Jehovah's Witnesses can be assumed. See *1934 Yearbook of Jehovah's Witnesses*, p. 101; *1974 Yearbook of Jehovah's Witnesses*, p. 109; Garbe, *Zwischen Widerstand und Martyrium*, p. 81.

7   Report by Karl R. Wittig, certified in Frankfurt on November 13, 1947. See *1974 Yearbook of Jehovah's Witnesses* (Wiesbaden, 1974), pp. 138f.; *Wachtturm* (August 1, 1955), pp. 462f.

8   Kater, *Die Ernsten Bibelforscher im Dritten Reich*, p. 218.

9   See Garbe, *Zwischen Widerstand und Martyrium*, pp. 405f.; idem, »Der lila Winkel,« *Dachauer Hefte* 10 (1994), p. 10; Andreas Müller, »›Ich hatte Mitleid mit den Nazis‹: Von Sachsenhausen bis Buchenwald; Die tragische Geschichte des Max Liebster aus Reichenbach im Odenwald,« in: »*Zukunft*« *Beruf* (February 5, 1997), p. 31. According to the report about Esterwegen concentration camp by Arthur Winkler, »the political inmates wore green, worn-out uniforms with yellow dots on the backs.« *Trost*, v. 16, no. 371 (Bern, March 1, 1938), p. 12; according to a report by a Jewish inmate in Buchenwald concentration camp, »political inmates wore red stripes.« *Trost*, v. 17, no. 395 (Bern, March 1, 1939), p. 14.

10   Jehovah's Witnesses were again banned by the German Democratic Republic on August 31, 1950. (*1974 Yearbook of Jehovah's Witnesses*, p. 225; see *1999 Yearbook of Jehovah's Witnesses* (New York, 1999), pp. 78f.); also, Peter Maser, *Glauben im Sozialismus* (Berlin, 1989), p. 20.

11   Wachtturm-Gesellschaft, History Archive. Thus, Ernst Seliger was imprisoned twice by the Nazis because he was a Jehovah's Witness. When after six months imprisonment he still refused to repudiate his connection with the Witnesses, he was remanded to Sachsenhausen concentration camp in July 1937. After the war he was released, and subsequently the Communists rearrested him and his wife Hildegard in November 1950 in Torgau; in July 1951, he was sentenced to 15 years in prison by a communist court in Leipzig because of his activities as a Witness. His wife Hildegard Seliger, who also spent many years in various Nazi concentration camps, was sentenced for the same reason to 10 years in prison. She was sent to Waldheim prison, where she spent one year in solitary confinement, and three weeks in an »unlighted« jail cell for smuggling parts of the Bible. In 1954, she was transferred to the Halle prison. Ernst and Hildegard Seliger spent a total of 40 years in Nazi concentration camps and in Nazi and Communist prisons. See *Watchtower*, v. 96, no. 14 (July 15, 1975), pp. 423–426. Other examples include: Friedrich Adler and Wilhelm Engel, who were incarcerated for nine years under the Nazis as Jehovah's Witnesses. In 1950, under the GDR regime, both were arrested again and received life sentences because of their religious beliefs. In the summer of 1964, they were released and expelled to West Germany. Each of them had endured nearly 23 years of imprisonment because of their beliefs. See *1974 Yearbook of Jehovah's Witnesses*, pp. 229f.; »*Then is finished the Mystery of God*,« pp. 121f. Non-German Jehovah's Witnesses suffered similarly: for example, Wilhelm Scheider (Poland), was in various concentration camps from 1939 to 1945 and spent the years from 1950 to 1956 and from 1960 to 1964 in prison under the Communist regime. (See *Jehovah's Witnesses— Proclaimers of God's Kingdom*, p. 453).

12   The final protocol of the seminar in Bad Urach names as victims groups: Jews, Sinti and Roma, victims of the »euthanasia« program, homosexuals, foreign labor, forced labor, and prisoners of war. A letter from the Public Affairs Office, Selters, to the Director of the Landeszentrale für politische Bildung, Dr. Siegfried Schiele, received in response a letter of apology, dated January 10, 1997: »You point to historical facts which are still not discussed enough in public. ... It is indeed a matter of concern for us to include the victims of religious persecution in the commemoration and to have them participate in the preparation for the commemoration on January 27. There is no doubt about this, although you indicate the omission of Jehovah's Witnesses in the report and presume a deliberate omission. ... We ask you to excuse this misleading omission.« See also Stiftung Lesen in cooperation with the Bundeszentrale für politische Bildung (Bonn) and the Börsenverein des Deutschen Buchhandels (Frankfurt), ed., *Verfolgung und Vernichtung unter nationalsozialistischer Herrschaft: Leseempfehlungen der Stiftung Lesen in Zusammenarbeit mit der Bundeszentrale für politische Bildung und dem Börsenverein des Deutschen Buchhandels* (Mainz, 1997); and the speech by former German President Roman Herzog on January 19, 1996, in the German Parliament on the occasion of January 27, Commemoration Day for the Victims of National Socialism. He names »Jews, Sinti, Roma, and homosexuals, to mention only the most important groups.« *Bulletin*, no. 6 (Bonn, January 23, 1996), p. 46.

13 Garbe's criteria include »that the history of these people ... is not widely known even today«; »in school books, there is at best marginal mention, there are no memorial sites which present a comprehensive documentation of their persecution, and in most cases there was neither restitution nor rehabilitation. The veil of the past lies on the fate of these people. ... One false interpretation of this concept can be that they are victims who were ›overlooked,‹ simply forgotten by mistake. This, however, is out of the question. Rather, their history was systematically suppressed for decades and deliberately forgotten. ... Thus, a deliberate strategy of ›organized forgetfulness‹ had been followed.« Detlef Garbe, »Die ›vergessenen‹ Opfer,« in: *Verachtet - verfolgt - vernichtet*, ed. Projektgruppe für die vergessenen Opfer des NS-Regimes (Hamburg, 1986/1988), p. 5. See Detlef Garbe, *Zwischen Widerstand und Martyrium*, p. 9; Brigitte Oleschinski, »Religiöse Gemeinschaften im Widerstand,« p. 193. Sybil Milton mentions four reasons why Jehovah's Witnesses have become »forgotten victims«: 1. »Intolerance or, at least, the disinterest of German and European society,« 2. »as a consequence of postwar memorial practices in handling the volatile subject of the holocaust,« 3. the »lack of published documentation about Jehovah's Witnesses,« and 4. »that important eye-witness testimony by surviving Witnesses has not been collected.« Sybil Milton, »Jehovah's Witnesses As Forgotten Victims,« pp. 143f. in this anthology.

14 Detlef Garbe, »Der lila Winkel,« pp. 7f.; idem, *Zwischen Widerstand und Martyrium*, pp. 402–407, 550; idem, »Sendboten des Jüdischen Bolschewismus,« p. 169; Michael Berenbaum, The World Must Know: *The History of the Holocaust as Told in the United States Holocaust Memorial Museum* (1993), pp. 51f., 129f. In Moringen concentration camp the female Jehovah's Witnesses, 22 percent, were the second largest group in size after communist women (24 percent). In 1937, they were the largest group with at least 35 percent. Jutta von Freyberg and Ursula Krause-Schmitt, *Moringen, Lichtenburg, Ravensbrück; Frauen im Konzentrationslager 1933–1945* (Frankfurt, 1997), pp. 16, 20; see Garbe, *Zwischen Widerstand und Martyrium*, p. 225. Nevertheless, Hans Hesse and Jürgen Harder have come to a different conclusion based on new research: »The largest group of women in Moringen concentration camp were Jehovah's Witnesses ... In absolute figures: we have the names of 310 women, that is 45.9 percent. This meant that nearly half of all the women whose names are known and who were in the concentration camp were Jehovah's Witnesses. These findings have not been taken into account in previous research. ... This statement, however, applies to the Moringen concentration camp for women but also to the successor camps, that is, Lichtenburg and Ravensbrück concentration camps until the outbreak of the war.« Lecture at Moringen City Hall on March 7, 1997; see *Der Tip für Sie!* (Northeim, May 14, 1997), p. 14; *Harz Kurier*, Südniedersachsen (May 19, 1997).

15 Zipfel, *Kirchenkampf in Deutschland*, pp. 175f.

16 Oleschinski, »Religiöse Gemeinschaften im Widerstand,« pp. 193f.

17 The clergy and members of the larger denominations resisting out of Christian conviction were usually given red triangles, also the marking for »politicals,« including Communists, Social Democrats, anarchists, middle-class democrats, or who were in opposition, Nazis who had fallen out of favor and the so-called »malcontents.« The purple triangle was also assigned to some prisoners who no longer belonged to the Jehovah's Witnesses (as for example, Freie Bibelforscher-Vereinigung, Menschenfreundliche Versammlung/ Engel Jehovas, and so-called apostates) as well as Seventh Day Adventists, whose numbers were very small. See Garbe, »Der lila Winkel,« pp. 9f.; idem, *Zwischen Widerstand und Martyrium*, pp. 12f., 405f. The purple triangle was usually a »full triangle,« that is, a triangle cut from a piece of purple cloth, made up of a single piece of cloth, and was sewn to the striped blue and white cloth jacket on the left side of the breast with the tip pointing downward. The jacket cloth (and also the men's pants) had a pattern with ca. 1.7 cm (0.67 inch) broad vertical stripes in blue and white from top to bottom. In addition to the solid triangle, there was also the so-called holow triangle. This was very uncommon. The hollow triangles in our possession are a strip, 30 cm (11.8 inches) long and 1.5 cm (0.6 inch) broad, cut out of one piece of purple cloth, obviously to save cloth. It was somewhat narrower than the blue and white stripes on the prisoner's jacket and was sewn on the jacket in the form of a triangle so that the horizontal top was about 9.5 cm (3.74 inches) and the two arms of the triangle pointing downward and touching at the tip were about 10 cm (3.94 inches) long. Almost directly under the tip of the purple triangle, right in the middle, a light-colored rectangular piece of cloth was sewn with the prisoner's number in waterproof ink or in black. This rectangular piece of cloth was generally longer than the horizontal side of the triangle and its width varied in size. With regard to the purple hollow triangle, the rectangle below it with the prisoner's number was often smaller (sometimes only 2.5 cm [0.98 inch] broad), obviously also in order to save material, and was about the same length as the horizontal side of the purple triangle which was attached above. The color of this rectangular fabric was sometimes much darker, almost a blackish color so that the deep black prisoner number written with ink or India ink

did not stand out as clearly as it did on the regular white rectangles. In some camps, the rectangle with the prisoner number was attached above the purple triangle as with female Jehovah's Witnesses in Ravensbrück or men in Sachsenhausen. There were light-colored rectangles with prisoner numbers written on them attached on the right side of the chest (in the direction away from the heart), and the solid purple triangle was attached to the rectangular piece of cloth with the prisoner's number. Moreover, men were often marked with a purple triangle on their trouser leg and women had a purple triangle attched to their jacket sleeves or dresses. For those Jehovah's Witnesses of Jewish origin, like other Jews, they had to have an additional yellow triangle with the tip pointing upwards so that both triangles made up a star of David. In SS records, these inmates were categorized as »Bible Student, Jew.« Their number was quite small. According to survivor accounts, during critical periods of the extermination of the Jews, some Jewish inmates tore off the yellow triangle so that only the other triangle was visible, and thus they survived. The purple triangle was first introduced as a marking for Jehovah's Witnesses about 1937-1938. Before that date, Jehovah's Witnesses in Lichtenburg concentration camp had to wear a blue circle on their chest; Sachsenhausen and Buchenwald concentration camps also used blue markings. Garbe, *Zwischen Widerstand und Martyrium*, p. 405; idem, »Der lila Winkel,« p. 9. According to the report of a Jewish prisoner in Buchenwald concentration camp, »the inmates had certain distinctive markings on their clothes. Political prisoners wore red stripes, Bible Students pink, ›work-shy‹ black. They stitched a star of David on a black and yellow background onto our jacket.« *Trost*, v. 17, no. 395 (Bern, March 1, 1939), p. 14.

18 Garbe, *Zwischen Widerstand und Martyrium*, p. 12.

19 Garbe, *Zwischen Widerstand und Martyrium*, p. 376, note 225, limits the figure of »about 6,000 to 7,000 Jehovah's Witnesses (who) refused military service« given by Röhm (Eberhard Röhm, *Sterben für den Frieden*, p. 213).

20 Garbe, *Zwischen Widerstand und Martyrium*, pp. 375f. Heinz Knobloch, *Berliner Grabsteine* (Berlin, 1989), p. 52.

21 Garbe, *Zwischen Widerstand und Martyrium*, p. 12.

22 Hanns Lilje, *Im finstern Tal* (Nuremberg, 1947), pp. 64f.

23 Jürgen Engert, ed., *Soldaten für Hitler* (Berlin, 1998), p. 179; the six part television series with the same title was broadcast by ARD (a German TV station) and the program »Widerstand« (resistance) was part 5, broadcast on April 24, 1998. It must be noted that Jehovah's Witnesses do not see themselves as pacifists, but as resisters of military service for reasons of conscience. See *Watchtower*, v. 44 (March 15, 1951), pp. 84-89.

24 *The Golden Age*, v. 14, no. 363 (New York, August 16, 1933), p. 734. In *Goldenes Zeitalter*, v. 12, no. 281 (Bern, June 1, 1934), pp. 3-15, a detailed report was published with the headline »Verfolgungen in Deutschland« [Persecutions in Germany], in which, among other things, attention was drawn to the fact that in Saxony alone, more than 500 fellow-believers were taken to concentration camps (p. 9); the report also publicized Nazi inhuman cruelties. In *The Golden Age*, v. 17, no. 419 (New York, October 9, 1935), p. 5, attention is drawn to Dachau concentration camp; on the same page, the number of prisoners (of all concentration camps) is stated as 300,000. Cf. *Wachtturm*, v. 42, no. 9 (May 1, 1937), pp. 139f. The number of incarcerated Jehovah's Witnesses at that time was »close to 4,000.« Alfred Antoni, »Report Concerning the Persecution in Germany,« in *The Golden Age*, v. 17, no. 427 (New York, January 29, 1936), pp. 274f. (Esterwegen concentration camp); Arthur Winkler, »Im Konzentrationslager Esterwegen,« in *Trost*, v. 16, no. 370 (Bern, February 15, 1938), pp. 12f. and no. 371 (March 1, 1938), pp. 12f.; no. 382 (August 15, 1938), pp. 15f.; v. 17, no. 395 (Bern, March 1, 1939), p. 14 (Buchenwald concentration camp); no. 401 (June 1, 1939), pp. 12f.; no. 404 (July 15, 1939), pp. 10ff. (Oranienburg concentration camp); no. 405 (August 1, 1939), p. 15; no. 407 (September 1, 1939), p. 15; Franz Zürcher, *Kreuzzug gegen das Christentum* (Zurich and New York, 1938), pages between p. 144 and 145, 149-168; *Consolation*, v. 20, no. 517, (New York, July 12, 1939), p. 10; *Awake!*, v. 76, no. 16 (August 22, 1995), pp. 3-15.

25 *Trost*, v. 17, no. 397 (Bern, April 1, 1939), p. 11; also see the statement by Thomas Mann, ibid., no. 391 (January 1, 1939), p. 6. Hitler still declared on January 30, 1939: »I solemnly declare before the whole German people: Nobody has been persecuted because of his religious beliefs so far, nor will anybody ever be persecuted on these grounds.« *Trost*, v. 17, no. 395 (Bern, March 1, 1939), p. 6.

26 Garbe, *Zwischen Widerstand und Martyrium*, p. 39.

27 See Gijsbert N. van der Bijl, »There Is Nothing Better Than the Truth,« in: *Watchtower*, v. 119, no. 1 (January 1, 1998), p. 27; Max Hollweg, *Es ist unmöglich von dem zu schweigen, was ich erlebt habe. Zivilcourage im Dritten Reich* (Bielefeld, 1997), p. 124.

28 Garbe, »Der lila Winkel,« p. 29.

29 Ibid., pp. 28ff.; see idem, *Zwischen Widerstand und Martyrium*, pp. 538-42.

30 A detailed bibliography is found at the end of this essay.

31 For example, the report by Erich Frost in *Watchtower*, v. 82, no. 8 (April 15, 1961), pp. 409-415, was printed in 3,800,000 copies and was published in 59 languages. The experiences of Charlotte Müller in *Watchtower*, v. 118, no. 9 (May 1, 1997), pp. 24-29 and Rudolf Graichen in *Watchtower*, v. 118, no. 15 (August 1, 1997), pp. 20-25 were published in 125 or 126 languages respectively and in 20,980,000 copies; both the report by Gijsbert N. van der Bijl in *Watchtower*, v. 119, no. 1 (January 1, 1998), pp. 25- 29, and by Éva Josefsson in *Watchtower*, v. 119, no. 11 (June 1, 1998), pp. 28-31 were respectively published in 128 languages, in an edition of 22,103,000 copies.

32 Garbe, *Zwischen Widerstand und Martyrium*, p. 39.

33 Ibid., pp. 30-41.

34 Thus, Margarete Buber-Neumann called Jehovah's Witnesses »voluntary prisoners.« Margarete Buber-Neumann, *Milena: Kafkas Freundin* (Berlin, 1990), p. 263. »By abandoning their faith and joining the ›racial community,‹ Jehovah's Witnesses could escape persecution; the Jews did not have this option.« See Garbe, »Sendboten des Jüdischen Bolschewismus,« p. 171; also Wolfgang Sofsky, *Die Ordnung des Terrors: Das Konzentrationslager* (Frankfurt, 1997), p. 35; United States Holocaust Memorial Museum, ed., *Jehovah's Witnesses: Victims of the Nazi Era 1933-1945* (Washington, D.C., n.d.), p. 1. At first, these »declarations« existed in different forms in various concentration camps and prisons which Jehovah's Witnesses could sign without moral difficulty. One example is the »Declaration of Commitment,« dated »Moringen, December 4, 1937,« which stated: »I agree to abstain from any subversive activity threatening the security of the state once I have been released from protective custody. I have been informed that I cannot claim compensation from the state for my protective custody. If my security is threatened, I can place myself in political custody. I have been ordered for the time being to report to the local police authorities every third workday after my release.« Instead of the last sentence, one declaration, dated Moringen, December 20, 1937, contained an addenda written especially for Jehovah's Witnesses: »The consequences of renewed activity for the IBSA have been pointed out to me. I have been informed that stopping propaganda is certainly not enough, but that a complete renunciation of the IBSA is expected from me. I have been informed that the warrant for arrest in protective custody is only nullified if my behavior is faultless and that otherwise I must expect my arrest for the slightest reason.« For these »Declarations of Commitment,« see the essay by Jürgen Harder and Hans Hesse in this anthology. For the texts of other declarations, see Zürcher, *Kreuzzug gegen das Christentum*, pp. 192ff.; Cole, *Jehovas Zeugen*, p. 198; Garbe, *Zwischen Widerstand und Martyrium*, p. 303; *Jehovah's Witnesses – Proclaimers of God's Kingdom*, p. 661. At the end of 1938, a standardized form was introduced, which provided for renunciation of faith and cooperation with the police against other Jehovah's Witnesses. Even if Jehovah's Witnesses had signed such declarations, which was the exception, the person was not immediately released but had to undergo a »test of credibility.« See Garbe, *Zwischen Widerstand und Martyrium*, pp. 302-315; idem, »Die Verfolgung der Zeugen Jehovas im nationalsozialistischen Deutschland – Ein Überblick,« in: *Widerstand aus christlicher Überzeugung – Jehovas Zeugen im Nationalsozialismus: Dokumentation einer Tagung*, p. 22; Gijsbert N. van der Bijl, »There Is Nothing Better Than the Truth,« *Watchtower* (Jan. 1, 1998), p. 27.

35 Matthew 24:14; Mark 13:10.

36 See *1974 Yearbook of Jehovah's Witnesses*, pp. 212-221. As with other victim groups, Jehovah's Witnesses who had not personally experienced the cruelties of the concentration camps often lacked understanding about these experiences. This was corroborated in my personal conversations with survivors. See Marianne Kröger, »Ravensbrück als Ort der Erfahrung: Leben und Werk der niederländischen Dichterin Sonja Prins,« *Dachauer Hefte* 10 (1994), pp. 63f.

37 Brigitte Bailer and Wolfgang Neugebauer, *Dreißig Jahre Dokumentationsarchiv des österreichischen Widerstandes (1963-1993)*, reprint from DÖW Jahrbuch (Vienna, 1993), p. 3.

38 Walther Hofer, *Der Nationalsozialismus: Dokumente 1933-1945* (Frankfurt, 1957, 1982), p. 124; Zipfel, *Kirchenkampf*, p. 473.

39 Martin Niemöller, *Ach Gott vom Himmel sieh darein. Sechs Predigten* (Munich, 1946), pp. 27f.

40 Hanns Lilje, *Im finstern Tal,* p. 64. Lilje was one of the signatories of the so-called Stuttgart Guilt Confession, which stated: »What we have often witnessed in our parishes, we now declare in the name of the entire church: For years we have indeed fought in the name of Jesus Christ against the spirit which found its terrible expression in the Nazi terror state; but we accuse ourselves for not having been more courageous in our convictions, more faithful in our prayers, more optimistic in our faith, and more zealous in our devotion.«

»Die Stuttgarter Erklärung,« *Verordnungs- und Nachrichtenblatt: Amtliches Organ der evangelischen Kirche in Deutschland*, published under permit US-W-1006 of military government control of news, no. 1 (January 1946).

41 Garbe, »Der lila Winkel,« p. 30; idem, *Zwischen Widerstand und Martyrium,* p. 40.

42 *Deutschland-Berichte der Sozialdemokratischen Partei Deutschlands (Sopade) 1934-1940*, reprint 6 vols. (Salzhausen and Frankfurt, 1980), v. 4 (1937), p. 707. See Garbe, *Zwischen Widerstand und Martyrium*, p. 406; idem, »Der lila Winkel,« p. 11.

43 *Das Goldene Zeitalter*, v. 10. no. 16 (August 15, 1932), pp. 247, 254; *1933 Yearbook of Jehovah's Witnesses*, p. 99; see Garbe, *Zwischen Widerstand und Martyrium*, pp. 83f.; idem, »Die Verfolgung der Zeugen Jehovas im nationalsozialistischen Deutschland: Ein Überblick,« pp. 16f.

44 Idem, *Zwischen Widerstand und Martyrium*, p. 84.

45 Ibid., pp. 96-102.

46 Garbe, »Sendboten des Jüdischen Bolschewismus,« p. 170; idem, »Die Verfolgung der Zeugen Jehovas im nationalsozialistischen Deutschland – Ein Überblick,« p. 16.

47 Guenter Lewy, *Die katholische Kirche und das Dritte Reich* (Munich, 1965), p. 58.

48 Garbe, *Zwischen Widerstand und Martyrium*, p. 82, note 170; idem, »Sendboten des Jüdischen Bolschewismus,« p. 151; *Der Staatsbürger.* Beilage der Bayerischen Staatszeitung, no. 2 (Munich, February 1997), pp. 1-6; »Protestant Church ... continuous trend of church membership withdrawals (withdrawals in West Germany from 1970 to 1993: about 3.9 million; annual rate of withdrawals starting in the mid–1990s: about 1 percent of the members) and the increase of the tax free allowance to 12,000 DM under the 1996 tax law, resulted in a loss of income from church taxes of about 440 million DM (-5.2 percent compared to 1995). ... Catholic Church ... Since the middle of the 1990s, the church has noticed an increase in the number of church membership withdrawals among 25 to 40 year olds with higher income.« (*Aktuell '98: Lexikon der Gegenwart*, v. 14 [Dortmund, 1997], pp. 221f.)

49 Jehovah's Witnesses do not consider themselves a sect. See *Reasoning From the Scriptures* (New York, 1985, 1989), pp. 202f.

50 Martin Kriele, »›Sekte‹ als Kampfbegriff,« *Frankfurter Allgemeine Zeitung*, no. 79 (April 6, 1994), p. 10; see Professor Dr. A. Freiherr v. Campenhausen, »Sekten, Scientology und der Rechtsstaat,« *Rheinischer Merkur*, no. 29 (July 18, 1997), p. 8; Professor Dr. Hartmut Zinser (member of the Enquete Commission on »So-called Sects and Psychogroups«), »Die Religionsfreiheit verteidigen, die Verantwortung fallenlassen,« *Badische Zeitung* (July 29, 1997); Zinser, *Der Markt der Religionen* (Munich, 1997), pp. 13f., 131ff.; Professor Dr. Hubert Seiwert, (also member of the above mentioned Enquete Commission), »Das ›Sektenproblem‹: Öffentliche Meinung, Wissenschaft und der Staat,« in: *Schluß mit den Sekten! Die Kontroverse über ›Sekten‹ und neue religiöse Bewegungen in Europa* (Marburg, 1998), pp. 12f.; *Zwischenbericht der Enquete-Kommission »Sogenannte Sekten und Psychogruppen,«* Deutscher Bundestag, Drucksache 13/8170 (July 7, 1997), p. 47.

51 Sybil Milton, »Jehovah's Witnesses As Forgotten Victims,« p. 143f., in this anthology. Willy Fautré, president of the organization »Human Rights Without Frontiers,« stated: »Outside their realm, the major world religions usually identify all other religious groups as ›sects‹ or ›cults‹ with all the bad connotations that this terminology implies. They use this term to qualify splinter groups inside their own ranks or new religious movements challenging their theology or their supremacy in certain parts of the world.« Human Rights Without Frontiers: European Magazine of Human Rights, v. 8, no. 2-3 (1996), »Bulgarian Helsinki Committee,« pp. 6f. Professor James T. Richardson, professor of sociology at the University of Nevada, has favored prohibiting the use of the term ›cult‹ in court cases: »The term cult should also be disallowed in legal proceedings where involvement in an exotic religious group is an issue. ... The term simply carries too much baggage to allow its casual use in proceedings designed to have rational judgments made about important issues.« See »Definition of Cult: From Sociological-Technical to Popular-Negative,« Review of Religious Research 34 (June 1993), pp. 348, 355.

52 *Königsberger Tageblatt*, no. 246 (September 3, 1936), p. 5.

53 *Stuttgarter NS-Kurier: Regierungsanzeiger für Württemberg*, no. 542 (November 19, 1935). See *Trost*, v. 17, no. 395 (Bern, March 1, 1939), pp. 3, 6f.

54 Nachrichten aus Nürnberg, *Völkischer Beobachter*, no. 325 (November 21, 1935).

55 For nine years Eimuth had been the sect expert of the Protestant Regional Association in Frankfurt. Since January 1, 1998, he has been the head of the office for public affairs of the association under which the almost 70 Protestant parishes in the city are organized. A new representative for questions of ideology has

not been hired yet. See *Frankfurter Allgemeine Zeitung,* no. 294 (December 18, 1997), p. 46.

56 See *Evangelisches Gemeindeblatt,* Württemberg (June 15, 1997); *die neue bildpost* (June 15, 1997). Eimuth also made the statement »to classify Jehovah's Witnesses as an anticonstitutional organization« in the program »Kinder in Sekten« in »Bayernmagazin,« *Bayern 1,* on June 3, 1997. The minority opinion of the commission members Dr. Angelika Köster-Loßack and Professor Dr. Hubert Seiwert regarding the interim report of the Enquete Commission »Sog. Sekten und Psychogruppen,« quotes by Eimuth in this connection with reference to epd, June 3, 1997. Dr. Angelika Köster-Loßack, however, warned »against hysteria when dealing with sects and at the same time opposed demands to classify Jehovah's Witnesses as anticonstitutional.« Epd 3759 (June 6, 1997).

57 *Nürnberger Zeitung,* issue *Fränkischer Kurier,* no. 125 (June 4, 1997), p. 16; *Landshuter Zeitung* (June 1997); *Fränkischer Tag* (Bamberg, June 4, 1997).

58 The Enquete Commission consisted of 12 members of political parties, represented in the German Parliament, and 12 experts who neither belonged to the Parliament nor to the German Government. The PDS had a non-voting member participating as an adviser. It named a non-voting expert. See Deutscher Bundestag, Drucksachen 13/4477 and 13/8170, p. 7f.

59 Deutscher Bundestag, Drucksache 13/8170, p. 20.

60 This is especially the case with the working groups 3 and 4, described in the interim report; see the reference to Jehovah's Witnesses on p. 100 and other pages, although on page 82 »Eimuth's general evaluations« are mentioned and the author even contradicts Eimuth's views on pp. 95f. See »Bundestags-Kommission soll Sekten untersuchen,« *Kieler Nachrichten* (March 1, 1996); »Über 82,000 Kinder und Jugendliche in Sekten,« *Saarbrücker Zeitung,* no. 52 (March 1, 1996), p. 12. Richard Singelenberg, social anthropologist at Utrecht University, an expert in cultural anthropology, with the specialty of religious movements, concludes in his review of Eimuth's book: »Throughout this essay, I have assumed that the author, because of his background, treated this controversial and extremely sensitive subject from a scientific point of view. This has not been done. Either he willfully chose to ignore such an approach or he does not grasp the elementary foundations of scientific reasoning. Concerning the former, one wonders why. Is it his association with an organization that has an outspoken religious identity, that causes him to disregard the fundamentals of his training? The reason I am bringing this point up is the suggestion of some German newspapers that Eimuth's book should serve as a basis for the parliamentiary Enquete Commission. ... Instead of providing an objective analysis of a very complicated social phenomenon and ill-understood public issue, the writer has resorted to a mere summation of clichés, thus adding just one more example to the existing reservoir of prejudices and stereotypes. One only hopes that the members of the Commission have the wisdom to judge for themselves.« Review of the book by Kurt-Helmuth Eimuth: »Die Sekten-Kinder,« Selters/Taunus 1997, p. 12; see also Richard Singelenberg, »Book Reviews: Die Sekten-Kinder,« *Journal of Contemporary Religion,* v. 13, no. 1 (January 1998), pp. 110f.

61 Deutscher Bundestag, Drucksache 13/8170, p. 41.

62 Gerhard Besier, »Religionsgesetze durch die Hintertür: Wie Staat und Kirchen den Psychomarkt aufräumen möchten,« *Focus,* 33 (1997), p. 64.

63 See footnote 50.

64 Zipfel, *Kirchenkampf,* pp. 174f.

65 The Council of Ministers, Office for Church Questions, issued this authorization on March 14, 1990, signed by State Secretary H. Kalb. See Religionsgemeinschaft der Zeugen Jehovas in Deutschland, ed., *Anerkennungsverfahren der Religionsgemeinschaft der Zeugen Jehovas in Deutschland 1990-1997* (Selters/Taunus, 1997), p. 69.

66 Informationsdienst der Zeugen Jehovas [Public Affairs Office], *Jehovas Zeugen — Antworten auf häufig gestellte Fragen* (Selters/Taunus, June 1996), p. 5.

67 Einkommensteuer-Kartei Berlin, 37. Erg. Lfg., Ersatzblatt V (September 1988). See Gottfried Held, »Die kleinen öffentlich-rechtlichen Religionsgemeinschaften im Staatskirchenrecht der Bundesrepublik,« *Jus Ecclesiasticum,* v. 22 (Munich, 1974), 150f. The accompanying letter of the Council of Ministers granting official recognition stated among other things: »It is an honor and a great pleasure to present to you ... the document recognizing the ›religious association of Jehovah's Witnesses in the GDR.‹ The association herewith joins more than 30 churches and religious associations which, on the basis of article 39 (2) of the Constitution and of other legal regulations of the GDR, exercise their activities independently in full freedom and have legal status.« Hermann Weber, »Körperschaftsstatus für die Religionsgemeinschaft der Zeugen Jehovas in Deutschland?,« in: *Zeitschrift für evangelisches Kirchenrecht,* v. 41, no. 2 (June 1996), p.

174; see also *Anerkennungsverfahren der Religionsgemeinschaft der Zeugen Jehovas in Deutschland 1990-1997*, p. 132.

68 VG 27 A 214.93; *Neue Zeitschrift für Verwaltungsrecht* (hereafter NVwZ), no. 6 (1994), pp. 609-612; see *Anerkennungsverfahren der Religionsgemeinschaft der Zeugen Jehovas in Deutschland 1990-1997*, pp. 95-112.

69 OVG 5 B 20.94; see *Anerkennungsverfahren der Religionsgemeinschaft der Zeugen Jehovas in Deutschland 1990-1997*, pp. 183-211.

70 BVerwG 7 B 117.96; BVerwG 7 C 11.96; see *Anerkennungsverfahren der Religionsgemeinschaft der Zeugen Jehovas in Deutschland 1990-1997*, pp. 214-238.

71 Zürcher, *Kreuzzug gegen das Christentum*, pp. 126-135; *1974 Yearbook of Jehovah's Witnesses*, pp. 115-117; Garbe, »Gott mehr gehorchen als den Menschen: Neuzeitliche Christenverfolgung im national-sozialistischen Hamburg,« in: *Verachtet, verfolgt, vernichtet*, ed. Projektgruppe für die vergessenen Opfer des NS-Regimes (Hamburg, 1986-1988), pp. 185f.; idem, *Zwischen Widerstand und Martyrium*, pp. 155-161, 177, 183, 352-402, 527.

72 *Frankfurter Allgemeine Zeitung*, no. 146 (June 27, 1997), p. 14.

73 »Zur Sache: Gründe für Respekt. Die Zeugen Jehovas – eine vergessene NS-Opfergruppe,« *Neues Deutschland* (July 14, 1997), p. 5. See Beatrice von Weizsäcker, »Mit zweifelhafter Methode,« *Der Tagesspiegel* (June 27, 1997), p. 6.

74 Case no. 2 BvR 1500/97.

75 *Frankfurter Allgemeine Zeitung*, no. 220 (September 21, 2000), p. 5; *Süddeutsche Zeitung*, no. 217 (September 20, 2000), p. 2; no. 218 (September 21, 2000), p. 6; *Die Welt* (September 21, 2000), p. 4; *Focus*, no. 38 (September 18, 2000), pp. 52f.

76 BVerfG 2 BvR 1500/97 of 12-19-2000; http://www.bverfg.de.

77 Christian Geyer, »Christian Neutrality,« *Frankfurter Allgemeine Zeitung*, English Edition, no. 220/51 (December 22, 2000), p. 7; compare also Katja Gelinsky, »Constitutional Court Defines Conditions For Religious Groups to Receive Tax Breaks,« *Frankfurter Allgemeine Zeitung*, English Edition, no. 218/51 (December 20, 2000), pp. 1f.

78 See Garbe, »Die Verfolgung der Zeugen Jehovas im nationalsozialistischen Deutschland – Ein Überblick,« pp. 25f.

79 Ibid., pp. 25f.

80 Program by Hans Meiser, »Gläubige oder Spinner? Zeugen Jehovas,« RTL, February 4, 1993.

81 Staatsanwaltschaft [State Attorney's Office] Neubrandenburg, St 725/95.

82 *Freie Presse, Chemnitzer Zeitung* (June 12, 1997). Probably with reference to the statement by Mrs. Jutta Birlenberg, President of KIDS e.V. in the RTL broadcast »Good Evening« (West Live) from May 2, 1997.

83 *Schweinfurter Tagblatt*, Gerolzhofen, no. 250 (October 30, 1997, p. L 3; *Der Steigerwald-Bote*, no. 253 (November 4, 1997), p. L 2; *Schweinfurter Tagblatt*, Gerolzhofen, no. 257 (November 8, 1997), p. L 4; *Der Steigerwald-Bote*, no. 259 (November 11, 1997), p. L 1; no. 260 (November 12, 1997), p. L 1; no. 275 (November 29, 1997), p. L 2; *Schweinfurter Tagblatt*, Gerolzhofen, no. 275 (November 29, 1997) p. L 5; *Der Steigerwald-Bote*, no. 277 (December 2, 1997), p. L 2; no. 300 (December 31, 1997), p. L 3, *Main-Post, Volkszeitung*, no. 259 (November 11, 1997), p. F 2, L 1; *Main-Post newsline* (November 12, 1997; November 3, 1997); *Main-Post, Volkszeitung*, no. 270 (November 24, 1997), p. L 3; *Schweinfurter Tagblatt*, Gerolzhofen, no. 275 (November 29, 1997), p. L 5.

84 Fax/message from the Samtgemeinde Eschede, March 4, 1998.

85 File 1605 11 XVII 9/94.

86 See, for example, the response of the State government of North Rhine-Westphalia from August 12, 1997, to the Kleine Anfrage (small written interpellation) 735, Drucksache 12/2300, in which the questions mentioned the religious association five times as a sect. In the answer there was no correction of this misuse of the term.

87 Kleine Anfrage No. 13/3340, March 4, 1998; the representative of the Senate mentioned among other false statements that »the religious association uses the same pressure to influence its followers to act in an unlawful way, namely to reject the obligatory acceptance of honorary posts (jurors).« This contradicts what Jehovah's Witnesses had already published in 1979: »Since the Bible does not pointedly discuss jury duty, each individual must personally decide what to do after considering all that is involved in jury service, as well as Bible principles and his own conscience.« See *Awake!*, v. 59, no. 23 (December 8, 1978), p. 28. »What if a Christian does not feel that his conscience permits him to serve on a particular jury? The Bible does not mention jury duty, so he cannot say, ›It is against my religion to serve on any jury.‹«... In the final analysis,

each Christian faced with jury duty must determine what course to follow, based on his understanding of the Bible and his own conscience. ... Each Christian has to decide for himself what he will do, and others should not criticize his decision.« Watchtower, v. 118, no. 7 (April 1, 1997), p. 29.

88 *Der Prignitzer* (February 3, 1999), p. 13.

89 Theodor Heuss, *Theodor Heuss, Politiker und Publizist: Aufsätze und Reden* (Tübingen, 1984), p. 303.

90 Karl Jaspers, *Vom Ursprung und Ziel der Geschichte* (Munich, 1949), p. 190.

91 See »Zivilcourage gegen Gewalt gefordert,« *Oranienburger Generalanzeiger* (January 28, 1998); *Der Prignitzer* (January 28, 1998), p. 4; *Neue Oranienburger Zeitung*, no. 23 (January 28, 1998), p. 16; *Märkische Oderzeitung* (January 28, 1998), p. 1; *Frankfurter Stadtbote: Märkische Oderzeitung*, v. 9, no. 23 (January 28, 1998); *Märkische Allgemeine*, no. 23 (January 28, 1998), p. 2; *Berliner Zeitung*, no. 23 (January 28, 1998), p. 30; *Siegerländer Morgenzeitung: Siegener Zeitung*, no. 23 (January 28, 1998), p. 2; *Berliner Morgenpost* (January 28, 1998), p. 17; *Cannstatter Zeitung, Untertürkheimer Zeitung, Stuttgarter Zeitung* (January 28, 1998), pp. 1f.; *Dosse-Kurier, Märkische Allgemeine* (February 3, 1998), p. 17; *Märker* (February 14-15, 1998).

92 See my essay, »›Jehovah's Witnesses Stand Firm Against Nazi Assault‹—Touring Exhibitions and Video Presentations, 1996-2000,« in this anthology.

93 Letter from Manfred Stolpe, Prime Minister of the State of Brandenburg, to the president of the Wachtturm-Gesellschaft, October 30, 1996.

94 See note 14.

95 Kreismuseum Wewelsburg, Fritz Bauer Institut, and Bundeszentrale für politische Bildung, ed., *Widerstand aus christlicher Überzeugung: Jehovas Zeugen im Nationalsozialismus; Dokumentation einer Tagung* (Essen, 1998). A similar academic conference, with the subject »Jehovah's Witnesses: Forgotten Victims of National Socialism?,« was held in Vienna on January 29, 1998. It was organized by the Dokumentationsarchiv des österreichischen Widerstandes (DÖW), as well as by the Institut für Wissenschaft und Kunst (IWK). See »Zeugen Jehovas: Vergessene Opfer des Nationalsozialismus?« in: *Mitteilungen Dokumentationsarchiv des österreichischen Widerstandes*, no. 134b (January 1998), and no. 135 (February 1998); *Der Standard*, no. 2776 (January 30, 1998), p. 8; *Wiener Zeitung* (January 30, 1998), p. 4; Dokumentationsarchiv des österreichischen Widerstandes, ed., *Zeugen Jehovas: Vergessene Opfer des Nationalsozialismus? Schriftenreihe des Dokumentationsarchivs des österreichischen Widerstandes zur Geschichte der NS-Gewaltverbrechen*, no. 3 (Vienna, 1998).

96 *Die Zeit,* no. 42 (October 10, 1997), p. 24; *Frankfurter Allgemeine Zeitung, Rhein-Main-Zeitung*, no. 236 (October 11, 1997), p. 64; *Frankfurter Rundschau* (October 6, 1997), p. 14; (October 9, 1997), p. 16 G. See my essay, »›Jehovah's Witnesses Stand Firm Against Nazi Assault‹ – Touring Exhibitions and Video Presentations, 1996-2000,« in this anthology for the exhibition concept.

97 *Die Welt* (October 23, 1997), p. 3; otz, *Ostthüringer Zeitung, Ostthüringer Nachrichten* (October 8, 1997), p. 1; (October 22, 1997); tlz, *Zeitung für Weimar* (October 10, 1997); (October 18, 1997); (October 22, 1997); tlz, *Thüringische Landeszeitung* (October 22, 1997), p. 4; *Weimarer Allgemeine* (October 22, 1997); *Neues Deutschland* (October 22, 1997), p. 4; *Thüringer Allgemeine, Weimarer Allgemeine* (October 8, 1997), p. 3; (October 21, 1997).

98 See note 88.

99 Niedersächsische Landeszentrale für politische Bildung, Gedenkstätte Bergen-Belsen: Veranstaltungen April 1998 bis September 1998; *Cellesche Zeitung*, v. 182, no. 91 (April 20, 1998), p. 14; *Hannoversche Allgemeine*, no. 91 (April 20, 1998), p. 4.

100 The watercolors are included in this anthology.

101 Karl Jaspers, *Vom Ursprung und Ziel der Geschichte*, p. 149.

Part B

History, Past and Present:
Jehovah's Witnesses in Germany[1]

History in Germany

For over 100 years now, Jehovah's[2] Witnesses[3] have been part of the religious scene in Germany. Since 1897, then known as Bible Students, they have proclaimed the gospel to their neighbors and friends. They have used the publications of the Watch Tower Society, namely, the magazine *The Watchtower*[4] and since 1922 *The Golden Age*,[5] today known as *Awake!*[6]

Augustine understands »religio« as »the bond of humans with God,«[7] and Jacob and Wilhelm Grimm define religion as »the subjective behavior towards God, the awe felt for him, and dedication to him.«[8] Jehovah's Witnesses do not want a new religion, as this would be incompatible with their reverence for God and devotion to him. On the contrary, they manifest a conscientious faithfulness to the old, as they are endeavoring to live the Christian way of life.[9]

For this reason Charles Taze Russell (1852–1916),[10] the first president of Zion's Watch Tower Tract Society, a non-commercial association devoted exclusively to Bible education,[11] advocated (old) Biblical truths, and refuted (newer) false religious doctrines and human philosophies which contradicted the Bible. Russell did not take any credit for having discovered new truths, but rather wrote: »Our work ... has been to bring together these long scattered fragments of truth and present them to the Lord's people — not as **new** (sic), not as our own **property** (sic), but as the Lord's. ... We must disclaim any credit even for the finding and rearrangement of the jewels of truth.«[12]

In July 1891, he remarked regarding Germany: »We saw ... nothing to encourage us to hope for any harvest in ... Germany« (meaning the ingathering of people belonging to Christ, who are also called »Christ's body parts« — author).[13]

In 1893, German immigrants, who had become Bible Students, returned from the United States to their native country.[14] The organized activity of the Watch Tower Society in Germany began in 1897 with a literature depot in Berlin (»Please contact Mrs. Margarete Giesecke, Nürnberger Strasse 66.«)[15] In the same year the magazine *Zion's Watch Tower and Herald of Christ's Presence* (»Zions Wacht Turm und Verkünder der Gegenwart Christi«) was published in German. In 1902, an office of the Watchtower Society was opened in Elberfeld (today part of the city of Wuppertal),[16] and in various places organized »classes« (parishes) laid the groundwork for congregations.

Until April 1905, arrangements were made to insert free sample copies of the *Watch Tower* into German newspapers. More than 1,500,000 of these *Watch Tower* samples were distributed — a great accomplishment for a very small group![17]

With the beginning of World War I in 1914, the Bible Students faced political and military disputes. Although at that time there was no consistent course of conduct, some took a firm stand. In what way?

In his book *Zwischen Widerstand und Martyrium*, the historian Detlef Garbe cites a report by pastors to the royal consistory of the church province of Westphalia. They reported with dismay that the Bible Students publicly propagate that it is a religious duty »for a soldier in war not to shoot at other human beings.«[18]

On December 7, 1921, the German Branch of the Watch Tower Society was recognized by a resolution of the Reich Council,[19] official recognition of their nonprofit status followed in 1922.[20] After June 1923, the International Bible Students Association and the headquarters in Germany, the Watch Tower Bible and Tract Society, had their official residence in Magdeburg.[21] It was the principal organization of the society called *Internationale Bibelforscher-Vereinigung, Deutscher Zweig* (International Bible Students Association, German Branch, or IBV) founded in 1926.[22]

On April 13, 1933, Bavaria banned the activities of Jehovah's Witnesses. Other German states passed similar measures in the following months.[23] Jehovah's Witnesses were the first religious organization to be banned by the Nazis.[24] On April 1, 1935, the Reich and Prussian Minister of the Interior provided formal notification to the State President in Magdeburg to dissolve the Watchtower Bible and Tract Society. This was carried out on April 27, 1935.[25] This prohibition throughout the Reich facilitated the legal expulsion of Witnesses from civil service positions throughout Germany. Some localities had already done this one year earlier. Ludwig Stickel was city accountant in Pforzheim. On March 29, 1934, he received a letter from the mayor, stating: »I am opening criminal proceedings against you with the purpose of dismissing you from your position. You are being charged with refusing to vote in the Reichstag elections of November 12, 1933.«[26]

Regarding the Nazi period, the historian Hans-Rainer Sandvoß noted that: »No other church or religious organization has, in comparison to their size, to mourn so many victims of their resistance, as the Jehovah's Witnesses.«[27]

Only after the end of World War II was it possible to activate the association. With the statute dated September 9, 1945, the International Bible Students Association, German Branch, Magdeburg was founded.[28] The change of the name to *Internationale Bibelforschervereinigung, Deutscher Zweig, e.V.* (Jehovah's Witnesses, International Bible Students Association, German Branch, registered association) was accepted with a resolution on June 8, 1946.[29]

On August 30, 1950, the branch in Magdeburg was closed a second time. In the GDR (former Soviet occupation zone), the activity of Jehovah's Witnesses was banned August 31, 1950, by decree of the Ministry of the Interior of the German Democratic Republic.[30] The Witnesses were accused of »systematic agitation against the present democratic order and its laws« as well as of espionage. The persecution was especially ruthless from 1950 until 1961. As far as it is known, more than 5,000 Jehovah's Witnesses had been imprisoned in GDR prisons and labor camps. In fifteen cases sentences for life imprisonment had been imposed.[31] (These sentences were later reduced to 15 years in prison.) While serving time in prison at least 58 of them died because of prison related mistreatment, illness, malnutrition, or advanced age.

Many of those who died in prison had already been imprisoned under Hitler.

Only after the fall of the Berlin Wall in November 1989 did the GDR cabinet council recognize the »religious organization of Jehovah's Witnesses in the GDR.« On March 14, 1990, they became a recognized religious organization with the same rights as all the other certified religious associations in the GDR.[32]

After the war, the preaching work in the Federal Republic of Germany was organized from Wiesbaden.[33] The *Wachtturm Bibel- und Traktat-Gesellschaft* administer the religious organization of Jehovah's Witnesses in Germany. Since 1983 the residence has been in Selters/Taunus.[34]

The Present Day

How do Jehovah's Witnesses define their message and community life?[35] They are Christians concerned with preserving early Christian teachings and virtues. Therefore, the complete Word of God, the Bible, is the basis and guide for their teachings, their organization, and for the conduct of each individual. They endeavor to follow Christ as their model. They do not follow any human leader, who propagates new teachings and unorthodox ceremonies,[36] and are therefore not a sect.[37]

Their self-image was confirmed by the European court for human rights in Strasbourg, which ruled: »Jehovah's Witnesses enjoy the status of a ›known religion‹ with the benefits that such a recognition brings.«[38] K. Dobbelaere, member of the Belgian Royal Academy, confirmed: »They (i.e., Jehovah's Witnesses) are not a sect. Their religion is established worldwide.«[39]

Compared with the major churches in Germany, they are a religious minority, similar to the Jews and other smaller religious organizations.[40] Jehovah's Witnesses number 192,000 members in Germany, more than 1.2 million in Europe, and more than 6 million in the world in more than 230 lands, islands, and territories.[41] As in other larger churches, during their services the gospel is read and sermons are given. Song and prayer, as well as wedding baptism, and funeral services also have an integral place.[42] Their services in about 2,100 congregations throughout Germany are open to the public. All family members are welcome to visit, or even participate, and to enjoy Christian fellowship.[43]

Many that come into personal contact with Jehovah's Witnesses, whether as neighbors, colleagues in the workplace, schoolmates, employers, or family members, consider them to be honest, decent, and hardworking members of society.[44]

Jehovah's Witnesses do not use questionable recruiting methods.[45] Instead, they speak to whomever may listen about their Bible based message of hope.[46] A recent survey in one European country revealed that on average each Jehovah's Witness had personally investigated the teachings of the Witnesses for three years before choosing to become a Witness.[47]

Jehovah's Witnesses use a method often encouraged by others for preaching. At a meeting of the World Council of Churches some 40 years ago, members were urged to »break out in a spirit of evangelism« and to teach their flocks to »go about evangelizing.« And in January 1994, Pope John Paul II said that it was »not the time to be ashamed of the Gospel, it's time to preach it from the rooftops.«[48]

In their efforts to reach everybody with the Gospel, they follow Jesus's words: »You received free, give free.«[49] All services of the church are free. There is no tithing, nor are collections made.[50]

Since the 1920s, Jehovah's Witnesses in Germany are recognized for serving the public welfare by their religious services. As laid out in their statutes all assets are used in agreement with the assignment in Matthew chapter 24, verse 14, *King James Version*: »And this gospel of the kingdom shall be preached in all the world for a witness unto all nations; and then shall the end come.«

One of their teachings is based on statements in the gospel according to which the Devil is the ruler of the »world,« e.g., in John, chapter 12, verse 31 and in the first letter of John, chapter 5, verse 19. This understanding influences their conduct in society and their relationship to the state.[51]

In the Bible the term »world« has a positive as well as a negative meaning. The positive refers to mankind in general, e.g., all people good or bad. This is the world that was loved by God and for which his son, Jesus Christ, died. Yet, Professor Walter Bauer refers to »world« also as that »which is at enmity with God, e.g., corrupted by sin, completely contradicting the godly way, doomed for destruction.«[52]

This is the world true Christians should be no part[53] of, as it is at enmity with God.[54] Therefore, worldwide Jehovah's Witnesses remain neutral in matters of politics and wars. A South African university professor said about them: »Here are people who see what others are inside, not just the color of the skin. Jehovah's Witnesses today form the only true brotherhood of mankind.«[55, 56]

To the best of their ability, they guard against any patterns of thinking, speech, and behavior which would contradict being a Christian like, for example, avidly pursuing material things and personal fame, or excessively indulging in pleasure.

They notice that the greater part of human society ›completely contradicts the godly way,‹ and they do not want to be influenced by this attitude.[57]

However, they do not literally isolate themselves as if they were hermits. Also, they do not feel that they are superior, and they are not presumptuous. The term »unbeliever« that the Bible occasionally uses for non-Christians is, therefore, not used as an official term or as an appellation. In their view, it would be very rude to speak disparagingly of fellow humans who are not Witnesses. They follow the Biblical advice: »A slave of the Lord ... needs to be gentle toward all.« (2 Timothy, chapter 2, verse 24, NW)

Furthermore, they believe that it would be wrong to assume that just because a person does not know Biblical truth,[58] he or she is indecent or immoral.

Just because the Bible calls the Devil »prince of the world« or »ruler of the world,«[59] Jehovah's Witnesses do not think that all persons with governmental power are pawns in the hands of God's enemy, as some people wrongly interpret it. Many officials have proven to be persons of principles. Because they were following the prompting of their conscience, some have courageously defended rights of minorities.[60]

Moreover, in a press release about the ruling of the Federal Administrative Court in Berlin, it states:[61] »Jehovah's Witnesses ... are not negatively inclined towards the state, but in principle have a positive attitude.«[62]

If governments uphold justice, law, and order, then Jehovah's Witnesses view them in line with Paul's words as »God's ministers« or »God's public servants.«[63] However, if they misuse their authority and suppress the people or persecute worshipers of God, then they obviously are not serving the interests of God, but those of his enemies.

Therefore, if humans demand something contrary to God's laws, or if humans forbid something that God demands, then Jehovah's Witnesses follow the example of the apostles, namely: »We must obey God as ruler rather than men.«[64, 65, 66]

Those familiar with their recent history are aware that individual members of their church even stick to their high moral standards when they are under intense pressure to give up their Christian conduct.[67, 68]

How should we view the statement of Jehovah's Witnesses that God will again step into human affairs?[69] What is connected with the dates of 1914,[70] 1925, and 1975?

Evidently great hopes were connected with these dates. From 1921 onward, the booklet *Millions Now Living Will Never Die* was distributed. According to the booklet, God's purpose, namely, the turning of the earth into a paradise and the resurrection of faithful men of old, like Noah or Abraham, would take place after 1925 onward.

The same was true for the year 1914.[71] Also for the year 1975, expectations were often too high.[72] On this subject statements were published and some were probably more definite than advisable.[73] This was acknowledged in *The Watchtower* in 1980.[74, 75]

How do Jehovah's Witnesses react when some of their expectations do not materialize? Their religion is for them »religio« as Augustine defined it, namely, a bond with God. Their personal bond with God is of utmost importance to them. Yes, to serve him is their purpose in life. They are motivated by the hope they derive from God's prophecies about the future. Furthermore, they are sure that attempts to explain Biblical prophecies were and are made out of sincere and unselfish intentions.[76] They are encouraged to keep in expectation of »the coming of the day of God« or »the presence of the day of Jehovah,«[77] not only because this is a valuable Christian tradition, but also because it is a Christian responsibility. Of course, they are aware that Christians from the times of the first followers and apostles have been eagerly waiting for the Kingdom of God. Therefore, they do not simply live from day to day, but they keep exerting themselves for God and their neighbors.

Although, they believe that the end could come tomorrow by means of God's intervention or even the end of their own life through illness or accident, they would still, like a pragmatist, plant an apple tree today.

Conclusion

Jehovah's Witnesses have been and are servants for the public welfare: They teach high moral standards and a Bible-based hope for the future.

— Worldwide they avoid wars, revolts, and revolutions.
— Although they follow the example of the early Christians and, therefore, desist from any political activities, they do not condemn any who think differently.
— They are tolerant. They do not try to hinder anyone from practicing his belief or being without religious affiliation.
— They desire to act according to their trained Christian conscience and wish that others would respect them in doing this.

Of course even in the future, faultlessness cannot be expected of them — even not when they reach the long-awaited perfection under the Kingdom of God, for the coming of which they earnestly pray.

Notes

1 This text was originally a 20-minute lecture at the scholarly symposium at Wewelsburg on October 5, 1997. It thus provides only an overview with the main dates. Consequently, the footnotes contain not only references but further basic information about the history and presence of Jehovah's Witnesses in Germany as well as additional details.

2 Jehovah (the causative form, the imperfect state, of the Heb. verb *hawah´* (become); meaning »He Causes to Become«). The personal name of God. (Isaiah 42:8; 54:5) Although also designated in the Bible by such descriptive titles as »God,« »Sovereign Lord,« »Creator,« »Father,« »the Almighty,« and »the Most High,« his personality and attributes — who and what he is — are fully summed up and expressed only in this personal name (Psalm 83:18). »Jehovah« is the best-known English pronunciation of the divine name, although »Yahweh« is favored by most Hebrew scholars. The oldest Hebrew manuscripts present the name in the form of four consonants, commonly called the Tetragram (from Greek *tetra-*, meaning »four,« and *gram'ma*, »letter«). These four letters may be transliterated into English as YHWH (or, JHVH).

3 Official name according to a resolution at conventions in 1931. Before (and sometimes also afterward), they were known as »Bible Students« or »Earnest Bible Students.«

4 The first issue was published in April and May 1897.

5 The first issue was on October 1, 1922, Bern, Switzerland; and on April 1, 1923, Barmen, Germany.

6 The first issue was on January 8, 1947.

7 W. Pfeifer, *Etymologisches Wörterbuch des Deutschen* (Berlin, 1989), p. 1409.

8 Jacob and Wilhelm Grimm, *Deutsches Wörterbuch,* vol. 14: (Munich, 1984), p. 51.

9 They consider themselves to be the revival of early Christianity in the sense of Jesus' parable of the world being the »field« on which sowing done by the early Christians leads to a greater harvest in the »time of the end.« Accordingly, even prominent personalities in their work take second place behind Christ. In 1870 something began which they call their »modern-day history.«

10 Russell was a deeply religious young man and founded one of the first independent Bible study groups. Although he had been raised in the Presbyterian Church, he still lacked an answer to important religious questions. According to Russell's own words, attending the meetings of other congregations, especially those of the Adventists, restored »his faith in the (divine) inspiration of the Bible.« But he was never closely connected to the Adventists. In 1877 after publishing some religious articles, he for the first time appeared as co-author of a book, *Three Worlds or Plan of Redemption*. The book focuses on themes of the Bible study group including the meaning of the redemption of mankind through the ransom sacrifice of Jesus Christ and also the widespread interest in the chronological-eschatological interpretation of biblical prophecies among protestant congregations in the United States. Therefore, they determined from biblical statements that the »end of the time of nations« would be in 1914. Then the theocracy with glorified Jesus as King would be established; later the restoration of Paradise on earth would take place. In July 1879 the first issue of the magazine *Zion's Watchtower and Herald of Christ's Presence* was published. Thereafter dozens of study groups were formed. Russell was constantly on the move as a preacher. Central themes of his speeches and writings were that Jesus would return invisibly and would not be visible during the »parousia«; that the widely spread »doctrine of hell« could not be reconciled with the love displayed by God through Jesus Christ; that the teaching of the immortality of the soul was diametrically opposed to the Biblical understanding of the term »soul,« and that a conscious, deliberate decision to serve God and his son was necessary in order to be a Christian.

11 Incorporated on December 15, 1884, in accordance with the law concerning nonprofit corporations of the commonwealth of Pennsylvania; the financial assets were contributed mostly by Russell himself, who thereby wished to use his inheritance as the son of a storeowner to honor God. The publishing and printing corporation of Jehovah's Witnesses was founded in order to give their missionary work a legal basis. It is recognized as a religious, nonprofit corporation. Despite its legal status this corporation has never been a business or commercial corporation, because profits or dividends have never been paid.

12 *Jehovah's Witnesses—Proclaimers of God's Kingdom* (New York, 1993), p. 49.

13 *1989 Yearbook of Jehovah's Witnesses*, p. 70.

14 *Watchtower* (June 1, 1893), p. 1539.

15 *Wachtturm* (Jan. 1898), pp. 39f.

16 *Wachtturm* (July/September 1902), pp. 1, 8.

17 *Jehovah's Witnesses–Proclaimers of God's Kingdom*, p. 410.

18 Detlef Garbe, *Zwischen Widerstand und Martyrium: Jehovas Zeugen im »Dritten Reich«* 3rd rev. ed. with an epilog (Munich, 1997), p. 46.

19 Letter from the Minister of the Interior to the Watchtower Bible and Tract Society in Barmen, reference IA 10153 2. Aug., dated December 7, 1921, in Watchtower Society Archive, Selters.

20 By the Prussian Minister of Science, Art, and Education transmitted by the mayor of Barmen. See the report of the Gesellschaft für Vermögenswahrung und -verwaltung (Treuhand und Revision) mbH, Berlin, about an investigation in 1932, in Watchtower Society Archive, Selters.

21 Certificate issued by Police President Magdeburg, September 14, 1932, in: Franz Zürcher, *Kreuzzug gegen das Christentum* (Zurich, 1938), p. 80.

22 Registration occurred on January 19, 1927, under no. 466, Watch Tower Society History Archive, Selters.

23 *Deutsche Justiz* (1934), p. 177 (the ban in Prussia on June 24, 1933, was based on §1 of the decree of the President of the German Reich for the protection of the people and the state of February 28, 1933).

24 Detlef Garbe, *Tel Aviver Jahrbuch für deutsche Geschichte*, vol. 23 (Gerlingen, 1994), p. 156.

25 Garbe, *Zwischen Widerstand und Martyrium*, pp. 133f.

26 *1974 Yearbook of Jehovah's Witnesses,* p. 116.

27 *Widerstand 1933-1945, Berlin*, vol. 8 of the series Resistance in Berlin from 1933-1945, *Widerstand in Mitte und Tiergarten* (Berlin, 1994), p. 282.

28 Registration of their statute of September 9, 1945, is found in the Associations Register, Magdeburg, entry no. 819 on September 22, 1945.

29 Registered in the Associations Register as entry no. 819 on July 1, 1946.

30 Letter from Dr. Steinhoff, Minister of the Interior of the GDR, to the branch office of Jehovah's Witnesses in Magdeburg, *DDR Handbuch*, vol. 2, 3rd ed. (1985), p. 1543.

31 Survey of the history of Jehovah's Witnesses in the GDR 1949-1990, July/September 1997, in Watch Tower Society History Archive, Selters; see Marley Cole, *Jehovas Zeugen* (Frankfurt, 1956), p. 209, which still reports on 14 cases.

32 Certificate of recognition from the Council of Ministers of the GDR, Department for church matters, in H. Weber, »Körperschaftsstatus für die Religionsgemeinschaft der Zeugen Jehovas in Deutschland?« in *Zeitschrift für evangelisches Kirchenrecht* vol. 41, no. 2 (June 1996), p. 172 (174).

33 Entered in the Associations Register, Wiesbaden, no. 792 (later no. 1439) as Jehovas Zeugen, Internationale Bibelforschervereinigung, Deutscher Zweig, e.V. (Jehovah's Witnesses, International Bible Students Association, German Branch, registered society), Wiesbaden on April 14, 1956. Change of name into Wachtturm Bibel-und Traktat-Gesellschaft, Deutscher Zweig, e.V. on May 28, 1956, at the Wiesbaden local court.

34 It is a Bible society. Only Bibles as well as magazines and publications for Bible education (including audio and video cassettes) are published. Association register of Limburg, no. 555, change of the location of headquarters in Germany entered on February 17, 1984.

35 Every Witness, true to his name, makes it the center of his life to witness to the honor of Jehovah and his son Jesus Christ. Every Witness realizes that he/she cannot »earn« salvation through evangelizing; the preaching activity, however, is part of the faithful fulfillment of the commission given by Jesus to all of his disciples. (Matthew 28:19). A prerequisite to their worship is a conscientious, voluntary dedication to God through his son, Jesus Christ. In his name they thank God for all the »undeserved kindness« (their way of expressing the traditional term »grace«). The son is subordinate to his father, Jehovah. The Witnesses reject the teaching of the trinity. Christ is sent by God as mediator of redemption, the only savior (Acts 4:12) and through his resurrection the guarantee of salvation (1. Corinthians 15:17, 20). In anticipation of theological interpretations during the last few decades, they put faith in the hope of resurrection and reject the platonic teaching of the immortality of the soul as well as the »doctrine of hell,« which is not consistent with the Bible. According to the early Christian example, they do not practice child baptism. Their whole life and not just their worship must be in accordance with God's direction found in the Bible which is accepted as God's inspired word and which is commented on in their publications. Evangelizing, the preaching of the »good news of God's Kingdom« (Matthew 24:14, »New World Translation of the Holy Scriptures,« hereafter abbreviated as NW, see also footnote 49), is an important part of their witnessing. They view this Kingdom, or God's Kingdom with the glorified Jesus as heavenly king, as the central means of salvation by God. This Kingdom will fulfill God's purpose to make everlasting life on a paradise earth possible for all humans: »Let your Kingdom come. Let your will take place, as in heaven, also upon earth.« (Matthew 6:9, 10, NW) Salvation through Christ is announced to all, but is fulfilled in two different ways: in heaven for

the »little flock« (Luke 12:32) of 144,000 heirs with Christ (Revelation 7, 14) who since the days of the apostles have been chosen by God throughout the centuries, and on earth for an unlimited number of people who appear during the time of the end (Revelation 7:9, 10).

36 Jehovah's Witnesses understand their organization to be theocratic according to the original meaning of the word (»rule by God,« »subjecting yourself to godly rule«) and this is a preview of the future of the »New World Society.« The headquarters are located in Brooklyn (New York); especially since 1975, the main responsibility rests collectively with the »Governing Body« (13 members in 2000), members of the Body are added by appointment. Neither individual members nor a class of persons, including members of the Governing Body, are viewed by Jehovah's Witnesses as a »direct channel« of God. As the Bible is the written Word of God, it could be called a channel of his thoughts. So if an organization loyally upholds and proclaims God's written Word, they can, therefore, serve in this general sense as God's channel of communication. In any case, neither do Jehovah's Witnesses, nor their Governing Body, or individual members thereof claim that they have a direct channel to God, be it through a personal conversation with God or in a vision, as the prophets of early Biblical times. The Governing Body or its members do not claim to receive revelations or to make decisions which would be considered infallible truths. Jehovah's Witnesses neither view the Governing Body nor any of its members as infallible. The responsibility for various countries (»branches«) is delegated to so-called Branch Committees. The branch territory is divided into several districts, every district consists of several circuits, each circuit contains several communities (»congregations«). Services are held three times a week, lasting altogether for about five hours. Most Jehovah's Witnesses attend the two regular services in the church of Jehovah's Witnesses, which is called a »Kingdom Hall« in harmony with their message of preaching work about the Kingdom. In general it is a simple, serviceable hall without candles, crosses, altars, etc. The third service is conducted in an informal setting, usually in the home of one of the members. Religious images do not have any importance in their services. These meetings, which begin and conclude with song and prayer emphasize teaching work. Also women and children actively participate in the program. Jehovah's Witnesses have no connections with miraculous healings of physical and mental ailments, nor with mysticism. They also refuse any part in esoteric beliefs, which have recently gained popularity. Conscientiously they look after responsibilities for pastoral care and care of the sick. Besides these devotional activities, their preaching work has priority in their community life. There is no specific time limit given as the maximum or minimum. According to individual circumstances, each person decides for himself how much time he can invest. According to the latest reports, active Jehovah's Witnesses have spent on the average nine hours a month in their preaching work. Reports are made to the local congregation about the time they spend in preaching the gospel. Compiled reports of all work are regularly published for individual countries and serve as spiritual encouragement as well as for planning and information. Their publishing activities are remarkable. Bible-based literature is published worldwide in more than 300 languages; their magazines *The Watchtower* and *Awake!* are probably the most widely distributed religious magazines in the world (in January 2001 with an edition of more than 23 million copies in 139 languages). In Germany, Bible-based literature has been given to all interested persons free of charge since September 1, 1991. Voluntary donations are usually given anonymously and provide what is necessary to finance the work. Tithes or any other obligations to contribute money are unknown in their organization. All overseers in their worldwide 91,000 communities are not paid and work as volunteers. No Witness in any way associates financial gain with the proclamation of their belief.

37 Jehovah's Witnesses reject this inappropriate designation. It does not surprise them, however, to be called a »sect,« since the same thing happened to the first-century Christians (Acts 24:14). But the following must be considered: Originally the word »sect« designated (more in a derogatory than in a neutral way) a group or community which had chosen a way of life or a religion that was different from that of the majority. Today this term designates religious groups with radical intentions and practices. They often practice their activities in secret and the members must be unconditionally devoted to a self-proclaimed leader. Absolutely none of this applies to Jehovah's Witnesses. The Witnesses expect to be respected as a Christian religion, which honestly and reasonably preserves and endeavors to practice the spirit of early Christianity as revealed in the Bible. Discussions about certain beliefs must be on a theological level. In its press release of May 28, 1998, after the completion of their two-year study, the Enquete Commission on »So-called Sects and Psychogroups« of the German Bundestag announced the decision » ... to no longer use the general and, therefore, stigmatizing term ›sect.‹«

38 The case »Manoussakis and others vs. Greece« (59/1995/565/651), Europäischer Gerichtshof für Menschenrechte (European Court of Human Rights).

39 Certificate November 12, 1996, in Watch Tower Society History Archive, Selters.

40 Cooperation: The more than one hundred branches work closely together; the missionary and humanitarian works in Africa, Eastern Europe, and in many parts of Asia owe a lot to the support from America and Western Europe. Other cooperative efforts, as, for example, with other churches are not cultivated by the Witnesses.

41 Addresses: Headquarters, Watch Tower Bible & Tract Society, 25 Columbia Heights, Brooklyn, NY 11201, USA. German Branch Office: D-65617 Selters/Taunus, Telephone 49- 64 83 - 41 31 10, Fax 49 - 64 83 - 41 31 00.

42 Aside from German, congregations have also been formed in the following languages: Arabic, Chinese, English, French, Greek, Italian, Croatian/Serbian, Persian, Polish, Portuguese, Russian, Spanish, Tamil, and Turkish. They all use the same church buildings of Jehovah's Witnesses (Kingdom Halls). There are no rituals; Jehovah's Witnesses only know two symbolic acts: baptism through immersion and the celebration of the Lord's supper. The Lord's supper is celebrated once a year according to the Passover festival of the old Biblical calendar. Jehovah's Witnesses do not smoke. They celebrate festivities, but none that their Bible-trained conscience would consider questionable, such as birthdays, Easter, Christmas. They do not see any Biblical basis for prohibiting drinking alcohol, coffee, or tea; moderation is their Biblical demand. There are no regulations regarding food except for the apostolic command to abstain from blood (Acts 15: 29).

43 For Jehovah's Witnesses, marriage and the family are the essential foundations of living together. That is why they are making an effort to contribute to the strengthening of family ties with the help of their publications and in their teaching work. They consider family planning to be the personal decision of every married couple. Out of respect for the holiness of life they reject abortions. Applying Bible principles contributes to stable marriages and harmonious families. Since about 30 percent of all marriages in Germany fail, an extensive survey revealed that among Jehovah's Witnesses about 5 percent are divorced or separated. This includes those who were already divorced before they became Jehovah's Witnesses. The Witnesses endeavor to be good communicators, companions, and teachers for their children. They follow the Bible's advice to be guided by love in raising children. Biblical love is a love guided by principles and not a »blind« love. When raising children this means striving for consistency so that the children and youths have enough room to develop their own personality while at the same time they are protected from harm through setting well-thought-out limitations. Verse 24 of Proverbs chapter 13 has given rise to discussion: »The one holding back his rod is hating his son, but the one loving him is he that does look for him with discipline.« Jehovah's Witnesses are convinced that the Biblical expression »rod« in no way means that a child may be beaten in anger or even mistreated. That is why the Bible also talks so often about »listening« to »discipline.« Jehovah's Witnesses reject violence as totally inappropriate and, therefore, an unacceptable means of child upbringing. To beat children is therefore not part of their concept of discipline.

44 In the *Münchener Merkur* of July 25, 1978, the following is stated about Jehovah's Witnesses: »They are the most honest and punctual tax payers in the Federal Republic. Their obedience to the laws can be seen in the way they drive as well as in crime statistics. ... They obey those in authority (parents, teachers, government). ... The Bible, the basis for all their actions, is their support.«

45 Without any commitment on the part of the person, they conduct free home Bible studies with persons who request it. This Bible study acquaints the student with the teachings of the Bible and the organization of the Witnesses without reducing their right to make a personal decision. Previous experience has shown that a number of Bible studies are discontinued. Newly-baptized Witnesses have often studied for a number of years before they decided to take the step of baptism. For those who want to leave the organization, a simple declaration of intent suffices.

46 Their Christian commitment is based on two things: thankful obedience to the Christian command to preach, and love of God and their fellow humans. The Witnesses are wholeheartedly thankful to Jehovah God and Christ: faithful insight into the purpose in life, salvation, and hope are precious gifts from God through Christ Jesus. Jesus himself gave the command that his followers were to »teach and baptize« others. (Matthew 28:19, 20). This worldwide activity is well described in the gospel according to Matthew, according to the King James Version, chapter 14, verse 14: »And this gospel of the kingdom shall be preached in all the world for a witness unto all nations; and then shall the end come.« When they bring this »invitation,« Jehovah's Witnesses endeavor to be polite and show respect for the convictions of others. That literature is offered not only takes into consideration the modern lifestyle with its greatly reduced time for conversations, but it also makes it possible to reach more people.

47 *Watchtower* (June 1, 1997), p. 7.

48 *Watchtower* (December 1, 1996), p. 32.

49 Matthew 10:8 according to the *New World Translation of the Holy Scriptures (NW)*: first complete publication in 1961, in the meantime more than 100 million copies have been distributed in more than 20 languages, among which are also African and Asian languages. There is only »one Bible« as the Holy Scriptures. Jehovah's Witnesses therefore do not have their »own Bible,« but rather a modern day Bible *translation*. In addition to other Bibles, the Witnesses have been printing and distributing the New World Translation of the Holy Scriptures for about forty years. It was prepared by Witnesses who remain anonymous. It was their desire to honor the name of God »Jehovah« in the same way as in the original texts. They consider it to be a disgrace toward God that so many Bibles have replaced the personal name of God by the title »Lord.« Besides this the Bible's message and teaching was to shine forth in fluent, modern language by means of a new and especially careful rendering of the original texts. This translation has often been criticized severely in religious circles, especially since it shows that the translators do not accept the teaching of the trinity. It must be acknowledged, though, that the translation is in accordance with all linguistic criteria and that even the rendering of the most criticized passages only shows the scope of meaning of the original text. Naturally this translation must also be open to factual discussion.

50 The opening of Eastern Europe has enabled tens of thousands of Witnesses, who had faithfully adhered to their faith despite communist persecution, to emerge from prohibitions. The whole community had to face the challenge of supplying these associates, as well as the many new ones who are now joining them, with Bibles, publications, Kingdom Halls, and also humanitarian help. Trusting in God, many Witnesses in the »old Federal states« (in the former Federal Republic of West Germany) have accepted restrictions and simplifications in order to be able to offer such help.

51 Jehovah's Witnesses consider it to be their Christian duty to support the state and its representatives. Their understanding of Christian neutrality, though, commands them to remain neutral in political and military questions and actions. Referring to Jesus's words »Pay back, therefore, Caesar's things to Caesar, but God's things to God,« they believe that he drew a line between what a Christian may do for the state and the unconditional devotion which he voluntarily and personally promised to God. Applying the words from Isaiah, chapter 2, verse 4, which are written on the »Wall of Peace« in front of the United Nations, »They [will] beat their swords into plowshares and will learn war no more.« Jehovah's Witnesses have been known, especially since World War II, for refusing to serve in the armed forces, be it with or without weapons. This position has earned them admiration but also inhumane persecution. Over the past decades, many hundreds of Jehovah's Witnesses have been condemned and punished for refusing to do military or alternate civilian service. This, however, has not impaired the respectful position of the Witnesses towards government authorities. Because God's Word commands them to »be in subjection to the superior authorities« (Romans 13:1), they would never consider participating in civil uprisings in order to protest against the politics of the government. The developments within the legislation of many countries during the last few decades has resulted in the viewpoint that performing services such as civilian service are now considered to be services detached from military service. *The Watchtower* of May 1, 1996, officially stated the possibility to respond to such efforts. Persons liable to military service consider and personally decide whether participating in civilian service can be reconciled with their conscience. The religious organization exerts no influence on this personal decision. In contrast to former years, many Jehovah's Witnesses now perform civilian service in Germany. This does not constitute an abandonment of their position of strict neutrality since these services are completely civilian and aimed at helping fellow human beings.

52 Walter Bauer, *Griechisch-Deutsches Wörterbuch zu den Schriften des Neuen Testaments und der übrigen urchristlichen Literatur* (Berlin, 1952), col. 809.

53 John, chapter 15, verse 19, *NW.*

54 James, chapter 4, verse 4.

55 *The Bible—God's Word or Man's?* (Watch Tower Society, 1989), pp. 182f., par. 19.

56 The Witnesses are not nationalistic, nor are the racist or antisemitic. In their missionary work they are free of prejudices and speak to people of all kinds.

57 See 2 Corinthians 6:14-17; Ephesians 4:18; 2 Peter 2:20.

58 There are no two truths. The Bible is very clear in essential matters of faith. Jesus himself said: »Narrow is the gate and cramped the road leading off into life, and few are the ones finding it.« (Matthew 7:14) Jehovah's Witnesses believe that they have found this road. Otherwise they would be looking for another religion. It would be intolerant to treat someone violently because of his convictions. Jehovah's Witnesses have experienced such intolerance from influental figures (in politics and in the churches) repeatedly. The

Witnesses, though, are determined to respect the responsibility and right of every individual to make a decision and to leave the judgement of individuals to God.

59 John, chapter 14, verse 30, *NW.*

60 »Thereby the New Testament reveals a truth which the mind of the understanding ones so often didn't want to see: in every kind of State there is a demon which is greedy for ever more power and that the state, therefore, if it wants to ensure discipline and order must be kept in check itself. Otherwise, it degenerates and becomes a curse for humans and an interplay of God on earth. It is the same with the State as with humans who are the image of God only as long as he remains in the discipline of God. Left up to himself he becomes a wild animal with strangely fast inevitability.« Dr. Otto Dibelius, then Protestant bishop of Berlin, in: *Grenzen des Staates* (Tübingen, 1949), pp. 15f.

61 Decision of June 26, 1997 – 7 C 11/96.

62 Press release from the Federal Administrative Court Press Office, no. 29/1997, June 26, 1997.

63 Romans, chapter 13, verse 6, *NW.*

64 Jehovah's Witnesses respect secular governments of the countries in which they live and follow Jesus' word: »Pay back, therefore, Caesar's things to Caesar, but God's things to God.« (Matthew, ch. 22, verse 21). In extreme situations, when governments have attempted to force Jehovah's Witnesses into unchristian behavior, they follow the apostolic example and believe ›that God must be obeyed more than men.‹ (Acts, ch. 5, verse 29, *NW*). There are no such laws in Germany at present.

65 They do not reject the state, but conscientiously weigh the command of being submissive according to Romans, chapter 13, against the apostolic command to »obey God rather than men« (Acts 5:29).

66 The refusal of blood transfusions can also be seen from this point of view. The main reason lies in the clearly-stated command in the Holy Scriptures. In Acts, chapter 15, verse 29, it is reported that the apostles commanded all Christians to »abstain from blood.« For centuries the meaning of this command was clear and important to Christians as all the other dictates stated in the aforementioned text, namely, not to lead an immoral way of life and to have no part in idolatry. In addition to this: The progress in medicine, especially during the last decade, has revealed a considerable number of risks involved with blood transfusions. Something else cannot be overlooked: the religiously motivated refusal to accept blood transfusions by Jehovah's Witnesses at no time meant a refusal of medical care, neither for themselves nor for their children. To the contrary, their willingness to cooperate for the purpose of developing, advancing, and applying ever more effective bloodless therapies was so great that at an international medical symposium in Paris, in February 1996, the following was stated about Jehovah's Witnesses: »Their unrelenting efforts to promote blood-free medicine by means of court decisions, education, and cooperation have benefited us all. They deserve our thanks.« As studies reveal, the mortality of Jehovah's Witnesses is not higher than the general population (B. von Bormann, S. Aulich, *Perioperative Anämie – wo sind die Grenzen für Hämoglobingehalt und Hämatokrit? Refresher Course: Aktuelles Wissen für Anästhesisten,* no. 22 [Nuremberg: Springer Verlag, 1996], pp. 1–8). For about seven years now there has been an auxiliary service for Jehovah's Witnesses in Germany who wish to have medical treatment without a blood transfusion. This auxiliary service located more than 4,200 cooperative doctors of different specialities who are willing to treat Jehovah's Witnesses without blood.

67 The fact that Jehovah's Witnesses expect salvation only from Jehovah and Jesus immediately brought them into conflict with Nazi ideology. Even the harshest persecution could not deter them from their conviction — a martyrdom which is now beginning to get well-deserved attention because of increased historical research. Persecutions of all kinds, which are altogether as intense and severe as those of the Nazi time, have marked the history of Jehovah's Witnesses down to our day. Such persecutions were seen especially in eastern European countries until the fall of the communist system, but also in a number of African states, where this growing religious organization uncompromisingly kept out of any tribal or political feuds and, therefore, often had to endure immeasurable distress. To the honor of Christianity their absolutely neutral and always humane conduct in Rwanda and Burundi stood, and still stands, in sharp contrast to that of members of several other denominations.

68 In the 1990s there were reasons to research the history of Jehovah's Witnesses, especially to secure survivor testimonies about Nazi Germany and Eastern Europe. Projects by historians and sociologists supported by Jehovah's Witnesses have opened up new perspectives.

69 It is said that Jehovah's Witnesses believe »only they alone will be saved«: Jehovah's Witnesses do not believe that. Because they are convinced that many others can be saved, they are very active in missionary work. They are also convinced that millions of humans who lived in past centuries and were not Witnesses

will be resurrected and receive the opportunity to gain everlasting life on earth under God's Kingdom (Acts 24:15). Besides this Jesus warned against judging others. Humans can only see outer appearances; God, though, sees the heart. He is a merciful judge and has given this responsibility to Jesus and not to Jehovah's Witnesses.

70   Our time, as Jehovah's Witnesses believe, since the enthronement of Christ in heaven in 1914, has been marked with all the features of the prophecy about the time of the end. Jehovah's Witnesses stand out because of their optimistic view of the future due to their Christian expectation of God's Kingdom, because of the ability to face problems in everyday life and within the family due to the power they derive from their faith, and because of their skeptical (but never aggressive) distance from the present world order. Jehovah's Witnesses attribute no special eschatological meaning to the turn of the Millennium. They do not expect the end of the world to be the end of planet earth, but rather the end of all evil, the complete removal of the present, wicked world order, which according to their opinion is under the influence of the Devil. God will be a righteous judge and decide who will survive and who will not. Jehovah's Witnesses unceasingly point to the parallel Jesus drew to the flood of Noah's day (Matthew 24:37-39), even though they do not expect another flood.

71   Expectations for 1914 were not fulfilled to the full extent, but there is no doubt for Jehovah's Witnesses that 1914 was a turning point in the history of mankind, which constituted the beginning of the Biblical »time of the end« (Daniel 8:17). Historians and statesmen have pointed to 1914 as a great turning point and, in many respects, the worst epoch in history began in that year. Years earlier, by the way, Russell had already warned against overemphasizing chronological elements.

72   Of the 6 million active Witnesses today more than 50 percent became Jehovah's Witnesses after 1975.

73   *Jehovah's Witnesses–Proclaimers of God's Kingdom* (1993), p. 104.

74   *Watchtower* (March 15, 1980), p. 17.

75   The article in *The Watchtower* of November 1, 1995, concerning the term »generation« and how Jesus Christ used it, is also of importance. The explanation shows that with the term »generation,« he was not specifying a certain time period, but rather a certain group of contemporaries. Jesus did not use the term »generation« chronologically, but sociologically. With this statement the basis for possible speculations on future calculations concerning the end (which is still expected in the »near future«) was withdrawn.

76   The Witnesses have learned from these mistakes. From their point of view, it was wrong to favor a certain point in time and not the feeling of expectancy and urgency itself. This was and still is maintained and proclaimed in the early Christian sense, sustained by the conviction that God's Kingdom with the resurrected and glorified Jesus as king is God's central means of salvation.

77   2 Peter, chapter 3, verse 12, *NW*.

Johannes Wrobel

The Video Documentary »Jehovah's Witnesses Stand Firm Against Nazi Assault«: Propaganda or Historical Document?

Introduction

The video documentary, »Jehovah's Witnesses Stand Firm Against Nazi Assault,« produced by the Watch Tower Society (Brooklyn, NY, USA), the nonprofit corporation of the religious association of Jehovah's Witnesses (known as »Bible Students« prior to 1931), is the focus of a factual controversy.[1]

It is extremely encouraging that the debate about this topic has been characterized by the attitude expressed in a letter from the Prime Minister of the State of Brandenburg to the German Branch of the Watch Tower Society (Wachtturm-Gesellschaft). On the occasion of the world premiere of this video documentary at the Ravensbrück memorial on November 6, 1996, he wrote: »[I] wish to assure you in this manner,... that it is with great admiration that I commemorate the Jehovah's Witnesses, who courageously resisted National Socialists and unselfishly assisted other prisoners. ... Your film screening is an important step toward informing the public about the role your religious association played under the Nazi regime.«[2]

Even critical consideration about the means and manner chosen by the Watch Tower Society for informing, on a worldwide scale, the public and the members of the religious association of Jehovah's Witnesses about Nazi persecution in Germany and neighboring countries, reveals that respect for the persecuted victims and factual argumentation were constantly maintained.[3]

And Dr. Stolpe's statement is correct: this film is indeed »an important step toward informing the public about the role (the) religious association played under the Nazi regime.« Information – not confrontation, agitation, or provocation – was, is, and remains the intent of this video documentary. Meanwhile, it has been made available, in addition to English and German, in Russian, Polish, French, Portuguese, Italian, and other languages. The video has been shown in the respective countries with positive reactions.[4]

»While informing the public,« the Watch Tower Society received praise, constructive criticism, and support from many public and private institutions. However, as expected, we have also received one-sided and biased criticism, especially from religious opponents.[5] This has been the manner and tradition in Germany since the 1920s and was thus to be expected. Then, in 1921, precursors of the »sect departments« in the major churches were created, along with their »defamatory literature,« as Detlef Garbe notes in his study, *Zwischen Widerstand und Martyrium: Die Zeugen Jehovas im »Dritten Reich«* (1997, p. 72); these publications are an example of »the errors that entered into theological science about Bible Students' teachings.«

All of our invitations for the world premiere of the video, sent to the Minister President of Brandenburg, the German President, and several other public figures, stated: »The film, its premiere in Ravensbrück, and the press conference in Berlin contain no religious preaching.«[6] During these events, no prayers were said, no Bible explanations given, and no religious songs sung, unlike the usual Jehovah's Witnesses' religious meetings. Instead, the program provided factual information, and commemorates the many victims of Nazism with the purple triangle and other imprisoned Witnesses.[7]

Nevertheless, religious opponents of Jehovah's Witnesses attacked the video documentary as »propaganda.«

This article examines the following questions:

— How did the video documentary come about? What was its goal?

— How are the terms »propaganda« and »religious preaching« understood?

— Does the video documentary »Stand Firm Against Nazi Assault« present the persecution of Jehovah's Witnesses in a historically accurate manner? Does it conceal essential facts? For example, did Jehovah's Witnesses in 1933 express antisemitism and attempt to ingratiate themselves with the Nazi regime, as was the case with the major churches and, long after 1945, has also been claimed about Jehovah's Witnesses?

Origin and Purpose of the Video Documentary

After the introduction, the video documentary begins with excerpts from an international seminar, »The Nazi Assault on Jehovah's Witnesses,« held at the United States Holocaust Memorial Museum in Washington, D.C., on September 29, 1994.[8] It was this seminar in distant America that actually gave the impetus for planning the video *Stand Firm Against Nazi Assault*, and not — as some inaccurately claim — the lawsuit seeking recognition of equal status for Jehovah's Witnesses with other churches recognized in Germany. The petition for recognition of equal religious status had already been accepted by two German courts, when in November and December 1995 and in the spring of 1996, the Watch Tower Society's film teams were conducting interviews with historians and Witness survivors in Germany, the United States, and Canada, as well as in Sweden and Denmark.

A total of ten historians from Europe and North America as well as twenty Witness survivors are heard in the film.[9] While shooting the film, conducting interviews, and editing the script, the multinational video team[10] adhered to the following guidelines: (1) To inform in general an international public, educational institutions, and the academic community about the persecution of Jehovah's Witnesses under the Nazi regime in a modern medium. (2) To show this dark chapter of history to members of their own religious community, using image and sound, a history known to them from numerous survivor accounts by persecuted Witnesses, published since the mid-1930s and especially after 1945, in Watchtower literature.[11]

The concept of the video is multi-functional, and can be shown in private homes, classrooms, lecture halls, or movie theaters in various countries. The effect of »Stand Firm Against Nazi Assault« may vary greatly from person to person: The historian will draw certain conclusions and gain knowledge for his work, whereas a Jehovah's Witness may feel inspired by the steadfastness of his/her fellow believers during the Third Reich.

We mostly filmed or documented individual statements about the theme, and have thus designated the film as a »video documentary.« (Since victims who can give testimony will soon no longer be among us, we recognize the importance of being able »to see the faces of the survivors, to hear their voices, to understand them,« as Steven Spielberg once stated.)[12]

Stand Firm Against Nazi Assault, therefore, claims to be a documentation, a »contemporary historical document,« and has been termed a »video documentary,« not a »documentary film,« and literally fulfills the definitions of »document« and »documentation« as convincing vivid testimony or evidence.[13] Evidence of what? First, of the undaunted, resolute, and steadfast spirit of individual Witnesses who followed their conscience. The documentary also shows the steadfastness of a great majority of the religious association and of a »faith without compromises,« as Detlef Garbe states. He also explains: »Large segments of the religious association were not to be intimidated by the increasing repression.«[14] We have concentrated on these »large segments of the religious association,« knowing that today, in an age of declining ethical and moral values, lesson may be learned from the way they responded to peer pressure, intolerance, and the voice of conscience.[15]

Were these ideals worth giving one's life for? That is not the issue here. At a time when newspapers in Germany were full of obituary announcements, when families lost fathers and sons at the front, people were also willing to die for their consciences for non-religious motives, for their opposing views. What importance did death then have in daily life, in the family? Susanne Zeller-Hirzel, who entered the political resistance in Stuttgart almost by accident and distributed leaflets by the White Rose, talks about Gestapo interrogations and the possibility of being executed, in a film called *Mut ohne Befehl* (Courage without Orders): »There were families that lost three sons. It was easy; dying was not the worst evil – if in the end you die for a good thing. But how was it for a soldier who had to fight despite his convictions and then be killed? Nobody thinks about this. This was also the case for many. And this too was terrible.«[16]

Both major churches, however, who had supported the anti-democratic, nationalistic spirit of the times in Germany during World Wars I and II[17], are mentioned only in passing in the video documentary *Stand Firm Against Nazi Assault*. And a positive image is presented in the context of historians' quotations, as well as a few well-known images about »the churches under National Socialism.« As German historian Garbe stated: »There is also evidence that Jehovah's Witnesses were aided by pastors ... but ... one has to say that evidence of such cases is rare.«

Of course, everyone has a right to imagine how he or she would have made an analytical documentary film about the history of Jehovah's Witnesses in Germany from the First World War and what information to include. However, an attempt to make a comparative criticism of *Stand Firm Against Nazi Assault* on this basis misreads the themes and form of our video. The video team, of course, tried to provide some background information on contemporary history, but this was not the main concern.[18] The Watch Tower Society did not aim to produce an inclusive documentary film about the history of Jehovah's Witnesses in Germany, nor did it intend to comment on all aspects of their history and the various statements made by its opponents. In many parts of the world, the erroneous assertions, such as the use of swastika flags, singing the national anthem,[19] or an attempt to ingratiate themselves to the Nazis at the convention in Berlin-Wilmersdorf on June 25, 1933, and the alleged betrayal by leading Jehovah's Witnesses, are unknown.[20]

The content and focus of the video documentary was decisively shaped by the experiences of people under the Nazi regime and the views of historians – not by current events. This has been well received and has met with great interest throughout the world.[21]

Recently, the impressive multi-media CD-ROM *Gegen das Vergessen: Eine Dokumentation des Holocaust* was released in Munich.[22] A computer magazine not only praised it, but also noted: »The CD-ROM would have been even better suited to include more survivor interviews and reports about individual experiences, since that is what ultimately makes history come alive.«[23] In *Stand Firm Against Nazi Assault*, religious individuals bring their pasts back to life! Is this really »propaganda«?

»Propaganda« or »No Religious Preaching«?

The term »propaganda,« which came into use in the nineteenth century and originated in the religious domain, became the short form of the name of the »Apostolic Congregation for Propagating the Faith,« established in Rome in 1622.[24] Nowadays it is used in a derogatory manner. If *Stand Firm Against Nazi Assault* were a »propaganda film,« it would serve propagandistic purposes; thus, in this case, the »ideas, facts, or allegations spread deliberately to further one's cause or to damage an opposing cause.«[25]

If this had been the aim of the film, it should be quantitatively provable. However, the opposite is true. Among the 118 statements by historians and camp survivors, only 11 statements (9.9 percent) include religious terms (e.g., God or prayer) or remarks pertaining to the beliefs of Jehovah's Witnesses (e.g., Bible study and refusal to perform military service).[26] Such statements, by themselves, are not an attempt to convert viewers, but reflect the religious conviction of the victims.

Schindler's List, Steven Spielberg's feature film with documentary features, in which actors portray Holocaust events, begins with a scene depicting a Jewish tradition. In the moving final scene, the real »Schindler Jews,« elderly individuals accompanied by the actors who played their characters, lay stones on the tombs of their rescuer following Jewish custom. Certainly, no one would think that Spielberg had intended to spread his Jewish faith or Jewish traditions with *Schindler's List*.[27]

Regarding a similar film, the documentary film *Fear Not* by Fritz Poppenberg (1997)[28] in which almost exclusively Jehovah's Witnesses speak out as victims of National Socialism, the Wiesbaden Film Evaluation office commented positively: »Persons appear for whom speaking always means giving witness.«[29] Nevertheless, the Witness survivors in *Stand Firm Against Nazi Assault* give »witness« without missionary intent. The film's producer and narrator did not try in any way either to »spread the faith« or propagate Jehovah's Witness religious beliefs in *Stand Firm Against Nazi Assault*, nor did they use it for advertising, propaganda, or similar purposes.

Since the derogatory word »propaganda« seemed inappropriate, the more appropriate phrase »no religious preaching« was coined for announcements of the video documentary. This language was appropriate for the following reason: To »preach« is a synonym for »evangelize,« and is linguistically connected with the preaching of the Gospel or God's Word.[30] *Stand Firm Against Nazi Assault* is far from preaching the Gospel or God's Word. If there are implicit or explicit statements in the film which non-Witnesses could regard as preaching, we are willing to discuss the matter. In any case, such statements were not included intentionally.

Criticism of *Stand Firm Against Nazi Assault* by the churches essentially amounts to that which the film does not mention or allegedly »conceals.« Is the video documentary to blame for perversion of history by concealing or leaving out something essential?

Falsification of History or Historical Accuracy?

In the third revised edition of his book *Zwischen Widerstand und Martyerium: Die Zeugen Jehovas im »Dritten Reich«* (Munich 1997), Detlef Garbe corrects the false statement that swastika flags were used during the Berlin convention on June 25, 1933, and that the national anthem was sung, as was originally spread by opponents of Jehovah's Witnesses.[31] Unfortunately, other historians also accepted this assertion uncritically.[32]

The assertion that the leading individuals among Jehovah's Witnesses had attempted to »ingratiate« themselves with the Nazi regime in 1933, received more publicity through a book entitled *Die Zeugen Jehovas: Eine Dokumentation über die Wachtturm-Gesellschaft*, published by Manfred Gebhard with Urania-Verlag in the German Democratic Republic (GDR) in 1970, and, surprisingly, published shortly thereafter in a licensed West German edition.[33] This »documentation« calls the June 25, 1933 assembly of Jehovah's Witnesses in Berlin-Wilmersdorf, an »antisemitic and pro-fascist convention.« It accuses the Wachtturm-Gesellschaft of »an unconscious falsification of the actual facts,« and asserts that Watch Tower directors first turned against Hitler in 1938, only after all attempts to reach a political compromise with Hitler had failed, and that they »drove their innocent fellow believers into Nazi prisons and concentration camps.«[34]

Similar accusations can be found in church literature against Jehovah's Witnesses for years now.[35] The authors adopt an ideological position similar to the Urania book, overlooking what Detlef Garbe describes: »This book, published under the name of Manfred Gebhard, but compiled by anonymous authors with the assistance of the Ministry for State Security, clearly takes prescribed ideological conclusions into account« and is characterized by a »selective use of sources« and »distorted quotations.«[36] (The work was commissioned by the GDR, where Jehovah's Witnesses had been persecuted for ideological reasons, and where more than 5,000 of them had been arrested, of whom at least 60 died. Many victims who died in the GDR had already also been persecuted and incarcerated by the Nazis!)[37]

Unfortunately, Gebhard's conclusions have been »uncritically espoused, in part, even today,« as Detlef Garbe explains.[38] Many professional historians still use Gebhard's biased book; this is proven by their source citations.[39]

Manfred Gebhard later expressly disassociated himself from this book and its »exaggerations and falsifications« (Garbe).[40] In a letter dated January 2, 1985, to Dieter Pape in Berlin, who had obviously worked as a ghost writer on the book, Manfred Gebhard stated: »I have already stated elsewhere that my role in the Urania book was mainly as editor (which is not identical to author). I let you know this, as you are frankly also concerned. Based on what I know today, I would *not* give my name for it again. (sic) I am accusing you of distorting history (probably because of the worst kind of toadying to your bosses). ... But also your citations on ›anti-Communism‹ also seem questionable to me.«[41]

It can only be hoped that the polemics in connection with the Berlin Jehovah's Witness convention on June 25, 1933, will soon come to an end.

It was legitimate that, in the spring of 1933, Jehovah's Witnesses headquarters in Magdeburg addressed the authorities and Reich Chancellor with petitions, explanations, and polite letters to make it clear that they were not enemies of the state and that existing prohibitions, based on paragraph 1 of the Emergency Decree of the Reich President for the Protection of Volk and State of February 28, 1933, actually for »protection« against communist subversive acts of violence,« were not justified. Jehovah's Witnesses were not communists, nor were they enemies of the state, and they were not at all politically active.[42]

Before the ban on Jehovah's Witnesses in 1933, church circles had tried, initially, to »fully utilize existing legal grounds for taking action against the Bible Students,« as Detlef Garbe states. This had resulted in more than 1,000 court cases against Bible Students for »unauthorized peddling« by the end of the 1920s,[43] as well as charges for disturbing the »express observance of Sundays and holidays.«[44] The legal department of the *Wachtturm Gesellschaft* (Watch Tower Society) in Magdeburg achieved acquittal in many cases, which proves that they likewise »fully utilized existing legal means,« but for the protection of religious freedom in Germany.[45]

In the United States, Jehovah's Witnesses had won outstanding decisions in American courts, which »have secured and broadened the religious-freedom guarantees of American citizens,« as one author stated. »Some thirty-one cases in which they were involved came before the Supreme Court in the five years from 1938 to 1943, and the decisions in these and later cases have greatly advanced the cause of the freedoms of the Bill of Rights in general, and the protection of religious freedom in particular.«[46]

Such legal victories were not granted to the religious association in Germany between 1933 and 1945, except for the sensational release of the confiscated printing plant by Prussian authorities on April 28, 1933,[47] and the remarkable decision of the Darmstadt Special Court on March 16, 1934, acquitting 29 Witnesses and declaring the prohibition of the »*International Bible Students' Association*« in Hesse (October 18, 1933) as »unconstitutional and without binding legal effect.«[48]

The efforts of the *Wachtturm-Gesellschaft* in 1933 must be seen in the context of contemporary history, namely, shortly after the »seizure of power« when German authorities restricted the rights of Jehovah's Witnesses in one German State after another, and issued bans, for example, in Bavaria and Saxony. The Witnesses fought in Prussia for their freedom of religion in Germany during the first few months of the legally established German government under Adolf Hitler and with state governments. These efforts cannot rightly be interpreted as an attempt to ingratiate themselves with the Nazi regime, as some have tried to claim by using a few sentences taken out of context from a declaration and a certain letter under discussion today.

Do all Governments Originate with the Devil?

One misunderstanding in connection with the Berlin convention may be due to the notion that Jehovah's Witnesses reject all governments, and believe that all governments originate with the Devil.[49] Jehovah's Witnesses did not and do not hold such a view. As in the case of the supposed presence of swastika flags and the alleged singing of the national anthem in June 1933, an incorrect understanding of the Bible Students' teachings found its way into specialized literature that had obviously been fostered by church attacks in the 1920s and 1930s.[50]

Jehovah's Witnesses pray for the coming of God's Kingdom, or his heavenly reign over the earth, according to the Lord's Prayer in Matthew, chapter 6, verse 10. Thus, »God's will may take place, as in heaven, also upon earth,« meaning that God grants governments only *temporary* legitimization. However, they view governments as »God's servant« (Romans, chapter 13, verse 4), which, with his permission, maintains law and order within human society.

These »superior authorities« merit their obedience and respect. (Romans, chapter 13, verse 1) But when a government breaks God's law and, for example, initiates the murder of Jews, Jehovah's Witnesses deny it (the authorities) their obedience and instead follow their Christian conscience. This seems to be a valuable lesson in loyalty toward the State. Since this view of relative obedience to the authorities is Biblically founded, it should not be surprising that similar positions can be found also in some Protestant and Catholic biblical commentaries and catechisms.[51] The difference between many members of the major churches and Jehovah's Witnesses is that the Witnesses have lived up to this ethical view by »standing firm despite persecution.«

Is this interpretation an anachronism, since, as is known, Jehovah's Witnesses considered God and Christ to be the »superior authorities« during the Hitler era? Not necessarily. Although Romans chapter 13, verse 1, was then interpreted that way, Jehovah's Witnesses normally treated officials with respect, based on the understanding that the authorities merit respect and honor. Note the following commentry in the Jehovah's Witness periodical, *Goldene Zeitalter* from February 1, 1937, published in Bern: Under the heading »Daily Life in Germany,« the perfidious machinations of the Nazi party and of Nazi officials are exposed in their hideousness. This is followed by the reamrk: »Such ›superior authorities‹ who are, no doubt, not ›God's representatives‹ (since they even blaspheme and despise God) have forfeited any right to speak of God the Almighty or to present themselves in any fashion as his representatives and to offer themselves to society as Christians in order to heal it; on the contrary, they are in an entirely obvious manner the ›beast,‹ the disgusting and hideous beast of prey that symbolizes government during the time of the end in Revelation (that is, the last book of the Bible, ed.).«[52]

The qualification must be added that the reference to »God's servant« was obviously meant sarcastically.[53]

This quotation came from a time when Jehovah's Witnesses experienced the head of the German government as an oppressive ruler in the *direct* service of the Devil, and they expressed this publicly.[54] In *Stand Firm Against Nazi Assault*, J.F. Rutherford said in 1938: »In Germany, the common people love peace. The Devil has put his representative, Hitler, in power.« Watchtower publications never held that all governments of that time were built by the Devil.

Comments on the 1933 Berlin Convention in the Video Documentary

The video documentary *Stand Firm Against Nazi Assault* quotes Dr. Christine King who accurately describes Jehovah's Witnesses' behavior toward the government: »From the first, Jehovah's Witnesses adopted a clear position, maintaining their political neutrality. ... In the first months, they attempted to explain to the authorities what this meant, and that this was not a political threat.«

And Willi Pohl, a member of the board of the Wachtturm-Gesellschaft explains in the film: »In this Declaration (of June 25, 1933), we explained that we had absolutely no political goals, that our activity was purely religious, and that we wished to make use of the freedom of belief and of religion as promised in the Nazi party platform and also by government officials, and that, therefore, the partial prohibition should be reexamined and withdrawn.«

The »Declaration« or convention resolution (petition) of June 25, 1933, which Witnesses distributed shortly thereafter as a four-page tract throughout the Reich, as well as the cover letter to the Reich Chancellor, which the Watch Tower Society addressed to public authorities and German state governments along with the petition, contained numerous references to the religious, nonpolitical, and nonthreatening nature of their activities. This clearly showed that the intention was not to ingratiate, but to inform. This is clear from the following excerpts from the resolution: »Our organization is not political in any sense... but we only ask for the freedom to believe and to teach what we conceive the Bible to teach, and then let the people decide which they wish to believe. ... Our organization seeks neither money nor members, but we are a company or organized body of Christian people engaged solely in the benevolent work of teaching the Word of God to the people at the least possible cost to them. ... The education, culture, and upbuilding of the people must and will come through the agency of God's kingdom concerning which we teach as set forth in the Bible. The salvation of the people depends upon the true knowledge of and obedience to Jehovah God and his righteous ways. ... The power of Jehovah God is supreme and there is no power that can successfully resist him. ... The hope for the world is God's kingdom...«

There are five references to the fact that Jehovah's Witnesses neither threaten nor endanger »the public order or security of the nation.«

The Witnesses implicitly protested against their persecution with the following words: »Jehovah God has emphatically expressed his anger against those who do persecute others who are trying to serve him; and this proves that those who persecute us do not represent God, but that they are incited so to do by the enemy of God and man. – Psalm 72:4.«

Attention is called to a »warning by Jehovah God, both to the rulers and to the people,« using a scriptural passage where the word »Zion« appears: »Yet have I set my king upon my holy hill Zion. ... Be wise now, O ye kings; be instructed, ye judges of the earth. Serve the LORD with fear, and rejoice with trembling. Kiss the Son, lest he be angry, and ye perish from the way, when his wrath is kindled but a little. Blessed are all they that put their trust in him! – Psalm 2:6, 10-12.« (This in no way sounds like »ingratiation« with those in power!)

Following are several excerpts from the cover letter addressed to the Reich Chancellor: »For this reason that which was decided in the conference was written down in the enclosed Declaration of the Watch Tower Bible & Tract Society, in order to submit it to you, Herr Reichskanzler, to the high officials of the German government and to the other local governments as a record of the fact that the Bible Students of Germany (the term ›Jehovah's Witnesses‹ being added in the first sentence of the letter, ed.) have as the only purpose of their work nothing else but this, to bring men back to God and to witness to the name of Jehovah, the Supreme One, the Father of our Lord and Saviour Jesus Christ, and to honour them. We know for a certainty that you, Herr Reichskanzler, will not allow such activity to be interfered with. ... Local police authorities will always confirm that Bible Students count among the order-loving and order-maintaining elements of the country and the nation. Their sole mission is to win human hearts for God. ... The conference of the 5,000 delegates finally manifested that the Bible Students and the Watch Tower organization respectively stand for upholding order and security of the State and also for the furtherance of the above-mentioned high ideals of the National Government in the religious domain.«

The last sentence quoted may have resulted in misunderstandings. The »Declaration« stated: »A careful examination of our books and literature will disclose the fact that the very high ideals held and promulgated by the present national government are set forth in and endorsed and strongly emphasized in our publications, and show that Jehovah God will see to it that these high ideals in due time will be attained by all persons who love righteousness and who obey the Most High. Instead, therefore, of our literature and our work's being a menace to the principles of the present government we are the strongest supporters of such high ideals. For this reason Satan, the enemy of all men who desire righteousness, has sought to misrepresent our work and prevent us from carrying it on in this land.«

What kind of »righteousness« was meant? What were the »high ideals held and promulgated by the present national government« with which Jehovah's Witnesses agreed? Here the care of the German people, such as employment, housing, health, and self-respect, and a generous old-age pension was not meant. The Nazi party platform of February 24, 1920, had demanded that such goals be reached.[55] The »Declaration« agreed in general with the »principles advocated by the German government,« but still made one point clear about their realization: »[We] point out that Jehovah God through Christ Jesus will bring about the full realization of these principles and will give to the people peace and prosperity and the greatest desire of every honest heart.«[56]

The high ideal of »righteousness« must be an allusion to points from Hitler's speeches or his program, which are clearly emphasized in the context of the »Declaration« and cover letter. The corresponding passage reads as follows: »The people of Germany have suffered great misery since 1914 and have been the victims of much injustice practiced upon them by others. The Nationalists have declared themselves against all such unrighteousness and announced: ›Our relationship to God is high and holy.‹ Since our organization fully endorses these righteous principles and is engaged solely in carrying forth the work of enlightening the people concerning the Word of Jehovah God, Satan subtly endeavors to set the government against our work and destroy it because we magnify the importance of knowing and serving God.«[57]

This comment may be an allusion to section 2 of the Nazi platform, which demanded »equality for the German people with other nations, as well as cancellation of the Versailles and St. Germain peace treaties.«

References to the misery of the people and population (and nations in general) after World War I are often found in Watch Tower literature before and after 1933, and are connected with the fulfillment of Bible prophecy.[58] Jehovah's Witnesses and the Nazis pointed to the same complaints or spoke about the same »illnesses,« but they had completely different diagnoses and therapies at hand and argued on different levels.[59] The following example makes this clear. The »Declaration« reads: »The present government of Germany has declared emphatically against Big Business oppressors and in opposition to the wrongful religious influence in the political affairs of the nation. Such is exactly our position; and we further state in our literature the reason for the existence of oppressive Big Business and the wrongful political religious influence, because the Holy Scriptures plainly declare that these oppressive instruments proceed from the Devil, and that the complete relief therefrom is God's kingdom under Christ. It is therefore impossible for our literature or our work to in any wise be a danger or a menace to the peace and safety of the state. Our organization is not political in any sense. We only insist on teaching the Word of Jehovah God to the people, and that without hindrance.«

This in no way sounds, despite so-called common »views,« like support or sympathy of Nazi ideology and its rulers.

The misinterpretation that Jehovah's Witnesses could see a solution to problems in National Socialism should be ruled out. Whereas the Bible Students argued on a religious level, the »national government« operated on a political level.

Apparently, the same »high ethical goals and ideals« were primarily a matter of religious values »which the National Government of the German Reich proclaimed regarding the relation of man to God, namely: honesty of the creature towards the creator!« Directly following this, it was again emphasized that this focused on »purely religious and unpolitical goals and efforts of Bible Students.«[60] The »Declaration« and the letter to the Reich Chancellor and state authorities explicitly and repeatedly drew attention to this fact.

The quotation from the Nazi party platform, which had only been quoted in the cover letter did not originate with the President of the Watch Tower Society, but with the German manager, can also be seen in this context.[61] It emphasized that the party »stands upon the ground of positive Christianity,« an expression that was not clearly outlined and that was viewed at that time as neutral by Jehovah's Witnesses and others.[62] Point 24 demanded »...the freedom of all religious denominations in the state so long as they do not endanger its existence or violate the sense of morality and morals of the Germanic race. The party as such stands upon the ground of positive Christianity without being bound to a certain denomination. It fights the Jewish materialistic spirit inside and outside us and is convinced that our people a durable recovery of the racial community can only come from *inside* (sic) based on public need before private greed.«

This quotation has also been completely misinterpreted.[63] In 1933, and also later, Jehovah's Witnesses quoted the Nazis to remind them of their own words, in which they ostensibly respected Christian values but not to ingratiate themselves.[64] Every edition of *Der Wachtturm* (Watchtower) published in Germany before the ban in Prussia, included a text adjacent to the imprint: »This periodical adheres strictly to the Bible as authority for its observations. It is independent and autonomous from all parties, sects or other secular organizations.«[65]

It can be acknowledged that some expressions in the cover letter are »quibbling terminology that at the same time allow for an interpretation in accord with the Bible Students' teachings,« as Detlef Garbe summarized.[66] This was related to the expectation of being able to »inform Hitler and other government representatives about their views and to convince them to change their position.«[67] (This expectation was illusory.) It is doubtful that the author then consciously »counted on the opposing side's misunderstanding it.«[68] I also disagree with Garbe when he states that it was a matter of »political calculation,« which left the »self-declared neutrality far behind.«[69] The wording was certainly not determined by political, but by legal calculations.

»The Association's Accommodation to National Conditions in Germany«

Just as Jehovah's Witness communities had developed structures to adjust to illegality during the ban, the legal department of the *Wachtturm-Gesellschaft* had tried to develop structures to adjust to legality already before June 1933. In the 1920s and especially at the beginning of Hitler's cabinet, they tried, as already mentioned, to negotiate with the German authorities and to inform government offices about the non-political, purely religious nature of their activities. To break down prejudices or to avoid giving unnecessary offense, the *Wachtturm-Gesellschaft* was prepared to make slight organizational changes, or adjustments, that were legal and in harmony with their religious beliefs. It thereby proved its flexibility, but was not willing to collaborate with the Nazis.

The *Wachtturm-Gesellschaft* in Magdeburg, representing the Internationale Bibelforscher-Vereinigung (International Bible Students Association), an additional religious corporation of Jehovah's Witnesses, proved, for example, to be flexible when it gave up the use of the word »International« in its letters. They, however, never considered calling the association »*Deutsche Bibelforscher-Vereinigung*« (German Bible Students Association). A regional designation, such as »North German or South German Bible Students Association,« as obviously desired by the legal adviser of the *Wachtturm-Gesellschaft* and approved by the authorities, was to be sure neutral and tolerable.[70]

Jehovah's Witnesses, however, refused to remove the word »Jehovah,« which they had adopted in 1931, from their name. One can only imagine how many times the antisemitic Nazis, who disparaged »Jehovah« as »God of the Jews,« were consequently forced to use the detested name![71] Furthermore, until the last issue of *Der Wachtturm* was published in Magdeburg on June 15, 1933, words that the Nazis loathed, such as »Jehovah's organization is called Zion,« could be found on the publisher's page.[72] This brings us to the question, whether the video documentary conceals antisemitic tendencies, which were supposedly evident at the Berlin convention on June 25, 1933.

Antisemitic Tendencies?

In the third edition of his book, Detlef Garbe stated: »Numerous judgments found in literature about the ›Wilmersdorf Declaration‹ include erroneous criticism, or rather, are not fair to the text and the situation. Therefore, one could not say that Jehovah's Witnesses had professed antisemitism… or promoted themselves ›as a possible ally.‹ Labels such as ›congress supporting the Nazis,‹ or the assertion that the Watch Tower management had attempted to ›conclude a pact with Hitler'… resulted from conclusions motivated by a desire to discredit [them] as in Gebhard's 1970 GDR documentation alleging the ›criminal support of the antisemitic Hitler policy‹ in the Declaration.«[73]

This statement is unambiguous. Nevertheless, I would like to go into more detail about this point.

Whereas critics today impute antisemitism to the Jehovah's Witnesses in 1933, antisemites, Nazis, and church representatives, especially »experts about sects,« have claimed just the opposite.[74] In 1935, the *Völkischer Beobachter* was even of the opinion that »Jehovah's Witnesses fought existing racial laws of the Third Reich with special animosity.«[75]

According to Detlef Garbe, already in the 1920s, »the teaching of the equality of the races« and the fact that the Bible Students spoke of the »creation of a reign of peace on earth without social and racial barriers« brought them »the hatred and merciless hostility of antisemitic groups.« Nazi ideologists and antisemites like Alfred Rosenberg accused Jehovah's Witnesses of »hypnotizing« the masses at the command of »Jewry« and of preparing them mentally for »Jewish world domination.« These accusations were »spread among the population not only by Nazi propagandists. German nationalist groups within the Protestant Church and some Catholic clergy behaved similarly. They respectively created new slogans. … Especially from 1921 to 1925, numerous church ›information pamphlets‹ about the Bible Students Association had been published… which were a church version of nationalist antisemitic defamatory pamphlets.«[76]

Again it must be emphasized that it can be documented that Jehovah's Witnesses did not support antisemitism (hatred of Jews) and racial hatred and considered Jews as »persons of equally high merit« in their literature.[77] Detlef Garbe, historian and director of the Neuengamme concentration camp memorial, states in the video documentary: »Antisemitism carries characteristics of racism, and the last thing Jehovah's Witnesses would do was to regard the Jews as being of less merit simply because of their origin. For them, all persons were of the same merit, were equal.«

The persecution of Jews was condemned as »inexcusable«[78] and as »racial obsession.«[79]

The fact that Watch Tower literature condemned the persecution of the Jews and called it »one of the blackest marks of shame in world history,«[80] was held publicly against Jehovah's Witnesses by the Nazis.[81]

The French doctor Odette Abadi, a former prisoner, remembers one Jehovah's Witness in Bergen-Belsen concentration camp: »A one-hundred-percent German Aryan woman, Ursula, has been living in our room and had been incarcerated because she belonged to the religion of Bible Students or Jehovah's Witnesses, a sect that searches for the truth in the Bible. They accept neither antisemitism nor fascism and Nazism, and their adherents refuse to perform work for war.«[82]

Jehovah's Witnesses, of course, also included Judaism along with Catholicism and Protestantism in their theological analysis of other religions, and, as a rule, criticized their religious leaders based on the Bible.[83] Similar criticism can be found in the Hebrew prophets of the Old Testament and in Jesus of Nazareth, and cannot be considered as equivalent to antisemitism or anti-Judaism.[84]

Use of the Words »Commercial Jews« and »Business Jews«

The use of the terms »commercial Jews« in the »Declaration« and »business Jews« in the cover letter may be viewed from the following perspectives:
— Consideration of the context (who is meant and why?)
— How often are the terms used? (one-time use)
— Consideration of Jehovah's Witnesses attitude towards Jews in general (no resentment; see above)
— Meaning and use of these terms in German (used since the nineteenth century; elimination of the word from dictionaries after 1933)

The term at issue is used in the »Declaration« as follows: »It is falsely charged by our enemies that we have received financial support for our work from the Jews. Nothing is farther from the truth. Up to this hour there never has been the slightest bit of money contributed to our work by Jews. We are the faithful followers of Christ Jesus and believe upon Him as the Savior of the world, whereas the Jews entirely reject Jesus Christ and emphatically deny that he is the Savior of the world sent of God for man's good. This of itself should be sufficient proof to show that we receive no support from Jews and that therefore the charges against us are maliciously false and could proceed only from Satan, our great enemy. The greatest and the most oppressive empire on earth is the Anglo-American empire. By that is meant the British Empire, of which the United States of America forms a part. It has been the *commercial Jews* of the British-American empire that have built up and carried on Big Business as a means of exploiting and oppressing the peoples of many nations. This fact particularly applies to the cities of London and New York, the stronghold of Big Business. This fact is so manifest in America that there is a proverb concerning the city of New York which says: ›The Jews own it, the Irish Catholics rule it, and the Americans pay the bills.‹ We have no fight with any of these persons mentioned, but, as the witnesses for Jehovah and in obedience to his commandment set forth in the Scriptures, we are compelled to call attention to the truth concerning the same order that the people may be enlightened concerning God and his purpose.«

The passage in the cover letter reads as follows: »In the same manner the President of our Society, during the last months, has not only refused to take part in the propaganda against Germany, but he has taken position even against it, as is also emphasized in the enclosed Declaration by calling attention to the fact that those who, in America, take the lead in the ›German cruelties‹ propaganda (namely *business Jews* and Catholics) are also the greatest persecutors of the work of our Society and of its President in America. *By these and other facts laid down in the Declaration, the slander that the Bible Students are supported by the Jews is to be refuted.«*

The cover letter was not composed by the President of the Watch Tower Society but by his manager in Magdeburg.[85] It explicitly states the reasons for the statement: Certain persons of Jewish origin who ran businesses in New York and London were the issue, not the Jews in general (hence, the Witnesses did not »distance themselves clearly from another hard-pressed group,« as Garbe states).[86] This is essential and is even emphasized by quoting an American proverb in the »Declaration.« The vehement attacks on Jehovah's Witnesses through opponents had already led to government prohibitions in Germany. They were accused of being financed by the »Jews,« so that they could set up a supposed Jewish world power. German Jehovah's Witnesses vehemently responded to this slander and emphatically repudiated it. They used clear language in order to distinguish between their non-commercial activities and the activities of their alleged Jewish sponsors. Their statement of that time can today be easily misunderstood as antisemitic, if one ignores the historical context and takes quotations out of context.

The use of the term »commercial Jews« in connection with big business[87] can be traced back to the nineteenth century as part of the standard German vocabulary of those days.[88] The term seems not to have disappeared from German dictionaries until 1933.[89] In any case, it is neither an indication of antisemitism, nor does it appear that Nazi terminology was taken into account.[90]

It is true that, today, after the horrible genocide of the Jews, people are more sensitive when using words or terms concerning Jews.[91] Nevertheless, if critics wish to read antisemitism (hatred of Jews) into comments made by Jehovah's Witnesses in 1933, they are overlooking the contemporaneous context and committing an anachronistic error. In the reverse cases, no one, for example, who forgot to place quotation marks (meaning so-called) around the then coined terms »Third Reich« (until 1938), »Crystal Night« (playing down), or »Seizure of Power« (heroization) can be called a Nazi.[92] There are more terms in German originally coined in Nazi Germany, but which are used today without hesitation.[93]

It is safe to say that Jehovah's Witnesses had neither hatred nor enmity toward Jews and that they never had any resentment toward them. The video documentary *Stand Firm Against Nazi Assault* is not guilty of misusing history and outlines the relationship of Jehovah's Witnesses to the Jews in a concrete historical context.

Conclusion

To reiterate: The church paper *Mainzer Bistumsnachrichten* of May 1997 accused *Stand Firm Against Nazi Assault* of having concealed the following:[94] »In a Declaration made at that time, the many common interests of the Watch Tower Society with goals of the Nazi leaders had been affirmed. In this letter, the ›commercial Jews of the Anglo-American empire‹ were also held responsible for the exploitation of peoples and had been denounced by Hitler. Jehovah's Witnesses also emphasized their rejection of ›commercial Jews and Catholics‹ in this letter to Hitler. The Declaration of 1933 is, however, briefly mentioned in the film but is played down, and the producers express neither regret nor admission of guilt, despite the renunciation of solidarity with the Jewish people.«

I believe that such incorrect polemical criticism will soon be a thing of the past.

Here it is again emphasized: It must be admitted that some formulations in the cover letter to the June 25, 1933 »Declaration« are written in a nitpicking fashion and thus give rise to misunderstandings. This is regrettable and would actually demand an apology if anyone had been harmed as a result.[95] The passages in question, however, were not influenced by political, antisemitic, or Nazi usage. It was, therefore, not necessary to go into further detail about the Wilmersdorf convention in Berlin in »*Stand Firm Against Nazi Assault* than has been done at present. The accounts of Witness survivors rightly receive much attention, making the film a document of contemporary history of a group of victims about whose persecution we know very little.

We sincerely hope that the critical viewer will similarly experience what critics described after watching Spielberg's film *Schindler's List*: »When the film ends, all objections have been forgotten.«[96]

Notes

1   This presentation was condensed and presented on October 5, 1997, at the Wewelsburg District Museum, on October 8 at the City Museum for Hamburg History, and on October 11 at the Frankfurt-Bornheim town hall. This manuscript includes additional revisions.

2   Letter from Dr. Manfred Stolpe, Minister-President of the State of Brandenburg, Potsdam, to the Wachtturm Bibel- und Traktat-Gesellschaft, Deutscher Zweig e.V., President Günter Künz, Am Steinfels, 65618 Selters, October 30, 1996. Original letter at the Wachtturm History Archives. See also Detlef Garbe, *Zwischen Widerstand und Martyrium: Die Zeugen Jehovas im »Dritten Reich«* (Munich, 1997), 546, note 13.

3   The panel discussion »Widerstand aus dem Glauben? Katholiken, Protestanten und Zeugen Jehovas im NS-Staat« at the Haus für Volksarbeit in Frankfurt/Main, on September 29, 1997, organized by Bishopric Limburg, Department for Ideological Issues and the Protestant Bureau for Ideological Questions. It was held in an objective atmosphere and was characterized by respect for Jehovah's Witnesses who had been Nazi victims. The historians present were Prof. Dr. Matthias Benad (Bethel Church Academy), Dr. Detlef Garbe (Neuengamme Concentration Camp Memorial), and Lutz Lemhöfer (Catholic Bishopric Limburg).

4   The titles of the video documentaries are as follows: Jehovah's Witnesses Stand Firm Against Nazi Assault (English, November 1996); Standhaft trotz Verfolgung – Jehovas Zeugen unter dem NS-Regime (German, November 1996); Muschestwo Swidetelj Jegowi pered lizom nazisma (Russian, May 1997); Niezlomni w obliczu przesladowan – Swiadkowie Jehowy a hitleryzm (Polish, September 1997); La fermeté des Témoins de Jéhova face à la persécution nazie (French, 1997); As Testamunhas de Jeová Resistem ao Ataque Nazista (Portugese, October 1997); I Testimoni di Geova, saldi di fronte all'attacco nazista (Italian, November 1997).

5   See Johannes Wrobel, Die Videodokumentation »Standhaft trotz Verfolgung – Jehovas Zeugen unter dem NS-Regime«: Eine Stellungnahme (Selters/Taunus: July 1997), Introduction 1.2, p. 1. Critics insinuate that the video documentary has a »missionary intent« and a »propaganda objective« (Mainzer Bistumsnachrichten, no. 16, May 7, 1997); pastor Joachim Keden (Protestant), Rev. Horst Neusius (Catholic), Renate Heers et al. in a report for the Rhineland-Palatinate Media Center, n. d. (spring 1997). Hans-Jürgen Twisselmann calls it a »professionally made video documentary« and also a »propaganda film« in the *Materialdienst der Evangelischen Zentralstelle für Weltanschauungsfragen* (May 1997), pp. 141–42.

6   In the letter from the Wachtturm-Gesellschaft to Prof. Dr. Roman Herzog, the Federal President of Germany, dated September 23, 1996, the paragraph from which the quotation was taken reads: »Today, there are proclamations for ›resistance to the spirit of the times‹ (Pope John Paul II in Berlin); Jehovah's Witnesses were surely not ›conformists who took the easy way out‹ during the Nazi regime. They steadfastly refused to use the greeting ›Heil Hitler!‹ or ›to accept even the smallest elements of National Socialism which didn't

correspond to their faith and their belief‹ (Dr. Christine King, vice-chancellor of Staffordshire University, UK). With good reason, the video documentary is entitled: »Jehovah's Witnesses Stand Firm Against Nazi Assault.« The film is 78 minutes long. It is produced by the Watchtower Bible and Tract Society, the religious nonprofit publishing society of Jehovah's Witnesses in New York. The film, the premiere in Ravensbrück, and the press conference in Berlin contain no religious preaching. The video, as all other publications of our society, will be distributed free of charge and is available as from January 1997.« On October 14, 1996, Ministry Councilor Wolfgang Käppler from the Office of the President, responded thanking us for the letter and assured us that the Federal President »attaches great importance to the commemoration of the victims of National Socialism. He is quite familiar with the fact that many ›Bible Students,‹ or Jehovah's Witnesses, were among these victims, and who, as all other victims, have his respect.« Attached to the letter was the President's January 19, 1996 Bundestag speech, »in remembrance of the victims of National Socialism« (Bulletin, January 23, 1996, no. 6, pp. 46–48), which, however, only mentioned »Jews, Sinti and Roma, the disabled, homosexuals, just to name the most important groups.« (Regrettably, Jehovah's Witnesses are still seldom mentioned as a victim group, although »before the war, about five to ten percent of all concentration camp inmates had been Jehovah's Witnesses.« [Detlef Garbe in »Stand Firm Against Nazi Assault«]; they formed a separate prisoner category [purple triangles] in the concentration camp system.)

7   The fact that the premiere on November 6, 1996, and the subsequent 400-plus similar events all over Germany contained no religious or missionary aspects was accepted by the print media, who reported about it in more than 1,000 newspaper articles. *Die Welt* on November 7, 1996 (»›Ein Lichtblick in dunkler Zeit‹; Film-Uraufführung: Die Zeugen Jehovas unter dem NS-Regime«) and *Der Tagesspiegel* on November 8, 1996, (»Ein neues Kapitel über ›vergessene Opfer des NS-Regimes‹: Die Zeugen Jehovas dokumentieren die Verfolgung der Bibelforscher im Dritten Reich. Historiker Garbe fordert: ›Desinteresse aufgeben‹«) were the first in this series of reports.

8   Historians from the United States, Great Britain, and Germany, as well as Jehovah's Witness survivors, participated in the seminar at the United States Holocaust Memorial Museum in Washington D. C. on September 29, 1994. James N. Pellechia represented the Watchtower Society and gave a slide presentation entitled: »The Spirit and the Sword: Jehovah's Witnesses Expose the Third Reich.« Garbe, *Zwischen Widerstand und Martyrium*, p. 550, note 27, refers to a bound copy of this slide lecture.

9   A description of the persons in the video is found in Wrobel 1997, Inhalt und Mitwirkende 3.2, pp. 4f.

10   In principal, the Watch Tower Society, which wants to bring honor to God in all its dealings, does not publish the names of authors, composers, and translators of their religious literature and songs. (cf. *The Watchtower*, February 1, 1991, p. 13; September 1, 1986, p. 30) Publications that are not of biblical nature are an exception. Thus, in 1995 the Watchtower Society had the slide presentation by James N. Pellechia at the U. S. Holocaust Memorial Museum on September 29, 1994, printed and stated his name (Garbe, *Zwischen Widerstand und Martyrium*, p. 550, note 27.) The names of the multinational video team who worked on »Stand Firm Against Nazi Assault« during the winter of 1995 and spring of 1996 have not been published.

11   The English (and German) periodicals *The Watchtower* (Der Wachtturm) and *Awake!* (Erwachet!), formerly *The Golden Age* (Das Goldene Zeitalter) and *Consolation* (Trost), include numerous personal narratives of victims before 1945 and until today. The quantity of published materials about the persecution of Jehovah's Witnesses is clear from *Watchtower Publications Index … 1930-1985*, New York 1986, and subsequent volumes (published in English, German, and other languages). See key words, such as »Germany (Nazi),« »concentration camps,« and ›Life Stories of Jehovah's Witnesses.« The 1959 history published in English by the association, *Jehovah's Witnesses in the Divine Purpose*, (published in German in 1960) which otherwise only dealt slightly with historical events in Germany, nevertheless contains a whole chapter on the Witnesses in Nazi concentration camps. The *1974 Yearbook of Jehovah's Witnesses* was produced as a historical report about the activities of the Wachtturm-Gesellschaft in Germany. The book includes a large number of biographical narratives. In the newer publication, *Jehovah's Witnesses–Proclaimers of God's Kingdom* (1993), there are numerous remarks and information about events in Nazi Germany, but the book is designed as a historical work on the worldwide activities of the religious association. See also bibliographic data in the appendix to Wolfram Slupina's essay »Persecuted and Almost Forgotten« in this volume.

12   *Das Beste Reader's Digest* (Stuttgart, September 1996), p. 94.

13   The word »document« (Latin documentum, documentary evidence that serves as proof or evidence) can mean »evidence, or proof.« The German »Dokumentation« (English: documentary) is a collection, arrange-

ment, and utilization of documents, evidence, or testimonies, and the term is defined as »detailed evidence.« The German word video-documentation is mostly used in its second meaning, namely »2. Expression of something, conclusive testimony, descriptive evidence.« (*DUDEN, Das große Wörterbuch der deutschen Sprache*, v. 2 (1993), p. 745) *Stand Firm* contains numerous documentary images, but is not called a documentary film. A documentary record, according to the above-mentioned lexicon, is a »record in image or sound that serves as a document (2).« (The second meaning of the German word »Dokument« is, as mentioned above, a »piece of evidence, proof: the film is a shocking d[ocument] of war.«) A documentary film is a »film using documentary records that tries to relate incidents and situations as precisely as possible, based on factual materials.« *Stand Firm* endeavors to be historically exact and to relate facts, but will not and cannot be an extensive »documentary film« about the history of persecution of Jehovah's Witnesses during the Nazi era. Since *Stand Firm* is literally not a film but a video (Betacam SP), the term »video documentary« and not »documentary film« was chosen from the beginning. The »film« can rightly be called with good reason a valuable video documentary of contemporary history on the subject.

14 Detlef Garbe, »Sendboten des jüdischen Bolschwismus: Antisemitismus als Motiv nationalsozialistischer Verfolgung der Zeugen Jehovas« (hereafter Garbe, Sendboten), *Tel Aviver Jahrbuch für deutsche Geschichte* 23 (1994), Nationalsozialismus aus heutiger Perspektive (Gerlingen, 1994), p. 168. The passage quoted is on pp. 163, 167, and 168.

15 The »myth of absolute uniformity,« as emphasized by Lutz Lemhöfer during the Frankfurt on Main conference on September 29, 1997, has never been presented in the historical writings of the Watch Tower Society, neither for 1933 nor for the bitter persecution period until 1945. *Jahrbuch der Zeugen Jehovas 1974* (*1974 Yearbook*) contains a report about the German persecution shortly after the »seizure of power« and in some concentration camps about individual and controversial conduct among Jehovah's Witnesses (cf. pp. 130f., 174f.). The *1974 Yearbook*, which relied substantially on subjective oral history testimonies must, however, be corrected in its negative assessment of the June 25, 1933 Berlin meeting. (cf. p. 110f.). The Watchtower Society stated more recently: »According to the account in the *1974 Yearbook of Jehovah's Witnesses*, some German Witnesses were disappointed that the language of the ›Declaration‹ was not more explicit in tone. Had the branch office manager, Paul Balzereit, weakened the text of the document? No, for a comparison of the German and the English texts show that this is not the case. Evidently, an impression to the contrary was based on the subjective observations of some who were not directly involved in the preparation of the ›Declaration.‹ Their conclusion may also have been influenced by the fact that Balzereit renounced his faith only two years later.« (*Awake!*, July 8, 1998, p. 14).

16 Film *Mut ohne Befehl: Widerstand und Verfolgung in Stuttgart 1933 bis 1945*, Stadtjugendring Stuttgart (1997). The film's accompanying brochure, p. 29.

17 Fritz Fischer, *Hitler war kein Betriebsunfall* (Munich, 1993), pp. 182ff.

18 Of the seven parts of the 78-minute video documentary, only two parts (or ten minutes, »Part II, Germany before 1933« and »Part III, Germany in 1933«) provide historical background information about how Hitler came to power, and that the religious association played a role in Germany that could not go unnoticed at that time. Historians talk five times and Witness survivors six times. (Wrobel 1997, Länge und Sequenzen der Dokumentation, 6.2, p. 8).

19 No swastika flags were used at the convention, as proven in indoor photographs. Furthermore, Jehovah's Witnesses did not sing the national anthem but the old Bible Student's song »Zion's Glorious Hope« (*Awake!*, July 8, 1998, pp. 12f.).

20 For the supposed betrayal by leading Jehovah's Witnesses, see Wrobel 1997, Erich Frost and Konrad Franke, 9.0, pp. 11-14.

21 Altogether, Jehovah's Witnesses and non-Witnesses speak 118 times (without interruption from a narrator.) Non-Witnesses and historians speak 44 times (38 percent), Jehovah's Witnesses 74 times (62 percent). (Wrobel 1997, Inhalt und Mitwirkende, 3.1, p. 5).

22 *Holocaust - Gegen das Vergessen*, Multimedia CD-ROM (ISBN 3-931293-47-5), Systhema/Navigo (Frankfurt/Main, 1997), academic advisor Professor Erika Weinzierl, Institute for Contemporary History of Vienna University.

23 *Computer BILD*, no. 19/97 (September 15, 1997), p. 66.

24 *Duden, Etymologie: Herkunftswörterbuch der deutschen Sprache* (1963), v. 7, p. 533; Webster's Ninth New Collegiate Dictionary (1991), p. 943.

25 *Duden, Das große Wörterbuch der deutschen Sprache* (1994), v. 6, p. 2637; *Webster's Ninth New Collegiate Dictionary* (1991), p. 943.

26 There is one passage where the narrator mentions God and salvation. He says: »But the Witnesses could not give to man what they believed belonged to God. Thus, a battle line was drawn over a simple greeting —Heil Hitler! – Jehovah's Witnesses refused to say »Heil Hitler!« because it meant ›salvation comes from Hitler.'« The point that Jehovah's Witnesses await salvation only from Christ was consciously left out. (Wrobel 1997, Wortbeiträge mit »religiösen« Inhalt, 4.2, p. 6).

27 Steven Spielberg, the most successful producer in the history of film, produced *Schindler's List* in 1993 and received worldwide acclaim. He received seven awards, including an Oscar for Best Film of the Year and one for Best Director. Thereafter, Steven Spielberg set up the »Survivors of the Shoah Visual History Foundation« in Los Angeles to »let survivors speak for themselves.« Linden Gross wrote that »Spielberg forms future history through eye-witness reports,« in his article, »Steven Spielberg: ein Starregisseur macht Geschichte.« (*Das Beste Reader's Digest*, [Stuttgart, September 1996], p. 94) That Steven Spielberg was raised as a Jew is clear from the following report: »As a small child, Steven Spielberg learned to count by means of a survivor's tattoo.« Despite such confrontations with Nazi atrocities, young Spielberg had conflicting emotions about his Jewish roots. Being a Jew often meant not belonging to the ›normal‹ world. Christmas was especially difficult for Steven as a boy. The family then lived in Haddonfield, New Jersey, in an area that won prizes for its Christmas decorations. His parents' home, however, stood without any decoration between brightly lighted houses. Steven called it »the black hole.« »Can't we decorate it a bit festively, as well?« he asked his father. »We are Jews,« replied Arnold Spielberg. »Be proud of what you are.« But Steven was not proud of this, since he felt isolated and alone. It became even worse when the family moved to Phoenix, Arizona, again a neighborhood where few Jews lived. Steven imagined a friend in whom he could confide – a small hairless creature from outer space.« (Ibid., p. 89)

28 »Fürchtet euch nicht«: Verfolgung und Widerstand der Zeugen Jehovas unter dem Nazi-Regime [Fear Not: Persecution and Resistance of Jehovah's Witnesses Under the Nazi Regime], documentary film by Stefanie Krug and Fritz Poppenberg, 92 min. (Berlin, 1996).

29 Steffen Wolff wrote in »Prädikatisierte Kinofilme: Die Bewertung der FBW (Filmbewertungsstelle Wiesbaden) – ›Wertvoll,‹ « JMS-Report, June 3, 1997, p. 51 about the film: »Fear Not. FRG, 1996. FBW: 08/04/1997–FSK okay above the age of 6. Excellent documentary material and impressive accounts characterize this thoroughly researched film about the resistance of Jehovah's Witnesses against the Nazi regime. The spirit of the film perfectly matches characters. People appear for whom speaking always means giving a witness. The careful camera work must also be emphasized.«

30 *Duden: Das große Wörterbuch der deutschen Sprache* (1995), vol. 8, p. 3680.

31 Garbe, p. 103, note 71: »The statements made in the first two editions of this book that the convention ›was opened with the German anthem‹ is based upon a misunderstanding. Also the assertion ›that the place was decorated with swastika flags‹ cannot and should not be maintained any longer, since – in contrast to this description which I had based on the tape-recorded transcript of a talk given by the former German Branch Servant Konrad Franke (passages published in the magazine *Christian Quest* 3 (1990), pp. 46f.) – there are doubts that do not permit further use of this account. Photos that obviously had been taken at the IBSA convention in the Wilmersdorf Tennis Hall prove what is also supported by other eyewitness reports (UaP Johannes Wrobel) that at least the interior [of the hall] had no swastika flags. It is quite possible that the sport hall rented by the WTG [Wachtturm-Gesellschaft] was decorated with swastika flags on the outside since the SA, SS, and other Nazi groups had celebrated the summer solstice. (See Christoffel, *Wilmersdorf*, p. 269).«

32 Francis L. Carsten wrote, in his otherwise remarkable essay about the religious association that, »among the opponents of the Nazi regime pride of place in many ways belongs to the religious sect which called itself Jehovah's Witnesses«: »A mass meeting held in Berlin in June with five to six thousand [Jehovah's Witness] participants began with the singing of the German national anthem and the hall was decorated with swastika flags.« (Carsten, *Widerstand gegen Hitler: Die deutsche Arbeiter und die Nazis*, Frankfurt and Leipzig, 1996 [English in 1995], ch. 7 »Jehovah's Witnesses.« F. L. Carsten based this statement on the first edition of Detlef Garbe's book *Zwischen Widerstand und Martyrium* (Munich, 1993), pp. 84f. Garbe, on the other hand, refers to an article in *The Christian Quest*, a dubious publication which is, undoubtedly, published by opponents of Jehovah's Witnesses but which could not be established as a publication in any North American library.

33 Cf. Wrobel 1997, Erich Frost und Konrad Franke 9.2, p. 11.

34 Gebhard 1970, pp. 158f., 170, 187.

35 Regarding the Berlin convention in 1933 the »Materialdienst of the Evangelische Zentrale für Weltanschauungs-

fragen« wrote under the heading »Facts That Have Been Concealed«: ›The site was decorated with swastika flags. ... When [Rutherford's] policy of accommodation did not seem to bear fruit, he reversed course and adopted a policy of confrontation.« (Hans-Jürgen Twisselmann, »Jehovas Zeugen im ›Dritten Reich': Zwischen Anpassung und Martyrium,« in: *Materialdienst der EZW:*, ed. Evangelische Zentralstelle für Weltanschauungsfragen (Stuttgart, no. 5/1997), pp. 143-44). The author gets further off course when he speaks of »marketing martyrs« in connection with the video documentary that is free of charge. He calls *Stand Firm Against Nazi Assault* a »propaganda film.« (p. 142) The *Mainzer Bistumsnachrichten* spread the idea that »not a single word is mentioned« in the Watch Tower Society video documentary about the following: »that the German leadership along with the international headquarters of the Watch Tower Society in 1933... tried to prevent persecution by currying favor with the ›Hochverehrten Reichskanzler Adolf Hitler‹ [Most Honorable Reich Chancellor Adolf Hitler] also seems to have been hidden under the seal of forgetfulness. On June 25, 1933,... the location for the convention was decorated with swastika flags. ... When Rutherford realized that attempts at conformity had not achieved the desired results, he formally called for martyrdom from the servile Jehovah's Witnesses in Germany. And most Jehovah's Witnesses accustomed to obedience, conformed to this request by their leadership.« (Eckhard Türk, MBN, »Unter dem NS-Regime verfolgt: Zeugen Jehovas zwischen Vergangenheitsbewältigung und Propaganda,« in: *Mainzer Bistumsnachrichten*, no. 16 (May 7, 1997), pp. 9-10). The cover letter to the »Declaration« of June 25, 1933, to the legally appointed head of State begins — with appropriate politeness — with the words »Sehr verehrter Herr Reichskanzler!« [Hon. Adolf Hitler, Chancellor of the Reich], not as stated by Türk. A caption about this letter, in the permanent exhibition of the Memorial to German Resistance in Berlin, reads: »Although the petition is addressed to Reich Chancellor Hitler, it avoids the salutation »Führer,« which was already common at that time. ... Just as representatives of the major denominations had done, leading Jehovah's Witnesses initially had hoped, in vain, to factually inform Hitler about their objectives. They had hoped that he would stop the persecution. Jehovah's Witnesses, however, left no room for doubt regarding their inner duty to serve only the Word of God.« (Exhibition text, copy: see Wrobel 1997, Der Berliner Kongreß am 25. Juni 1933, 10.3, p. 15).

36 Garbe, *Zwischen Widerstand und Martyrium*, pp. 20f.

37 There were over 23,000 Jehovah's Witnesses active for their faith in East Germany when the GDR government (1949-1989) banned their activities in August 1950. Among the 6,000 arrested Witnesses in East Germany were over 300 persons who had already been in concentration camps or prisons during the Nazi period. At least 60 Witnesses died in custody, mainly in the 1950s, because of mistreatment, illness, malnutrition, and advanced age. Based on Geschichtsarchiv der Zeugen Jehovas, (History Archive of Jehovah's Witnesses in Germany) Wachtturm-Gesellschaft, 65617 Selters/Taunus, Germany. See the GDR essays in this volume and Richard Singelenberg's book review *Zeugen Jehovas in der DDR. Verfolgung und Verhalten einer religiösen Minderheit* (Jehovah's Witnesses in the GDR. Persecution and Response of a Religious Minority), by Gerald Hacke, series »Berichte und Studien,« no. 24, Dresden, Hannah-Arendt-Institut, 2000, in: *Journal of Church and State*, vol. 42, no. 3, 2000, pp. 574ff.

38 Garbe, *Zwischen Widerstand und Martyrium*, p. 22.

39 The use of Gebhard diminishes the value of Manfred Koch's essay (»Julius Engelhard: Drucker, Kurier und Organisator der Zeugen Jehovas« in *Der Widerstand im deutschen Südwesten 1933 - 1945*, [Stuttgart,1984], p. 99): »An attempt at winning the favor of the Nazis seemed opportune in order to survive as an organization. They recommended themselves as a possible ally because of their own religiously motivated differences from Judaism. But attempts at ingratiation remained unsuccessful (Gebhard, 1971, p. 161).« Elke Imberger also bases her otherwise well-researched book on Manfred Gebhard's publication and on Günther Pape, *Die Wahrheit über Jehovas Zeugen: Problematik, Dokumentation* (Rottweil, 1970), probably also involved as co-author of the Urania book. Ralph Angermund, *Deutsche Richterschaft 1919-1945* (Frankfurt, 1990), p. 152 noted: »Although 5,000 Bible Students declared their loyalty toward the Nazi government and their agreement with the antisemitic principles of the Nazi party at a convention in Berlin on June 25, 1933, the sect was banned that same month«; the source cited in the footnote »Mammach, p. 39. Thereafter prohibitions followed at the request of the Episcopate.« Klaus Mammach utilized information from the Manfred Gebhard book published by Urania in his study, *Widerstand 1933-1939: Geschichte der deutschen antifaschistischen Widerstandsbewegung im Inland und in der Emigration* (Berlin, 1984), p. 39: »Other religious associations also accepted the regime. Five thousand so-called Bible Students, also known as called Jehovah's Witnesses, declared at a conference in Berlin on June 25, 1933, one day after the State banned the sect at the request of the Catholic church, that there ›were no contradictions‹ in their relation ›to the

national government of the German Reich‹ [Mammach does not consider the context since the additional remark from the original is missing here: ›but on the contrary–regarding the purely religious and unpolitical goals and efforts of the Bible Students–it is to be said that these are in full accord with the goals of the National Government of Germany regarding this matter,‹ ed.] that they would ›stand for the order and safety of this land‹ and also for the ›high ideals of the national Government in the religious domain.‹«

40 Garbe, *Zwischen Widerstand und Martyrium*, p. 20, note 44. See also Wrobel 1997, Erich Frost und Konrad Franke, 9.1 and 9.2. On December 26, 1984, Manfred Gebhard wrote: »The Urania book should be pulped, or placed in paper mills! I am fully aware that these are harsh words, particularly since I am involved in the Urania book.« (photocopy in possession of author)

41 Photocopy of this letter in the possession of author.

42 The Emergency Decree of the Reich President for the Protection of Volk and State (also known as the Reichstag fire decree) of February 28, 1933 (RGBL. I, p. 83) stipulated: »Based on Article 48, para. 2 of the Reich Constitution, the following is ordered for protection against communist acts of violence endangering the State: §1, articles 114, 115, 117, 118, 123, and 153 of the Constitution of the German Reich are suspended until further notice. Thus, restrictions on personal freedom, on the right to free expression of opinion, including freedom of the press, on the right of assembly and association, and violations of the privacy of postal, telegraphic, and telephonic communications, warrants for house searches, and orders for confiscations as well as restrictions on property rights are permissable beyond the legal limits otherwise prescribed. §2. In any German state the measures for the restoration of public security and order are not taken, the Reich government may temporarily take over the powers of the supreme authority in such a state in order to restore security.« (Quoted in *Deutsche Verfassung*, edited by Prof. Dr. Rudolf Schuster [Munich: 1992].) The prohibitions of Jehovah's Witnesses in Germany were based on this Reichstag Fire decree. Thus on April 18, 1933, Saxony »prohibited Earnest Bible Students based on the Reich President's decree for the protection of the people and the state of February 28, 1933« (photocopy in author's collection). Similarly, the ban for Prussia on June 24, 1933, also referred to the first article of the Reichstag Fire decree. (Garbe, *Zwischen Widerstand und Martyrium*, pp. 100f.) The decree of February 28, 1933, originally for »protection against communist acts of violence endangering the State« was, according to Wolf-Dieter Mechler, »utilized until the end of the Third Reich against ›intractable‹ members or followers of prohibited organizations, although scant documentation —especially for the war years — allows one to conclude that it was not the classical political opponents of the Nazis who were affected, but members of religious sects especially the Jehovah's Witnesses.« Wolf-Dieter Mechler, »Kriegsalltag and der ›Heimatfront‹: Das Sondergericht Hannover im Einsatz gegen ›Rundfunkverbrecher,‹ ›Schwarzschlachter,‹ ›Volksschädinge‹ und andere ›Straftäter‹ 1939 bis 1945,« in: *Hannoversche Studien*, Schriftreihe des Stadtarchivs Hannover, vol. 4 (Hanover, 1997), p. 73.

43 Garbe, Sendboten, p. 154.

44 *1974 Yearbook of Jehovah's Witnesses*, pp. 102, 105.

45 By fall 1926, 897 Bible Students had been taken to court. Of these cases, 460 had been closed, while 437 cases were pending (acquittal in 421 cases; in 25 cases, Bible Students were fined due to failures of the attorneys to appeal on time.) A legal department was instituted at the Magdeburg branch office of the Watch Tower Society (*1927 Yearbook of the International Bible Students Association*, pp. 69f.) Two years later, the legal department reported that in 1928, 1,660 legal proceedings were brought against the Society's colporteurs. Of these, 762 were completed (729 cases ended in acquittal, 33 in sentences, mainly because of dilatory filing of appeals); 898 cases were still pending (*1929 Yearbook of the International Bible Students Association*, p. 121).

46 Anson Phelps Stokes, *Church and State in the United States*, vol. 3 (1950), p. 546, quoted in: *Jehovah's Witnesses-Proclaimers of God's Kingdom* (1993), p. 699.

47 Prussian authorities were compelled to release the occupied printing plant, offices, and residences of the Wachtturm-Gesellschaft in Magdeburg, on April 28, 1933, which was a legal victory for Jehovah's Witnesses and, therefore, for religious freedom in Germany. Jehovah's Witnesses were determined to fight for their rights as granted in the German Constitution. For background on the release of the Magdeburg property, see Garbe, *Zwischen Widerstand und Martyrium*, pp. 92f.

48 The court stated: »The decrees in question are therefore legally invalid since they violate article 137, par. 2 of the Reich Constitution of August 11, 1919, which is still valid and in existence. ... The measures taken in the Hesse decrees are... unconstitutional and without binding legal effect.« (*Das Goldene Zeitalter*, Bern edition, June 1, 1934, pp. 7f. The section is missing in the equivalent article in *The Golden Age*, Brooklyn, N. Y., April 25, 1945, pp. 451-463.)

49 An »expert on sects« wrote the following in the *Materialdienst der Evanglischen Zentralstelle für Weltan-schauungsfragen*: »According to official Watch Tower Society teachings, not only the Nazi party striving for power ›originated with the Devil,‹ but **all** (sic) governments in this world.« (*Materialdienst*, 5/97, p. 144) This misinterpretation leads to misunderstandings about the attitude of Jehovah's Witnesses to the state and requires revision. When analyzing remarks regarding the influence of the Devil on human governments based on older Bible Student literature, two analytical textual criteria must be taken into consideration: 1. The language in which Rutherford's books were written. The German letter to the Chancellor of the Reich, dated June 1933, already complains: »On account of the alleged harsh language in our literature some of our books were forbidden.« Further, it stated in the »Declaration«: »We respectfully call attention to the fact that these books and other literature were written originally in America and the language therein used has been adapted to the American style of plainness of speech and, when translated into the German, the same appears to be harsh. We admit that the same truths might be stated in a less blunt and more pleasing phrase.« 2. The context and purpose of statement concerning Bible teaching of Jehovah's Witnesses. Thus, the »Declara-tion« complained that »our books and other literature have not been carefully examined by the rulers and hence are not properly understood.« The covering letter assumed that »probably because of the great amount of literature published by us or edited and because of the officials being burdened with much work, the contents of our literature and the purpose of our movement are largely misjudged, because they are judged according to that which our religious opponents bring forth and which causes prejudice.« Rutherford's book *Government* (1928) states: »The kingdoms and governments of this world have been cruel, harsh and oppressive upon the people. Every government of the world has thus been dominated by Satan, even though the rulers and the people did not understand or believe it.« (p. 45); the Devil (Lucifer) is also called »the invisible ruler of all the nations« (p. 246) and »the invisible ruler of the peoples« (p. 252). The Biblical teaching of the reign of the Devil over the earth, or rather of his influence on the world including all human institutions and governments, can generally also be found in Protestant and Catholic textbooks. The Protestant *Stuttgarter Jubiläumsbibel*, 1934, comments about Revelation 12:4: »Satan is specified... as prince of this world (John 14:30) who has all the power of the earth (chap. 13:1; 17:3, 9-13) at hand to accomplish his purpose.« If the Devil has »all power of the earth« at hand, it could imply that all governments »originate with the Devil,« yet neither the Protestants nor the Bible Students had intended to state this. The Biblical »truth« in question is based, except for clear Biblical statements mentioned in the quotation above, on the point that the Devil has a certain guilt and responsibility for the evil on earth, whereas the almighty God (Jehovah or Yaweh) having universal sovereignty as the creator of the universe, is not to blame for temporarily permitting the evil. (see *Government*, 1928, pp. 31, 34f.) The book, *Government*, emphasizes: »It is also true that in all these nations there have been a few men of good intention who have striven to better their fellow man.« (pp. 44f.) »In all these forms of government there have been many men who have endeavored to establish a just and equitable rule, but have failed« (p. 243 deals with a final solution for poverty, crime, sickness, etc.) and »the founders of the American government said that all men are created equal and that all men should stand equal before the law. They said well, but their sayings have not been put into action. On the contrary, the common people have not stood equal and have not had an equal show. They have been exploited and the fruits of their labor spoiled.« (p. 296; cf. pp. 158, 206f., 280f., 330ff.) Since early statements had lead to misunderstandings, the view that all governments are to be considered as »God's servants,« in Romans, ch. 13, verse 4, has been emphasized in modern times.

50 Unfortunately the misinterpretation about Jehovah's Witnesses understanding of the State has entered academic literature. Thus Koch comes to the wrong conclusion: »Jehovah's Witnesses refused adherence to any worldly authority based on their interpretation of the Bible.« (Koch, 1993, p. 82) This erroneous and thus perhaps disastrous interpretation is also found in the work of Helga Grebing and Christl Wickert distributed by the Hesse State Central Office for Political Education: »The deliberate rejection of any worldly order made them enemies of the German racial community, and nuisances to the Volk.« (Helga Grebing and Christel Wickert, *Frauen im Nationalsozialismus. Widerstand von Frauen gegen den Nationalsozialismus*, publ. by Konrad Schacht, Wiesbaden, 1994, p. 40) Stefanie Reichelt is just as wrong in her analysis of Jehovah's Witnesses: »Their belief did and still does dictate that they must acknowledge God as the only and absolute authority under all circumstances.« (Stefanie Reichelt, *»Für mich ist der Krieg aus!«: Deserteure und Kriegsdienstverweigerer des Zweiten Weltkriegs in München*, Munich, 1995, p. 51)

51 The standpoint of relative obedience to the State according to the Biblical understanding of Jehovah's Witnesses is not unknown in theological literature and dogma. The Protestant *Stuttgarter Jubiläumsbibel* of 1934 comments on Romans chapter 13 verses 4 and 7, as follows: »Therefore, it is called God's servant. And

if the highest authorities, emperors and kings, write ›by grace of God,‹ it thus should remind them that the highest rulers are also subordinate to the one God and Lord, to his high standing and law; but also that they should not be dependent on status and laws made by men which are in conflict with God's order and majesty. ... Christians obey the authorities for the sake of conscience, and they refuse compliance when something that is against God's Word is required of them. (Acts 5:29)« The Catholic catechism, *Katholische Katechismus der Bistümer Deutschlands* (Mainz, 1955), p. 225, similarly states: »If the authorities demand something that is a sin, one must not acquiesce. Holy Peter says: ›We must obey God rather than men.‹ (Acts 5:29)«

52 *Das Goldene Zeitalter* (Bern), of February 1, 1937, points out that a government that blasphemes God, despises, or behaves devilishly or in opposition to his laws can, according to the Bible, be classified as a »wild beast« in the *direct* service of the Devil and not as »God's minister,« which was meant sarcastically here. When it was a matter of Christian obedience, the term »superior authorities« mentioned in Romans 13 was obviously exclusively applied to God and his Son, Jesus Christ, starting with the *Watchtower* issue of June 1 and 15, 1929, onwards. It was this interpretation of Scripture that was not changed until publication of the article series in *The Watchtower* articles of November 1 to December 1, 1962, (*Wachtturm* of January 1 to February 1, 1963) but the fundamental attitude of Jehovah's Witnesses towards the state, or the principles or truths on which this was based, continued: »Before those articles were published, we knew and taught that Jehovah is the Most High, and that Jesus is the second to Him in power and authority. We knew that we should be law-abiding persons, but that, when there was a conflict between man's law and that of God, we would obey God as ruler rather than men. Those basic truths are the same today as they were before; they have not changed. ... Our viewpoint toward God and toward the State is the same as before.« (*Watchtower,* October 1, 1966, p. 608) This statement is correct, since already in 1912 an explanation of Romans 13:1 read: »Every soul be subject, etc.... Except when they conflict with God's laws.« (King James Version, Bible Students Edition [Berean Bible], 1907, p. 354) Even today, Jehovah's Witnesses still have a balanced attitude toward secular governments and are law-abiding, as the following Watchtower comment shows: »It would be incorrect to conclude that all humans in governmental authority are Satan's tools. ... The political ›superior authorities‹ are God's ›minister‹ when they fulfill their God-approved role, which includes authority ›to inflict punishment on evildoers but to praise doers of good.‹ (1 Peter 2:13, 14) Jehovah's servants conscientiously pay back to Caesar what he legitimately demands in the way of taxes, and they go as far as their Bible-trained conscience will allow them to go in being ›obedient to governments and authorities as rulers, ... ready for every good work.‹ (Titus 3:1)« (»In the World but No Part of It,« in: *The Watchtower,* November 1, 1997, pp. 16ff.)

53 This explanation must have been meant sarcastically with a view to the Bible Students' former understanding. *The Watchtower* of May 15, 1933, stated: »The time was when even consecrated [anointed Jehovah's Witnesses] believed that the ›higher powers‹ [›superior authorities‹] are the earthly rulers. The enlightened ones now know that that is not true, but that the ›higher powers‹ are Jehovah and his great officer Christ Jesus, to whom is committed all judgment, and that all consecrated must be found obedient unto Christ before being fully approved and taken into the Kingdom.« (p. 150)

54 After the persecution of Jehovah's Witnesses did not abade and Hitler's mask of deception and propaganda was revealed, many Watch Tower publications bluntly denounced the outrages of Nazism. This included, for example, the above-mentioned article from *Das Goldene Zeitalter* (Bern), February 1, 1937. See also »The Holocaust–Who Spoke Out? 50th Anniversary of Liberating the Camps,« *Awake!,* August 22, 1995 (New York).

55 Point 7 of the NSDAP party platform demanded that the state be required »primarily to provide employment and housing for its citizens.« Point 10 stated: »The activity of the individual must not infringe upon the interests of the community, but must be for the benefit of all.« Point 12 called »personal enrichment through war as a crime against the people.« Point 14 called for »sharing in the profit of big business«; point 15 asked for »a generous extension of old age pensions«; point 18 called for »the ruthless fight« against those »who harm common interest through their activity.« Point 20 advocated »an extension of the national education system. ... We call for the education of specially gifted children with poor parents, regardless of their position or profession, at the expense of the state.« Point 21 mentioned the »protection of mother and child« and the »prohibition of work by minors.« Point 23 called for »the legal fight against *conscious* (sic) lies spread through the press.« (»Programm der Nationalsozialistischen Deutschen Arbeiterpartei,« in: *Meyers Kleines Lexikon*, 9th rev. ed., 3 vols., Leipzig, 1933, vol. 2, p. 1604)

56 The complete quotation reads: »Instead of being against the principles advocated by the government of

Germany, we stand squarely for such principles, and point out that Jehovah God through Christ Jesus will bring about the full realization of these principles and will give to the people peace and prosperity and the greatest desire of every honest heart.«

57 The quotation continues as follows: »Instead of our organization's being a menace to the peace and safety of the government, it is the one organization standing for the peace and safety of this land. We beg to remind all that the great crisis is upon the world because the transition period from bad to good is at hand, and the hope of the world is God's kingdom under Christ, for which Jesus taught his followers to constantly pray: ›Thy kingdom come. Thy will be done on earth, as it is done in heaven.‹ The power of Jehovah God is supreme and there is no power that can successfully resist him. His time to exercise his power in the interest of humanity and to the vindication of his great name is here.«

58 A passage in the Watchtower book *Deliverance* (1926) reads: »The scripture says: ›Woe to the inhabiters of the earth, and of the sea! For the devil is come downs unto you, having great wrath, because he knoweth that he hath but a short time.‹ (Rev 12: 12) Since the World War the burdens and trials of the people continue to increase. They are now experiencing some of the woes foretold in this scripture, but not all of them yet. The expenses of governments increase. Some of the people's money must be taken to prepare for another great war. The wicked are set up, and the proud appear to be happy, even though they are not. While this is going on the faithful witnesses for God are carrying out the command given them by the Lord, who said: ›This gospel of the kingdom shall be preached in all the world for a witness unto all nations: and then shall the end come.‹ (Mt 24:14)« (p. 267)

59 Jehovah's Witnesses repeatedly condemned injustice in the world, the exploitation, and the false teaching of the masses without departing from their position of »Christian neutrality« (observation of events worldwide according to Biblical aspects but without taking sides with or influencing politics). J. F. Rutherford remarked after he had spoken of grievances in the government of the United States on June 26, 1932: »I am not taking sides in politics. I am merely calling attention to the facts, that I may in a moment cite Jehovah God's prophecy applying at this very hour and which discloses the cause of the present trouble and what is the only possible remedy. (*The Crisis*, booklet, 1933, p. 11) Jehovah's Witnesses noticed that the German government had also emphatically spoken out »against Big Business oppressors and in opposition to the wrongful religious influence in the political affairs of the nation.« And »such is exactly our position,« was stated in Berlin. But Jehovah's Witnesses immediately added that they named other reasons »for the existence of oppressive Big Business and the wrongful political religious influence.«

60 The corresponding passage in the cover letter states: »At the conference it was ascertained that in the relation of the Bible Students of Germany to the National Government of Germany there is no contradiction, but on the contrary-*regarding the purely religious and unpolitical goals and efforts of the Bible Students*-it is to be said that these are in full accord with the goals of the National Government of Germany regarding these matters.« (sic)

61 Garbe, *Zwischen Widerstand und Martyrium*, p. 89 refers to my uncompleted and unpublished draft manuscript entitled »Anbiederung oder Glaubenszeugnis? Die Petition der Zeugen Jehovas vom 25. Juni 1933 und der Kongreßbericht an den Reichskanzler: Eine Dokumentation« (Selters/Taunus, February 1997), which I have used for this essay.

62 The acknowledgement of »positive Christianity« was one of the »cleverest propaganda strategies in the early [Nazi] party program« and blinded »many Christians to the true nature of the NSDAP.« (Klaus Goebel in book review in *Frankfurter Allgemeine Zeitung*, January 26, 1989, p. 8) The *Lexikon für Theologie und Kirche* (1962) noted: »The slogan of ›positive Christianity‹ in Article 24 of the party platform obscured the views of leading Nazis toward Christianity and the churches during the first few months of 1933, which they considered to be outdated but still tolerated for tactical reasons and attempted to find a modus vivendi.« (LfTK, 1962, vol. 7, p. 803) The term »positive Christianity« was not clearly outlined and was open to interpretation. The historian Friedrich Zipfel commented: »The position ›of positive Christianity‹ called for by the Nazis was not clear, but linked to the slogan ›the welfare of all above private greed,‹ it could be interpreted as active Christianity dominated by a moral and social sense of responsibility.« (Friedrich Zipfel, *Kirchenkampf in Deutschland 1933-1945*, Berlin, 1965, p. 1) Jehovah's Witnesses, no doubt, could have agreed to such an interpretation then. They obviously understood »positive Christianity« to be the early Christianity or »true Christianity« that, in their opinion, differed from »negative« Christianity or Christianity watered down by the traditions and pagan philosophies of the state churches. Later, Jehovah's Witnesses became enraged that Nazism spoke about »positive Christianity,« but meant something completely different, thus resembling an unpredictable »Janus-faced being.« The *Goldene Zeitalter* published in Bern (No-

vember 15, 1938, p. 14) complained: »In the Reichstag, they claimed to stand upon the ground of positive Christianity but in reality they considered it a crime to read the Bible or to own or distribute Bible literature.« The periodical quoted Reich Minister without portfolio and Prussian Interior Minister Hans Kerrl from Fulda: »The state and movement do not, in any case, consider getting involved in a church or denominational quarrel about dogmas. They support instead positive Christianity. ...« The Swiss edition of the Witness periodical *Das Goldene Zeitalter* commented about this statement: »Until then, one could believe he was a Christian really believing in the Bible, whose statements could be endorsed and emphasized. ... But again there was a ›Janus-faced person‹ with its two faces plainly before us. Again ›positive Christianity‹ can move mountains, but, in reality, it meant the Nazi state [and] Nazi party, and the Bible for the party platforms. ... They imitate Catholic and Protestant religions when they hypocritically used the names ›God,‹ ›Jesus Christ,‹ and ›positive Christianity‹ with the selfish intention of attaining their goal: bringing the entire nation completely and absolutely into conformity (Gleichschaltung) with the party platform.« (p. 15) The statement by the Watch Tower Society showed that Jehovah's Witnesses supported »positive Christianity« in the summer of 1933, without expressing their approval of Nazism or the entire party platform.

63   The NSDAP party program, including point 24, had been proclaimed by Hitler on February 24, 1920. That Jehovah's Witnesses referred to point 24 in the cover letter has been misinterpreted in academic literature and misused against the Witnesses. A passage in Manfred Gebhard's »documentation,« subsidized by the Ministry for State Security of the former GDR, read: »No doubt, the focus is the statement by the ›conference of Witness representatives in Germany to be in complete harmony with the Nazi party platform point 24 and its designated fight against the Jewish spirit and with the request to Hitler to apply Nazi guidelines as a standard for the Watch Tower Society and Jehovah's Witnesses to avoid conflict with Hitler's state.« (p. 164) Historian Elke Imberger commented on this passage without quoting from the cover letter: »The conference referred to point 24 of the Nazi party platform. In this plank, the Nazi party pretended to be a representative of ›positive Christianity,‹ declaring war on the ›Jewish materialistic spirit.‹ Thus, the letter was a declaration of loyalty by the International Bible Students Association to the Nazi regime and consequently the sect gave up its self-declared neutrality.« (Elke Imberger, *Widerstand »von unten«: Widerstand und Dissens aus den Reihen der Arbeiterbewegung und der Zeugen Jehovas in Lübeck und Schleswig-Holstein 1933–1945*, Neumünster, 1991, pp. 258f.) Why did Jehovah's Witnesses quote from the 1920 party platform? Facutal information for the Reich Chancellor (and his representatives) should not be damaged by »religious prejudices« (i.e., church influence), and thus, Hitler was reminded of his own party platform. (In the »Declaration« the word »remind« is repeatedly used in specific contexts.) For Jehovah's Witnesses at that time, the basic message of this part of the party platform was religious autonomy and tolerance and hope for an »open-minded« hearing of their case. Friedrich Zipfel remarked about Nazi party platform point 24: »The contradictions in this plank was not completely obvious or recognized much too late by the majority of Christian Germans in those years. ›The freedom for all religious denominations in the State‹ might be considered as an expression of religious tolerance as in the traditions of the past two centuries. It was no doubt the legitimate right of the secular state that it turned against religious beliefs that might endanger its existence. It was, however, a truism that religious denominations should not violate the ›moral sense and norms.‹« (Zipfel, p. 1) The cover letter by the German branch of the Watch Tower Society in Magdeburg went further than the »Declaration« of the president of the movement. The »Declaration« did not refer to Nazi party platform point 24, although the Nazis, called »the Nationalists,« were also quoted there (as already mentioned above): »The Nationalists have declared themselves against all such unrighteousness and announced that ›Our relationship to God is high and holy‹. Since our organization fully endorses these righteous principles...Satan by subtilty endeavors to set the government against our work and destroy it because we magnify the importance of knowing and serving God.« After June 1933, Jehovah's Witnesses quoted the Nazis in their literature more than once without intending to express the slightest approval of Nazism or having done so. The purpose of using such quotations was to remind the addressed party of the principles that he had himself proclaimed. Thus, the *Goldene Zeitalter* of June 1, 1934 (Bern), page 7 (the English equivalent was published in *The Golden Age* of April 25, 1934, p. 455) stated: »This is in defense of our brethren in Christ who are suffering innocently. For a whole year we have waited and have suffered the unjustified and cruel measures of the German government; we have waited (in vain) for a release [of the bans] because the treaty between America and Germany guaranteed that our activity could be carried on without hindrance, and because, according to many public utterances of the present leaders in Germany, who claim to be sent of God, liberty of faith and conscience was supposed to be safeguarded in the Third Reich. For

example: Reichskanzler Adolf Hitler, in April 1933, said: ›Nationally and racially thinking men have the holy obligation to take care that everyone in his own religion should not only speak outwardly of God's will, but he should really fulfill God's will and see to it that God's work is not dishonored. Whoever destroys God's work is therefore fighting against God's will and the creation of the Lord.‹ Thus he and his officials are judged by his own words. He also said that if a man knows a thing, sees a danger and a possibility of help, ›then it is his damned duty and obligation, not to work quietly, but to stand publicly against the evil and for its remedy; and if he does not do it, then he is a coward and a weakling.‹ Reichsminister Rudolf Hess, Hitler's right-hand man, said, in October, 1933: ›Confession and faith, or no confession, is every man's own and private affair, which he must account for to his own conscience. Coercion of conscience must not be exercised.‹ Reichskanzler Hitler also said in his book *Mein Kampf*: ›Man's relation to his God is holy and must be respected,‹ and that political power and religious matters must be kept separate. In view of these utterances, which we accepted as truthful statements, many letters and requests were submitted to the German authorities regarding the unlawful and oppressive measures against our Society and against our brethren in Germany, but these requests were neither heeded nor answered.« In June 1933, Jehovah's Witnesses quoted from the 1920 Nazi party platform for the same reason their Society in the United States and Switzerland quoted Rudolf Hess and Adolf Hitler one year later. One difference was that in summer 1933 they still considered the statements by the Nazis »as truthful statements.« They judged the German Reich Chancellor by his own party platform. Why should Jehovah's Witnesses »give up their self-declared political neutrality« in connection with this reminder? Such a conclusion is not based on facts and may be attributed to the fact that non-Witnesses do not fully understand the Witness doctrine of »Christian neutrality.«

64 Even the *Materialdienst der Evangelischen Zentralstelle für Weltanschauungsfragen* admits: »Watch Tower Society literature never had any common ground with the Nazi platform and its ›high ideals.‹ On the contrary: as pointed out in the film, the Watch Tower Society had already discredited National Socialism as a movement active in the service of mankind's enemy, the Devil, in its journal *Das Goldene Zeitalter* (today *ERWACHET!*).« (5/97, p. 144)

65 *Der Wachtturm*, (June 15, 1933), p. 178.

66 Garbe, *Zwischen Widerstand und Martyrium*, p. 107.

67 Ibid.

68 Ibid.

69 Ibid., p. 105.

70 The »adaptation of the association to the national conditions in Germany« (Garbe, *Zwischen Widerstand und Martyrium*, pp. 87f.) by establishing a North German and the South German Bible Students Association in April 1933 has been called evidence for »a policy of accomodation« with concessions and as a »strategy for rescue.« But this overlooks then as now that Jehovah's Witnesses as a religious association have the right, in every country, to take legal steps and to make lawful changes within their legal corporation if they consider this necessary for the defense of religious rights. The release of the Magdeburg buildings on April 28-29, 1933, that had been closed by the police, clearly shows how the religious association, represented by the Watch Tower Society, fully used various legal means to protect communally valuable property and the Magdeburg branch office. In 1934, the Society still pointed out clearly that it was a religious association protected by article 137 of the Constitution, that had not been suspended by the Nazi ›revolution‹ as confirmed by a special tribunal in the Circuit (Appeals) court in the district of Darmstadt on March 16, 1934. (*Das Goldene Zeitalter*, June 1, 1934, pp. 7f.) *Das Goldene Zeitalter*, April 25, 1934, p. 452, stated retrospectively: »Jehovah's Witnesses in Germany have made every possible effort to present their case before the German authorities, asking that all restrictions and impediments be removed and that they be allowed, without restrictions, to continue their worship of God and their service to Him according to His commandments, as guaranteed by the Constitution of Germany. All their efforts in this matter have failed.« The tactical measures by the Watch Tower Society's legal department in Magdeburg to establish new legal corporations are to be seen in this context.

71 In the articles Hans Hauptmann, »Hinter den Kulissen der Zeugen Jehovas,« *Heilbronner Tagblatt*, no. 161 (July 14, 1933), p. 6, and »Ernste Bibelforscher!« in *Drehscheibe: Das Blatt der denkenden Menschen*, 5, no. 7, (February 10, 1935), Jehovah is called »God of the Jews.«

72 On the publisher's page of each issue, including the last legal issue printed in Magdeburg, it stated: »The Scriptures clearly teach that *Jehovah* is the only true God. ... that the Logos is now the Lord Jesus Christ in glory, clothed with all power in heaven and earth, and the Chief Executive Officer of Jehovah. ... That

Jehovah's organization is called Zion, and that Christ Jesus is the Chief Officer thereof and is the rightful King of the world; that the anointed and faithful followers of Christ Jesus are children of Zion, members of Jehovah's organization, and are his witnesses whose duty and privilege it is to testify to the supremacy of Jehovah, declare his purposes toward mankind as expressed in the Bible, and to bear the fruits of the kingdom before all who will hear. ... That the relief and blessings of the peoples of earth can come only by and through Jehovah's kingdom under Christ which has now begun; that the Lord's next great act is the destruction of Satan's organization and the establishment of righteousness in the earth, and that under the kingdom all those who will obey its righteous laws shall be restored and live on earth forever. ... It [this journal] adheres strictly to the Bible as authority for its utterances. It is entirely free and separate from all parties, sects or other worldly organizations. It is wholly and without reservation for the kingdom of Jehovah God under Christ his Beloved King. It is not dogmatic, but invites careful and critical examination of its contents in the light of the Scriptures. It does not indulge in controversy, and its columns are not open to personalities.« (*Der Wachtturm,* June 15, 1933, Magdeburg, p. 178)

73 Garbe, *Zwischen Widerstand und Martyrium,* p. 106, note 82.

74 In August 1933, the Lutheran Pastor Seifert-Reichenbach from Saxony entitled one article with inescapable hypocrisy: »Wie kam man auf die Vermutung, daß die Lehre der Bibelforscher als judenfreundlich anzusehen ist?« (What makes one assume that the Bible Students' teachings are philo-semitic?) in *Heimatklänge-Wernesgrün,* no. 8 (August 1933), p. 5.

75 *Völkischer Beobachter,* no. 325 (November 21, 1935), »Nachrichten aus Nürnberg,« no page.

76 Garbe, *Sendboten,* pp. 149–152.

77 *Das Goldene Zeitalter* (April 14, 1930), p. 124.

78 *Trost* (previously *Das Goldene Zeitalter*) (Bern, November 15), 1938, p. 12.

79 *Trost* (Bern, January 1, 1940), p. 10.

80 *Life,* Watch Tower Society (1929), p. 206.

81 In 1935, an article »Der Gipfel der Gemeinheit« in the *Wilhelmshavener Zeitung* quoted from the book *Leben* (1929, pp. 205f.): »Further the book, »Life,« committed the following sordid blasphemy: ›Fortunately for the Jews, the Devil was never able to induce them to believe in the doctrine of conscious torment in hell-fire and brimstone. ... The persecution of the Jews by so-called Christians is one of the blackest marks of shame in world history.« (2. Beilage *Wilhelmshavener Zeitung,* no. 165, July 18, 1935, article »Der Führer – des Teufels besonderer Vertreter. Der Gipfel der Gemeinheit. Vom ›Wirken‹ der Bibelforscher, die sich ›die Zeugen Jehovas‹ nennen.«

82 Odette Abadi, *Terre de détresse: Birkenau – Bergen-Belsen* (Paris, 1995), p. 141.

83 A passage in the book *Government* (1928, p. 253) reads: »In the Scriptures ›The Stone‹ is used to symbolize God's Anointed King. All government-builders, including the clergy both of the Jews and of so-called ›Christendom,‹ have rejected him. ›The stone which the builders refused is become the head stone of the corner. This is the Lord's doing; it is marvelous in our eyes.‹ (Ps. 118:22, 23)«

84 Garbe, *Zwischen Widerstand und Martyrium,* p. 107, note 89.

85 Garbe, *Zwischen Widerstand und Martyrium,* p. 107, note 89.

86 Ibid., p. 104.

87 The Watchtower publications of those days were full of references to Big Business and the interference of religion in politics. J. F. Rutherford saw »the biggest catastrophe for the world in–using his words–›unholy trinity,‹ meaning the influences in alliance of church, politics, and finance« in the 1926 *Goldene Zeitalter* (July 15, 1926, pp. 215f.). In the brochure *Die Krise [The Crisis]* (1933) he wrote: »The three visible elements of men that rule the nation are, to wit, the commercial, the political, and the religious, and of these three the commercial is the most powerful. Among the earlier statesmen of America there were some God-fearing men who foresaw the advance of a mighty and selfish power and gave warning that the greedy would some day destroy the liberties of the people. This warning was unheeded, and the selfish, commercial element, which is otherwise called ›Big Business,‹ has stealthily and constantly moved forward to its goal.« (p. 6)

88 *Deutsches Wörterbuch* by Jacob Grimm und Wilhelm Grimm (1877, reprinted 1984), vol. 10 (H-Juzen) col. 382: »HANDELSJUDE, m. handel treibender Jude, besonders hausierer: ein armer handelsjude und mäkler.« The original term »commercial Jews,« however, refers to »Geldjudentum« (monied Jews). On September 1, 1897, the Bern newspaper *Der Bund* reported about a speech by Max Nordau at the first Zionist congress of August 1897 in Bern. Besides Herzl, Nordau was a prominent representative of political Zionism. »In his speech on Sunday, Max Nordau... made a ruthless attack on the Geldjudentum which resulted in loud applause in the assembly.«... About the ›100 or 150 overly-rich Jews,‹ Nordau said: »They never contributed

to true Judaism except for throwing in some alms in a fit of flamboyant generosity. For centuries, there has been the legend that the Jews would have all the power and rulership in the world, being the personification of the Mammon, while the majority of our nation has to cope with the most bitter hardships day by day.« (Der Bund, Bern, »So schrieb der ›Bund‹ vor hundert Jahren,« September 1, 1997, n. p.)

89 The word »Handelsjude« cannot be found in Nazi usage. *»Selbstverständliche« Begriffe und Schlagwörter aus der Zeit des Nationalsozialismus* (cited hereafter: NS-Deutsch) (Straelen/Niederrhein: 1988), nor in *DUDEN* of 1937 or 1942.

90 While Detlef Garbe observed (*Zwischen Widerstand und Martyrium*, p. 106, note 82) that it could be said that Jehovah's Witnesses were not antisemitic, to this I agree, but I cannot follow him (ibid., p. 105) if he means that the sentence using the words »commercial Jews« shows »their willingness to conform to the prevailing usage.« The remarks on the Anglo-American empire are already found in Rutherford's books before 1933. (See chap. 1 in the German book *Regierung* [1928] and its English equivalent *Government* [1928].)

91 The saying »Tut nichts! Der Jude wird verbrannt!« by the Patriarch of Jerusalem in Lessing's dramatic poem *Nathan the Wise* (1779) is »seldom used today and only in situations in which it cannot be misunderstood as an expression of antisemitic offense,« according to *Duden*. This reference work states that the quotation »Haust du meinen Juden, hau' ich deinen Juden« which is used similar to »tit for tat,« became a standard quotation during the nineteenth century. »Today after the mass murder of the Jews during the Third Reich, the use of the quotation can be deemed objectionable.« (*Duden Zitate und Aussprüche*, Duden, Mannheim, 1993, vol. 2, pp. 431, 200)

92 NS-Deutsch, pp. 54, 117, 125.

93 The concept »Doppelverdiener« (ibid., p. 53; until 1933-34 was a Nazi insult for a married couple with a double income) and »asozial« (p. 26 meant »alien to the society«). Since the word »sozial« (social) but not »asozial« (antisocial) can be found in A. Pinloche, *Etymologischen Wörterbuch der deutschen Sprache* (Paris, 1930), one might conclude that »asozial« is a Nazi term. *Meyers kleines Lexikon*, 9th ed., (Leipzig 1933 [1934]) explains: »Asozial [antisocial] (lat.) people – People who cannot adapt themselves to society: alcoholics, vagabonds, prostitutes, idlers, criminals« (p. 112). Today »asozial« is defined as follows: »unsocial, incapable of living in human society, harmful to society; ant. social.« (*Wahrig Fremdwörterlexikon*, Ranate Wahrig-Burfeind, Gütersloh, 1991, p. 79)

94 Not much remained of the following points in the critique of the theologian Lutz Lehmhöfer, Diocese of Limburg, department for ideological questions, as indicated at the event on September 29, 1997, and the conference of October 5, 1997. Although Lemhöfer concentrated on the things »not mentioned in the film« or what the film »conceals,« he primarily complained about a lack of critical analysis in historical self-presentation of Jehovah's Witnesses. But he was not sparing in his praise of the video documentary. At the event in Frankfurt on September 29, 1997, Lemhöfer explicitly pointed out that the established churches had designed their image in the historical analysis of the Nazi period. The *Frankfurter Rundschau* of October 9, 1997, page 16 (G) reported: »After 1945, the Protestant as well as the Catholic Church endeavored to achieve a positive presentation of their role. ... ›I know this form of myth-making well,‹ said Benad. ›After the war, the Confessing Church became ever larger. Actually, there had been only a few individuals who had resisted because of their own, not religiously motivated, ethics.‹ The Protestant professor of history stated that a differentiated presentation of Protestant history during the Nazi era was not possible until the 1980s. Lemhöfer added: ›Catholic historiography also had a strong affirmative character until the 1970s which did not correspond much with historical facts.‹«

95 A statement by the Watch Tower Society about the Berlin Convention on June 25, 1933, which was published after this lecture, said with regard to the phrase »commercial Jews«: »This statement clearly did not refer to the Jewish people in general, and it is regrettable if it has been misunderstood and has given cause for any offense. Some have claimed that Jehovah's Witnesses shared the hostility toward the Jews that was commonly taught in the German churches at the time. This is absolutely untrue. By their literature and conduct during the Nazi era, the Witnesses rejected anti-Semitic views and condemned the Nazi mistreatment of the Jews. Certainly, their kindness toward Jews who shared their lot in the concentration camps provides a resounding rebuttal to this false accusation.«(*Awake!*, July 8, 1998, »Jehovah's Witnesses Courageous in the Face of Nazi Peril,« p. 14)

96 Jörg von Uthmann, »Vom Lebemann zum Lebensretter. Premiere im Klima antisemitscher Mißgunst: ›Schindler's List,‹ Steven Spielbergs neuer Film,« *Frankfurter Allgemeine Zeitung*, December 14, 1993, p. 33.

Gabriele Yonan

History, Past and Present: Jehovah's Witnesses in Germany

An Analysis of the Documentary »Stand Firm Against Nazi Assault« From the Perspective of Religious Studies

Who Are Jehovah's Witnesses? – Their Theological Classification

Jehovah's Witnesses are an independent Christian denomination whose eschatological teaching points to the »Kingdom« of God. This »kingdom« is understood as God's government in heaven which, under the administration of Jesus Christ, will solve mankind's problems through his peaceful reign over the earth. In terms of religious studies, this denomination can be described as »chiliastic,« that is, characterized by the expectation of Christ's thousand-year reign, his millennium.

This Christian group which began in America in the last third of the nineteenth century sprang from the then widespread belief in the closeness of Christ's return (parousia) and the creation of a New Jerusalem. According to the beliefs of Jehovah's Witnesses, before the dawn of God's kingdom on earth there will be a decisive battle (Armageddon[1]) by which God himself will defeat the wicked powers of the Devil and destroy them.

Around 1870 the American businessman Charles Taze Russell (1852–1916) gathered about him a small group of people who were interested in studying the Bible. Known as »Earnest Bible Students,« they read the Bible with special attention to its statements about the last days. Starting in 1879 the magazine *Zion's Watch Tower* was published, and one year later the Watch Tower Bible and Tract Society was established. Since 1909 this society has had its headquarters in Brooklyn, New York.

In 1931 this Christian group adopted the name »Jehovah's Witnesses.« This use of God's name was based on a Hebrew text from the Old Testament, Isaiah 43:10, 12. The name appears about 7,000 times in the Hebrew scriptures of the Bible in the form of the tetragram (meaning »four characters«) JHVH.

Jehovah's Witnesses see themselves as part of the biblical tradition of witnesses from ancient times and especially from the New Testament, based, for example, on Bible texts like those with the words of Jesus to Pontius Pilate: »To this end was I born, and for this cause came I into the world, that I should bear witness unto the truth.« (John 18:37)

In Germany Jehovah's Witnesses have been active since 1896, and were known until 1931 as »Ernste Bibelforscher« (Earnest Bible Students). Their religion now totals 192,000 members in Germany in more than 2,000 local congregations. Worldwide there are now over 6 million members (that is, active preachers) in 235 countries. Their most important journal is *The Watchtower*, with a circulation of more than 23 million. In 2000, their annual memorial of the death of Christ was attended by more than 14 million persons globally.

Recapitulation: Facts and Recognition of Their Resistance

During the Nazi regime, Jehovah's Witnesses as a religious group almost unanimously resisted Nazism. Of the more than 20,000 Jehovah's Witnesses [in Germany] in 1933, almost one in two was arrested. »A total of 6,019 had been arrested, ... 8,917 arrests were registered. ... A total of 2,000 brothers and sisters had been put into concentration camps, ... 253 had been sentenced to death and 203 of these had actually been executed.«[2]

The exemplary position of Jehovah's Witnesses has been acknowledged and honored by important church representatives and historians in Germany and other countries. Two examples:

— Hanns Lilje, Bishop of the Protestant-Lutheran Lower Saxon State Church in Hanover, wrote in his memoirs shortly after the war, that »... no Christian community can stand even the slightest comparison with the numbers of their [Jehovah's Witnesses] martyrs.«[3]

— The Protestant theologian Kurt Hutten, who built and directed the former »Apologetic Center of the Protestant Church in Germany« under the new name *Evangelische Zentrale für Weltanschauungsfragen* [Protestant headquarters for ideological questions] in Stuttgart, wrote in his book »Seher, Grübler, Enthusiasten« [Visionaries, Ponderers, Enthusiasts], which is still acknowledged as a standard work: »In the Nazi state Jehovah's Witnesses were banned and cruelly persecuted already in 1933. In numerous court cases they were given heavy sentences. Thousands of them were in prison because they had continued their activity, they had refused military service, and for other reasons. Testimonies from former concentration camp prisoners confirm their uncompromising determination and courageous attitude; when given the tempting offer of freedom in exchange for a denial of their principles they refused, and accepted all the consequences. Around 1,000 were executed, and another 1,000 died in prisons or concentration camps; members of Jehovah's Witnesses were sentenced to more than 20,000 years in prison.«[4]

And in 1989 the Canadian jurist William Kaplan from the University of Ottawa stated: »The courage of Jehovah's Witnesses, the way they endured their oppression and kept fighting for what they believed, is a credit to the human spirit.«

Failure of the Major Churches During the Nazi Regime

Shortly after the end of the war, the German Protestant Church made a public declaration of its failures under National Socialism, known as the »Stuttgarter Schuldbekenntnis,« the Stuttgart Confession of Guilt, in 1945. This confession included the tacit acceptance and condonement of persecution, especially of the Jews, which resulted in the most massive genocide in history. It also included accepting the war of aggression and destruction to which Hitler had subjected the world, resulting in 55 million dead with destruction and devastation all over Europe.

The two major churches proceeded from distinct positions. Protestantism had influenced Germany through the imperial regime and Bismarck's Prussia. Since the Weimar Republic had introduced a process of secularization – the recognition of other denominations as equals and rejection of the concept of sects (1919) – it met with disapproval by parts of the church. The Protestant Church was hoping for a restoration of its own privileges through a new political and national power. Many Protestant clergymen saw in Hitler a »great man sent by God,« a man who would introduce the rebirth of a new Protestant Germany.

The Catholic Church had suffered further losses of power in Germany after Bismarck's defeat of their political party, the Center Party, under the imperial government of Wilhelm II. That is why the Catholic Center Party had supported the creation of the Weimar Republic after World War I. Before 1933, the Catholic Church had disapproved of the Nazis. Catholics were forbidden to join the Nazi party, and the racial ideology was condemned in church. But shortly after Hitler's assumption of power on January 30, 1933, the church changed its course. On March 24, 1933, the Catholic bishops wrote an encyclical in which they encouraged all German Catholics to be loyal to all »rightful authorities,« to carefully fulfill their duties as citizens, and refrain from all illegal and seditious activity. It was now permitted to wear a uniform while attending a religious service. Church representatives celebrated this as »the greatness of the times« and called for joyful and wholehearted readiness for cooperation in the new authoritarian state.

Soon after this, on July 20, 1933, Hitler's government and the Vatican completed the »concordat,« an agreement of special protection which guaranteed the rights of the Catholic Church to operate its own schools, religious orders, religious education, etc. in Germany. In exchange for this the Catholic Church was obliged to make its political party, the Center, vote for the Enabling Act of March 1933. On March 28, 1933, bishops of the Catholic Church openly spoke for Hitler and the leadership of his Nazi party and urged »loyalty towards legal authority.«

After the signing of the concordat, Catholic Cardinal von Faulhaber wrote to Hitler: »This handshake with the Papacy means a grand deed of immeasurable blessing. ... May God preserve our Reich Chancellor for our people.«

The Catholic Church believed it could secure its existence by establishing an arrangement with the new regime. This was a fallacy, since Hitler had no intention of keeping any agreements. The numerous appeals made by Catholic dignitaries to Hitler, calling him »a most honorable Chancellor,« did nothing to change this.

What the Protestant Church did was even worse. The German Protestant Church held its national synod on September 27, 1933, in which Rev. Ludwig Müller was appointed Bishop of the Reich.

His speech reflected his adoption of Hitler's totalitarian ideology: »... As he has done for every people, so the eternal God has also given our people its own particular native law. This has unfolded through the Führer Adolf Hitler. ... This law speaks to us through the history of our people as it has grown from blood and soil. ... From this community of German Christians in the Nazi state of Adolf Hitler shall grow the German Christian national church which will include all German people. One people! One God! One Reich! One church!«

The church movement called German Christians (*Deutsche Christen*) demanded the expulsion of Protestant Christians of »foreign blood« (baptized Jews) and the removal of »all non-German elements from church service and confession.« This group had been active since the autumn of 1932 under the direction of Nazi clergymen, and won a 70 percent victory in the church elections of July 1933.

When it became clear that even the concordat did not bring the Catholic church in Germany the protection anticipated within the totalitarian Nazi state, a new papal encyclical in 1937 »With Burning Concern« (*Mit brennender Sorge*) was a reminder of the promised special privileges: »With burning concern and growing displeasure, we have observed for some time the sufferings of the church and the growing trials of the men and women in this land and people who have stayed loyal to her in both mind and deed.«

»Those who separate the race, the people, the state, the form of government, the persons in power, or other fundamental elements of human society — elements which rightfully claim an important and honorable position within the earthly order — from the realm of such earthly values and elevate them to the highest norm of all, including religious values in worshiplike adoration, he or she distorts and falsifies the God-given and God-commanded order of things.«[5]

There are two places in which this encyclical criticizes Nazi racial ideology, but not the antisemitic agitation and persecution of the Jews. It reprimands the supremacy of the Germanic race, which was not in harmony with the Christian understanding of the Holy Scriptures of the Bible, especially the Old Testament.

Although the Jews or other victim groups are still not mentioned, the Pope now criticized Nazi racial ideology. The encyclical was read in all Catholic churches but met with very little response among the German Catholic bishops. Only two bishops, Konrad Graf Preysing in Berlin and Clemens August Graf von Galen in Münster, called — in vain — for a more decisive church policy.

The Confessional Church: Resistance on its Own Behalf

In May 1934, the Confessional Church, as an opposition movement within the Protestant Church of Germany, issued a theological declaration which stated: »... the destruction of the confession and thus of the Protestant Church in Germany both in faith and unity must be resisted. The Confessional Synod will resist the attempts to bring about the unity of the German Protestant Church through false teachings and the use of force or unclean methods. The unity of the Protestant Church of Germany can only come about through the word of God in faith through holy spirit. ... We reject the false teaching that the state, over and above its special mission, should be the only and complete arrangement of human life and thus also fulfill the role of church.«[6]

On October 20, 1934, the Barmen Declaration was followed by the Dahlem Confessional Synod.

On examining the texts it becomes clear that their concern was primarily an internal dispute about the national church (*Reichskirche*), the unity of the church, and the purity of its teachings. Not a single word is mentioned about antisemitic attacks against Jews, the oppression of Jehovah's Witnesses, communists, socialists, or other persecuted groups, thousands of whom were already confined to prisons and concentration camps, nor about how many Jews were on their way to emigration. Critical resistance was offered only by a few responsible church individuals, persons who could not count on support from their church leaders.

One minority criticized the unification of the 28 independent Protestant state churches in 1934 to make »one state church (*Reichskirche*) under one Reich bishop.«

»Only a minority — more or less the members of the second preliminary leadership of the Confessional Church — ventured to go beyond this internal church dispute. This protest within the Confessional Church should not be concealed but noted as a matter of fact. Research about the resistance of the Confessional Church has shown how heterogeneous it was and that its readiness to be critical against the regime in attitude and action varied a great deal.«[7]

In 1935, those Protestant Churches that were part of the Confessional Church preached from their pulpits against »racial-national ideology,« but in the end believers were mostly admonished to obedience to secular authority. Only in a paper written by the »radical wing« of the Confessional Church — and not by the Confessional Church as a whole — is condemnation of antisemitism, arbitrary Gestapo actions, and the existence of concentration camps expressed.

There were protests against German neo-paganism and the ideology of a *völkisch* religion and Germanic-pagan deism, or a deification of Hitler. Subsequently 500 clergymen were temporarily arrested.

The researcher on antisemitism, Wolfgang Benz, reached the following conclusion in his study *Widerstand im Nationalsozialismus* [Resistance under National Socialism] (Bundeszentrale für politische Bildung, 1994): »Neither when the Nuremberg laws in September 1935 deprived German Jews of their civil rights, nor during the 1938 November pogrom (Crystal Night on November 9), did the churches as public institutions protest in a united and powerful way.«

Altogether, during the entire Nazi regime, about 900 Protestant Christians (clergy as well as laity) were arrested and sentenced because of faith-based resistance. They were put in prisons or in concentration camps, and twelve individuals were executed for religious reasons.

To this day, a small group of Protestant Christians around the minister and theologian Martin Niemöller (1892–1984), a leading member of the Confessional Church, stand out. In the autumn of 1933, when the so-called Aryan paragraph was also introduced in the churches, he founded the *Pfarrernotbund*, an organization to aid fellow clergymen, which 6,000 ministers joined by the end of the year. In 1937 he was sent to a concentration camp where he remained incarcerated until the end of the Nazi regime. This is where he witnessed the steadfastness of Jehovah's Witnesses. He remembers this in his book »*Ach Gott vom Himmel sieh darein: Sechs Predigten*« [Oh God, Look Down From Heaven: Six Sermons][8] published shortly after the war: »And we Christians of today stand ashamed before a so-called sect like the Earnest Bible Students [Jehovah's Witnesses], who by the hundreds and thousands went into concentration camps and [even] died because they declined service in war and refused to fire on humans. In this, as in many other matters, it should now be clear that precisely we, the Church and Christians, today are called to penance and repentance if we would continue to preach God's word and represent his cause!«

Another solitary warrior was the Catholic priest, Max Joseph Metzger, who in 1943 wrote a »manifesto for a new Germany« demanding the reconciliation of peoples, world peace, and a democratic, Christian, antimilitary and socially committed Germany. However, nothing is mentioned in this manifesto for the defense of Jews.

In all, it can be said that the protest of the two major churches was articulated especially in their own cause, and only individual clergymen explicitly spoke up in public against the persecution of the Jews. In the first place, their concern was the defense of institutional and religious claims of the two established churches against the totalitarian state. Personalities like the Catholic dean of the Berlin cathedral Bernhard Lichtenberg, the Protestant theologian Dietrich Bonhoeffer, and the priest Heinrich Grüber, who openly fought for persecuted Jews, remained exceptions. The great majority of Protestant Christians joined the Nazi regime.

Political and religious resistance groups like communists, socialists, Pfarrernotbund, and the Confessional Church were first of all fighting for their own interests, their own existence, and their own bid for power.

Thus, Wolfgang Benz concludes in his above-mentioned study *Widerstand im Nationalsozialismus*: »Resistance in the political sense, with the intention of overthrowing the Nazi regime, was never implemented by the Confessional Church as a whole. It was fighting first for the integrity of its own organizational structure, and then for the independence of its church teaching, according to which the Christian commandments could never be subjected to Nazi ideology.«

Religious Persecution in History

There was one Christian group which rejected the Nazi state without compromise: Jehovah's Witnesses, or Earnest Bible Students as they were then known. This Christian denomination, which totaled 25,000 members in Germany, was already banned in 1933, but about half of the members continued their »preaching work« underground. Jehovah's Witnesses refused to say »Heil Hitler,« refused to participate in marches, refused to sing the national anthem and the Horst Wessel song, and, above all, refused military service, oath to the flag, and all activities connected with the military establishment. For this, they were bitterly persecuted from the beginning of the Nazi regime. About 10,000 Jehovah's Witnesses were incarcerated. This small Christian group attempted through large-scale leaflet campaigns in 1936 and 1937 to open the eyes of the German population to the criminal character of the Nazi state and thus defend their religious interests against an unjust regime. Their religious resistance resulted in a death toll of 1,200 victims.

The persecution of Jehovah's Witnesses in the Third Reich belongs to the tradition of religious persecution in history. The very early cruel persecution of Christians in the polytheistic Roman empire and under the Persian Sasanids who had Zoroastrianism as their state religion belong to the same tradition. Later came persecutions of Christians who were against the doctrines of the early councils of the imperial church (Arians, Nestorians, Monophysites).

Another example of religious persecution is the persecution of Jews as a religious community in Europe in the late middle ages and their expulsion from Spain in the fifteenth century. The Spanish Inquisition, as well as the historical persecution of Christian sects before and after the time of German Reformation aiming at the Bogomils, Waldensians, Albigensians, Baptist movements, Unitarians, Mennonites, Quakers, and Methodists are to be mentioned in this line of religious persecutions. Since the seventeenth century, many of them emigrated to gain religious freedom in the New World of America.

Religious Resistance Interpreted and Evaluated

A religious model of interpretation can be found in the eschatological beliefs of Jehovah's Witnesses. They saw Hitler's Reich as the demonic advancement of Satan and his army. Their resistance against this was a battle against Satan for Jehovah — and they saw themselves as Jehovah's apostles, witnesses, and disciples. God had given them the mission to resist. The apocalypse (Revelation of John) had predicted the battle against evil, and now they saw the fulfillment of biblical prophecy. They did not consider the persecution directed against them as divine justice, but as the final battle (Armageddon) before the heralded Thousand Year Reign. It was a battle of the righteous against anti-Christ and against his proclaimed thousand year reign of darkness — another reflection of Satan and a test from him that had to be resisted.

Another test from Satan for these biblically fundamentalist Witnesses was the offer of signing a declaration which required one to renounce one's beliefs in return for release from the concentration camp. To them such an offer had to seem like Satans' temptation by Jesus in the New Testament, where Satan demands: »If you recognize me and reject Jehovah, you will be able to live in the earthly world, otherwise, you will remain in my power.«

In contrast to the Jews, who were God's chosen people by virtue of the old covenant, Jehovah's Witnesses saw themselves as chosen because they had accepted the true faith by an act of their own choice, which served as grounds for the new covenant.

In this fact lies the difference to the Jewish interpretation of the Holocaust as an unfathomable trial and an inescapable punishment from God.

When in 1943 and 1944 German cities were carpet-bombed and reduced to rubble, when at the end of the war the atrocities of Hitler and his followers were revealed, and when the surviving inmates of the liberated concentration camps, the horror of the gas chambers and furnaces, mountains of human hair, teeth, and bones were publicly shown to the world in international newsreels in front of the smoking ruins of the destroyed German cities, it was then that the apocalyptic idea of the Jehovah's Witnesses had become reality. The destruction of Germany, the extermination of six million Jews, had reached a metaphysical dimension.

For the surviving Jehovah's Witnesses the final battle, Armageddon, had been won. From their point of view, they had victoriously and steadfastly fought for Jehovah. Hitler and his demons had been defeated with Jehovah's help. Contrary to the established churches they had only served »one master,« and despite the many victims they had emerged from the chaos of destruction. In contrast to the Jews they saw a meaning in their persecution, their suffering, and their active but nonviolent religious battle. Their religious community had survived the Nazi regime in complete moral integrity.

A document written shortly after the collapse of the Nazi regime shows that this corresponded with the point of view of Jehovah's Witnesses themselves. The German Witness Franz Kusserow (1882–1950), who had been imprisoned by the Nazis for seven years and four months and was liberated only in 1945, wrote shortly after the end of the war to the Nazi judge of guardianship court, which had deprived him of custody of his three children: »Thus two religious and ideological creeds were facing each other: On one side, the Nazi idea built on imperfect laws made by imperfect people; on the other side, the faith of people who were loyally dedicated to God on the basis of the perfect laws of God. Which faith or ideology would win, win the final victory? Well, National Socialism is already in ruins. Those who spoke for it in bombastic and glorious terms are now branded as cowards and criminals. They were the lawmakers who stamped the study of the Holy Scriptures as a crime and put faithful men of God into prisons and concentration camps only because they were thinking and acting in obedience to the guidelines of God. Which faith will win? The answer of the Holy Scriptures is: ›The faith that has conquered the world.‹«[9]

The Declaration of June 25, 1933: A Textual Analysis

Only a few months after Hitler's assumption of power, the activities of Jehovah's Witnesses were banned in various states of the Reich (e.g., Bavaria and Saxony) on the basis of the decree of February 28, 1933, for »the prevention of communist acts of violence dangerous to the State« and for »the restoration of public security and order.«

On April 24 to 29, 1933, the German police and the SA seized the Watchtower printing plant in Magdeburg (Prussia). This seizure was briefly discontinued, but by the end of June the premises were again shut down — permanently. A few weeks later, twenty-five truck loads of Bibles and Bible literature printed there were publicly burned by the Nazis.

As the situation for Jehovah's Witnesses clearly continued to grow worse (on June 24, 1933,

Prussia also issued a ban on their activities), the Watch Tower Society, together with its German branch office, decided to hold a large convention in Berlin-Wilmersdorf. The 7,000 delegates in attendance adopted a Declaration which spoke out against the false charges of seditious activity and emphasized the political neutrality of Jehovah's Witnesses. This resolution was addressed to Reich Chancellor Adolf Hitler in the form of a petition, an appeal.

The churches in Germany today criticize the Witnesses that this Declaration represented an attempt by Jehovah's Witnesses to »curry the favor« of Hitler and the Nazi state, and that it included antisemitic statements. They claim that it was only after the failure of this attempt that Jehovah's Witnesses rebelled against the Nazi regime. The charges climax in the accusation that the American Watch Tower Office and its president, J. F. Rutherford, had knowingly sacrificed the German Jehovah's Witnesses and pushed them onto a road that would inevitably lead to martyrdom.

A textual analysis of the actual document examines these charges:

The excerpts and passages quoted from the Declaration create the impression that it is primarily a justification, conforming to the Nazi system, and an expression of their anti-Jewish attitude. This, however, is a falsification of the facts. From a secular point of view, the document is a »sermon« or pronouncement directed to the addressee, Reich Chancellor Hitler himself. It was a clear renunciation of secular power but assumed suggestively that surely even Hitler sought the good, that he had to seek the good. But it also proclaimed that if this should prove not to be the case, then the Reich Chancellor and Führer of the German people belonged to Satan's kingdom. Then Hitler was an enemy of Jehovah and his Witnesses. These straightforward statements left the Reich Chancellor with only two possible conclusions: Either the Declaration was the product of collective delusions by a religious group, or it was a crazy, brazen declaration of war from a Biblical David against a Goliath.

While the powerful, universal Roman Catholic Church had given the Dictator a handshake in the form of a highly political gentlemen's agreement, the concordat, here a minute Christian splinter group was blowing the trumpet of Jericho and demanded in sermon-like style, and in all seriousness, that Hitler should subject himself completely to the will of Jehovah — with the promise that they would then maintain their neutrality as they did in all other states. And although Hitler was still addressed in politely neutral terms, this small group did not hesitate to label his solvent business partner, the Roman Catholic Church, a tool of »Satan, our great enemy.«

The Witnesses repudiated the charges that they were supported by Jews or Bolsheviks — accusations whispered into the Chancellor's ears by the Church, »Satans« tool. And, in fact, the churches had long been pushing for an official ban on this »sectarian« but, above all, zealously preaching Christian denomination. Under the Weimar Republic such attempts had failed.

»Because Jehovah's Witnesses advocate only one government, God's Kingdom, some have viewed them as subversive. But nothing could be further from the truth. In imitation of Jesus' apostles, ›they are no part of this world.‹ (John 17:16) They are politically neutral. Because of their loyalty to God, they obey the laws of the respective human governments. Indeed, they are exemplary in their ›subjection to superior authorities.‹ (Romans 13:1) Never have they advocated rebellion against any human government! There is, however, a line that cannot be crossed under any circumstances. It is the line between the duty of Jehovah's Witnesses to man and their duty to God. They render to Caesar, or governments, what belongs to Caesar but to God what belongs to Him. (Matthew 22:21)«[10]

The passages from this Declaration which the churches today single out for quotation cannot rightfully be termed antisemitic or anti-Jewish; rather, they are anti-American, yet, basically anti-secular. The polemic against the Anglo-American world power with its big business and enterprises built up by »commercial« Jews must be seen in its entire context, and in judging its German version it must be kept in mind that it is a translation from the American original.

Jehovah's Witnesses were not prepared to submit to any earthly government. They maintained »strict neutrality,« and this position certainly left no room for »currying Hitler's favor.« Observe, too, that the Declaration does not address him as »Führer« and does not conclude with the words »Heil Hitler« — as was the case at that time on most official church documents addressed to state authorities.

The Declaration of June 25, 1933, contains the following clear statements:

1. refutation of the accusation that the Witnesses were financed by Jews or Communists,
2. declaration of their absolute neutrality in politics and that their activity was purely religious,
3. opposition to the (Catholic) church because it is seen as a political institution, and
4. the statement of being true followers of Jesus Christ and his disciples.

Each point is supported by quotations from the Bible as the only authority and guide for the Witnesses' behavior.

It is also interesting to note the emphatic statement from Jehovah's Witnesses that their criticism is not directed against any »honest religious teacher«; what they criticize is »wrongful religious influence in the political affairs of the state.« They cannot even be charged with disputing the teachings of other churches: »We do not object to or try to hinder anyone's teaching or believing what he desires.«

However, the anti-clerical attitude of Jehovah's Witnesses is quite clear. They explicitly mention the Catholic church and the Jesuits as their enemies. Almost naively they advertise that their »American brethren have greatly assisted in (their) work in Germany,« but that the secularization of the churches in America is reprehensible. Their seeming agreement with Hitler in their attitude towards the League of Nations, too, is rooted in their own religious world concept.

The fact that the Witnesses included end-of-the-world prophesies in their Declaration as a central teaching at a time when Hitler endeavored to build his own Millennium must have seemed, in his eyes, to be nothing less than a declaration of war.

The absence of influence by the antisemitic terminology of that time is evident from the Declaration's free and unabashed use of Old Testament quotations that include the term »Zion.« The Declaration culminates in the statement that since Jehovah's Witnesses have placed themselves on God's side, all who fight against them are bound to lose. »... but as for us, we will serve Jehovah forever.«

If Hitler ever read this Declaration personally, the result must certainly have been one of his renowned fits of rage. The words, »This brood will be exterminated in Germany!,« which according to the Witnesses he exclaimed in such a moment, have the ring of authenticity.

When the entire text of the Declaration of June 25, 1933, and the letter to Hitler are seen today in the context of the history of Jehovah's Witnesses in Nazi Germany, the history of their religious resistance, and their stand during the Holocaust, then the text does not reveal itself as an »antisemitic statement« or an attempt at »currying Hitler's favor.« These accusations emanate from contemporary church circles and are deliberate manipulations and falsifications of history, seemingly motivated by discomfort about their moral mediocrity.

At the time of the 1933 convention and much later, governments, statesmen, and diplomats from all countries had freely negotiated with Hitler and revealed their respect and reverence.

Even in 1936, when thousands had already been put into concentration camps (with Jehovah's Witnesses among the very first), the International Olympic Games were held under the emblem of the swastika.

It is possible to view, from a human point of view, the Declaration as absurd or ridiculous in its completely unrealistic judgment of the political situation. This seems to be the case with those critics from church circles who speak of strategic control of the resistance through the American headquarters of the Watch Tower Society. This is an entirely secular evaluation which reveals more about the churches' own internal condition than it contributes to the search for truth. The churches were, and are, so firmly tied up with the political and social matters of state that are themselves an integral part of the secular world. As religious institutions during the Nazi era, they were unfit to follow the commands of the Bible in a literal way, or to motivate a majority of their members to do so. Only a few persons from the two major churches, acting as individuals, were exceptions to this path.

Summary

The logic of Jehovah's Witnesses did not fit into the logic of the »rational human mind« — if it did, they would have been told that one cannot resist Hitler's dictatorship and that a nonviolent resistance on the part of a small religious group would lead to its elimination. It was the »logic of absolute faith« of a fundamentalist biblical Christian group that made possible this resistance based on faith.

It is amazing that today the churches, of all groups, are forcing a religious community to justify the resistance it made in those times, when irrefutable evidence proves that this religious group did show unique steadfastness and had to make extraordinary sacrifices.

The resistance of Jehovah's Witnesses proves two things: That even a larger group was, after all, not able to achieve something, but also, that pacifist resistance in the form of refusal was possible — and that the price for this was one's own life. That is an answer to give to those later generations who ask: Why did you not do anything?

One thing stands out clearly from the moving survivor accounts in the video documentary: There were no directions from the headquarters of the Watch Tower Society. The commands all came from the Holy Scriptures, both the Old and the New Testament.

Jehovah's Witnesses can rightfully claim to have resisted »evil.« In a literal sense of this Biblical calling they have fulfilled their own claim of being true followers of Jesus Christ, while both of the two major churches have, as they openly admit, failed terribly. It should now, six decades later, be time to show them due respect in the name of Christianity.

Without the example of this steadfast Christian group under the Nazi dictatorship, we would — after Auschwitz and the Holocaust — have to doubt whether it was possible at all to fulfill the Christian teachings of Jesus.

Notes

1 Harmagedon or Armageddon, mentioned only one time in the Revelation of John [Revelation (16:15): »And they gathered them together to the place called in Hebrew, Armageddon.«], Greek version of Hebr. »Har Meghiddohn«–Mountain of Megiddo or Mountain of Assembly of Troops.

2 *1974 Yearbook of Jehovah's Witnesses* (New York, 1973), p. 212.

3 *Im finstern Tal* (Nuremberg, 1947), p. 47.

4 Kurt Hutten, *Seher, Grübler, Enthusiasten* (Stuttgart, 1954), p. 69.

5 Cited in Georg Denzler and Volker Fabricius, eds., *Die Kirchen im Dritten Reich* (Munich, 1987), p. 124.

6 Barmen Declaration.

7 Archive report no. 7 (1997), EK Berlin-Brandenburg, *Widerstand in Berlin von 1933-1945*, p. 26.

8 Published Munich, 1946.

9 Letter from Franz Kusserow to Dr. Isphording, Salzkotten, December 3, 1945.

10 »The Holocaust. Who Spoke Out?,« *Awake!* (August 22, 1995), pp. 5f.

Dietrich Hellmund

Critical Reflection on the Video Documentary »Stand Firm Against Nazi Assault«: Propaganda or Historical Documentation?

My lecture deals with the subject of »Critical Reflection on the Video Documentary »Stand Firm Against Nazi Assault«: Propaganda or Historical Documentation?«[1]

First of all, I would like to express my thanks for being allowed to stand here at this meeting and as a Protestant Christian and Church historian, to state my views about a painful chapter of the Third Reich, which has unjustly fallen into obscurity. It has not always been the case that my opinion was sought. In 1965, when I was first interested in the history of Jehovah's Witnesses during the Nazi years, I inquired of the Watch Tower Society in New York as well as with the German branch of Jehovah's Witnesses, at that time located in Wiesbaden-Dotzheim. They did everything in their power to prevent me from getting access to the publications of the Watch Tower Society, although at first I was only interested in seeing or borrowing literature that the Society itself had published in the past decades.

Other authors, besides myself, who wanted to do research on Jehovah's Witnesses, had similar experiences.

If today I can stand and speak here on the initiative of Jehovah's Witnesses, then this may perhaps be the beginning of their opening up and also becoming more receptive towards critics on the outside. This criticism on my part is not intended to and should not demean an opposing opinion, but is rather intended as a thoughtful, helpful contribution to understand what happened at that time during the gruesome »thousand years« — a time of dictatorship, during which all who were able to act, speak, and write became guilty or ambiguous. I expressly welcome and support this beginning of cooperative research and interpretation of that dreadful time.

It should be mentioned from the first that I am speaking here not only as a church historian, who wants to shed light on the past, but also as a Christian and I recognize you, Jehovah's Witnesses, also as Christians. Please believe this. Both points. Also that which is said here »for we shall all stand before the judgment seat of God.« (Romans 14: 10-12)

With grief and melancholy and deep understanding, I thus see the sufferings of many Jehovah's Witnesses, whom the inhumane Hitler state had forced into unbelievable sufferings. In my book about the history of Jehovah's Witnesses, a dissertation published in 1972, I worded it as follows: »Jehovah's Witnesses report in gruesome detail about the unimaginable suffering in the concentration camps. Of the harassment by guards, of hunger and pestilence, of being gnawed by rats, of infestation with lice, and of the death of patient Christian sufferers. It is impossible to read this without sympathy and commiseration.«[2]

I am now assuming the prerogative, as one whose »critical reflection« is requested by the organizers, to examine this documentary critically. I will do this with seven statements, that will be documented.

Hypothesis 1: Already before 1933, the Watch Tower Society with its Jehovah's Witnesses had brought itself into a situation of explicit conflict with the state and the church.

This statement is necessary, because in literature and illustrations (including caricature) often an almost incomprehensible astonishment prevails about state and church representatives, who, with or without instructions, proceeded against individual Witnesses or the Watchtower Society.

I will begin with conflicts with the churches. In the 1920s, president Rutherford had Jehovah's Witnesses walk through the streets with sandwich-board signs. Messages such as »Religion is a Snare and a Racket« were written on those placards.[3] Whoever challenges those of a different religious opinion in this manner, must not be surprised by counter-measures by the police and courts and — even worse — about mob violence and lynching. Jehovah's Witnesses were immediately persecuted. Basically, volume 7 of *Studies in the Scriptures* by Charles Taze Russell, the first president of the Watch Tower Society, had already set the course. That was 1917! There, the church and churches were called »Babylon the Harlot,« or »daughters of harlots.« It also contained many other attacks especially against the church.

Thereafter, in this rapidly developing war-like situation against Jehovah's Witnesses much was also said and written by the churches, which can only be regretted. I do not want to comment further on the polemical literature of the Watch Tower Society, nor on the defamatory pamphlets of governmental or ideological authors. However, regarding church literature of this kind (there were also thank God tracts of a different nature), I would like to say something: I cannot apologize for it, because I did not write these outrages. But I can say to you: I am deeply ashamed of these statements.

More important for understanding the documentary »Stand Firm Against Nazi Assault« and the critical evaluation which I demand, is that the Watchtower Society under their president Rutherford had maneuvered itself long before 1933 into a situation of outright conflict and strife with *all* states, even such peaceful ones as Switzerland or Sweden, or such problematic ones as Nazi Germany.

According to Rutherford's teaching, Satan uses the financial, political, and religious power blocs for his plans. Big business, politics, and churches are said to be his compliant tools. By 1929 at the latest, the valid teaching was: A Witness is to obey only Jehovah God and Christ Jesus, but not governmental authorities. Consequently, there were situations in many countries that resulted in persecution and arrests. I maintain that if the teaching proclaimed as new light in *The Watchtower* of May 1, 1996, had been valid in 1933, which was not the religious doctrine at that time, then persecution of Jehovah's Witnesses would not have hit them as quickly or as radically. However, it would have taken place in any case because this new pagan Nazi ideology did not tolerate any other religion besides itself. The Churches soon got a taste of this somewhat later.

Hypothesis 2: In the beginnings of the Third Reich, the Watch Tower Society, i.e. the management of Jehovah's Witnesses, tried to conform to the ruling ideology, thus endeavoring to defuse the conflict which had begun to emerge. This is not stated in the documentation »Stand Firm Against Nazi Assault,« although it mentions the resolution of June 25, 1933.

Willi Pohl discusses the campaign of June 25, 1933, in »Stand Firm Against Nazi Assault«: »In this declaration we explained that we had absolutely no political goals, that our activity was purely religious, and that we wished to make use of the freedom of religion in accordance with the promise made in the party platform and also by government officials, and that, therefore, this matter of partial bans should be investigated, and they should be relifted.«

My understanding of this resolution is completely different. I read it as an attempt to compromise with the goal of making coexistence possible, to negotiate bearable conditions. At that time, not only the Jehovah's Witnesses tried this. So that you can form your own opinion, I will read several sentences from Watch Tower Society's text accompanying this document addressed to »the Honorable Chancellor,« i.e. Hitler.[4]

Quotation 1: »The presiding office of the Watch Tower Society in Brooklyn is and always was to a large degree friendly to Germany. It was for this reason that in 1918 the President of the Society and the seven members of the Board of Directors were condemned in America to 80 years imprisonment, because the President refused to use two of his journals in America for war propaganda against Germany. These two journals, The »Watch Tower« and »Bible Student,« were the only two periodicals in America which refused to engage in war propaganda against Germany and for this reason they were forbidden and suppressed in America during the war [i.e. World War I].

In the same manner the President of our Society, during the last months, has not only refused to take part in the propaganda against Germany, but he has taken position even against it, as is also emphasized in the enclosed Declaration by calling attention to the fact that those who, in America, take the lead in ›German cruelties‹ propaganda (namely business Jews and Catholics) are also the greatest persecutors of the work of our Society and of its President in America.«

Quotation 2: »At the conference it was ascertained that in relation the Bible Students of Germany the National Government of Germany there is no contradiction, but on the contrary — regarding the purely religious and unpolitical goals and efforts of the Bible Students — it is to be said that these are in full accord with the goals of the National Government of Germany regarding these matters.«

Quotation 3: »The conference of the 5,000 delegates finally manifested that the Bible Students and the Watch Tower organization respectively stand for upholding order and security of the State as well as for the furtherance of the above-mentioned high ideals of the National Government in the religious domain.«

In my opinion, this resolution is anything but a »protest against the Hitler government for their highhanded interference with the witness work of the Society.« Although this is »only« the text accompanying the resolution, and not the resolution itself, both texts together (since they were also mailed together) are not blazing protests – as interpreted in a Jehovah's Witness historical work. (*Jehovah's Witnesses in the Divine Purpose*, p. 130)[5]

For me, the resolution is a document of conformity and ingratiation. Moreover, it proves that Dr. King is *not* correct, when she is quoted on the cover blurb of the video stating: »... Jehovah's Witnesses spoke out from the beginning. They spoke out with one voice. And they spoke out with tremendous courage.« With tremendous courage — yes. With one voice? I am not certain.

Hypothesis 3: Religious associations which split away from the Watch Tower Society and no longer wanted to have anything to do with Rutherford, were also dragged into the persecution of Jehovah's Witnesses.

Only briefly: I am referring to splinter groups such as the Church of the Kingdom of God, Dawn, and the Free Bible Association (Free Bible Students). They, too, have their martyrs, although their religious convictions were not a matter of conflict as in the case of Jehovah's

Witnesses (e.g. refusal of military service and »Heil Hitler« greeting). But their persecutors treated them as Bible Students, just like the Jehovah's Witnesses, without making any differentiation. By the way, the GDR upheld these bans. »A man is judged by the company he keeps.«[6]

Hypothesis 4: A milder and more sympathetic judgment of those Jehovah's Witnesses willing to compromise and those so-called »losers« is necessary.

Two Witnesses who had special responsibilities during this time were not mentioned in the »documentary«: Balzereit and Frost.

Around 1920, Paul Balzereit became the manager of the German branch office, and in 1933 president of the German Watchtower Society. At that time, just like Rutherford, he represented the policy of conformity and willingness to compromise. He continued this in the Wilmersdorf Declaration, which was approved by the adherents. Able to escape, he organized the illegal work from Prague. In May 1935 he was arrested, and while still in prison, he was removed by Rutherford because he had not liked his behavior during the trial. He had also signed a declaration [renouncing his faith], but nevertheless was only released from Sachsenhausen concentration camp in 1938.

In my opinion, Balzereit rendered great services to the Watch Tower Society. So he deserved something better than this treatment by Rutherford.

Also Erich Frost, branch servant after 1945, deserves empathy. He stated in *The Watchtower* that he had been able to remain silent during his arrest in 1937 despite SS tortures and abuse, and that he did not betray any important information to the police. He could protect the lives and freedom of coreligionists. However, Gestapo interrogation protocols discovered after the war reveal that: Frost revealed the meeting places and tasks of his eight district servants; consequently, one of them, Karl Siebeneichler, lost his life in Sachsenhausen concentration camp. (*Der Spiegel*, July 19, 1961)

Also Frost deserves our compassion, not our contempt, based on understanding, because of his many services for the Watch Tower Society. Who is there among us who could say: I can resist the torture of the Gestapo!? By the way, in the case of Frost, we have testimony from a survivor. As a historical document, it has worn out. Who would swear that this is only an isolated example?[7]

This also applies to a considerable group of unnamed Jehovah's Witnesses, who had been faithful for a long time, but then, for example, by their signature, succumbed to pressure. Parents, for example, who shortly before being sent to the concentration camp also confronted the loss of their right to raise their own children! Their own children, forcibly adopted by Nazi parents, a ghastly idea. [I urge you to] have more understanding for these parents who became weak! Of how much value is a religious witness to the outside if I can no longer tell it to my own children anymore?! There there was no decision between good and evil — that is easy — but between bad and worse. Both behavior patterns can be Biblically substantiated! In my understanding of the Bible, in such cases only the conscience of the affected person can decide; no religious association can relieve a person from such deliberation and decision.

I am deeply touched by the fate of one person that was told to me at the Wewelsburg conference a couple of days ago. It is described in a letter to the Watchtower Society written by Mr. Hans Eduard Winkler on September 18, 1995: There was a political prisoner in a work crew to which several Jehovah's Witnesses had also been assigned. Again, it was April 20, Hitler's birthday. For this festive occasion, the SS improved the extremely scarce food provisions a little bit. Each person was to receive a piece of blood sausage! Jehovah's Witnesses refused to accept this feast from the SS, because of Hitler's birthday and because it was blood sausage. The SS guards became furious. For several days all the food was taken away from the entire work crew, not only from Jehovah's Witnesses, and fed to pigs.

Many who did not share this religious decision of conscience suffered, this is certainly not an isolated case. Was that wise, was it Christian, was this brotherly love? — the »political prisoners« and criminals asked themselves. If you did not want to eat blood sausage, you could have given it to us, your fellow prisoners. Where is brotherly love? Here, showing no consideration, other political prisoners, already on the verge of starving to death, were made to suffer even more hardships!

Let me make this clear: I am interested in the *external impact* of this »firm stand against Nazi assault.« If being a Christian in the concentration camps entails disastrous as well as unintentional side effects for others, we make our love of neighbors and love for God utterly pointless for outsiders. These proceedings, known to the Watch Tower Society, and their omission, clearly shows the bias of this film documentary. It certainly is not a propaganda movie, but for me, it is a skillfully documented apologia: a document of rationalization, a defense film.[8]

Hypothesis 5: It is essential to retract incorrect estimates of the ideology of the Third Reich. For example, Watchtower publications talk »about gruesome treatment of Jehovah's Witnesses by the Roman Catholic Hierarchy and their allies in Germany« or »The Hitler government, which was supported and influenced by the Roman Catholic Hierarchy ...« The truth is that National Socialism was a dictatorial ideology in its own right, a personality cult of the purest kind, the godlike veneration of a psychopath who had come to power. »Heil Hitler!« — is all that needs to be said! Salvation by Hitler!

Hypotheses 6: We do not yet have all available sources.

The history of Jehovah's Witnesses in the Third Reich is still only partially researched. We still do not know all the records left from the Third Reich (for example on the subject of art plundered by the Russians). Also we still do not know the considerations and models which the Watch Tower Society in New York, and especially their president Rutherford, had planned and attempted.

In short: Nearly 60 to 70 years after these events, the Governing Body of Jehovah's Witnesses is called upon to open their archives in New York in order to make their protocols and records available for historical research. Finally because of this long time, none of the responsible individuals, who participated in decision-making or about whom decisions were made, would still be alive anyway. So I ask the Watch Tower Society: Open your archives!

Hypothesis 7: Also incorrect retroactive interpretations about operations during the Nazi period need to be revised in the history of Jehovah's Witnesses.

Those who suffered even more than Jehovah's Witnesses were the Jews. There was only one judgement for them: The »Final Solution,« meant the extermination of Jews for racial reasons. Despite explicit knowledge of these circumstances, the Jehovah's Witness book *Let God Be True,* English edition 1946, (German edition 1948), stated about the Jews: »Many of their sufferings they inflicted upon themselves by their profit-seeking and rebellious conduct.« (page 224) This sentence after the Holocaust! It is then far too little when this sentence is silently deleted in the (probably compelled) second edition of this book. That is far too little for me.

Here, the historiography of Jehovah's Witnesses does great wrong to those who were imprisoned with them in the concentration camps. This should be openly stated fifty years afterwards and admit one's guilt! This was done by my own Protestant church, of necessity, in the form of the Stuttgart Declaration of Guilt (with comparable statements and omissions).[9]

In conclusion, I would like to quote a few sentences from my book about the ›History of Jehovah's Witnesses,‹ published in 1972. I used these lines as my conclusion about the sufferings of Jehovah's Witnesses during the Third Reich: »Their religious steadfastness in the camps received general admiration, as well as special privileges from the SS. They were known for being willing, honest, reliable, and easy to direct. Thus, their guards often liked to use them as cheap, reliable workers in their homes.

»In these special privileges lay the secret of the high number of survivors, because these jobs as trusties in the homes of SS officers often meant better labor conditions than usual, and a little extra food rations from time to time.

»Thus, despite the high mortality rate in the concentration camps, statistics reveal ›only‹ a maximum of 2,000 deaths among Jehovah's Witnesses. And this among a group that had been imprisoned since 1934. In comparison the survival rate of the Jews is much lower. And that, although their persecution first became acute with Kristallnacht (i.e., in 1938!).

»With these statements I do not wish to challenge the tremendous sufferings of Jehovah's Witnesses in the concentration camps. They were so great, that in the eyes of many, the opinion was: ›According to the consensus of fellow prisoners, Jehovah's Witnesses were subject to the worst treatment in the camps.‹ (*Jehovah's Witnesses in the Divine Purpose*, p. 171)

»This is the opinion of one eyewitness. It is understandable, but wrong. There was never a command to exterminate them as there was for the Jews, Sinti and Roma (›Gypsies‹), and mentally ill persons. There were millions who fared worse, and who could report about much greater martyrdom, if this crowd of witnesses would not be forever silent. These millions were gassed, a fate from which almost all Jehovah's Witnesses had been spared.

»However, if we would attribute the protection of so many Jehovah's Witnesses to small privileges and extermination commands that were never issued, we would close our eyes to a decisive fact. It is the Lord God, who protected these Jehovah's Witnesses. It is Jesus Christ who acknowledges those who are His. *All* of his Christians.«

I would like to add: No matter to which religious community they belong.

Notes

1 Slightly revised manuscript of my presentation at the Hamburg City Historical Museum, October 8, 1997.

2 Dietrich Hellmund, *Geschichte der Zeugen Jehovas in der Zeit von 1870 bis 1920*, with an appendix *Geschichte der Zeugen Jehovas in Deutschland bis 1970*. Theology dissertation, Hamburg, 1972.

3 Based on W. J. Schnell, *Falsche Zeugen stehen wider mich*, 2nd ed. (Konstanz, 1960), 105ff.

4 Quotations based on Günther Pape, *Die Wahrheit über Zeugen Jehovas: Problematik, Dokumentation* (Rottweil, 1970), 137ff.

5 Spokesmen for the Public Affairs Office of Jehovah's Witnesses emphasized that the text discussed was the accompanying letter and not the resolution itself. I can confirm the facts and have included it in this essay. But the problem is that this doesn't resolve the content problem: the contrast of both texts reveals that the leadership of Jehovah's Witnesses uses another language with those in power than with its members, who never realized the content of the accompanying letter. Moreover, we must keep in mind that this accompanying letter was at first and perhaps only read to interpret the resolution.

6 Jehovah's Witnesses place special significance that because of their characteristics, they were the only religious association to receive special markings, the purple triangle, in concentration camps. Criminals were assigned a green triangle, political prisoners a red triangle. Protestants in the camps, such as Niemöller, Lilje, and Bonhoeffer, were included with the »politicals« and wore a red triangle. These facts mean that Jehovah's Witnesses were not the only religious association given a purple marking, but that also the Free Bible Students (Freien Bibelforscher) received this marking. These facts must still be researched in detail. But if these facts are corroborated: the others were only a very small marginal group.

7 In subsequent private conversation, I received information from the Public Affairs Office of Jehovah's Witnesses that the Gestapo interrogation protocol was possibly distorted by the Stasi. In my opinion, this unproven possibility is relevant. My source received the Gestapo protocol anonymously by mail. Perhaps this also applies to *Der Spiegel*, who first published this material.

8 In contrast to today's standard Marxist usage (as, for example, »the apologists of capitalism«), I am using the term »apology« in a positive way as in Christian theology: First century Christians – the apologists – wrote defense texts, »apologetics,« in which they attempted to make their beliefs clear to non-Christian contemporaries. Moreover, there is a famous Protestant declaration of faith, »Apologia for the Augsburg confession.« (Every priest is required to take this oath on installation in office.) Therefore, this is an appropriate label for the »documentary.«

9 In the subsequent podium discussion, I was astonished at the silence about this antisemitic sentence by the two participating Holocaust specialists. Sybil Milton and Henry Friedlander presented papers and were also present during my presentation.

Lutz Lemhöfer

Between Historical Documentation and Public Promotion of One's Image

Comments About the Watch Tower Society Film: »Stand Firm Against Nazi Assault«

During the past few years, historical research has to a greater extent turned its attention to smaller, formerly rarely considered, groups of Nazi victims. Among them are Jehovah's Witnesses, who suffered especially severe persecution by the Nazi state. In addition to regional studies, which describe the fate of Jehovah's Witnesses in individual regions or in individual concentration camps, the unparalleled precision of the study by Detlef Garbe must be mentioned: *Zwischen Widerstand und Martyrium: Die Zeugen Jehovas im »Dritten Reich,«* [Between Resistance and Martyrdom: Jehovah's Witnesses in the Third Reich] published in Munich in 1993. This volume is unsurpassed in its accuracy and extensive treatment of the subject. But also Jehovah's Witnesses themselves, or rather their organization, the Watch Tower Society, has taken charge of a wide presentation of their persecution and fate during the Nazi period. The traveling exhibition »Jehovah's Witnesses Stand Firm Against Nazi Assault« was produced by the Watch Tower Society. This exhibition and a video bearing the same title are part of these presentations. The video was and still is shown in connection with this exhibition, and is also offered as a historical documentary to schools and other educational institutions. Just like the exhibition, the film wants to inform the general public about the sufferings and the courage of Jehovah's Witnesses in prisons and concentration camps. It achieves this successfully and is partly very poignant when individual survivors share their past experiences. However, the film has obvious deficiencies in analysis. If these are now specified, they should not and must not detract from respect for the victims.

1. The Stylization of a Unified Resistance

Throughout the film, Jehovah's Witnesses are presented as a completely unified and unanimous group, acting and reacting heroically. This interpretation can also be found in some historical literature and, thus, is voiced in the film as well. The British historian, Christine King, for example, is quoted as saying that Jehovah's Witnesses resisted the Nazis »from the beginning...with one voice. And they spoke out with tremendous courage,« their position was »very clear right from the very beginning.« However, researchers also hold another viewpoint. Especially during the first months after the Nazi assumption of power, both the headquarters of the Watch Tower Society in Brooklyn and the German branch office in Magdeburg made an attempt to protect the religious activities of Jehovah's Witnesses through verbal conformity. On the other hand, many Jehovah's Witnesses considered the Nazi state — like all other forms of government — to be satanic, and displayed correspondingly uncompromising attitude and conduct. The former Witness, Günther Pape (*Ich war Zeuge Jehovas*, Augsburg 1993, pp. 8f), for example, remembers how in his home village of Thale/Harz, the local congregation was divided after a quarrel over the question of whether or not Jehovah's Witnesses should continue to be active in missionary work. »In Thale, the local overseer spoke out against it, my father, however, spoke for it. He took over as head of the congregation. The result — a further split.« Also Detlef Garbe observed in his study that this was not an isolated case: »Now, the movement faced a gruelling test: the management acting according to the maxim ›save what can be saved‹ of loyal communities of Bible Students, warning against any provocation of the authorities; on the other hand, those with uncompromising beliefs who intended to openly oppose Satan's powers. In several International Bible Student Association communities, supporters confronted opponents of the Madgeburg headquarters' conciliatory course. Subsequently they separated. For example, this was the case in Flensburg, Kiel, and Neumünster.« (Garbe, p. 115) However, the video conceals this sort of differentiation; interpretations by academics, such as that quoted from Garbe are not included. Here, historical accuracy is sacrificed in favor of the myth of *complete* uniformity. And yet, the initial uncertainty of the Witnesses regarding the proper tactical conduct towards the Nazis is by no means shameful. Various social groups, including the trade unions and even the major churches, initially evaluated Nazism in an inconsistent and partly naive manner. Nobody born later should blame persons for misjudgments in 1933, because these can only be definitely evaluated afterwards from a historical distance. Also, during the first years of the Nazi dictatorship, many members of the political resistance underestimated Nazi viciousness and aggressiveness. Thus Jehovah's Witnesses are not to be blamed for their uncertainty, but for their refusal to address this openly in the video.

2. Concealed Attempts at Conformity

Something similar applies to the sympathetic presentation of the large mass meeting of Jehovah's Witnesses in Berlin on June 25, 1933. The German office and the president of the Watchtower Society, Rutherford, had prepared this mass event with about 5,000 to 7,000 Witnesses attending. They adopted a declaration urging government authorities to end discrimination against Jehovah's Witnesses since, as it explicitly states, »political clergy, priests, and Jesuits« had unjustly accused them. According to the document, the charge that Jehovah's Witnesses were hostile to the state was inaccurate. Instead the declaration pointed out similarities with the new rulers: »A careful examination of our books and literature will disclose the fact that the highest ideals held and promulgated by the present national government are set forth in and endorsed, and strongly emphasized in our publications. ... Instead, therefore, of our literature and our work's being a menace to the principles of the present government we are the strongest supporters of such high ideals.« Further it explained that Jehovah's Witnesses did not receive support from the Jews as was falsely claimed by Nazi propaganda. This clarification, however, is followed by comments, which attempt to adapt to Nazi anti-Jewish and anti-American indignation. »The greatest and the most oppressive empire on earth is the Anglo-American Empire. ... It has been the commercial Jews of the British-American Empire who have built up and carried on Big Business as a means of exploiting and oppressing the peoples of many nations.« Similarly, the letter addressed to Hitler that accompanied the Declaration, also pointed to the overwhelmingly pro-German attitude of the international Watch Tower Society. At the same time, other groups were blamed for the anti-German »atrocity propaganda in America«: »commercial Jews and Catholics.« On April 26, 1933, in the name of the *Norddeutsche Bibelforschervereinigung* [North German Bible Students Association] and the *Süddeutsche Bibelforschervereinigung* [South German Bible Students Association], the legal adviser of the Watch Tower Society had already deemed it necessary to point out that in the new name of the association (with the deletion of the title »International Bible Students Association«) »only German citizens were members and held leading positions.« In the same letter, a clear distinction was drawn between them and Communism, in line with religious beliefs of Jehovah's Witnesses, but no longer exhibiting much political neutrality. According to Detlef Garbe, »it became clear that the course of conformity did not leave their former religious self-image undamaged, but rather affected its substance: Everyone who intended to get on good terms with the high and mighty of the ›old world‹ through such actions had left their self-stated ›neutrality‹ far behind.« (Garbe, p. 100) In the *1974 Yearbook of Jehovah's Witnesses*, the Declaration of June 25, 1933, was still presented as controversial. (pp. 110f.) It stated there: »Many in attendance were disappointed in the ›declaration,‹ since in many points it failed to be as strong as the brothers had hoped. ... It was not the first time that Brother Balzereit had watered down the clear and unmistakable language of the Society's publications to avoid difficulties with government agencies. A large number of brothers refused to adopt it just for this reason. ... The conventioneers returned home tired and many were disappointed. ... Even though the declaration had been weakened and many of the brothers could not wholeheartedly agree to its adoption, yet the government was enraged and started a wave of persecution against those who had distributed it.« The video does not speak of this controversy. Instead, the declaration is plainly interpreted as an act of resistance. This would be totally legitimate in an apologetic self-depiction. But in a documentary, which claims to be scientific, different existing interpretations should be contrasted so that the observer can reach his own conclusion. Again: The point is not to reproach the protagonists of that time from a subsequent secure and safe place. Other social groups, particularly the major churches, also made attempts to secure greater concessions by partial conformity. For example, this applies to the concordat between the German Reich and the Holy See on July 20, 1933, which many have interpreted as moral recognition of Hitler's regime. But other historians still claim it was an example of nonconformity to secure legal positions. This interpretation had already been controversial among the contemporaries within the church, and is still contested today. Thus it is all the more important to present both positions, to open the way for discussion. Despite this partial attempt at conformity, it remains undisputed that the persecution of Jehovah's Witnesses started more rapidly, proceeded more brutally, and ended more bloodily than was the case with any other religious group. And it is unquestioned that attempts for conformity by the Watch Tower Society did not occur after 1933.

3. The Churches as a Dark Background for a Dazzling Self-portrayal

In contrast to the consistent heroic portrayal of Jehovah's Witnesses, the major churches are also consistently depicted as forerunners and agents of Nazi dictatorship. Although the film does not focus on this, it is nevertheless a subliminal background theme. If reference is made to the churches, it is done with exclusively negative undertones. It portrays the war sermons of 1914–1918 as driving disappointed soldiers into Hitler's arms. This is, no doubt, one mosaic in the development of the Nazi movement, but certainly not the only one. At another point, an interview with an historian about the church's approval of prohibitions against Jehovah's Witnesses is underlined with photographic stills of clergy raising their hands in the Hitler salute. The date and circumstances of the picture are not given. The unspoken message is: Not only in connection with prohibitions against Jehovah's Witnesses but also more broadly, the churches were in agreement with the ›brown‹ rulers. Individuals from the church's resistance are only quoted if they have words of praise for the Witnesses. Reprehensible blunders by the churches are mentioned, such as the official authorities' silence about the November pogrom in 1938. Not a single word is mentioned to show that from 1933 to 1938, conflicts between the Nazi State and the Catholic as well as the confessing Protestant church had increased enormously. For example, Pope Pius XI condemned Nazi racial ideology in 1937 with the encyclical »With Burning Anxiety« (*Mit brennender Sorge*), although it was expressed in roundabout ecclesiastic and theological language. Here, by using individual, absolutely legitimate points of criticism, a distorted overall picture of the relationship of the main Christian churches to the Nazi state is presented. The open-minded viewer of this film gets the impression that Jehovah's Witnesses were not only the most determined, but also the only religiously motivated resistance group. And the main churches not only seem to be weak and mealy-mouthed, but appear to be compliant agents of the regime. This point of view is traditional with the Watch Tower Society. In a complete misreading of the real historical context, the Catholic church was presented particularly as directly pulling the strings of Nazi machinations during the 1930s. Consequently, in September 1936 a convention of Jehovah's Witnesses in Lucerne protested against the »cruel treatment of Jehovah's Witnesses by the Roman Catholic hierarchy and their allies in Germany and in all parts of the earth.« A few months later, the president of the Watch Tower Society, Rutherford, published a book with the straighforward title *Enemies*. Detlef Garbe wrote about this: »The president of the Watchtower Society completely subordinated current events to his dichotomous view of the world and the idea that the decisive final battle had already started: Everything centered only around the great contradiction, the one between Jehovah's organization and that of Satan's organization led by the ›Roman Catholic hierarchy,‹ since ›the inhabitants of the earth‹ were ›subject to either one or the other of both these organizations.‹« (Garbe, p. 242) The fact that at the same time the Nazi state also limited the Catholic churches sphere of action, and that priests were also brought before the same special courts as Jehovah's Witnesses because of »disloyalty« (*Heimtücke*) did not prevent [the Witnesses] from viewing Hitler's government as being ›in full agreement with the Vatican in Rome‹ and to explain the Jesuits who had been disqualified as ›unfit for military service‹ and defamed by the Nazis, as secret manipulators of Hitler as their puppet. *The Watchtower* of August 22, 1995, without any explanation, reprinted a contemporary caricature from the 1930s illustrating a voluptuous, dolled-up beauty with the Pope's crown on her head, who is cuddling and cooing with a Devil in an SS uniform, recognizable by horns, and a sword with the inscription »terrorism« in his hand. (At least to interested visitors of the exhibition in Frankfurt, this issue of *The Watchtower* was made available instead of a catalog.) Also in the book »Jehovas Zeugen – Verkündiger des Königreiches Gottes« [Jehovah's Witnesses – Proclaimers of God's Kingdom] published in German in 1993, this legend is developed further without a clear bibliographical reference. Thus, on pp. 659f. an (anonymous) Catholic priest is quoted who reported requests from German bishops to Hitler to suppress Jehovah's Witnesses; Hitler ostensibly complied with these wishes and emphasized that he would not tolerate besmirching German Catholics by the American judge Rutherford. The newspaper quoted, *Der Deutsche Weg*, is not a church periodical, but the journal of the German minority in Poland sympathetic to Nazi ideology. Neither the priest's statement nor Hitler's alleged declaration are documented in any way. Nevertheless, these weak historical sources are supposed to support a historical assessment.

The video »Stand Firm Against Nazi Assault« presents a stereotyped portrayal of the history of the 1930s in what it says and conceals about the churches. This is historically incorrect. However, it offers the possibility of presenting one's own resistance in a brighter light and in sharper contrast against the dark antithesis of the churches. At this point less would have been more, since the courage of the Witnesses against Nazi dictatorship, frequently and impressively documented in this film, does not require such artifice.

4. Legitimate Function of Writing History

Historical self-portrayal of a group seldom springs only from interest in finding out what really occurred. Often history is used as a justification for current claims and demands. This is true not only for Jehovah's Witnesses. In the former GDR, historical research and museum education blatantly attempted to prove the leading role of the working class, and also their supposed major role in antifascist resistance. Because of opposite interests in the Federal Republic of Germany, West German historiography recognized and acknowledged the significance and role of the Communist resistance against the Nazi regime only belatedly. And it was not before the 1960s and 1970s that the major churches wrote about their contradictory position between involvement and protest under Nazi dictatorship. Immediately after the war, the Catholic church wrote their own history, seeing particularly heroes and saints among its own ranks. Despite the Stuttgart Declaration of Guilt, the Protestant church to a large extent simply adopted the tradition of the Confessional Church, although the Confessional church had been a minority between 1933 and 1945. Without a doubt, this presentation (by no means used as a tactic, but out of belief) served to buttress church claims for leading positions in rebuilding a democracy in Germany and to have a lasting influence on the legislation. The past had shown where a godless and antichurch policy leads. Therefore, it is not unusual that the first extensive and publicly effective self-portrayal of the history of the persecution of Jehovah's Witnesses is accompanied and characterized by a similar undertone of justification. References to the victims of the past is intended to promote a more positive attitude toward Jehovah's Witnesses in the present. At the same time, there are undertones in the public presentations of the exhibition as well as in the video which relate the present criticism of Jehovah's Witnesses to past persecution in order to silence today's critics. Some critics probably have this in mind when they speak of »instrumentalizing (using) the victims.« Of course, this criticism is not directed against the contents of the film »Stand Firm Against Nazi Assault,« but against the way it is used in public.

It would be necessary to hold this debate publicly, rather than hidden, and thereby make the distinction between honoring the victims and reflecting on their motives. All opponents and victims of the Nazis deserve high esteem and respect — even if one does not share their motives and goals. In the torture chambers, the Nazis mistreated political opponents of differing views: monarchists, democrats, stalinists, and many others. Honoring their resistance against the Nazi dictatorship does not mean approving monarchist and stalinist positions. This also applies to the religiously motivated opponents of National Socialism. The uncompromising refusal of Jehovah's Witnesses to the Nazi state (after the previously mentioned short phase of accommodation and hesitancy) is to be honored. The men and women who suffered for their refusal are also to be honored. Nevertheless, room must be allowed for discussion as to whether or not the strict neutrality claimed by Jehovah's Witnesses, which at the same time excluded participation in any political revolutionary attempts or political resistance, represents an appropriate Christian position.

5. Conclusion

The video documentary »Stand Firm Against Nazi Assault« is important because it preserves the history of a small but unusually courageous group of persecutees from oblivion. It is important to let the voices of survivors speak, since they will no longer be able to testify in a few years. It is important to remember the cruelty of the Nazi dictatorship toward a comparatively small and helpless minority, which can hardly be understood by the rational mind. The film contributes to this. Nevertheless, it still must be stressed that this is not a critical-analytic work, but a historical self-portrayal of a group with explicit apologetic tendencies. The fact that also non-Witnesses speak, when their statements support the self-image of the group, does not change this. Critical statements, including those from the academics quoted in the film, are not mentioned. No room is given to controversies or even to different interpretations of the events that are shown. This clearly reduces the value of the documentary. This is to be regretted, especially since a presentation of the history of persecution of Jehovah's Witnesses, with so many touching details and individual fates, has not existed until now. Perhaps a later documentary will succeed in bringing sensitive empathy and the necessary critical distance into a more balanced relationship.

Wolfram Slupina

»Jehovah's Witnesses Stand Firm Against Nazi Assault«—Touring Exhibitions and Video Presentations, 1996–2000

Increased public interest in the religious association of Jehovah's Witnesses has been seen, especially since the ruling of the Administrative Court in Berlin on October 25, 1993, about defining the legal status of Jehovah's Witnesses and the appeal by the Berlin Senate; the original ruling was confirmed by the Berlin Higher Administrative Court on December 14, 1995, and again appealed by the Berlin Senate.[1]

In order to meet these expectations the Public Affairs Department of Jehovah's Witnesses in Selters was formed on January 5, 1996.[2] It was to serve as the contact point for special themes and questions by the public.[3]

To increase and centralize their own historical research about Jehovah's Witnesses in Europe, a historical archive was created in April 1996 in the German branch at Selters/Taunus. One year later, this department was attached to the Public Affairs Office. The History Archive of the Watch Tower Society strives to cooperate with other archives and memorials.

The Public Affairs Departement participated in the 1996 world premiere of the documentary video »Jehovah's Witnesses Stand Firm Against Nazi Assault« at the Ravensbrück Memorial, 60 km north of Berlin, on November 6, 1996, which was attended by numerous public officials and survivors.[4] Before this event, the press was invited to attend a press conference in Sorat, Hotel Humboldt-Mühle, in Berlin-Tegel. In addition to a 20-minute excerpt from the »Stand Firm« documentary and brief presentations by the historian and Director of the Neuengamme Memorial, Detlef Garbe, and the historian and Director of the Wewelsburg District Museum, Wulff Brebeck, the focus was on the survivors Simone Liebster and Franz Wohlfahrt, who were also interviewed in the video.[5]

During the premiere that followed that afternoon, Angelika Peter, Minister for Education, Youth, and Sport in Brandenburg, stated: »Jehovah's Witnesses were prohibited by the Nazis even in 1933, because they utterly rejected any oath to the Third Reich and refused military service. This meant under the then prevailing beliefs that they refused loyalty to the Nazi state and its leader. Consequently, they became vulnerable to persecution and tribulations. ... There were repeated attempts to compel them to perform military service. Most of them remained steadfast and refused, despite coercion, to serve the Third Reich in any way. It is correct and necessary that we remember them today. We should not remain silent about their suffering, nor–worse still–simply forget. It is just and important that today we remember the exemplary unwavering stand of Jehovah's Witnesses. Because it was right to reject that unjust system under all circumstances, and this applies to us, even more so if we have reasons not to share the beliefs of Jehovah's Witnesses.«

An audience of 350 attended the premiere at Ravensbrück. This occasion was reported by the press and television. One hundred articles appeared throughout Germany.[6] Claudia Lepping reported in the Berlin *Tagesspiegel* under the headline »A New Chapter About Forgotten

Victims of the Nazi Regime: Jehovah's Witness Document the Persecution of Bible Students in the Third Reich.« She stated: »The historian Garbe, who as Director of the Hamburg-Neuengamme Memorial has tried to research the many smaller groups of victims … demanded that his colleagues give up their longstanding disinterest about this subject. Jehovah's Witnesses shared the fate of other groups of Nazi victims, who like them–even after 1945 were socially marginalized, as for example the Sinti and Roma. In this way, they are ›forgotten victims‹ of the Nazi regime.«[7]

Up to January 16, 1997, nearly two and a half months later, newspapers still wrote about the video premiere, particularly if historical research with survivors established a local connection.[8] The premiere also resulted in the television program »Witnesses Under the Swastika: Stand Firm Against Nazi Assault,« on Deutsche Welle Berlin on November 16, 1996.[9]

One day after the video premiere in Ravensbrück, i.e., on November 7, 1996, a video screening was held at the Technical University of Berlin, attracting an audience of 220 people. The host was the Center for Antisemitism of the Technical University. Uni-radio in Berlin reported about this event on November 7, 1996.[10]

This film documentary enabled a wider audience to learn about survivor experiences in various concentration camps, supplemented by valuable background information by internationally recognized historians and academics, without religious indoctrination.

The topicality of this subject was emphasized by the Bundestag event on January 19, 1996, for the establishment of the future Memorial Day for the Victims of National Socialism. The date of January 27, the liberation of Auschwitz, was chosen. On the occasion of this event, former President of the German Bundestag, Professor Dr. Rita Süssmuth, stated: »Memorial days provide no guarantee against amnesia. Whether they influence what one expects, depends on whether it is personally important for us and whether it can be transmitted to subsequent generations. … In remembering the dignity of the victims, we are challenged to increase future generations' conscience for justice and injustice, for tolerance and intolerance, for the value of every life, its dignity, and right to freedom. … In remembering the years of inhumanity in Germany, we are alerted against complacency. … If we have learned anything from the Nazi era of dictatorship, it is that above all we must decisively resist every form of barbarism, latent in all communities, and its greatest allies, namely, indifference, laziness, cowardice, and the absence of individual courage.«[11]

Former Federal President Professor Dr. Roman Herzog emphatically recalled on the occasion of this event that »today we might actually forget, since survivors are dying, and there are fewer victims who can personally describe the horror of their sufferings. History fades rapidly if it was not part of one's own personal experiences. Therefore we must make the memory part of a vivid future. We do not want to conserve our horror, we want to learn lessons that can serve as direction for future generations. … If we were to delete these memories, then we would be the first victims of our own self-deception.«[12] In order to combat this danger, the U.S. Holocaust Memorial Museum in Washington, D.C., suggested research about the persecution of Jehovah's Witnesses in Nazi Germany; this resulted in the Watchtower Bible and Tract Society 78-minute video documentary »Jehovah's Witnesses Stand Firm Against Nazi Assault.« This video is now available in 28 languages and has a circulation of more than 1,085,000 copies.[13] Manufacture in eight additional languages is planned.

The *Newsletter* of the Association of Holocaust organizations states: »This excellent film on the courageous role of the Jehovah's Witnesses in protesting against the Nazi regime with great sacrifice, often with their lives, belongs in every video collection. Ten historians from Europe and North America, and more than 20 Witness survivors relate this story of courage and triumph.«[14] Steven Spielberg's Visual History of the Shoah Foundation uses »Stand Firm« as a training video for interviewers of Witness survivors. The U. S. Holocaust Memorial Museum carries this video documentary in its museum shop.

In order to prevent amnesia, both officials and the public, particularly the younger generation, requested the self-depiction of victim groups. Jehovah's Witnesses had long enough been one of the »forgotten victim groups« of the Nazi regime.[15]

A recent study in Sweden[16] revealed that a majority of students were not certain whether the Holocaust had occured as described by historians.[17] Therefore, the Swedish government in cooperation with the Swedish Teachers Association (Lärarnas Riksförbund) and school authorities began a national educational campaign with the slogan »Living History,« where Jehovah's Witnesses were also asked for support. In a catalog with the same name »Living History,« the video »Jehovah's Witnesses Stand Firm Against Nazi Assault« as well as »Purple Triangles«[18] and the film documentation »Fear Not«[19] were also recommended.[20]

Even in Germany, students knew frighteningly little about the Nazi era. The results of a Forsa survey showed that only 7 percent of the youngsters surveyed between the ages of 14 and 18 knew what had been decided at the Wannsee Conference. Only 13 percent of the students had an idea of the contents of the Nuremberg Laws, and the word Auschwitz did not mean a thing to one student in three. About half of the students had little or virtually no interest in the subject »National Socialism« and the »Third Reich.« Ca. 12 percent of those surveyed felt that information received about these topics in schools was not believable.[21]

Former Federal President Professor Dr. Roman Herzog insisted on the necessity of explaining this part of history for a younger generation in his Bundestag speech on January 19, 1996, commemorating the victims of National Socialism. He stated: »It is especially important to reach our youngsters and to intensify their understanding of potential future dangers. I am counting on the assistance of the media and especially the teachers and also the contributions of all other groups in society.«[22]

In order to explicitly illuminate these themes for younger generations, Jehovah's Witnesses have produced a 28-minute short version of the video »Jehovah's Witnesses Stand Firm Against Nazi Assault« with texts and teaching suggestions.[23] The premiere of the English version took place on January 28, 1998, in Sony Pictures Europe House in London, including survivors and historians as Professor Christine King (Vice-Chancellor of Staffordshire University), Professor of Religion Dr. Roger Homan of the University of Brighton, and representatives of the Imperial War Museum in London. The German version was released in 1999.

This »Stand Firm« video documentary is recommended for educational use as quoted in the *School Library Journal*: »This edited version ... is designed for educational use. The selected excerpts give viewers a cohesive explanation of why the Witnesses were persecuted by the Nazis, their religious beliefs, and the impact of their stand against the treatment of the Jews. Although this version is less detailed than the original, students will be able to understand it because it uses the same excellent quality film footage, photos, and documents to illustrate the historical background beginning with pre-1933. The male narrator presents a good chronological overview of the Holocaust, especially as it pertains to the Jehovah's Witnesses. Several historians and Jehovah's Witnesses survivors give testimony to that time period. Non-English dialogue is simultaneously translated by voice-over. The video presents many individual acts of courage, and contains an excellent segment on other churches' non-reaction to Kristallnacht[24] and other

Holocaust events. ... This is a good, concise presentation for middle and high school classes of a not-often studied aspect of the Holocaust.«[25]

Similarly in January 1998, a 55-minute English version of the documentary video became available for broadcast via satellite to more than 300 television stations in North America. Any station with interest ca »pull down« the program and store its for future broadcasting.

In its publication »»...die vielen Morde...‹. Dem Gedenken an die Opfer des National-sozialismus« the Berlin Institute for Advanced Educational Training [Berliner Institut für Lehrerfort- und -weiterbildung und Schulentwicklung, BIL] made the follwing interesting statement about the video documentation: »This documentation has been criticized as religious propaganda on various past occasions. However, the Landesbildstelle Berlin (Berlin State Picture and Movie Board) has come to the conclusion that the way of presentation does not differ from that of other groups of victims.«[26]

As a result of the positive response by academic experts as well as by the public to the events in Ravensbrück and Berlin, similar programs are being planned and implemented throughout Germany. The core of the program is the documentary video, connected with survivor interviews and contributions from historians and individuals in the public sector. The programs were limited strictly to historical information and deliberately excluded religious content.

A member of a South German memorials initiative, who is also a teacher of religion, wrote to the Public Affairs Department about the program he had attended at Leonberg on January 27, 1997, which drew an audience of 160 persons. »I would like to tell you about that I was pleased by the introductory and concluding presentations. ... I found the program very impressive without being pushy! The program has changed my negative prejudices toward Jehovah's Witnesses. I say this openly, even though as a teacher of religion I feel quite at home in my Protestant church. Whenever I teach about the theme of the churches who base themselves on Jesus Christ, I mention this event about the Witnesses and show excerpts of the video.«

Similar presentations occurred in many other larger cities, such as, Frankfurt am Main, Dresden, Würzburg, Stuttgart, Wiesbaden, Hanover, Kaiserslautern, Kassel, Bayreuth, Heidelberg, Kiel, Nuremberg, Karlsruhe, Hamburg, Lübeck, Mainz, Munich, Regensburg, Saarbrücken, Rosenheim, Bremen, to name but a few of the places where programs were held: until 2001, more than 500 presentations with ca. 550,000 visitors had taken place after the premiere at Ravensbrück on November 6, 1996. Jehovah's Witnesses also organized about 70 presentations throughout Germany around the remembrance day of January 27, 1997. About 30 further programs are planned for the coming months.

A Traveling Exhibition Accompanying the Documentary Video »Jehovah's Witnesses Stand Firm Against Nazi Assault«

Over 330 of the more than 500 presentations included a traveling exhibition about »Forgotten Victims.« An historical exhibition had been installed in the mid-1970s in the German headquarters of the Jehovah's Witnesses. Display cases with artifacts from former concentration camps and documents showing Witnesses as a persecuted victim group were viewed by tens of thousands of visitors. In addition to the documentation, there were statistics of the various victim groups as well as historical documents from survivors. One particular artifact was a miniature edition of the book »Jehovah« that could be concealed inside a normal box of matches,[27] and had been used for study purposes by Witnesses under Nazi persecution.[28] It was made by Richard Blümel, who had later been incarcerated by the Nazis.[29]

At the dedication of the expanded Witness headquarters in Selters/Taunus on May 14–15, 1994, the exhibition was revised and newly conceived. The history of the persecution of Jehovah's Witnesses in the Nazi era was presented on fifteen panels.

On September 29, 1994, the U.S. Holocaust Memorial Museum in Washington held a symposium about Jehovah's Witnesses under National Socialism. In France, there were two large commemorations with survivors of the concentration camps, on March 28, 1995, in Strasbourg and on March 30 in Paris. This was historically appropriate, since 1995 was the fiftieth anniversary of the liberation of the concentration camps.

Accompanying the commemorative program in France was the exhibition entitled »In Remembrance of the Witnesses 1933–1945,« designed by the European Association for Remembering Deported and Interned Jehovah's Witnesses (CETJAD) that had been founded in Paris in 1990.[30] This exhibition included 70 panels (each 108 cm x 89.5 cm in size), starting with a timetable of events—the opening of the camps in Dachau and Oranienburg, in March 1933; the Nuremberg Laws to »protect the German blood,« in September 1935; the »Anschluss« (or annexation) of Austria to Germany, in March 1938; »Kristallnacht,«[31] in November 1938; the gradual ban on Jehovah's Witnesses; the invasion of the Soviet Union, in June 1941; and the euthanasia of the mentally sick, from 1939 to 1941. Some of these panels highlighted the indoctrination of the young in the Hitler Youth and the fascination that the huge Nazi rallies in Nuremberg held for the masses. Other panels showed how Jehovah's Witnesses were the victims of disinformation and how, as of 1935, they distributed magazines and tracts exposing Nazi excesses.

From May 1995 to April 1996, this traveling exhibition was seen in 48 cities in France and Belgium as well as in French-language parts of Switzerland. It was seen by more than 100,000 people and thus found a wide acclaim among broad segments of the population.[32]

The French exhibition about Jehovah's Witnesses persecuted in the Nazi era was used as a model for the documentary exhibition produced by the Watch Tower Society in Selters/Taunus. It was first shown in the restaurant »Zur Friedenseiche« in Brandenburg from April 27–30, 1995. The official commemorative event by the state of Brandenburg was the fiftieth anniversary of the liberation of Brandenburg prison on April 27.

On November 6, 1996, about 50 panels were used to decorate the room at the Ravensbrück memorial and museum, where the world premiere of the documentary video »Jehovah's Witnesses Stand Firm Against Nazi Assault,« took place attended by numerous survivors, historians, staff of the memorial, and German public officials.

Words of greeting were sent by Minister President Manfred Stolpe of Brandenburg. Professor Dr. Jürgen Dittberner, then director of the Foundation for Memorials in Brandenburg, stated in acknowledgment: »We hold in all honor the memory of these people who did not betray their faith and who had to suffer or even die as a result.«

The exhibition panels included reproductions of documents, photographs, and statements, and include headings like »Chronology 1933–1945,« »Victims of the Nazi regime,« »Prisoner markings,« »Concentration camps,« »Brandenburg penitentiary,« »Sachsenhausen,« »Auschwitz,« »Family tragedies,« and »Evacuating the camps.«

The steel frames (200 cm x 97 cm) for the 50 exhibition panels (each 108 cm x 89.5 cm) and the lighting (12 volt halogen lamps) came originally from France. The contents of the German panels were changed and expanded. Three glass exhibition cases (concentration camp uniform with purple triangle; a cello made in a concentration camp by the survivor Georg Klohe,[33] and tools) completed the information presented on panels.

Based on the positive response, three sets of this exhibition each with 50 panels have since been produced and can be lent to accompany public film showings or other programs (as for example, at memorials). A fourth traveling exhibition with 16 panels emphasizing the persecution of Jehovah's Witnesses in Schleswig-Holstein and Hamburg also serves the same purpose. In the meantime 33 panels have been produced in electronic form, highlighting the persecution of Jehovah's Witnesses under National Socialism, accompanied by 10 additional panels describing the oppression of Jehovah's Witnesses in the GDR. These panels have been used especially for exhibitions in Switzerland. They have further been translated into Italian and Japanese.

A similar concept was used in the Watch Tower Society traveling exhibit in Russian for the video premiere on May 15, 1997, in the Moscow World Trade Center, attended by 500 people. At this event, there were ten Witness survivors from Russia, the Ukraine, and Germany. Two German and Ukrainian survivors of the Stutthof concentration camp have stayed in touch by letter since their liberation in May 1945. Fifty-two years later they met again in Moscow at this event.[34]

An additional complete set of panels in German language was prepared for the Austrian premiere and special exhibition at the Mauthausen concentration camp on June 18, 1997. This special exhibition with the topic »The Forgotten Victims« found substantial public interest, when it was shown at the Mauthausen memorial from June 18 to July 13, 1997; similar interest has been evident at other domestic and foreign events. In Austria, this exhibition together with an independent exhibit designed in Austria was viewed by more than 110,000 persons until summer 1999 in over 70 cities. In Brazil, Denmark, England, Israel, Italy, Japan, Norway, Russia, Spain, Sweden, and Switzerland similar exhibitions have been presented by Jehovah's Witnesses.

The »Stand Firm« events in Denmark were premiered in the 18th century »Odd Fellows Hall« in Copenhagen on March 30, 1998. This event was a video premiere as well as an exhibition opening. Altogether 23 exhibitions have been organized with a total of 50,000 in attendance. The events were well received by the news media. The exhibitions have been dealt with in about 100 newspaper articles. Among the hosts have been the universities of Copenhagen and Odense; also the universities of Aalborg and Roskilde have agreed to show the exhibition in 1999. In March 1999, it was also shown in the Faeroe Islands. Four percent of the population there visited the exhibition. In February 2000, it was shown in Nuuk in Greenland. One in every six of the city's inhabitants visited the exhibition. The video presentation and the exhibition will be presented also in Iceland.

After having received the video documentary »Jehovah's Witnesses Stand Firm Against Nazi Assault,« Ritt Bjerregaard, Denmark's member of the European Commission, wrote the following statement: »Without doubt your material has historical value and will be useful for education. After all, such experiences are best related by the ones who suffered them personally. The Second World War was a cruel period with unimaginable costs for both countries and populations, but it is not a time to be forgotten or silenced to death. Hopefully, future generations will learn a lesson from the mistakes of that time, and in that connection it is important to remember that from the very start the idea behind the European Union was the desire to preserve peace—a no lesser task with the future enlargement of the Union. Your film gives fine and thorough information about a group of people who stood firm. Something for which there is a need in our time as well.«[35]

Video presentations and exhibitions on a larger scale have now been held in Sweden in over 160 cities with, so far, more than 201,000 visitors.

In Spain, 31 large Holocaust exhibitions entitled »A Witness Testimony« have been arranged until March 2001 with a total of more than 130,000 visitors. Three of the 31 exhibitions were organized at the Canary Islands. Two hundred and thirty newspaper articles, 150 radio programs and 80 TV programs reported on these events. In addition, 40 »Stand Firm« video showings have been organized—four of them at university centers—with 8,215 persons in attendance and six TV stations have broadcast the condensed version of the »Stand Firm« video.

The more than 500 presentations in Germany included over 100 accompanying press conferences, enabling journalists to explore special questions with the historians, survivors, and representatives of the Public Affairs Department of Jehovah's Witnesses. In Germany alone, more than 2,800 newspaper articles have dealt with this subject in conjunction with presentations of the video and traveling exhibitions. The reports often had a local emphasis, interviewing survivors from a specific place or publishing research by Jehovah's Witnesses and historians. Television stations have reported about this more than 150 times, and over 130 programs have appeared on the radio.

The presentation at Glauchau from February 14 to March 3, 1997, stands out, and was seen by 10,850 persons. Fourteen survivors accompanied the exhibition. The city historian of Meerane wrote the following comment in the guest book: »I want to thank you for the interesting film report and also for the discussion at the exhibition. This too contributes to our understanding of German history.« A member of the Saxon Landtag (state parliament) wrote on February 20: »The fate of individuals from 1933 to 1945 is impressively presented. Unfortunately, in the past, there has been little or no attention given to the fate of Jehovah's Witnesses. This exhibition is therefore all the more proof that in the Nazi era, crimes were committed not only against communists, social democrats, and Jews. This exhibition has a special value even today. Increasing right-wing tendencies in Germany and throughout the world show that today we must do everything to prevent the reemergence of fascism. Education is the best tool. I wish the initiators of the exhibition continued success and hope that the exhibition can be shown in other places.«

At many presentations, between 15 and 50 percent of the audience were not Jehovah's Witnesses. The exhibition in the town hall of Aschaffenburg from May 11–19, 1997, was visited by 4,870 persons, and 1,300 persons saw the related film showing of »Stand Firm.« A guest book was also available here; furthermore, a survey of visitors was completed. Nearly 273 visitors, or about 6 percent of those attending (182 Witnesses and 91 non-Witnesses) participated. The average age of those surveyed was 33.5 years, although a group of youngsters and young adults between 12 and 19 years old were noticeable. Of the Witnesses surveyed:
- 40 percent had information only from the literature of the Watch Tower Society about the persecution of Jehovah's Witnesses in the Nazi era;
- 42 percent received new information; and
- 35 percent were strongly impressed by conversations with survivors.

The non-Witnesses responded that:
- 35 percent had received new information;
- 100 percent found the exhibition to be honest;
- 52 percent were moved;
- 30 percent had spoken to survivors and 37 percent had seen survivors; and
- 22 percent thought that their opinions about Jehovah's Witnesses had changed in a positive way.

A total of 500 visitors wrote entries in the guest book. Eleventh grade students from high school wrote: »We would like to thank you for the extremely informative exhibition, which certainly required a great deal of work. It is important to bring this subject closer to today's youth. The idea of having survivors speak provided finishing touches for the exhibition.« Their teacher added: »I can fully support what my class wrote. For us teachers this is also obligatory.«

Planing the exhibition in different locations also intensified research about the local history of Witnesses during the Nazi era. This enabled Jehovah's Witnesses in the last several months to transcribe about 100 individual biographies every week that were not always known to our History Archive at the Watch Tower Society in Selters/Taunus.

In conjunction with the exhibition at the old town hall at Lorsch from September 9–14, 1997, intensive research was conducted about the persecution of Jehovah's Witnesses by the Nazis. We thus discovered sixteen new individual Witness biographies, previously not known to the Watch Tower Society. In seven additional cases, we only had the names of individuals, but could not find further information about their individual persecution in the Nazi period.[36] This new data was established by intensive research. The Bensheim History Workshop Jakob Kindinger e.V. participated in this project. The chairperson Gert Helbling said about the exhibit: »Although we may not share the religious or socio-political views of the Witnesses, we nevertheless welcome that the persecution of Jehovah's Witnesses by the Nazis is explained to the public.«[37]

Naturally there are also critics. Renate Rennebach, member of the German Bundestag in the Enquete Commission about »So-called Sects and Psychogroups,« »had the impression that Witnesses sought to use their victimization to improve attitudes about them. ... They used persecution as a ›certificate of innocence‹ (Persilschein)[38] for everything else they did.«[39] The CDU state parliamentary deputy and expert on sect matters in Baden-Württemberg, Dr. Paul-Stefan Mauz, considered the exhibition »Jehovah's Witnesses Stand Firm Against Nazi Assault« shown at the Kursaal in Stuttgart-Bad Canstatt from January 23 until February 1, 1998, with opening presentations by the historians Dr. Detlef Garbe, Prof. Dr. Eberhard Jäckel, and Dr. Siegfried Schiele (director of the State Agency for Political Education in Baden-Württemberg) to be »a scandalous campaign of sympathy for a sect.«[40] He also criticized that »Jehovah's Witnesses clearly wanted to snare people with the exhibition.«[41]

These opinions are in strong disagreement with the opinions of politicians and church representatives immediately after the Second World War, who acknowledged and honored the victim role of Jehovah's Witnesses.[42] Thus the historian Detlef Garbe warns: »Tendencies to instrumentalize the past are also evident by many critics of the Witnesses, who do not engage in a critical analysis of historical findings, but begin with negative opinions in advance, feeling bound to contest today's activities by Jehovah's Witnesses. ... The results of research that confirm the extraordinary intensity of persecution that the Witnesses faced, are not fraudulent because the Watch Tower Society seeks to use them today (unlike in the past) to improve their public acceptance. Witness victims, who suffered persecution because of their beliefs and accepted death rather than killing others while wearing the uniform of the Hitler army, deserve our respect and admiration; and our society would do well not to refuse this to them. ... The recognition that actually those ›pious fanatics,‹ as they are still often called, systematically rejected serving a criminal government, whereas others—such as the churches, with few exceptions—did not have the will or force to resist, is for many an exasperating idea that is difficult to accept. Finally, even those who reject the beliefs of Jehovah's Witnesses need the ›provocation‹ of remembering the courageous evidence of Jehovah's Witnesses during the Nazi era.«[43]

On the occasion of a podium discussion on September 29, 1997, in the Frankfurt Haus der Volksarbeit, Garbe stated that the Watch Tower Society legitimately demanded recognition of the victim status of the Witnesses. The speaker Lutz Lemhöfer of the bishopric Limburg commented that the Witnesses deserved recognition as victims and that the discussion about this had to be civil. The former German President Richard von Weizsäcker stated aptly: »It is not a matter of conquering the past. One cannot do that. It cannot be changed afterwards or be undone. Whoever closes his eyes to the past will be blind to the present. Whoever does not want to remember the inhumanity, is open to danger from new infections.«[44] The documentation about Jehovah's Witnesses under the Nazis remind us of these concerns.

Meanwhile, this exhibition is recommended in the journal for public relations by libraries *PR-Koffer. Öffentlichkeitsarbeit für Bibliotheken* under the section »Exhibitions« with reference to the presentation in the »Niedersächsische Staats- und Universitätsbibliothek« from October 16 to November 13, 1998: »The exhibition reminds us of the forgotten history of this religious minority. The collection displays death sentences and farewell letters, prisoner identification cards, photos and drawings of the camp life, inflammatory articles from the Nazi period, and information about the religious group. It highlights the fate of individuals and proves the uncompromising determination with which Jehovah's Witnesses refused the Nazi system. And it shows the brutality the Hitler dictatorship used against these people. The exhibition provided material for discussion in public. The library offered an accompanying program—this is also recommended for other exhibitors.«[45]

Notes

1   See my essay »Persecuted and Almost Forgotten« in this anthology concerning the legal status.

2   Informationsdienst der Zeugen Jehovas, *Jehovas Zeugen: Antworten auf häufig gestellten Fragen*, 6/96, p. 3. See Detlef Garbe, *Zwischen Widerstand und Martyrium: die Zeugen Jehovas im »Dritten Reich*,« 3rd ed. (Munich, 1997), postscript, pp. 545, 548f.; »Dokumentation: Bericht über die Tätigkeit des ›Informationsdienstes der Zeugen Jehovas,‹« *Materialdienst der EZW* 8/97, pp. 249–252; *Spektrum: Evangelische Nachrichten und Meinungen* (August 13, 1997); *1998 Yearbook of Jehovah's Witnesses* (New York, 1997), p. 44.

3   Public Affairs Departments also exist in Denmark, France, Italy, Austria, Russia, Spain, Switzerland, and other countries. On January 17, 1997, in the Brooklyn headquarters of the Watch Tower Society, Public Affairs Office was founded, and began work on February 1, 1997, coordinating the individual Public Affairs Departments. In February 2001 the name of the office in Brooklynwas changed to »Office of Public Information.« This office was first under the jurisdiction of the Writing Commitee and is now under the jurisdiction of the Chairman's Committee in Brooklyn. See *1998 Yearbook of Jehovah's Witnesses*, p. 44.

4   *Jahresbericht der Stiftung Brandenburgische Gedenkstätten* (1996), p. 28; *1998 Yearbook of Jehovah's Witnesses*, pp. 46f.

5   »A Beam of Light in a Dark Age,« *Awake!* v. 78, no. 12 (June 22, 1997), pp. 14f.

6   *1998 Yearbook of Jehovah's Witnesses*, p. 46 mentioned 99 newspapers; subsequent coverage means that 100 papers covered this premiere.

7   *Der Tagesspiegel*, v. 52, no. 15799 (November 8, 1996), p. 5.

8   »Video über Verfolgung Zeugen Jehovas,« *Neue Westfälische* (January 14, 1997); »Video über Verfolgung Jehovas Zeugen: Erinnerung an Opfer des Nazi-Regimes,« *Bad Oeynhausener Anzeiger (Westfalen-Blatt)*, no. 12 (January 15, 1997); »Selber Zeugen Jehovas erhielten Video über Verfolgung in der NS-Zeit. ›Einzigartige Zivilcourage,‹ *Selber Tagblatt, Schönwalder Anzeiger* (Frankenpost), January 16, 1997, p. 2.

9   Interview with the survivor Horst Schmidt and Detlef Garbe.

10   Uni-Radio Berlin (radio channel for universities, higher education institutes, and special academies), November 7, 1996, interview with Johannes Heil.

11   Bulletin no. 6, Press and Information Service of the German Federal Government, Bonn, January 23, 1996, p. 45.

12   Ibid., p. 46.

13 It is available in Chinese (Cantonese and Mandarin), Croatian, Czech, Danish, Dutch, English, Finnish, French, German, Greek, Hebrew, Hungarian, Italian, Japanese, Korean, Latvian, Lithuanian, Norwegian, Polish, Portuguese (European and Brazilian versions), Romanian, Russian, Serbian, Slovenian, Slowakian, Spanish, Swedish (as of April 2001). The different versions were produced in Argentinia, Brazil, Corea, India, Japan, the Netherlands, and the USA. The premier for the Hebrew version was launched in the King David Hotel in Jerusalem (Israel) on April 11, 1999. Participating in the program besides two survivors were Judith Buber Agassi, Professor of Sociology, researching femal Jewish prisoners from Ravensbrück, and Shulamit Imber, Pedagogical Director of Yad Vashem.

14 *Newsletter*, Association of Holocaust Organizations, vol. 8, no. 4 (November 1996).

15 Detlef Garbe, »Die ›vergessenen‹ Opfer,« in: *Verachtet - verfolgt - vernichtet*, ed. Projektgruppe für die vergessenen Opfer des NS-Regimes (Hamburg, 1986-1988), pp. 5-13; idem, *Zwischen Widerstand und Martyrium*, p. 9; Brigitte Oleschinski, »Religiöse Gemeinschaften im Widerstand,« in: *Widerstand gegen den Nationalsozialismus*, ed. Bundeszentrale für politische Bildung, v. 323 of their series (Bonn, 1994), p. 193; Sybil Milton, »Zeugen Jehovas - vergessene Opfer?,« in: *Widerstand aus christlicher Überzeugung: Jehovas Zeugen im Nationalsozialismus; Dokumentation einer Tagung* (Essen, 1998), pp. 30ff.; see my essay »Persecuted and Almost Forgotten« in this anthology.

16 The media was informed that 60 percent of Swedish youngsters were not certain that the Holocaust had really occurred as described by historians.

17 Andreas Lange, Heléne Lööw, Stéphanie Bruchfeld, and Ebba Hedlund, *Utsatthet för etniskt och politiskt telaterat vald m. m. spridning av rasistisk och antirasistisk propaganda, samt attiyder till demokrati m. m.*, bland skolever. CEIFO (Immigration Center), Stockholm University, BRA (Council for Prevention of Crimes), Stockholm, June 1997. Nearly 8,000 students throughout Sweden were surveyed between February and April 1997.

18 A Starlock Pictures Production, 1991.

19 92-minute long film documentary by Stefanie Krug and Fritz Poppenberg, Drei Linden Media, Berlin.

20 *Levande historia* (Stockholm, 1998), pp. 29, 38, 42, 44. On January 14 and 15, 1998, the Nordiska Museum in Stockholm hosted the Swedish premiere of the documentary video »Jehovah's Witnesses Stand Firm Against Nazi Assault.« There was also a press conference and a 20-minute public screening of the short version of the video as well as survivor interviews. Present were Thage G. Petersson, Coordinating Minister for the Swedish government and former Minister of Defense, and Anna-Karin Johansson, coordinator for the government commission. A supplementary exhibition about this subject was viewed by about 1,000 persons in the museum. On January 16, 1998, Jehovah's Witnesses showed the exhibition in the assembly hall in Strängnäs together with a program focused on survivor interviews. An audience of 8,464 was counted. After this event, an additional 2,500-3,000 persons had the chance to view the exhibition. See *Aarboga Tidning*, v. 148, no. 8 (January 14, 1998), pp. 1, 6f.; *Strengnäs Tidning*, no. 11 (January 15, 1998), pp. 1, 7.

21 *Die Woche* (July 10, 1998); *BZ,* Berlin (July 2, 1998).

22 Bulletin no. 6, Bonn (January 23, 1996), p. 47.

23 *1998 Yearbook of Jehovah's Witnesses*, p. 46.

24 *Kristallnacht* (Crystal Night) or *Reichskristallnacht* are terms that make reference to the massive pogrom against the Jews organized by the Nazis on November 9 and 10, 1938. The terms have come to be regarded as a euphemistic way to refer to the broken windows of synagogues, Jewish-owned stores, communal centers, and homes that were plundered. It is estimated that about 7,000 shops that were owned by Jews were ransacked and destroyed, and some 26,000 Jews were arrested and afterwards deported. (Cf. Wolfgang Benz et al. [ed.], *Enzyklopädie des Nationalsozialismus*, 2nd ed. [Munich, 1998], pp. 679f.; *Historical Atlas of the Holocaust*, United States Holocaust Memorial Museum [New York, 1996], pp. 24f.)

25 *School Library Journal* (February 1998), *p. 70*.

26 Berliner Institut für Lehrerfort- und -weiterbildung und Schulentwicklung (Ed.): »...die vielen Morde...«. Dem Gedenken an die Opfer des Nationalsozialismus, 1999, p. 177.

27 Joseph P. Rutherford, *Jehovah*, ed. Watch Tower Bible and Tract Society, German edition (Bern, 1934). The miniature edition contained sections of this book.

28 *Awake!*, v. 79, no. 11 (April 22, 1998), p. 14.

29 *Watchtower*, v. 88, no. 21 (August 1, 1967), pp. 472-475.

30 Cercle Européen des Témoins de Jéhovah Anciens Déportés et Internés, ed., *Mémoire de Témoins 1933-1945* (Louviers, 1995).

31 See ftn. no. 25.

32 *Awake!*, v. 77, no. 11 (June 8, 1996), pp. 16–19.

33 Kirsten John, »*Mein Vater wird gesucht ...«: Häftlinge des Konzentrationslagers in Wewelsburg* (Essen, 1996), p. 125.

34 *1998 Yearbook of Jehovah's Witnesses*, p. 47.

35 Original in Danish dated April 23, 1998; author is in possession of a photocopy.

36 See the essay »Rescued From Oblivion: The Case of Hans Gärtner« in this anthology.

37 »Die Zeugen Jehovas als ›vergessene Opfer‹ der Nazis,« *Bergsträßer Anzeiger* (September 9, 1997), p. 3; »Vergessene Opfer der Nazis,« *Mannheimer Morgen* (September 9, 1997).

38 *Persilschein* (essentially, certificates of virtue or white-washing named for the detergent Persil) had been issued after 1945 by denazification authorities as certificates of non-objection for individuals who had more or less been involved with the Nazi regime.« (Brockhaus-Wahrig, *Deutsches Wörterbuch* [Wiesbaden, 1983], v. 5, p. 96) This insinuation is even more incomprehensible if linked to the suffering of individual victims.

39 »Zeugen Jehovas: Umstrittener Umgang mit Opferrolle,« *Hersfelder Zeitung*, no. 40 (February 17, 1997), p. 3; *Waldeckische Allgemeine*, HNA, no. 40 (February 17, 1997).

40 *Stuttgarter Nachrichten* (February 29, 1998), p. 22; *Winnender Zeitung* (January 29, 1998); *Fellbacher Zeitung* (January 29, 1998), p. 19; *Waiblinger Kreiszeitung*, no. 23 (January 29, 1998); and *Remszeitung* (January 29, 1998).

41 *Stuttgarter Zeitung* (January 24, 1998), p. 29; *Cannstatter Zeitung*, *Untertürkheimer Zeitung* (January 26, 1998), p. 4.

42 Martin Niemöller, *Ach Gott vom Himmel sieh darein: Sechs Predigten* (Munich, 1946), pp. 27–28; Hanns Lilje, *Im finstern Tal* (Nuremberg, 1947), pp. 64f.; Detlef Garbe, »Der lila Winkel,« *Dachauer Hefte* 10 (1994), pp. 11, 30; idem, *Zwischen Widerstand und Martyrium*, pp. 40, 406.

43 Detlef Garbe, »Die Verfolgung der Zeugen Jehovas im nationalsozialistischen Deutschland: Ein Überblick,« in: *Widerstand aus christlicher Überzeugung* (Essen, 1998), pp. 26f.

44 Richard von Weizsäcker's speech on May 8, 1985, on the 40th anniversary of the end of the Second World War. See Richard von Weizsäcker, *Brücken zur Verständigung. Reden* (Berlin, 1990), p. 36.

45 1/1999 issue, p. 30, published by the Deutsche Bibliotheksinstitut, Berlin, with support of the Federal government and the states.

Jolene Chu

From Marginalization to Martyrdom

In Warsaw, there stands a Gestapo prison where the condemned awaited execution. Down in a basement cell, scratched on a wall, are barely visible words in Polish: »Nobody thinks of me and nobody knows. I am so alone.« It is signed, »Girl, 21 years, and must die – guiltless.«[1]

This poignant epitaph bespeaks the disastrous success of the Nazi strategy of marginalization. In a step-by-step process, victims were isolated so completely that millions of faceless humans ceased to exist in the minds and hearts of their fellow man long before they perished behind the barbed-wire fences. On reflection, was it really true that »Nobody knows«? Or was it rather the case that »Nobody *wants* to know«?

The regime's systematic attack on its civilian enemies followed a familiar continuum of stereotyping, devaluation, segregation, depersonalization, incarceration, and annihilation. Sometimes the processes ran concurrently. Each step was designed to cut emotional, social, moral, and finally, physical ties between the victims and the general population. As the atrocities escalated, sympathetic reaction was feeble. Public outcry was virtually non-existent, a calamitous tribute to the effectiveness of the process.

In retrospect, it is a sad and sobering fact that the Nazi regime executed a brilliant and ruthless war against the Jews, and nearly won. As the nation underwent rapid transformation into a terror state, the regime also launched attacks on other enemies of the state for various reasons and with varying degrees of success. The rationales and victims were diverse, but the mechanisms of marginalization, persecution, and annihilation all too often were very much the same.

In some cases the attacks on smaller groups predated the war against the Jews. The regime's pilot programs, used to hone the machinery of murder and to test the waters of public opinion,[2] reappeared in more monstrous and terrifying incarnations as the Nazis undertook the crusade that would go on to eclipse in scope and intensity all such smaller campaigns.

As one of the earliest targets of the Hitler regime, the religious community of Jehovah's Witnesses were to experience, seemingly in time-lapse fashion, the process of marginalization that would soon thereafter be brought to bear on the Jews of Europe. A brief summary of Nazi measures against the small population of Witnesses will bear out certain similarities to what would become in time the Nazi's overall campaign.

Despite any mechanical similarities, however, the battle against the Witnesses took on an entirely different character at the behest of its initiators. In some ways this blunted the success of the campaign, for had the Nazi policy of extermination extended to the Witnesses, it would likely have succeeded in large measure. The Gestapo and SS had in their grip nearly half of the Witnesses of Germany at one time or another.[3]

Instead of genocide, the Hitler regime determined to wage a contest of wills with the Witnesses. It sought to destroy, not a people, but a religion, a rival loyalty. It used the weapons that it knew best: humiliation, terror, threats, and torture. Therefore, it created a number of martyrs, as many Witnesses died clinging to their convictions. Eventually the regime resorted to strategic executions, but these also had a minimal effect in intimidating the Witnesses into submission.

Long before January 1933, hostile political and religious media effectively branded the Witnesses as dangerous, a subversive sect funded by Jews or Bolsheviks.[4] The Witnesses' proselytism, criticism of mainstream churches, and position of political neutrality earned them few friends in popular political and religious circles. With the accession of Hitler's regime, the Nazi propaganda machine picked up and enlarged the theme of »subversive foreign sect« and used the charge of »Jewish tendencies« as one pretext to proscribe the group.[5] The media variously labeled the Witnesses as »Marxists,« anti-Christian »Bible Twisters,« and the »Jewish worm.«[6]

One by one, the remaining civil and human rights of the Witnesses were legally removed. The SA and the police broke up religious services and seized private property.[7] For refusal to vote in the election held on November 12, 1933, Witnesses were subjected to job dismissal, beatings, and public humiliation. They were paraded through the streets with placards that read, »We are traitors to the Fatherland! We did not vote!«[8] Witnesses were also denied unemployment and pension benefits.

On April 7, 1933, the Civil Service Law that banned non-Aryans from civil service jobs, including teaching positions, was promulgated.[9] Measures against Jehovah's Witnesses in civil service positions were formalized in June 1934. Dismissal became common on the grounds that the Witnesses had refused to give the Hitler salutation and did not vote.[10] Before long, simply being an Jehovah's Witness was sufficient grounds for arrest and incarceration. House searches, confiscations, and beatings increased.[11] In this early period, hundreds of Witnesses spent time in Nazi prisons and camps.[12]

On May 10, 1933, the infamous book burnings evoked scenes from Dante's Inferno. Some 20,000 pieces of »un-German writing« were fed to the flames in Berlin alone.[13] The regime also went after Witness books. The SA seized and burned 25 truckloads of Bibles and Bible literature from the Witnesses' Magdeburg printing plant on August 21 to 24, 1933.[14]

Because the Witnesses were an unpopular minority both inside and outside Germany, there was little public protest over these abuses, except by the Witnesses' own international community.[15]

The Nazi process of marginalization accelerated in 1935 with further legal encroachments on the Witnesses' public, private, and religious life. They became virtually unemployable. Like the Nuremberg law prohibiting marriage to a non-Aryan, marriage to a Witness also became grounds for divorce in 1935.[16] Witness teachers were not permitted to teach in state schools, and their children were denied the right to be taught. Starting in 1935, children of Witnesses were expelled from school. Some 860 Witness children were taken from their parents to be raised as »proper Nazis« in reeducation homes.[17] The institution of mandatory military service presented a special problem for the politically neutral Witnesses. Arrests and incarcerations rose dramatically, and the Witnesses made up a significant proportion of the pre-war camp population.[18]

Immediately following *the November 1938 Kristallnacht pogrom*, 30,000 Jewish men swelled the concentration camp population. Six thousand Witnesses prisoners, many of them veterans of the camp system, were on hand to greet the unfortunates.[19]

The typical experience for camp inmates may have varied little in physical conditions, in terms of crushing labor, putrid food, filth, and torture.[20] There were, however, important differences between the Witness experience and that of the Jews, as well as most other victim groups. The Witnesses faced persecution, the Jews faced genocide. The Witnesses were viewed as ideological or spiritual enemies of the regime; the Jews were primarily targeted as biological enemies.

In the eyes of the Nazis, the biological enemy had to be exterminated, while the ideological enemy had to be converted, although death was often the penalty for refusal to convert. In the end, then, millions of Jews became victims of Nazism's unyielding racial agenda, given only the option to die or be killed. Some established their own terms of victory by choosing to die with dignity or to resist no matter how slender the odds. Thousands of Jehovah's Witnesses were also victimized. However, because the Nazis gave them the option to relinquish their principles as a means of obtaining their freedom, the Witnesses may be designated martyrs.

In analyzing this ideological conflict, we draw on Professor Ervin Staub's summary of National Socialism's three basic components:

1) racial purity, the racial superiority of Germans, and racial antisemitism;

2) nationalism; and

3) the Führer principle, which required unquestioning obedience to Hitler.[21]

In almost exact counterpoint, historian Brian Dunn names the three points of incompatibility between the Witnesses and the Nazis:

1) The Witnesses are opposed to racism. They could not accept the »Übermensch/ Untermensch« concept (the idea of superior and inferior persons);

2) Their movement is international in scope and outlook; and

3) The Witnesses are politically neutral toward secular governments, which in practice meant that Jesus is their »Führer.«[22]

It is little wonder that the Nazis and Jehovah's Witnesses clashed from the very beginning. These principles became the basis both for ideological resistance to the regime and, paradoxically, for increased chances for survival. Let us examine this further.

1) The Witnesses oppose racism. Their doctrine left no room for the concept of the *Volk* (racial community) as a dominating group and the devaluation of specific racial groups and of human life in general. This core belief in the brotherhood of man immunized the Witnesses as a group against Nazi racial propaganda, and it governed their relationship with Witnesses and non-Witnesses inside and outside the camps.

Non-Witness survivors testify that the Witness camp population was noted for its caring behavior toward other victim groups. The Witnesses in Buchenwald shared their rations with starving Jews rounded up during Kristallnacht and went without food themselves for up to four days.[23] Although such altruistic acts jeopardized their own physical health, it likely had a beneficial effect on their morale. Bruno Bettelheim's and Tzvetan Todorov's analyses of camp life show that such moral acts kept the spark of life alive.[24] It was evidence that camp life had not succeeded in stripping away their Christian values and sense of decency. According to Bettelheim, »they were the only group of prisoners who never abused or mistreated other prisoners.«[25]

2) The Witnesses are international. This connection to a worldwide brotherhood of fellow believers gave the Witness inmates a vital feeling of solidarity and connection. Unlike the young Polish woman in the Gestapo prison, the Witnesses were confident that »somebody knew, somebody cared, and they were not alone« in their plight. Some Witnesses risked their lives to smuggle reports of camp life to the outside knowing that their reports would be believed and publicized. Witness literature smuggled into the camp confirmed this, often carrying stinging firsthand exposés of Nazi atrocities.

The group solidarity of the Witnesses, as with members of other groups, did much to improve their chances for survival.[26] Eugen Kogon said that »membership in a group was perhaps the finest experience in the camp.«[27] The Witnesses exhibited family-like caring behavior among their supranational community, sharing food parcels, and nurturing the sick.

At the same time, it must be admitted that their internationalism put the Witnesses in an often fatal position. They categorically refused military service, conscientiously refusing to take up arms against fellow humans and especially against fellow believers in other lands. Hundreds of Witnesses were tortured and executed, martyred for their unbending neutrality.[28]

3) The Witnesses refused to accept Hitler as *Führer*. Jesus was their *Führer* (leader). They maintained their self-respect and autonomy, refusing to »heil« as savior the man responsible for their plight. Refusal to »heil« brought terrible retribution in and out of the camps. Of course, Germany's *Führer* demanded much more of his followers than a perfunctory greeting. Because Jehovah's Witnesses as a group measured every Nazi demand against their obligations to Christian standards, they refused to take even the first steps that led many fellow citizens down the road from passive bystander to active participant in Nazi crimes.

By adhering to their principles, the Witnesses succeeded in turning Nazi tactics to their advantage. The SS humiliated random prisoners by asking, Why are you here? and demanding the demeaning response, »I am a filthy Communist,« or »I am a dirty Jew.« When the Witnesses were asked, Why are you here? they seized the opportunity to witness for their faith and their God.[29]

The SS denied them full correspondence privileges and marked their censored letters as coming from »a stubborn Bible Student.« Rather than feel deprived, they believed that family members at home who received such letters took courage in the implied message that their loved one was holding steadfast.

The SS staged public executions to intimidate the Witnesses. These often produced martyrs for the cause who affirmed their belief in ultimate rewards and solidified the convictions of their fellow believers.[30]

The Witnesses were the only Christian group designated by their own prisoner symbol — the purple triangle. Intended by the SS as a stigma of shame, the triangle became an important symbol of identification to the Witnesses, a badge of their faith, bringing them instant recognition of each other and the clear advantage of belonging to a group. The symbol crossed national and ethnic lines so that individual prisoners of different nationalities were adopted and cared for despite language and cultural differences.

The Witnesses made the most of changing circumstances. At first in the larger camps they were kept as a isolated group. They bonded with and helped one another to survive physically and spiritually. In order to disrupt their solidarity, the prison or camp officials sometimes separated the group. Then they commenced their incessant preaching, and their numbers multiplied.

Among the Nazis' greatest tactical failures was the *Erklärung* (»Declaration«) that gave each Witness the chance for freedom in exchange for his signature renouncing his faith and affiliation.[31] Few Witness prisoners accepted the offer, which was often accompanied by specially selected tortures.[32] This document tested their convictions to the limit, but it also afforded each Witness an opportunity to exercise free choice, to take pride in adhering to principles, and to perform an act of faith and loyalty for his heavenly Sovereign.[33]

Some have interpreted the consistent conduct of Jehovah's Witnesses as a response to totalitarian peer pressure from within their religious community. Arguing against this interpretation is the fact that similar conscientious decisions, such as the decision not to sign the declaration, were made by Witnesses whether they were in isolation or in a peer group. Moreover, a totalitarian system characteristically depersonalizes both its victims and its supporters.

The victim is made to feel powerless to make a difference by dissident action, and the obedient supporter of a totalitarian regime is told that he is a mere cog in the machinery, thus relieving him of the pangs of personal responsibility and the burden of personal decision.[34] Neither description can apply to members of the Witness community, whose belief system moved the vast majority of them to make their choices, whether in the presence of peers or not, precisely because they retained their human identity, exercised their conscientious choice, and took personal responsibility for their actions.

Sad to say, totalitarianism did not die with Adolf Hitler. But we have in the Witnesses a story of victory over despotism. The Witnesses whose legacy we scrutinize today did not see themselves as heroes. They were only living their faith. However, in doing so, they left for future generations a model of the moral power of conscience and the triumph of the human spirit.

Notes

1   Transcript of lecture by Plater Robinson, Holocaust Education Specialist at the Southern Institute for Education and Research, Tulane University, New Orleans, Louisiana, at the March 6, 1997 teachers' workshop, »The Nazi Assault on Jehovah's Witnesses.«
2   For example, Michael Berenbaum calls the T-4 program (the so-called euthanasia program) »a prefiguration of the Holocaust.« See Michael Berenbaum, *The World Must Know* (Boston: Little, Brown and Company, 1993), p. 65.
3   Proportions of Witness victimization and incarceration in other Nazi-occupied countries are similar.
4   According to historian Christine King, the Witnesses even earned mention in an 1923 edition of the infamous Protocols of the Elders of Zion. Christine Elizabeth King, *The Nazi State and the New Religions: Five Case Studies in Non-Conformity* (New York: The Edwin Mellen Press, 1982), p. 149. Later characterizations by Nazi sources then are not surprising. As Doris Bergen has written of the Nazi German Christian movement, they »tarred all opponents with the brush of Jewishness.« Dorris L. Bergen, *Twisted Cross: The German Christian Movement in the Third Reich* (Chapel Hill: The University of North Carolina Press, 1996), p. 32.
5   See the court opinion reprinted in *The Golden Age* (February 27, 1935), pp. 323–327, describing the Witnesses as subject to »foreign influences« and as showing »Jewish tendencies.« The frequent charges of links with purported Jewish-Bolshevik movements may explain, in part, statements in the resolution adopted by Witnesses at the June 25, 1933, Berlin convention. The *Erklärung*, the four-page resolution affirming the Witnesses' neutral position, contained a clear denial of financial connections with Jews. Indicating that such denials constituted an effort to disprove the allegations of conspiracy, the *Erklärung* stated that »there never has been the slightest bit of money contributed to our work by Jews« and that »the charges against us are maliciously false.«
6   Celebrating the June 24, 1933 ban on the Witnesses, the *Westdeutscher Beobachter* article of July 4, 1933, combined all three charges: »Zum Verbot der ernsten Bibelverdreher: Was sich hinter den frommen Biedermännern verbarg« (»The Prohibition of the Earnest Bible-Twisters: What Was Hidden Behind Those Pious Worthies«). Translation: »The International Bible Students Association was one of those organizations that one might call the embodiment of the antichrist. This foreign Jewish firm, financed with American money, deliberately planned to destroy the harmonious life of the people, state, and family by religiously fanaticizing its adherents in an unheard of manner.
     »The literature, sold everywhere, shows an abysmal, religiously moral degradation, joining hands in every way with communism. Under a professedly scientific mask, the entire Bible was turned upside down and changed into just the contrary; and above all the redemption of man by Judaism was preached.

»The Bible Students assisted communism not only in a spiritual way, but, by admitting former communists, made it possible for them to continue to organize in spite of all measures taken by the national government. On the other hand, harmless people were taken advantage of to further these political aims, and the family life of many people was destroyed by this senseless religious fanaticism. For this reason it has proven unavoidable to prohibit the International Bible Students Association, the New Apostolic Sect, [not to be mistaken for the New Apostolic Congregation], and the Watch Tower Bible & Tract Society in the state of Prussia. We cannot suffer the moral standard of a people to be lowered by such irresponsible people to a degree that we would have to be ashamed of our spiritual inheritance, handed down to us. The glory of the communist Bible distorters and Jehovah's Witnesses has come to an inglorious end in Prussia.«

7   Private property losses at this early stage was estimated at two to three million marks. *1974 Yearbook of Jehovah's Witnesses* (Brooklyn, NY: Watch Tower Bible and Tract Society, 1973), pp. 108, 112. See also King, p. 19, and *The Golden Age* (April 25, 1934), pp. 151, 153.

8   Franz Zürcher, *Kreuzzug gegen das Christentum* (Crusade Against Christianity) (Zurich: Europa Verlag), p. 128a; *The Golden Age* (April 25, 1934), pp. 456-461.

9   Berenbaum, p. 22.

10 King, pp. 153-54; Ernst Christian Helmreich, *The German Churches Under Hitler: Background, Struggle, and Epilogue* (Detroit: Wayne State University Press, 1979), p. 395.

11 Report dated April 10, 1934, to Martin Harbeck at the Bern, Switzerland, Watch Tower Office, on file with the Watch Tower History Archive, Selters, Germany. See also *The Golden Age* (April 25, 1934), pp. 456-61, for numerous examples.

12 *The Golden Age* (April 25, 1934), pp. 456, 461.

13 Berenbaum, p. 24.

14 *The Golden Age* (April 25, 1934), p. 456; *1974 Yearbook of Jehovah's Witnesses*, p. 112.

15 The Witness community did what it could to publicize Nazi atrocities, regularly publishing detailed reports about the crimes against their own members, as well as the persecution of European Jews, the Slavs, political prisoners, dissident ministers, and others. See »Watchtower Holocaust Reprints 1933-46 and *Index* in 13 volumes,« United States Holocaust Memorial Museum Center for Advanced Holocaust Studies library collections.

16 King, p. 155; *1974 Yearbook of Jehovah's Witnesses*, p. 212.

17 *1974 Yearbook of Jehovah's Witnesses*, p. 212.

18 King, pp. 154f.

19 *Papers Concerning the Treatment of German Nationals in Germany 1938-1939* (London: His Majesty's Stationery Office), Germany No. 2, 1939, pp. 10, 12, 14, 35.

20 Many times the caprices of individual commandants determined who would be the favorite target group of SS sport. Occasionally the Jews and Witnesses were thrown together, as with one labor detail in Neuengamme, because they all believed in the Hebrew God, Jehovah. This is according to the Jewish survivor Max Liebster, who was part of the 30-man labor detail.

21 Ervin Staub, *The Roots of Evil: The Origins of Genocide and Other Group Violence* (New York: Cambridge University Press, 1989), p. 98.

22 Brian Dunn, »Jehovah's Witnesses in the Holocaust Kingdom,« in *The Churches' Response to the Holocaust*, v. 2 *Holocaust Studies Annual* (Greenwood, Fl: The Penkevill Publishing Company, 1986,) p. 158.

23 *The Watchtower* (August 15, 1945), p. 256; Eugen Kogon, *The Theory and Practice of Hell*, pp. 41ff.

24 Bruno Bettelheim, *The Informed Heart: Autonomy in a Mass Age* (Glencoe, Illinois: The Free Press of Glencoe, 1963), p. 20.

25 Bettelheim, pp. 122f. Bettelheim shows that an integrated personality, strong inner convictions nourished by satisfying personal relations, along with an intellectual mastery of events as they happen are one's best protection against oppressive controls. Bettelheim, pp. 104f.

26 Bettelheim, p. 182. Although discredited as a psychoanalyst in later years, Bettelheim's first-hand observations on camp life and the response of various types of prisoners may still be valid.

27 Kogon, p. 280: »Group allegiance meant joining a small group of friends or co-religionists. ... In such groups men again became human beings, after the humiliation suffered in the toil of the day, after punishment and roll call and barracks life. Despite prison stripes and shorn skulls, they were able to look their fellows in the face, beholding the same sorrow and the same pride, and drawing renewed strength. Hope was revived, helping them to be ready to proceed on the appointed path, step by step. Membership in such a group was perhaps the finest experience in a concentration camp.«

28 See Kogon, pp. 41ff.

29 An amusing anecdote is related by the Dutch Witness survivor Arie Kaldenberg. He relates that in Vught concentration camp at the roll call, the Witnesses had decided that they would not answer to the name »Bibelforscher« (Bible Students) since the organization had adopted the name Jehovah's Witnesses in 1931. The SS officer twice called in vain for the »Bibelforscher« prisoners to step forward. After no reaction, one of the Witnesses approached the frustrated officer and explained that they would only answer to »Jehovah's Witnesses.« He relented, and the Witnesses stepped forward responsively. »We made him say the name,« gloats Kaldenberg. Video interview, October 12, 1995, Netherlands.

30 In the documentary video *Jehovah's Witnesses Stand Firm Against Nazi Assault* (produced by the Watch Tower Bible and Tract Society, 1996), survivors Heinrich Dickmann and Josef Rehwald describe the execution by firing squad of Dickmann's brother, August, on September 15, 1939. Immediately after the shooting, Sachsenhausen Commandant Hermann Baranowski threatened other Witness prisoners, about 500, with a similar fate if they refused to sign a renunciation of their religious affiliation and beliefs. Not one Witness prisoner yielded. See also Detlef Garbe, »Der lila Winkel: Die ›Bibelforscher‹ (Zeugen Jehovas) in den Konzentrationslagern,« *Dachauer Hefte* 10 (1994), pp. 3-31.

31 Few others Nazi victims were offered such an escape option. One such individual was Protestant minister Paul Schneider in Buchenwald, who was offered a similar document certifying his agreement to Nazi restrictions on his church activities. See Claude R. Foster, Jr., *Paul Schneider, The Buchenwald Apostle* (West Chester, PA: SSI Bookstore, West Chester University, 1995), pp. 773f.

32 According to historian Detlef Garbe, no more than a few dozen Witness prisoners were released from concentration camps after signing the document. See Detlef Garbe, *Zwischen Widerstand und Martyrium: Die Zeugen Jehovas im Dritten Reich* (Munich: Oldenbourg, 1994), p. 417. Survivor accounts indicate that a few of those who had signed the document did so in order to gain their freedom, with the intention of resuming their religious activity.

33 Other episodes in connection with the *Erklärung* illustrate the Nazi intention to wield it as part of their psychological arsenal. One survivor (name withheld by request) relates how his Witness father was returned home by the SS after eight years in camp, handcuffed to the bed, and left to be with the family for a few days. He was then presented with the document, which he refused to sign, and was then returned to the camp. The man survived liberation only to be rearrested by the Stasi and sent to an East German prison, where he died.

34 Staub, pp. 83ff. and 162-165. Staub analyzes the developmental process of genocidal mentality, particularly the tendency toward compartmentalization and integration, and the »deindividuation« that »freed perpetrators from moral constraints.«

James N. Pellechia

Teaching Tolerance: A Case Study

»Moral instruction and education are inseparable.«[1] This was Lev Nikolaevich Tolstoy's conclusion after a lifetime of reflection and experience. By this he meant that education includes the
inculcation of moral values.

Holocaust history shows the catastrophic consequences of education devoid of positive
moral training. In the words of Dr. Franklin Littell, we run the risk of producing »technically
competent barbarians, immune to the pangs of conscience, the claims of religion, the rules of
professional ethics.«[2]

Because many Holocaust scholars and educators are acutely aware of this danger, they look
for positive models amidst the horror of Holocaust history. For this reason, they asked the
Watch Tower Society for teaching materials on the history of Jehovah's Witnesses — a minority
Christian group that stood up to Nazism and spoke out against its cruelties. One result of
these requests is a documentary called »Jehovah's Witnesses Stand Firm Against Nazi Assault«
and its supplementary Teaching Guide. Through archival footage, historical commentary by
Holocaust scholars, and survivor testimony, this video tells a story of the power of moral
education. Sociologist Anna Pawelcynska described the Witnesses as »a tiny island of unflag-
ging resistance existing in the bosom of a terrorized nation.«[3] In the words of historian Christine King, the Witnesses »spoke out from the start. They spoke out with *one* voice. And they
spoke out with tremendous courage, which has a message for all of us.«[4]

This history also provides important additional evidence of the Shoah. The Witnesses were
virtually all non-Jews, but they were eyewitnesses to the crimes against the Jewish people. They
unite their voices in response against those who would deny the Holocaust.

To explain the usefulness of this history to teachers of tolerance training, we will give a brief
outline of the twelve-year persecution of the Witnesses. Even before Hitler assumed power, the
Witnesses warned about the threat of rising militarism. In 1929, their periodical »Das Goldene
Zeitalter« [The Golden Age], now known as »Erwachet!« [Awake!], stated that »National socialism is a movement that is acting directly in the service of mankind's enemy, the Devil.«[5]
Although the Witnesses were politically neutral, the extremist Nazi ideology forced them into
a position of confrontation with the new regime. The Witnesses pledged loyalty to God and
his dominion, an allegiance that a totalitarian regime would not tolerate. The Witnesses refused
to say »Heil Hitler,« as if he were Germany's savior.[6] The Nazis falsely branded Jehovah's
Witnesses as Communists, a threat to the state, and conspirators of the Jews. On June 28, 1933,
a band of SA men and local police stormed the Watch Tower office, seized the printing
facilities, and officially banned the Witnesses. From August 21–25 truckloads of Watch Tower
literature were confiscated and burned.[7]

Despite the growing pressure, the Witnesses felt a moral obligation to expose and speak out
about the dangers of Nazism. In the issue of August 16, 1933, the journal »The Golden Age«
first mentioned the existence of concentration camps.[8] Many Witnesses had firsthand knowledge of the camps. By 1934, 1,000 German Witnesses had been arrested, and 400 of them had
been sent to the camps. On April 1, 1935, Witnesses were banned from all civil service jobs and

arrested throughout Germany. Their pensions and unemployment benefits were denied, marriage to a Witness became legal grounds for divorce, Witness children were excluded from attending school, and some were removed from their Witness parents to be raised in Nazi re-education homes.[9] By 1937, there were 6,000 Witnesses in the camps.[10] They were the only religious group to be designated by their own symbol – the purple triangle.

Despite Gestapo efforts to shut down the Witnesses' activities, a persistent underground organization continued to function. On small hand-operated mimeograph machines, they published scathing exposés of Nazi atrocities and distributed them by the thousands in daring nighttime operations.[11] The historian and author Claudia Koonz wrote that the Witnesses, »practically to a person, unequivocally refused to render any form of obedience to the Nazi state.«[12] They did not join political resistance movements, but »waged passive resistance for their beliefs, which prohibited all war and violence.«[13] Koonz also commented, »Sustained by religion, they were the most cohesive group of resisters.«[14]

Whereas other victims were mainly the Nazis' biological enemies, the Witnesses were their ideological enemies. Historian Brian Dunn wrote that »the SS goal in dealing with the Witnesses was not to kill them, but to break their spirit and commitment.«[15] By threats and torture, the SS tried to coerce the Witnesses to sign a declaration renouncing Witness doctrines and swearing loyalty to Hitler. If they signed, they could go free. The vast majority of Witnesses held firm to their moral values, a number of them at the cost of their lives.

What was the relationship of the Witnesses to the Jews? Dr. Detlef Garbe, director of the Neuengamme Memorial, states: »The last thing Jehovah's Witnesses would do was to regard Jews as being of less merit simply because of their origin. For them, all human beings had the same significance, were equal.«[16] The sociologist and author Helen Fein described the process by which the Nazis excluded the Jews from their »universe of obligation,« marginalizing them step by step, from boycotts to ghettos to gas chambers. By the time plans for the Final Solution were formalized, the general populace had long since ceased to feel any moral responsibility for the victims as »those toward to whom obligations are owed, to whom rules apply, and whose injuries call for [redress].«[17] Because of their moral training, Jehovah's Witnesses as a religious community and as individuals refused to accept the Nazi ideology of hate. Historian Dunn cites this as a basic reason for the Nazi persecution of the group. He wrote: »The Witnesses are opposed to racism in any form. .... The Witnesses' interpretation of one verse of scripture, Acts 17:26 ›And he hath made of one blood all the nations of men for to dwell on the face of the Earth‹ abolished racial or ethnic discrimination for them. They could not accept the concept of superior and inferior beings (Übermensch/Untermensch).«[18]

Witness doctrine and practice stood in sharp contrast to the strong antisemitic tradition of many churches. The Witnesses' beliefs immunized them against racist indoctrination. Their belief in the brotherhood of man translated into concrete acts of altruism. Historian Christine King cited sources about assistance to Jews. It shows that Jehovah's Witnesses, along with Adventists and Quakers, »were outstanding in their care and in the risks they were prepared to take.«[19] Professor King notes that Holocaust survivors remember the Witnesses for their willingness to share food, care, and comfort with other prisoners. In Chelmina's book, *Women in USSR Prisons*, a survivor of a Soviet prison wrote: »Jehovah's Witnesses regard it as their personal obligation to help everybody, regardless of their religion or nationality.«[20]

For the Witnesses, a pattern of community service was a part of their religious tradition long before the Nazis assumed power. Their public ministry and social work were ways of expressing their love of their neighbor and helping others to improve their quality of life through application of Bible principles. Amidst the privation and desperation of camp life, their expressions of neighborly love came to include sharing food, clothing, and other acts of caring. In the »Stand Firm« film, the survivor Max Hollweg dispassionately describes a near-fatal beating that he received on arrival in Buchenwald. He only survived the night because of the care of a rescuer, a fellow Witness. This »brother« embraced Hollweg's cold body and warmed him through the night. In a later segment of the film, Hollweg is one of several dozen Witnesses in the Wewelsburg concentration camp. They had refused military service. One »brother« is brutally beaten and left for dead by the SS. Now Hollweg became the rescuer and this at great risk to himself. With obvious pride, he relates that the near-dead prisoner recovered and was standing for rollcall the next morning.

This kind of caring, according to Professor Ervin Staub, can halt the cycle of group violence: »To reduce the probability of genocide and war, helping must be inclusive,... so that the evolving values of caring and connection ultimately include all human beings. We devalue those we harm and value those we help.«[21]

Conclusion

Holocaust education must be taught in a way to assist the student to learn from the past and connect what he has learned to the present. He must first ask, »What would I have done?« And then, »What will I do?« But how can the student answer these questions positively unless he has positive examples of moral and altruistic behavior from the history of the Nazi period? If we only present what Joseph Brodsky called the »human negative potential,«[22] we run a great risk.

The filmmaker Pierre Sauvage, who told the story of his family's rescuers in Le Chambon, France,[23] stated: »If we remember solely the horror of the Holocaust, we will pass on no perspective from which meaningfully to confront and learn from that very horror. If we remember solely the horror of the Holocaust, it is we who will bear the responsibility for having created the most dangerous alibi of all: that it was beyond man's capacity to know and care.«[24]

The history of Jehovah's Witnesses has much to contribute to Holocaust education. As a group, they showed that resistance to evil was possible. They provide a reply to the bystanders who ask, »What could we have done?« Their program of moral education, based on love for God and neighbor, led them to stand up against Nazism. Professor Lance Hill of Tulane University stated that »history shows that if the major religions had taken the stand that the Witnesses did, the Holocaust never would have happened.«[25]

Holocaust history raises issues vital to the development of moral consciousness. It shows the tragic result of the abdication of personal accountability, and challenges all to scrutinize their current ethical choices. Samuel and Pearl Oliner, prominent in the field of altruism research, called on parents, community, and schools to prepare our youth for social responsibility, »preparation,« they state, »that can not only help individuals resist the destructive impulses in society, but also empower them to accept the obligation to do so.«[26]

Teaching the Holocaust requires enormous pedagogical skill. A teacher presents a unique event with universal lessons. He takes the incomprehensible and strives to make it real. He describes mankind at its worst to motivate his students to be their best. The noxious elements that ignited the Holocaust still hang heavy in the air. Our imperative is to teach young people to understand these forces historically, to identify them in the present, and to know that people can have the moral courage to stand up—and speak out—for what is right.

Notes

1 Leo Tolstoy, *Polnoe sobranie socinenij*, v. 38, p. 62. Tolstoy did not always hold this view. For instance, in the periodical *Yasnaya Polyana*, 1858, he maintained that »school should have one goal—the transmission of information and knowledge, without trying to cross over into the area of moral convictions.« (*Polnoe sobranie socinenij*, v. 38, p. 62.)

2 Franklin H. Littell, »Holocaust Education After ›40 Years in the Wilderness,‹« in Marcia Sachs Littell, Richard Libowitz, and Evelyn Bodek Rosen, eds., *The Holocaust Forty Years After* (Lewiston, Queenston, Lampeter: Edwin Mellen Press, 1989), p. 3.

3 Anna Pawelczynska, Values and Violence in Auschwitz: A Sociological Analysis (Berkeley, CA: University of California Press, 1979) [translated from the Polish »Wartosci A Przemoc, Zarys socjologicznej problematyki Oswięcimia«], p. 88.

4 Transcript of Professor King's lecture at the seminar, »The Nazi Assault on Jehovah's Witnesses,« September 29, 1994, United States Holocaust Memorial Museum, Washington, D.C. Professor King is Vice-Chancellor of Staffordshire University, Staffordshire, United Kingdom.

5 *Das Goldene Zeitalter*, Magdeburg, German edition (October 15, 1929), p. 316.

6 *The Watchtower* (August 1, 1935), p. 267.

7 *1934 Yearbook of Jehovah's Witnesses* (1933), p. 129; »Persecution in Germany,« in: *The Golden Age* (April 25, 1934), p. 451.

8 *The Golden Age* (August 16, 1933), p. 734.

9 *Teaching about the Holocaust: A Resource Book for Educators* (Washington, D.C.: United States Holocaust Memorial Museum, n.d.), p. 91.

10 Helmut Krausnick and Martin Broszat, Anatomy of the SS State (London: Granada Publishing, 1968) [translated from the German, Anatomie des SS-Staates], p. 196.

11 *Der Wachtturm* (May 1, 1937), p. 139f.; *Jehovah's Witnesses—Proclaimers of God's Kingdom* (New York: Watchtower Bible and Tract Society, 1993), p. 448.

12 Claudia Koonz, *Mothers in the Fatherland: Women, the Family, and Nazi Politics* (New York: St. Martin's Press, 1987), p. 312.

13 Pawelcynska, p. 89.

14 Koonz, p. 331.

15 Brian R. Dunn, »Jehovah's Witnesses in the Holocaust Kingdom,« in *Holocaust Studies Annual*, v. 2, eds. Fischel and Sanford Pinsker (Greenwood, FL: Penkeville Publishing Company, 1986), p. 159.

16 Manuscript of the video documentary »Jehovah's Witnesses Stand Firm Against Nazi Assault.« The »Deutsche Christen« (German Christian) movement led the charge for a liturgy »free of Jews,« even producing several altered versions of the Bible such as *Die Botschaft Gottes*. The Witness periodicals, *Das Goldene Zeitalter*, June 1, 1934, p. 15, and October 9, 1935 (English edition), p. 15, and *Consolation* (English edition), July 12, 1939, p. 10, indicate that the Witnesses were well aware of Nazi antipathy to the name Jehovah. See also Christine Elizabeth King, *The Nazi State and the New Religions: Five Case Studies in Non-Conformity* (New York: The Edwin Mellen Press), p. 190, and Doris L. Bergen, *Twisted Cross: The German Christian Movement in the Third Reich* (Chapel Hill, North Carolina: University of North Carolina Press, 1996), chapter 2. The Witnesses resisted pressure to expunge their texts and hymns of Hebraic references, such as »Zion,« »Jerusalem,« and »Jehovah.« This commonly led to the charge that the Witnesses were politically linked to Jewish-Bolshevik movement. See King, The Nazi State, pp. 148f. See also *The Golden Age* (April 25, 1934), p. 451, where the charge of Jewish-Marxist connections was used as a pretext to ban the Witnesses in April 1933; Hans Jonak von Freyenwald, *Die Zeugen Jehovas: Pioniere für ein jüdisches Weltreich; Die Politischen Ziele der Internationalen Vereinigung Ernster Bibelforscher* [Jehovah's Witnesses: Pioneers of a Jewish Empire; The political goals of the International Association of Earnest Bible Students] (Berlin: Germania, 1936); and caricature in *Der Stürmer*, May 1935.

17 Helen Fein, *Accounting for Genocide* (New York: Free Press, 1979), p. 4; Pearl M. and Samuel P. Oliner use the term »extensivity« in a similar way, meaning »the tendency to assume commitments and responsibilities toward diverse groups of people,« including attachment in committed interpersonal relationships and inclusiveness of diverse individuals and groups as those for whom one assumes responsibility. See Pearl M. Oliner, and others, eds., *Embracing the Other: Philosophical, Psychological, and Historical Perspectives on Altruism* (New York: New York University Press, 1992), pp. 369f.

18 Dunn, p. 158.

19 King, *The Nazi State*, p. 102. Anecdotal evidence confirms these statements. For example, in New York City, a Polish Jew met a Watch Tower staff member at a business meeting in May 1995. He said to the Witness: »I have a warm place in my heart for Jehovah's Witnesses. You saved my life as a young boy.« He went on to relate that in his village the Nazis would pay one kilo of sugar to anyone who turned in a young Jewish boy. His neighbors who were Witnesses hid him from the Nazis.

20 Helena Celmina, *Women in USSR Prisons* (Stockholm, 1980).

21 Ervin Staub, *The Roots of Evil: The Origins of Genocide and Other Group Violence* (New York: Cambridge University Press, 1989), pp. 276f.

22 Facing History and Ourselves, *Holocaust and Human Behavior Resource Book* (Brookline, MA: Facing History and Ourselves Foundation, 1994), p. xiv.

23 Sauvage's film is called »Weapons of the Spirit.«

24 C. Rittner and S. Myers, eds., *Courage to Care*, p. 102, quoted in Facing History Resource Book, p. 386.

25 Interview on WWL-TV, New Orleans, on March 6, 1997. Hill is director of Tulane's Southern Institute for Education and Research, a teacher training organization that specializes in prejudice-reduction workshops.

26 Samuel P. and Pearl M. Oliner, *The Altruistic Personality: Rescuers of Jews in Nazi Europe* (New York: Free Press, 1988), p. 258.

Hans-Hermann Dirksen, Jürgen Harder,
Hans Hesse, and Johannes Wrobel

Chronology: Development and Persecution of Jehovah's Witnesses

The religious association of Bible Students or Jehovah's Witnesses, as they renamed themselves in 1931, was created by Charles Taze Russell in the 1880s.

1876	Charles Taze Russell is appointed pastor by the »Bible Study Group« he founded.
1879	Establishment of the magazine *Zion's Watch Tower and Herald of Christ's Presence* which becomes the central journal of the new movement.
1879	Beginning of intensive missionary work and establishment of the religious association by a lecture series in various cities, by studying the Bible and publications, and by setting up reading groups, from which communities later develop (in 1899 there were supposedly ca. 2,500 followers in the United States).
1886–1904	C.T. Russell publishes his *Study of the Scriptures* in 6 volumes, establishing the core of his community.
1909	Transfer of the Society's headquarters to Brooklyn, New York.
Oct. 31, 1916	C.T. Russell dies during a lecture tour in the United States.
January 6, 1917	Joseph Franklin Rutherford, an attorney, is appointed as new president of the Watch Tower Society. He immediately restructures the religious association. Individual communities no longer appoint representatives themselves, but are appointed by the leadership of the Society.

Bible Students in Germany

1902	As a result of expanding the missionary efforts of Jehovah's Witnesses in foreign countries in the 1890s, the first office in Germany is opened in Elberfeld, near Wuppertal, in 1902. Growth of followers in Germany:
1905	About 1,000 regular subscribers for the *Wachtturm*.
1918	3,868 »active persons« are counted.
1919	Their number increases to 5,545.
Until 1926	The Association of the Bible Students in Germany with 22,535 followers becomes the largest branch of the religious association outside the United States.
Until 1933	The community expands; there are ca. 25,000 »active persons« and ca. 10,000 sympathizers.
July 26, 1931	At a convention in Columbus (Ohio) the »International Association of Earnest Bible Students« is renamed »Jehovah's Witnesses.« In Germany it

takes a few more years until the new name is accepted, so that for a long time in public Jehovah's Witnesses are still known by the name »Bible Students« or »Earnest Bible Students.«

Persecution of Jehovah's Witnesses Under National Socialism

Jan. 30, 1933	Adolf Hitler is appointed Reich Chancellor.
Feb. 28, 1933	The so-called Reichstag Fire Decree is passed.
Mar. 5, 1933	Out of their religious conviction Jehovah's Witnesses decline to participate in Reichtag elections, resulting in harassment and mistreatment in many places. Jehovah's Witnesses refuse to give the Hitler salute or to pledge allegiance. Later they refuse to participate in any state organization, such as the Hitler Youth, the Nazi People's Welfare, the Reich Air-raid Association, and the German Labor Front. The Nazis view their refusal to perform military service as especially »hostile to the state.«
March 1933	The German branch of the religious association is restructured and new societies are formed: the »*Norddeutsche Bibelforschervereinigung*« (North German Association of Bible Students) and the »*Süddeutsche Bibelforschervereinigung*« (South German Association of Bible Students.) Paul Balzereit becomes the head of the German section.
	Attempts by Jehovah's Witnesses to negotiate with the German government to continue their religious activities fail, and various states ban the Bible Students' Association.
April 7, 1933	The »Law for Restoration of the Career Civil Service« is passed. Apart from the Witnesses' refusal to join the German Labor Front, this law results in the loss of work for many and destroys their livelihood.
Apr. 10, 1933	Ban of the Bible Students' Association in Mecklenburg.
Apr. 13, 1933	Ban of the Association in Bavaria.
Apr. 18, 1933	Ban of the Association in Saxony.
Apr. 19, 1933	Ban of the Association in Hesse.
Apr. 24, 1933	The police and SA occupy and search the offices and printing plant at the Association's headquarters in Magdeburg.
Apr. 26, 1933	Ban of the Association in Lippe and Thuringia.
Apr. 28, 1933	Intercession of the Brooklyn headquarters with the American government results in the temporary recovery of the Magdeburg office from German authorities. However, confiscated material is destroyed.
May 15, 1933	Ban of the Association in Baden.
May 17, 1933	Ban of the Association in Oldenburg.
May 19, 1933	Ban of the Association in Braunschweig.
June 6, 1933	Ban of the Association in Lübeck.
June 24, 1933	Ban of the Association in Prussia.
June 25, 1933	Mass rally in Berlin-Wilmersdorf by invitation of the Magdeburg headquarters, attended by ca. 7,000 Jehovah's Witnesses. Passed »Declaration« to invalidate accusations against the association, and reveals leadership attempts at reaching an agreement with the new rulers in Germany. This course fails.

June 28, 1933	Ban of the Association in Bremen.
June 28, 1933	Second occupation of the Magdeburg headquarters.
June 28, 1933	Ban of the Association in Hamburg.
Sept. 7-9, 1934	Reacting to increasing persecution of Jehovah's Witnesses, the religious association organizes an international convention in Basel, which is also attended by ca. 1,000 followers from Germany despite the ban. Attempts to negotiate with the German government have failed. The unrestricted resumption of missionary and propaganda activities as well as establishing an illegal organization are decided.
Oct. 7, 1934	Massive campaign of foreign protest letters by Jehovah's Witnesses inundate German officials.
Jan. 9, 1935	The first documented case of a Witness, Anna Seifert, incarcerated in Moringen concentration camp.
Apr. 1, 1935	Nonuniform measures in German states hinder systematic suppression of activities by Jehovah's Witnesses. This results in Reich prohibition on April 1, 1935. Simultaneously, the Watch Tower and Tract Society in Magdeburg is dissolved and state and local governments are instructed to confiscate the assets of the association via circular decree of July 13, 1935.
Spring 1936	From this time onward, the persecuting authorities make use of a further means to force the followers of the »teachings of the Bible Students« to surrender their convictions. Many times custody is taken away from parents via court decision to stop a »subversive« influence. Between 1936 and 1946, at least 860 children were affected by this measure according to Jehovah's Witness sources.
June 1936	The Gestapo forms a special unit for surveillance of Jehovah's Witnesses.
Aug.-Sept. 1936	The first mass arrests of Jehovah's Witnesses throughout the Reich are implemented. Despite increasing persecution (up to mid–1937, at least 17 Witnesses die during interrogations and in prisons) and the loss of the organization's leadership, the association is able to reorganize.
Sept. 4-7, 1936	Lucerne convention of Jehovah's Witnesses passes a resolution denouncing the persecution of Jehovah's Witnesses in Nazi Germany.
Dec. 12, 1936	About 100,000 copies of the Lucerne protest resolution are distributed in various German cities; the campaign is repeated in February and March 1937.
Dec. 1936	In Moringen concentration camp, female Jehovah's Witnesses refuse to work for the Winter Relief Campaign, resulting in isolation as well as prohibitions on receipt of all mail and packages for months.
1937	During the year Jehovah's Witnesses in concentration camps are included in instructions for »recidivist offenders.« They are penalized with heavy labor assignments and growing harassment. In Dachau concentration camp they are imprisoned in »Isolation,« a barrack separated by barbed wire from the rest of the camp. This »model« is later implemented in Sachsenhausen concentration camp.
Apr. 22, 1937	Circular decree from Gestapo Berlin: »All International Bible Students Association followers released from prisons after serving their sentence

are to be taken into protective custody; their transfer to a concentration camp can be requested if an explanation of the facts is submitted.« Thereafter, hundreds of Jehovah's Witnesses are remanded to concentration camps. For example, in Moringen, the percentage of Jehovah's Witnesses increases from 17 percent in June to 89 percent in December 1937. In other concentration camps, Jehovah's Witnesses make up on average 5 to 10 percent of camp inmates in prewar years. Only in the women's camps of Moringen, Lichtenburg, and Ravensbrück (until the beginning of the war) are Jehovah's Witnesses the largest prisoner group. After the beginning of war, their proportion decreases drastically: Mauthausen concentration camp 5.2 percent (at the end of 1944: 0.12 percent), Buchenwald concentration camp 3.3 percent (at the end of 1944: 0.3 percent).

June 20, 1937	In the first half of 1937, a detailed report about persecution in Germany is assembled in Bern using information from Witnesses in Germany. The flyer is titled: »Open Letter – To Germans who believe in the Bible and love Christ.« This »open letter« is distributed on June 20, 1937, in a mass operation throughout Germany.
Fall 1937	Second wave of mass arrests of Jehovah's Witnesses. Despite regional successes in reorganizing local groups, Jehovah's Witness activities stop throughout the Reich.
Dec. 20, 1937	In Moringen concentration camp for women, a »declaration« is introduced only for Jehovah's Witnesses. After 1935 »declarations« were used in concentration camps as well as in prisons. After 1937, this is institutionalized by imposing subsequent detention (*Nachhaft* = protective custody arrest after completing a prison sentence) if the declaration is not signed. Before the war, this »declaration« was ostensibly signed more frequently. Estimates are that about 10 percent of Witnesses incarcerated in concentration camps signed and up to 50 percent in prisons. On December 21, 1937, this »declaration« is standardized on Himmler's orders. It states: »Declaration. I have come to know that the International Bible Students Association is proclaiming erroneous teachings and under the cloak of religion follows hostile purposes against the State. I therefore left the organization entirely and made myself absolutely free from the teachings of this sect. I herewith give assurance that I will never again take any part in the activity of the International Bible Students Association. Any persons approaching me with the teachings of the Bible Students, or who in any manner reveal their connections with them, I will denounce immediately. All literature from the Bible Students that should be sent to my address I will at once deliver to the nearest police station. I will in the future esteem the laws of the State and join in every way the community of the people. I have been informed that I will at once be taken again into protective custody if I should act against the declaration given today.«
1938	Standardized color symbols are introduced for concentration camp inmates. Jehovah's Witnesses receive the »purple triangle.«
March 1938	Total mail ban for Jehovah's Witnesses in concentration camps. Restric-

	tions on receiving and sending letters are stamped by the camp postal censor: »The prisoner remains, as before, a stubborn Bible Student and refuses to reject the Bible Students' false teachings. For this reason the usual privileges of correspondence have been denied him.«
Oct. 6, 1938	Jehovah's Witnesses in Lichtenburg concentration camp for women refuse to listen to a radio speech by Adolf Hitler on the occasion of occupying the Sudetenland. The SS drive the women out of their cell with water hoses. Many women do not recover from this torture.
1939–1940	During these two years, SS terror rages against Jehovah's Witnesses in the concentration camps.
Sept. 15, 1939	August Dickmann, a Jehovah's Witness, is publicly shot in Sachsenhausen concentration camp. The news of his execution is announced on the radio.
Dec. 19, 1939	In Ravensbrück concentration camp, female Jehovah's Witnesses refuse to sew bags which they assume are to be used as gun holsters, and therefore war-related work. The SS unsuccessfully tries to break the women's resistance with punishments such as standing at attention for days, withdrawal of food, and detention in darkness. This harassment continues until March 1940.
After 1942	Conditions improve for Jehovah's Witnesses in the concentration camps. For example, female Witnesses are »very sought after« as domestic help by SS leaders. They are even entrusted with childcare, although in many cases their own children had been removed from their custody.
March 6, 1944	Dr. Robert Ritter announces in a letter to the President of the Reich Research Council (*Reichsforschungsrat*) his plan to begin »genealogical investigations of the racial and genetic ancestry of Jehovah's Witnesses in Ravensbrück concentration camp.«
July 21, 1944	Himmler mentions in a letter his plan to settle Jehovah's Witnesses after the war in the border zone adjacent to the Soviet Union, because their pacifist influence would result in Soviet »defenselessness.«
1933–1945	Of about 25,000 Jehovah's Witnesses, ca. 10,000 had been imprisoned for a various lengths of time; 2,000 of them in concentration camps; 1,200 had died or were murdered, including ca. 250 Jehovah's Witnesses who had been executed for refusing military service.

Persecution of Jehovah's Witnesses in the SBZ (SOZ)/GDR 1945-1990

9/9/1945	Organization meeting of the »International Bible Students Association, German Branch« in Magdeburg; in the same month, registered with the Register of Associations (Vereinsregister) at the Magistrate's Court in Magdeburg.

4/4/1946	The Information Service Department of the Main Aministrative Office (Hauptverwaltungsamt) of the City of Leipzig asks the outdoor service a question concerning the religious services of a community called »Jehovah.« Expressed should be »how the activity of religious groups is carried out.«
7/1/1946	Registry of the change of name »Jehovah's Witnesses, International Bible Students Association, German Branch« with the Register of Associations (Vereinsregister) in Magdeburg.
7/24/1947	Confirmation by the Soviet Military Administration Germany (SMAD) that Jehovah's Witnesses are registered.
8/27-29/1948	The Soviet authorities refuse permission for a convention in Leipzig. Thereupon Jehovah's Witnesses hold their convention in the Waldbühne in West Berlin.
9/22/1948	Bruno Haid, member of the SED central secretariat, personnel department, wrote to the vice president of the German Administration for Internal Affairs (Deutsche Verwaltung des Innern, DvdI), Erich Mielke, requesting all material about the activities of religious sects (Jehovah's Witnesses) and all political activities by the church. A national monitoring of Jehovah's Witnesses begins.
12/6/1948	The head of the Thuringia Department K5 verifies that no anti-democratic propaganda is carried out at the meetings of Jehovah's Witnesses, the »recruits,« however, »get lost for our assignment.«
Early 1949	In the K5's report, terms such as »activity hostile to the state« or »sect hostile to reconstruction« appear.
7/29-31/1949	A further Waldbühne convention in West Berlin. Adoption of a resolution. Therein, among other things, it is protested against the undemocratic and unconstitutional bans and restrictions of the religious services in Saxony, against the political and religious hostility, against the designating of Jehovah's Witnesses as warmongers and enemies of peace. It is declared that Jehovah's Witnesses keep neutral towards all political and ideological questions. It reads literally: »Under no circumstances, not even under the pressure of dictatorial measures, will Jehovah's Witnesses get involved in the global conflict between East and West.« Without warning, the authorities of the Soviet Occupation Zone (SBZ) cancel the provision of the already approved special trains and block the approach roads to Berlin. Nevertheless, about 33,000 persons visit the convention.
9/13/1949	Meeting of the Politburo. Drawing up of a plan of action against Jehovah's Witnesses.
10/7/1949	The SBZ becomes the German Democratic Republic. The number of Jehovah's Witnesses lies between 12,000 (average) and 17,000 (peak).
Autumn 1949/Spring 1950	Defamatory articles appear in various newspapers.
February 1950	Petition of Jehovah's Witnesses to the state leadership drawing attention to the deplorable state of affairs. On July 10 this petition was again sent numerously to West and East Germany.

Spring and Summer 1950	Pressure on Jehovah's Witnesses by the GDR authorities increases. The People's Police break up numerous circuit assemblies and arrest platform speakers. During the last week in August, a craftily conducted press campaign, peppered with slander, prepares the populace for the planned ban on Jehovah's Witnesses.
8/30/1950	Occupation and confiscation of the administration building of the Watch Tower Society in Magdeburg by the Ministry for State Security (Ministerium für Staatssicherheit, MfS), most of the workers are arrested. During this time, at least 300 Witnesses of Jehovah are arrested nationwide. Several Witnesses of Jehovah, such as Erich Poppe from Meißen, die as a result of the severe abuse suffered whilst held in the custody of the state security.
8/31/1950	Ban decreed by the GDR Minister of the Interior, Dr. Steinhoff. He orders that Jehovah's Witnesses be »removed from the list of authorized religious organizations and thus are banned.« These are accused of »systematic agitation against the existing democratic order and its laws« as well as espionage. Up until the erection of the Berlin Wall in 1961, Watch Tower literature reaches the GDR via West Berlin.
10/4/1950	Pronouncement of judgment at the public trial against Willi Heinicke, Fritz Adler and seven other Jehovah's Witnesses. »Heinicke and Adler receive life imprisonment, the rest 8-15 years,« reports the »Frankfurter Neue Presse.« Other large trials ensue in the territory throughout the GDR. This wave of trials continued on to approximately summer/autumn 1951.
1/9/1951	In a directive Erich Mielke lays stress on the work of recruiting informers in order to »discover the foremost functionaries and the most dangerous agents of the sect.«
6/18/1955	Bruno Sarfert dies in the Brandenburg-Görden penitentiary. Cause of death: »Circulatory problems.« About a year previously, on 3/15/1954, Bruno Seifert, another Witness of Jehovah, was so badly beaten that he died shortly after in a Dresden hospital.
8/13/1961	West Berlin becomes divided from East Berlin and the GDR. At first only single Watch Tower articles reach the congregations (parishes). Articles are typed with up to 8 carbon copies on a typewriter and studied in small groups. Soon simple devices are made for duplicating the articles. Later, the Witnesses are provided with India (light)paper editions from West Germany.
8/6/1962	Carsten Möller collapses and dies following strenuous work in the Brandenburg penitentiary. This Witness of Jehovah was imprisoned for 10 years by the Nazis and for 11 years by the communists.
March 1963	The Ministry for State Security makes it its goal to arrest the whole leadership of Jehovah's Witnesses in the GDR (operational procedure »swamp« [Sumpf]). During the following years, informers, house searches, interrogations and bugging devices are some of the common practices of the State Security Service.

11/15/1964	In one fell swoop, 142 young Jehovah's Witnesses are arrested on account of conscientious objection – (General military service had been instituted in December 1962). They are later consigned to hard labor.
11/23/1965	House searches take place nationwide. Seventeen Jehovah's Witnesses are arrested.
7/25/1966	The series of trials against the so-called illegal leadership of Jehovah's Witnesses begins. Fifteen Witnesses in prominent positions receive prison sentences of up to 12 years.
August 1966	New work directive of the MfS in the central operational procedure »swamp« (ZOV »Sumpf«), whereby in particular unofficial collaborators (Inoffizielle Mitarbeiter, IM) in responsible positions are to be won over. The work of undermining is to be intensified.
May 1971	The Walter Ulbricht era comes to an end (1950-1971); start of the Honecker era (until 1989). From now on the People's Police impose administrative fines (»Ordnungsstrafen«) on Jehovah's Witnesses who publicly spread their belief.
1985	Jehovah's Witnesses are no longer to be penalized on account of conscientious objection.
11/9/1989	Fall of the Berlin Wall. The East German Jehovah's Witnesses are now able to travel to the West without impediment in order to obtain Watch Tower literature.
3/14/1990	The »Religious community of Jehovah's Witnesses in the GDR« receives state recognition.
1945-1990	From 1950 until 1961 (construction of the Berlin Wall), 3,006 Jehovah's Witnesses were arrested by the GDR authorities. Of these, 2,170 (including 641 women) received prison sentences (on an average 5.7 years) In fifteen cases a life term was imposed. Following 1961 the number of judgments declined.
	At least 250 of the Witnesses of Jehovah who were imprisoned, mostly in the 50s, had already been incarcerated under National Socialism.
	Presumably (status August 1998) a total of over 5,000 Jehovah's Witnesses were imprisoned in various penitentiaries and work camps. Of them, at least 57 (43 men and 14 women) died in prison or from the consequences of imprisonment, from abuses, sickness, malnutrition and old age.

Bibliography

(The pages inside parentheses mention Jehovah's Witnesses)

1. Surveys

Benz, Wolfgang. »Die Zeugen Jehovas.« In: *Informationen zur politischen Bildung: Deutscher Widerstand 1933-1945*, no. 243. Bonn, 1994 (pp. 21, 49)

Benz, Wolfgang and Walter H. Pehle, ed. *Lexikon des deutschen Widerstandes.* Stuttgart, 1997 (pp. 321-325)

Benz, Wolfgang, Hermann Graml, and Hermann Weiß. *Enzyklopädie des Nationalsozialismus.* Stuttgart, 1997 (pp. 192, 280, 287, 405, 412, 439, 449, 450, 710, 726)

Canonici, Guy. *Les Témoins de Jéhovah face à Hitler.* Paris, 1998

Carsten, Francis L. *Widerstand gegen Hitler: Die deutschen Arbeiter und die Nazis.* Frankfurt am Main and Leipzig, 1996 (pp. 166-176)

Cercle Européen des Témoins de Jéhovah Anciens Déportés et Internés (CETJAD). *Mémoire de Témoins 1933-1945.* Boulogne-Billancourt, 1995

Cole, Marley. *Jehovas Zeugen: Die Neue-Welt-Gesellschaft: Geschichte und Organisation einer Religionsbewegung.* Frankfurt am Main, 1956 (pp. 188-206, 231-235)

Conway, John S. *The Nazi Persecution of the Churches 1933-1945.* New York, 1968 (pp. 195-199, 371, 373, 431)

Garbe, Detlef. »›Sendboten des jüdischen Bolschewismus‹: Antisemitismus als Motiv nationalsozialistischer Verfolgung der Zeugen Jehovas.« In: *Tel Aviver Jahrbuch für deutsche Geschichte 23*, Gerlingen, 1994 (pp. 145-171)

Garbe, Detlef. *Zwischen Widerstand und Martyrium: Die Zeugen Jehovas im »Dritten Reich.«* Munich, 1997

Graffard, Sylvie and Léo Tristan. *Die Bibelforscher und der Nationalsozialismus (1933-1945): Die Vergessenen der Geschichte.* Translated from the French. Paris, 1998

Grünberg, Wolfgang and others, ed. *Lexikon der Hamburger Religionsgemeinschaften: Religionsvielfalt in der Stadt von A-Z.* Seminar für praktische Theologie der Universität Hamburg. Hamburg, 1995 (pp. 121-124, 203, 233)

Hellmund, Dietrich. *Geschichte der Zeugen Jehovas (in der Zeit von 1870 bis 1920).* Ph.D. dissertation, Lutheran Theological Faculty of the University Hamburg. Hamburg, 1971. (Postscript includes history of Jehovas Witnesses up to 1970)

Helmreich, Ernst Christian. *The German Churches under Hitler: Background, Struggle, and Epilogue.* Detroit, 1979 (pp. 29, 91f., 129, 287, 338, 389-399, 409, 561)

Kater, Michael H. »Die Ernsten Bibelforscher im Dritten Reich.« In: *Vierteljahrshefte für Zeitgeschichte 17*, no. 2, April 1969 (pp. 181-218)

King, Christine E. »Jehovah's Witnesses under Nazism.« In: *A Mosaic of Victims: Non-Jews Persecuted and Murdered by the Nazis*, edited by Michael Berenbaum. New York, 1990 (pp. 188-193)

King, Christine E. *The Nazi State and the New Religions: Five Case Studies in Non-Conformity.* New York and Toronto, 1982 (pp. 91, 107, 123, 136, 147-203)

Kolarz, Walter. *Die Religionen in der Sowjetunion.* Freiburg i. B., 1963 (pp. 335-342)

Krug, Stefanie, and Fritz Poppenberg. *Fear not. Persecution and Resistance of Jehovah's Witnesses under the Nazi regime.* Video, 92 minutes. Berlin, 1996

Loofs, Friedrich. *Die »Internationale Vereinigung Ernster Bibelforscher.«* Leizpig, 1921

Mehringer, Hartmut. *Widerstand und Emigration: Das NS-Regime und seine Gegner.* Munich, 1997 (pp. 102-107, 137f., 236ff.)

Oleschinski, Brigitte. »Religiöse Gemeinschaften im Widerstand.« In: *Widerstand gegen den Nationalsozialismus,* edited by Peter Steinbach and Johannes Tuchel. Bonn, 1994 (pp. 193-201)

Pierro, Matteo. *Fra Martirio e Resistenza: La Persecuzione nazista e fascista di Testimoni di Geova.* Como, 1997

Ruppel, Helmut, Ingrid Schmidt, and Wolfgang Wippermann. *... stosset nicht um weltlich Regiment? Ein Erzähl- und Arbeitsbuch vom Widerstehen im Nationalsozialismus.* (Wege des Lernens) 1986

United States Holocaust Memorial Museum. *Jehovah's Witnesses: Victims of the Nazi Era 1933-1945.* Washington, D.C., 1995

Watch Tower Bible and Tract Society. *Jehovah's Witnesses—Proclaimers of God's Kingdom.* New York, 1993

Watch Tower Bible and Tract Society. *1974 Yearbook of Jehovah's Witnesses.* New York, 1973 (pp. 65-253)

Wachtturm-Gesellschaft. *Jehovah's Witnesses Stand Firm Against Nazi Assault.* Video, 78 minutes. Selters/Ts., 1996

Wachtturm-Gesellschaft. *Jehovah's Witnesses Stand Firm Against Nazi Assault.* Video, short version for schools, with study guide. 28 minutes. New York, 1997

Zipfel, Friedrich. *Kirchenkampf in Deutschland 1933-1945: Religionsverfolgung und Selbstbehauptung der Kirchen in der nationalsozialistischen Zeit.* Berlin, 1965 (pp. 44, 175-201, 352-358, 363-371, 411-417, 484, 527-533)

Zürcher, Franz. *Kreuzzug gegen das Christentum: Moderne Christenverfolgung. Eine Dokumentation.* Zurich and New York, 1938.

Religious Survey
Ruttmann, Hermann. *Vielfalt der Religionen am Beispiel der Glaubensgemeinschaften im Landkreis Marburg-Biedenkopf.* Marburg, 1995 (pp. 106-109)

Bibliography
Bergmann, Jerry. *Jehovah's Witnesses and Kindred Groups: A Historical Compendium and Bibliography.* New York and London, 1984

Nazi and GDR Periods
Garbe, Detlef. »Im Westen vergessen, im Osten verschmäht: Verweigerung und Widerstand der Zeugen Jehovas in der Geschichtsschreibung.« In: *Informationen Studienkreis deutscher Widerstand,* 22, no. 46. Frankfurt, November 1997 (pp. 27-30)

2. Local History Studies

Hoffmann, Werner, and Reinhard Hildebrandt. *Streiflichter aus Verfolgung und Widerstand 1933-1945.* Issue no. 5 edited by VVN Kreisvereinigung Ludwigsburg. Ludwigsburg, 1993 (pp. 40-52)

Kessel, Joseph. *Medizinalrat Kersten.* Translated from the French. Munich, 1961 (pp. 161-173)

Pavlicic, Michael. *Lippspringe: Beiträge zur Geschichte,* edited by Stadt und Heimatverein Lippspringe. Paderborn, 1995 (pp. 535-538)

Ahlen
Stadt Ahlen, The Mayor, ed. *Die Verfolgung der Zeugen Jehovas in Ahlen von 1933-1945: Rede von Horst Rösling während der »Woche der Brüderlichkeit.«* Ahlen, 1995

Augsburg

Hetzer, Gerhard. »Ernste Bibelforscher in Augsburg.« In: Broszat, Martin, Elke Fröhlich, and Anton Gorssmann, eds., *Bayern in der NS-Zeit: Herrschaft und Gesellschaft im Konflikt*. Munich and Vienna, 1981, v. 4 (pp. 621–643)

Baden

Schadt, Jörg. *Verfolgung und Widerstand unter dem Nationalsozialismus in Baden. Die Lageberichte der Gestapo und des Generalstaatsanwalts Karlsruhe 1933–1940*, ed. by Stadtarchiv Mannheim. Stuttgart, 1976 (pp. 48, 55, 58f., 64f., 79, 92f., 100, 143, 156, 184, 204, 238, 241f., 246, 250, 253–256, 260–266)

Baden-Württemberg

Roser, Hubert, ed. *Widerstand als Bekenntnis: Die Zeugen Jehovas und das NS-Regime in Baden und Württemberg*. Konstanz, 1999

Bavaria

Broszat, Martin, Elke Fröhlich, and Anton Grossmann. *Bayern in der NS-Zeit. Vol. 4: Herrschaft und Gesellschaft im Konflikt*. Munich and Vienna, 1981 (pp. 448, 450, 459, 621–643)

Berlin

Sandvoß, Hans-Rainer. *Widerstand in Berlin 1933–1945: Widerstand in einem Arbeiterbezirk*. Issue no. 1: *Wedding*. Berlin, 1983 (pp. 75f.)

Sandvoß, Hans-Rainer. *Widerstand in Berlin 1933–1945*. Issue no. 3: *Widerstand in Spandau*. Berlin, 1988 (pp. 153–159)

Sandvoß, Hans-Rainer. *Widerstand in Berlin 1933–1945*. Issue no. 4: *Widerstand in Neukölln*. Berlin, 1990 (pp. 222–225)

Sandvoß, Hans-Rainer. *Widerstand in Berlin 1933–1945*. Issue no. 6: *Widerstand in Pankow und Reinickendorf*. Berlin, 1994 (pp. 201–205)

Sandvoß, Hans-Rainer. *Widerstand in Berlin 1933–1945*. Issue no. 8: *Widerstand in Mitte und Tiergarten*. Berlin, 1994 (pp. 292–286)

Sandvoß, Hans-Rainer. *Widerstand in Berlin 1933–1945*. Issue no. 10: *Widerstand im Kreuzberg*. Berlin, 1996 (pp. 224–228)

Wörmann, Heinrich-Wilhelm. *Widerstand 1933–1945, Berlin*. Issue no. 5: *Widerstand in Charlottenburg*. Berlin, 1991 (pp. 231, 254)

Wörmann, Heinrich-Wilhelm. *Widerstand 1933–1945, Berlin*. Issue no. 9: *Widerstand in Köpenick und Treptow*. Berlin, 1995

Bielefeld

Knobelsdorf, Andreas, Monika Minninger, and Bärbel Sunderbrink. »Das Recht wurzelt im Volk: NS-Justiz im Landgerichtsbezirk Bielefeld.« In: *Bielefelder Beiträge zur Stadt- und Regionalgeschichte*, ed. Stadtarchiv and Landesgeschichtliche Bibliothek Bielefeld, no. 11, 1992 (pp. 59–68)

Bochum, Wattenscheid

Zehnter, Annette. *Widerstand und Verfolgung in Bochum und Wattenscheid 1933–1945*. Essen, 1992 (pp. 210–216)

Bremen

Marßolek, Inge and René Ott. »Die Ernsten Bibelforscher (Jehovas Zeugen).« In: *Bremen im Dritten Reich: Anpassung – Widerstand – Verfolgung*. Bremen, 1986 (pp. 303–308, 312)

Celle

Hermann, Reiner. *Jehovas Zeugen in Celle 1922-1997.* Celle, 1997

Delmenhorst

Glöckner, Paul Wilhelm. »Der Widerstand der ›Ernsten Bibelforscher.‹« In: *Delmenhorst unter dem Hakenkreuz*, v. 2: *Der Widerstand.* Delmenhorst, 1983 (pp. 46–61)

Detmold

Riechert, Hansjörg. *Nationalsozialismus in Detmold*, edited by Hermann Niebuhr and Andreas Ruppert. 1998 (pp. 723ff.)

Dorsten

Stegemann, Wolf and Dirk Hartwich, ed. *Dorsten unter dem Hakenkreuz: Kirche zwischen Anpassung und Widerstand. Eine Dokumentation zur Zeitgeschichte.* V. 2. Dorstem, 1984 (pp. 128–139)

Duisburg

Bludau, Kuno. »*Gestapo-geheim!*«: *Widerstand und Verfolgung in Duisburg 1933–1945.* V. 98, Schriftenreihe des Forschungsinstituts der Friedrich-Ebert-Stiftung. Bonn-Bad Godesberg, 1973 (pp. 223f., 289f., 292ff.)

Düsseldorf

Moß, Christoph, and Angela Kawell. *Verfolgung und Widerstand der »Ernsten Bibelforscher« (Zeugen Jehovas) während der NS-Zeit in Düsseldorf.* Mahn- und Gedenkstätte Düsseldorf, ed. Düsseldorf, 2000.

Wickert, Christl. »Frauen im Hintergrund – das Beispiel von Kommunistinnen und Bibelforscherinnen.« In: *Das »andere Deutschland« im Widerstand gegen den Nationalsozialismus: Beiträge zur politischen Überwindung der nationalsozialistischen Diktatur im Exil und im Dritten Reich.* Essen, 1994 (pp. 200–222).

Essen

Schmidt, Ernst. *Lichter in der Finsternis: Widerstand und Verfolgung in Essen 1933–1945. Erlebnisse – Berichte – Forschungen – Gespräche.* Frankfurt am Main, 1980 (pp. 174–78, 382–385)

Schmidt, Ernst. *Essen unter Bomben: Märztage 1943*, edited by Alte Synagoge Essen. Essen, 1984 (pp. 62–65)

Steinberg, Hans-Josef. *Widerstand und Verfolgung in Essen 1933–1945.* V. 7, Schriftenreihe des Forschungsinstituts der Friedrich-Ebert-Stiftung. Bonn-Bad Godesberg, 1972 (pp. 374–401)

Eutin

Stokes, Lawrence D. *Kleinstadt und Nationalsozialismus: Ausgewählte Dokumente zur Geschichte von Eutin 1918–1945.* V. 82, Quellen und Forschungen zur Geschichte Schleswig-Holsteins, Gesellschaft für Schleswig-Holsteinische Geschichte. Neumünster, 1984 (pp. 515, 530, 567, 697–716)

Frankfurt

Wipppermann, Wolfgang. *Das Leben in Frankfurt zur NS-Zeit IV. Der Widerstand: Darstellung, Dokumente, didaktische Hinweise.* Frankfurt am Main, 1996 (pp. 73–76, 136f.)

Friedrichstadt

Kühl, Reiner W. »Widerstand im Dritten Reich: Die Ernsten Bibelforscher in Friedrichstadt.« In: *Unterhaltung für Friedrichstadt und die angränzende Gegend: Mitteilungsblatt der Gesellschaft für Friedrichstädter Stadtgeschichte,* no. 27, 1985 (pp. 165–190)

Gerresheim

Augustin, Uwe. »Die Internationale Vereinigung Ernster Bibelforscher (Zeugen Jehovas).« In: Angela Genger, ed., *Erlebtes und Erlittenes: Gerresheim unter dem Nationalsozialismus: Berichte — Dokumente — Erzählungen.* Düsseldorf, 1993 (pp. 202-209)

Göppingen

Storr, Matthias. »Die Verfolgung der Zeugen Jehovas. Das Tausendjährige Reich Adolf Hitlers gegen das Tausendjährige Königreich Gottes.« In: *Göppingen unterm Hakenkreuz*, v. 32. Veröffentlichungen des Stadtarchivs Göppingen. Göppingen, 1994 (pp. 230-235)

Gruibingen

Gemeinde Gruibingen, Kreis Göppingen, ed. *Gruibinger Heimatbuch.* »Geschichte der Zeugen Jehovas in Gruibingen.« Göppingen, 1986

Hamburg

Garbe, Detlef. »Gott mehr gehorchen als den Menschen: Neuzeitliche Christenverfolgung im nationalsozialistischen Hamburg.« In: *Verachtet — verfolgt — vernichtet*, edited by Projektgruppe für die vergessenen Opfer des NS-Regimes in Hamburg e.V. Hamburg, 1988 (pp. 171-203)

Herne, Wanne-Eickel

Dorn, Barbara, and Michael Zimmermann. *Bewährungsprobe Herne und Wanne-Eickel 1933-1945*, edited by Stadt Herne. Bochum, 1987 (pp. 236-240, 338-342, 373)

Hessen

Hessisches Hauptstaatsarchiv, ed. *Quellen zu Widerstand und Verfolgung unter der NS-Diktatur in hessischen Archiven: Übersicht über die Bestände in Archiven und Dokumentationsstellen.* Wiesbaden, 1995 (pp. 17, 61, 66, 70, 74, 96, 110, 154)

Itzehoe

No author. »Die Verfolgung der Ernsten Bibelforscher.« In: *Itzehoe: Geschichte einer Stadt in Schleswig-Holstein*, v. 2. Itzehoe, 1991

Karlsruhe

Koch, Manfred. »Die Veröffentlichung einer Todesanzeige ist unzulässig«: Zum Widerstand gegen den Nationalsozialismus in Karlsruhe. In: *Aufstieg der NSDAP und Widerstand*, Stadtarchiv Karlsruhe. Karlsruhe, 1993 (pp. 82-85)

Kassel

Knigge-Tesche, Renate, and Axel Ulrich. *Verfolgung und Widerstand 1933-1945 in Hessen.* Frankfurt am Main, 1996 (pp. 128ff., 132, 451, 527, 529, 532)

Lübeck, Schleswig-Holstein

Imberger, Elke. *Widerstand »von unten«: Widerstand und Dissens aus den Reihen der Arbeiterbewegung und der Zeugen Jehovas in Lübeck und Schleswig-Holstein 1933-1945.* Neumünster, 1991 (pp. 243-376)

Mannheim, Biography

Matthias, Erich, and Hermann Weber. *Widerstand gegen den Nationalsozialismus in Mannheim.* Mannheim, 1984 (pp. 425-431)

Moers

Schmidt, Bernhard, and others. *Tatort Moers: Widerstand und Nationalsozialismus im südlichen Altkreis Moers*. Moers, 1994 (pp. 486ff.)

Niedersachsen (Lower Saxony)

Mlynek, Klaus, ed. *Gestapo Hannover meldet ... Polizei und Regierungsberichte für das mittlere und südliche Niedersachsen 1933 und 1937*. V. 29, Veröffentlichungen der historischen Kommission für Niedersachsen und Bremen. V. 1, Hildesheim, 1986 (pp. 63, 116, 166, 177, 188, 212, 260, 306, 331, 341, 355, 358, 367, 381, 404, 439, 494, 522, 526)

Oberhausen

Emig, Erik. *Jahre des Terrors: Der Nationalsozialismus in Oberhausen. Gedenkbuch für die Opfer des Faschismus*. Oberhausen, 1967 (pp. 96ff., 250–257)

Oldenburger Land

Heuzeroth, Günter, and Sylvia Wille. »Die unter dem lila Winkel litten: Die Verweigerung der Zeugen Jehovas und ihre Verfolgung.« In: *Verfolgte aus religiösen Gründen*, edited by Universität Oldenburg, editor Franz-Josef Endel. V. 3 of the series *Unter der Gewaltherrschaft des Nationalsozialismus 1933-1945: Dargestellt an den Ereignissen im Oldenburger Land*. Oldenburg, 1985 (pp. 167–214)

Osnabrück

Steinwascher, Gerd, ed. *Gestapo Osnabrück meldet ... Polizei- und Regierungsberichte aus dem Regierungsbezirk Osnabrück aus den Jahren 1933 bis 1936*. V. 36, Osnabrücker Geschichtsquellen und Forschungen. Osnabrück, 1995 (pp. 137, 155, 175, 187, 209, 238, 297, 309, 330, 346, 397, 435, 437, 440, 444, 447, 450)

Osterode am Harz

Struve, Walter. »Die Zeugen Jehovas in Osterode am Harz: Ein Fallstudie über Widerstand und Unterdrückung in einer kleinen Industriestadt im Dritten Reich.« In: *Niedersächsisches Jahrbuch für Landesgeschichte*, v. 62. Hanover, 1990 (pp. 265–295)

Struve, Walter. *Aufstieg und Herrschaft des Nationalsozialismus in einer industriellen Kleinstadt: Osterode am Harz 1918-1945*. Essen, 1992 (pp. 242–274)

Ostwestfalen and Lippe

Minninger, Monika. *Zur Verfolgung von Zeugen Jehovas in Ostwestfalen und Lippe, 1933-1945*. Bielefeld, 2001.

Paderborner Land

Königes, Jona, Markus Moors, and Schäferjohann-Bursian. *Endlich Frieden!? Das Ende des Zweiten Weltkriegs im Paderborner Land*, Kreismuseum Wewelsburg, Wewelsburg, 1995 (pp. 25ff., 30)

Ruhr-Lippe

Dittgen, Willi. *Zwischen den Kriegen 1919-1939: Unruhige Zeiten zwischen Ruhr und Lippe*. V. 12 »Dinslakener Beiträge.« Dinslaken, 1977 (pp. 141f.)

Schwabach

Aumer, Manuela, and Martin Aumer. »Die ›Ernsten Bibelforscher‹: Eine religiöse Minderheit in Zeiten großer Bedrängnis.« In: *Vergessen und verdrängt? Schwabach 1918-1945*, edited by Sabine Weigand-Karg and others, exhibition in Stadtmuseum Schwabach, Oct. 19 – Dec. 14, 1997. Schwabach, 1998

Sulzfeld

Breitkopf, Bernd. *Sulzfeld: von Bauern, Steinhauern und Edelleuten*. Ubstadt-Weiher, 1997 (pp. 259–262, 410)

Traunstein

Niederlöhner, Edmund. *Verfolgung und Widerstand in der NS-Zeit im Landkreis Traunstein 1933–1945*, edited by Kreisjugendring Traunstein. Traunstein, 1994 (pp. 67–73)

Tyrol

Maislinger, Andreas. »Die Zeugen Jehovas (Ernste Bibelforscher).« In: *Widerstand und Verfolgung in Tirol 1934–1945: Eine Dokumentation*, V. 2 edited by Dokumnentationsarchiv des österreichischen Widerstandes. Vienna, 1984 (pp. 369–383)

Wiesbaden

Bembeneck, Lother, and Axel Ulrich. *Widerstand und Verfolgung in Wiesbaden 1933–1945: Eine Dokumentation*, edited by Magistrat der Landeshauptstadt Wiesbaden, Stadtarchiv. Giessen, 1990 (pp. 248–251, 284ff.)

Zwingenberg

Kilthau, Fritz. »Verfolgung der Zwingenberger Zeugen Jehovas.« In: *mitten unter uns: Zwingenberg an der Bergstraße von 1933 bis 1945*. Heppenheim, 2000 (pp. 154-171)

Refusal of Military Service

Beplate, Ernst. »Ich bin kein Deutscher!« In: *Der Bürgermeister im Hundeloch: Bederkesaer Geschichten und Begebenheiten quer durch die Jahrhunderte*, Schriften der Burggesellschaft Bederkesa, no. 8. Stade, 1993 (pp. 51–54)

Wichmann, Ehrhardt. *Vergessene Opfer, verdrängter Widerstand*. Minden, 1998 (pp. 16–21)

3. Biographies

Gollnick, Rüdiger, and others. *Dinslaken in der NS Zeit: Vergessene Geschichte 1933–1945*. Kleve, 1983 (pp. 285–295)

Högl, Günther. »Widerstand aus christlicher Verantwortung: Die Zeugen Jehovas.« In: *Widerstand und Verfolgung in Dortmund 1933–1945: Katalog zur ständigen Ausstellung des Stadtarchivs Dortmund in der Mahn- und Gedenkstätte Steinwache*. Dortmund, 1992 (pp. 297ff.)

Hollweg, Max. *Es ist unmöglich von dem zu schweigen, was ich erlebt habe: Zivilcourage im Dritten Reich*. Bielefeld, 1997

Jobst, Vinzenz. *Anton Uran: Verfolgt, vergessen, hingerichtet*. Klagenfurt, 1997

Koch, Manfred, and Julius Engelhard. »Drucker, Kurier und Organisator der Zeugen Jehovas.« In: *Der Widerstand im deutschen Südwesten 1933–1945*, edited by Michael Bosch and Wolfgang Niess. V. 10, Schriften zur politischen Landeskunde Baden-Württemberg, Landeszentrale für politische Bildung. Stuttgart, 1984 (pp. 94–103)

Kusserow, Hans-Werner. *Der lila Winkel: Die Familie Kusserow — Zeugen Jehovas unter der Nazidiktatur*. Bonn, 1998

Pavlicic, Michael. *Lippspringe: Beiträge zur Geschichte*, edited by Stadt und Heimatverein Lippspringe. Paderborn, 1995 (pp. 535–538)

Philipsen, Bernd. »Für den Glauben in den Tod. Martyrium einer Süderbraruper Familie in der NS-Zeit.« In: *Kreis-Chronik: Handbuch für den Kreis Schleswig-Flensburg*, edited by Spagat Kulturmagazin. Schleswig 1993-1994 (pp. 39–43)

Poelchau, Harald. *Die Ordnung der Bedrängten*. Berlin, 1962 (pp. 76f.)

Schröder, Karl. »Vom Leben und Sterben des Bibel-Forschers Ludwig Cyranek aus Adscheid, Gemeinde Hennef. Ein Beitrag zur Verfolgung der Zeugen Jehovas im Dritten Reich.« In: *Die Vierziger Jahre: Der Siegburger Raum zwischen Kriegsausbruch und Währungsreform*, edited by Stadtmuseum Siegburg. Siegburg, 1988 (pp. 34-41)

Schumann, Walter. *Nur vierzehn Tage: Ein Tatsachenbericht*. Stuttgart, 1945 (pp. 87, 107ff., 141, 147)

Struckmeier, Ingo. »Die Verfolgung der Zeugen Jehovas: Martin Heinel aus Eickhorst.« In: *Die Kriegsjahre in Deutschland 1939 bis 1945: Schülerwettbewerb Deutsche Geschichte um den Preis des Bundespräsidenten*, edited by Dieter Galinski and Wolf Schmidt. Hamburg, 1985 (pp. 159–179)

Wachtturm-Gesellschaft. *Purple Triangles*. Video, 28 minutes. Selters/Ts., 1991

Walz, Loretta. *Spurensuche mit Gertrud Pötzinger*. Video, 8 minutes. Berlin, 1993

Biography: Simone Arnold Liebster

Arnold Liebster, Simone. *Facing the Lion: Memoirs of a Young Girl in Nazi Europe*. New Orleans, 2000

Biography: Hans Gärtner

Kilthau, Fritz. »Hans Gärtner – Ein Zeuge Jehovas verhungert in Dachau.« In: *Mitten unter uns: Zwingenberg an der Bergstraße von 1933 bis 1945*. Heppenheim, 2000 (pp. 172-180)

Biography: Karl Henning

Hansen, Hans Peter. »Die Zeugen Jehovas: Unvereinbarkeit religiöser Überzeugung mit den Ansprüchen des totalitären Staates.« In: *Bespitzelt und verfolgt: Krefelder Lebensläufe aus den Akten der Gestapo*, v. 4. Krefeld, 1994 (pp. 37, 45-48)

Biography: Max Liebster

Müller, Andreas. »Ich hatte Mitleid mit den Nazis.« In: *Zukunft Beruf: Fachmagazin für Aus- und Fortbildung*, edition for Karlsruhe, Baden-Baden, Rastatt and Pforzheim. February 5, 1997. Weinheim, 1997 (pp. 29-36)

Müller, Andreas. *Auschwitz. Endstation. »Ich hatte Mitleid mit den Nazis.«* Weinheim, 1998

Bayer, Ingeborg, ed. *Ehe alles Legende wird: Das 3. Reich in Erzählungen, Berichten, Dokumenten*. Baden-Baden, 1979 (pp. 201ff.)

Biography: Gerhard Steinacher

Schachendorfer Kulturkreis, ed. *Gerhard Steinacher: Er starb für Gottes Ehre. Wie der Mensch und die Akte Gerhard Steinacher vernichtet wurde*. Documentation by Gyula Varga. Schachendorf, 1998

Biography: Ilse Unterdörfer and Elfriede Löhr

Poppenberg, Fritz. *Unter Jehovas Schutz*. Video, 28 minutes. Berlin, 1998

Biography: Franz Wohlfahrt

Wölbitsch, Lieselotte. *In tiefer Nacht beginnt der Morgen: Franz Wohlfahrt überlebt den NS-Terror*. Klagenfurt, Ljubljana, Vienna, 2000

4. Concentration Camps

Bergmann, Jerry. »The Jehovah's Witnesses' Experience in the Nazi Concentration Camps: A History of Their Conflicts with the Nazi State.« In: *Journal of Church and State*, v. 38, 1996 (pp. 87-113)

Daxelmüller, Christoph, ed. *Zeugen Jehovas im KZ*. Bayerische Blätter für Volkskunde. Neue Folge, NF1 (1999). Würzburg, 2000

Drobisch, Klaus and Günther Wieland. *System der NS-Konzentrationslager 1933-1939*. Berlin, 1993 (p. 202)

Garbe, Detlef. »Der lila Winkel: Die ›Bibelforscher‹ (Zeugen Jehovas) in den Konzentrationslagern.« In: *Dachauer Hefte*, v. 10, 1994 (pp. 3-31)

Högl, Günther. »Widerstand aus christlicher Verantwortung: Die Zeugen Jehovas.« In: *Widerstand und Verfolgung in Dortmund 1933-1945*. Katalog zur ständigen Ausstellung des Stadtarchivs Dortmund in der Mahn- und Gedenkstätte Steinwache. Dortmund, 1992 (pp. 297ff.)

Kammler, Jörg. »Ich habe die Metzelei satt und laufe über ... ‚« v. 6 der Schriftenreihe des Magistrats der Stadt Kassel: Kasseler Soldaten zwischen Verweigerung und Widerstand (1939-1945). In: *Kasseler Quellen und Studien*. Fuldabrück, 1997 (pp. 11ff., 19, 54-58, 135-148, 228)

Kogon, Eugen. *Der SS-Staat: Das System der deutschen Konzentrationslager*. Munich, 1988 (pp. 264-267)

Kogon, Eugen. *The Theory and Practice of Hell: The German Concentration Camps and the System Behind Them*. New York, n. d. (pp. 40-45, 50f., 122f., 219, 273)

Langbein, Hermann. »... nicht wie die Schafe zur Schlachtbank«: Widerstand in den nationalsozialistischen Konzentrationslagern 1938-1945*. Frankfurt am Main, 1995 (pp. 188-191)

Lilje, Hanns. *Im finstern Tal*. Nuremberg, 1947 (pp. 62-65)

Sofsky, Wolfgang. *Die Ordnung des Terrors: Das Konzentrationslager*. Frankfurt am Main, 1993 (pp. 140, 143, 146, 150)

Haaest, Erik. *Aktion Prammen*. Copenhagen, 1995 (pp. 50-57)

Concentration Camp Trials

Broszat, Martin. Nationalsozialistische Konzentrationslager 1933-1945. In: Hans Buchheim and others, *Anatomie des SS-Staates*, v. 2. Olten and Freiburg, 1967 (pp. 66, 72f., 85f.)

Fricke, Kurt. *Die Justizvollzugsanstalt »Roter Ochse« Halle/Saale 1933-1945: Eine Dokumentation*. Magdeburg, 1997 (pp. 64-67)

Auschwitz

Broszat, Martin, ed. *Rudolf Höss: Kommandant in Auschwitz*. Stuttgart, 1958 (pp. 75-78, 184)

Czech, Danuta. *Kalendarium der Ereignisse im Konzentrationslager Auschwitz-Birkenau 1939-1945*. Reinbek bei Hamburg, 1989 (pp. 113, 194, 481, 488f., 492, 495, 891, 895, 923, 960, 1022)

Pawelczynska, Anna. *Values and Violence in Auschwitz: A Sociological Analysis*. Berkeley and Los Angeles, 1998 (pp. 85-89)

Schafft, G. E. and Gerhard Zeidler. *Die KZ-Mahn- und Gedenkstätten in Deutschland*. Berlin, 1996 (pp. 77, 105, 186, 188, 226, 239, 314)

Auschwitz: Children

Wohl, Tibor. *Arbeit macht tot: Eine Jugend in Auschwitz*. Frankfurt am Main, 1990 (pp. 76f., 93)

Bergen-Belsen

Hermann, Reiner. *Jehovas Zeugen in Bergen-Belsen*. Celle, 1998

Buchenwald

Berke, Hanns. *Buchenwald: Eine Erinnerung an Mörder*. Salzburg, 1946 (pp. 26, 29f., 59f., 106, 108)

Busse, Ernst. *KLBu Konzentrationslager Buchenwald: Bericht des internationalen Lagerkomitees Buchenwald*. Weimar, n. d. (pp. 110f.)

Hackett, David A., ed. *Der Buchenwald-Report: Bericht über das Konzentrationslager Buchenwald bei Weimar*. Munich, 1996 (pp. 21, 48, 54, 56, 69, 81, 212-216)

Nationale Mahn- und Gedenkstätte Buchenwald, ed. *Konzentrationslager Buchenwald: Katalog zu der Ausstellung aus der Deutschen Demokratischen Republik*. 1990 (pp. 34ff.)

Buchenwald, Sachsenhausen

Müller, Andreas. *Auschwitz. Endstation. »Ich hatte Mitleid mit den Nazis.«* Weinheim, 1998

Dachau

Schaeper-Wimmer, Sylvia. *Das Unbegreifliche berichten: Zeitzeugenberichte ehemaliger Häftlinge des Konzentrationslagers Dachau*, edited by Museumspädagogisches Zentrum München. Munich, 1997 (pp. 55-61)

Wandel, Fritz. *Ein Weg durch die Hölle ... Dachau, wie es wirklich war*. GMZFW no. 208, Reutlingen (pp. 19ff.)

Dachau, Gusen, Mauthausen

Gostner, Erwin. *1000 Tage im KZ: Ein Erlebnisbericht aus den Konzentrationslagern Dachau, Mauthausen und Gusen*. Mit authentischem Bildmaterial und Dokumenten sowie einem zeitgeschichtlichen Nachwort von Christoph von Hartungen und Georg J. Anker. Reihe Dokumente 01. Innsbruck, 1947, 1986 (pp. 26f., 42-45, 50f., 60f., 82f., 98f., 102-109, 142f., 198-211)

Dachau, Ravensbrück, Lichtenburg

Benz, Wolfgang and Barbara Distel, eds. *Dachauer Hefte* 3: Frauen, Verfolgung und Widerstand. Brussels, 1993 (pp. 4f., 14, 131, 138f., 170, 181f.)

Emslandlager

Ausländer, Fietje, and Norbert Haase, eds. *Hans Frese. Bremsklötze am Siegeswagen der Nation: Erinnerungen eines Deserteurs an Militärgefängnisse, Zuchthäuser und Moorlager in den Jahren 1941-1945*. DIZ-Schriften, v. 1. Bremen, 1989 (pp. 79f.)

Mauthausen

Jäckel, Eberhard, and others, eds. *Enzyklopädie des Holocaust*, v. 1-3. Tel Aviv and Berlin, 1990, 1993

Marsálek, Hans. *Die Geschichte des Konzentrationslagers Mauthausen*. Vienna and Linz, 1995 (pp. 109, 128-131, 139f., 281f.)

Moringen

(see Jehovah's Witnesses: Women)

Neuengamme

Bauche, Ulrich, and others. *Arbeit und Vernichtung: Das Konzentrationslager Neuengamme 1938–1945*: Katalog zur Ausstellung im Dokumentenhaus der KZ-Gedenkstätte Neuengamme. Hamburg, 1991 (pp. 30, 34, 197)

Kupfer-Koberwitz, Edgar. *Als Häftling in Dachau ... geschrieben von 1942 bis 1945 im Konzentrationslager Dachau*, v. 19, Schriftenreihe der Bundeszentrale für Heimatdienst. Bonn, 1956 (pp. 40, 41, 284-296)

Kaienburg, Hermann. *Das Konzentrationslager Neuengamme 1938-1945*. Bonn, 1997 (pp. 24, 50, 77, 82, 145, 161, 225, 235, 310f.)

Ravensbrück

Poppenberg, Fritz. *Unter Jehovas Schutz.* Video, 28 minutes. Berlin, 1998

Wewelsburg

Brebeck, Wulff E. and Karl Hüser. *Wewelsburg 1933–1945. Das Konzentrationslager.* Westfalen im Bild: Eine Bildmediensammlung zur westfälischen Landeskunde. Münster, 1995 (pp. 20ff., 47, 54f.)

John, Kirsten. *»Mein Vater wird gesucht ...«: Häftlinge des Konzentrationslagers in Wewelsburg.* Essen, 1996 (pp. 136–165)

5. Jehovah's Witnesses: Women

Buber-Neumann, Margarete. *Als Gefangene bei Stalin und Hitler: Eine Welt im Dunkel.* Frankfurt am Main and Berlin, 1993 (pp. 194–210, 199f., 205, 211, 227, 235, 241–244, 246–259, 271, 278f., 308, 330, 377)

Garbe, Detlef. »Kompromißlose Bekennerinnen: Selbstbehauptung und Verweigerung von Bibelforscherinnen.« In: Christl Wickert, ed., *Frauen gegen die Diktatur: Widerstand und Verfolgung im nationalsozialistischen Deutschland.* Berlin, 1995 (pp. 52–73)

Grebing, Helga and Christl Wickert, eds. »Frauen im Hintergrund — das Beispiel von Kommunistinnen und Bibelforscherinnen.« In: *Das »andere Deutschland« im Widerstand gegen den Nationalsozialismus: Beiträge zur politischen Überwindung der nationalsozialistischen Dikatur im Exil und im Dritten Reich.* Essen, 1994 (pp. 10, 200ff.)

Haaest, Erik. *Aktion Prammen.* Copenhagen, 1995 (pp. 50–57)

Koonz, Claudia. *Mothers in the Fatherland: Woman, the Family, and Nazi Politics.* New York, 1987 (pp. 312, 331–334, 342f., 406)

Biographies: Emmy Zehden

Göbel, Wolfgang. *»... für immer ehrlos«: Aus der Praxis des Volksgerichtshofes,* edited by Gedenkstätte deutscher Widerstand. Berlin, 1985 (pp. 22–32)

Women, KZ

Geve, Thomas. *Youth in Chains.* Jerusalem, 1958

Women, KZ: Bergen-Belsen, Ravensbrück

Füllberg-Stolberg, Claus and others, eds. *Frauen in Konzentrationslagern: Bergen-Belsen — Ravensbrück.* Bremen, 1994 (pp. 321–332)

Women, KZ: Moringen

Harder, Jürgen. *Widerstand und Verfolgung von Bibelforscherinnen im Frauen-KZ Moringen.* Master's degree essay, University Göttingen, 1997

Harder, Jürgen, and Hans Hesse. »Zeuginnen Jehovas aus Baden und Württemberg im Frauen-Konzentrationslager Moringen.« In: Hubert Roser, ed., *Widerstand als Bekenntnis: Die Zeugen Jehovas und das NS-Regime in Baden und Württemberg.* V. 7 of the series Portraits des Widerstands. Konstanz, 1998

Hesse, Hans. »Zwischenbericht zum Forschungsprojekt ›Geschichte des Frauen-KZ in Moringen.‹ In: Kurt Buck and others, eds., *Die frühen Nachkriegsprozesse: Beiträge zur Geschichte der nationalsozialistischen Verfolgung in Norddeutschland* 3. Bremen, 1997 (pp. 195ff.)

Hesse, Hans. *Das Frauen-KZ Moringen 1933-1938.* Göttingen 2000

Women, KZ: Moringen, Lichtenburg, Ravensbrück

Freyburg, Jutta von, and Ursula Krause-Schmitt. *Moringen – Lichtenburg – Ravensbrück: Frauen im Konzentrationslager 1933-1945*. Frankfurt, 1997 (pp. 15ff., 20f., 49-52, 59f.)

Hesse, Hans, and Harder, Jürgen. *»... und wenn ich lebenslang in einem KZ bleiben müßte ...« Die Zeuginnen Jehovas in den Frauen-Konzentrationslagern Moringen, Lichtenburg und Ravensbrück.* Essen 2001.

Women, KZ: Ravensbrück

Brümann-Güdther, Elisabeth, and Sigrid Jacobeit, eds. *Ravensbrückerinnen*. V. 4, Schriftenreihe der Stiftung Brandenburgische Gedenkstätten. Brandenburg, 1995 (pp. 60-63)

Women, KZ: Ravensbrück, Bergen-Belsen

Brandes, Ulrike, Claus Füllberg-Stolberg, and Sylvia Kempe. »Arbeiten im KZ Ravensbrück.« In: *Frauen in Konzentrationslagern: Bergen-Belsen, Ravensbrück*. Bremen, 1994 (pp. 58f., 61)

Women, Local History Bonn

Hix, Iris-Maria. Vergessener Frauenwiderstand. In: Annette Kuhn and Valentine Rothe, eds., *Frauenleben im NS-Alltag: Bonner Studien zur Frauengeschichte*, v. 2. Pfaffenweiler, 1994 (pp. 150-154)

6. Trials

Angermund, Ralph. »Die geprellten ›Richterkönige‹: Zum Niedergang der Justiz im NS-Staat.« In: Hans Mommsen, ed., *Herrschaftsalltag im Dritten Reich: Studien und Texte*. Düsseldorf, 1988

Beckert, Ruth. *Die erste und letzte Instanz: Schau und Geheimprozesse vor dem Obersten Gericht der DDR*. Goldbach b. Aschaffenburg, 1995 (pp. 223-227)

Buck, Kurt, ed. *Die frühen Nachkriegsprozesse. Beiträge zur Geschichte der nationalsozialistischen Verfolgung in Norddeutschland*, no. 3 (1997). Bremen, 1997 (pp. 70, 195ff.)

Dittrich, Irene. *Heimatgeschichtlicher Wegweiser zu den Stätten des Widerstandes und der Verfolgung 1933-1945. V. 7: Schleswig-Holstein. part 1: Nördlicher Landesteil*. Frankfurt, 1993 (pp. 34f., 98f., 113f., 123, 136, 146, 189, 201, 214)

Dokumentationsarchiv des österreichischen Widerstandes, ed. *Widerstand und Verfolgung in Wien 1934-1945*. Vienna, 1984 (pp. 161-185)

Kammler, Jörg. »Ich habe die Metzelei satt und laufe über ...« V. 6 der Schriftenreihe des Magistrats der Stadt Kassel: *Kasseler Soldaten zwischen Verweigerung und Widerstand, 1939-1945*, in: *Kasseler Quellen und Studien*. Fuldabrück, 1997 (pp. 11-13, 19, 544-558, 135-138, 228)

Maislinger, Andreas. »Andere religiöse Gruppen.« In: *Widerstand und Verfolgung in Salzburg 1934-1943: Eine Dokumentation*, edited by Dokumentationsarchiv des österreichischen Widerstandes, v. 2. Vienna, 1991 (pp. 323-351)

Mechler, Wolf-Dieter. »Kriegsalltag an der ›Heimatfront‹: Das Sondergericht Hannover im Einsatz gegen ›Rundfunkverbecher,‹ ›Schwarzschlachter,‹ ›Volksschädlinge‹ und andere ›Straftäter‹ 1939 bis 1945.« In: *Hannoversche Studien*, edited by Klaus Mlynek. Schriftenreihe des Stadtarchivs Hannover. Hanover, 1997 (pp. 70-73)

Müller, Manfred. *Neuss unterm Hakenkreuz: Die NSDAP und ihre Gegner in einer katholischen Stadt des Rheinlandes*. Essen, 1988 (pp. 121f.)

Neugebauer, Wolfgang, ed. *Widerstand und Verfolgung in Wien 1934-1945*, v. 3. Vienna, 1984 (pp. 161-185)

Niermann, Hans-Eckhard. »Die Durchsetzung politischer und politisierter Strafjustiz im Dritten Reich: Ihre Entwicklung aufgezeigt am Beispiel des OLG-Bezirks Hamm.« In: Justizministerium des Landes Nordrhein-Westfalen, ed., *Juristische Zeitgeschichte*, v. 3, »Strafjustiz im Dritten Reich.« Düsseldorf, 1995 (pp. 252-309)

Rüter-Ehlermann, Adelheid. *Justiz und NS-Verbrechen: Sammlung deutscher Strafurteile wegen nationalsozialistischer Tötungsverbrechen 1945-1966*, v. 5. Amsterdam, 1970 (pp. 127-138)

Schlüer, Jochen, and Karl-Heinz Lange. »Wir werden nun mal nicht verstanden: Schicksale von Zeugen Jehovas im Raum Herford 1933 bis 1945.« In: *Historisches Jahrbuch für den Kreis Herford*. Bielefeld, 1997 (pp. 115-132)

Schreiber, Jürgen. »Wehrmachtjustiz und Kriegsdienstverweigerung.« In: *Wehrwissenschaftliche Rundschau*, no. 31, 1982 (pp. 145f.)

Warmbrunn, Paul. »Strafgerichtsbarkeit in der Pfalz und in Rheinhessen im Dritten Reich.« In: *Justiz im Dritten Reich: Justizverwaltung, Rechtsprechung und Strafvollzug auf dem Gebiet des heutigen Landes Rheinland-Pfalz*, part 1, edited by Ministerium der Justiz Rheinland-Pfalz. Frankfurt am Main, 1993 (pp. 372-376, 832)

Trials: Refusal of Military Service

Hartmann, Albrecht, and Heidi Hartmann. *Kriegsdienstverweigerung im Dritten Reich*. Frankfurt am Main, 1986 (pp. 54-99)

7. Children

Facing History and Ourselves National Foundation, Inc. *Resource Book: Facing History and Ourselves, Holocaust and Human Behavior*. Massachusetts, 1994 (pp. 188f., 232f.)

8. Refusal of Military Service

Ausländer, Fietje. *Verräter oder Vorbilder? Deserteure und ungehorsame Soldaten im Nationalsozialismus*, v. 2, DIZ Schriften. Bremen, 1990 (pp. 121, 187, 192)

Bredemeier, Karsten. *Kriegsdienstverweigerung im Dritten Reich: Ausgewählte Beispiele*. Baden-Baden, 1991 (pp. 60, 69, 76-79, 84ff., 199f.)

Elbert, Harald and Klaus Fröbe. *Beck-Rechtsberater: Kriegsdienstverweigerung und Zivildienst*. Munich, 1989 (pp. 83, 86, 133, 216)

Fahle, Günter. *Verweigern – Weglaufen – Zersetzen: Deutsche Militärjustiz und ungehorsame Soldaten 1939-1945. Das Beispiel Ems-Jade*, v. 3, DIZ-Schriften. Bremen, 1990 (pp. 153-158)

Freyberg, Jutta von, Barbara Bromberger, and Hans Mausbach. *»Wir hatten andere Träume«: Kinder und Jugendliche unter der NS-Diktatur*; mit Interviews, Zeitzeugenberichten, Dokumenten und Beiträgen von Jefim Brodski. Frankfurt am Main, 1995 (pp. 78, 95, 148f., 168)

Haase, Norbert. »Desertion – Kriegsdienstverweigerung – Widerstand.« In: Peter Steinbach and Johannes Tuchel, eds., *Widerstand gegen den Nationalsozialismus*. Bonn, 1994 (pp. 526-536)

Kossack, Kristan. *Vergessene Opfer, Verdrängter Widerstand: Wehrmachtdeserteure, Wehrkraftzersetzer und Kriegsdienstverweigerer im Altkreis Minden 1939-1945*. Edited by Versöhnungsbund – Gruppe Minden. Minden, 1998 (pp. 16-21)

Lilje, Hanns. *Im finstern Tal*. Nuremberg, 1947 (pp. 62-65)

Reichelt, Stefanie. »Für mich ist der Krieg aus«: *Deserteure und Kriegsdienstverweigerer des Zweiten Weltkriegs in München*. Munich, 1995 (pp. 51-97)

Wieben, Uwe. *Keiner ist vergessen, nichts ist vergessen! Verfolgung, Opposition und Widerstand in Boizenburg*. Rostock, 1997 (pp. 27ff.)

Kammler, Jörg. »Ich habe die Metzelei satt und lauf über ...« V. 6 der Schriftenreihe des Magistrats der Stadt Kassel: *Kasseler Soldaten zwischen Verweigerung und Widerstand, 1939-1945*, in: *Kasseler Quellen und Studien*. Fuldabrück, 1997 (pp. 11-13, 19, 54-58, 135-148, 228)

9. Special Tribunals

Bajohr, Frank, ed. *Norddeutschland im Nationalsozialismus*. Forum Zeitgeschichte, v. 1. Hamburg, 1993 (pp. 203-207)

Garbe, Detlef. »Radikale Verweigerung aus Prinzipientreue und Gewissensgehorsam,« in: Landesbildstelle Berlin, ed., *Der Fall Jägerstätter: Kriegsdienstverweigerung im Dritten Reich*. Begleitheft zur Videokassette 42 54574. Berlin, 1996 (pp. 39-47)

Bundesminister der Justiz, ed. *Im Namen des Deutschen Volkes: Justiz und Nationalsozialismus*. Katalog zur Ausstellung. Cologne, 1994 (pp. 168, 237, 254f., 263ff., 292)

10. Documentation of Symposia

Benz, Wolfgang, and others. *Erinnerung und Begegnung: Gedenken im Land Brandenburg zum 50. Jahrestag der Befreiung*. Published by Ministerium für Wissenschaft, Forschung und Kultur des Landes Brandenburg. Potsdam, 1996 (pp. 38-41, 68f., 82-87, 90-93, 116-119)

Dokumentationsarchiv des österreichischen Widerstandes, ed. *Zeugen Jehovas: Vergessene Opfer des Nationalsozialismus?* Vienna, 1998

Kreismuseum Wewelsburg, Fritz Bauer Institut, and Bundeszentrale für politische Bildung, eds. *Widerstand aus christlicher Überzeugung: Jehovas Zeugen im Nationalsozialismus. Dokumentation einer Tagung*. Essen, 1998

11. German Democratic Republic

Bästlein, Klaus, and others. *Politische Strafjustiz in der früheren DDR, dargestellt an ausgewählten Einzelschicksalen*. Hohenleuben, 1996 (pp. 53-67)

Besier, Gerhard, and Stephan Wolf, ed. »*Pfarrer, Christen und Katholiken«: Das Ministerium für Staatssicherheit der ehemaligen DDR und die Kirchen*. Neukirchen-Vluyn, 1992 (pp. 81, 84, 149f., 152f., 154f., 280f., 286, 290, 292f., 295, 788, 800)

Bundesministerium für gesamtdeutsche Fragen, ed. *Unrecht als System: Dokumente über planmäßige Rechtsverletzungen im sowjetischen Besatzungsgebiet*, part I. Bonn, 1952 (pp. 21-34)

Bundesministerium für gesamtdeutsche Fragen, ed. *Unrecht als System: Dokumente über planmäßige Rechtsverletzungen im sowjetischen Besatzungsgebiet*, part II. Bonn, 1955 (pp. 143f.)

Dirksen, Hans-Hermann. »*Keine Gnade den Feinden unserer Republik«. Die Verfolgung der Zeugen Jehovas in der SBZ/DDR 1945-1990*. Berlin, 2001

Hacke, Gerald. *Zeugen Jehovas in der DDR: Verfolgung und Verhalten einer religiösen Minderheit*. Berichte und Studien Nr. 24. Dresden, 2000.

Lahrtz, Jens-Uwe. »»Maulwürfe unter religiöser Tarnung.«« In: *Sächsische Justizgeschichte*. Schriftenreihe des Sächsischen Staatsministeriums der Justiz, v. 8. Dresden, 1998 (pp. 59-92)

Obst, Helmut. *Apostel und Propheten der Neuzeit: Gründer christlicher Religionsgemeinschaften des 19./20. Jahrhunderts*. Berlin (Ost), 1981

Schuller, Wolfgang. *Geschichte und Struktur des politischen Strafrechts der DDR bis 1958*. Ebelsbach, 1980 (pp. 36f., 41-47, 56f., 61ff., 67, 81, 85ff., 97ff., 127, 170f., 187, 205, 233, 277ff., 315, 320, 323f.)

Worst, Anne. *Das Ende eines Geheimdienstes. Oder: Wie lebendig ist die Stasi?* Berlin, 1991 (pp. 199, 247)

Yonan, Gabriele, ed. *Im Visier der Stasi: Jehovas Zeugen in der DDR*. Niedersteinbach, 2000

Yonan, Gabriele. *Jehovas Zeugen: Opfer unter zwei deutschen Diktaturen 1933-1945; 1949-1989.* Religion und Zeitgeschichte, v. 1. Berlin, 1999

German Democratic Republic: Trials

Haase, Norbert, and Brigitte Oleschinski, eds. *Das Torgau-Tabu: Wehrmachtsstrafsystem, NKWD-Speziallager, DDR-Strafvollzug.* Leipzig, 1993 (pp. 115ff., 243f.)

Bundesministerium für gesamtdeutsche Fragen, ed. *Partei-Justiz: Eine vergleichende Dokumentation über den nationalsozialistischen und kommunistischen Rechtsmißbrauch in Deutschland 1933-1963.* Bonn and Berlin, 1964 (pp. 64-70)

German Democratic Republic: Trials, Women

Haase, Norbert. *Das Reichskriegsgericht und der Widerstand gegen die nationalsozialistische Herrschaft.* Katalog zur Sonderausstellung der Gedenkstätte Deutscher Widerstand in Zusammenarbeit mit der Neuen Richtervereinigung. Berlin, 1993 (pp. 13, 19, 47, 49f., 95-99, 271)

German Democratic Republic: Divorce, Custody Law

Gräf, Dieter. *Im Namen der Republik: Rechtsalltag in der DDR.* Munich and Berlin, 1988 (pp. 192-232)

Contributors

Michael Berenbaum

b. 1945. Michael Berenbaum is a writer, lecturer, and teacher consulting in the conceptual development of museums and the historical development of films. He is also an [adjunct] Professor of Theology at the University of Judaism in Los Angeles. In the past he has served as President and Chief Executive Officer of the Survivors of the Shoah Visual History Foundation. Prior to that he was the Director of the United States Holocaust Research Institute at the U.S. Holocaust Memorial Museum and the Hymen Goldman Adjunct Professor of Theology at Georgetown University in Washington, D.C. From 1988-93 he served as Project Director of the United States Holocaust Memorial Museum, overseeing its creation. Berenbaum is the author and editor of twelve books, scores of scholarly articles and hundreds of journalistic pieces. His most recent work is The Bombing of Auschwitz Should the Allies Have Attempted It? co-edited with Michael Neufeldd

Jolene Chu

b. 1957, studied social history at New York University, researcher specializing in the history of Jehovah's Witnesses in the Nazi era, at the international offices of the Watch Tower Society; project coordinator of Holocaust-related education programs and cooperative efforts with the Survivors of the Shoah Visual History Foundation, Facing History and Ourselves, the Imperial War Museum Holocaust Exhibition, and numerous other Holocaust education and research facilities; serves on the advisory board for the Journal of Genocide Research.

Christoph Daxelmüller

b. 1948, Professor for Folklore Studies at the University of Würzburg and project director »Culture in Nazi concentration camps: Culture as a survival strategy.« Studies in folklore, cuneiform writing, and Semitic studies at Munich and Würzburg.

Hans-Hermann Dirksen

b. 1966, attorney, studied at Kiel University, and has specialized in criminal law since 1995. LLD at Law Faculty of Greifswald University 1999. Publications include: »Keine Gnade den Feinden unserer Republik« Die Verfolgung der Zeugen Jehovas in der SBZ/DDR 1945-1990 (Berlin, 2001). Research projects about the criminal prosecution of religious minorities in communist regimes.

Henry Friedlander

b. 1930, Professor of History in the Department of Judaic Studies at Brooklyn College of the City University of New York. Deported 1941 from Berlin to Lodz ghetto and 1944 to Auschwitz-Birkenau, Neuegamme, Ravensbrück men's camp, emigrated to the United States in 1947. In addition to articles on the historiography of the Holocaust, Nazi concentration camps, and postwar war crimes trials, he is the author of The Origins of Nazi Genocide: From Euthanasia to the Final Solution (Chapel Hill, 1995). He is coeditor of 7 volumes of the Simon Wiesenthal Center Annual (New York, 1984-1990) and the 26 volume documentary series, Archives of the Holocaust (New York, 1990-1995).

Detlef Garbe

b. 1956, Head of the Neuengamme Concentration Camp Memorial and Museum in Hamburg since 1989. Numerous publications about the history of concentration camps, Jehovah's Witnesses, other forgotten victim groups, military justice, and postwar confrontations with the Nazi past. Editor of *Beiträge zur Geschichte der nationalsozialistischen Verfolgung in Norddeutschland*, and author of *Zwischen Widerstand und Martyrium: Die Zeugen Jehovas im »Dritten Reich«* (Munich, 1997).

Martin Guse

b. 1961, social worker and educator, employed in juvenile education and social work. Research focus is the history of the Moringen and Uckermark concentration camps. Author of the exhibition catalog, *»Wir hatten noch gar nicht angefangen zu leben«: zur Geschichte der Jugend-KZ Moringen und Uckermark 1940-1945* (Moringen and Liebenau, 1992 and 3d exp. ed. 1997), and the exhibition *KZ Moringen 1933 und Frauen-KZ Moringen 1933 bis 1938* at the Moringen Memorial Museum.

Jürgen Harder

b. 1967, master's degree in history; studied history, German language and literature, and communication at Göttingen University. Staff member of the Göttingen History Workshop, with research specialty on Nazi persecution of Jehovah's Witnesses.

Dietrich Hellmund

b. 1934, Protestant pastor in Hanover and Hamburg; 1971, Ph.D. in theology at Erlangen University with monograph about history of the Jehovah's Witnesses. From 1969–1998, member of the project »religious communities« in the United German Lutheran-Evangelical church (Vereinigte Evangelisch-lutherischen Kirche Deutschlands); contributor to handbook *Religiöse Gemeinschaften*; chairman and member of the commission on ideologies of the North Elbe Church directorate.

Hans Hesse

b. 1961, master's degree in history, freelance author; studied ancient history, contemporary history, and communications at the Free University Berlin. Author of *Hoffnung ist ein ewiges Begräbnis: Edition des Briefwechsels von Hannah Vogt aus dem KZ Moringen 1933* (Bremen, 1998); research projects about the persecution of Sinti and Roma in Bremen and the Moringen concentration camp.

Kirsten John-Stucke

b. 1966, master's degree in history, is a researcher at the Wewelsburg District Museum. She studied contemporary history, German language and literature, and communications at Münster University; and interned at the Morgenstern Museum in Bremerhaven. Author of various articles and books on Wewelsburg concentration camp, prisoner biographies, and persecution of Jehovah's Witnesses in the Nazi era.

Walter Köbe

b. 1943, since 1979 volunteer associate of the Watch Tower Bible and Tract Society in Selters/Taunus; head of the Public Affairs Office for Jehovah's Witnesses in Germany.

Ursula Krause-Schmitt

b. 1942, historian, since 1975 responsible for archival and library development at the Studienkreis Deutscher Widerstand in Frankfurt. Publications include: co-author with Jutta von Freyberg of the exhibition catalog, *Moringen – Lichtenburg – Ravensbrück: Frauen im Konzentrationslager 1933-1945* (Frankfurt, 1997); and co-author in the series *Heimatgeschichtlicher Wegweise zu den Stätten des Widerstandes und der Verfolgung 1933-1945*.

Lutz Lemhöfer

b. 1948, studied Catholic theology, sociology, and political science; since 1991, specialist in ideological questions for the Catholic Bishopric Limburg. Publications include: *Katholische Kirche und NS-Staat – aus der Vergangenheit lernen?*, co-author with Monika Kringels-Kemen (Frankfurt, 1981); *Die braune Machtergreifung: Universität Frankfurt 1930-1945*, co-author with Christoph Dorner and others (Frankfurt, 1989); and *Was gehen uns die Sekten an?*, co-author with Kurt-Helmuth Eimuth (Frankfurt, 1998).

Sybil Milton

b. 1941, dec. October 16, 2000, independent historian, since 1997 affiliated as Vice-President with the Independent Experts Commission: Switzerland – World War II. She served as Senior Historian of the U.S. Holocaust Memorial Museum from 1988 to 1997 and Director of the Archives of the Leo Baeck Institute in New York from 1974 to 1984. Her books include the coedited volumes: *The Holocaust: Ideology, Bureaucracy, and Genocide* (New York, 1981); 7 volumes of the *Simon Wiesenthal Center Annual* (New York, 1984-1990) and the 26 volume documentary series, *Archives of the Holocaust* (New York, 1990-1995). She also co-authored *Art of the Holocaust*, which won the National Jewish Book Award in 1982. She has published numerous articles about Nazi Germany and the Holocaust, including about the use of photographic evidence as historical documentation; women and the Holocaust; the politics of postwar memorials; the fate of Sinti and Roma in Germany and occupied Europe between 1933 and 1945. Her most recent books are *In Fitting Memory: The Art and Politics of Holocaust Memorials* (Detroit, 1991) and guest co-editor of the special issue »Photography and the Holocaust« of the journal *History of Photography* (Winter 1999). She has also drafted the entry for »Jehovah's Witnesses« for the Walter Laqueur and Judith Baumel, eds., *Encyclopedia of the Holocaust* (New Haven, in press).

Angela Nerlich

b. 1966, member of research staff at the history archive of Jehovah's Witnesses, Selters/Taunus, Germany.

James N. Pellechia

b. 1944, studied journalism and communications at Columbia University; associate editor of the periodical *Awake!* (Erwachet!); author of *The Spirit and the Sword—Jehovah's Witnesses Expose the Third Reich*; producer of the video documentary *Jehovah's Witnesses Stand Firm Against Nazi Assault*.

Thomas Rahe

b. 1957, studied history and Catholic theology, Ph.D. 1987; since 1987, academic and research director of the Bergen-Belsen Memorial Museum. Numerous articles and publications about Jewish history, social history of the concentration camps, and most recently, the essay »Rabbiner im Konzentrationslager Bergen-Belsen,« in *Memora* 9 (1998).

Hubert Roser

b. 1957, studied history, geography, and political science in Mannheim; Ph.D. 1996, dissertation »NS-Beamtenpolitik und regionale Verwaltung in Baden und Württemberg, 1933–1939.« Since 1997, researcher at the University of Karlsruhe for the research project »Resistance against National Socialism in the German Southwest.« Editor and contributor to *Widerstand als Bekenntnis: Die Zeugen Jehovas und das NS-Regime in Baden und Württemberg* (Konstanz, 1998).

Wolfram Slupina

b. 1947, since 1967 senior staff at the German headquarters of the Watch Tower Society in Wiesbaden, and after 1984 in Selters/Taunus; since January 1996, in charge of public affairs division for schools, education, and memorials.

Göran Westphal

b. 1966, doublemajored in German Studies and Protestant Theology at Schiller University Jena, Germany, and Nottingham University, Great Britain; 1996-97 on a scholarship at Concordia College, Moorhead, Minnesota, USA.

Johannes Wrobel

b. 1953, since 1979 researcher and author on the writing staff of the Watch Tower Society; head of the history archive of Jehovah's Witnesses, Selters/Taunus, Germany. Writing and research staff for the video documentary *Jehovah's Witnesses Stand Firm Against Nazi Assault* (1996); presentations in Austria, England, Germany, Russia, Sweden, and Israel on the Nazi and Communist persecution of Jehovah's Witnesses.

Gabriele Yonan

b. 1944, Ph.D. in oriental studies and history of religion at the Free University, Berlin. Lecturer for oriental languages, literatures, and religions. Publications include *Ein vergessener Holocaust: Die Vernichtung der christlichen Assyer in der Turkei* (Göttingen, 1989), also translated into English and Turkish language editions.

Antje Zeiger

b. 1963, teacher's certificate; research staff member at the Sachsenhausen Memorial Museum and director of the satellite museum on Sachsenhausen »death marches.« Her research focuses on death marches and liberation and Jehovah's Witnesses in Sachsenhausen.